Ian Budge • Ivor Crewe • David McKay • Ken Newton

with contributions from
David Robertson, Nigel South, Maurice Sunkin and Albert Weale

The new British Politics

© Addison Wesley Longman 1998

Addison Wesley Longman Ltd
Edinburgh Gate
Harlow
Essex CM20 2JE

and Associated Companies throughout the World.

Published in the United States of America by Addison Wesley Longman Inc.,
New York.

Illustrations by Margaret Macknelly
Typeset by 42
Typeset in 10pt Times
Produced by Addison Wesley Longman Singapore Pte Ltd
Printed in Singapore

First printed 1998

ISBN 0582-28925-4

British Library Cataloguing-in-Publication Data
A catalogue record for this book is available from the British Library

CONTENTS

PART II – GOVERNMENT

PART III – PARTICIPATION

PART IV – REPRESENTATION

PART V – ORDER

PART VI – POLICY

PART VII – THE NEW BRITISH POLITICS

PREFACE

For over a century the most visible features of British politics have remained the same: the monarchy, the unwritten constitution, the unelected House of Lords, the Government's domination of the House of Commons, the Conservative and Labour parties, a large London-based Civil Service and an influential national press.

In the 1990s everything seems to be changing. State power was centralised under Margaret Thatcher in the 1980s and under John Major in the 1990s. Now, under a New Labour Government, radical plans for devolution and other political reforms are being planned and even a coalition government of Labour and Liberal Democrats in 2002 has been mooted. The Thatcher decade seems far back in history.

This book asks how far British politics have really changed. Do the reforms amount to the policy revolution touted first by Margaret Thatcher and now by Tony Blair? Or are they more apparent than real? Have they left the British people worse or better off? Have they enhanced or eroded their rights and liberties? Is Great Britain PLC better able to cope with the modern world? Assessing how recent developments have affected the quality of British democracy is one of the main aims of the book. Another is to trace the increasing integration of Britain and Europe and to ask if there is really any realistic alternative left for Britain outside a federal European Union.

We have aimed to answer these questions with the most comprehensive and up-to-date evidence yet assembled, presented through text, tables, graphs, photographs and cartoons in the clearest and most direct way possible. Each chapter has a similar structure with an introduction, frequent 'briefings' in the text, a chronology ('milestones') at the end, suggestions for essays and projects, a chapter summary and further reading. Key terms are defined in the margins of the text and consolidated into a full glossary at the end of the book. Altogether a vast amount of information is provided about the workings of contemporary politics and about Britain's links with the rest of the world.

In preparing this book we have received assistance from many friends and colleagues. Colin Rallings of the University of Plymouth gave us election statistics with his typical generosity. Our colleague David Sanders provided a large amount of material and kindly allowed us to cite his predictive 'Essex Model' of British general elections. Deborah Davies, Dylan Griffiths, Sean McKeown, Ian S. Wood and Robert Wood collected information and compiled tables for us. Jackie Mutlow undertook numerous office tasks including liaison between the scattered authors and the publishers. With great speed and efficiency Julie Lord transformed over 700 pages of almost illegible script and oddly formatted files into a presentable typescript. Jenny Roberts was eagle-eyed and indefatigable in her copy editing. And Chris Harrison, Kevin Ancient, Jane Toettcher and Christian Turner of our publishers, Addison Wesley Longman, were models of encouragement, tact and support. We are indebted to them all.

Ian Budge
Ivor Crewe
David McKay
Kenneth Newton

Colchester, Essex

The publisher has made every attempt to obtain permission to reproduce material in this book from the appropriate source. If there are any omissions please contact the publisher who will make suitable acknowledgement in the reprint.

We are grateful to the following for permission to reproduce photographs, cartoons, figures and tables:

Central Office of Information for Plates 1.1, 6.1, 6.7, 7.1, 9.1, 19.1, 22.1 and 25.3; Getty Images for Plates 3.1 and 3.2; Telegraph Group/Nicholas Garland for cartoons 3.3, 4.3 and 25.4, and Telegraph Group/Matt for cartoons 16.2 and 27.2; Vicky for cartoon 4.1 and Vicky/*Evening Standard* for cartoon 4.2; European Parliament for Plate 5.1; Steve Bell for cartoons 5.2 and 7.2; Bill McArthur for cartoon 6.2; Peter Brookes/*The Times* for cartoons 8.1 and 19.2; MacDiarmid/*The Independent* for Plate 8.2; Chris Riddell/*The Independent* for cartoon 11.1; PA News for Plates 12.1 and 12.2; Mirror Syndication International for Plate 12.3; News International/*The Sun* for Plate 13.1; The Wire Station for Internet page, Plate 14.1; Popperfoto for Plate 14.2; *The Guardian* for Plate 14.3; *The Manchester Evening News*/Dick Graham for cartoon 15.1; Michael Cummings/*Daily Express* for cartoon 16.1; MAC/*Daily Mail* for cartoon 20.1; Dave Brown/*The Independent* for cartoon 17.1; Peter Schrank/*The Independent* for cartoon 21.1; British Nuclear Fuels for Plate 24.1; Michael Cummings/*The Times* for cartoon 23.1; Lloyd's of London for Plate 25.1; Popperfoto for Plate 25.2; Steve Fricker/*Daily Telegraph* for cartoon 27.1; Cassell for Fig 1.1; Macmillan Press Ltd for Figures 1.3, 25.2, 25.3, 25.4 and Tables 1.1, 10.1 and 15.1. Crown copyright is reproduced with the permission of the Controller of Her Majesty's Stationery Office. We are also grateful to the Centre for Caricature and Cartoon at the University of Kent, Canterbury for their assistance.

LIST OF ABBREVIATIONS

ABC	Aubrey, Berry, Campbell (Trial, 1977)
AC	Appeal Cases
ACAS	Advisory, Conciliation, and Arbitration Service
ACPO	Association of Chief Police Officers
AEA	Atomic Energy Authority
AEEU	Amalgamated Electrical Engineering Union
All ER	All England Reports
Art	Article
ASH	Action on Smoking and Health
BAOR	British Army of the Rhine
BBC	British Broadcasting Corporation
BCC	Broadcasting Complaints Commission
BCS	British Crime Survey
BMA	The British Medical Association
BP	British Petroleum
BPBNC	Both Parents Born New Commonwealth
BSB	British Satellite Broadcasting
BSC	Broadcasting Standards Council
CAP	Common Agricultural Policy
CBI	Confederation of British Industries
CEPS	Central Economic Planning Staff
CFSP	Common Foreign and Security Policy
CFC	Chlorofluorocarbon
CGT	Capital Gains Tax
CJHA	Committee on Justice and Home Affairs
CLA	Country Landowners' Association
Cm	Command
CND	Campaign for Nuclear Disarmament
CNN	Cable News Network
CON	Conservative
CONVOTE	Conservative voting support in the current month
COPA	Committee of Professional Agricultural Organisations

COREPER	Committee of Permanent Representatives (Ambassadors)
CPRS	Central Policy Review Staff
CPS	Crown Prosecution Service
CRE	Commission for Racial Equality
CSA	Child Support Agency
CSC	Civil Service College
CSD	Civil Service Department
CWU	Communications Workers Union
DEA	Department of Economic Affairs
DES	Departments of Education and Science
DHA	District Health Authorities
DIS	Defence Intelligence Staff
DM	Deutschmark
DoE	Department of the Environment
DoT	Department of Transport
DSS	Department of Social Security
DTI	Department of Trade and Industry
EC	European Community
ECHR	European Convention on Human Rights and Fundamental Freedoms
ECJ	European Court of Justice
ECR	European Court Regulation
ECSC	European Coal and Steel Community
EDC	European Defence Community
EDP	Economic and Domestic Policy
EEC	European Economic Community
EGOs	Extra Government Organisations
EJ	European Justice
EMS	European Monetary System
EMU	European Monetary Union
EOC	Equal Opportunities Commission
EP	European Parliament
ERM	Exchange Rate Mechanism
ETUC	European Trade Union Confederation
EU	European Union
FCO	Foreign and Commonwealth Office
FHA	Food and Health Authority
FMI	Financial Management Initiative
G7	Group of 7
GATT	General Agreement on Trade and Tariffs
GCHQ	Government Communications Headquarters
GCSE	General Certificate of Secondary Education
GDP	Gross Domestic Product
GEC	General Electric Company
GLC	Greater London Council
GMB	General and Municipal
GMG	Glasgow Media Group
GNP	Gross National Product

GPMU	General Public and Municipal Workers
HMI	Her Majesty's Inspectorate
HMIC	Her Majesty's Inspectorate of Constabulary
HMSO	Her Majesty's Stationery Office
IBA	Independent Broadcasting Authority
ID	Identification
ID cards	Identity cards
ILEA	Inner London Education Authority
ILO	International Labour Organisation
IMF	International Monetary Fund
IRA	Irish Republican Army
ITC	Independent Television Commission
ITN	International Television Network
ITV	Independent Television
JIC	Joint Intelligence Committee
JP	Justice of the Peace
LAB	Labour
Lib Dem	Liberal Democrat
LTE	London Transport Executive
MAFF	Ministry of Agriculture and Fisheries
MEPs	Members of the European Parliament
MINIS	Management Information Systems for Ministers
MoD	Ministry of Defence
MPO	Management Personnel Office
MPs	Members of Parliament
MSFU	Managerial Scientific and Financial Union
MTV	Music Television
NASUWT	National Association of Schoolmasters Union of Women Teachers
NATO	The North Atlantic Treaty Organisation
NBPI	National Board for Prices and Incomes
NCIS	National Criminal Intelligence Service
NDPBs	Non-Department Public Bodies
NE	North East
NEB	National Enterprise Board
NEDC	National Economic Development Council
Neddy	National Economic Development Council
NFU	National Farmers Union
NHS	National Health Service
NRC	National Reporting Centre
NSPCC	National Society for Prevention for Cruelty to Children
NUM	National Union of Miners
NUS	National Union of Students
NUT	National Union of Teachers
NW	North West
ODM	Ministry of Overseas Development
OECD	Organisation for Economic Co-operation and Development
Ofgas	Office of Gas Supply

Oftel	Office of Telecommunications
OFWAT	Office of Water Regulation
OMCS	Office of the Minister for the Civil Service
OPEC	Organisation of Petroleum-Exporting Countries
OPS	Office of Public Service
OPSS	Office of Public Service and Science
PAC	Public Accounts Committee
PACE	Police and Criminal Evidence Act
PC	Plaid Cymru
PCA	Parliamentary Commissioner for Administration
PCA	Police Complaints Authority
PCB	Police Complaints Board
PESC	Public Expenditure Survey Committee
PFI	Private Finance Initiative
PLC	Public Limited Company
PM	Prime Minister
PPSs	Private Parliamentary Secretaries
PR	Proportional Representation
PRT	Petroleum Revenue Tax
PSBR	Public Sector Borrowing Requirement
QBD	Queen's Bench Division
QMV	Qualified Majority Voting
R & D	research and development
RAF	Royal Air Force
RFSR	Russian Federal Socialist Republic
RSG	Rate Support Grant
RSPB	Royal Society for the Protection of Birds
SDLP	Social Democratic and Labour Party
SDP	Social Democratic Party
SEA	Single European Act
SERPS	State Earnings Related Pension Scheme
SMSP	Single-Member Simple Plurality System
SNP	Scottish National Party
SOGAT	Society of Graphical and Allied Trades
STV	Scottish Television
STV	Single Transferable Vote
TECs	Training and Education Councils
TGWU	Transport and General Workers Union
TUC	Trades Union Congress
TV	Television
UDF	Ulster Defence Force
UHT	Ultra Heat Treated
UK	United Kingdom
UKREP	United Kingdom Representative
UN	United Nations
UNIEU	Union of Industries of the European Union
USA	United States of America

USDAW	Union of Shop, Distributive and Allied Workers
USSR	Union of Soviet Socialist Republics
UVF	Ulster Volunteer Force
VAT	Value Added Tax
WDM	World Development Movement
WEU	West European Union
WLR	Weekly Law Reports

PART I

Background

CHAPTER 1

Explaining British politics: **international, social, and historical contexts**

This chapter reviews key features of British politics. Some of these are shared with other democracies in Europe and overseas, while some are unique to Britain. They are all affected, however, by moves to European integration and globalisation. Current British politics are not simply an internal affair. Some of the most important influences are international ones, and these are imposing new strains on political parties and on territorial relationships with Ireland, Scotland and Wales.

Uniquely, British institutions and political practices were 'fixed' in the mid-nineteenth century and continue in many ways to operate as they did then. They coexist uneasily with a society in continual and rapid change under the impact of world developments. Are British institutions well adapted to respond to social demands? Or to handle the political and economic problems of the twenty-first century? How far will the Blair Government go in its attempts to reform Britain's political structure? Answering these questions helps us assess the quality of British democracy, a major aim of this book.

The specific features covered in this chapter are:

- Liberal democracy and the Westminster model of government
- The international context and its impact on promoting social change in postwar Britain
- Demands and constraints on British government
- The class/territorial division in Britain
- The British 'Establishment'
- 'Europe' and Britain
- Britain: decline or adaptation?

LIBERAL DEMOCRACY

Britain is a liberal-democratic state. Liberal democracy (see Briefing 1.1) means that institutions such as the civil service and army, which administer and defend the national territory, operate under the supervision of a regularly elected government

BRIEFINGS

1.1 LIBERAL DEMOCRACY

Liberal democracy exists in states that have regular elections for choosing the Government, in which all residents are entitled to vote, *and* which guarantee rights for individuals and groups which cannot be taken away. There have been liberal states that guaranteed legal rights without being full democracies (for example, Britain between 1832 and 1868). And there have been democracies that infringed group rights, although examples of these are harder to think of.

Elections are important for maximising the probability that the Government will act in accordance with majority wishes. This characteristic is important in defining a country as a democracy. However, most people would agree that minorities also need to be protected, even to be protected against the majority if the majority want to discriminate against them. It is important for minorities to be allowed to persuade others of the correctness of their view and perhaps become the majority later. This possibility has to be left open if democracy is to function properly, so the protection of minorities is as important in its way as majority rule. Liberalism has traditionally stressed individual rights (freedoms of speech, assembly, religion, movement). That is why democracies that incorporate such guarantees are called liberal democracies.

Key term

Liberal democracy – The form of government practised in the West which tries to combine representative institutions of government, such as regular and free elections, with liberal values about individual rights and responsibilities.

---

and parliament. These arrangements guarantee citizens certain rights and freedoms. Free elections to choose governments define Britain as a democracy, while the liberal element comes in the form of restrictions on the power of politicians and the state to interfere in the lives of private individuals and families.

Making comparisons

Key term

Government – a general term which refers either to the body which forms the political executive (as in 'the Labour government'), or the institutions of the state (as in 'the British system of government').

Britain is one of about 20 fully liberal democracies in Europe and about 40 elsewhere in the world. British institutions, such as Parliament and political parties, are broadly similar to those that operate in other democracies. This is particularly so where other countries are 'parliamentary democracies' like Britain and not 'presidential democracies' like the United States or Russia. In a 'parliamentary democracy' the members of the government are drawn from parliament, and the government itself depends on the support of parliament. This contrasts with the United States, where the head of government is separately elected and independent of the elected legislature.

Britain was the first parliamentary democracy in Europe. Many of the other European countries modelled their political institutions and ways of doing things on Britain when they too introduced responsible governments and elected parliaments. In the 1950s and 1960s the British system (known as the 'Westminster model', see Briefing 1.2) was exported to many of the colonies and territories of Britain's old Empire when these countries became independent. As a result many British procedures and practices exist in other liberal democracies too. Good examples are the way local government is organised, and some of the ways in which political parties operate.

However, some unique features of British politics were not copied elsewhere. A good example is Britain's unwritten constitution: there is no one basic document that specifies the relationships between Government, Parliament, the courts and the ordinary citizen.

BRIEFINGS

1.2 THE WESTMINSTER MODEL OF RESPONSIBLE PARTY GOVERNMENT

Britain is a 'representative democracy' because popular votes are usually cast for party candidates who advocate a policy programme, rather than for individual policies themselves (a practice termed 'direct democracy'). The party which gets a majority of candidates elected to the House of Commons then forms the Government, until the next election.

The 'Westminster Model', so-called after the area of London where the Houses of Parliament stand, is the term used to describe this form of representative democracy. Its most important feature is the fusion of legislative and executive power in the hands of the majority or largest party in the parliament.

The majority party leader becomes Prime Minister and nominates close party colleagues and supporters to form the Cabinet and Government. They make national policy and law which their majority in the House of Commons can be guaranteed to support, owing to the strict discipline which the party leadership in the Government enforces on the majority party. All members of the Government should support its policy (in public anyway). All MPs (Members of Parliament) of the ruling party vote for government policy. The opposition parties can only oppose, as the 'Westminster Model' denies them any direct power.

This system is supported by many commentators on the grounds that it makes for decisive, strong government and fixes responsibility for government actions on the party in power. The fact that one or other of the two main parties will form the next government gives voters a clear-cut choice between their policy programmes.

The 'Westminster Model' has been criticised, however, for making the ruling party *too* strong. It creates an 'elective dictatorship' of the majority party leadership, who can ignore all opposition and criticism, however justified, of what they propose to do. Moreover, the fact that an election may transfer total power in a matter of days from a party with one set of policies to another which opposes them (as with Conservatives and Labour in the 1997 general election) creates uncertainty and instability for business and for people in general, who have no secure guidelines on what the future will look like after a change of government.

Key term

Westminster Model – the form of liberal democracy which is modelled on the British government in Westminster – the part of London where the Houses of Parliament are located.

Plate 1.1 The Houses of Parliament, Westminster: the Seat of British Government. Built between 1840 and 1852 by Sir Charles Barry with designs by Augustus Pugin

When other countries made the transition to democracy, often after an internal revolution or defeat in war, they had to make a blueprint of the way their new democratic politics should operate. British institutions and practices evolved more gradually, so there was never a definite turning point at which people thought political practices should be written down in one document. (Chapter 7 discusses the constitution in more detail.)

This difference from most other democracies does not make Britain less democratic. Having regular elections and the opportunity to vote governments in or out is what counts. In many respects, however, it does make British politics different. For example, given the absence of a written document that specifies precisely what governments can and cannot do, it is more difficult in Britain to claim that a government has acted unconstitutionally.

Some groups, like 'Charter 88', a group of reforming lawyers and academics, claim that Britain needs a written constitution for precisely that reason. Most elected governments, on the other hand, feel that they exercise their powers in a reasonable way and that a written constitution would be unnecessarily restrictive and cumbersome.

We can see which side is right by looking at liberal democracies which do have written constitutions and seeing whether these documents are indeed important in safeguarding individuals and minorities, as Charter 88 would claim, or whether they are unnecessarily restrictive, as most British governments have claimed.

Comparisons with experience in other democracies help us to answer important questions about British politics on a factual basis, instead of just advancing our own opinions. Would a change in the methods of electing MPs lead to parties not having a majority in the House of Commons, and thus having to combine to form coalition governments? Would coalition governments be more representative than single-party ones or would they instead be weak and helpless? Again we can look at other countries such as Germany or Italy to see if such consequences necessarily follow when coalition governments emerge.

THE INTERNATIONAL CONTEXT

Making comparisons is useful because it highlights the ways in which British politics resemble those of other countries, and the ways in which they are unique. They also help us to put British politics in an international context. This is important because we cannot really understand British politics unless we take account of developments outside the country. It is easy to lose sight of this during political debates that focus on things British governments can do on their own, like regulating or deregulating industry or raising and lowering taxes. However, even these actions are often defended as improving British economic competitiveness in relation to other countries.

One only needs to think of the two world wars of the twentieth century, with their more than one and a half million British deaths, to appreciate the fact that politics in Britain cannot be isolated from what goes on elsewhere in the world. Britain's close involvement in the military alliance that dominates power relations between the world's major military powers (NATO – The North Atlantic Treaty Organization) makes this even truer, as does Britain's growing integration into the European Union of 15 states, including all of Britain's neighbours. Whether or not Britain goes on to form a federal union with the other European countries, or stands apart, the EU and its decisions will affect it ever more closely, often more so than decisions taken by British governments alone.

THE HISTORICAL CONTEXT

Attitudes to Europe, to British institutions, and to political processes, all emerge from history. This is even truer of Britain than of other liberal democracies. Britain was the first country in the world to base itself on a wholly industrial and commercial economy, to see the bulk of the population shift from the countryside into cities, and to evolve social and political institutions to deal with that situation. As a result the key British institutions – Parliament, political parties, the Cabinet, Civil Service, local government, trade unions, and financial institutions in the City of London – all took on their modern shape at that time.

Such institutions have adapted to some modern developments but remain basically unchanged. In the course of the twentieth century other European countries were taken over by dictatorships, or defeated in war and occupied. Only Britain, owing partly to its island position, managed to avoid this. Most continental European countries thus experienced a sharp break with their political past, which pushed them into changing and updating their political practices. Only Britain had no immediate need to do this.

As a result, extreme stability and continuity have marked British political institutions since the mid-nineteenth century. To take one example, two out of the three big political parties – the Conservatives and Liberal Democrats – date back to the 1870s in their modern form. The third, Labour, is only slightly younger, having been founded in 1900.

Such stability and continuity may be welcomed as evidence of the maturity and deep-rootedness of British democracy. Particularly during and after the Second World War, British institutions and traditions stood out like an island of stability and a beacon of hope in a shifting and chaotic world. At a time when Europe was divided and its democracies were threatened by Communist subversion within and Russian aggression without, Britain seemed admirably free from internal divisions and was perceived as democratic and strong. These characteristics made Britain the chief ally of the United States in the military and political confrontation with the Soviet Union known as the Cold War (1948–90).

The flipside of continuity and stability, however, was a reluctance to change so as to keep up with new developments, internationally and internally. The other European democracies stabilised themselves and replanned their institutions, recovered economically from the devastation of the Second World War, and spearheaded a move to European integration from which Britain initially stood aloof. West Germany gained a large share of world trade and challenged Britain for the position of leading ally of the United States. As the Cold War declined in intensity, world bases were abandoned and the Empire was given independence. Britain's position on the international scene became less and less important. In such a situation parliamentary debates over foreign policy, conducted in the grand style of earlier days, began to seem more like a charade designed to bolster pretensions than the world-shaking decisions of the old days.

Indeed, British world preoccupations began increasingly to look like excuses for not tackling basic problems nearer to hand, like Europe and its own social and economic problems. Such preoccupations stopped Britain from joining the European Community until 1973. At home they diverted attention from the ever-accelerating social changes which started with the creation of the welfare state in the late 1940s, and carried on with economic affluence and immigration in the 1950s, and growing social and economic difficulties thereafter. The inability or reluctance of the political institutions to deal with these changes form the stage on which recent British politics have been played out.

BRIEFINGS

1.3 THE WELFARE STATE

This is a generic term for the provision by the state of collective goods and services to its citizens: health, education, housing, income support and personal social services for children, the old, the sick, and the unemployed. The state uses public funds to provide a minimum standard of living, or safety net, for its citizens. There are many different forms of welfare intervention: some work primarily through cash benefits, others by providing services directly; some provide universal benefits, others selective benefits; some try to redistribute incomes and resources, others are more concerned with raising sufficient funds for basic services; some are highly developed, some are more minimal. The proportion of national wealth spent in Britain on the welfare state rose particularly rapidly from 1950 to 1980. The term 'welfare state' also refers very often to the array of institutions – hospitals, health trusts, insurance, employment and training agencies – set up to care for those in need.

Social change in postwar Britain

The postwar Labour governments (1945–51) consolidated all the existing schemes for health care and social protection into a unified body of legislation, along with institutions to implement it. Collectively these went under the name of the welfare state (see Briefing 1.3).

The basic aim was to ensure that all British residents could get support in all the major crises of life: poverty, sickness, old age and unemployment. State help was to be provided whether or not the recipients could pay. In this sense the welfare state was based on the notion of *universal* rather than *selective* benefits: *all* citizens, irrespective of their financial position, were to be provided with welfare state support. This basic support was supplemented by schemes to provide everyone with decent housing and education.

In themselves these welfare reforms would have produced major social changes. They allowed poorer groups – generally urban manual workers – to improve their basic standards of living and to get better jobs as a result of education. This contributed to breaking down class barriers and produced more geographical and social mobility (see Table 1.1).[1]

---

[1] The major 'class' division is between manual occupations often involving hard physical effort and nonmanual occupations which usually involve desk or computer work. Table 1.1, based on social surveys done in the 1970s, shows that 18.8 per cent of the population had fathers in manual work but are themselves in nonmanual jobs (or had husbands in nonmanual jobs). That is to say that almost a fifth of the old manual working class had 'risen' to the non-manual middle class. This is balanced by the 7.8 per cent who had fathers in nonmanual work but are themselves now in manual work (or have husbands who are). Even taking this into account, however, the general movement between generations in the middle of the postwar period is 'up', both in terms of the relative magnitude of these percentages and the fact that the working class was much larger than the nonmanual groups.

Table 1.1 Increasing social mobility in Britain in the 1970s

Father's Occupational class	Sons or Sons-in-law in Occupational Class		
	Nonmanual	**Manual**	**Total**
Nonmanual	16.8	7.8	24.6
Manual	18.8	56.6	75.4
Total	35.6	64.4	100%

Source: A.H. Halsey, *Trends in British Society Since 1900* (London: Macmillan), p. 146

Economic expansion and change also encouraged this, however. In the first half of the postwar period (1950–65) the traditional industries expanded and some prospered. New service sectors like tourism and personal finance developed. Many of the new jobs were nonmanual but attracted sons (and increasingly daughters) from the working class.

Unemployment was low, partly because governments made it a major priority to expand employment. The economy also grew every year and provided more jobs. This situation made it easy to absorb refugees from Eastern Europe after the end of the war. The prospect of a job attracted growing numbers of immigrants during the 1950s and 1960s, at first from Ireland, then from the colonies in the West Indies, and from the Indian sub-continent.

The arrival of these groups gave Britain for the first time a section of the population who obviously differed from the rest in terms of appearance and, in the case of Asians, in religion and many of their social customs too. Although restrictions on immigration were imposed from 1962 onwards, by the later 1990s around 3 per cent of the population were classified as Asian, just over 1 per cent as of Caribbean and African origin and 1 per cent (Southern) Irish.

This adds up to a total of just under 3 million people of foreign origin, out of a total British population of 58 million. This is not enormous, but of course the job seekers naturally concentrated in the more prosperous and populous areas, notably London, Birmingham and the northern textile towns (see Table 1.2). Their growing presence was sometimes followed by tensions with the native population, which from the 1960s erupted in sporadic rioting and sometimes encouraged racial appeals in elections.

It must be said, however, that Britain is not unique in this respect. On the whole, compared with some countries, restraint and goodwill on both sides have marked British race relations. This held true even when economic and social conditions deteriorated in the later 1970s and early 1980s. This downturn pressed more heavily on the Afro-Caribbean and Bangladeshi communities whose members were largely in manual jobs, than on the business and service-oriented Indians and Pakistanis, creating social and political divisions among immigrant groups themselves.

The presence of immigrants stresses the fact that Britain is a multiethnic society (see Figure 1.1). Awareness of this was heightened by the claims of territorial minorities inside Britain – the Scots, Welsh and (Catholic) Northern Irish – to recognition. The overwhelming majority (just over 83 per cent) of the British

Table 1.2 Percentage of
population who belong to
minority ethnic groups

Northern England	1
Yorkshire and Humberside	4
North-West England	4
East Midlands	5
West Midlands	8
East Anglia	2
Greater London	20
Rest of South-East England	3
South-West England	1
Wales	2
Scotland	1

Source: Central Statistical Office, *Social Trends 24* (1994) (London: HMSO, 1994) Table 1.9, p. 25.
Note: Minority ethnic groups include mainly West Indians, Guyanese, Indians, Pakistanis, Bangladeshis, Africans and Chinese.

population live in England. However, the Scots (just over 9 per cent or five million), the Welsh (nearly 5 per cent or two million) and Northern Irish (3 per cent) dominate their own areas of Britain. Each group has generated nationalist parties who seek greater political autonomy and, in some cases, total secession from the British state. Their claims have been fuelled by the fact that the peripheries have been much less prosperous than the London and South-East area over the postwar period. Hence, some sections of their populations feel they can do better on their own (see Chapter 6 for a detailed discussion).

Figure 1.1 Current ethnic
composition of the British
population

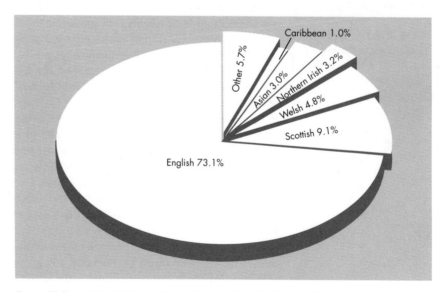

Source: H. Drost, *What's What in Europe* (London: Cassell, 1995), p. 275

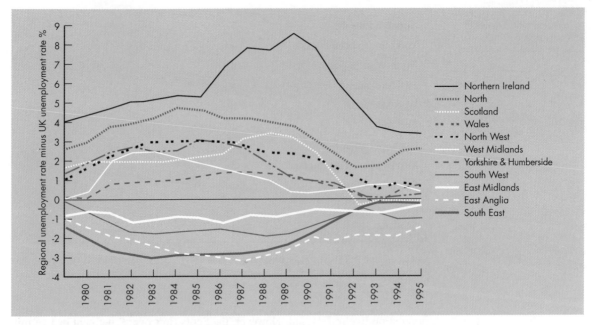

Figure 1.2 Regional unemployment compared wth the British average 1979–95
Source: Employment Gazette; Labour Market Trends, Table 2.3

Key term

New Right – the
politicians and theorists of
the 1980s who believed in
the efficacy of market
competition as the best
means of guaranteeing
political freedom and
economic growth.

There was a general economic downturn in Britain after the early 1970s. Just as prosperity had been unevenly shared among the various regions in the earlier postwar period, so the suffering fell unevenly, mostly on the peripheries – including the North and the Midlands of England – in the 1980s (see Figure 1.2).

The main reason was that traditional industries such as textiles, coal mining, steel and shipbuilding were heavily concentrated in the North and Wales and newer light industries such as car manufacture were concentrated in the English Midlands. By the 1980s these industries were facing huge pressure from competitors around the world, particularly East Asia. Thousands of jobs were lost as firms introduced cost-saving measures to improve their efficiency. Meanwhile, the Government, committed to 'New Right' economic policies (see Briefing 1.4), refused to intervene to try to save factories and mines from closing, believing that it was up to the management of the industries themselves to respond to the pressures of the market by becoming more efficient. As a result, unemployment reached 12 per cent in the mid-1980s and a comparable level in the mid-1990s, never declining after 1980 below 6 per cent of those looking for work. Figure 1.3 shows how the percentage of unemployed peaked in the early 1980s and 1990s. British unemployment rates have sometimes been higher and sometimes lower than the average for European Union (EU) countries. They have been lower than this average recently, particularly in the 1990s. In 1997 unemployment in all OECD countries was 7.7 per cent, in the EU it averaged 11.3 per cent and in the UK it was 7.4 per cent.

Economic change was not confined to the unemployed. Many men, for example, dropped out of the labour force altogether, taking early retirement on the basis of

Figure 1.3 Unemployment in Britain compared with other European and developed countries 1975–96

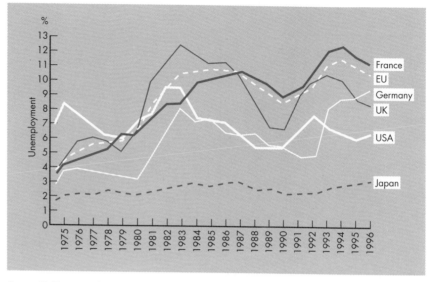

Source: P. Curwen (ed.), *Understanding the UK Economy* (London: Macmillan, 1997), p. 355

BRIEFINGS

1.4 THATCHERISM AND THE NEW RIGHT

'Thatcherism' is a term used to describe the attitudes and policies of the Conservative governments from 1979–90, when Margaret Thatcher was party leader and Prime Minister. These attitudes have been summed up in the words 'free market, strong state'. On the economic side, the object was to 'get the government out of business' and restore individual initiative. This was achieved by 'privatisation' (selling off) government enterprises like electricity, water, gas and public housing. Many regulations were abolished and serious attempts made to reduce the number of government employees (from 700,000 to 590,000 in the course of the 1980s).

Strong and authoritative state action was needed, however, to break trade union resistance to these changes or even to initiate them in the first place against internal Conservative party opposition, parts of the Civil Service, local governments and other groups. Mrs Thatcher and her supporters built up state power by, for example, strengthening police and security forces (see Chapter 21) and taking powers away from local government (see Chapter 18).

The emphasis of Thatcherism on freeing markets tied in with the thinking of 'neo-liberal' or 'New Right' economists, who saw the market as more efficient than the state (including the welfare state) at providing everyone with goods and services. Mrs Thatcher is therefore often described as a 'neoliberal' or 'New Right' politician. (For more on these ideas see Chapters 2 and 16.)

Figure 1.4 Women and the workforce

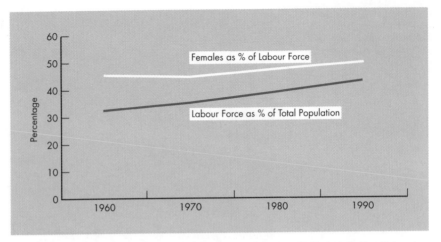

Source: J-E Lane, D. McKay and K. Newton, *Political Data Handbook* (Oxford: Oxford University Press, 2nd rev. edn 1997), pp. 36–7

their savings or pensions. Many more women took jobs outside the home, until the numbers of women working approached those of men. Women tended to be more flexible and to take the service and part-time jobs that now became available.

Unemployment and a changing pattern of family and life cycle employment created new demands on the welfare state at the same time as the Conservative Government wanted to cut social spending and strengthen citizens' self-reliance. As the eligibility criteria for unemployment and social benefits were tightened in order to reduce expenditure and cut taxation, disparities between rich and poor increased (see Table 1.3)[2].

Postwar Britain therefore remains a remarkably unequal society. In contrast to the immediate postwar period, however, the middle classes are much more numerous than in the past. A vote of 40 per cent is enough to give a national party a majority in Parliament and to sustain a government. Thus groups which benefit from the current distribution of income and wealth are numerous enough to vote a government in, regardless of the situation of the approximately 20 per cent living in poverty. These social developments partly account for the long tenure of Conservative Governments under Mrs Thatcher (1979–90) and John Major (1990–97) which were committed to tax cutting and reducing government spending on the social services.

---

[2] Table 1.3, based on what people leave when they die, shows the amount of wealth owned by the most wealthy 1 per cent, 5 per cent etc. of the population. The distribution is obviously not proportionate: the most wealthy owned 17 per cent of the marketable wealth in 1993, and the top 50 per cent a staggering 92 per cent. Only 8 per cent of national wealth therefore is owned by the bottom half of the population! Pension schemes, which give an entitlement to income when people retire, are also a form of wealth. The bottom table shows that entitlement under state pension schemes does reduce inequality in wealth, giving the bottom half 18 per cent of wealth in 1992 compared with only 8 per cent in the top table. However, the figures for different years show that their share has gone down slightly from 1976 (from 20 per cent to 18 per cent).

Table 1.3 The distribution of wealth in Britain

	Percentages				
	1976	1981	1986	1991	1993
Marketable wealth					
Percentage of wealth owned by:					
Most wealthy 1%	21	18	18	17	17
Most wealthy 5%	38	36	36	35	36
Most wealthy 10%	50	50	50	47	48
Most wealthy 25%	71	73	73	71	72
Most wealthy 50%	92	92	90	92	92
Total marketable wealth (£ billion)	280	565	955	1,171	1,809
Marketable wealth plus occupational and state pension rights					
Percentage of wealth owned by:					
Most wealthy 1%	13	11	10	10	10
Most wealthy 5%	26	24	24	23	23
Most wealthy 10%	36	34	35	33	33
Most wealthy 25%	57	56	58	57	56
Most wealthy 50%	80	79	82	83	82
Total marketable wealth (£ billion)	472	1,036	1,784	3,014	3,383

Source: Central Statistical Office *Social Trends 26* (London: HMSO, 1996) Table 5.21, p. 111

POLITICAL DEMANDS AND INSTITUTIONAL CONSTRAINTS

Some critics have argued that this situation does not seem very healthy or stable. If groups which are suffering deprivation, partly as a result of government policy, see no way of changing this through peaceful persuasion and elections, they are liable to react in ways which are undesirable for a democracy. Either they can back parties with more extreme demands – in the most extreme case revolutionary parties which threaten the electoral process itself – or they can threaten to secede from the United Kingdom if they live in a particular area like Ireland or Scotland.

Of course, the election of an alternative government can bring relief and hopes of reintegrating the marginal groups into society. This is why democracies, which offer such an escape mechanism through elections, are strong and stable. British institutions have shown they can produce the promise of change, with the landslide election of the new Labour Government in May 1997.

It remains to be seen, however, how far a Labour government will find itself boxed in by having to retain the support of previous Conservative voters who feel they have done well out of the social changes of the postwar decades and do not want them to be substantially reversed. Fears about losing new-won gains may account for the fact that the Conservatives have governed Britain for 35 of the last 50 years.

Not only electoral considerations but international and institutional constraints limit what a British government can do. The two come together in the financial institutions and markets of the City of London (see Briefing 1.5). As we shall see in the next chapter, Britain historically was more dependent than other countries

BRIEFINGS

1.5 THE CITY

This is a geographical area, referring to the old core of London within the medieval city wall, between the modern centre and the residential East End. Most of the head offices of the financial institutions of Britain, including the Stock Exchange and Bank of England, are physically located there. The term is used metaphorically to refer to British financial institutions in general.

These institutions dominate the British economy for two reasons. The first is that collectively they own most of the large businesses and firms through their shareholdings. Second, manufacturing industry borrows from them to finance production and expansion. Bank decisions about whether to make loans and how much to charge for them thus affect the activity of the whole economy. However, governments in turn can influence this by setting the general rate of interest for loans through the 'bank rate'.

The City is also one of the three or four leading financial centres of the world, for reasons we investigate in Chapter 2. Thus, its collective judgements about how well the British economy is performing, and whether to hold on to British currency, influence foreign investors as well. If the City's judgement is negative, money markets across the world will sell pounds for ever-decreasing amounts of foreign currency, thus effectively reducing the value of savings in Britain and of sales overseas.

on the goodwill of financial, rather than commercial, markets. The major British financial institutions, such as banks, trust funds and insurance companies conduct their worldwide business from the City of London. Much of their business consists in buying and selling shares in British and international companies and in lending governments money. The City is a major influence on what foreign lenders think about British prospects, as well as having a direct impact on them itself.

The major way in which its influence is felt is through the price it and other lenders charge the Government for loans, or whether the City is even prepared to lend money for the day-to-day operations of government in the first place! British governments habitually spend more than they take in revenue. Any improvement in educational or health standards costs money, which has to be borrowed. So it is clear that a Labour government is heavily dependent on the goodwill of the financial markets. A loss of goodwill can result in a reduction in the value of the British currency, through the loss of world financial confidence in it. This could plunge not only the British government but the whole of the economy into crisis.

In the past, City influence pressed particularly upon Labour governments because financiers naturally wanted their shares to become more valuable, and Labour governments were traditionally high spenders and taxers. Plans to take more money in taxes rather than letting it emerge in higher profits reduces the

Social Democratic – the ideology of that part of the political left which holds that political and social change can and should be achieved by means of peaceful reform rather than revolutionary violence.

value of shares. Since the mid-1990s, however, the Labour Party, along with other Social Democratic parties in Europe, has abandoned high tax, high spending policies in favour of fiscal rectitude (i.e. low taxation and restraints on public spending and inflation). This sea change in policy is likely to have important consequences for British politics and for the British economy.

THE CENTRAL CONFLICT IN BRITISH POLITICS: THE CLASS/TERRITORIAL DIVISION

The financial markets' desire for expenditure cuts, limited taxation and hence generally limited government tied in very well with Conservative policies of the 1979–97 period. Financial services directly or indirectly employ millions of the new middle class in South-East England. So the views of the financial markets and the new middle classes form one side of a political division which separates the Conservative and Labour parties. Labour's core support has traditionally come from groups which by and large have been disadvantaged by recent social changes: the unemployed, the shrinking numbers of manual workers represented by trade unions, immigrants and all those dependent on and working in old industries. Only when Labour adopts a more centrist position which broadens its appeal beyond its core supporters to the mass of middle-class voters can it win elections. This is precisely what happened in May 1997.

Because of the way industry developed in Britain these social divisions are also reflected in a territorial division of political opinion. The availability of water power and coal meant that the manufacturing industries of the Industrial Revolution – textiles, coal mining, steel and shipbuilding – were located in the 'Celtic Fringe' – Scotland, Northern Ireland and Wales – and in the north of England (see Briefing 1.6).

The large new nineteenth century cities – Glasgow, Manchester, Liverpool, Leeds, Cardiff, Belfast – developed in these regions, along with Birmingham in the Midlands. They housed the new industrial class of manual labourers and

BRIEFINGS

1.6 THE 'CELTIC FRINGE'

The term 'Celtic Fringe' was coined around 1900 to describe the northern and western peripheries of the British Isles (Scotland, Wales and Ireland) which voted Liberal, Labour or Nationalist rather than Conservative. However, the north of Ireland, which gave strong support to the Conservatives at that time, was not included. Almost a century later there is still a different voting pattern in the Celtic Fringe, although Labour has replaced the Liberals (or Liberal Democrats) as the leading party.

Map 1.1 The British Isles with regions

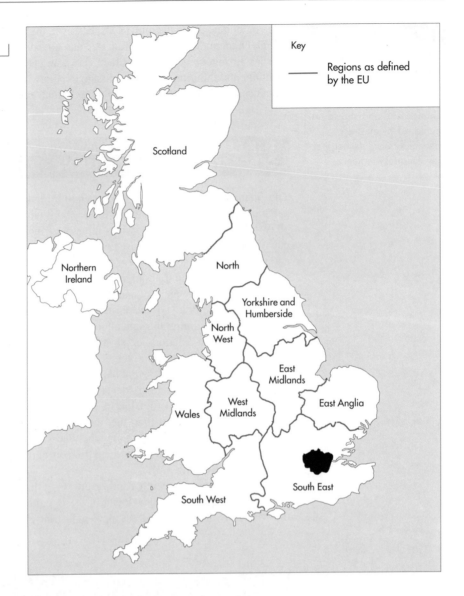

Key

—— Regions as defined by the EU

Scotland

Northern Ireland

North

Yorkshire and Humberside

North West

East Midlands

West Midlands

East Anglia

Wales

South East

South West

factory workers, often in appalling conditions. These cities and their inhabitants depended on manufacturing and extractive industries, unlike London which remained the seat of government, administration, commerce and finance. Although a large working class grew up in Central and East London, the capital and its surrounding area (the 'Home Counties') was the centre of an even larger and more prosperous middle class.

Class contrasts between manual and 'white-collar' workers were thus reinforced in Britain by a territorial division between the geographical areas in which each predominated. From this point of view the Labour (and Liberal) parties have often seemed more like coalitions of the British peripheries against London and South-East England, than class-based parties. This is particularly true now when, following the Labour victory in the 1997 election, 124 out of 165 Conservative MPs come from South-East England. Also significant is the fact that in 1997 not one Conservative MP was elected in Wales or Scotland.

Divisions between these two territorial class coalitions go beyond party politics. Financial interests trading worldwide from the City of London need above all a stable currency and low inflation to preserve the value of their cash and investments. This need has often conflicted with the requirement of manufacturing industry for devaluation of the currency to help their exports, and for mildly rising inflation to give people more money to buy their products. In turn this situation stimulates investment and employment (see Chapter 3 for a discussion of these ideas).

Government policy has usually favoured financial interests, since failure to consider these provokes an immediate financial crisis, with both national and international repercussions. Industrial consequences are long-term: over time the financial bias of government policy has speeded the decline of the old manufacturing industries. This was particularly marked in the early 1980s, when the Thatcher Government made money expensive to borrow and kept the exchange rate of the pound high in relation to other currencies. In turn this made British goods expensive to buy abroad and depressed exports, while firms found it difficult to borrow to tide themselves over at home. As a result many firms, predominantly located outside the South-East, went bankrupt or had to dismiss much of their workforce.

By the mid-1990s, the Labour Party had reconciled itself to the fact that, to achieve electoral success, it was obliged to follow a policy of fiscal and monetary responsibility. This meant keeping taxes low, attempting to balance the national budget and, above all, keeping strict controls on inflation. With the abolition of restrictions on the movement of capital across national borders during the 1980s and 1990s, governments in all countries felt pressure to control inflation and thus prevent a decline in the values of currencies. In this sense, the values represented by the City of London throughout the postwar period (low taxes, balanced budgets and low inflation) became the economic orthodoxy almost everywhere. As we shall see, this development has had the effect of putting strict limits on what governments of all political complexions can do in terms of public expenditure.

Key term

State – the set of public bodies and institutions within a given territory which exercise a monopoly of the legitimate use of physical force. In Britain the state consists mainly of Parliament, the military, the courts, the police, the Civil Service, and local government.

THE BRITISH STATE AND THE BRITISH 'ESTABLISHMENT'

The class/territorial division is at the heart of the Left–Right cleavage between the British parties, which we shall discuss in Chapter 16. Labour wants help for disadvantaged groups and regions, the Liberal Democrats desire their greater empowerment, while Conservatives want a strengthening of the existing order and of the disciplines underpinning it. As we have seen, important institutions like the City of London as well as many business people and business groups have historically sided with the Conservatives. Many analysts of British politics were thus led to conclude that leading British institutions, including state institutions like the Civil Service and the security services, were biased against the Left and

Key term

The Establishment – a vague term referring to the elite of public and private life which, some claim, run Britain irrespective of which party is in government.

would covertly do their best to thwart them when they were in power. Some variants of these 'conspiracy' theories saw the whole set of central institutions, including the Crown, judges and even the clergy of the Church of England, as lined up to thwart any left-wing threats to their privileges and position (see Briefing 1.7 on 'the Establishment').

This perspective was always too far-fetched. Bishops have figured among the major critics of recent Conservative policies on the grounds that they were hurting the weak. Civil servants and government departments rarely agree among themselves. If the Treasury favoured City financiers, the Department of Employment often supported trade unions.

Nevertheless the Treasury and the Home Office are the most powerful and central of the departments dealing with internal affairs. Spending departments, like Employment, Education, the Scottish and Welsh Offices, do not deal with core policies. The Treasury has close links with the City of London, and supports their preferences for tight expenditure controls and tax cutting, putting the maintenance of financial confidence at the top of its list of priorities. A certain structural bias is thus built into British central institutions, which favours the private versus the public, tax cutting against services, London and the Home Counties against the peripheries. However, low inflation and fiscal rectitude have become the orthodoxy for all political parties. Put another way, they determine the limits of what even the most radical governments can do in the taxing and spending domain. In areas largely independent of economic policy, and especially constitutional reform, major changes can still be achieved. But the acceptance of economic orthodoxy by all political parties has significantly changed the nature of British politics, as we shall see.

BRIEFINGS

1.7 THE 'ESTABLISHMENT'

This was a term coined in the 1960s to describe the British equivalent of the 'power elite' felt to exist in most countries, that is to say, powerful figures in business, the Civil Service and the armed forces who ran the country regardless of what party was elected to government. The term 'Establishment' was borrowed from ecclesiastical terminology where it referred to the bishops and higher clergy of the State Church (of England). They were felt to epitomise the fuddy-duddy and inert nature of the traditional British elite, deriving from exclusive private schools and Oxford and Cambridge Universities. Radicals in the 1960s depicted these people as powerful enough to thwart necessary change, and to contribute to the snobbery and hierarchical nature of British society. However, they were represented as not knowing how to use their power constructively as they were influenced by old-fashioned ideas of Empire and of British world dominance.

Ideas of this kind were quickly discredited when Mrs Thatcher came to power in 1979 and started ruthlessly to change British institutions and practices without effective resistance from anyone. Ironically, the Church of England 'Establishment' then emerged as among her most socially minded critics.

EUROPEAN INTERVENTION

How British institutions emerged in the form they have today will be examined in the next chapter. They were heavily shaped in the mid-nineteenth century by Britain's then position as the leading industrial country, dominant in world trade.

New international influences are emerging, however, which may redress the balance of the old. These stem in part from Britain's increasing integration into the European Union. By creating additional pressures from outside the existing set of British institutions, the European Union may give the Labour Government an opportunity to call on countervailing forces which would tip the balance towards its own preferred policies.

This opportunity exists because most other members of the EU have better social protection than Britain. Paying less for social benefits does, of course, enable firms to cut prices, particularly if there is no legislation enforcing a minimum wage (as was true in Britain until recently) or the minimum wage is set at a low level in comparison with other EU states. Other EU governments are therefore afraid that in the Single European Market, which they are creating, British firms will have a competitive advantage because of lower wage and welfare costs.

Precisely for this reason the Treaty of Maastricht, which envisaged an emerging federal union between member states, had a 'Social Chapter' binding all governments to give social rights to workers to ensure a 'level playing ground' for competition. However, the Conservative Government of John Major 'opted out' of the Social Chapter, the only one of the member governments to do so.

The Major Government also reserved its position on the question of whether to enter a currency union with the other member states. Such a union would have the advantage of creating a strong stable European currency that would command international confidence and avoid financial crises better than a purely British pound. But it would remove control of most financial policy from the British Government and Treasury and place it in the hands of a European Central Bank.

Large sections of the Conservative Party see this as an unacceptable surrender of British national sovereignty to the union. Hence it is very doubtful if any Conservative government would now agree to European Monetary Union (EMU). However, a large number of Conservatives do want to enter. In this they agree with most financial and industrial interests, who see British firms being excluded from a lucrative and expanding market if they stand aloof.

This situation provides an unprecedented opportunity for the Labour Government to pursue its policies with the consent of both industrial and financial interests. By accepting both EMU as well as the Social Chapter, Labour would advance its social policies without creating a crisis of confidence.

The price would be a diminution of British autonomy over monetary policy. No longer would British governments be able to 'fine-tune' the economy by adjusting interest rates to promote activity, or raise them independently of its European partners as a way of coping with inflation. At the moment the value of the pound changes roughly in line with the objective performance of the British economy and thus provides an automatic guide to the value of exported and imported goods. With monetary union, British goods would be valued in terms of a

European-wide currency, which might not be as sensitive to British conditions as the pound sterling is.

There is, however, a question of how valuable this autonomy has been. Governments have often disastrously misjudged the needs of the economy, lowering interest rates when inflation was going up, in the 1970s, or raising them in a way which crippled most of industry in the early 1980s. Similarly, British governments have often been forced into damaging devaluations, which have undermined confidence in the British economy. It is quite possible that a European Central Bank would do as well, or better, for British firms than British governments.

Moreover, the freedom to encourage economic activity by making money cheap has often been abused. Governments have created an economic boom before an election in order to make people feel good and collect votes, only to provoke a crisis immediately after the election. Indeed, in recognition of this fact, one of the first actions of the present Labour Government was to grant the Bank of England the power to set interest rates without direct government interference.

BRITAIN: DECLINE OR ADAPTATION?

Whether we think the European influence is a good or bad thing, British politics cannot be explained without taking it into account. This would be the case whether Britain was in or out of the EU. So closely are its economy and defence now bound up with Europe that they will be vitally affected by European Union decisions. That is not a choice. The only real question is whether the Government chooses to try to influence European policy from outside or inside. In the case of the Labour Government there seems much to be gained from going in and little from staying out.

The inability of Britain to go it alone, evident in the case of Europe and in Britain's relationships with the world superpower, the United States, seems a far cry from its position in the mid-nineteenth century when it was at the centre of a worldwide empire and an even more extended trading network. The contrast has prompted many critics to see postwar British politics as a series of unsuccessful attempts to cope with national decline.

'Decline' is an emotive word with all sorts of implications beyond the specific area to which it applies. It has undertones of moral and spiritual decay, which did indeed inform certain analyses of the British situation in the 1980s. A more neutral characterisation of British politics is that they have been concerned with adaptation to an unstable and shifting world environment, in which the British position has also changed quite radically.

Clearly, the British state is much less powerful militarily and economically at the end of the twentieth century than it was in the mid-nineteenth century (from 1850 to 1870). Then it was far and away the leading naval power in the world. This power enabled it to trade everywhere and to build up an empire which at its height covered a quarter of the land area of the world. At the same time Britain produced a half to one third of the goods used in world trade, and many sectors of British industry were the only ones which then existed, a fact that further consolidated its commercial predominance.

All this was due to the fact that the Industrial Revolution was carried through first in Britain, making British firms the undisputed leaders in a variety of manufactures ranging from textiles to steel. This unique situation could not last. Even to sell their goods abroad, British entrepreneurs had to invest in overseas infrastructures such as railways, which then provided the basis for other countries to industrialise too. Their doing so was a precondition for Britain to continue its industrial expansion, as purely agricultural societies could take only a limited supply of British exports.

These 20 years or so of unchallenged naval and commercial predominance in the mid-nineteenth century were important in many ways. The major British institutions took shape in this period, a fact which continues to affect modern-day politics. It would be unrealistic, however, to treat this period as the baseline against which current performance should be measured. Britain could never have continued to be the only technologically advanced nation in the world. When other nations caught up and then overtook Britain, however, diagnoses of national decline inevitably followed.

Clearly, Britain no longer enjoys the commercial and military pre-eminence that it did then. However, it has been on the winning side in the two world wars and in the Cold War, and it disengaged from its colonies relatively painlessly. The British were able to recognise the formidable power of local nationalism, and avoided becoming embroiled in the sort of long and corrosive wars fought by France and Portugal in the 1950s and 1960s. Britain has kept its options open in Europe up to the present time. All this looks less like decline than like an astute adaptation to a changing world situation.

Much of the debate on decline has, however, focused on the economy rather than directly on foreign affairs. Discussion has concentrated on the fact that the British share in world trade has consistently fallen over the last 150 years from one third in 1899, to one quarter in 1950, to around a twentieth today. The British economy has, at least until the 1990s, proved less dynamic than many others. Gross Domestic Product (GDP, the total value of goods and services produced in a country) has grown by only 2.4 per cent a year on average over the postwar period (see Table 1.4 and Figure 1.5).[3]

On the face of it, such steady growth might be taken as a considerable achievement. In the context of a developed economy it means that each year there are more resources to support desirable purposes, such as education, health and welfare, and to raise the living standards of the whole population.

What worries proponents of the decline thesis is that British economic growth has been slower, often markedly slower, than that of France and particularly Germany and Japan (Table 1.4). A special phrase, '*relative* economic decline', has been coined to record this fact, somewhat paradoxically as it in fact refers

---

[3] Figure 1.5 takes the GDP for 1990 as 100 per cent and then calculates GDP for other years as a percentage of this. So GDP for 1951 was only 35 per cent or just over a third of GDP in 1990. By 1997, estimated GDP had increased to about 110 per cent of GDP in 1990. Thus the graph shows quite dramatically how British economic resources have increased over the postwar period in absolute terms.

Table 1.4 Economic growth in leading industrial democracies 1962–97 (Average Annual Percentage Growth in GDP)

	1962–72	1977–88	1989–96	1997*
France	4.7	1.6	1.7	2.6
Germany	3.6	1.3	2.0	2.5
Italy	3.9	2.2	1.9	2.5
Britain	2.2	1.8	1.4	3.2
United States	3.0	2.3	2.3	2.2
Japan	9.2	3.9	2.5	2.3

* Partly projected

Source: First two columns Ian Budge, 'Relative Decline as a Political Issue' *Contemporary Record*, 7 (1993), pp.1-23; third column, *Keesing's Contemporary Archives*; fourth column, *The Economist*, May-June 1997

to the steady economic *growth* that Britain has enjoyed since the Second World War.

One might well ask, why should higher German, Japanese (and sometimes French and Italian) growth concern Britain? It does not affect the increasing resource base that British governments can tap into for worthy purposes like extending welfare, or reducing taxes. Nor are national economies directly in competition like individual firms, so that the more trade one country takes the less there is for others. National economies are conglomerations of very different enterprises, whose only common factor is that they are located in the same country. Some British firms do well in international competition, others lose out, but there is no Great Britain plc which competes as such on world markets.

The main reason why commentators have been concerned with the lower rate of British economic growth is that they see the economy as a basis for interna-

Figure 1.5 Growth of British gross domestic product over the postwar period 1951–94

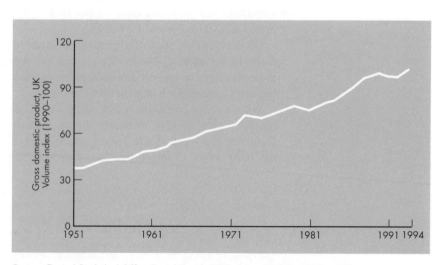

Source: Central Statistical Office *Social Trends 26* (London: HMSO, 1996), p.112

tional influence and power, rather than for internal well-being. If they were worried about having extra resources to redistribute internally, the steady and constant British economic expansion would provide them. Concern that the expansion is not as rapid as that of other countries really implies that it weakens Britain in dealing with other countries.

Whether this is really true is debatable. For a medium-sized country Britain has played a remarkably large part in world affairs, even during the 1980s and 1990s. Growing by one or two per cent more per annum would hardly have affected this. Moreover, since the early 1990s Britain's performance has improved. Indeed, as Chapter 3 will show, by the late 1990s the British economy was recognised as one of the most dynamic in the EU. Inside the EU, Britain's failure to acquire more influence is mostly due to its opposition to greater integration in Europe. This leaves it isolated from its partners and unable to exert much influence. Recent economic improvement has not changed the nature of this stand-off.

So-called 'relative economic decline' does not provide an illuminating focus on British politics. Where it has been important, however, is in providing politicians with an additional argument in favour of ideologically inspired projects which they wished to carry through anyway.

The most obvious example is the Thatcherite programme of the 1980s. Essentially this aimed at reducing the size and expenditures of government, particularly on welfare and other services, reducing taxes at the upper levels, and selling off government-owned industries and firms to private investors. This programme was part of the 'New Right' or 'new liberal' ideology to which Mrs Thatcher and her supporters subscribed. This gave individuals the maximum possible scope economically, by 'getting government out of business' and abolishing as many controls on economic activity as possible (including the costs incurred from welfare and taxes).

One of the major arguments used in support of these massive changes (which were accompanied by higher unemployment and increasing income and wealth inequality) was that they were necessary to avert Britain's 'relative economic decline'. Many people accepted the ensuing hardships for this reason. In the event, the comparative performance of the British economy hardly changed in the 1979 to 1991 period, and whether the improvement since then is attributable to 'Thatcherite' policies or to other factors is much debated. What does seem to be the case is that by the century's end the UK had made the long and difficult adjustment from Empire and world leader to that of a moderately successful but medium-sized economic and military power.

GEOGRAPHY: BETWEEN TWO CONTINENTS

If there has been a decline in British influence over the last 50 years it has had as much to do with government mistakes and political miscalculations as with economics. However, these do not simply result from stupidity or ideological rigidity. They also reflect structural factors springing out of Britain's geographical and cultural location.

Geographically Britain is an island group off the Northwestern shore of Europe. Its proximity to Europe means that it has always been involved in

European affairs. Its strategic location on the Atlantic means, however, that it was always in a position to expand westwards. British emigration and trade, therefore, have been predominantly overseas, away from Europe. They ended up creating new English-speaking countries in North America and Australasia, with which Britain has closer cultural links than with France and Germany, despite being geographically much closer to those countries.

Since 1960 British governments have therefore been pulled in two directions, often proving unable to make up their minds between them. The European Union, particularly under the influence of France, has wanted to create a strong European block of countries with external barriers against the rest of the world. Britain, with strong commercial and particularly financial links overseas, has wanted the EU to pursue relatively liberal, open trading policies. It has also wanted the EU to co-operate with the United States rather than rival it.

These conflicting pulls are behind British membership of the EU on the one hand, and its opposition to an exclusive, federal, largely autonomous and self-sufficient EU on the other. Britain would maximise its influence and prosperity by pressing ahead with integration into the EU, which increasingly seems likely to emerge as a world superpower. Yet this would weaken its overseas links, particularly with the United States, with which it shares a language and – to some extent – a culture. The choice is hard. As an American observer, Dean Acheson, acutely observed in the 1950s, 'Britain had lost an empire but not yet found a role'. It is still hesitating between two roles: that of world free trader, and that of good European. The victory of New Labour seems likely to tip it towards the latter, largely because of the social gains involved. If so, it will resolve the conflicting external pulls which Britain has felt for most of the postwar period.

SUMMARY

- Britain is a liberal democracy. As such it shares many political characteristics with other countries which are also liberal democracies, both in Europe and overseas. The most obvious are regular, free competitive elections, and parliaments and governments chosen by popular vote.

- However, Britain also has unique characteristics deriving from its own particular history and geography. Some of the most important of these are associated with the Industrial Revolution which was pioneered in Britain. As a result, Britain became the first European country to create institutions such as mass parties, a representative parliament, popular press, trade unions, international exchanges and markets.

- These still exist, largely in their original form. A central question of this book is how well such unchanging institutions serve the needs of a continually changing society, divided between different ethnic groups, classes and regions.

- A further question is how well they can cope with the international pressures which Britain, like all countries, continually faces. It has become hard to distinguish between purely national politics and foreign relations, particularly with the move to European integration. Britain now has to decide between committing itself fully to Europe or remaining in its present uneasy position between Europe and the rest of the world.

ESSAYS

1. What is the nature of the constraints that the financial markets impose on British politics? How have these changed over recent years?

2. What is meant by the British 'Establishment?' What role does it play in British politics?

3. What is meant by the class/territorial divide in Britain? How important is this divide in accounting for the distribution of wealth and income in Britain?

- The Labour Government, now committed to free market principles, is likely to decide in favour of Europe as a way of securing long-term economic growth while helping to protect citizens and consumers from some of the harsher aspects of the free market economy. In this way it may end the long series of hesitations and fudges which have contributed to the sense of economic and social crisis which has characterised British politics over the last 30 years.

- British politics need to be explained by a combination of national and international factors, set within a unique historical and geographical context. Historical influences are mainly channelled through the institutions which the country inherited from the mid-nineteenth century. Their importance is such that we need to start our detailed explanation by seeing how they originated and developed, and we do this in Chapter 2.

FURTHER READING

A provocative account of some of the general themes discussed in this chapter is Will Hutton, *The State We're In* (London: Jonathan Cape, 1995). Andrew Gamble, *The Free Economy and the Strong State* (London: Macmillan 1988) assessed the 1980s in Britain. On 'decline' versus 'adaptation' see Ian Budge, 'Relative Decline as a Political Issue', *Contemporary Record*, 7 (1993), pp. 1–23. For the British role in Europe and the world, see Ian Budge, Kenneth Newton et al., *The Politics of the New Europe* (London: Addison Wesley Longman, 1997), Chapters 1 and 2.

CHAPTER 2

'Fixing' institutions and relationships: the British world system 1850–1930

Britain's development into an industrialised and urbanised society was well advanced before any other country came near to making their own 'Great Transformation'. The fact that Britain was the first industrialised country had profound effects for the future development of society and politics. Internally, a series of reforms created or reshaped institutions to deal with the consequences of people massing together in towns and cities and these institutions – such as Parliament, the Civil Service, local government, courts and police – remained substantially unchanged until recently. Externally, Britain got locked into a pattern of relationships with the rest of the world which also persists, even though both Britain and the world have changed in the meantime.

Does this represent an admirable stability or British inability to cope with the modern world? Are we seeing incremental adaptation or national decline? These are questions already raised in Chapter 1, which will be considered throughout the book. We cannot finally answer them until we have looked in detail at how British politics and institutions function in practice. To understand them fully we also need to look at the critical formative period in which they emerged and see what influences shaped them. We do this in this chapter, before going on to postwar developments in Chapter 3.

This chapter covers:

- The 'great transformation' of British politics 1830–50

- The British world system 1850–90

- Internal change and reform 1840–1900

- Free markets and industry 1890–1939

- Protection against free trade 1890–1939

- Internal defence against the free market 1890–1939

THE 'GREAT TRANSFORMATION' 1830–50

Key term

The Glorious Revolution 1688 – established the King's dependence upon the support of parliament. It was thus a first step towards parliamentary and constitutional government.

The mid-nineteenth century was the critical period in which various developments came together to shape modern Britain. These developments, however, went even further back in time. The 'Glorious Revolution' of 1688 (see Briefing 2.1) had ensured that Parliament, representing country landowners and wealthy burgesses, had to be consulted in all important matters of state. In effect, the royal government depended on the support of both Parliament and the sovereign.

During the eighteenth century this led to an opening up of political life. Political opposition by the wealthy and privileged was no longer automatically equated with disloyalty. This allowed the commercial and industrial middle class, based in the growing towns and cities, a political opening when they agitated for full representation in Parliament. Movements for reform began in the eighteenth century but attained an irresistible force in the 1820s and the early 1830s. The expanding middle class wanted reforms to promote free trade and urban development, to which the dominant landowners were indifferent or hostile. These questions had become so central because of the quickening pace of industrialisation – the growth of manufacturing, factories and mechanisation. These trends had been slowly developing over a hundred years, but accelerated tremendously in the early nineteenth century (see Briefing 2.2).

The development of factory machinery powered by steam meant the concentration of manufacturing in towns, to maximise the advantages of transport and markets. The emergence of an industrial working class clustered around the factories expanded older towns tremendously and created new towns where previously there had been villages. By 1850 a quarter of the British population lived

BRIEFINGS

2.1 THE 'GLORIOUS REVOLUTION' OF 1688

The revolt of the Protestant nobility and gentry against the centralising, Catholic monarch James II in 1688 was the decisive act that set the shape of political events and constitutional relationships for the next century and a half. The English nobles invited the anti-French ruler of the Netherlands, William III, to take over the throne, provided he agreed to respect their position and give Parliament (which they controlled) a veto over money matters.

This led to British involvement in a series of wars with France which established their overseas dominance. Internally it meant that the King's government had also to be supported by a majority in Parliament, a first step towards constitutional government. The crucial second stage was that Parliament had to be genuinely elected; this was accomplished through the Great Reform Act of 1832 and subsequent reform acts.

BRIEFINGS

2.2 THE INDUSTRIAL REVOLUTION

During the eighteenth century, technology was increasingly applied to manufacturing processes, from cloth to iron, which had previously been carried out by hand in scattered artisan workshops. The most notable development was the use of mill machinery which utilised water and steam power to spin and weave cloth and to shape metal. As a result, a large number of unskilled workers could produce more, better quality goods at a lower price. The use of a single power source and of a large, concentrated labour force prompted the invention of the modern factory. When steam was substituted for water power, factories were grouped near to coalfields and close to each other. These groupings of factories and associated workers' housing produced industrial towns and cities, which developed an infrastructure of canals, roads, transport and services. By 1850 more than half the population of Britain lived in such settlements and Britain had become the first urbanised society. The factory owners, professionals and merchants who dominated the new cities formed a new political grouping which wanted a share in political power, and eventually the organised working class also wanted representation to improve their conditions. Thus the economic changes associated with the Industrial Revolution destabilised the old political order in which landed aristocrats and gentry dominated Parliament.

in cities of over 100,000 and more than a half in conglomerations which could be described as urban.

However, most of these areas had no political authority to police, regulate or represent them. Even where an old borough council existed it was either indifferent to new urban problems or incapable of tackling them. The new middle class which lived in the urban areas felt personally threatened by disorder and disease, and wanted in any case to have a healthier and more disciplined workforce in the factories.

Political reform was not a simple matter, however. Votes were regarded as property, even when this led to such bizarre consequences as a landowner simply nominating two MPs to represent a defunct borough that was now his estate. Even where a borough was not extinct, the unelected council's most important function was often to nominate MPs. In return for support of the Government, many MPs and councillors received money and favours. Thus the reform of local councils involved much else. It was an attack on property rights, as councillors had often bought their seat on the council and MPs had bought their seat in Parliament. This system was justified as ensuring that nobody without a substantial stake in the country occupied positions of authority.

The reform of local councils therefore meant the reform of parliamentary elections and thus changing Parliament itself. The new middle class was quite prepared to accept this as it wanted other policy changes which only Parliament could legislate, for example, a more economical way of providing welfare and an end to taxes on imports, notably of food.

Middle class agitation produced the 'Great Reform Act' of 1832 (see Briefing 2.3) and the repeal of the Corn Laws in 1846. The repeal of the Corn Laws reflected the shift in political power produced by the Reform Act, as MPs responded to the concerns of their urban electors.

The 'Great Reform Act' of 1832 was in fact a very limited measure, abolishing some of the worst 'rotten' and 'pocket' boroughs, transferring their seats to new cities, and creating uniform qualifications for voters based on possession of property. In effect it extended voting rights to the wealthy and the upper-middle class. Parliamentary reform was followed by municipal reform which set up new councils in urban areas which were able, where they wished, to tackle local health and

BRIEFINGS

2.3 THE REFORM ACTS 1832–1928

The 'Great' (First) Reform Act of 1832 was passed by the unreformed Parliament under pressure from the politically mobilised middle class (industrialists, merchants, and their supporters and dependants). It was a limited measure, abolishing most 'rotten boroughs' (constituencies with very few electors) and 'pocket boroughs' (constituencies controlled by one big landowner), where MPs could buy their seat from electors or obtain it from a landed proprietor. These seats were redistributed to counties or to the large new industrial towns. Inside the redrawn constituencies the vote was given to property holders, resulting in limited numbers of electors in each constituency.

The Great Reform Act was not a very radical measure, but it did show that the electoral system could be changed peacefully in favour of previously excluded groups. Further agitation later in the century brought about:

- the Second Reform Act (1867) which gave the vote to the wealthier workmen in towns;

- the Third Reform Act (1884) which extended the franchise in towns and gave it to agricultural labourers;

- the extension of the vote to about a third of adult males who were still excluded, along with women over 30, in 1919;

- finally, in 1928, the granting of the vote to women on the same terms as men.

These changes were accompanied by reforms of the constituency system which ensured that constituencies were relatively equal in size, thus weighting votes more equally. It was typical of the cautious and incremental nature of political change in Britain, however, that all the reforms left intact the 'first past the post system', in which the individual candidates compete in small constituencies and the one with the most votes wins, whether or not he or she gets a majority.

crime. The New Poor Law created uniform, minimal and often harsh facilities for those in desperate need.

The new middle classes followed up these successes by abolishing all protective taxes on imports, notably of food (the Repeal of the Corn Laws, 1846). The reason they wanted this was logical and simple. British industry was incomparably bigger and more efficient than that in other countries and therefore had nothing to fear from competition or imports. What manufacturers did want, however, was cheap food for their workforce, so that wages and prices could be kept down. Protective tariffs on imports of food left food prices high, to the benefit of British farmers and country dwellers in general. The abolition of tariffs on wheat signalled the end of all such protective measures, marking the dominance of urban interests over rural and of the new middle class (the 'bourgeoisie') over the landed gentry.

The abolition of protective tariffs produced the 'Great Transformation' of British society and of Britain's place in the world. For the first time a country took the gamble of making itself dependent on foreign imports for its basic survival. By the beginning of the twentieth century half of what the British ate was imported, much of it from the Americas and Australasia. This meant in turn that Britain had to export to survive. (It also rendered it particularly vulnerable in the First and Second World Wars to submarine attacks, which sank the ships carrying food.)

This military consequence was not foreseen by agitators like John Bright and Richard Cobden who attacked protection. They were, however, quite prepared to gamble on manufactured exports paying for food imports. Given British industrial supremacy this seemed a safe bet. In support of Corn Law Repeal they developed a series of interlocking arguments for free trade, that is, the abolition of all protective tariffs on a worldwide basis (see Briefing 2.4).

The free trade advocates believed that without 'artificial' tariffs the pressure of competition would force each area of the world to concentrate on what it produced most efficiently. Efficiency might be linked to natural advantages such as the presence of minerals or a beneficent climate. It was marked in practice by the ability to produce and market the good at a lower price than elsewhere in the world, provided political barriers like tariffs did not distort market judgements. Hence the importance of eliminating them.

In this way universal free markets would stimulate the production of goods, and distribute them at the lowest possible prices, thereby maximising human well-being. They also reduced the possibility of war, whose prime cause was thought to be poverty or covetousness. Now the populations of all countries would enjoy all the benefits which were humanly attainable, or so the argument went.

The free traders argued that Britain was uniquely placed to ensure the spread of open markets, in three ways. First, it could set a potent example as the dominant trading nation. Second, it could enforce free trade throughout its extensive colonial empire and even force other less developed countries, like China and Latin America, to open up their markets. Third, its unchallengeable navy could police markets and trade routes to ensure that free trade was not threatened by selfish practices on the part of other countries.

Key term

Free trade – the idea that international trade should not be restricted by protection in the form of tariffs, custom duties, or import quotas which are designed to protect the domestic economy from foreign competition.

Key term

Liberalism – with a small 'l', liberalism is the political belief that individual rights should be protected by strictly limiting the powers of government.

Key term

Liberalism – Liberalism (with a capital 'L') refers to the beliefs and policies of the Liberal Party.

Key term

Neo-liberalism – the ideas associated with the New Right of the 1980s that market competition is the best means of guaranteeing political freedom and economic growth.

BRIEFINGS

2.4 FREE TRADE, FREE MARKETS, PROTECTIONISM AND CLASSICAL (NEO) LIBERALISM

Classical economics (the ideas of Adam Smith, David Ricardo and Jeremy Bentham) concluded that trade and well-being would be maximised in a market of independent producers who could trade freely with each other. Although they put many practical qualifications on this argument, politicians like Richard Cobden and John Bright adopted it enthusiastically on behalf of the new middle class. They believed that once free trade was extended, both nationally and internationally, it would eliminate the causes of war, since everybody would receive the maximum benefits possible from the operation of the market, and this would remove the causes of conflict between nations.

Although this summary of the argument may seem a little naive, belief in free markets and free trade has gained new force in recent years from adherents such as Margaret Thatcher and Leon Brittan (a Conservative MP who held various ministerial posts from 1979 to 1986 and is now responsible for competition policy in the European Commission). Many countries have accordingly tried to sweep away their own barriers to trade and continue to eliminate them internationally through the General Agreement on Trade and Tariffs (GATT).

In the nineteenth century the new free trade ideas seemed to provide an answer to most modern dilemmas and were taken up enthusiastically by reformers and liberals everywhere, hence their label of classical or neo-liberalism. The antithesis of free trade was protection, where special taxes or tariffs were applied to goods to keep another country's products out. The classic example of this were the Corn Laws in Britain, which excluded cheaper foreign grain in the interests of British farmers and were abolished in 1846.

THE BRITISH WORLD SYSTEM 1850–90

Free trade, free markets and free competition constitute a set of ideas to which British politicians and parties have been strongly attached ever since the 1850s. Concrete examples of their continuing influence today are British entry into the European Union (conceived as an extended 'Common Market'), support for the Single European Act of 1986 and enthusiasm for opening up world trade in the GATT negotiations of 1993. World trading conditions and British economic competitiveness have changed enormously since the mid-nineteenth century. Regardless of such changes, British policy makers have opened up the country to foreign trade, and done their best to abolish protection internationally, apart from a brief period during the economic recession of the 1930s.

The explanation for this steadfast adherence to free trade and economic liberalism is not simply historical and cultural but is also institutional and structural. In the period of its industrial and commercial supremacy Britain created institutions such as the financial markets in the 'City', and made enormous overseas investments which depended on world free trade and the unhampered flow of money.

These developments followed naturally from Britain's overwhelming dominance in the world economy from 1850 to 1870. With industrial products which nobody else was producing, and which could not all be absorbed by the domestic market, manufacturers depended on overseas outlets. But clearly something needed to be traded for manufactured goods. Other countries could go into debt, of course, and many did, contributing to a massive growth of British assets overseas. Ultimately, however, they needed to balance their imports with exports.

The abolition of protection in Britain, under the influence of free trade ideas, helped solve the problem. Increasingly, Britain imported food and raw materials for industry (such as raw cotton, timber, and mineral ores). The most plentiful supplies of these were in the less developed world, notably North and especially South America, and Australasia.

As a result, British trade turned increasingly towards these areas. In line with free trade ideas about each country doing what it did best, Britain manufactured, while overseas trading partners raised animals and crops, or dug and quarried, exploiting the extensive natural resources which they had and Britain did not.

There was a snag, however. Often the natural resources were inaccessible, or under the control of hostile governments or indigenous peoples who had no desire to trade. To deal with the latter Britain rapidly expanded its direct control of likely territories, converting them into 'colonies'. It used its Navy to protect trade routes and the Army to destroy indigenous opposition.

In other cases it supported like-minded governments who could subdue the indigenous inhabitants. In terms of transport, British banks could supply capital for building railways for the transport of settlers and crops. These were usually built by British-owned companies, which used British iron for the rails, imported locomotives and rolling stock from Britain and employed British personnel, thus creating another British asset overseas.

British banks and financial institutions thus traded and invested on a world scale long before any other country did. They were driven on by the logic of an expanding economy which demanded outlets overseas and gave them immense resources for investment. The profits generated internally by British industry were such that industrial expansion up to the late nineteenth century was self-financed from profits and sales of shares rather than by direct borrowing from banks. Hence, to use their deposits profitably, financial institutions increasingly found it expedient to invest overseas.

Free trade ideas fitted these arrangements very well, justifying the world movement of capital and payment of interest back to Britain. They underpinned a situation in which investment in British industry was simply one of a number of alternative options for banks and finance houses, to be weighed against US railways, Chinese textile factories or Argentinean cattle ranches. The City naturally chose the one whose return was higher, claiming that it would be failing in its duty to maximise returns to shareholders if it did otherwise. These attitudes are still prevalent today.

Britain was able to accept universal free trade in the nineteenth century because its industry and commerce could take on the world. This was an attitude typical of the first industrialised country but which was obviously much harder for later ones to accept. Primary producers overseas of food and raw materials could accept it for a while. They had products to export which Britain wanted, and by accepting the role of British suppliers they could attract investment and build up their economic infrastructure of roads, railways, houses, and supporting facilities.

However, other European countries had interests which directly conflicted with those of Britain. Military monarchies, like Germany and Russia, wanted to build up an industrial base in order to service their armies. It was intolerable to them that the steel they needed to make guns should not be under their control; nor that the railways needed for rapid mobilisation should be maintained and run by foreign contractors. Quite apart from their military concerns, these countries also wanted to develop an industrial base for tax and revenue. By becoming richer they were able to afford bigger and better equipped armies, which they could then use to build up their power or to defend themselves from their neighbours.

Most European countries, therefore, had strong incentives to develop their own industry. In order to do this they had to subsidise and protect them from British competition, which would (initially at any rate) have driven their products from the market. These governments, therefore, embarked on a series of measures collectively known as 'protectionism', which went directly counter to all the doctrines of free trade. Banks were directed to support national industries and close links were created between them and firms, to the extent that they even nominated their own senior staff to the firms' boards of directors. Taxes were imposed on imports, above all on British goods, to ensure that their price was higher than that of the national product. Instead of allowing market demand to determine which products would be supplied, governments indicated which industrial sectors were to be developed and in which competition could be allowed.

Germany was the major exponent of protectionism in the late nineteenth century, but all the developed countries apart from Britain followed suit. The United States adopted a halfway policy. It protected products like steel, where it wanted to build up its own industry, but it welcomed British investment in railways and transport, and was happy to supply primary products, like raw cotton or tobacco from the South, where there was a British demand.

Thus, the free trade system – with London at its centre – which Britain managed to impose on most of the world in the second half of the nineteenth century, had its exceptions and dissenters. For a time, however, these were not too important in the British scheme of things. Free trade as we have described it operated without much impediment until the 1890s, and survived, although with increasing difficulty, until the great world recession of the 1930s. Meanwhile free trade ideas and their supporters generated internal developments, to which we turn in the next section.

INTERNAL CHANGE AND REFORM 1840–1900

The reform of Parliament and the municipalities, creation of the New Poor Law (see Briefing 2.5) and abolition of protective tariffs clearly demonstrated the dominance of the industrial, commercial and professional classes over the old landed

BRIEFINGS

2.5 THE NEW POOR LAW AND THE NINETEENTH CENTURY WELFARE SYSTEM

The New Poor Law, passed in 1834, was a measure to deal with the poor, and those unable to support themselves, in an efficient and economical way. The major innovation was the setting up of 'workhouses' in each district of the country, into which those who wanted 'relief' had to go. The conditions under which they lived were severe and authoritarian and often harsh. Men were kept separate from women and children, but all had to work as ordered. The level of support was supposed to be kept below the minimal level obtainable by working in the lowest paid employment, in order to keep as many in gainful employment as possible.

The workhouse took not only the unemployed but the mentally deficient, sick and dying: it was the universal last resort of the neighbourhood. It was administered by boards elected by the local taxpayers, who had an interest in keeping expenses low. The system of election did provide a basis, however, for later elected local government. Gradually the system was modified along more humane lines. Clearly, however, its harshness and limitations gave the working class and poor good reason to organise politically in order to obtain better treatment from the state.

The New Poor Law regarded unemployment and disability as the moral fault of individuals, who had failed to make proper provision for themselves, and not as a collective problem beyond the scope of any one person, for which humane communal help should be given. Nevertheless, workhouses remained an important part of the welfare system up to the creation of the welfare state after the Second World War.

aristocracy (see Briefing 2.6). In the middle years of the nineteenth century this dominance was reinforced through the reform or foundation of a whole series of cultural, economic and political institutions which reflected the values of the Victorian middle classes and catered to their interests.

> **Key term**
>
> **Franchise** – in its political sense, the right to vote.

These ranged from the reform of the armed forces and Civil Service, which began to recruit on the basis of open competition and merit rather than the ability to buy a position, to the creation of schools, institutes and later universities in the industrial provinces which trained the children of the new middle classes and 'respectable' skilled working class for positions in trade, business and the professions. The social and geographical extension of the franchise led to the election of many more businessmen and professionals to the House of Commons. The reform of the Stock Exchange and commodity exchanges expanded trade and finance, to the benefit of the commercial middle class. The emergence of a national, mass circulation press and book publishing industry disseminated middle-class values more widely in a society with rapidly improving literacy rates.

BRIEFINGS

2.6 CLASS AND ITS IMPORTANCE IN BRITAIN

Britain is often regarded as a particularly class-conscious society. This is partly because social, and particularly geographical, mobility has been less than in comparable industrialised societies. Britain has not experienced the sweeping social and political changes brought about by revolution and war in most other European countries, nor the mass immigration which opened channels of mobility in the United States. Thus the class divisions fixed by the Industrial Revolution still remain, although very much modified by economic and industrial changes after the 1950s.

The strength of class in Britain lies in the fact that it is reinforced by a whole series of social characteristics and life opportunities. In the industrial cities of the nineteenth century there was a clear demarcation between the areas and type of housing occupied by industrial workers and those of both the lower-middle and upper-middle class. Each had its own type of school, club, church; each had its own social habits and lifestyle. Manual workers left school at the minimum age, went straight into work, spoke with a particular accent and even looked different from the prosperous middle class. They would travel little, marry and die young, earn minimal wages, be subject to unemployment, and probably live in the industrial cities of Britain.

Of course, there were many exceptions to this pattern and many variations within the working and middle classes. But large blocks of the population were marked out by these cumulative differences. The working class relied on collective action to improve their situation while the middle class were more disposed to adopt individualistic solutions, which their better resources and education made possible. A corollary of this was that the working class increasingly supported Labour, with its message that state intervention could help them, while the 'solid' middle class became increasingly Conservative from the 1880s onwards. Social differences were thus reinforced by political ones.

In the discussion here we shall concentrate on the more directly political institutions. But Table 2.1 lists and briefly describes the whole range of institutions founded or reformed in the nineteenth century, with a note on the interconnections between them. You will find that most of them are quite familiar because they all exist and function in broadly the same way today. As we noted in the last chapter, an important explanation for the present-day form of British politics is that the institutions which shape it are essentially inherited from the mid-nineteenth century and, until recently, have remained largely unchanged. This may testify to their usefulness and adaptability, or to the inability of the British to get away from their past. We shall have a clearer idea of this after we have examined that past in detail.

Table 2.1 Major nineteenth century institutions still functioning today

Name	Area of life	Prominent examples	Period of reform, modernisation and reinvention	Salient features	Purpose	Links with other institutions
Reformed public schools (actually very exclusive private schools)	Educational and cultural	Eton, Rugby, Harrow	1830–60	All-male schools, mainly with a classical and arts bias	Mould pupils for leadership roles, particularly as administrators	Ex-pupils dominate political parties, Parliament, Civil Service, finance, Army, law and Church
State secondary schools	Educational, vocational	Town grammar schools, technical colleges	1850–90	Usually male with relatively specialised curriculum	Give broad foundation for local business and professions	Ex-pupils go into industry, local business, lower reaches of professions
Ancient universities	Educational, cultural	Oxford, Cambridge	1870s	Advanced classical and arts-based education but also house important specialised institutes particularly in pure science	Give public school pupils broader contacts and assimilate best pupils from state schools	Graduates dominate political parties, Parliament, Civil Service, law and Church
Provincial universities	Educational, vocational	Manchester, Birmingham	1880–1980	Relatively vocational and professional curriculum	Technical and applied training for professions	Some graduates get to higher levels. Most supply middle and lower ranks of professions and activists for Liberal and Labour parties
Stock exchanges	Financial, economic	London Stock Exchange	1800 onwards	Market in ownership of firms	Allow company shares to be bought and sold without involving purchasers in management	Close links with banks, insurance companies, and other financial institutions with money to invest, many MPs
Commodity exchanges	Commercial	Baltic exchange, London metal market	1850 onwards	Britain is main importer of much food and raw material so exchanges set world price	Give stability to buying and selling raw products and helps spread risk, aids British dominance of market	Banks specialising in overseas investment, many MPs

Army	Political, military	Infantry regiments	1870s	Professional force organised in regiments	Fights limited wars and garrisons foreign stations	Officers come mainly from public schools
Navy	Political, military	Reorganised to cope with metal steamships from 1870s	1870s	Increasingly professional and technical, organised in major fleets	Safeguards British sea-routes	Officers come mainly from public schools
Police	Political, social	Metropolitan Police (London)	1840–60	Controlled locally but all forces have the same hierarchical organisation	Ensure social order and stability	Officers come mainly from state schools
Town councils	Political	Birmingham, Glasgow	1840–60	Relatively non-partisan organisation of services by elected local representatives	Ensure efficient physical management of designated areas	Local industry, business, and schools
Civil Service	Political	Home Office, Foreign Office	1873	Nonpartisan hierarchical organisation divided into functionally differentiated ministries	Ensures legislation and government policies are carried out	Upper levels dominated by Oxbridge graduates
Parliament	Political	House of Commons	1868–80	Strict government control of proceedings, use of select committees for investigation	Forum for political confrontation of two major parties, and recruiting ground for government	Majority of MPs from public schools and involved in business and finance
Political parties	Political	Conservative, Liberal, Labour	1870–1906	Tie together local organisations, linking the country to leadership in Parliament	To put or keep party leadership in government by increasing the party vote in elections	Conservatives with business, Labour with trade unions
Trade unions	Economic, political	Teachers, miners	1890s	Hierarchical organisations, each covering a wide variety of industries and firms	Improve workers' conditions by industrial and political action	Labour Party after 1906
Mass press	Social, political	Daily Mail	1890s	Privately owned, mass circulation all over country	Sell papers and influence voters	Mainly with Conservative Party

The institutions listed in Table 2.1 are only a selection of those founded or re-founded by the Victorians. Among those not listed are banks and insurance companies, prisons, hospitals, museums, cultural and scientific institutes, art galleries, charities, pressure groups, professional associations and many more. The list is almost endless and covers almost all aspects of our lives, even now. Such institutions operate in other parts of the world too of course; Britain is not unique in having them. What does characterise British institutions, however, is that in many cases they were first invented here and have changed less than in other countries in response to modern pressures.

This is clear above all in the case of Parliament. The political struggles of the nineteenth century between reformers and the old landed interest led politicians to group themselves in two major parties: Liberals (reformers) and Conservatives (defenders of established interests). By the 1870s both had organised themselves on a country-wide basis and were imposing party discipline on their members.

This meant that the House of Commons, the popularly elected chamber, was regarded as a national forum for the confrontation of two great political parties. All its procedures were arranged so as to focus and enhance this confrontation, from the physical arrangements of the debating chamber which forced MPs of different parties to confront each other and choose sides, rather than mingle, to the procedures for debates and committees which also allowed Government and Opposition to confront each other.

The state of the parties from 1868 to 1878, in the first really reformed Parliaments, was thus built into the arrangements still prevailing in the 1990s. When Labour came to the fore in the 1920s it simply squeezed out the Liberals as a serious competitor for government power.

These consequences of Britain's parliamentary institutions were reinforced by the single member constituency system which Britain has inherited for electing MPs (Chapter 15). MPs can be elected if they receive more votes than any of their competitors. This gives an advantage to large parties with strong regional support rather than to a small party with a wide national appeal, and is why today governments are formed by either the Labour or Conservative parties rather than the Liberal Democrats.

Another Victorian institution which was to have a strong, if diffuse, influence over national life was the 'public school' (in fact, a particularly exclusive private school open only to the wealthy). Such schools had developed in the eighteenth century to educate aristocrats. From the 1830s onwards they were reformed and opened to the wealthy middle classes. Their aim was redefined as producing Christian gentlemen with a strong moral sense and commitment to public duty. This was to be achieved through the study of Latin and Greek, with literature and history thrown in, and an emphasis on competitive sport.

A by-product of this was the fusion of aristocracy, gentry and upper-middle class in a single upper class marked out by accent, background and lifestyle. The contacts made at public school rendered entry to politics and business easier and helped secure advancement. To an extraordinary degree, therefore, most institutions founded in Victorian times were – and still are – dominated by graduates of public schools and of the exclusive universities, Oxford and Cambridge.

Plate 2.1 The House of Commons. The Conservative and Labour Parliamentary parties face each other on confrontational lines in the debating chamber during Prime Minister's Question Time

This makes contacts between the people at the top easier, as they share a common background. Links are reinforced by the fact that many MPs, particularly in the Conservative Party, came from and continue in business after they are elected. The Victorians approved of MPs having personal wealth, because it made them independent, and of MPs engaging in activities outside Parliament, because it kept them in touch with the broader society. Although MPs were paid from 1911 onwards (a reform which opened the way for those without inherited wealth or high incomes to serve in Parliament) the practice remains of taking directorships, consultancies and other jobs to supplement this. The fact that business links increasingly involve the financial corporations of the City of London reinforces the latter's influence over political decisions. This is something already commented on in Chapter 1.

Looking over the array of institutions listed in Table 2.1, a distinction emerges between institutions important at the national level – Parliament, political parties, the Civil Service, the armed forces, London-based finance – and those serving the localities, such as town councils, the police and trade unions. The former deal with 'high politics' – diplomacy, legislation, finance – the latter with 'low politics', that is, public health, welfare, crime. 'High politics' tend to be conducted by public schoolboys, 'low politics' by products of state education. Nowadays 'high' and 'low' politics are not so sharply separated, of course. But many of these contrasts continue in modern Britain.

FREE MARKET AND INDUSTRY 1890–1939

The Victorians also modernised the Stock Exchange, where company shares were bought and sold. By extending the idea of a limited liability company – where the maximum individual investors could lose was the value of their holding in the company – they increased the incentives for individuals with money to buy and sell shares as their price fluctuated. Such individuals were not actively concerned with the development of the company they bought into. They were simply concerned with the price they could sell the share for. If it fell, they sold rapidly, causing a general collapse of the price.

This development could bankrupt a company by preventing its raising money through share sales or bank loans (since banks would not lend to a company in trouble). Share prices might fall for many reasons other than bad management, for example, a temporary fall in demand which, given time, a firm might overcome. Or companies might wish to invest more of their profits in better machinery to increase profits in later years.

The divorce between investment and management meant, however, that the predominant concern of investors was the current share price, not the underlying performance and prospects of the company. If it failed to pay out high returns each year it would be in trouble, regardless of whether it could envisage an upturn the next year.

Such 'short-termism' on the part of investors has often been criticised and seen as a weakness in the British economy. As a result, manufacturing firms are always tied to immediate results and hampered from making long-term plans for modernisation and investment to deal effectively with competition. One can see, however, that British investors are simply following the logic of a free market, in which shares are necessarily a product to be bought and sold. In such a market investors themselves would be in trouble if they let considerations other than immediate profit and loss enter in.

This was particularly true for British financial markets as the world was opened up from 1850 onwards, largely through their investments. Banks, insurance companies and individual investors had an increasing choice between various overseas outlets, with high and immediate rates of return. These were guaranteed by British naval and military power over the world free-trade system centred in London.

British industrial shares in fact came late into the financial markets in any large quantity. This was because it was easier financing expansion from their high rate of profits rather than from loans or share sales. The development of more and more sophisticated technology increasingly ruled this option out. Profits themselves were cut into by a slow-down in the rate of growth during the 'Great Depression' of 1870–92. Firms amalgamated in order to survive. The new conglomerates turned to banks and the Stock Exchange to finance development, by selling their shares.

In doing so, however, they made themselves subject to the short-term pressures of the financial markets. It is in this development that we can trace the structural impact of Britain's primacy in the Industrial Revolution on the present-day situation. Had Britain not been the first to industrialise, had its investors not developed a free international financial market on the basis of British dominance, banks and finance might have co-operated with home industry rather than simply trading in it, against other options. Once such relationships took root, however, attempts to overturn them were likely to provoke a financial crisis.

Britain inherited, from the nineteenth century, financial markets that are highly efficient, internationally oriented and in part divorced from British industry. A better appreciation of the consequences can be obtained by comparing them with the very different path other countries, particularly Germany and Japan, took towards industrialisation.

PROTECTION AGAINST FREE TRADE 1890–1939

The second, third and fourth industrialising nations could not follow the free trade path marked out by Britain. To open their markets to free competition simply meant that cheaper British products would ruin their home industry. If they wanted to build their own industrial base they had to protect developing industries by imposing taxes on any incoming products that threatened them. This meant that the home consumer had to pay higher prices. On the other hand, the industries protected in this way also provided growing opportunities for employment and domestic prosperity.

The move to protection in these countries also gained strength from their desire to safeguard agriculture and home supplies of food. This was because countries like France and Germany viewed the economy above all from a military point of view. They wanted industrialisation to provide steel and guns, uniforms and equipment for the army. They wanted railways to speed general mobilisation and to take troops more quickly where they were needed. A productive home agricultural base was necessary for two reasons: to maintain a large, peasant population which could provide army conscripts and to ensure food supplies in time of war.

The economic policies adopted by the Continental countries were thus in complete antithesis to Britain's internationally focused free trade, where home industry had to compete with foreign imports and investment opportunities. The concern was rather to protect and nurture home industry and agriculture and to allow international competition only when these were strong enough to sustain themselves.

This contrast in attitudes affects present-day relationships, particularly between Britain and its partners in the European Union. For Britain, the attraction of the Union has always been the prospect of abolishing tariffs and extending free markets across Europe, as a preliminary to extending them to the rest of the world. France and Germany, on the other hand, have always seen the Union primarily in terms of building a strong Europe which can protect and develop its industries on a Continental rather than a national scale. The British preference for a looser economic association rather than a federal union stems from the structure and functioning of its financial markets inherited from the nineteenth century.

Building up industry inside one's own country rather than through international competition also involved a different relationship with banks and financial institutions. The latter did not have the overseas investment opportunities open to the City of London, which had already monopolised them. Developing domestic industry thus offered the best way for French and German banks to make money. However, this had to be a long-term process, since the firms needed to build themselves up. In return for investments and loans firms could not offer quick profits. Instead they provided seats on their boards for bank representatives and other shareholders and involved them in the day-to-day management of the business.

Instead of 'short-termism', therefore, second-stage industrialisation encouraged 'long-termism'. Shares were not bought and traded as commodities but conserved as part of a permanent relationship between shareholders and managers, and profits were to be taken only after the business could afford it. Investment and modernisation were seen as a continuing process necessary for future development and continuing viability.

Long-term planning was encouraged through the active intervention of the government in these relationships. Economic strength was seen as a national priority, even as a prerequisite for national survival. This encouraged a much more active role for government than in Britain, where free trade doctrines limited government intervention as much as possible, in order to allow markets to operate at maximum efficiency.

It is important to see these contrasts between Britain and other countries not just as accidental, but as rooted in the structures and institutions that followed from the sequence of industrialisation in the world. Being first, British practices and attitudes necessarily differed from most of those countries which developed later. What has shaped society, economics, and politics cannot be reversed without fundamental revolution, which Britain has never had, and is unlikely to have.

Like all complex historical developments, this one had both positive and negative effects. British attachment to free trade has rendered the financial sector notably competitive at a world level. The City of London is one of four leading financial markets in the world (along with New York, Frankfurt, and Tokyo). On the negative side, British industry has been unprotected and undercapitalised. As manufacturing industry generally employs more people than finance, this meant that the bulk of the population, particularly in regions outside the South-East of England, suffered greatly from closures and unemployment, leading to insecurity and poverty in their lives.

INTERNAL DEFENCE AGAINST THE FREE MARKET 1890–1939

Such insecurity grew as British industry suffered increasingly from foreign competition from the 1880s onwards. Foreign firms operating from a protected home base took full advantage of free trade to penetrate both the British and colonial markets. Ideological and structural constraints meant that British governments resisted internal pressures to impose protective tariffs until the 1930s, when it became obvious that the First World War had completely disrupted the old world trading arrangements.

For the unskilled working class, these developments exacerbated the general precariousness of their position in an unregulated free market. They had no savings to fall back on and no particular skills to make them especially valued. They were employed on a weekly or even a daily basis, and when there was no work they had no money to pay the rent or even to buy the next meal. Prolonged unemployment would force them into a New Poor Law workhouse where their family would be split up and there they would live under conditions deliberately made harder than those of the poorest paid worker outside, to discourage 'dependency' and reduce the tax burden on the working population.

In this situation workers naturally sought security through organised action. Their first successful attempt was through consumer co-operatives which reduced prices and shared out profits to their members. Other collective organisations like funeral and sickness clubs followed. These all operated on the basis that large numbers of tiny contributions could finance a strong collective organisation, which then protected individuals in times of need. Such organisations were often associated with churches, particularly Nonconformist churches and the Catholic Church, the majority of whose adherents were working class (see Briefing 2.7).

BRIEFINGS

2.7 NONCONFORMISTS, CATHOLICS AND POLITICS

Up to the First World War (1914–18) religion was probably more important than social class in shaping British politics. Developments in the nineteenth century encouraged the growth of Protestant churches outside the established state churches: the Church of England (episcopalian, governed by bishops) and the Church of Scotland (presbyterian, governed by elders). Nonconformists (to the state Church) were decreasingly discriminated against. Thus churches like the Methodists, Baptists and Congregationalists could conduct mass conversions and place a chapel in every town. They appealed particularly to the new working class, offering another collective organisation to look after their spiritual and often material well-being. Thus they tended to be stronger in the peripheries of Britain than in the centre. Non-conformists had a natural interest in reform, to remove the remaining discrimination against themselves and reduce the privileges of the state Church. They tended to support the Liberals against the Conservatives.

The Roman Catholic Church catered mainly for Irish immigrants who provided new labour for the industries of mainland Britain. Catholics tended to be even more discriminated against than Nonconformists and were generally poorer. They had little cause to support either of the main British parties but were attracted by the Irish Nationalists, who wanted a devolved parliament in Ireland. Around 1910 the Catholic Church withdrew its opposition to the newly formed Labour Party, which was also attractive to Catholics because of its proposals for social reform and state help for the poor. This paved the way for widespread Labour voting among Catholics, which continues to the present time.

In spite of this, co-operatives were often resented by the middle class. Small shop-keepers and professionals saw them as offering unfair inducements which undermined the free market in goods and services.

This was even more true when workers banded themselves together to bargain about the price of their labour. Employers saw this as an unfair attempt to raise their costs, which in a competitive market would drive them out of business. They much preferred to deal with individuals where they could offer what they felt they could afford on a take it or leave it basis. Workers on their side saw this as an inherently unequal bargain, in which their sole source of support could be reduced or cut off according to the vagaries of employers and markets.

The remedy was to join collective organisations – trade unions – which could bargain on a more powerful basis than any individual. If a trade union could persuade the whole workforce of a particular factory or firm to withhold their labour, profits would be severely hit and so it would be worthwhile for an employer to

BRIEFINGS

2.8 BUSINESS CARTELS VERSUS LABOUR CARTELS

A 'cartel' is an organisation, usually of firms or manufacturers, which aims to establish monopoly control of a particular product, so as to regulate its price. In this way market demand by consumers and competition among producers will not determine the price, which will be decided by what producers think is a reasonable profit over and above their costs of production. The temptation for producers, especially if they face no competition and their product is a necessity of life, is to set the price and their profits very high.

A cartel is a direct attack on the free market, since it undermines or dominates competition. With the growth of big firms and multinational companies, many semi-cartels exist today. As they tend to drive prices up and stifle innovation, governments try to regulate them, for example, through the Monopolies Commission and regulators such as OFWAT (the office of water regulation) in Britain.

Trade unions can also be seen as cartels, trying to ensure that no worker undercuts another in terms of wages, and thus driving the price of labour up. Late nineteenth century liberals and business people regarded them as such and tended to oppose them or regulate them closely. Margaret Thatcher and her Conservative Governments (1979–90) also looked on unions this way.

Trade unions would argue, however, that workers' wages are not just a price to be set by the market. Individual workers competing against each other, and helpless against wealthy companies which can afford to pick and choose, would drive their own wages down. The saving in 'labour costs', however, would be counter-balanced by increasing human misery in terms of poverty, health, family stability and crime, problems which would affect the rest of society and eventually incur costs in social security, health care and policing.

make a better offer, even though this cut into profits to a certain extent. Worker co-operatives were regarded as unfair, even though they bought and sold on the market like everybody else. This was even more true of trade unions, aiming at a monopoly of labour in order to bargain more effectively (see Briefing 2.8). This seemed a direct attack on the free market, and in the first half of the nineteenth century trade unions were outlawed. In the second half they were severely regulated and restricted by, for example, being made liable for damages caused by anyone who could be regarded as acting as their agent (e.g. a worker on strike).

Employers often brought in nonunion labour to break a strike by the existing workforce. 'Pickets' of striking workers confronted these and violence sometimes ensued. Thus, the collective responsibility of unions for damage caused by their members was a serious liability for them, rendering them ultra-cautious in their actions and weakening their finances. The police normally took the side of the employers, protecting their property and maintaining free access for strike-breakers to the factory premises.

Trade unions and their supporters wanted to change the balance of power in the workplace by getting Parliament to absolve them from collective responsibility for individual actions (see Briefing 2.9). They also wanted governments to act more neutrally in industrial disputes.

To achieve both objectives they had to gain more political power. The Second Reform Act (1867) and the Third Reform Act (1884) gave the vote to substantial numbers of working-class men. In order to attract their votes both the Conservatives and Liberals passed legislation favouring trade unions. Various attempts were also made to organise a specifically 'Labour Party', which eventually emerged in 1900 as an alliance of trade unions, co-operatives and some of the small Socialist parties which had already elected a few MPs.

At the same time employers and landowners had been steadily leaving the Liberal Party and joining the Conservatives, whom they saw as more likely to protect their interests at home and abroad. The Liberals became more dependent on working-class votes and Labour Party support in Parliament. This accompanied a radical shift in the political views of many of their MPs and parliamentary leaders. Retaining individual freedom as a central value, they began to feel that political and social freedom was not attainable unless individuals had a reasonable economic basis from which to pursue it. If they did not know where the next meal would come from, they could hardly pay attention to politics or decide political questions rationally.

In line with these ideas a Liberal Government passed, with Labour support, the National Insurance Act of 1911. This provided for contributions by employees, employers and the state towards the provision of health and unemployment insurance. What this meant was that everyone who had worked would get free healthcare when they were sick, from payments guaranteed by the state. The same applied to unemployment: all who lost their job would be entitled to weekly payments until they found another. When there was a Labour Government supported by Liberals (1923–24), a Housing Act was passed to help local councils build subsidised houses for rent to those with little money.

Technological developments made it increasingly expensive to build and equip factories, which resulted in firms becoming larger and larger over this period.

BRIEFINGS

2.9 THE RISE AND FALL OF UNION POWER: TRADE UNION LEGISLATION 1868–1997

In 1868 the various small trade unions (mainly of craftsmen) which had been locally organised in Britain held a joint meeting which resulted in a federation with a governing council, the Trades Union Congress (TUC). The Liberal Government's Trades Unions Act (1871) gave them legal recognition and protection of funds against embezzlement. The Conservative Conspiracy Act (1875) declared that no trade union could be prosecuted for anything that would not be illegal if done by an individual. On this foundation trade unions grew, most importantly by organising unskilled labourers as well as (relatively well-off) craftsmen (the 'New Trade Unionism' of the 1890s). Trade unions also began to use their funds to send 'Labour' candidates to Parliament. This helped the foundation of the fully fledged Labour Party in 1900.

One stimulus to taking more direct political action was the Taff Vale decision by the courts (1901) which decided that a trade union could be held responsible and sued for the actions of members during strikes. The Liberal Government's Trades Disputes Act (1906) effectively reversed this decision. Only an individual could be sued for illegal actions. The Trade Union Act (1913) stated that unions could use funds for political purposes if they were separated from general funds, and members who objected would not be forced to pay into them.

On this legal basis trade unions grew rapidly from 1906 to 1926, mounting direct actions and strikes with considerable success against employers. Adverse economic conditions after the First World War produced more industrial action, culminating in the general strike of 1926. All trade unionists were called upon to strike, basically in support of miners' attempts to avoid wage cuts and dismissals. The Conservative Government defeated the strike after a week but took relatively restrained action against the trade unions, stipulating that members had to 'opt in' to paying the political fund rather than 'opt out'.

With the election of the Labour Government in 1945, trade unions secured a reversal of this measure. More importantly, they were consulted on all issues relating to labour and industrial relations by the Government and the 'closed shop' and factory negotiating committees were recognised as normal practice. Neither Conservative governments nor Labour governments from 1951 to 1970 challenged the legal powers of trade unions. The Conservative Government of Edward Heath (1970–74) tried to regulate trade unions through a special code of industrial law and a special court, the Industrial Relations Tribunal. The miners' strike in 1973–74 precipitated a general strike which brought down the government. The Labour Governments of Harold Wilson and James Callaghan (1974–79) tried to conciliate trade unions by reaching formal agreements with them on prices and wages. A failure to agree on wage restraint in 1978 led to a near general strike in 1979 (the 'Winter of Discontent'). This rendered Labour so unpopular that it lost the general election of 1979.

2.9 THE RISE AND FALL OF UNION POWER: TRADE UNION LEGISLATION 1868–1997 (continued)

The 'New Right' Conservative Government of Margaret Thatcher regarded trade unions as a major impediment to the free market, echoing the views of free market economists of the late nineteenth century. In a series of legislative measures the 1979–83 and 1983–87 governments:

- required regular trade union ballots on whether they should keep a political fund,

- required regular re-election of trade union leaders,

- required ballots of members before strike action could be taken,

- perhaps most importantly, outlawed secondary picketing, that is, industrial action against any firm not directly involved in an industrial dispute. Thus strikers could picket a newspaper, for example, if they were in dispute with it. But they could not stop another firm delivering newspapers, even if this was vital to keep the newspaper going. Enterprising employers could thus split their companies into two to avoid union reprisals since the law would hold that the one not in direct dispute should not be picketed in any way.

Concurrent developments also weakened trade unions. A growth in unemployment reduced their membership from 12 million to 7.5 million in the course of the 1980s. In a set-piece confrontation the Government defeated a year-long miners' strike in 1984–85, brought about by the closures of mines. The media proprietor, Rupert Murdoch, also broke the print and journalists' unions' power in the Wapping dispute (1986–87), with the help of the secondary picketing legislation.

In a curious way, however, the reforms imposed on the unions also helped them, making them internally more democratic, leaner and fitter. In their glory days from 1950 to 1979 they had become very bureaucratised, with policy and leadership chosen by agreement among leaders and little contact with the rank and file. Having to submit themselves to democratic election actually strengthened leaders' claims to represent their members. This was reflected in a cautious return to industrial action in the 1990s, especially as economic conditions became gradually more favourable after 1995. Even though the 'New Labour' party of Tony Blair distanced itself from too close a connection with the trade unions, the unions worked hard for its return to office in 1997. They have been rewarded by British adoption of the European Social Charter (1997) and the upholding of a minimum statutory wage for all workers.

Foreign competition also resulted in firms amalgamating in order to have more resources and to cut costs. Increasingly companies operated not one but many factories. Correspondingly, trade unions became larger as well. It was no longer enough to stop work at one factory in order to get better offers from employers. Firms could always shift work from one factory to another, or even close down factories affected by a strike. What was necessary was to disrupt all the factories controlled by a firm in order to induce it to negotiate.

However, in seeking more members, unions did not grow in accordance with any very rational plan. Although they initially based themselves upon one particular group of craftsmen or workers, the desire to reinforce themselves in one factory or inside one company often led to recruitment of very different types of workers.

Moreover, two, three, four, or even more unions might operate inside one factory. They might put different demands to management and one might go on strike when others did not, because workers were, and are, not an undifferentiated group. Trade unions representing skilled workers were anxious to maintain 'differentials' between their members' wages and those of unskilled workers. So when one union obtained its demands another might well strike to obtain more for its members in order to maintain their 'differential'.

The messy nature of British trade unionism, with large unions often overlapping each other in terms of workers represented, and with multiple unions represented in the same factory, is illustrated in Table 2.2. This lists the major unions operating in Britain today. The size of the largest unions is quite striking: the 10 largest account for three quarters of the 6.5 million members in the country as a whole. Union activity is co-ordinated by the Trades Union Congress (TUC), a committee and annual delegate conference supported by a permanent bureaucracy. But its powers are very limited compared with those of individual unions.

Table 2.2 Major trade unions in Britain

Name	Number of members in 1995	Industrial or service sector covered
UNISON	1,400,000	Public employees including health workers
TGWU (Transport and General Workers)	900,000	All sectors of industry including communications
GMB (General and Municipal)	790,000	Distributive sector and local government
AEEU (Amalgamated Electrical Engineering Union)	750,000	All sectors of industry
MSFU (Managerial Scientific and Financial Union)	452,000	Managers and specialists across all sectors of industry
CWU (Communications Workers Union)	280,000	Electronics, particularly communications
USDAW (Shop, Distributive and Allied Trades)	290,000	Shops and stores, transport
GPMU (General Public and Municipal Workers)	200,000	Mainly local government
NUT (National Union of Teachers)	179,000	Teachers in state schools, particularly primary schools
NASUWT (National Association of Schoolmasters/Union of Women Teachers)	157,000	Teachers mainly in state schools

ON THE RECORD

WHAT ARE THE CHANCES OF GENTLEMANLY CAPITALISM PREVAILING IN THE 1990s?

If the future was simply an extrapolation of the past, we would all be rich or dead – or both. Nevertheless, we can be sure that capitalism will prevail in the fore-seeable future. This is not to say that we have reached 'the end of ideology': dead prophets have a habit of rising again. But the socialist experiment has ceased to yield political or economic returns and will not be re-run unless capitalist alternatives fail. Moreover, we can be confident from what we know of the changing structure of contemporary capitalism that the advanced economies will continue to shift resources into finance and services. As recent research has shown these sectors were not simply the outcrop of a 'post-industrial society', but were bound up with the very process of modernisation, in Britain at least, during the past three centuries. By fusing tradition with progress they made the modern English gentleman, generating new forms of wealth that were, exceptionally, both sizeable and acceptable, consolidating political power in hands that were both familiar and clean, and fending off the claims of the industrial bourgeoisie.

The nature of the social contract has now changed: the English gentleman traded privilege for duty; the ethos of public service upheld the state, the monarch and the empire. The end of the empire diminished the state and the monarchy; the incursion of transnational companies, not least in the City, reduced the economic importance of the gentlemanly elite; the *petit bourgeois* revolution promoted by Margaret Thatcher destroyed the concept of public service. The City of London continues to thrive, but the super-rich who man the upper reaches of the financial and service sectors are now, as Defoe put it, the 'mere outsides of gentlemen'. In embracing the market, the new elite has jetti-soned the notion of civic duty, but, knowing no history, wonders why the ties that used to bind the nation have loosened, and regrets, in an age of unrestraint, that manners no longer maketh man – or woman.

A. G. Hopkins, FBA, is the Smuts Professor of Commonwealth History at the University of Cambridge and a Fellow of Pembroke College. He was previously Professor of International History at the University of Geneva, and, before that, Professor of Economic History at the University of Birmingham. He has two main academic interests, one the economic history of Africa and the other the history of British imperialism.

The untidy nature of union organisation is another legacy from the nineteenth century. Britain was the first country to have trade unions. They grew up sponta-neously and incrementally in response to local initiatives, without an overall blue-print. Once they had emerged as large composite bodies it was hard to change them. There has been no dictatorship, war, or occupation to force a more rational industry-based organisation as in Germany, for example.

Another legacy from the nineteenth century is the atmosphere of 'short-termism' within which negotiations between trade unions and management take place. The managers' immediate concern must be to satisfy the financial markets that good profits are being made. This keeps the share price up and ensures the firm's continuing survival. Faced with this, the trade union's concern is to safeguard members' standards of living for the current year. Neither is able to look beyond the current year to possible long-term co-operation, as prospects are so uncertain. When one side simply seeks to hold wages as they are and the other to increase them, the situation is set for a confrontation and trial of strength, and in fact encounters between unions and employers in Britain often take confrontational form. That helps to account for the bad state of industrial relations in Britain, which has been a problem for many governments of the modern period.

ESSAYS

1. Describe the main electoral reforms of the period from 1867 to 1884. What impact did these reforms have on party politics?

2. Why did Britain pursue a policy of free trade for much of the nineteenth and early twentieth centuries? What were the political and economic effects of this policy?

3. Account for the rise of the trade union movement in Britain from 1860 to 1914. How did the trade union movement affect party politics?

4. What effect did overseas expansion have on British economic and political life down to 1914?

SUMMARY

This chapter has concentrated on the many features of British politics which derive from Britain's experience as the first urbanised and industrialised nation in the world. To put these developments in their historical setting the Milestones chart the key events, both nationally and internationally, up to 1945.

The legacy of the mid-nineteenth century and Britain's dominance of the world industrially and commercially are:

- a deep attachment on the part of most policy makers to free trade and the ideal of a free competitive market;
- financial markets (the 'City of London') which trade internationally and give no special preference to British industry;
- many political and other institutions which continue in an essentially nineteenth century form today (e.g. Parliament, the political parties, the Civil Service, local government);
- a working class defence against the free market which relies on collective action, focused particularly on trade unions and the Labour Party.

MILESTONES

MILESTONES IN BRITISH HISTORY 1867–1945

BRITAIN	WORLD
CONSERVATIVE–LIBERAL ALTERNATION IN GOVERNMENT 1867–86	
Home rule for Canada, 1867	
Second reform bill extends franchise, 1867	
Great Economic Depression, 1870–1892	Franco-Prussian War, 1870–1871 makes newly united Germany dominant on the continent of Europe
Liberal reforms in health, civil service, army, 1868–74	
Trades Union Act, 1871	

MILESTONES IN BRITISH HISTORY 1867–1945 (continued)

BRITAIN

Unions protected from liability for individual members' acts, 1875

Control of Suez Canal and Egypt secures sea-route to India. Indian Empire consolidated, 1878

Expansion in South Africa, 1879–80

80 Irish Nationalist MPs elected to House of Commons and disrupt parliamentary proceedings, 1874–80

Irish 'Land War', 1879–83

Third Reform Act extends franchise further, 1884

First Home Rule Bill for Ireland splits Liberal Government, which is defeated, 1886

CONSERVATIVE PREDOMINANCE IN GOVERNMENT 1886–1905 (Liberals, 1892–95)

Local Government Act extends elected councils to counties, 1888

Second Irish Home Rule Bill defeated, 1893

Home rule movements grow in Scotland and Wales during 1890s. Scottish Office centralises Scottish administration

Labour Party founded 1900 with support of trade unions

Home rule for Australia and New Zealand, 1901

LIBERAL PREDOMINANCE IN GOVERNMENT 1905–16

Trade Union Acts, 1906 and 1913, strengthen unions

Home rule for South Africa, 1909

Parliament Act, 1911, strengthens power of House of Commons (elected) against House of Lords (unelected)

National Health Insurance Act – extensive government intervention to protect and pay sick, unemployed and old, 1911

Third Irish Home Rule Bill initiated 1912 – Lords' now limited veto can only block it until 1914

Rising violence by Irish Protestants, paramilitary organisations founded, 1912–14. 'Curragh Mutiny' of army officers in Dublin against having to enforce home rule, 1914. Home rule postponed

1915–18: submarine attacks almost cut off British food supplies

WORLD

1884–1905: The 'Grab for Africa': European powers set out to conquer as much territory as possible. Most falls to France and Britain

Boer War, 1899–1902. Britain conquers independent white republics of South Africa with difficulty

Anglo-French military co-operation initiated 1904; extended to Russia, 1907. This creates an informal alliance against Germany

Naval arms race between Britain and Germany for dominance of North Sea, 1906–14

First World War begins 1914 – Britain, France and Russia against Germany, Austria–Hungary and Turkey

US enters war against Germany, 1917

German defeat, 1918

MILESTONES IN BRITISH HISTORY 1867–1945 (continued)

BRITAIN

WORLD

1916–22 COALITION GOVERNMENTS BETWEEN LIBERALS AND CONSERVATIVES
Franchise extended to almost all adult males and women over 30, 1918
Civil War in Ireland, 1918–22

Ireland partitioned between Irish Free State and Northern Ireland, 1922
Home rule for both parts of Ireland

1919–23 Treaties of Versailles and Trianon reduce and disarm Germany, break up Austria–Hungary, create Poland and other new central and eastern European countries and extend French and British control of Arab Middle East
League of Nations set up without USA
Russian Revolution, 1917–22
Communist Government takes over (reduced) Russian empire

CONSERVATIVE PREDOMINANCE IN GOVERNMENT, 1922–29
(first Labour minority Government 1923–24)
Housing Act provides for subsidised housing, 1924
General Economic Depression from 1920 –
many strikes by individual unions
General Strike fails, 1926

LABOUR GOVERNMENT 1929–31
Labour splits over cutting social payments, 1931

Wall Street Crash (collapse of American share values) ushers in Great Depression of 1930s: world trade slumps, millions unemployed in all countries

NATIONAL COALITION GOVERNMENTS OF RUMP LABOUR AND LIBERALS DOMINATED BY CONSERVATIVES 1931–40
Cuts in social benefits, abandonment of free trade, protectionist measures create cartels and monopolies to regulate market
Government of India Act 1936 gives India limited home rule as a response to growing nationalist agitation

1933–39 rise and consolidation of Nazi regime in Germany, rearmament and takeover of adjoining territories. Leads to Second World War, 1939

COALITION GOVERNMENTS OF CONSERVATIVES, LABOUR AND LIBERALS 1940–45
Full wartime planning and control of society and economy

Germans conquer most of European mainland except for Russia, 1940

Germany attacks Russia, 1941
US enters war on British side, 1941
Defeat of Germany and Allies, 1945

PROJECTS

1. Assess the arguments for and against giving workers any special protection against the free market.

2. Obtain statistical evidence for the proposition that Germany or the United States rapidly caught up with Britain as an economic power in the last quarter of the nineteenth century.

3. Investigate the origins of any local institution such as a library, school, college or museum established in the period 1830–80. Who established it and why? How was it established? How does its foundation reflect the prevailing values and interests of the time?

FURTHER READING

Karl Polanyi, *The Great Transformation* (Boston: Beacon Press, 1957) is the classic account of the triumph of free trade in Britain. Eric Hobsbawm's three volume history traces out the social and economic consequences of the Industrial Revolution. The one most relevant to this chapter is Eric Hobsbawm, *Industry and Empire* (Harmondsworth: Penguin, 1968). Andrew Gamble, *Britain in Decline* (London: Macmillan, 1989) reviews many of the developments discussed in this chapter from a rather pessimistic point of view. P. J. Cain and A. G. Hopkins, *British Imperialism* (Harlow: Longman, 1993) is a hugely influential two-volume account of the role of 'gentlemanly capitalism' in Britain's imperial and commercial history.

http://www.awl-he.com/politics/newbritpol

Internet resources – visit *The New British Politics* Webpage for links to a specially-chosen selection of Internet resources relevant to this Chapter.

http://www.awl-he.com/politics/newbritpol

CHAPTER 3

From protection back to free trade 1931–98

By the early 1930s the whole system of world free trade to which British industry and finance had adapted had broken down. This was partly due to competition from other industrial economies like the United States, Germany and Japan. But the breakdown stemmed primarily from the effects of the First World War where the leading trading nations had fought each other to a standstill. The destructive effects on Germany in particular destabilised international trade and finance, illustrating incidentally that relationships between national economies are not so much competitive as interdependent.

The final breakdown of the old trading system was signalled by the World Depression, which began with a general collapse of financial confidence from 1929 to 1931 and continued for most of the 1930s. This chapter discusses how that led to an initial abandonment of free trade ideas and to massive government intervention in economy and society. This was designed both to protect British industry and to guarantee minimum living standards for the population. The reforms initiated by the National Governments of the 1930s were carried much further by the Labour Governments of 1945–51.

The end of the long postwar boom in the 1970s demonstrated the limits of government intervention. Free trade and free markets reasserted themselves vigorously under the Conservative Governments led by Margaret Thatcher (1979–90), replacing the earlier 'social democratic consensus' with a 'neo-liberal' one. Many of the policies and issues of the 1980s and 1990s in Britain thus hark back to the mid-nineteenth century rather than to the 1930s and 1940s. The new element is the relationship with Europe. This chapter shows how controversy about the nature and extent of government intervention has been at the core of modern British politics, and remains the central issue dividing the Conservative Party from Labour today.

The chapter describes:

- The rise of government intervention from 1931–45

- Labour's creation of the welfare state and nationalisation of basic industries 1945–51

- Diminishing industrial competitiveness and increasing economic conflict 1951–77

- The return to market principles in the 1980s

- The economic consensus of the 1990s

THE RISE OF GOVERNMENT INTERVENTION 1931–45

Contrary to usual belief, government economic management did not become firmly established during the Second World War but following the world crisis of 1931. World economic dislocation exposed the weakness of major British industries such as steel making, coal mining, shipbuilding and textile manufacture. It radically increased the number of unemployed to a quarter or a third of the workforce in many regions. Finally it forced the abandonment of the Gold Standard, the link between the value of the pound and the price of gold, symbolic of the unquestioned integrity and value of the currency.

Governments of the ensuing eight years reacted to these alarming developments with a new economic strategy. Although this fell short of full economic planning it did represent a fundamental break from the orthodox liberal tradition which had dominated policies until then. The new policy was inspired by the need to protect British industry and agriculture from foreign competition. This required both the imposing of tariffs on imports and encouragement for the reconstruction of ailing industries. A contemporary comment on the introduction of the (Protectionist) Import Duties Bill shows how interventionist the new policy was:

> [The Bill] does provide us with such a lever as has never been possessed
> before by a government for inducing, or if you like, forcing industry to set its
> house in order. I have in my mind particularly iron and steel and cotton: and
> my belief in the advantages of protection is not so fanatical as to close my
> eyes to the vital importance of a thorough reorganisation of such industries
> as these, if they are even to keep their heads above water in the future.[1]

During the 1930s the Government encouraged reorganisation in the basic industries (mainly through the creation of private cartels and monopolies), provided central marketing schemes for agricultural products (the marketing boards) and began a policy of regional revival (via the Special Areas Acts of 1935, 1936 and 1937). The Government also pursued a policy of monetary expansionism based on low interest rates, although the motivations here were probably as much a desire to reduce the national debt as to fuel economic growth.

It would be misleading to characterise the National Government as benevolent either in relation to industrial recovery or social policy: by modern standards it was neither. On the social side it cut welfare and unemployment benefits and applied means tests, which excluded many people from benefit.

The protection of industry from foreign competition combined with reorganisation was a radical change. But there was no indicative planning in the sense of pointing the general direction in which economic and social change should go (see Briefing 3.1). Administrative innovations were few and far between (the marketing boards being the main exception). But a regulatory framework for unsystematic, special-purpose developments was laid down, and for the first time applied to industrial protection.

Key term

Indicative planning – the practice of the state indicating targets or goals for such things as employment, inflation, output, without necessarily taking action of its own to achieve them.

---

[1] S.H. Beer, *Modern British Politics* (London: Faber, 1965), p. 293

BRIEFINGS

3.1 NATIONAL ECONOMIC PLANNING: INDICATIVE AND POSITIVE

Following the experience of the Great Depression of the 1930s, which seemed to demonstrate the failure of capitalism and the apparent success of the massive state intervention characteristic of the Second World War, it became fashionable in the immediate postwar period to favour economic planning over the free market as a means of economic organisation. Very generally, two varieties of planning were available: *positive planning*, where the state takes responsibility for investment, production and for the setting of prices and wages; and *indicative planning* where the state indicates investment, production and price targets and intervenes directly only when the market fails to reach these. Positive planning, which is most often associated with Communist states, has never been a realistic option in Britain except in wartime. Indicative planning was tried extensively in France in the postwar period, and from 1959 to 1976 various British governments attempted to emulate the apparently successful French experience. On two occasions Labour governments set up the machinery for indicative planning: the Department of Economic Affairs (DEA) in 1965 and the planning agreements with industry in 1975. On both occasions, however, immediate economic pressures, most notably the need to defend the value of sterling on the foreign exchanges, led to the abandonment of planning. By the late 1980s planning had slipped from the agenda and today it is not considered an efficient or appropriate means of controlling the economy.

Key term

Positive planning – direct state action to achieve planning goals. Keynesian policies involve positive planning.

Towards the end of the decade, support for more comprehensive regulation and planning was mounting, and manifested itself in a number of policy areas. In land use, the Government legislated to control the urban sprawl, which was occurring in the still prosperous Midlands and South East, as newly protected light industries (such as the manufacture of cars and electrical goods) developed to supply the home market.

More significantly, the Government set up the Barlow Commission on the Distribution of the Industrial Population. In 1940 this recommended a two-pronged attack on the twin problems of regional unemployment and the continuing sprawl caused by rapid population drift to London and the Midlands. Growth in the prosperous cities should be contained with rigid controls on industrial location, while industry should be given incentives to locate in the distressed North and West. These were radical proposals indeed, and clearly demanded some central co-ordinating authority if they were to be implemented effectively.

Between 1937 and 1942 a number of other commissions were initiated to provide recommendations on new towns (Reith Report), land values (Uthwatt Report), land utilisation in rural areas and national parks (Dower and Hobhouse Reports) and social security (Beveridge Report). Many of the commissions were concerned with the physical environment, reflecting the growing influence of the town planning lobby during the 1930s. Beveridge was given a very wide brief – all income maintenance (unemployment benefit, pensions, national assistance, welfare services and health) – as was Barlow. But it is notable that no commission on the reorganisation of industry or on industrial relations was created.

We can sum up the growth of state intervention under the Conservative-dominated governments of the 1930s in terms of two major developments. First, an acceptance by the Government of a role in regulating industrial and agricultural production. Second, the beginnings of planning, with some recognition that the problems of society and economy could be solved only through increased government action.

These changes came about in response to the near collapse of international capitalism in the 1930s. But, crucially, the government saw recovery in terms of reviving old industries (iron and steel, mining, textiles, shipbuilding) and regions which were assumed to be victims of international forces. It devoted little thought to the restructuring of industry or to channelling investment into high-productivity, high-growth industries. Physical planning apart, the enhanced role for the state was perceived solely in terms of how to help declining traditional industries and, in embryo form at least, how to ameliorate the social evils of industrial decline. The same attitudes dominated within the Labour Party. However, Labour supported more draconian solutions: more government ownership and control of industry. Labour also wanted the state to set up comprehensive welfare and health services.

Between 1936 and 1945 public and elite attitudes towards state intervention were transformed by two events: the acceptance of Keynesian economics and the total modification of the economy during the Second World War (see Briefing 3.2). The monetarist orthodoxy accepted by the National Governments of the 1930s held that industrial development could only take place if there was general confidence in the currency, maintained by government budgets in which revenues equalled or surpassed expenditures. Keynes showed that the economy could function under these conditions well below the level it might attain with full use of available resources. Since the main underused resource was labour, this implied long-term unemployment for large sections of the workforce. Governments could, however, raise the economy to nearly full capacity by increasing government expenditure and therefore stimulating demand.

The war seemed to confirm the validity of this assumption. Spending on armaments was massively increased in the late 1930s. By June 1943 only 60,000 people were registered as unemployed, and by 1945 few political leaders opposed Keynesian demand management. The war also gave planning an enormous boost, both in theory and practice. Central committees strictly controlled prices, incomes, industrial relations and production. Never before or since has the British economy been so rigidly disciplined.

Being both authoritarian and comprehensive, wartime controls were always seen by civil servants and many politicians as temporary. This fact was reflected in the ad hoc nature of administrative reforms. The old prewar ministries remained intact, ready to resume their traditional roles once hostilities ceased. Labour politicians were less antipathetic to controls. Even they, however, were

Key term

Orthodox economics – the dominant economic approach before Keynesian theory which argued for minimal state intervention in the economy.

Key term

Keynesianism – economic theory or policy derived from the writings of J. M. Keynes (1883–1946) which advocates some government economic intervention to achieve economic stability, growth, and full employment.

BRIEFINGS

3.2 ORTHODOX ECONOMICS AND KEYNESIAN ECONOMICS

Orthodox economics assumes that the most efficient system of economic organisation is based on minimal government intervention and free markets. National accounts – the relationship between income (taxes) and expenditure (government spending) – should always be in balance. For a government to spend more than it receives in taxation leads to inflation. During the 1930s, however, tax revenues fell as a result of the Depression, leading governments to cut expenditure including unemployment and other benefits. The Cambridge economist John Maynard Keynes (later Lord Keynes) noted that the effect of this was to reduce the level of total demand in the economy and therefore to depress it even further. He demonstrated that it was possible for the economy to reach equilibrium (that is, when supply matches demand) at a level far below full capacity with resulting high levels of unemployment. The Government therefore needed to stimulate demand by increasing expenditure, the precise opposite of what governments actually did for most of the 1930s. Budget deficits were acceptable, therefore, when the economy was operating below full capacity. Once full capacity had been reached, government accounts should once again be brought into balance. If they were not, inflation would return.

The experience of the Second World War seemed to confirm this thesis: massive government spending led to full employment and eventually to labour shortages and inflation. After the War, all British governments accepted Keynesian thinking: governments had a duty to intervene to maintain full employment via government spending. Not until the 1970s, when rising inflation and rising unemployment occurred at the same time, were the basic principles of Keynesian economics challenged. As a result, orthodox economics became again a feasible alternative for policy makers.

highly ambivalent about centralised planning of the positive variety (where the state took all important economic decisions, leaving only a residual role to the market). We can see in this a lingering survival of free trade ideas which otherwise seemed wholly abandoned.

However, the Keynesian revolution and the war destroyed the minimal state spending policies of previous eras. Towards its end the earlier reports, plus further White Papers on employment and education, laid the foundations for greatly increased state spending in society and economy. However, state planning through a central planning agency was rejected by the Conservatives and won little sympathy among Labour politicians. Neither party had devoted much intellectual energy to the question of industrial reorganisation and planned industrial investment. The emphasis was on production rather than on productivity: increasing total output, irrespective of how efficiently this was achieved, was the primary concern.

THE NEW LABOUR ORDER 1945-51

Key term

Welfare state – a state in which the government ensures the basic social and economic necessities of its citizens by financing and providing goods and services such as education, health care, housing, and social security.

The Labour Government elected in 1945 passed a remarkable volume of legislation. Basic industries were nationalised, the welfare state was created, regional policy strengthened dramatically and physical planning by local authorities established as mandatory. All these policies remained in place until the 1980s. Only then did Conservative governments challenge them through privatisation, the dramatic scaling down of regional policy, and the creation of 'internal markets' in education and health.

Postwar policy was dominated by a driving desire to maintain full employment. Keynesian demand management, nationalisation and regional policy were either primarily or partly designed to achieve this and, combined with a generally favourable international trading position, did so until 1951. Industry readapted to peacetime conditions quite efficiently and Britain's share of world trade actually increased during these years.

Plate 3.1 Festival of Britain. General view of the River Walk showing The Islanders and part of the Skylon. The Festival came to symbolise national postwar hopes for modernisation

Full employment and industrial recovery were achieved quickly, but little was done in the field of industrial organisation. Various wartime reports had pleaded for a close co-ordination of industrial location and industrial policy (Barlow) and for comprehensive economic planning (Beveridge, 1944, in his 'unofficial' report on employment). Neither was effected, however. This was partly because of opposition from established bureaucracies – and in particular the Treasury – to a new central planning agency. (There was even opposition to calling the new Ministry of Town and Country Planning just plain 'Planning' for fear it might assume a more comprehensive role.)

More important was the absence of Labour support for industrial reorganisation. In the first year after the war there was talk about a national plan plus all the administrative machinery necessary to implement it. But instead the new Government opted to retain the wartime planning machinery. The 1947 fuel crisis came as a rude shock, bringing severe shortages of coal and other raw materials. In response, the Government created a Central Economic Planning Staff (CEPS) who would implement an annual Economic Survey – really a short-term plan – for labour resources and economic growth.

Under the guidance of Stafford Cripps, Chancellor of the Exchequer at that time, a limited and short-term form of planning actually prevailed during 1947 and 1948. Some reassertion of direct control over labour and an effective wage freeze were part of the strategy, as was voluntary price restraint by manufacturers. From late 1948 onwards, however, enthusiasm for planning declined and was effectively abandoned by Labour. The unions objected to wage restraint and the new austerity of 1946–48 was electorally unpopular. More importantly, perhaps, the administrative innovations were never more than ad hoc in nature. Existing departments continued much as before, the Economic Surveys were for one year only, and opposition within the Cabinet to yet more controls and planning was mounting. Moreover, state intervention to help industry was always framed in terms of more centralisation. Not surprisingly in the context of the wartime experience, this attracted considerable opposition. More creative and less authoritarian means of improving economic performance were not on the agenda.

Yet we should not underestimate Labour's achievement of these years. In social policy a comprehensive welfare system was created, providing free health care and secondary education for all, public housing, and a wide range of income maintenance payments for the disadvantaged. Similarly, in land use planning, a comprehensive approach had been adopted, although there was a notable failure to co-ordinate physical with economic planning. In the economic area, indeed, Labour's efforts depended more on improvisation and persuasion than on radical reforms.

Labour leaders quite failed to see the possibilities of using the new public sector as a way of steering the whole economy in the direction they desired. They behaved as if, while carrying through their plans for nationalisation, they had no understanding of the real meaning of what they had done. Ownership changed; power did not. It had long since ceased to be true, if indeed it ever was, that the shareholders in industries like the mines and railways exercised any real [management] power over them.[2]

---

[2] J. Leruez, *Economic Planning and Politics in Britain* (Oxford: Martin Robertson, 1975), p. 76

Nationalisation was thus the only economic legacy left by Labour to successive governments. Keynesian demand management had already been accepted by the late 1930s, and continued as government policy through to the late 1970s.

When the Conservatives came to power in 1951, the basic relationships between government, unions, finance and industry were almost unchanged from the prewar years. The trade unions played no integrated role in economic or industrial policy. Big business was quite happy to accept a regulative government role, especially in foreign trade, but they too were excluded from central economic policy making. Administrative changes were largely confined to the creation of new bureaucracies to implement the programmes of a burgeoning welfare state. The public sector had expanded enormously, but the basic tools available to governments to guide and control the public sector changed very little. The divorce between industrial and financial sectors, and between both of these and government, continued to be almost as wide as in the earlier free trade era.

DIMINISHING INDUSTRIAL COMPETITIVENESS AND INCREASING ECONOMIC CONFLICT 1951–77

The Conservatives and the state 1951–64

The Conservatives fought the 1951 election on the twin themes of preservation of the welfare state and decontrol of the economy. Decontrol meant lower income and purchase taxes (in 1951 they remained very high); an end to rationing, especially of building and other materials (see Briefing 3.3); abolition of the prohibitive tax (100 per cent) on land development profits; relaxation of exchange controls; and the denationalisation of certain industries (notably road transport and steel). All of these were achieved by 1959, and decontrol almost certainly contributed to the growing prosperity of the 1950s.

The Conservatives also preserved the essentials of the welfare state, for which there was always great public support. Some small changes were made, mainly by tinkering with some services (notably housing and charges for health services) so as to make their availability somewhat more selective. But the changes were small.

If the Conservatives did not dismantle the welfare state nor privatise the nationalised industries, what part did they play in controlling or guiding public intervention? To answer this we have to divide the period into two parts. Until about 1960, government intervention in industry was minimal but Keynesian demand management of expenditure and interest rates continued. After 1960, Keynesian methods were combined with incomes policy and some embryonic planning devices both to control inflation and to achieve a higher rate of economic growth. The transition from the minimalist role to something approaching indicative planning, with government stipulation of general goals and priorities, was inspired by an increasing disenchantment with Britain's economic performance, which was falling behind that of West Germany and France.

Using fiscal and monetary policy to stimulate or depress economic activity in the Keynesian fashion, the Government soon found itself in a vicious 'stop–go'

BRIEFINGS

3.3 WARTIME RATIONING

Very soon after the outbreak of war in September 1939 the Government introduced petrol rationing, followed in January 1940 by food rationing. Few British citizens expected rationing to last for long, partly because few expected the war to last for long. In the event almost every commodity, including clothes, fuel and food, was subject to rationing by the end of the war. On most items rationing lasted until the late 1940s and was not completely removed until 1952. Every household was issued with a ration book, containing stamps which had to accompany money purchases. Ration allowances were meagre – for example, as late as 1951 the meat ration was a mere four ounces per person per week – and designed to provide the very minimum necessary to feed, clothe and heat a family. Rationing was necessary because Britain depended on imports of fuel, food, textiles and other commodities. Shortages in all of these developed as production was disrupted by war and enemy action, and as resources were diverted to the armed forces. After the war, shortages actually worsened as the demand for food and fuel in war-ravaged Europe soared. In 1947 the fuel quota was reduced in the context of a severe winter, and in 1949 some of the most restrictive rationing was introduced because Britain was running out of the dollars needed to buy goods on the international markets. Most commentators agree that the continuing austerity of the 1940s and early 1950s contributed to the defeat of the Labour Government in 1951.

Key term

Stop–go cycle – a pattern in which the economy swings between growth and recession. If growth becomes inflationary and 'over-heated', deflationary policies are introduced to slow growth and stabilise the economy.

cycle. To protect financial markets it felt it must defend the value of the currency, and so it had to avoid recurring balance of payments deficits (an imbalance of imports over exports which affected confidence in sterling). As the economy expanded, so imports increased and the trade deficit widened. The Bank of England was then forced to buy more pounds with its foreign currency reserves to maintain exchange rates at their declared values. With reserves falling and the deficit continuing, governments felt obliged to depress economic activity by raising taxes and restricting credit in order to reduce imports and solve the balance of payment crises. But this brought a rise in unemployment and a fall in output causing governments once more to inflate the economy and to precipitate yet another sterling crisis (see Briefing 3.4).

Such 'stop–go' tactics became common between 1953 and 1970. A related problem was inflation which accelerated during 'go' periods and declined during 'stop' periods. In today's terms both the inflation and unemployment rates were low (Figure 3.1) but, crucially, they were higher than those of comparable countries. Indeed, as the decade wore on, the fundamental problem with the economy was increasingly defined as failure to achieve a rate of economic growth comparable to other major industrial countries. Measured by almost any criteria – industrial investment, productivity, gross national product per capita – Britain was

BRIEFINGS

3.4 'STOP-GO' AND THE BRITISH ECONOMIC CYCLE

During much of the postwar period, British economic management was characterised by periodic rounds of economic growth followed by government-induced deflation to stem the inflationary effects of growth. Typically, the cycle went something like this: in year one, the Government would reduce taxation and interest rates in order to stimulate employment and growth. This in turn led in year two to an upsurge in imports on which the expansion of the British economy depended. With a growing balance of payments deficit, the pound would come under pressure on the foreign exchanges, forcing the Government in year three to dampen demand by raising interest rates and taxation. This resulted in increased unemployment, and pressure by the trade unions for government action. Given the commitment of all governments to full employment (see Briefing 3.2), chancellors of the exchequer would then be obliged in year four to stimulate the economy in order to reduce unemployment. The cycle would then begin again. Most economists agree that this pattern led to a vicious cycle of underinvestment in British industry: it was because British industry was uncompetitive that growth in the economy led to import-led inflation, but, without a period of steady increase in demand with sustained investment, industry could not catch up with its foreign competitors. In other words, as soon as the conditions for sustained investment appeared they were undermined by the Government's need to protect the pound.

Not until the 1980s, when the pound was bolstered by North Sea oil revenues, did conditions change in ways which allowed the cycle to be broken, and it was not until the post-1992 period that British industry had become sufficiently competitive to support a period of sustained growth. By the late 1990s, however, there were new fears that an overvalued pound might undermine growth.

being outstripped by other countries and in particular by Germany, Italy and France. At the same time there was an increasing perception that high rates of economic growth could only be achieved if, as was the case in all these countries and particularly in France, the Government actively intervened in the economy.

By the late 1950s sympathy for more state intervention in industry and economy was mounting within the Conservative Government. Infatuated with the French experience, Selwyn Lloyd, the Chancellor of the Exchequer, and Harold Macmillan, the Prime Minister, launched a limited form of indicative planning in 1961. Their main planning device was the National Economic Development Council (NEDC or 'Neddy'), which brought together members of government, industry and the unions. Its main function was to identify the obstacles to faster growth and then recommend ways in which these could be removed.

In its first report, Neddy estimated that an annual growth rate of 4 per cent per annum between 1961 and 1966 was possible if there was a change in the relationship between government and industry, if public expenditure could be

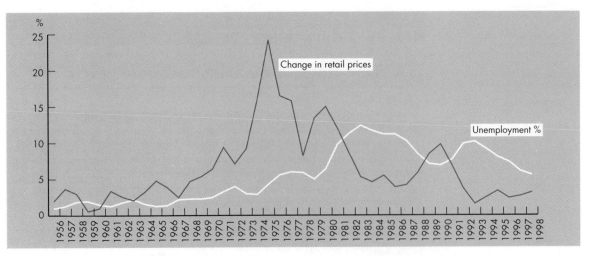

Figure 3.1 Unemployment and Inflation, UK 1956–98
Note: Figures for 1997 and 1998 are projected

projected ahead accurately over the next five years, and if prices and incomes could be held down and, through this, balance of payments crises avoided.

Neddy's recommendations in this and subsequent reports were carefully worked out. However, in spite of the fact that the Government accepted the 4 per cent target, few of the recommendations were implemented. Neddy faced other government departments, particularly the Treasury, antipathetic to planning and eager to defend sterling and pursue monetary orthodoxy. The Government did go so far as to reorganise the Treasury in 1962 and create a new section on the National Economy, whose job would be to liaise with Neddy. Also, for a short period between 1962 and 1964, Neddy did constitute a real rival to the Treasury and, with the Chancellor (by then Reginald Maudling) on its side, led the way towards economic expansion.

What Neddy and the Chancellor were unable to do was to control prices, wages and, perhaps most importantly, public expenditure. Failure with prices and incomes was understandable given the absence of a long-term legislative frame-work to control either (although Selwyn Lloyd had introduced a 'pay pause' during a sterling crisis in 1961). As the economy expanded, so labour became scarcer and unions were better able to bargain for higher wages and to oppose more efficient, but disruptive, work practices.

Public expenditure was viewed in a way dramatically different from before and since, as exerting mostly beneficial economic effects. The growth of the welfare state and nationalisation had been accompanied by remarkably few administrative reforms. The system of control over expenditure in the 1950s was largely unchanged since the mid-nineteenth century. In sum it was approved annually in the budget, never surveyed systematically and never planned more than one year ahead. With the publication of the Plowden Report in 1961 (*Control of Public Expenditure*, Cmnd 1432) and Neddy's call for five-year expenditure planning, the Government at last accepted the need for expenditure surveys which eventually became regular and annual in 1969 (the Public Expenditure Survey Committee or PESC). But in the early 1960s, when the prevailing view was that the Government could spend its way out of trouble, very few systematic controls on expenditure existed.

In sum, the later Conservative years were characterised by a new enthusiasm for economic planning and by some quite ambitious experiments. However, the Government failed to institute the detailed changes needed to make planning work. On the production side, targets were broad and macro, and planning within specific sectors of industry was quite primitive. Incomes, prices and expenditure were at least partly beyond the Government's control. Thus, as expansion set in, so inflation and trade deficits worsened yet again.

Labour and planning 1964–70

Serious overheating of the economy together with the usual sterling crisis occurred before the 1964 general election. Labour therefore inherited a difficult economic position on coming to power. As a Labour Government which emerged from 13 years in opposition, the Prime Minister Harold Wilson and his Cabinet were eager to pursue reforms in social policy – mainly in housing, pensions, education and transport – all of which were expensive; to renationalise steel (also expensive), as well as to continue the Conservative policy of rapid economic growth.

Significantly, however, Labour's ideas about how to produce growth had developed very little in opposition. Their main innovation, the creation of the Department of Economic Affairs (DEA) in 1965, was inspired by a deep mistrust of the Treasury and a perception that Neddy's role was by necessity limited because it was outside the main machinery of government. Hence the DEA was a full-blown government department assigned the job of long-term economic planning, while the Treasury was confined to its traditional role as short-term controller of expenditure. The DEA's brief was extensive: to devise a longer term National Plan; to revitalise industry and improve efficiency, working partly through the 'little Neddies'; to work out a prices and incomes policy; and to reorganise regional policy.

As it turned out, this most radical administrative change lasted just four years, and as an effective policy institution the DEA was operational for less than two. Two major reasons for its failure can be identified. First and foremost was the accelerating rate of economic crisis from 1965 to 1967. Britain's competitive position had been deteriorating for some years and balance of payments deficits were slowly increasing. Sterling was clearly overvalued, mainly because of the need to maintain the stability of the pound as an international reserve currency (see Briefing 3.5). The Labour Government was committed to economic growth and the expansion of public services and found it impossible to reconcile its policy objectives with economic reality. An already bad situation was aggravated by the Government's deference to the official Treasury and City line of giving

BRIEFINGS

3.5 THE CHANGING FORTUNES OF THE POUND STERLING

When the leading industrial countries established a fixed exchange rate regime for postwar trade at Bretton Woods in 1944, it was agreed that the United States dollar would be the main currency of international trade. In addition, however, the pound sterling would also perform this role. In other words, when countries traded with each other they would use either dollars or pounds as a medium of exchange. The pound was accorded this status because a large number of countries used pounds as their main reserve. These included British colonies and dominions but also some Latin American, Middle Eastern and Scandinavian states. Bretton Woods allowed for devaluations but only under emergency circumstances. Britain was, therefore, expected to maintain the value of the pound in relation to the dollar. Any forced devaluation would undermine confidence in the whole sterling area. Under the worst circumstances, a flight from the pound would lead to a collapse in its value. From 1945 until the end of the Bretton Woods system in 1971, successive British governments were under pressure to maintain the value of sterling. The two forced devaluations in 1949 and 1967 were regarded as major government failures, and these pressures intensified the problems of the stop–go cycle (see Briefing 3.4). Most countries gradually moved out of the sterling area during the 1950s and the 1960s. Even after 1971, when currencies floated freely in relation to one another, the problem of currency weakness remained, but this was mainly because the lack of competitiveness of British industry led speculators to believe that the pound was a poor long-term prospect. In 1976 such sentiments led to a run on the currency, and only large loans to the Government and the intervention from the International Monetary Fund (IMF) prevented economic collapse.

Since then the value of sterling has not been so central to government economic policy, partly because governments have acted more responsibly in fiscal matters and partly because of the existence of a floating exchange rate regime. One major exception was the British involvement with the Exchange Rate Mechanism (ERM) of the European Monetary System (EMS) between 1990 and 1992. (This subject is covered extensively in Chapter 4.)

priority to the value of sterling. In 1966 a serious payments crisis and a crippling seamen's strike coincided, inducing investors to sell pounds, and the Government opted to abandon national planning for industrial expansion, and instead to safeguard the currency by restricting credit.

The second reason for the DEA's demise was precisely its organisational isolation from the Treasury, the institution responsible for providing immediate advice in crisis situations. Deflation in order to defend sterling was not the only policy option open to Harold Wilson in 1966. He could have devalued and solved the immediate crisis, an option actually taken a year later in 1967, or he could have cut public expenditure. But with Keynesian economics still very much alive and a host of election commitments to honour, this was never a realistic alternative. Finally, he could have frozen prices and incomes in order to cut costs,

Plate 3.2 Minister of Technology Anthony Wedgwood Benn opens Oceanology International, the world's first fully international conference on underwater technology at Brighton. The Labour Government had come to power on a modernising platform, with Harold Wilson famously speaking of the 'white heat' of technology

improve industry's productivity and reduce inflation. In fact prices and incomes policies were gaining in popularity as a possible solution to the country's problems. In 1965 a new independent body, the National Board for Prices and Incomes (NBPI), was created to investigate income and prices increases and to arbitrate on their fairness. But a total wage and price freeze would have been unpopular with the unions as well as with industry. So it was avoided, at least for the time being.

Economic planning was effectively laid to rest after 1967. The DEA, together with the institutions it fostered, fell into disuse. The Industrial Reorganisation Corporation, which had been set up to provide loans to industry to speed improvements in efficiency, found it could not operate in the absence of a secure and predictable economic climate. The NBPI and an incomes policy were also effectively abandoned. Instead, under the guidance of the new Chancellor of the Exchequer, Roy Jenkins, economic policy reverted almost to a pre-Keynesian strategy: some government expenditure was cut (mainly in defence), foreign loans were repaid and taxes increased. Interestingly, the Jenkins deflation was not so damaging to employment as might have been expected (Figure 3.1), largely because the 1967 devaluation did produce something of an investment boom.

Labour's six years in office were characterised by continual economic crises. The reconstruction of industry and achievement of a high growth rate eluded the Government. In fact, Britain's share of world trade fell from 13.9 per cent to 10.8 per cent during these years.

In spite of this, some important reforms and election pledges were carried through. Comprehensive education was launched, and public transport and physical planning reorganised. Public expenditure also increased, notably in education, health and local government. However, in comparison with the 1945–50 period, Labour had hardly been a radical reforming government. Rather than institute reforms, the Government simply increased spending on existing programmes. Taxation increased dramatically from 32 per cent of gross domestic product (GDP) in 1964 to 43 per cent in 1970. (Gross domestic product is the total value of all the goods and services bought and sold in the domestic economy.) Moreover, the Government's failure to carry through a radical programme alienated many supporters within the Labour movement. By 1970 increasingly militant trade unions were demanding more fundamental reforms and were prepared to use their bargaining muscle to extract higher wages from employers.

While the 1960s were years of periodic economic difficulties, the 1970s were years of unremitting economic crisis. For present purposes we can divide them into four quite distinct periods, each representing a sharp change in the role of the state in economy and society.

Conservative expansionism 1970–72

The first thing the new Conservative Government of Edward Heath did on coming unexpectedly to office in 1970 was to dismantle the NBPI and the Industrial Reorganisation Corporation. It thus, apparently, disavowed both an incomes policy and a strong state role in guiding industry. It combined this with abandoning a fixed exchange rate for the pound and letting international financial markets determine its value.

The Government was also intent on reforming industrial relations, to render the introduction of more efficient working practices easier, by imposing a more rigid framework of law on trade union activity. What transpired was the 1971 Industrial Relations Act which sought to make unions accept certain legal restrictions on their activities, notably on their right to strike, and to submit themselves to a special court. From its inception this inspired the fiercest hostility from the unions.

Another plank in government policy was to negotiate British entry to the European Community (now the European Union). This it successfully did in 1972. Entry was expected to stimulate British industry by exposing it to new competitive pressures while at the same time opening up new markets.

In the absence of an incomes policy and industrial strategy, how were inflation and balance of payments crises to be solved? Strangely, and in spite of some reforms in the control of public expenditure, not by reducing expenditure! Instead, a policy of economic expansion via reduced taxation and increased public spending was followed. With no controls on incomes and expenditure, inflation took off, soaring from 6.4 per cent in 1970 to 9.4 per cent in 1971, by far the highest figure since 1950 (Figure 3.1). This situation could not last long. The rapid increases were bound to undermine the balance of payments and Britain's trading position, especially with a floating exchange rate. In a famous 'U-turn' of November 1972, Edward Heath announced a prices and incomes freeze.

Incomes policy and union confrontation 1972–74

Key term

Incomes policy – government policy designed to secure economic growth and stability by regulating incomes and wages, on the grounds that excess wage and salary demands may be inflationary.

Phase I of the Heath freeze lasted until March 1973 when, under Phase II, all employees were to be subject to an annual increase of £1.00 per week plus 4 per cent per annum. The new system was to be policed by a Pay Board, and price increases were also to be carefully controlled by a newly established Price Commission. Phase II represented a highly significant break with past Conservative principles. Machinery was created to control prices and incomes for a minimum of three years. This implied acceptance of a permanent incomes policy. The Conservatives thus endorsed a highly interventionist economic policy.

Although opposed by the trade unions, Phase II was generally adhered to. Not so with Phase III, which provoked confrontation by the unions and eventually brought the Government down. In fact Phase III was really quite flexible. It permitted a maximum 7 per cent increase, plus extra amounts as a productivity payment and for working 'unsocial' hours. The miners demanded more than the norm on the grounds that they were a special case. They initiated extensive picketing, not only of collieries but of power stations and other energy supplies, causing hardship and short-term working throughout the country. Railway workers also went on strike. Public disenchantment with statutory wages policy grew. By October 1973 only 37 per cent of the public considered Stage III fair. Heath decided to call a general election.

The Government's 'U-turn' on incomes policy in 1972 was accompanied by another change of heart on industrial policy. In spite of the liberalism and minimal state intervention which apparently prevailed in 1970, Heath very soon began to indulge in a range of policies to aid, succour and guide industrial recovery. Bankrupt companies such as Rolls Royce and Upper Clyde Shipbuilders were bailed out, regional incentives and development grants were strengthened, a Minister for Industrial Development was attached to the new Department of Trade and Industry, and workforce retraining was organised and greatly strengthened. All this did not amount to planning in the sense of economic targets being set over a fixed time period, but it did represent a new institutionalised liaison between government and industry.

Finally, after 1972 the Government promised to cut public expenditure. However, by 1973 the pressures to increase expenditure, partly to compensate for the effects of incomes policy, were mounting. When they left office, the Conservatives were actually presiding over a larger public sector than in 1970, in

Figure 3.2 Government outlays as a percentage of GDP, selected countries 1978–97

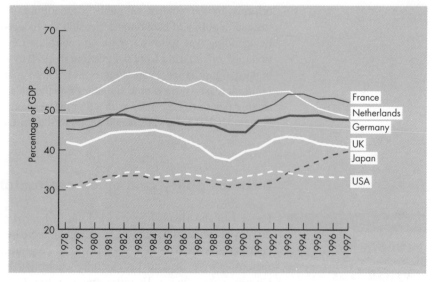

Source: Christopher D. Foster and Francis J. Plowden, *State Under Stress* (Buckingham, Open University Press, 1996), Figure 1.1.

terms of the government share of gross domestic product, and number of enterprises owned by government. This demonstrates how much the Heath Government was relying on incomes policy to harness inflation. Talk of controlling the money supply, which dominated the policy agenda in the late 1970s, was almost completely absent.

A return to planning 1974–75?

While in opposition, the left wing of the Labour party converted its disenchantment with the 1964–70 period into a set of alternative policies which were eventually published as the Labour Programme 1973. They called for a dominant role for the state in the British economy and claimed that Britain's industrial recovery could be facilitated only by further nationalisation, the creation of a National Enterprise Board (NEB), the introduction of planning agreements between the Government and individual industries, a new deal for workers in industrial relations and the management of firms, and the protection of vulnerable industries from foreign competition.

Many of these ideas formed the basis of the 1974 election manifesto. On coming to power the Labour Government set about implementing at least some of them. The Industrial Relations Act was repealed; a National Enterprise Board, whose job would be to act as a state holding company to encourage investment and improve productivity, was created, and a system of planning agreements between industries and state was established. A new 'Social Contract' would bind both government and trade unions to moderate wage demands. In fact, the Social Contract resulted in anything but moderation. Weekly wage increases jumped from 12.2 per cent in 1973 to 29.4 per cent in 1974. Inflation too bounded ahead, reaching 16.1 per cent in 1974 and a staggering 24.2 per cent in 1975 (Figure 3.1). Finally, the Conservatives' quite generous public expenditure targets for 1974 and 1975 were met in full.

1974 was a bad year for all the developed countries. The quadrupling of oil prices by the Organisation of Petroleum Exporting Countries (OPEC) in late 1973 precipitated a sharp down-turn in world trade and an acceleration of inflation everywhere (see Briefing 3.6). A good part of the 1974–75 inflation can be attributed to these international forces.

However, Britain suffered from additional problems and its industrial competitiveness continued to decline. British trade unions were more successful than those in many other countries in keeping wage rates up to or beyond the rate of inflation. In fact until the end of the 1970s, in spite of general economic difficulties,

BRIEFINGS

3.6 OPEC AND THE OIL CRISES OF THE 1970S

Partly as a result of the increased economic activity associated with US intervention in the Vietnam War (1964–72), oil and other commodity prices increased rapidly during the late 1960s and early 1970s. As a result, the bargaining power of commodity producers increased substantially. Most of the world's oil came from Arab states and poorer Third World countries who formed a cartel (a price and production fixing arrangement among producers) called the Organisation of Petroleum Exporting Countries (OPEC), to increase the price of oil by bargaining. When Israel went to war with Egypt and Syria in 1973, OPEC decided to increase the price of oil in order to punish Israel and its Western backers. Within a year oil prices increased fivefold on the world markets, bringing severe inflation to the industrialised countries. Countries such as Britain were particularly hard hit, having no indigenous oil supplies. In addition, powerful trade unions were able to insist that wages kept up with or exceeded price increases, thus fuelling further inflation. The disruptive effects of this inflation were considerable and led indirectly to the bailing out of the British economy in 1976 by the IMF (see Briefing 3.5). Later in the decade a second oil crisis with accompanying price increases was caused by the Iranian revolution. The new regime in Iran was deeply hostile to the West and persuaded OPEC to precipitate another price rise. By 1979–80, however, Britain's North Sea oil began to be extracted. As a result, Britain benefited from the increased oil price and the pound sterling appreciated rapidly on the foreign exchange markets. Since the early 1980s OPEC has been in disarray as a result of conservation measures in the West, increases in oil production in such areas as Alaska and the North Sea, and internal divisions within the original OPEC countries.

the majority of the British population enjoyed growing prosperity and a rising standard of living.

From a general economic and business point of view, however, the combination of low industrial productivity, accelerating rates of inflation and wages, and a high level of public expenditure could not go on. Moreover, unemployment was rising fast. The assumptions of Keynesian demand management seemed no longer to apply. According to Keynesian orthodoxy, unemployment or under-capacity occurred only when prices and interest rates were low. Inflation was a product of rapid growth and labour shortages. Now, however, most countries experienced both inflation and high rates of unemployment at the same time. This fact, above all others, was responsible for the revival both of incomes policies and, crucially, of traditional monetary policies.

Monetarism and incomes policy 1975–79

The Labour left's policies for radical surgery on the British economy came to very little: the surgery turned out to be of a conservative rather than socialist variety. The first change came in July 1975 when a government now dominated by Labour's right wing announced a new incomes policy which granted £6 a week for all workers earning up to £8,500 and nothing for those earning over this figure. This was not a statutory policy but an agreement worked out between the Government and the Trades Union Congress. It was remarkably successful (strikes fell to a 22-year low during the £6 a week period) and demonstrated the growing strength of the TUC. In April 1976 the Labour PM, Harold Wilson, resigned to be replaced by James Callaghan, but this did not affect economic policy. In July 1976 the informal agreement was renewed and a 5 per cent limit agreed, and again in 1977 when a 10 per cent limit was accepted. In 1978, 5 per cent was proposed but effectively rejected by the trade unions. Their resentment at government imposition of this 'ceiling' was shown by widespread transport and public service strikes in the 'Winter of Discontent' (1978–79) which almost certainly lost Labour the May 1979 election.

Just as important as incomes policy was the Government's conversion to a limited form of monetarism. During 1976 the selling of sterling reached panic proportions. Fixed exchange rates (the Bank of England commitment to buy sterling for fixed sums in other currencies) had been abandoned in 1971 and left free to fall. And fall the pound did, to a low of $1.57 at one point. Britain was approaching the point where the Government could not meet immediate payments on outstanding debts. In exchange for massive loans from the International Monetary Fund, Denis Healey, the Chancellor, agreed to new controls on the money supply. Interest rates rose to a record 15.5 per cent and public expenditure was cut. After complex negotiations, the International Monetary Fund (IMF) and the Treasury agreed that the Public Sector Borrowing Requirement, the amount needed by the Government to cover the gap between resources and expenditure (see Briefing 3.7), should be trimmed by £3 billion over two years. In fact, public spending did not fall quite as rapidly as planned. But the very idea of using public sector spending

Key term

Monetarism – a revised version of neo-classical economics which, contrary to Keynesianism, argues that government should minimise its involvement in economic matters, except for controlling the money supply as a way of holding down inflation.

Key term

Public Sector Borrowing Requirement (PSBR) – the amount borrowed by government to help finance its annual expenditure.

BRIEFINGS

3.7 THE PUBLIC SECTOR BORROWING REQUIREMENT (PSBR)

Put simply, the PSBR is the difference between government revenue and expenditure. As was noted in Briefing 3.2, British governments after the Second World War were committed to full employment and running up the national debt was deemed necessary for this end. Note that the annual public debt in Britain is labelled a *requirement* rather than an option. With the intervention of the IMF to bail out the economy in 1976, holding down public spending became a priority (see Briefing 3.5), and the Conservative Government elected in 1979 was determined to make a reduction in the PBSR a top priority. In 1980 the Government launched its Medium Term Financial Strategy which aimed to reduce the PBSR in stages from 4.8 per cent of GDP in 1979–80 to under 3 per cent by 1983–84. In the event the PSBR increased to 5.7 per cent of GDP in 1980–81 and induced the government to produce a very deflationary budget in 1981. This, together with a period of sustained economic growth from 1983, reduced the PSBR to 0.9 per cent of GDP in 1986–87 and gave a surplus in the following two years, which was helped by proceeds from privatisation during the period. By the early 1990s, however, recession took its toll on government revenues and the PSBR once again moved into deficit, reaching over 5 per cent of GDP by 1996. The Labour Government elected in 1997 pledged to reduce this figure to well below 3 per cent over a five-year period. Note that the Maastricht convergence criteria require governments to keep their annual debt liability to below 3 per cent of GDP.

as the major instrument of economic policy was new, notwithstanding Roy Jenkins' more limited efforts in this direction between 1968 and 1970.

The combination of incomes policy and public expenditure cuts reduced inflation quite quickly to a low of around 8 per cent between 1978 and 1979 (Figure 3.1). However, unemployment remained stubbornly high. Labour's plans both for industrial reorganisation and social reform were rendered ineffective by the spending cuts. As with its predecessor, crisis management rather than social reform became the Government's overriding preoccupation, and more and more problems focused on the reaction of the trade unions to government intervention.

THE 1980s: BACK TO THE MARKET

In fact, government intervention, whether of the Labour or the old Conservative variety, seemed increasingly to create more problems than it solved. Perhaps the solution lay in a return to the free trading and free market ideas associated with the Golden Age of the mid-nineteenth century? These were particularly attractive as they had also encouraged hard work, thrift, saving and respect for authority, virtues which many thought the country had lost in the preceding 20 years and which were traditional sources of support for the Conservative Party.

In fact the Conservatives under Margaret Thatcher won the general election of May 1979 amid a wave of popular revulsion against the strikes and trade union excesses of the 'Winter of Discontent'. The new Prime Minister and her closest associates had been converted to the belief that Britain was suffering from political and moral breakdown, traceable to the excessive government intervention fostered by socialism. They believed that the 'Nanny State', as they called it, gave everybody an assurance that they would be bailed out if things went wrong for them. Consequently they engaged in all sorts of irresponsible behaviour, since they did not have to suffer the consequences of their actions.

According to Thatcher's ideology, those who suffered were the solid moral majority who did behave responsibly, saved for old age and worked hard. These were denied the fruits of their labour by a swollen state apparatus which took away their savings in taxation, depressed their initiative by over-regulation, while rewarding 'scroungers' and going soft on criminals.

A major imperative, therefore, was to cut government down to size and limit its intervention in society. By doing so it could distance itself from those who had usurped its authority, particularly trade unions, and act with force where it had to intervene, notably in support of law and order and free-market reform. A strong government could also assert British interests abroad, in collaboration with like-minded American administrations. Bolstered by the enhanced economic growth which these policies would bring it could also push the European Union in a free trade direction.

These leading ideas inspired government action both under Margaret Thatcher (1979–90) and her successor as Conservative Prime Minister, John Major (1991–97). However, their actual application varied under different Conservative governments and at different points during this 18-year period. We can divide it into four phases which we examine in detail below.

The new monetarism 1979–83

The new Conservative Government of 1979 was determined to avoid the expediency and pragmatism of the 1970–74 Heath Government. The Conservatives were pledged to solve Britain's economic problems not by planning or incomes policies, but through rigid adherence to monetarist orthodoxy. Once given a stable operating climate of low inflation and taxes, the market would bring about recovery. The Government's role in industrial revival would be minimal.

To achieve a low rate of inflation the money supply would have to be carefully controlled. So on coming to office the Conservatives attempted to cut projected public expenditure quite dramatically and raised interest rates to record levels. In order to finance lower income taxes, the indirect tax on sales (VAT or value-added tax) was also raised, a fact which partly accounted for a quickly rising rate of inflation during 1979–80. Unleashed from incomes policy, wage rates also increased rapidly, although little higher than the rate of inflation.

The reduction in money supply in combination with the world downturn in economic activity which occurred between 1978 and 1981 quickly lowered the level of activity in the British economy. Unemployment increased from an already high 5.3 per cent in 1979 to over 11 per cent in 1982. It would be over-simple to claim that the Government's main *strategy* was to use unemployment to reduce wage rates and therefore inflation. Undoubtedly, however, this was the *result* of government policy.

On the industrial front the NEB, while not disbanded, was quickly reduced in resources and status. The nationalised industries were required to operate strictly according to commercial criteria. Any idea of social planning or reforms involving increased expenditure was put into cold storage to await economic recovery. Unfortunately this was not even faintly visible until 1982.

As a strategy for the rapid revitalisation of British industry, the new policy was hardly successful. It is important to stress, however, that at least one component (a policy of high interest rates and expenditure cuts) had been pioneered by the Labour Government between 1976 and 1979. The major change was the new devotion to market principles, which naturally meant rejection of a prices and incomes policy. But from 1981 this crept back in various forms, notably by imposing cash limits on what government departments, public authorities and nationalised industries were allowed to offer to their employees. The need for some kind of incomes policy was in line with developments under previous governments. Similarly in the field of industrial policy, even during its first year of office, the Thatcher Government was prepared to continue support for lame duck industries such as British Leyland and British Steel. Moreover, it actually strengthened the industrial retraining programmes inherited from Labour. This, together with increasing state payments to the unemployed, prevented the Government from reducing public expenditure as a percentage of GDP. The bottom of the very deep 1980–81 recession occurred in late 1981 and thereafter the economy began to show signs of improvement. However, recovery was from a very low base and unemployment continued to rise until 1985.

Privatisation and deregulation 1983–87

Key term
Privatisation – the opposite of nationalisation, privatisation is the returning of nationalised industries wholly or partly to the private sector.

Until 1983 the Thatcher Government favoured monetarism: a belief that control of the amount of money circulating in the economy would alone improve general economic efficiency. From 1983, however, monetary targets were rarely met and ministers became less and less dependent on the theory. They did not, however, abandon their free market philosophy. Denationalisation (or 'privatisation'), reducing trade union power, and increasing economic incentives in the public sector all remained central to government policy. The British National Oil Corporation, Jaguar Cars, British Leyland, British Telecom, the Trustee Savings Bank, British Gas and British Airways, Rolls Royce and many council-owned homes were sold. In the late 1980s water companies, electricity supply and other 'natural monopolies' traditionally within the public sector were also privatised.

Major legislation in 1980, 1982 and 1984 all but transformed industrial relations law. 'Closed shops' (i.e. factories where all the workforce have to join a union) had to be approved in a secret ballot by four-fifths of the workers; secondary picketing (i.e. the picketing of firms not themselves party to an industrial dispute) was outlawed; secret ballots were introduced to endorse industrial action, to elect top union officials, and to approve the collection of union political funds. These laws, together with continuing high unemployment, substantially weakened the trade unions. From 1979–95 their membership in most cases halved. They were further debilitated by the costly and often violent miners' strike of 1984–85, which ended with a split in the National Union of Mineworkers and an effective victory for the Government. Many mines were closed and the remnants of the industry were sold off in the mid-1990s.

Unemployment remained the Thatcher Government's Achilles' heel. By 1987 the number and scope of youth employment schemes, retraining programmes and other employment creation devices had increased considerably. Through all of this, however, the Government never entertained the possibility of a return to an official incomes policy or to an overtly interventionist industrial policy, let alone anything that could be called economic planning. By 1985, although the world price of oil had declined, so reducing vital revenue from North Sea oil, the economy began to expand very rapidly by British standards, culminating in the frenetic 'boom' of 1987–88.

Plate 3.3 Nicholas Garland cartoon in the *Daily Telegraph*, 23.9.81 showing unemployment about to go through the 3 million mark under Thatcher

Free markets and renewed problems 1987–92

In spite of its overwhelming victory in the general election of June 1987, the third Thatcher administration was acutely aware of the political dangers from those left out of free market prosperity, above all minority ethnic groups, inner-city residents, and particularly members of these groups living in the Midlands and North. They had all suffered more than anyone else from the accumulated problems of nineteenth- and twentieth-century industrialisation, and from accelerated deindustrialisation in the 1980s. Intervention in these areas had traditionally involved high levels of public expenditure on housing, transport and social services, with central Government relying on locally elected councils to effect its policies. The Conservatives, in line with their free market philosophy, sought instead to remove what they saw as the dead hand of Labour-dominated local government through various measures tried out in the mid-1980s and now intensified. The centrally controlled Youth Training Scheme, channelling the energies of the young unemployed, was extended and made semicompulsory; enterprise zones with suspension of normal planning regulations were set up under nominated boards; council house sales continued and private renting of houses was encouraged. State schools were given the right to opt entirely out of local authority control and thus gain much greater autonomy. Subsidies for public transport were effectively removed and competition was encouraged. Meanwhile moral and administrative pressure was applied to those receiving unemployment benefit to take any form of work available, however low-paid and unattractive. Vigorous attempts were also initiated to break away from national pay settlements, so that firms operating in areas of high unemployment could pay less.

By such means the Government hoped to render the depressed areas more attractive to private enterprise by capitalising on their potential reserves of cheap labour. Paradoxically, however, this attempt to free the local economy involved the use of considerable coercive power by central Government, particularly on local Government and trade unions, the major centres of opposition to its policies. Central direction also extended to individuals, particularly the young and the unemployed. To a considerable extent, Conservative policies could be seen as changing the forms and focus of government intervention, rather than reducing the extent of intervention overall.

The attempt to get government out of the economy appeared by the end of the 1980s to have had real but limited success. In areas of traditional strength – finance and services centred on South-East England – free enterprise policies had strengthened Britain's competitive position in an era of growing interdependence and internationalisation of markets. They had not averted the industrial decline of the outlying areas, but no previous policies had done that either. By 1991, however, it had become clear that the recovery was temporary and linked to special conditions such as the upsurge in world trade in the mid-1980s and, above all, the peaking of oil revenues. These would have freed any government from the balance of payment problems which had dogged previous economic initiatives.

The stock market 'crash' of October 1987 convinced the Government that in order to avert a recession it was necessary to stimulate the economy by lowering interest rates. At the same time, the third Thatcher Government was less intent on holding down public expenditure. It had a surplus of revenues over expenditures and had eliminated the annual Public Sector Borrowing Requirement (PSBR) by 1987. But the expected downturn in economic activity following the collapse of world stock prices in October 1987 never transpired. As a result, the economy became seriously overheated in 1988, culminating in an inflation rate of close to 10 per cent (Figure 3.1). Remedial action in the form of punitively high interest rates followed rapidly, which in turn depressed the housing and property markets and helped precipitate the 1990–92 recession.

A number of other countries went through a similar boom/slump cycle during the late 1980s and early 1990s. In few others was the initial stimulus to growth and inflation so great or the subsequent deflationary reaction so draconian. Britain therefore experienced a longer and deeper recession than any comparable country.

THE 1990s: RETURN TO CONSENSUS

A new consensus 1992–97

The Conservatives' surprise election victory in 1992, giving them a record fourth term, was not just a confirmation of the Thatcher policies of the 1980s. Some of the Thatcher agenda remained: lower taxes on incomes and profits, privatisation and increasing competition and self-management within the public sector. But some was dropped: most importantly, the Major Governments no longer pursued orthodoxy in the national accounts. Public expenditure was allowed to rise to a point where by 1995 the Public Sector Borrowing Requirement rose above 6 per cent of GDP. Money was initially pumped into health, education, transport and a range of other areas before further cuts were imposed from 1994 onwards to finance reductions in income tax.

The Major Government's domestic policy might therefore be characterised as a more relaxed and pragmatic form of Thatcherism. Indeed it seemed to be running out of policy ideas. Labour accepted many of the Thatcherite changes while emphasising some of its own traditional priorities like welfare and education. From 1995 the British economy recovered ahead of its European partners and much of the Government's energy went into managing the boom so as to sustain steady growth and avoid a subsequent recession.

Much of the Major Government's attention had also to be given to British relationships with the European Union. Mrs Thatcher had been a strong upholder of British sovereignty – the idea that the British Government should always have the last say on what was done on British territory. This had caused tensions with other countries in the European Union, particularly France and Germany, who were strong supporters of a closer (and even a federal) European Union.

The single most important move towards European Union in the 1980s was the Single European Act (SEA). This aimed to abolish all restraints to trade within the European Union by 1992. To speed up progress it gave the European Commission and European Court greater powers of regulation and intervention, independent of national governments. It also introduced majority voting, on matters related to the development of the market, among Member States in the Council of Ministers. (For more detail on the European Union see Chapter 4.)

Moves towards a European Free Market were wholly in line with Thatcherite thinking. Her warm endorsement of the economic aims of the SEA seems to have blinded her to its political consequences. Opening up markets demands strong political intervention, as her own experience in Britain might have warned her. In delegating greater powers to the 'Brussels bureaucracy', even to enforce free trade, she was undermining the autonomy of the British Government and Parliament.

This was masked up to 1991 by the fact that British commissioners and advisers and many neoliberal economists were at the forefront in striking down protectionist measures in countries like France and Germany. Under John Major, however, it became clear that the free market was simply a stage on the road to closer political union. The Treaty of Maastricht (1992) committed countries of the European Union to closer integration of social and economic policies, and to collective decision making in many areas. Britain reserved the right to opt out of the creation of a single currency if it wished, and refused to accept the 'Social Chapter' on minimal working conditions for European employees.

Even so, the treaty seemed to a substantial body of 'Eurosceptics' in the Conservative Party to go too far. Their scepticism was reinforced by the improvement in the British economy after the country was forced out of the European Monetary System (EMS), which obliged members to keep their currencies within narrow limits in relation to each other (see Chapter 4 for a detailed account of the events of 'Black Wednesday', 1992, which forced Britain and Italy out of the EMS).

As France and Germany powered ahead with their project of a Federal Union, and as the European institutions became more active in Britain, the persistent opposition of the Conservative Eurosceptics spread to other aspects of government activity. They objected to the slackening pace of Thatcherite reform and threatened to vote against a whole series of government measures unrelated to Europe.

With a miniscule majority in Parliament, the Major Government (itself split internally) took an increasingly negative stance in Europe to retain Eurosceptic support. This in turn alienated the pro-European Conservatives. Supported by most of industry and the City, they wanted to go along with European monetary union (EMU), either because they feared the consequences if Britain was left out, or because they saw positive benefits for London as the financial centre of a more integrated Union. Divisions both in Cabinet and in Parliament contributed to the impression of an indecisive, do-nothing government which helped lose them the election of 1997.

New Labour?

The Labour Party returned to office in May 1997, for the first time in nearly 18 years. Much has changed since it was defeated in 1979. In particular, Labour has accepted most of the Thatcherite agenda, including the need for strict financial discipline and tax reductions. How far this will square with spending more on welfare and education – Labour's traditional priorities – remains to be seen.

Significant policy initiatives have been taken, however, without spending money. Labour has a much more positive attitude towards EU intervention to secure social rights and has, therefore, accepted the social provisions of the Treaty of Maastricht. It is also more positive than were the Conservatives over monetary union, although on coming to power the new Labour Government confirmed that Britain would not be in the first group of EMU members in 1999. As membership is supported by the City and most of industry, Labour has a rare chance to win over the business interests which usually oppose it. With its acceptance of the privatisations and of the free market, it might conceivably end up as a generally more attractive option for business than a divided Conservative Party.

Goodwill earned in this way may carry over to the constitutional reforms Labour is carrying through. The most important of these is setting up a parliament to oversee Scottish affairs and establishing an Assembly, with more limited powers, for Wales (see Chapter 6). These measures could, however, trigger a more general review of the British constitution as a whole, with particular emphasis on the protection of individual and group rights and a change in the electoral system, the rules for translating party votes into parliamentary seats. Any change would have to increase Liberal Democratic representation in the House of Commons. This could result in an era of coalition or minority governments, thus finally breaking the two-party monopoly on power which has endured since 1868.

AN OVERVIEW OF POSTWAR EVENTS

To provide a general background to postwar developments, our 'Milestones' give a chronology of the main events, international as well as domestic. At some points in this period attention was deflected from economic problems to alarming foreign developments and the danger of nuclear war. In the 1950s, when the economy enjoyed a modest postwar boom and trade unions could be placated with a share of increasing profits, both the Korean War and disengagement from most remaining territories of the prewar colonial empire preoccupied successive Conservative governments. With diminishing commitments elsewhere, entry to the European Community seemed increasingly attractive as a cure for the ills of British industry, by opening wider markets and intensifying domestic competition. After ignoring the actual formation of the Community in 1956, abortive negotiations for entry occurred in 1962 and 1968 before they succeeded under Edward Heath in 1972 and were reluctantly endorsed by the Labour Government in 1975 following a national referendum on the subject (see Chapter 4).

The eruption of communal strife in Northern Ireland and intensified demands for some form of autonomy in Wales and Scotland also took up considerable political energy in the 1970s. By the end of that decade, however, even these movements were being seen as tensions generated at least in part by economic malaise. As membership of the Community failed to exert any visible economic effects and governments took increasingly far-ranging actions to boost economic growth, they provoked ever more extensive reactions against their policies. Thus the moderate Labour Government of Callaghan, with its muted interventionist policy, fired radical left-wing demands for control over the parliamentary leadership to ensure the enactment of social reforms and supporting measures of government economic control. Their success in getting such demands accepted in the Labour Party after 1979 prompted a secession by some established leaders and MPs to form the Social Democratic Party, which in alliance with the Liberals won just over a quarter of the votes in the General Election of 1983 and over one-fifth in 1987, undermining Labour's established electoral base.

Labour support for more extensive intervention prompted the Thatcherite reaction to get government out of business and industrial relations altogether. Even so, the trade unions felt the Government was responsible for the three million unemployed and must be forced to help the jobless through subsidies and programmes of job creation. 'Nonintervention' was almost as much a recipe for political confrontation in the industrial field as earlier governments' positive intervention had been.

The overall consequence of a shrinking industrial base and uneven prosperity was an intensification of political conflict at many levels of society. At the bottom, violent rioting in many urban centres in 1981, 1985 and 1991 was a warning that socially deprived groups could not just be left to bear the consequences of unemployment on their own. Although trade unions were weakened by legislation and unemployment, the 1984–85 miners' strike, a bitter teachers' dispute in 1985–86, and violent picketing of News International's Wapping plant in 1986–87, showed that serious industrial problems remained, even if masked and at times deflected by increased prosperity among those in work. Industrial relations may have been transformed by weakening the trade unions and imposing tighter work discipline in highly competitive conditions, but the British Airways' strike and lockout of 1997 showed that strife in the workplace had not disappeared.

ESSAYS

1. In what ways was the role of government enhanced during the 1933 to 1951 period? What legacy remains of these changes in the late 1990s?

2. What were the main differences in economic policy between Conservative and Labour governments during the 1951 to 1970 period?

3. Why was there an apparent breakdown of the postwar consensus after 1970? Have we returned to an economic consensus in the late 1990s?

4. Was there a decline of the British economy from 1950 to 1980? Has the situation changed in the 1990s?

SUMMARY

This chapter has shown how British governments broke away from Free Trade doctrines in the 1930s and 1940s by protecting industry and society from the rigours of full competition. In particular governments intervened to:

- Nationalise basic industries (coal, steel, transport, and public utilities) so as to guarantee price and production levels and a minimum level of service.

- Use monetary policy to achieve a high level of activity in the economy with top priority being given to full employment.

- Use regional and land use planning laws to direct investment and employment towards reviving older industrial regions and alleviate crowding in the inner cities.

- Create a comprehensive welfare state to provide all citizens with basic health care, education and adequate housing.

From the 1950s to the late 1970s few governments challenged these policies. However, it became increasingly difficult to fund them because:

PROJECTS

1. Using statistical and other sources trace the relative performance of the British economy since 1930. Why, in this period, have manufacturing and mining declined so dramatically?

2. Identify the main trade unions in modern Britain. Trace the fortunes of the trade union movement since 1945.

3. Catalogue government policies of nationalisation, denationalisation and privatisation since 1945. Account for the changes in policy over time.

- Britain suffered from chronic balance of payments problems which led to repeated bouts of 'stop–go', i.e. overheating of the economy followed by the need for deflation.

- The international economic environment became more difficult during the 1970s with the abandonment of fixed exchange rates and the rapid increase in commodity prices.

- Britain's economic performance was poor compared with other countries as strikes and low productivity led to an ever present sense of economic crisis. The preferred solutions to these problems – incomes policy and economic planning – gradually became discredited.

- By the mid-1970s, intellectual and political opinion moved in favour of market solutions to economic problems, although sections of the Labour Party continued to support strong state intervention.

- Since the 1980s a combination of market solutions to economic problems together with fiscal and monetary discipline have dominated the political agenda. Full employment has been given a lower priority, although the Labour Party remains more concerned than the Conservative Party with employment problems. Similarly, both parties now accept that welfare state benefits have to be selective rather than universal. The major difference between the parties is on the degree of selectivity, with Labour favouring higher benefit levels.

- By the late 1990s the performance of the British economy seemed to have recovered to reach the average (or by some measures, above the average) of the developed countries.

- By the late 1990s, the major tensions in economic policy revolved around Britain's relationship with Europe. This issue was not only the source of major conflict within the Conservative Party but also between the Conservative and Labour parties, with Labour accepting the social provisions of the Maastricht Treaty, and the Conservatives rejecting them.

MILESTONES

MILESTONES: EVENTS, POLICIES AND GOVERNMENTS 1931–97

BRITAIN	WORLD
'National' Governments, 1931–40 *(MacDonald, Baldwin, Chamberlain)* *Conservative-dominated*	World Depression, 1928–39
Abandonment of gold standard, 1931	Rise of Hitler in Germany
Massive unemployment, 1930–38	
Tariffs on foreign imports, 1931–35	Nazi annexations:
Formation of industrial cartels, 1931–38	Austria (1938), Czechoslovakia, 1939
Marketing boards for Agriculture	Attack on Poland, 1939, precipitates war
Special Areas Acts, 1935, 1936, 1937	
Rearmament, 1936–40	
Series of Reports on land use, town planning, population distribution, 1938–40	

MILESTONES: EVENTS, POLICIES AND GOVERNMENTS 1931–97 (continued)

BRITAIN

WORLD

Wartime Coalition, 1940–45 (Churchill)
Unprecedented control of labour, supplies, food, production, 1940–45
Beveridge Report on social insurance 1942

Second World War, 1939–45

Labour Government, 1945–51 (Attlee)
National Health Service Act, 1946
National Insurance Act, 1946
State ownership of coal industry, gas, electricity, transport and steel
Town and Country Planning Act, 1947
Full employment policy, wage and dividends freeze, control of production in many areas, rationing
Independence of India, Pakistan, Burma and Ceylon, 1948

German surrender, 1945
Japanese surrender, 1945
Dislocation of international trade after Second World War
Berlin crisis, 1948–49, marks start of Cold War with Soviet Union and intensification of Western Alliance (NATO)

Conservative Governments, 1951–59 (Churchill, Eden, Macmillan)
Deregulation of trade and financial controls
Limited denationalisation of iron and steel industry, and road transport
Invasion of Suez, 1956

Korean War, 1950–53
World economic growth

Formation of European Community, 1956

Conservative Governments, 1959–64 (Macmillan, Home)
Independence of most African colonies
Wage and price freeze, 1962–63
Unsuccessful application to join EC, 1962

Détente with Soviet Union, 1960–79
Relaxation of Cold War and arms race

Labour Governments, 1964–70 (Wilson)
Balance of payments crisis, 1964–66
National economic plan effectively abandoned, 1966–67
Increasing credit, wage and dividend restrictions, 1966–69
Devaluation of £ sterling, 1966
Unsuccessful application to join EC, 1968
Plan to regulate trade union and industrial relations, 1969–70 (revealed in Green Paper *In Place of Strife*, 1969) defeated by trade union and internal Labour opposition
Intervention of British troops in Northern Ireland, 1969

US involvment in Vietnam War, 1964–73
Increasing liberalisation of world trade under GATT (General Agreement on Trade and Tariffs)

MILESTONES: EVENTS, POLICIES AND GOVERNMENTS 1931–97 (continued)

BRITAIN	WORLD
Conservative Governments, 1970–74 (Heath)	
Floating exchange rate for £ sterling, 1971	
Industrial Relations Act, 1971 (legal regulation of trade unions)	
'U-turn' from not interfering in industry or wage negotiations to restrictions on wage and salary increases	
Suspension of Northern Ireland Parliament and Direct Rule, 1972	
Reorganisation of local government units into larger ones, 1972–75	
Entry to EEC, 1973	
Easy credit and high inflation, 1973–74	
Successful strikes by National Union of Mineworkers, 1972 and 1974, which disrupt entire country	
Discovery of oil in British North Sea	Rise in world oil prices, 1973–74
Labour Governments, 1974–79 (mostly in minority) (Wilson, Callaghan)	
Major election gains by Scottish and Welsh Nationalists, 1974	
High inflation, 1974 onwards	
Social Contract with trade unions, involving limits on prices and incomes and legal concessions, 1975–78	
Referendum for continuing membership of EC, 1975	
Balance of payments crisis, 1976	
Severe credit restrictions and increasing cuts in projected government expenditure, 1976–79	
High and increasing unemployment, 1975 onwards	
'Winter of discontent', 1979 (strikes by numerous groups of workers including transport strike)	British oil revenues from North Sea equal payments for foreign oil
Defeat of government proposals for Scottish and Welsh devolution, 1979	
Conservative Governments, 1979–97 (Thatcher, Major)	
Policy of restricting stock of money to bring down inflation involves further cuts in government expenditure, 1979–82, and central restrictions on local government expenditure	Increasing friction between Soviet Union and West from 1979
Legal restrictions on union's rights to picket during strikes and to extend scope of stoppage	World economic depression intensifying up to 1981
Falling inflation and greatly increasing unemployment, 1980–82	
Savage and extensive urban riots, 1981	

MILESTONES: EVENTS, POLICIES AND GOVERNMENTS 1931–97 (continued)

BRITAIN	WORLD
Foundation of Social Democratic Party and leadership defections from Labour, 1981	
Falklands War, 1982	World economic recovery, 1982–86
Re-election of Conservatives with large majority, Liberal–Social Democratic Alliance comes close to Labour in terms of votes but not seats, 1983	
Miners' strike, 1984–85: most bitter industrial dispute since war	Oil and other commodity prices fall, 1986
Renewed urban riots, 1985	
Unemployment reaches 13 per cent, then begins to fall	
Renewed balance of payments problems with drop in oil revenues, 1988–97	Relaxation of Soviet–Western relations, 1986–87, serious disarmament negotiations between the USSR and USA
'Privatisation' of many nationalised industries including gas	Single European market planned for mid-1990s
Re-election of Conservatives with large majority, 1987, Labour fails to recover significantly and Alliance fails to break through	
Economic boom, 1987–89, followed by severe recession,1990–94	Break-up of Soviet Union follows peaceful liberation of East European states, 1989–91
Britain joins Exchange Rate Mechanism (ERM), 1990	
Replacement of local rates by Community Charge (poll tax) provokes massive non-payments and riots, 1989–90	Gulf War, 1991
Replacement of Mrs Thatcher as Prime Minister by John Major, 1990	Maastricht Treaty on further European Union, Britain opts out of Social Charter and reserves decision on monetary union
Conservatives returned with a majority of 21 with John Major as Prime Minister, 1992	
Britain forced out of ERM by currency crisis, 1992	
Increasing internal conflict in Conservative Party between 'Eurosceptics' and pro-Europeans	
Government forced into increasing opposition to 'Europe'	
Slow economic recovery, 1994–96	Intergovernmental Conference on closer European Union, 1997
'New Labour' wins general election, 1997	
Labour Government, 1997 (Blair)	Russia accepts eastward expansion of NATO
Bank of England given autonomy to act on interest rates	
Labour endorses strict financial orthodoxy	
British economic performance among EU countries improves	
Referenda approve a Scottish assembly and a degree of devolution for Wales, September 1997	France, Germany and some other EU states find it increasingly difficult to meet EU convergence criteria but remain determined to have monetary union in 1999

FURTHER READING

A very large literature on British economic policy exists. Among the best recent accounts of economic decline are those by David Coates, *The Question of UK Decline* (London: Harvester Wheatsheaf, 1994) and Andrew Gamble, *Britain in Decline* (London: Macmillan, 4th edn. 1994).

On the politics of economic change, see, for the early period, Samuel H. Beer, *Modern British Politics* (London: Faber, 1965) and for the 1970s, Keith Middlemas, *Politics in Industrial Society* (London: Deutsch, 1979).

On the Thatcher era, see David Marsh (ed.), *Implementing Thatcherite Policies* (Milton Keynes: Open University Press, 1992). A longer term cultural perspective is provided by Martin Weiner, *English Culture and the Decline of the Industrial Spirit 1850 to 1980* (Cambridge: Cambridge University Press, 1981).

http://www.awl-he.com/politics/newbritpol

Internet resources – visit *The New British Politics* Webpage for links to a specially-chosen selection of Internet resources relevant to this Chapter.

http://www.awl-he.com/politics/newbritpol

Britain in Europe

By the 1990s, British politics were increasingly dominated by the question of European Union. The former European (Economic) Community (EC, EEC) had changed its name to the 'European Union' (EU) by the Treaty of Maastricht (1992). This symbolised the intention of its Member States, particularly France and Germany, to transform it into a federal union.

The British Government's reservations were signalled by its opt-out (uniquely among Member States) from the 'Social Chapter' of the Treaty, which set minimum working conditions. Conservatives saw these as jeopardising British economic competitiveness, which was based upon work flexibility and low wages. Labour agreed with other Member States in interpreting the opt-out as an attempt to turn Britain into the 'sweatshop of Europe'.

Britain further reserved its position on whether to have a common European currency and this possibility triggered furious domestic controversy within the Conservative Party. The inseparability of European from domestic politics was shown by the limitation of maximum working hours through a decision by the European Court in 1996.

The fact that European bodies could now legislate for Britain independently of the Government and even against its expressed wishes showed that national sovereignty was being eroded. By the same token a new federal entity, in which Britain constituted just one unit, was clearly emerging. The decision whether to go ahead and accept the single currency is clearly the most crucial to be taken by any British government in the late 1990s.

This chapter traces the history and institutional development of the European Union and examines British relationships with it. The fact that the EU is now as much part of British life as local government illustrates that one cannot separate domestic from foreign relationships in explaining British politics.

This chapter covers:

- The origins of the European Union
- Britain and Europe in the early years
- The Gaullist vetoes: Britain rebuffed
- British accession to the EU
- The Single European Act and Maastricht: towards federalism?
- The Conservatives and the currency crisis of 1992
- Europe as a crisis issue in British politics

ORIGINS OF EUROPEAN UNION: THE AFTERMATH OF WAR

The countries of Europe emerged from the Second World War (1939–45) traumatised and divided. Many had been devastated by military action, and almost all had suffered severe economic and social dislocation. Of 26 states existing before the war, three had been annexed by 1941, ten occupied by aggressors, one occupied against its wishes and four occupied and then divided up. During the war, more than 20 million people died, with many millions more injured or displaced. The trauma did not end in 1945. In the three years following the war, the whole of Eastern Europe was occupied by the Soviet Union, civil rights and liberties were suspended, and the subjugated populations forced to adhere to Soviet values in all aspects of economic and social life.

It is not surprising, therefore, that the politicians responsible for rebuilding Western Europe aimed at the closest possible co-operation between countries, leading eventually to some form of economic and political union. The key to successful co-operation was the relationship between Germany and France, the largest of the West European powers. Although they had a long history of mistrust and conflict, which had been the root cause of both world wars, their combined strength could provide a crucial bulwark against Soviet expansionism.

From the very beginning, however, important differences were apparent between the British attitude to European co-operation and that of the Continental powers. The British, while supporting co-operation between the Continental states, were not themselves keen to integrate with other European countries. Instead, the British saw their interests in terms of three overlapping spheres of influence: those of the Empire, the USA and Europe. In this sense they still considered themselves a world power with a status far above that of France and the defeated Axis countries. Quite apart from this, their financial interests and trading relationships gave them stronger overseas links than the continental countries. Britain would certainly encourage France, Germany and the other continental states to co-operate, but it would remain detached from the process.

In contrast, Continental politicians were committed not just to co-operation between France and Germany, but to a much wider project, involving the political and economic integration of all the European states. In this sense pioneers like Jean Monnet (the Planning Commissioner responsible for the modernisation of France), Robert Schuman (France's Foreign Minister) and Konrad Adenauer (Chancellor of the Federal Republic of Germany) were advocates of a European government with powers independent of those of constituent states. Only through total integration would French–German hostility be buried and the family of European nations be guaranteed peace and stability for generations to come.

Although British and Continental attitudes to European co-operation have varied over the half century since the end of the Second World War, the generally enthusiastic approach of Continental Europeans and the sceptical approach of the British have been constants throughout. Underlying this contrast has been the British commitment to free trade and thus to a purely economic Common Market, as distinct from the Continental project for full-blooded political union.

Plate 4.1 Vicky cartoon from the *Daily Express*, 1961, showing Harold Macmillan's reluctance to join the European Union: 'If they want us they will have to make it easy for us'. Charles de Gaulle and Konrad Adenauer lead on their bicycles

"IF THEY WANT US THEY WILL HAVE TO MAKE IT EASY FOR US" —MR. MACMILLAN

Plate 4.1 Vicky cartoon from the *Daily Express*, 1961, showing Harold Macmillan's reluctance to join the European Union: 'If they want us they will have to make it easy for us'. Charles de Gaulle and Konrad Adenauer lead on their bicycles

BRITAIN AND EUROPE: THE EARLY YEARS

From the late 1940s until the mid 1950s there were three distinct initiatives on European co-operation. In 1949 the Council of Europe was created (see Briefing 4.1). This established a 50-year pact 'for collective collaboration in economic, social and cultural matters, and for collective self-defence'. This high-sounding objective was not backed up with legislative powers, however. The Council remained little more than a talking shop during subsequent decades. Originally 10 states joined the Council, but by 1996 this number had expanded to 38. Early attempts to give the organisation real teeth were blocked by those members intent on the defence of national sovereignty, most notably Britain, Ireland and the Scandinavian countries.

Much more ambitious was the attempt to create a European Defence Community (EDC) in the early 1950s, which would establish a European army (see Briefing 4.2). With the rise of Soviet power in Eastern Europe, the need for a pan-European military force was clear. The French, in particular, saw it as a way of making use of German labour while retaining political control over a resurgent German state. At the insistence of the British, the EDC would also have had representative institutions, so the initiative envisaged an incipient European government and assembly.

From the very beginning, however, the British remained on the sidelines. They broadly supported the community idea for the Continental countries but would accept only an 'associated' status for their own forces, which would remain under British command. Participation in traditional treaty arrangements such as the North Atlantic Treaty Organisation (NATO) was one thing; merging British armed forces with those of other powers was quite another. In the event, the

BRIEFINGS

4.1 THE COUNCIL OF EUROPE

The Council of Europe was set up in 1949 as an intergovernmental consultative organisation designed to advance co-operation between members and help encourage democracy and human rights throughout Europe. The Council meets in Strasbourg, France, and is made up of a Committee of Ministers, a Parliamentary Assembly and a Congress of Local and Regional Authorities. Meeting four times a year, the Assembly adopts resolutions and the Council then makes recommendations to members. In spite of this statelike structure, the Council of Europe has no legislative powers. Decisions are taken by consensus of all the members. Until recently the most important function of the Council was the operation of the European Convention on Human Rights which was created in 1954 and whose rules are enforced by the Court of Human Rights. Note that this Court, whose decisions are binding on members, is *not* an EU institution.

By 1996, the Council of Europe had 38 members with another six countries accorded 'guest status'. Since the fall of Communism, the Council's role as a forum for advancing democracy has increased substantially. A newly created European Commission for Democracy through Law advises emerging democratic countries on constitutional and other matters. In addition, membership of the Council is seen as a first step towards membership of the EU.

Plate 4.2 Vicky cartoon in *Evening Standard*, 1962 showing Britain (personified by Harold Macmillan) caught in a dilemma between its Commonwealth commitments and a new European future

"BUT MY DEAR, YOU KNOW — ALL THESE RUMOURS OF OUR BREAK-UP ARE RIDICULOUS!"

BRIEFINGS

4.2 THE EUROPEAN DEFENCE COMMUNITY (EDC) AND THE WEST EUROPEAN UNION (WEU)

Following the outbreak of the Korean War in 1950, with the Soviet threat continuing, the Allies agreed that it was necessary to rearm West Germany. The French Government therefore proposed that the six countries (France, Italy, Belgium, the Netherlands, Luxembourg and West Germany) that had agreed to the European Coal and Steel Community should create a parallel European Defence Community. The EDC was seen at the time as a first step towards the creation of a European army and a European state. In the event, however, both left-wing and right-wing members of the French National Assembly feared a resurgent Germany and refused to ratify the agreement. In addition, the British disliked the idea of a European army, and the Americans wanted German participation in NATO immediately, rather than the several years it would take to work out the details of a European army.

Created in 1955, the West European Union was a compromise solution whereby West Germany was permitted to rearm but could not possess nuclear or biological weapons. In return the Allied occupation of Germany ended, although NATO troops, including a substantial British presence, were to be based on German soil. WEU membership originally consisted of the Six plus the UK. Since then Portugal, Spain and Greece have joined and a number of other countries have associate status. The Council of the WEU, composed of foreign and defence ministers of the Member States, meets twice a year, with the secretariat based in Paris. Increasingly the WEU is viewed as the defence wing of the EU, and during the 1990s, plans were adopted to transform the WEU into a common EU defence organisation.

Key term

Functional integration – integration based upon pragmatic co-operation between states in specific areas of (usually) economic activity. In the European context, functional integration is often contrasted with deeper and wider political integration of a federal kind.

initiative came to nothing. The French General Assembly, fearful of a loss of French sovereignty, refused to ratify the proposal.

Only the third attempt at European integration was to bear fruit. By the 1951 Treaty of Paris, France, West Germany, the Netherlands, Luxembourg, Italy and Belgium (collectively known as the Six, see Map 4.1) created the European Coal and Steel Community (ECSC) with the aim of integrating the administration of the most important industrial raw materials. The British excluded themselves, largely because they continued to see their trade relations in terms of the Empire and North America rather than Europe. The ECSC is important because it established the principle of *functional integration* (integrating specific industrial or economic sectors) under a supranational institutional authority responsible for policing a European policy (see Briefing 4.3).

The ECSC was the precursor of the European Economic Community (EEC) created by the Treaty of Rome in 1957. In turn this was to develop into the European Union in the 1990s. From its very beginning the EEC opened up the possibility of evolving from a loose confederation of countries concerned only with integration in certain functional economic sectors into a much tighter

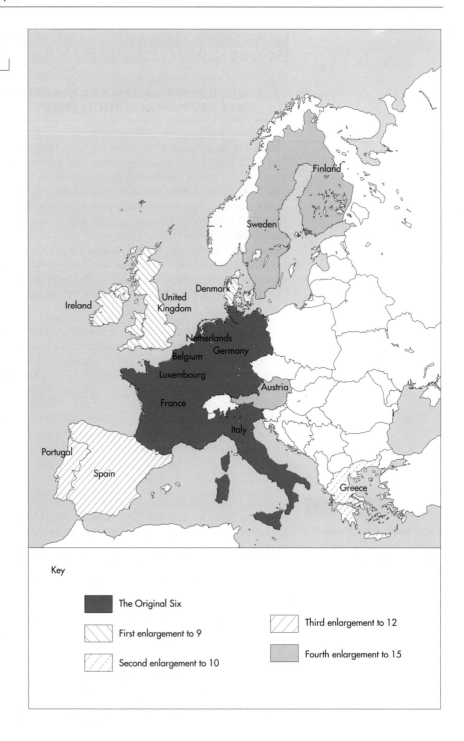

Map 4.1 The enlargement of the European Union 1957–95

Key

The Original Six

First enlargement to 9

Second enlargement to 10

Third enlargement to 12

Fourth enlargement to 15

organisation resembling a federal state. Aware of this ultimate objective, the founding fathers of the EEC created a comprehensive institutional structure which resembled that of a national government. The European Commission acted

BRIEFINGS

4.3 FUNCTIONAL INTEGRATION AND THE COMMON AGRICULTURAL POLICY (CAP)

Following the failure to create a European state, European leaders decided that *functional integration* would make the members of the EC interdependent economically and that this would encourage political integration. The reasoning was that, if the countries of the Six shared common production and pricing policies in such essential goods as coal, steel, atomic power and agriculture, they would be locked into economic interdependence and would therefore have every incentive to co-operate on other matters (a phenomenon which social scientists have called spillover). This would then eliminate the sort of competition and conflict which led to the Second World War.

As an economic project, functional integration proved less than successful. By the late 1950s, national rather than Community priorities dominated policy in coal, steel and in the generation of atomic energy. Only in agriculture did co-operation flourish, mainly because of the political benefits of pleasing large numbers of small farmers in France, Germany and Italy. The Common Agricultural Policy (CAP) set artificial prices for all the major agricultural products. Whenever the world market price of a product fell below this price, the EC imposed tariffs on imports to make up the difference between the market price and the CAP price. Inefficient farmers were, therefore, given an incentive to remain inefficient. Consumers were paying above market prices for food and in addition a surplus was built up which had to be stored. These surpluses – the 'butter mountains' and 'wine lakes' – resulted in a widespread ridiculing of the CAP.

During the 1980s and the 1990s, a number of reforms were initiated, all of which were designed to reduce the level of price support and eventually to replace the intervention price mechanism with direct income supports. While the proportion of the EU budget devoted to the CAP has declined in recent years – as indeed has the agricultural population which at around 5 per cent is just one third of the 1958 figure – there is general agreement that the inefficiencies of the CAP will have to be addressed in future years.

like a government, although for many years its powers were strictly circum-scribed. (Figure 4.1 shows the institutional structure of the EU in the 1990s which is broadly similar to the original design laid down by the Treaty of Rome.[1])

---

[1] Decision-making procedures in the EU are complex and can only be provided schematically in Figure 4.1. The most important relationship is between the citizens of the individual Member States, national governments, the Council of Ministers and the Commission. For major policy and political initiatives the Council remains the key body. For the details of implementation the Commission is centrally placed. These relationships are shown in emphasis in the figure. A secondary, but increasingly important body is the European Parliament which, via the codecision-making procedures introduced by the Maastricht Treaty, now plays a role in a range of policy areas. Finally, the meetings of government leaders (the European Council, not to be confused with the Council of Ministers) can launch major initiatives which are later endorsed by the Council of Ministers.

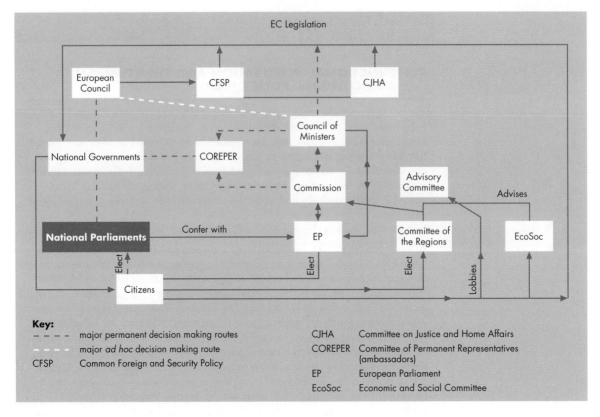

Figure 4.1 Decision making in the European Union
Source: Adapted from Church and Phinnemore (eds), *European Union and European Community* (London: Harvester 1994), Figure 9

Aware of these longer term commitments to integration, the British declined to join the new organisation. It was enthusiastic about the EEC's immediate economic objectives: the creation of a customs union or common market in goods and services among the Member States. But it feared that membership would jeopardise Britain's trading relationships with the Empire and Commonwealth countries, and North America.

The early years of the EEC were dominated by the Common Agricultural Policy (CAP) and the looming presence of the French President, General de Gaulle, who was the prime mover in both European and EEC politics from 1958 to 1969. The CAP was a system of guaranteed price supports for the numerous and generally inefficient farmers of France, Italy and other member states. CAP payments dominated the EEC budget, which gave the EEC the reputation of a protectionist agricultural grouping rather than a promoter of free trade and open markets. General de Gaulle aggravated this problem by refusing to let the organisation proceed on other fronts. He was highly suspicious of those officials and politicians intent on moving the countries of Europe towards federalism. For de Gaulle, individual nation states, not the EEC, should always be the basic unit of governance.

BRITAIN AT THE DOOR: DE GAULLE's VETOES

The European stance of the British changed substantially during these years. By the early 1960s it was clear that British trade was shifting from overseas and towards Europe. In addition, the economies of the Six were performing well and the British were keen to share their new-found prosperity. Finally, changes in both the Conservative and Labour parties encouraged a more pro-European position. Under the leadership of Harold Macmillan the Conservatives had become a modernising, centrist party committed to rapid economic growth and technological change. Similarly, the Labour Party under Harold Wilson was intent on modernisation. For both leaders, participation in an economically dynamic Europe looked attractive. However, both the Conservative Government's application for EC membership in 1963 and the Labour application in 1967 were vetoed by General de Gaulle (see Briefing 4.4).

The vetoes stemmed from de Gaulle's fear that British membership would lead to the EEC's being dominated by Anglo-American interests, but he was wrong about the immediate effects of the Anglo-American relationship. Britain may have had something resembling a special relationship with the USA but this did not equate to an anti-French alliance. In the long run, however, de Gaulle may have been correct in thinking that Britain's overseas interests would produce a structural conflict of interest with the Continental members whose trade and culture were much more centred on Europe itself.

BRIEFINGS

4.4 PRESIDENT DE GAULLE ON THE BRITISH APPLICATION TO JOIN THE EEC 1963

It must be agreed that the entry first of Great Britain, and of [other] states, will completely change the series of adjustments, agreements, compensations and regulations already established between the Six. We would then have to envisage the construction of another Common Market which ... would without any doubt no longer resemble the one the Six have built. Moreover, the Community, growing in that way, would be confronted with all the problems of the economic relations with a crowd of other states, and first of all with the United States ... in the end there would be a colossal Atlantic Community under American domination.

Speech given in Paris, January 1963

BRITAIN JOINS THE COMMUNITY

De Gaulle's rejections of British membership helped rekindle scepticism over Europe among certain sections of both the Conservative and Labour parties. This would come to full fruition during the 1970s and the 1980s. Following the defeat of Labour in the 1970 general election, Edward Heath became prime minister. Heath was an enthusiastic supporter of British membership, and following de Gaulle's resignation in 1969, he successfully negotiated Britain's third application in 1972. Along with Ireland and Denmark, Britain became a member of the European Community (EC) in 1973 (see Map 4.1). Among many Conservative MPs, British participation in Europe was acceptable only so long as the EC confined itself to extending free trade. There was always the possibility of conflict once European integration went beyond that.

Meanwhile most of the opposition to the EC came, not from the Conservatives, but from the Labour Party. Following the defeat of the Wilson Government in 1970, the party moved perceptibly to the left. The narrow Labour victories in the general elections of 1974 brought with them an influx of Labour MPs committed to a radical socialist agenda. Many saw this as being impeded by membership of a 'capitalist', free trade, European Union. In opposition, Labour had therefore pledged itself to 'renegotiating' British membership, a pledge which was to culminate in a national referendum on EC membership in June 1975, the first nationwide referendum ever held in Britain. Like subsequent referendums it was a way for a divided government to shift responsibility for making a difficult decision and avoid tearing itself apart.

The Labour left were convinced that the EC was a 'rich man's club' dominated by German capitalism. Moreover, serious economic dislocation had been caused by global inflation and the oil crisis of 1973 and 1974. Many left-wingers thought that free trade would bring high unemployment, and that the interests of the working class would therefore best be served by a policy of protectionism and state-sponsored industrial investment. At that time, the EC seemed to represent the very antithesis of this sort of economic nationalism.

The centrist Labour leadership put itself firmly behind continuing membership. In the referendum in 1975, 17,378,581 electors voted 'yes' (67.2%) and 8,470,073 voted 'no' (32.8%) (see Table 4.1). Continuing moves towards European integration will generate other referendums in the late 1990s.

'Europe' as an issue in British politics was to remain relatively dormant until the early 1980s, mainly because the British accession was followed by a period of inertia at the European level. Within the EC a crisis of identity emerged as attempts at further integration faltered. In the face of the economic dislocations of the 1970s, national governments tended to rely on national rather than collective solutions to their problems. At the same time, the CAP was increasingly perceived as excessively expensive, wasteful and inefficient. By the late 1970s, agricultural surpluses in the form of food 'mountains' had built up, through the inability of European farmers to sell their produce at the market-determined world price. Instead, the EC bought the produce at a higher price and stored it for

Table 4.1 Referendums held
in European countries on
EC/EU related matters,
1972–94

Country	Issue	Date	Result % Yes	No
France	EC enlargement	21 April 1972	67.7	32.3
Ireland	EC membership	10 May 1972	83.0	17.0
Norway	EC membership	25 September 1972	46.5	53.5
Denmark	EC membership	3 October 1972	63.3	36.7
United Kingdom	Staying in EC	5 June 1975	67.2	32.8
Greenland	Staying in EC	23 February 1982	48.0	52.0
Denmark	Single European Act	27 February 1986	56.2	43.8
Ireland	Single European Act	26 May 1987	70.0	30.0
Denmark	Maastricht Treaty	2 June 1992	49.3	50.7
Ireland	Maastricht Treaty	18 June 1992	67.0	33.0
France	Maastricht Treaty	20 September 1992	51.0	49.0
Denmark	Maastricht Treaty	18 May 1993	56.8	43.2
Austria	EU membership	19 June 1994	66.4	33.6
Finland	EU membership	16 October 1994	56.9	43.1
Sweden	EU membership	13 November 1994	52.2	46.9
Norway	EU membership	28 November 1994	47.5	52.5

Source: T. Bainbridge and A. Teasdale, *The Penguin Companion to the European Union* (London: Penguin, 1996), p. 389

future use. These 'mountains' emphasised the protectionist and interventionist side of the Community and helped bring it into opprobrium on the Conservative right.

The British budget problem

From the time the UK joined, British politicians expressed disquiet at the unfairness of the British financial contribution to the EC, which arose from the structure of EC finances. EC income was based on national governments' revenue from tariffs and levies on imports from outside states, and as Britain was the largest importer in the community the British contribution was high. However, as a relatively efficient agricultural producer, Britain's income from the EC, via the CAP, was low. In relation to Gross Domestic Product, therefore, the UK was a substantial net contributor to the EC. This problem was recognised very early and a seven-year transitional period was negotiated at the time of British membership.

Thereafter it was accepted that Britain would receive a disproportionate share of EC development and other funds.

The problem was that these funds never amounted to much. By the early 1980s, the 'British budget problem' was recognised as a substantial anomaly. It was at this juncture that Margaret Thatcher came on the scene, determined to see justice done. She was able to bargain hard because the agreement of all Member States was necessary for substantial changes in the budget. At that time the EC received 1 per cent of all national value added tax (VAT) receipts. Without an increase to a proposed 1.4 per cent the organisation would run out of money.

Early negotiations came to nothing. Following the decision to admit three new member states (Portugal, Greece and Spain), all of whom were likely to be net recipients of EC funds, the budget deadlock looked set to reach crisis proportions. In June 1984 the Fontainebleau Agreement was signed. This provided a rebate (or abatement as it was called) for the British, which would be calculated annually. By 1995 some £16 billion had been repaid.

Much more important than the sums involved, which were relatively small in relation to GDP, was the intransigent negotiating stance of the British, and in particular the steely determination of the Prime Minister, Margaret Thatcher. The Prime Minister saw it as part of her mission to achieve justice for Britain. In so doing she reinforced a belief that she was highly sceptical about the whole European project, and damaged the reputation of the EC with the British public.

The budget negotiations of the early 1980s also helped establish an image of Britain as a 'bad European' among the officials and politicians of the other Member States. Events since then have reinforced, rather than challenged, this reputation.

THE SINGLE EUROPEAN ACT AND MAASTRICHT: QUANTUM LEAPS FORWARD FOR THE EC

Key term

Intergovernmental organisations –
international organisations which allow national states to co-operate on specific matters while maintaining their national sovereignty.

Until the mid-1980s the EC was an *intergovernmental* organisation with responsibilities mainly in agriculture, environmental protection, regional and competition policy (see Briefing 4.5). For important decisions such as enlargement, major budget and policy changes, a unanimous vote in the Council of Ministers was required (see Table 4.2). And although the European Parliament (EP) had been directly elected by voters since 1979, its powers were confined to approving or rejecting the budget as a whole. From 1985 to 1992, all this was to change as the EC evolved into an embryonic federal state.

The impetus came from a growing perception that the Member States could not compete successfully in an increasingly interdependent world unless they were truly integrated. In addition, the experience of the 1970s and the early 1980s had convinced many European politicians and officials that national governments on their own would find it increasingly difficult to control inflation. The solution to these problems lay in a single economy with a single currency (see Briefing 4.6).

Key term

Federal – a political structure which combines a central authority with a degree of constitutionally defined autonomy for sub-central units of government – usually states, regions, or provinces.

BRIEFINGS

4.5 INTERGOVERNMENTAL AND FEDERAL ORGANISATIONS

When discussing forms of international organisation it is common to characterise them in terms of a continuum ranging from loose organisations which have no power to impose rules or sanctions on members, to full-blown federal governments which can oblige a member (or constituent state) to adhere to legislation and punish it for noncompliance. One of the loosest intergovernmental organisations is the United Nations: members can leave at will and there are effectively no sanctions that the Security Council can impose on them.

Since the late 1990s, the EU has developed into what might be called a 'strong' intergovernmental organisation. The Council of Ministers can, by majority vote, oblige members to follow certain policies. (Although on major matters, such as enlargement of the Union, unanimity is still required.) Moreover, the EU has all the trappings of a state including a legislature, courts and a bureaucracy. Most scholars agree that, for a true federation to exist, the central government should have control over defence and macro-economic policy. Should the single currency be adopted, therefore, the EU will have taken a significant step towards federalism. Note, however, that compared with other federations the EU would have a weak central government. In federal countries such as the USA, Australia and Canada, the central government controls defence, the economy and a vast range of social policies. No one expects the EU to take on equivalent roles for many years, although proponents of a united Europe clearly want such a transformation. Note also that in the strongest federations the central government is often prepared to go to war to keep the federation together, as was the case in the American Civil War and more recently with Russia's intervention in Chechnya. Membership of the EU is effectively voluntary: if a country wanted to leave, serious economic consequences may follow, but the other members would respect the right of that state to secede. In this sense the EU resembles a *confederation*, where membership of the collection of states is voluntary, more than a *federation*, where membership is considered irreversible.

Such arrangements would also require a degree of political integration so as to hold European-wide institutions accountable to electors. Political integration was also seen, not least by Chancellor Kohl, the German leader, and François Mitterrand, the French President, as a way of binding an enlarged Germany into Europe, and preventing it from threatening its neighbours.

The first step in this transformation was the Single European Act (SEA) signed in 1986. Its main objective was to achieve, by 1992, the original aim of the 1957 Treaty of Rome: the creation of a single market in goods, capital and labour. In addition, the Act strengthened the federal as opposed to intergovernmental nature of EC decision making. Unanimity in the Council of Ministers remained for major issues such as enlargement. But the details of implementation could be

BRIEFINGS

4.6 THE CHANGED INTERNATIONAL SITUATION DURING THE 1980s AND THE IMPETUS TOWARDS MONETARY CO-OPERATION

Competing theories exist to explain the acceleration of moves towards European union during the 1980s, but most agree that monetary co-operation is a key factor. From the late 1970s most OECD countries agreed to abolish exchange and other controls on the movement of capital across national borders. As a result, investors from around the globe could move their money to those countries which were likely to produce the best return. The key factors determining where to invest are the stability of exchange rates, interest rates and political and social stability. With the internationalisation of capital movements, governments in all the EU countries had an incentive to keep their investment environments as attractive as possible. Previously they could literally stop money from leaving the country, but with the abolition of controls they had no power to do so. Moreover, during the 1970s and 1980s a number of governments (including Britain, France, Belgium and Italy) had been unable to stop the export of capital by raising interest rates and had been forced into humiliating devaluations. As a result, opinion started to harden around the idea of pooling currencies in a European Monetary System (EMS) which, through the operation of an Exchange Rate Mechanism (ERM), would oblige governments to keep their currencies within specified bands around a central rate. During the early 1980s the ERM did not work well as many countries failed to keep within the specified bands. However, during the 1983 to 1989 period things improved, so much so that the ERM was increasingly viewed as a precursor to full monetary union. During 1992 and 1993, however, the system unravelled as the international markets decided that the currencies of the vulnerable economies (in particular Britain and Italy) were overvalued and ripe for mass selling. German unification had forced the Germans to raise interest rates to hold down inflation, so capital moved rapidly to Germany and out of other Member States' currencies. Governments proved incapable of stemming the outward flow of capital and were forced to leave the ERM, effectively devaluing their currencies.

Since the events of the early 1990s, two schools of thought have emerged about monetary co-operation. One school, represented by the right wing of the Conservative Party, sees these events as evidence of the folly of trying to link currencies together. It argues that a single currency would be even more dangerous, because it would remove an individual country's ability to devalue and would, in the worst possible circumstances, lead to high unemployment and economic recession. The second and dominant school argues that the problems with the ERM in 1992 and 1993 are evidence of the need for a single currency which would stabilise all of Europe's currencies at one level, with the Euro (the new currency unit) emerging as a strong and highly sought-after international currency.

Table 4.2 Arrangements for qualified majority voting (QMV) in the EU

Country	Weighting	Country	Weighting
France	10	Austria	4
Germany	10	Sweden	4
UK	10	Denmark	3
Italy	10	Finland	3
Spain	8	Ireland	3
Belgium	5	Luxembourg	2
Greece	5	TOTAL	87
Netherlands	5		
Portugal	5		

expedited through 'qualified' majority voting (this is explained in Table 4.2).[2] The powers of the European Parliament were also strengthened, although not dramatically so, and the Treaty made bold declarations on the need for greater political (i.e. defence) co-operation.

Margaret Thatcher and the British Government enthusiastically supported the economic provisions in the SEA, but they were critical of the political changes. Achieving a genuine common market in goods and services had long been an objective of Conservative governments. It was the marriage of this objective to political integration which was unacceptable to many members of the party.

Their objections paled into insignificance beside Conservative reactions to The Treaty on European Union (the Maastricht Treaty) which was signed on 7 February 1992. Maastricht represented a radical departure from preceding initiatives because of its ambitious economic and political objectives. The most important of these were:

- creation of a European Union with a common citizenship;

- creation of a single currency by 1999 under the control of a European Central Bank;

- strict 'convergence criteria' for joining the currency (see Briefing 4.7);

[2] Each country represented in the Council of Ministers is given a weighting as shown; for a measure to be adopted a total of 62 votes is necessary. The Single European Act and the Maastricht Treaty greatly extended the number of areas covered by QMV (they had previously required unanimity). Great controversy has surrounded the size of the blocking minority required under QMV. The British, in particular, were concerned that with enlargement the position of the bigger states would be weakened. From the very beginning the Community gave to smaller states a weighted vote greater than they would have been given in proportion to their populations. The present arrangement is a compromise. Following the 1995 enlargement the British wanted the blocking minority to be set at 23. For a discussion, see T. Bainbridge and A. Teasdale, *The Penguin Companion to the European Union* (London: Penguin Books, 1996), pp. 378–83.

BRIEFINGS

4.7 THE CONVERGENCE CRITERIA FOR EUROPEAN MONETARY UNION (EMU)

Before the formal adoption of monetary union (EMU), the Maastricht Treaty stipulated that there be a 'sustainable convergence of the economies of the member states'. This is because the currencies cannot be united unless countries experience reasonably similar economic conditions and pursue similar economic policies. To qualify, therefore, countries should meet the following criteria:

- price stability or a rate of inflation close to that of the three best performing states;
- the achievement of a public sector deficit of not more than 3 per cent of GDP in any year and not more than 60 per cent accumulated debt as a percentage of GDP;
- stability of a member's currency in the ERM for two years with no devaluations within two years;
- the achievement of a level of long-term interest rates as low as the average of the three best performing states in the EU.

These criteria proved very difficult to achieve in the 1992 to 1998 period when many member states experienced economic recession. In both 1996 and 1997 the *interpretation*, if not the wording, of the criteria was loosened so as to accommodate the particular problems of Germany and Italy, neither of whom looked likely to meet the strict interpretation of the criteria by 1999, when EMU was scheduled to take effect.

- acceptance of a Social Protocol (sometimes also known as the 'Social Chapter') on minimum working and social conditions for all citizens of the European Union;
- creation of a Cohesion Fund to help the poorer states and regions adjust to economic change;
- co-decision making between the Council and the Parliament in selected areas so as to strengthen the role of the European Parliament. Decisions resulting from this procedure were subject to qualified majority voting (QMV) in the Council of Ministers. The treaty also extended the number of policy areas subject to QMV (see Table 4.2).

The new British Prime Minister, John Major, eventually signed the Treaty. But he did so only after extensive negotiations which secured an opt-out for Britain from the final stage of the single currency if this was desired. The Government also refused to accept the Social Protocol and had serious misgivings about the extension of QMV.

British objections were partly political and partly ideological. Politically, John Major was vulnerable to the vociferous and significant minority of 'Eurosceptics'

Plate 4.3 Garland cartoon in the *Daily Telegraph*, 1992: Margaret Thatcher warns that the EU is headed for severe problems unless plans for a centralised economy and political union are drastically changed. Her bow is aimed at Jacques Delors, European Commissioner, who is flanked by Douglas Hurd, John Major, François Mitterrand and Helmut Kohl

---

Key term

Sovereignty – the exclusive right to wield legitimate power within a territory. A sovereign state has complete control over its own affairs.

---

within the parliamentary Conservative Party. Their influence grew substantially following Major's relatively narrow victory in the April 1992 general election, which made him dependent on their support in Parliament. The dissenters were convinced that the adoption of a single currency – and indeed the extension of the QMV principle in the Council – would signify the end of British sovereignty.

The Prime Minister, together with his Chancellor and top officials, assumed a more pragmatic line: that membership of a single currency would be in Britain's interests 'when the time was right'. Top government officials, as well as central bankers and the Chancellor, believed that a single currency would keep inflation down once and for all. If there has been a constant in British economic policy since 1979, it has been a commitment to keeping inflation low. The failure to achieve this during the late 1980s eventually persuaded Margaret Thatcher to join the European Monetary System (EMS). EMS membership was widely perceived as an essential precursor to full monetary integration.

Ideologically, the Social Protocol flew in the face of attempts by successive Conservative governments to deregulate the labour market. Almost all Conservatives, including the Prime Minister, were convinced that controls such as a minimum wage, maximum working week and employment rights for part-time workers would increase employers' costs and lead them to take on fewer workers, thus producing higher unemployment.

John Major returned from Maastricht claiming a substantial victory. He boasted not only of his opt-out from the Social Protocol and potential opt-out from the single currency, but also about the very name of the new European organisation. For it was John Major who insisted on the word 'Union' rather than 'Federation'.

Not until 12 October 1993 was the Treaty accepted by all Member States. In the meantime ratification had proved long and acrimonious. It was narrowly approved by referendums in Denmark and France, although it took two attempts for the Danes to get popular acceptance (see Table 4.1).

In Britain, the debate over the treaty centred on the House of Commons and created deep divisions within the Conservative Party. Labour and the Liberal Democrats supported the Treaty. Indeed the Labour Party was fiercely critical of the Government's rejection of the Social Protocol. In the end, only a threat to dissolve Parliament and call an election persuaded some of the Conservative Eurosceptics to toe the party line, and the Treaty was narrowly approved on 24 July 1993.

THE CONSERVATIVES AND THE CURRENCY CRISES OF 1992

Given the events that intervened between the signing of the Treaty in February 1992 and the formal parliamentary vote of approval in July 1993, John Major's parliamentary success was quite an achievement. For during these months Britain experienced a serious and politically damaging currency crisis arising from its membership of the European Monetary System (EMS).

As early as 1970 the EC Member States had held discussions on the possibility of a single currency. The economic traumas of the 1970s postponed any move towards monetary union. In 1979, however, most of the members agreed on the creation of a European Monetary System which would keep currency values constant in relation to one another through co-ordinated central bank intervention. Margaret Thatcher's Conservative Government of 1979–83 declined to join the system, since it believed in market forces, not only in the provision of goods and services but also on the foreign exchanges.

British membership remained a side issue for the next eight years. In part this was because of ideological distaste for controls, in part because controls did not seem to be working very well. Members' currencies had to be devalued repeatedly against an ever stronger Deutschmark (the German currency). However, after 1987 the system settled down. The pound sterling had long been a target for speculators on the foreign exchange markets, a fact which had led to continual 'stop–go' policies in the British economy (see Chapter 3). EMS offered the prospect of stabilising the situation, so pressure slowly built up for British membership.

From March 1987 the Treasury and Bank of England had pursued a policy of 'shadowing' the Deutschmark (DM), maintaining the value of sterling at around DM 3.0. Threatened by a revolt in her cabinet led by the Chancellor, Nigel Lawson, Margaret Thatcher eventually – but only very reluctantly – agreed to join the EMS in October 1990. Sterling was allowed to fluctuate in relation to other currencies in the system by up to 6 per cent on either side of its 1990 value.

All went well for the next two years. The pound's value was maintained and interest rates were gradually reduced. By 1992 the Maastricht Treaty had been signed, and EMS membership was increasingly seen as a first step towards full monetary union. The British, while maintaining the right not to participate in a single currency, also refused to rule out the possibility of joining.

By mid-1992 serious strains in the EMS were apparent. In the wake of reunification, the Germans were deflating their economy and raising interest rates. In

Table 4.3 Chronology of the ERM crisis, 1992–93

Date	Event
8 September 1992	Finland floats the mark
13 September 1992	Italy devalues the lira by 7 per cent
16 September 1992	UK withdraws from the ERM
16 September 1992	Italy suspends intervention agreement in the ERM
16 September 1992	Spain devalues the peseta by 5 per cent
19 November 1992	Sweden floats the krona
22 November 1992	Spain and Portugal devalue by 6 per cent
10 December 1992	Norway floats the krona
30 January 1993	Ireland devalues the punt by 10 per cent
13 May 1993	Spain devalues the peseta by 8 per cent
13 May 1993	Portugal devalues the escudo by 6.5 per cent
2 August 1993	All ERM currencies move to the broader bands of ±15 per cent around unchanged central rates. Separate agreement between Germany and Netherlands to maintain 2.25 per cent bands

Source: David McKay, *Rush to Union* (Oxford: Clarendon Press, 1996), Table 5.1

response, speculative money was flowing into the Deutschmark and out of the other currencies in the system. In the summer of 1992 the pound fell out of its 6 per cent band and in September 1992 the Bank of England spent nearly £20 billion on the foreign exchanges in defence of the current exchange rate. The Chancellor and Prime Minister gave the strongest possible commitments to maintaining EMS membership, but in the end they were powerless in the face of market pressures. Following a panic 5 per cent increase in interest rates which did nothing to stem the run on sterling, Britain finally left the EMS on 16 September, the day that came to be known as Black Wednesday.

Britain was not alone. By the summer of 1993 almost every EMS member, including France, had been forced to devalue (see Table 4.3). The events of September 1992 have great historical significance. For the first time since 1945 an incumbent Conservative Government was widely perceived as incompetent in its handling of the economy. The political fallout continued for several years thereafter. The Major Government was never again as popular as at the time of the 1992 general election. The debacle of September 1992 was thus a major contribution to the eventual electoral defeat of the Government in the spring of 1997.

EUROPE AS A CRISIS ISSUE IN BRITISH POLITICS

Gradually, over the last 20 years, the responsibilities of the European Union have increased, and EU policies now affect many aspects of British economic and social life. However, for most of the population the European Union remains remote. In their everyday lives people feel much more directly affected by the activities of local councils and the Westminster Government. This claim is backed up by the large number (29 per cent in 1994, Table 4.4) who continue to hold 'no opinion' about membership of the EU. However, antipathy to Europe among the British is higher than among all the other European populations except the Danish (Table 4.4). Moreover, at 36.4 per cent in 1994, turnout in the European parliamentary election was less than half that at the 1992 general election, and was one of the lowest turnout figures in the EU.

There are, therefore, deep divisions over Europe among many sections of the public and in particular among British political leaders. While this affects both the major political parties, the deepest divisions exist within the Conservative Party. These derive from a broader cleavage between internationalists and nationalists. The former, well represented by such party grandees as the former prime minister Edward Heath, Douglas Hurd and Geoffrey Howe (both former Foreign Secretaries), see Britain's future as an active but by no means dominant *partner* in a multicultural Europe. The nationalists, represented by such oppositional figures as Enoch Powell (former Conservative Minister, then Ulster Unionist MP 1974–87), Margaret Thatcher and John Redwood (Eurosceptic Minister in the Major Government), see Britain essentially as an *independent* economic and political force in an increasingly complex global economy. This division underlies

Table 4.4 Public opinion on membership of the European Union in constituent countries

Country	1973 Good	Bad	No opinion/ No reply	1980 Good	Bad	No opinion/ No reply	1990 Good	Bad	No opinion/ No reply	1994 Good	Bad	No opinion/ No reply
Belgium	57	5	38	57	2	41	69	5	26	56	10	36
Denmark	42	30	28	33	29	38	49	25	26	53	26	21
Germany	63	4	33	65	6	29	62	7	31	50	12	38
Greece				42	22	36	75	5	20	64	9	27
Spain				58	5	37	65	8	27	50	14	36
France	61	5	34	51	9	40	63	7	30	50	13	37
Ireland	56	15	29	52	19	29	74	8	18	72	7	21
Italy	69	2	29	74	3	23	75	3	22	68	5	27
Luxembourg	67	3	30	84	3	13	72	8	20	71	9	20
Netherlands	63	4	33	75	3	22	82	3	15	77	5	18
Portugal				24	6	70	62	4	34	54	13	33
United Kingdom	31	34	33	21	55	24	52	19	29	43	22	35
AVERAGES	56.5	11.3	32.2	53	13.5	33.5	66.6	8.5	24.9	59	12.1	28.9

Source: Commission of the European Communities, Brussels

attitudes towards EU institutions and in particular the European Parliament. The internationalists accept the interdependence of Britain with Europe and the rest of the world, and adopt an essentially pragmatic stance towards the increasing power of supranational institutions: they agree with them if they bring concrete benefits. For the Eurosceptics, any attempt to strengthen EU institutions is a direct affront to the sovereignty of Parliament and must be resisted at every turn. The depth of these feelings is clear in speeches by Enoch Powell and Margaret Thatcher (Briefing 4.8).

The 'controversy' sums up the arguments for and against further integration of Britain with the Union. The depth of these divisions and the continuing impetus within the EU for ever closer union, mean that the European question now dominates the politics of the Conservative Party. This was amply demonstrated in the aftermath of the Labour landslide in the 1997 election. In the ensuing leadership election, only one candidate, Kenneth Clarke, was a pro-European, while three, John Redwood, Peter Lilley and Michael Howard, were deeply hostile to the EU. Moreover, the eventual winner, William Hague, while not overtly a Eurosceptic, was recognised as a leader who would delay British entry into EMU for many years if he could.

BRIEFINGS

4.8 ENOCH POWELL AND MARGARET THATCHER ON EUROPE

Our Parliament is a homogeneous body. It wills a single nation which elects the disparate members who sit together in the House. It is the Parliament of the United Kingdom. The Parliament which assembles at Strasbourg is an assembly of those who have been elected in different nations ... They do not come together as the representatives of a single self-recognising community... We are performing a type of solecism in attributing the term Parliament to that Assembly... [it] is not a 'Parliament' and it is not the wish of the people of this country that it should ever be a Parliament in the sense of being the ultimate repository of the legislative and executive powers under which the people of the United Kingdom are to live.

Enoch Powell, speech to the House of Commons, 26 June 1986

To try and suppress nationhood and concentrate power at the centre of a European conglomerate would be highly damaging and would jeopardise the objectives we seek to achieve. Europe will be stronger precisely because it has France as France, Spain as Spain, Britain as Britain, each with its own customs, traditions and identity... We have not successfully rolled back the frontiers of the state in Britain only to see them reimposed at a European level with a European superstate exercising a new dominance from Brussels.

Margaret Thatcher, speech at Bruges, 20 September 1988

CONTROVERSY

SHOULD BRITAIN AGREE TO CLOSER EUROPEAN UNION?

The case for Britain strengthening and deepening the EU

The danger from Germany

The EEC transformed Franco-German relations but Germany – especially a united Germany – is still the dominant economic power in Europe. Any possible threat from this is best thwarted or pre-empted by locking Germany into closer political union with the rest of Europe.

The danger from outside

The collapse of the Soviet Union and the increased uncertainties of the post-Cold War era mean that Europe needs to meet any new threats or challenges that might emerge from Asia, the Middle East or even Africa. Europe needs to move towards a common foreign and defence policy, which can only be achieved by strengthening the central institutions of the European Union.

World economic competition

Changes in technology and the growing economic power of the countries of the Pacific Rim are creating an increasingly competitive global economic system. Deepening the Union in *economic* and *financial* terms – for example, by introducing a common currency – will enable European producers to compete more effectively in the internal Union market and strengthen the European Union's bargaining position in world markets more generally.

The democratic deficit

EU policy makers are subject to very limited popular control. The Council of Ministers is not answerable to the European Parliament and the unelected and largely unaccountable Commission has far greater decision-making autonomy than any national civil service. Greater democratic accountability within the EU's institutions is accordingly necessary.

The bicycle analogy

Unless the Union keeps moving forward – towards ever closer integration – it will atrophy. (This argument is frequently stated but never demonstrated.)

The case for Britain resisting or not participating in the strengthening and deepening of the EU

Dangers of a common currency

It is too risky to have a common currency when 'real' economic convergence has not occurred among the economies of the Union's Member States. The Maastricht convergence criteria (inflation, interest rates, debt/GDP

SHOULD BRITAIN AGREE TO CLOSER EUROPEAN UNION? (continued)

ratios) are inappropriate. The important criteria are employment rates, economic activity and growth rates. The EU structural adjustment fund' and EU regional policy do not possess anything approaching the resources needed to make the kind of regional transfer payments that will be necessary if low economic activity rates persistently afflict a sizeable number of EU regions. The key danger of a common currency is that poor areas will remain depressed because they will be unable to devalue themselves into activity and the EU will not possess sufficient central funds to stimulate economic activity there. A common currency could be a recipe for continuing recession and depression in certain regions.

The democratic deficit

The process of EU integration needs to proceed at a rate that has the full (overwhelming majority) support of electorates in the Member States. 'Real democracy' may be impossible in such a large and diverse community: there may always be a *perceived* democratic deficit.

The dangers of judicial legislation

Judicial legislation (judges in effect creating new law by interpreting established legal principles or commitments in the light of new situations) is dangerous because the decisions of the judiciary are by definition not susceptible to political control, and are therefore not accountable to electors.

Injustices in EU rule operation

Uneven rule implementation in different Member States makes for huge injustices in the operation of EC law/rules. These injustices will increase in the future and in time will produce popular resentment.

Foreign and defence policy

A common EU foreign and defence policy is a recipe for inaction and impotence. The indecisiveness of the EU over the collapse of Yugoslavia foreshadows the likely dithering that will characterise EU foreign and defence policy in the future as diverse interests and diverse perceptions compete with one another for supremacy in policy determination.

Fortress Europe versus global market

The common market element of the EU – which will be further strengthened by the introduction of a common currency – will.operate to the long-term detriment of EU producers. The real market of the future is the global market. An insulated EU market – economic fortress Europe – will atrophy.

Flexibility

British interests, as in the past, are best served by retaining maximum strategic flexibility in terms of trade patterns and political-military alliances. Circumstances constantly change. The EU will be too unwieldy to respond effectively to new economic, political, ecological and military challenges.

ESSAYS

1. Why was there a drive towards European integration after the Second World War? Why were the early efforts unsuccessful?

2. Account for the sceptical attitude among many British governments towards European union. Have these attitudes damaged British interests?

3. Why was the Treaty of Maastricht considered so radical? If fully implemented would it result in a European federal state?

4. What is the Common Agricultural Policy? Why has it been so controversial?

SUMMARY

- Britain has traditionally been sceptical about European integration, because of its stake in world markets and its links with English-speaking countries overseas. It suffers from a structural and cultural dilemma which other countries do not encounter and which have caused it to be seen as a 'bad European'.

- The British eventually joined in 1973 in the hope of sharing in the increasing prosperity of the EEC states. The early years of membership were overshadowed by a national referendum in 1975 on whether to remain, and by disputes over the fairness of the British financial contribution.

- Margaret Thatcher supported the Single European Act (1986) creating a single market in goods, labour and capital but was suspicious about a move towards full political integration.

- John Major signed the Maastricht Treaty (1992) but insisted on opt-outs from the Social Protocol and the Single Currency. The British Government also had serious doubts about strengthening the European Parliament and moves towards a federal Europe.

- Turmoil on the foreign exchange markets in September 1992 led Britain to leave the European Monetary System ('Black Wednesday') and resulted in serious political problems for the Major Government.

- Eurosceptics within the Conservative Party gained in strength. By the mid-1990s, divisions within the party were threatening the very survival of the Government. In this sense Europe had become a longstanding crisis issue in British politics. This is illustrated in our 'Milestones'.

- New Labour is reasonably united round a pragmatic attitude to Europe: they support it if there are clear benefits. This is still far removed from the political commitment of the continental states to union.

FURTHER READING

A good account of British foreign policy is David Sanders, *Losing an Empire, Finding a Role: British Foreign Policy Since 1945* (London: Macmillan, 1990). For the United Kingdom and Europe, see Stephen George, *Britain and European Integration Since 1945,* (Oxford: Basil Blackwell, 2nd edn 1994). See also Ian Budge, Kenneth Newton et al., *The Politics of the New Europe* (London: Addison Wesley Longman, 1997), Chapter 2. A history of the growth of European unity is provided by Derek W. Urwin, *The Community Of Europe: A History of European Integration Since 1945* (London: Longman, 1994). On this theme, see also David Arter, *The Politics of European Integration in the Twentieth Century* (Aldershot: Dartmouth, 1993). Specialised studies of the Single European Act, the Commission and the Council are provided by Robert O. Keohane and Stanley Hoffmann (eds), *The New European Community: Decision Making and Institutional Change* (Boulder, Colorado: Westview Press, 1991). A specialised study of monetary integration is Paul De Grauwe, *The Economics of Monetary Integration* (Oxford: Oxford University Press, 1994). Useful reference works include Clive H. Church and David Phinnemore (eds), *European Union and European Community: A Handbook and Commentary on the Post Maastricht Treaties* (London: Harvester 1994) and Timothy Bainbridge and Anthony Teasdale, *The Penguin Companion to European Union* (London: Penguin Books, 1996).

PROJECTS

1. Write a historical account of the British relationship with Europe since 1945. Does the election of a Labour Government in 1997 mark a turn-around in the British relationship with Europe?

2. Analyse the events leading up to the collapse of the Exchange Rate Mechanism in 1992 and 1993. Why did Britain join the ERM in 1990 and why was it forced out in 1992?

3. Account for the signing of the Treaty of Maastricht in 1991. Provide an analysis of the ratification process in the signatory countries. Why did this process vary so much from state to state?

MILESTONES

MILESTONES IN CONSERVATIVE AND LABOUR DIVISIONS ON EUROPE

1967 36 Labour MPs defy their party and vote against joining the EEC

1971 39 Conservative and 69 Labour MPs defy their parties on a vote on joining the EEC

1974 The Conservative ex-Cabinet Minister, Enoch Powell, advises Conservatives to vote Labour in the February general election in order to support Labour's anti-European policy

1975 A deeply split Labour Government uses the European referendum to extricate itself from its political dilemma over whether to stay in the EEC

1981 The 'Gang of Four' (Roy Jenkins, David Owen, Shirley Williams, Bill Rogers) leaves the Labour Party to form the rival Social Democratic Party (SDP), partly in reaction to Labour's growing anti-European policy

1983 Labour adopts an anti-Europe position for the general election and loses heavily

1986 Michael Heseltine resigns his Cabinet post as Defence Secretary in protest over the sale of Westland Helicopters to an American rather than a European firm. Leon Brittan (who was Trade and Industry Secretary) leaves the Government over the quarrel

1989 The Chancellor of the Exchequer, Nigel Lawson, resigns partly because of a running battle with Margaret Thatcher over joining the EMS, and partly because of remarks by her economic advisor, Professor Sir Alan Walters, about the ERM

1990 Nicolas Ridley (a close ally of Margaret Thatcher's) is forced to resign over anti-German remarks

1990 Sir Geoffrey Howe resigns as deputy Prime Minister and Leader of the House of Commons, partly over Margaret Thatcher's European policy

1992 Both parties try to avoid election campaign statements about Europe for fear of opening wounds

1992 Britain withdraws from the EMS after heavy selling of sterling. The popularity of the Major Government declines and never recovers

1994 The Conservative Whip is withdrawn from eight Conservative backbench Eurosceptics

1994/5 The Government's small majority is threatened by Conservative Eurosceptics

1997 Sir James Goldsmith's breakaway Referendum Party (campaigning on the single issue of a Referendum on Europe) threatens the Conservative Party's election chances. It fails to gain any seats but makes inroads into Conservative support

CHAPTER 5

Europe in Britain

Chapter 4 looked at the part Britain has played within Europe and the European Union (the former European Community). This chapter will examine the other side of the coin: the impact of the EU on government and politics within Britain. It will discuss the decisions British governments have to take about Europe in the later 1990s, the constitutional effects of membership up to the present, how the EU itself makes decisions and what effects this has in Britain. In addition we shall see how membership of the European Union has affected the machinery of government and the ways in which public policy is made inside Britain. The chapter will also discuss the problem of the 'democratic deficit' of the EU and tackle the question of 'subsidiarity', that is, which level of government is best equipped to deal with particular responsibilities.

This chapter discusses:

- The centrality of the EU to British politics in the 1990s

- The EU and the British constitution

- How the EU is governed and Britain's part in this

- How British civil servants interact with their EU counterparts

- How British interest groups deal with EU policies

- How the EU affects public policy

- The nature of the 'democratic deficit'

- Subsidiarity: which level of government should be responsible for which policy area inside Britain

UNION OR SECESSION? THE BRITISH DILEMMA

The most important decisions the British Government has to take in the late 1990s are about its relationship with Europe. This is not just a matter of foreign policy, for such decisions will crucially affect Britain's own power and standing inside the national territory, what is commonly termed its 'sovereignty'. What the Government has to decide is how far it is prepared to become a constituent part of a European federation. In such a federation a European government in Brussels, only partly elected from Britain, would decide British social policy, for example, and largely regulate the economy. Perhaps it may even direct foreign policy and deal with matters of peace and war involving British lives.

Put this way, it seems as though the Conservative 'Eurosceptics' are right in claiming that British national sovereignty will disappear. They argue that British industry and finance will be constrained by European regulations, and achievements of the Thatcher period, such as the taming of trade unions, will be undermined by officials from Brussels. British competitiveness based on the availability of cheap labour will be eliminated by the imposition of European minimum standards, with the danger that investments will go elsewhere.

Eurosceptics see no benefits arising from these developments, since their ideal is an autonomous British state regulating all its own internal and external affairs. Pro-Europeans, on the other hand, see the loss of autonomy as a price worth paying for the influence British governments and individuals can exert in a much larger political unit. Better to be part of a new superpower, they argue, than an independent but third-class state on the fringe of world developments. They cite the new opportunities available for finance and industry within the European Union, and claim that British economic and social development will be faster and smoother within a more dynamic economy, in which British financial expertise is joined with German industrial strength.

The pro-Europeans believe that loss of political autonomy would be balanced by the British share in electing a European Parliament and government. European institutions would not be 'foreign' but representative of European citizens in Britain as much as they would be of European citizens in Spain, France, Italy, Scandinavia and the Low Countries. Only if one thinks of the British Parliament and Government, as Enoch Powell and Margaret Thatcher do, as the sole bodies authorised to represent the British people, could one regard a wider European democracy as threatening.

As the quotes in Chapter 4 illustrate, this is exactly what Conservative Eurosceptics do think. Many groups in Britain, however, are positively attracted by Europeanisation. Scottish, Welsh and Irish nationalists see it as a way of easing the stranglehold of the British state on their own countries (see Chapter 6). The Labour Party is reassured by the social protection the European Union offers to vulnerable groups like low-paid workers. From the trade unions' point of view, undermining Thatcherite reforms might be no bad thing. Employers' competitiveness is their employees' poverty. Constitutional reformers see in the guarantees offered by the European treaties a protection for the civil liberties threatened by British governments. Even Conservatives like Kenneth Clarke, the former Chancellor of the Exchequer, see Europeanisation as a necessary step to consolidating Britain's world trading position, rather than as a threat to it.

These issues are not theoretical ones likely to affect us only in the next millennium. For the European Union already operates in Britain, parallel to but independently of the British Government and Parliament. On a range of questions British courts take their precedents from the European Court in Luxembourg, just as British civil servants and local councils follow directives from Brussels. The EU does not have (and is not likely to have) its own administration in Britain to enforce decisions directly. It relies on British institutions to do that. But as the example of the courts shows, this can be quite effective.

Once the legitimacy of European intervention is accepted, British judges and officials can be very efficient in enforcing it. In local government, the European institutions have potential allies whose administrative network covers the country and could be utilised under the doctrine of 'subsidiarity' (see Briefing 5.1) to by-pass central Government in London.

This chapter looks at the way in which EU institutions operate in Britain and the way in which their presence has already changed British political practices and structures. We can expect more changes as the Labour Government supports closer integration and federal union. On the other hand, the EU will always rely more on indirect rather than direct means of intervention. Thus, what we may expect to see in the next millennium is continuing adaptation of the British Civil Service and local government to the European dimension, rather than any immediate restructuring to meet EU needs. Adaptation has already gone a long way, as we shall see when we examine the European presence in Britain more closely.

Key term

Subsidiarity – the principle whereby decisions should be taken at the lowest possible level of the political system.

BRIEFINGS

5.1 SUBSIDIARITY AND ITS POSSIBLE CONSEQUENCES IN BRITAIN

The principle of subsidiarity states that public policy should be made and implemented at the lowest appropriate level of government, that is, at the point closest to ordinary citizens. Only decisions which *have* to be taken at the European level should be made there; all others should be made by national, regional or local government. In the (clumsy and vague) words of Article 3B of the Maastricht Treaty:

> In areas which do not fall within its exclusive competence, the Community shall take action, in accordance with the principle of subsidiarity, only if and insofar as the objectives of the proposed action cannot be sufficiently achieved by the Member States, and can, therefore, by reason of the scale or effects of the proposed action, be better achieved by the Community.

The subsidiarity principle therefore protects the interests and powers of nation states where there is no good reason to take decisions at the European level. However, it can easily be extended within Member States to relations between the centre and the regions or localities. It is therefore something of a two-edged sword so far as protecting existing state power is concerned and may serve to empower Scotland or Wales, for example, in relation to the UK as a whole.

EUROPE AND THE BRITISH CONSTITUTION

Practical and parliamentary sovereignty

Key term

Parliamentary sovereignty – the power of parliament to make or repeal any law it wishes.

The main constitutional issue raised by membership of the European Union concerns parliamentary sovereignty. In Britain, legal sovereignty is vested in Parliament. The concept of parliamentary sovereignty means that Parliament can pass any law it wants.

From the mid-nineteenth century until 1973, parliamentary sovereignty was one of the cornerstones of the British constitution. Joining the European Community – and therefore accepting the 43 volumes of legislation and more than 3,000 regulations and directives already passed – changed all that. British law must now be consistent with European law, and British courts must both accept and enforce European law. In cases of disagreement, the European Court of Justice in Luxembourg has the final word, and British citizens may appeal to the European Court if they believe the British government is acting unlawfully. The British Government may even have to compensate citizens for actions judged by the European Court to exceed its powers. It was clear that European law would take precedence over British law when Britain joined the EC, but the principle was underlined strongly by the Factortame Case of 1991. This required British law to fall into line with European law on the registration of shipping, a matter which had been jealously controlled by the sovereign British state for centuries. More recently, in 1996, the Conservative majority in Parliament was forced by decisions of the European Commission and the Court to accept the right of employees to opt for a 48-hour week, even though the Government resisted this strongly and had in fact declared it would not accept it. Loss of sovereignty could hardly go further than that.

In a practical sense Britain has long since ceased to have exclusive and total control over its own affairs (if, indeed, any country ever does have total control). Joining NATO or signing the GATT treaties on free trade, for example, requires agreement with other nations and the loss of some national autonomy. To this extent practical sovereignty is limited in even the most powerful modern state.

But the question of constitutional sovereignty and the EU is more complicated than this. Membership of the EU hugely limits practical sovereignty, but it also formally and legally limits parliamentary sovereignty. This makes the issue supremely important in the minds of some politicians.

Others contend that this loss of sovereignty is neither final nor absolute. They argue that Parliament could, if it wished, revoke membership of the EU tomorrow, so regaining its old sovereign status. The process of leaving the EU would, of course, be long, messy, disruptive and expensive. Thus for all practical purposes it may be impossible. To the extent that British secession remains theoretically possible, however, Parliament has not lost its legal sovereignty. To the extent that it is in practice unlikely, absolute parliamentary sovereignty no longer exists in Britain.

Executive power

Paradoxically, another consequence of EU membership is an increase in the political power of the Government and Cabinet. This is because the main centres of power in the EU are not accountable to the British Parliament, nor to any other national parliament, for that matter. The Council of Ministers, the main executive body in Brussels, is composed of representatives of national *governments*. It cannot become embroiled in the domestic politics of its Member States. Thus any influence the British Parliament brings to bear upon the Council must pass through the British Government. And this, of course, gives the Government a crucial role.

Parliamentary approval is not required for EU legislation (see Briefing 5.2). On the contrary, the British Parliament may only scrutinise legislation on a 'take note' basis, and even then it may only deal with proposed, future legislation. 'Taking note' means recording legislation and the action it requires, but doing nothing to change it in any way. Officers of the EU do not attend parliamentary meetings, and neither explain nor justify their actions to Parliament. Parliament can only advise ministers about the policy they should adopt and await the outcome. Ministers may take note of parliamentary opinion, but they may also ignore it if they please.

Other aspects of the constitution

Membership of the EU has so far had little effect on other aspects of the British constitution. Britain resisted attempts to implement a common electoral system for European Parliament elections, insisting on its traditional single member, simple majority system (see Chapter 15). Nor have other constitutional features been much affected. The two-tier structure of government (central and local) has been retained, as has the same set of central ministries. The highest court in the land remains the House of Lords and there is still no written constitution or Bill of Rights. The same rules of parliamentary procedure apply and much the same parliamentary timetable is followed. In these respects EU membership has changed British practices very little.

HOW THE EU IS GOVERNED

Before seeing how the EU has affected government in Britain, we need to see how it manages itself. The most important Union institutions are located at Brussels in Belgium (see Map 4.1), about an hour's flight from London. The European Court sits further away in Luxembourg City, and the European Parliament is located even further away at Strasbourg on the French–German border (but its committees operate in Brussels close to the other centres of EU power).

BRIEFINGS

5.2 BRITISH PARLIAMENTARY SCRUTINY OF EUROPEAN LEGISLATION

The best that Parliament can do to control EU legislation is to exert control over the British Government's negotiating position within the European bodies. In practice, this has been difficult. When Britain joined the European Community, the Committee on European Secondary Legislation was formed (May 1974). From the beginning, it was clear that the Committee would be hard pressed to fulfil its functions of scrutiny. The Committee had a right to examine draft proposals submitted by the Commission or the Council of Ministers and these documents were supplied by the relevant Whitehall departments. However, the Committee had extremely limited powers once it received the documents. It was *not* empowered to debate the merits or demerits of a Commission proposal. All it could do was to recommend that it be referred for debate to a standing committee or, in certain important cases, to the House as a whole. With 30 to 40 documents arriving at the Committee every day, there were few that could be given further consideration.

Once an issue is earmarked for debate, there remains the problem of how Parliament is to influence the Government's Council negotiating position. No specific amendments are allowed to be made to the Commission proposals, and the House or Standing Committee may only debate on a 'take note' motion. Additional problems arise from the fact that a maximum of 90 minutes is allowed for a debate, and even this small amount of time is not made available until two hours before midnight.

Initially the Government was prepared to listen to the views of Parliament on EC legislation, although it would not submit its own views to scrutiny. By 1976, however, the Government was no longer prepared to grant even this meagre concession in all circumstances. Michael Foot, then Leader of the House, stated on behalf of the Government:

Ministers will not give agreement to any legislative proposal recommended by the Scrutiny Committee for further consideration by the House before the House has given it that consideration, unless the Committee has indicated that agreement need not be withheld, or *the Minister concerned is satisfied that agreement should not be withheld for reasons which he will at the first opportunity explain to the House.*

The italic type emphasises the considerable freedom of action which the British Government has been able to reserve for itself. The Committee faced further scrutiny problems when the Commons was in recess as no debate could be called and the Committee could not even meet, although the chairperson could act on his or her own initiative to scrutinise legislation. The fact that the parliamentary timetable is not co-ordinated with the timetable of the Council of Ministers meant that the Committee was often in a position where it could not carry out its functions. When an instrument was adopted in Council before it reached the Committee, the limit of the Government's obligation was 'that the Committee should be informed, by deposit of the relevant document and by submission of an explanatory memorandum, of instances where fast-moving documents go for adoption before scrutiny can take place'.

In view of the unfavourable procedures for adequate Commons supervision of EU legislation, it is hardly surprising that there was little competition among MPs to serve on the Scrutiny Committee. There were persistent calls for an improvement in the scrutiny procedures, which were met when the House of Commons reorganised its procedures in 1991. The Select Committee on European Legislation now considers all proposed legislation and refers matters needing further scrutiny to one of two standing committees. They report to the House of Commons but parliamentary approval is still not required for European legislation. The Government may note parliamentary opinion but may also ignore it if it wants.

Figure 5.1 identifies the central institutions of the EU and British participation in them. Decision making in the EU is complicated by the fact that it has two executives and governments, rather than just one.

Figure 5.1 British participation in the central European Union institutions

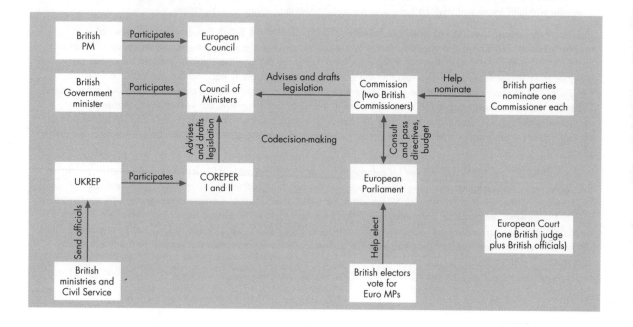

The body that might become the European Government if the EU becomes a truly federal state is the European Commission. This is a body of 20 politicians nominated by each member country (two each by the bigger members, Britain, France, Spain, Italy and Germany; one each by Sweden, Finland, Denmark, Ireland, Netherlands, Belgium, Luxembourg, Portugal, Austria and Greece). The Commission as a whole is scrutinised and approved by the European Parliament at the beginning of its term of office.

This procedure emphasises that Commissioners' loyalties are not to their home country but to the EU. The Commission has increasing powers to act autonomously in implementing the Single European Market and the general industrial and trade policies of the Community. We have already seen how action under its Work, Health and Safety powers, in allowing workers to opt for a 48-hour minimum week, cut across Conservative Government policy in 1996. The Commission runs the EU's central bureaucracy, divided into 25 directorates–general. These resemble the functional ministries of Member States which act in each separate policy area.

However, the Commission and its civil service are not autonomous. In many areas their function is to prepare policy proposals for decision by the Council of Ministers. The latter is the parallel, second and in most respects more powerful organ of the EU. Because it consists of representatives of national governments it is easy to think of the Council as an executive. In fact, however, as the ultimate source and approver of policy initiatives, the Council performs many of the functions carried out by legislatures in other political systems.

The Council consists of a General Affairs Council and various technical councils. The foreign ministers of Member States meet in the General Affairs Council, while ministers for particular policy areas such as agriculture meet in the technical councils. Associated with the ministerial councils is the Committee of Permanent Representatives (COREPER in Community jargon). COREPER I 'shadows' the foreign ministers and consists of the national ambassadors to the Community, while COREPER II consists of the deputy ambassadors. There are numerous committees and working parties of appropriately qualified national civil servants associated with it. All these bodies carry out detailed preparatory work for the meetings of corresponding ministers.

Thus the Council of Ministers also has a civil service working for it, which in many respects overshadows the permanent 'Eurocrats', just as the Council overshadows the Commission. Most new initiatives come from it or from the European Council (not to be confused with the Council of Europe, see Chapter 4, p. 92), which is the meeting of prime ministers and heads of governments of the Member States which often has to take decisions over matters on which the Council of Ministers cannot agree. Any major new initiative or proposals for the extension of EU powers have to be agreed here. It is only the ministers who can commit national governments to courses of action not already agreed in the founding treaties.

Because of the powers of the Council of Ministers and of the European Council, it has often been said that the EU is more of an intergovernmental than a truly federal structure. Decisions have to be negotiated and agreed between the governments of the Member States rather than autonomously by the supranational bodies. It is here that the British Government can hold out for what they consider to be British interests.

This was reinforced by the original practice of taking decisions in the Council unanimously. Every country had a veto, so by withholding its consent any national government could block any proposal. This is how British governments would have liked the situation to continue, so that they could veto any action affecting Britain with which they did not agree.

Since the Single European Act of 1986, however, and even more under the Treaty of Maastricht (1992), qualified majority voting (QMV) has been introduced into the Council of Ministers for all but very major policy decisions such as the enlargement of the EU. Under this procedure not even two of the larger countries, acting together, can block proceedings. This has put the initiative – even in the intergovernmental Council of Ministers – into the hands of France, Germany and the smaller countries, which want to speed up integration. As a result the Council of Ministers has increasingly become a profederal body whose decisions accelerate rather than slow down progress to full integration.

Increasingly in the 1990s, therefore, an antifederalist British government has found itself isolated even on the body which might have been expected to protect its interests. Its position has also been undermined by the decisions of the European Court, which tends to support the Commission. Meanwhile, the European Parliament has also proved itself prointegrationist. It has often carried with it not only British Labour and Liberals but also British Conservative 'Euro MPs', who have thus found themselves at loggerheads with their own party at Westminster.

Of course, as Figure 5.1 also shows, stand-offs between British and European institutions are not a simple matter of 'us' versus 'them'. This is because British MPs and civil servants participate in EU institutions and shape EU policy just as much as any other national group. In fact, as one of the four leading Member States in the EU, the British play a disproportionate part compared with most others. This was particularly true of the framing and implementation of the Single European Act (1986) with its free market principles, which the ex-Conservative Commissioner Leon Brittan pushed through with the help of British economic advisers.

THE EU AND THE BRITISH CIVIL SERVICE

In spite of spreading integration, membership of the EU has had little impact on the way government actually works in Britain. As we pointed out, the Union has no direct administration of its own within Member States. Instead it relies on the existing national machinery to carry through its directives and legislation.

Thus no special ministry has had to be created in Britain to look after EU affairs. Instead, the European Secretariat of the Cabinet Office and the Foreign and Commonwealth Office (FCO) co-ordinate the work of Whitehall ministries, and of the British staff in Brussels (UKREP) through a constant round of inter-departmental meetings. Whitehall departments which are most deeply embedded in European affairs – the Treasury, Trade and Industry, Agriculture, the

Environment – have special European divisions within them. The rest deal with matters on an ad hoc basis as required.

The implementation of EU policy is thus handled by central ministries and departments, very much like the implementation of national policy. This is because it now *is* national policy, in a sense, even if decided by European bodies. What has called for more of an administrative effort is the fact that Britain, through its membership of the Council of Ministers, and its associated committees (COREPER I and II) is now heavily involved in the process of preparing and passing European legislation in the first place.

Such legislation is not wholly, or even largely, 'political' in nature. However, the fact that policy is decided through negotiations between national governments, and that there are, on occasion, questions which arouse considerable controversy, pervades the entire policy-formulation process. The British Government has to define and defend its interests in relation to the EU as a whole and to the other Member States. The result is that the Foreign and Commonwealth Office, which traditionally represents British interests abroad, has become the central co-ordinating ministry for EU policy. It organises the UK Permanent Representation in Brussels and acts as the link between the home civil servants based in Brussels and their counterparts in the Whitehall ministries. The European Communities Section in the FCO is responsible for most of the co-ordinating work. It consists of several deskworkers covering different EU policy areas.

Although the FCO plays a co-ordinating role in formulating Britain's EU policy, it does not have the technical competence to determine that policy by itself. The specification for an industrial product, for example, is hardly within its competence. So there is considerable reliance on the functional ministries which do possess such expertise. Departments closely involved in formulating British EU policy in their areas of competence are the Treasury, MAFF (Agriculture and Fisheries), DoE (Environment), Trade and Industry, and Energy, most of which have EU sections co-ordinating their involvement with the EU. Departmental representatives liaise with the FCO, but also participate directly in meetings of specialists held under the aegis of the Commission, in the working parties and associated committees of COREPER, and also in ad hoc British civil service committees shadowing COREPER European Council meetings. The functional departments also play a major role in the preparation of briefs for Council meetings.

Co-ordination of British policy is achieved for the most part through a series of informal telephone contacts among officials from interested government departments. But there is also a committee system through which EU policy can be discussed. At a basic level, there are a series of interdepartmental committees in the major policy areas. There are also temporary committees, bringing together the people most immediately concerned with a particular policy issue, and usually organised at the instigation of one of the functional departments. Their composition varies widely. A committee meeting on shipbuilding subsidies, for instance, would be chaired by a representative from the Board of Trade, and include officials from the Treasury, the Board of Trade, the FCO, and possibly the Welsh, Scottish or Northern Irish Offices. Only the FCO would be represented on every committee. Above the specialist policy committees is a European Union Committee that oversees the preparation of briefs for the Permanent

Representation and the Council meetings, and is generally responsible for the co-ordination of Britain's EU policy.

In its capacity as a central co-ordinating body, the Cabinet Office also plays a significant role in the formulation of British policy. Officials from the Cabinet Office attend the regular committee meetings of the EU and are very closely involved in the more controversial issues. They also play a mediating role in ironing out differences between British government departments. Such a mediating role is especially important in the European context, where the Government tries to present its views in terms of a national consensus.

Besides all the interdepartmental Civil Service committees concerned with formulating Britain's EU policies, there are also political interministerial committees. These include a cabinet committee composed of the ministers most affected by EU activities, which regularly discusses EU issues and which is chaired by the Foreign Secretary.

Many of these arrangements for co-ordinating policy form an extension of interdepartmental committees and negotiating sessions inside Britain itself. What is new is the central co-ordinating role of the Foreign and Commonwealth Office, and the opportunities for civil servants from different ministries to work closely within the same organisation in Brussels, at the British Permanent Representation (UKREP).

Indeed, the major effect of the EU on the British Civil Service is the addition of a major European dimension to every civil servant's work. Most departments are involved one way or another with European policy matters, and most home civil servants have to keep a careful eye on developments in Brussels. Many have to attend the London meetings or travel regularly to EU meetings, apart from being seconded to UKREP. This means that many civil servants have to incorporate the European dimension into their daily working lives, and attend frequent training or refresher courses to keep them abreast of developments.

This creates a huge workload for politicians and civil servants. Every week tons of documents arrive from Brussels, Strasbourg and Luxembourg. Almost every week there is a high level EU meeting involving the Prime Minister and/or other ministers. Apart from the Council of Ministers there are many other political meetings, and civil servants may spend as much time in Brussels as in London. There is also a meeting every week or so of the Cabinet EU Committee. Even without the EU, pressure on senior politicians and civil servants is enormous. With it, demands on their time and energy are even greater.

THE EU AND BRITISH PRESSURE GROUPS

Pressure or interest groups are organisations representing groups of people with some condition or activity in common which might be affected by politics (see Briefing 5.3). The most obvious of these are trade unions, grouping manual workers, craftspeople, or white-collar workers. But there are thousands of others: churches, sports and professional organisations, animal and environmental protection groups and many more. Almost any activity or interest one can think of has an organisation to protect or advance it.

BRIEFINGS

5.3 PRESSURE GROUPS AND INTEREST REPRESENTATION

Pressure groups

Pressure groups are formed voluntarily by people who wish to protect or promote a common interest or cause. Unlike political parties, most pressure groups have no wish to become the government of their country, and compared with parties they have a fairly narrow range of concerns. Many pressure groups are not primarily political at all. But if their interests and aspirations are affected by government they will organise themselves politically in order to influence public policy. The term 'pressure' does not necessarily imply the use of negative sanctions, such as strikes or the withdrawal of co-operation. It may simply involve passing on information to the government and the general public. Indeed, depending upon circumstances, pressure groups use a wide variety of means to exercise influence, from mass demonstrations to writing letters to representatives. There are two main types of pressure groups: sectional or interest groups, and cause or promotional groups.

Interest groups or sectional groups

Interest groups represent people in their occupational capacity and are, therefore, mainly concerned with economic interests. The three main kinds of interest groups are business, professional, and trade union organisations. People join interest groups, therefore, because of their occupation.

Cause groups

Cause groups are formed to promote or protect an idea, goal, or principle which is not directly related to the personal or material interests of their members. In other words they are voluntary organisations formed by people who have some common aspiration, apart from their jobs. The category is a broad one and covers all sorts of voluntary organisations and associations: churches; educational, cultural and leisure organisations, charities and welfare organisations; community associations; sports, social and youth clubs; and scientific organisations.

Peak associations

Similar types of interest groups are often brought together by a peak, or umbrella, organisation in order to co-ordinate activity. Peak associations are thus large organisations whose members consist of smaller organisations. Most notable are the confederations that bring together business interests under one roof and try to speak for them all, and the parallel organisations of trade unions. Peak organisations do not stop with a particular country but are often organised up to the European or even world level. Nor are peak associations limited to interest groups: they cover all types of pressure groups.

Politics inevitably affects these aspects of life. Any proposal for regulation or intervention affects somebody who either wants intervention to take an advantageous form or to be left alone. In either case groups exist or are formed to affect the political outcome.

Traditionally, interest groups in Britain have enjoyed close relationships with particular ministries. The extent to which they have shifted their 'lobbying' to Brussels is a good indication of how far British policy is now being decided there rather than in London.

Among the pressure groups whose interests are affected by the EU, the larger ones are now organised at both national and international levels. They operate in Brussels, as in London, maintaining offices in both places in order to keep a close watch on policy developments and to lobby for their interests. At the European level, groups act mainly on the Commission and Parliament, both of which are fairly open to outside interests. However, both also try to simplify life by dealing with only one or two large organisations in the same policy field. Therefore, British pressure groups look for close working relations with their European partners. They are more likely to get a hearing if they act together, and more likely to be successful if they pool resources and speak with one voice. For example, the National Farmers Union is part of the Committee of Professional Agricultural Organisations (COPA) which maintains a strong presence in Brussels. So also do other umbrella groups such as the European Trade Union Confederation (ETUC) and the Union of Industries of the European Union (UNIEU).

PUBLIC POLICY

Policy development in pursuit of European integration has often been patchy, and implementation of policy has often been erratic, as the budget and the bureaucracy of the EU are relatively small. Between 1993 and 1997, the budget was fixed at no more than 1.37 per cent of the combined GNP of Member States. The EU employs approximately 15,000 people in Brussels and Luxembourg, which is smaller than a medium-sized department of central Government in Britain or the administration of a large city such as Amsterdam or Barcelona. Nevertheless, the EU already has an enormously powerful and wide-ranging policy impact, covering almost everything from the routines of daily life all the way up to the grand issues of monetary union and foreign policy. Every year the EU issues more than 12,000 legal instruments in the form of regulations, directives, decisions, recommendations and opinions (see Briefing 5.4).

Economic affairs

This is probably the most important single area so far as national policies are concerned. The Single European Act, passed in 1986 and planned for full implementation in 1992 (but still delayed) intends there to be free movement of goods, services, capital, and people throughout the EU. Among other things, this means

BRIEFINGS

5.4 HOW POLICY IS IMPLEMENTED BY THE EU

Decisions in the EU are implemented by means of five types of 'legal instruments', as follows:

1. *Regulations* are general and, since they have the force of EU law, they are directly binding on all Member States.

2. *Directives* are more frequently used than regulations and, like them, are binding on all Member States. Unlike regulations, however, directives leave it open for Member States to decide how best to achieve the desired goal. For example, the Community directive of 1979 on direct elections to the European Parliament required the British Government to make provision for direct elections, but left it open to the Government to decide which electoral system to use. It chose the same system used for parliamentary elections – the single member, simple majority system – rather than the proportional representation system more commonly used in EU countries.

3. *Decisions* are binding on all those to whom they are addressed.

4. *Recommendations* have no binding force, and are sometimes not defined as 'legal instruments'.

5. *Opinions* have the same characteristics as recommendations.

Key term

Harmonisation – the attempt of the EU to create common product standards and specifications among its Member States in the interests of a free and genuinely common market.

---

the free movement of university students (promoted by the ERASMUS programme which pays the extra expenses). Many technical specifications in manufacturing and services have been standardised (the EU term is 'harmonisation'). And since the EU itself is funded by each nation paying a proportion (1.21% of its receipts from value added tax), VAT rates have also been partly standardised. The plan to introduce a common European currency (the Euro) is probably the most ambitious, difficult, and controversial part of the whole agenda.

National governments are no longer permitted directly to subsidise industries. But the EU provides money for industrial restructuring and technological development, offering loans at special interest rates through the European Investment Bank. The basic principle is that public subsidies should be distributed on an EU basis to strengthen the EU economy, and not by national governments in a way that interferes with a free market. There are also rules about public procurement. Public bodies, like governments, are obliged to seek tenders for large contracts on the open market across the EU. Finally, attempts have been made to regulate conditions of work, including minimum pay, employment laws, and such things as the enforced use of tachographs (monitoring machines) in the cabs of long distance trucks, a measure the European Court forced on an unwilling British Government in 1979.

By and large, the EU has been successful in its attempts to create a single, integrated market, although its difficulties and failures have often attracted more attention than its successes. Examples of difficulties involving British interests are: the export of British lamb to France (blocked by French farmers); the ruling in 1990 that British Aerospace had to pay back the illegal subsidy of £44 million it received when it bought Rover cars from the Government; ending the practice in some countries of favouring home-produced spirits, a decision which helped the Scottish whisky industry. Once again, these examples show how deeply EU policy reaches into national economic affairs. EU authority is supreme in competition policy (the EU policy of encouraging free competition between firms in the same sector and discouraging monopoly practices), although few mergers or acquisitions of note have been blocked by the Commission. Similarly, although the Maastricht Treaty speaks optimistically about a free labour market, linguistic, cultural and other barriers have resulted in low levels of mobility between Member States.

Regional aid

Britain receives substantial grants from the European Regional Development Fund, created in 1975 to help poor or industrially run-down areas. Of the 50 million people in the EU living in such regions, 20 million are in Britain (Wales, Scotland, Northern Ireland and the North of England). The standard of living in Britain as a whole is almost exactly the EU average, but only in the South-East of England is it higher (by about 20 per cent), while in Northern Ireland it is 25 per cent lower. The special regions of Britain benefit from funds and policy initiatives aimed at building up small businesses and the tourist trade, retraining workers in declining agricultural areas, restructuring industry and retraining workers, rebuilding urban infrastructure and revitalising the economy in areas of industrial decline. Merseyside alone now receives about 1.3 billion pounds from London and Brussels.

Consumer affairs

Common standards for the labelling and selling of foods have been adopted. Well-publicised examples in Britain involve the production of icecream, sausages and beer, but EU regulations cover a large proportion of the goods sold in shops. The EU has ruled that tobacco products must not be advertised on television, and it carefully regulates the amount and the timing of television advertising. Recently, it has also taken action to block British beef exports as a result of 'mad cow disease'.

Agriculture and fishing

The Common Agricultural Policy (CAP) is the largest single item on the EU's annual budget, accounting for almost half the total, although it used to be three-quarters. It is intended to give some economic security to the large number of poor farmers and agricultural communities in Western Europe. This has involved higher

Plate 5.2 Steve Bell cartoon in *The Guardian*, 20.9.96: Mr Major and Minister for Agriculture, Mr Hogg. The Conservative Government threatened to block progress on EU reform talks unless blocks on British beef exports as a result of 'mad cow disease' were lifted

farm prices and created the infamous 'wine lakes' and 'butter mountains'. Although British farmers benefit very substantially from CAP, the country as a whole pays more than it gets because British farms are relatively large and efficient. Currently the EU's fishing policy is even more controversial because, in trying to preserve fish stocks, it has affected the livelihoods of fishing communities in Britain.

Environmental policy

The EU has developed a wide range of policies to protect the environment involving, among other things, forests, birds, plants, animals, drinking water, waste disposal, bathing beaches, and recreational areas. Many of these have caused difficulties for the British Government: substandard water supplies and bathing beaches, inadequate industrial pollution controls, new roads which fail environmental impact norms (the M3 at Twyford Down, for example), and new conifer forests which are inconsistent with EU standards (see Chapter 24). In 1993 Lancashire County Council successfully prosecuted the British Government in the European Court for its failure to clean up three bathing beaches. EU policy in these matters may be embarrassing for the Government but serves to protect British consumers.

Social policy

The EU has enacted a broad range of social measures. For example, industrial training has been financed by the European Social Fund since 1972, and the policing of international crime is well established. Some policies have attracted much publicity, such as the case of Smith v. Macarthy, in which the European Court forced a British employer to observe equal pay rules. More recently, the controversial Social Chapter of the Maastricht Agreement laid down a broad range of regulations on, among other things, social conditions, working hours, minimum wages, and health and safety standards. The Chapter was not signed by the Conservative Government of the time, but has been accepted by the Labour Government.

Foreign affairs and security

On economic matters the EU has been relatively successful in framing a common European policy. It now acts for its members in the vitally important GATT (General Agreement on Tariffs and Trade) negotiations, and appears alongside the most powerful nations in world economic meetings. But on diplomatic and defence matters its success is limited. Some Member States, including Britain, jealously guard the power to decide their own foreign and defence policies, or else prefer to work through NATO. Consequently, Europe failed to provide international leadership during the Gulf War (1990–91), and the different policies of Member States over Bosnia (1992–95) made that situation worse.

Two points should be noted about the impact of the EU on public policy. First, some of the rules and regulations on paper are only partially enforced, if at all. There are many ways of breaking, bending or ignoring them. This means that large areas of public policy remain largely unaffected by EU directives and law (law and order, for example). Also unaffected are all those very important areas – agriculture apart – where the nation state provides direct cash payments for individuals: pensions, social and unemployment benefits. In other words EU competence is mainly confined to *regulation* rather than the direct *distribution* of benefits. This may, of course, change with further integration and monetary union and consequent pressures to redistribute across countries and regions to help adjustment. Figure 5.2 shows the budget of the Community in 1996. Note the continuing importance of agricultural subsidies and of structural funds used to help poorer regions 'catch up' with the more affluent regions of the Community.

The rules on public procurement are complex, and can be easily twisted and evaded. Britain has a good record of compliance with EU directives. In 1991 only Denmark, Luxembourg, and the Netherlands were found to be more compliant, and some countries were much worse. Figure 5.3 shows the degree of compliance with Single Market laws as of December 1995 and the number of complaints against countries for flouting the trade rules. Again, Britain's performance is relatively good compared with many Member States, and in particular Germany. However, Britain continues to have some of the worst ice cream and the best beer in Europe, despite EU attempts to change both!

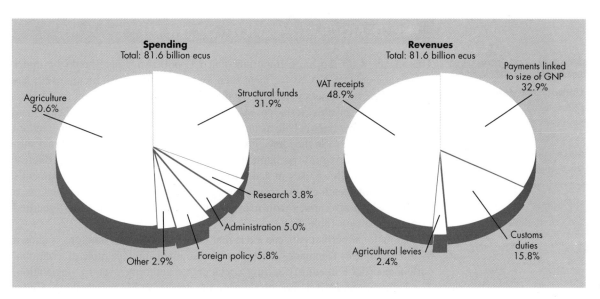

Figure 5.2 The 1996 European Union budget
Source: *The Budget of the European Union* (Brussels: EC, 1996)

Whatever the actual impact of EU policy, the fact remains that many of the policy areas previously controlled by national government are now partially or even wholly in the hands of European decision makers. To this extent it is certainly true that EU policy has an important and expanding effect on daily life in Britain.

Figure 5.3 Single Market laws enacted by national governments, 31 December 1995, and complaints against countries for rule violation, 1995

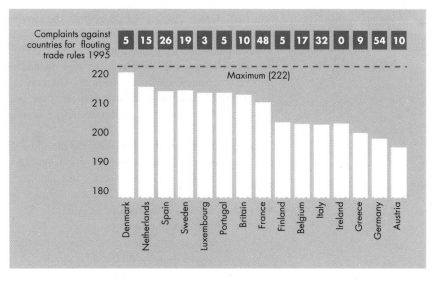

Source: Commission of the European Communities, *Report on Implementation of the Commission's Work Programme in 1995* (Brussels: European Commission, 1995)

THE 'DEMOCRATIC DEFICIT' OF THE EU

This makes it all the more important that EU policy making should be under democratic control. Yet, as we have seen, one effect of British membership has been to place much policy making outside the scrutiny of Parliament (p. 117).

The blame for this rests on successive British governments. They have regarded parliamentary debate as an unnecessary interference with their freedom of action in the EU. So they have given no lead that might have resulted in a substantial restructuring of parliamentary procedures to give the EU effective scrutiny. This failure raises in acute form the question of whether Parliament's essentially nineteenth-century procedures can cope with modern developments, a question which also arises with many of the other British institutions inherited from the past (see Table 2.1).

That national parliaments can exert real power over EU negotiations is shown by the example of Denmark, which provides an interesting example of a national parliament (the Folketing) exerting considerable authority over EU legislation. The Folketing secured its position during the debate on EU membership. Under the Danish Act of Accession, the Government is required to make an annual report to the Folketing and to keep Parliament informed of Council business. General debates on the EU are held at regular intervals, and special debates also take place.

The main mechanism, however, by which the Folketing controls the Danish Government's negotiating position in the Council of Ministers is through the Market Relations Committee. The committee system is extremely well developed and committees enjoy considerable authority. The Market Relations Committee is the most authoritative of all and also the most prestigious: its 17 members, elected proportionately from the various political parties, include many former cabinet ministers. Under the rules of procedure, the Government is committed to consult with the Market Relations Committee on all Council business. The Committee meets weekly and may question ministers and civil servants involved in EU policy. The Government is obliged to seek mandates from the Committee before important Council decisions. In many Council sessions, Danish ministers have had extremely narrow mandates and on some occasions they have had to seek new mandates from the Committee before reaching agreement on a particular issue.

In the light of Danish experience, the inability of the British Parliament to control its government's negotiating position may be part of a general decline in its power, attributable to the dominance of a single party in Government at any one time, Government control of the parliamentary agenda, and the poor access of MPs and peers to information. In Chapter 18 we shall consider the general question of parliamentary power.

In the European area, however, there is another body which might be able to hold governments to account: the directly elected European Parliament itself (see Briefing 5.5). It holds its legislative meetings in the French city of Strasbourg, far away from the real centres of power in Brussels, and meets in full session for only one week a month.

BRIEFINGS

5.5 THE EUROPEAN PARLIAMENT

Until 1979 members of the European Parliament (EP) were appointed by national governments from the membership of their own elected assemblies. After 1979 the EP was directly elected, as agreed by the Treaty of Rome, every four years. Seats in the EP are allocated amongst Member States in rough proportion to their population.

Although the EP is charged with the duty of supervising the Commission and the Council of Ministers it lacks power and has mainly a secondary and advisory role. Although its jurisdiction has expanded, the Parliament is still primarily a delaying or amending body with limited powers of veto, especially on budgetary matters. It is logistically and bureaucratically hampered by having to meet in Brussels for committees and in Luxembourg and Strasbourg for plenary sessions. Moreover, the main secretariat is located in Luxembourg. Business is conducted in all the official languages of the EU, which necessitates a huge burden of translation.

Members of the European Parliament (MEPs) sit in international party groups. There are nine main groups, with the Socialists and the Christian Democrats being the largest; compared with national legislatures party organisation is relatively weak. Much parliamentary work is carried out in committees.

This indicates that its influence is strictly limited. The Parliament is the least weighty of the four major European bodies (Council of Ministers, Commission, Court, Parliament). However, it is not quite so limited as its peripheral position and short legislative sessions might suggest.

For one thing, it does most of its work in specialised committees, and these meet in Brussels where they cross-question Commissioners and European civil servants on all aspects of European policy. Increasingly these meetings receive press coverage, especially when they uncover frauds or anomalies in Community Policy.

The EP has also been given increased powers in every revision of the original treaty (Treaty of Rome, 1958), so it can reject the Budget or national nominees to the Commission (but only as a whole). Parliament has to be consulted on a whole range of social and economic policy (Single European Act 1986) and it has positively to approve policy, or at least not reject it, in other areas, under the Treaty of Maastricht (1992).

The weakness of the European Parliament is that it mainly controls the Commission. The body they *should* want to control is the Council of Ministers, since that is where initiatives on most EU matters originate. Until they can affect the Council's decisions, or until its governmental powers are mostly transferred to the Commission, much of what the EP does seems like shadow-boxing.

Parliament really has no desire to punish or hamper the Commission when it is its ally in campaigning for a transfer of power from national to EU level.

This fact also mutes party conflict within the European Parliament. In 1997 MEPs were organised into nine main party groups: Left, Socialists (with British Labour included), Liberals (including British Liberal Democrats), European People's Party (Christian Democrats), Forza Italia, Democratic Alliance, Radical Antifederalist and Greens. British Conservatives are attached to, but not members of, the European People's Party. The major groupings are Socialists and Christian Democrats, who compete for parliamentary control with each other. However, most politicians who get themselves elected to the Parliament are naturally Europhile and federalist. Hence party conflict is muted, rendering parliamentary proceedings rather dull as well as irrelevant to core decision making.

The European Parliament's one significant asset is that it is the only elected European body. Direct elections are held every four years, more or less simultaneously across all the countries of the EU. Hence it can claim to have more of a democratic, popular mandate for what it says than the Commission or the Court.

However, the Council of Ministers can also claim that its members, chosen to represent their country by their respective national governments, owe their position ultimately to popular election. In Britain, general elections are clearly regarded as more important than Euroelections as evidenced by the fact that they attract about double the number of voters.

Indeed, as campaigning in Euroelections is in the hands of the British parties rather than an all-European Socialist or Conservative organisation, they often appear like a pale reflection of the general election. European issues only enter in a negative way (e.g. 'resisting Brussels bureaucracy') and elections are fought mostly on issues of domestic politics. It is difficult, therefore, for British members of the European Parliament (MEPs) to claim a very convincing mandate for wresting power from the Council of Ministers, when they have been elected on the basis of (or as a protest against) the British Government's domestic record (see Briefing 5.6).

The powerlessness of the British Parliament in European affairs is not counterbalanced, therefore, by any greater authority or effectiveness of the European Parliament. The latter has only marginally greater power of scrutiny over European legislation and no greater control over the Council of Ministers. This detracts even from its direct election, by lowering its visibility to electors and ultimately their turnout. The EP has the potential for democratic control should the EU become a real federation. Until that day, however, it remains the weakest of all the European institutions and the most limited in its functions.

SUBSIDIARITY AND LOCAL GOVERNMENT

This 'democratic deficit' might be made up within the structure of the EU – at least to some extent – by implementing the idea of 'subsidiarity', which is frequently talked about and is even written into the Treaty of Maastricht as a vague

BRIEFINGS

5.6 RELATIONS BETWEEN EURO MPs (MEPs) AND BRITISH MEMBERS OF PARLIAMENT (MPs)

Many Conservative MPs like the free-market aspect of the EU, but hate the loss of national sovereignty necessary to achieve it. Some reject the social aspects of EU policy (the Social Chapter, for example). Others claim that Brussels stands for the remote and stifling bureaucracy of a European superstate. On the Labour side some feel that the EU is a club for wealthy countries, while others also resent the loss of sovereignty. The fact that both main parties have their pro- and anti-Europe wings makes the issue difficult for them to handle, and the issue being so highly charged increases the problem. Only the Liberal Democrats are united, having always been strongly pro-European. In short, Europe has been a persistent source of rancorous conflict within the two main parties for three decades, and the conflict shows no sign of going away.

Relations between the party groups in the European Parliament and in Westminster are not particularly good, particularly on the Conservative side where Margaret Thatcher's legacy of distrust remains. Conservative members of the European Parliament (MEPs) are allowed to attend the Backbenchers' Committee in Westminster (the 1922 Committee) but there are few other direct connections. There are stronger ties on the Labour side: MPs and MEPs frequently meet, and the latter have rights and powers within the national organisation. For example, the leader of the Labour Group in the European Parliament sits on the Party's National Executive Committee, and Labour MEPs can vote in the national leadership elections.

Europe was a significant factor in Margaret Thatcher's fall from power in 1990, and the issue posed severe difficulties for the Major Government of 1992–97 throughout its life. Splits were not particularly evident in the Labour Opposition from 1992–97, but they are likely to open up in the New Labour Government when it has to take important and controversial decisions about further integration.

commitment. 'Subsidiarity' means that policy should be made and implemented at the lowest possible level of government compatible with efficiency and accountability. One reason for doing so is to make decision making more open and accessible to those whom it affects.

'Subsidiarity' has been seen by 'Eurosceptical' countries like Britain as a way of limiting future transfers of power from London to Brussels, or even of getting some powers back. As we have seen, however, this hardly guarantees democratic control, given the weakness of parliamentary scrutiny.

A better idea might be to go all the way and transfer some European and some central British powers to local and regional governments, the third set of directly elected bodies in Britain. They have the advantage of being much closer to their electors than either the European or British governments and parliaments.

Traditionally, many 'personal' services which were centralised in other European countries – education, police, public health – have been controlled by local authorities in Britain. The tendency under Conservative governments from 1979–97 has been quite the opposite however. Such services have either been taken over by central government or given to unelected 'quangos' nominated by the Government (for a discussion of quangos, see Chapter 10, pp. 255–57).

Such centralisation has been justified in terms of controlling public expenditure, benefiting from the 'economies of scale' of larger, if nonelected, units, and of introducing competition. An unstated reason, arising from the election cycle in Britain (which ensures that most local councillors are elected at the Government's midterm, when its popularity is low), is that most councils are controlled by the Liberal Democrats or Labour. Conservative governments thus found it easier to work with nominated bodies whose members were more likely to be 'one of us' (in Margaret Thatcher's phrase).

This erosion of local democracy has been one factor stimulating demands for local autonomy in Scotland, Wales and Northern Ireland. We shall discuss these regions and their local Nationalist parties in the next chapter. Here we need only note that regional elected assemblies will be boosted by the doctrine of subsidiarity. There are few tasks outside foreign affairs and defence which government at this level would not be fitted to do. Even if Scottish and Welsh independence became an option it would be easier to contemplate within the Single Market and the structure of the EU.

Hence, the Scottish National Party uses the slogan: 'Scotland in Europe'. Paradoxically, therefore, the centralisation of Western Europe under the EU also helps towards its decentralisation, a point noted in our discussion of regionalism in the next chapter.

Quite apart from the possibility of carrying 'subsidiarity' to its logical conclusion, the EU has already had an effect on the British regions and local government. The EU has substantial regional funds and many of its policies have a direct impact on local services. As a result, a large and increasing number of local and regional bodies have built their own special links with Brussels. Some maintain an office and staff there to keep close watch on events, to try to influence European bodies, and to raise money. Others employ consultants in Brussels to act on their behalf. Some authorities group together to form consortia, but the larger ones act separately.

It often suits both local interests and Brussels to work directly with one another, thereby short-circuiting the Government in London. This is consistent with subsidiarity, but it is also a convenient political device which allows the localities and Brussels to build political alliances independently of national governments. This is notably true for Britain where the Government has the reputation of being the 'awkward partner'. As a result, the EU strengthens the position of local and regional government as against the central Government in London. This is a concrete example of centralisation in Brussels developing hand-in-hand with the decentralisation of power to the local and regional levels, something which is taken up within the context of regionalism in the next chapter.

ESSAYS

1. Why is the issue of European Union so divisive in British party politics? Is it likely to become less divisive in the next 10 years or so?

2. What organisational impact has membership of the EU had on Whitehall and Westminster? Have they restructured around Europe or adapted existing organisations? Why?

3. The EU's main areas of policy interest are economics, the environment, consumer affairs, regional policy, agriculture and fisheries, and security and foreign policy. Pick any three and trace the impact of EU policy on British affairs.

PROJECTS

1. Identify the main effects of membership of the EU on the executive, legislative, and judicial branches of British government. Where does most power and influence lie?

2. Imagine you are the leader of a major European pressure group. How would you try to influence EU policy on a matter of interest to your group? Answer with reference to:

(a) agricultural policy
(b) environmental policy
(c) competition policy.

3. Locate the interests of Scotland and Wales in relation to the EU. Does British membership of the EU make the devolution of legislative powers to Wales and Scotland more or less likely?

SUMMARY

This chapter has examined the impact of the European Union on government and politics in Britain. The effects have been deep and profound but they also vary considerably, as follows:

- Constitutional effects have been slight, with the single and major exception of parliamentary sovereignty. Parliament must accept EU law, and cannot change, repeal or even debate it. Legal sovereignty in relevant policy areas has therefore shifted from Westminster to the EU. With this important exception, the British constitution has changed little.

- In terms of the machinery of central government the UK has adapted existing structures rather than change them. There is no special Ministry for European Affairs, as there is in many countries. Instead European affairs are handled by a series of interdepartmental committees, co-ordinated by the Cabinet Office, and by the Foreign and Commonwealth Office. Nonetheless, the sheer volume of EU work has added enormously to the pressures on leading politicians and civil servants. They have also had to develop a European awareness in almost everything they do.

- Pressure groups whose interests are affected by the EU have responded by moving into Brussels where they have replicated their London lobbying activities and organisations. They often join forces with other European partners to form 'umbrella' organisations which represent many national organisations with similar interests. It is estimated that about 500 'Euro-groups' are recognised by policy makers in Brussels, and that over 3,000 full-time lobbyists operate in the city. British groups are fully involved with both.

- Local governments and regional organisations have followed suit and made direct contact with European decision makers in Brussels. The advisory 'Committee of the Regions' (Figure 4.1) gives them an institutional basis inside the structures of the Union.

- The impact of the EU varies considerably in different policy areas. In some its effects are pervasive, in others, less so. But EU policies now affect many aspects of daily life in Britain, and their influence is likely to grow.

FURTHER READING

For the fullest accounts of the impact of the European Union on the government, politics and policy of the UK see S. Bulmer, S. George, and A. Scott (eds), *The United Kingdom and EC Membership Evaluated* (London: Pinter, 1992); C. Pilkington, *Britain in the European Union Today* (Manchester: Manchester University Press, 1995). Also useful is S. George, *Britain and European Integration Since 1945* (Oxford: Blackwell, 1991), Chapter 4. The issue of sovereignty is discussed in some depth by P. Norton, 'Europe and the Constitution', *Talking Politics*, 6(**3**), (1994).

CHAPTER 6

The (dis)United Kingdom? Ireland, Scotland and Wales

The last chapter showed how the EU operates as a third layer of government in Britain, challenging traditional ideas about the exclusive sovereignty of the British state over its national territory. Not only does the central state face challenges from Europe, there are also demands for greater autonomy in Scotland, Wales and Northern Ireland. This chapter will examine the general environment, European and British, within which regional political movements have developed. It will also look at the economic and social disparities between the British regions, which fuel demands for a change in territorial relationships, and the cultural and institutional differences which provide a focus for the nationalist movements in Scotland and Wales. Particular attention will be given to the special case of Northern Ireland, and the general influence which a political settlement there could have on territorial relationships within the UK as a whole. Finally, the prospects for reform of the centralised British state under the New Labour Government will be discussed.

This chapter therefore covers:

- Minority nationalism and state building in Britain and Europe
- Regional disparities and the nature of territory and ethnicity in the British Isles
- Wales: cultural distinctiveness but political fragmentation
- Scotland: some cultural, but more institutional, distinctiveness
- Northern Ireland: rival claims of nationhood
- The constitutional implications of regional autonomy

MINORITY NATIONALISM AND STATE-BUILDING IN BRITAIN AND EUROPE

Britain (see Briefing 6.1) is unique among the countries of the EU in having had part of its national territory secede in a violent struggle for independence in the twentieth century. The present-day Republic of Ireland broke away from the

BRIEFINGS

6.1 ENGLAND, BRITAIN, GREAT BRITAIN, THE UNITED KINGDOM, AND THE BRITISH ISLES

There is often confusion between the terms England, Britain, Great Britain, the United Kingdom and the British Isles. This is partly because geographical entities get mixed up with political ones. The largest geographical entity, *The British Isles*, consists of the two main islands and many smaller ones. The larger island, *Great Britain*, contains England, Wales, and Scotland, and the smaller one, *Ireland*, comprises *Northern Ireland* and the *Republic of Ireland*. The largest political entity is the *United Kingdom of Great Britain and Northern Ireland* which consists of England, Scotland, Wales, and Northern Ireland. This is often shortened to the *UK*. The largest part of the UK is England, often confused with Great Britain or even the UK by the English. The *Republic of Ireland* was part of the UK until 1922 when it broke away after the War of Independence.

Key term

Nationalism – the belief that the people identified as belonging to a national community should form their own sovereign state.

United Kingdom in 1922 by force of arms. Irish nationalists have continued the guerrilla war in Northern Ireland and on the British mainland through a series of terrorist acts. Only Spain among the Member States of the EU has experienced anything similar to this, in the form of Basque terrorism.

Minority nationalism (see Briefing 6.2) on the other hand – the demand for political autonomy on the part of cultural or religious minorities – is quite common throughout Western Europe. Belgium has effectively split itself between Dutch-speaking Flemings and French-speaking Walloons. Italy and Spain have granted extensive powers to regional minorities, and Bavaria has its own political party inside Germany.

Scottish and Welsh nationalism are thus not anomalies on the European scene; on the contrary they are a familiar phenomenon. That is in part why the EU has created its advisory 'Committee of the Regions' to represent minority groups, bypassing the claims of the existing Member States to be homogeneous nations.

Indeed, there are some European Federalists who advocate a 'Europe of the Homelands' (*Europe des Patries*) which would cut out existing nation-states altogether and base a European Federation on the traditional regions. One does not have to go this far to see that regional aspirations might well be a useful ally in the EU's attempts to take power away from the Member States.

The reason why so many regional minorities exist goes back to the very formation of European states, most of which were created by powerful rulers expanding out from their fortified capital to seize surrounding territories. Sometimes these were inhabited by people speaking the same language and sharing a similar way of life to the original subjects, but sometimes they were very different. Whatever the case, they could be taxed and used to support an even more powerful army for further territorial expansion.

BRIEFINGS

6.2 STATE NATIONALISM AND MINORITY NATIONALISM: ARE NATION-STATES REALLY NATIONS?

'State' is another word used to describe a 'country' or 'polity'. It refers first to a territorial unit governed by a single supreme (or 'sovereign') authority and secondly to the military and administrative institutions that defend and organise that unit. In the context of international relations the idea of an autonomous territorial unit is usually uppermost. References to the activities of the 'state' inside Britain usually mean the executive and its administrative apparatus.

The British state was consolidated through the actions of English kings and rulers, based around London, who conquered the outlying regions of England from 800–1200, then Wales and Ireland. They tried but failed to conquer Scotland, which was, however, incorporated by negotiation through the dynastic Union of the Crowns in 1603, and the Union of Parliaments in 1707. Southern and Western Ireland broke away violently from the British state at the end of the First World War (1919–22) and set up a separate state, the Republic of Ireland. The 'Six Counties' of Northern Ireland are still disputed between the British and Irish states and violence continues. The Scottish Nationalist Party (SNP), which gained 22 per cent of the Scottish vote in the 1997 general election, advocates Scottish independence through peaceful means.

The growth of independence movements stems from the influence of nationalism, the idea, which originated in the nineteenth century, that each 'people' defined by a particular language and culture should have its own state. In practice, this often meant that the dominant group in each existing state imposed its own language and culture on the minorities. 'Unionists' therefore often claim that Britain is a nation-state as most 'Britons' speak English and have a common culture. Welsh, Scottish, and Irish nationalists oppose this, arguing that the existence of a separate culture in their country justifies an independent state for them. Nationalism is thus a two-edged sword. Depending on what groups are identified as important, it can be used either to argue for the legitimacy of the existing 'nation-states' such as the United Kingdom, or for the right of secession of the Scots, Welsh and Irish.

The traditional state tried to impose the same religion on all its subjects but did not concern itself with their culture or language. After the French Revolution, however, the idea that the state should be 'one and indivisible' – all citizens should be equal to each other but also similar – gained ground. This was the origin of the dominant ideology of nationalism, according to which every people or nation should have its own state. Universal education gave those in control of existing states an opportunity to create a corresponding nation by imposing the state language on all schools and educating all children in it. The growth of a mass press, and later radio and television – all using the majority language – aided this process.

State attempts to impose a single and dominant language provoked resistance from minorities who saw their own culture and language disappearing under state pressure. Their remedy was to create their own political institutions in order to sustain, rather than depress, their culture. Thus they too found support in the ideas of nationalism. One only had to recognise the minority as a separate nation to argue that it should have its own state. However, minority secession or even autonomy was resisted by the majority, who saw this as splitting 'their' nation, and redoubled their attempts at assimilation of the minorities. What these conflicts call into question is what constitutes the nation: the region, or the state in which it has become embedded?

These conflicts have worked their way through British politics. The core of the British state is clearly formed by South-East England, which conquered or assimilated the other parts of the islands in a process lasting a thousand years (up to the parliamentary union with Ireland in 1801).

In some respects state formation in Britain was more permissive than in other European countries. Because of its island position it had less need to exert an iron control over its borders. It could afford to leave local leaders in charge (in mainland Britain at least); provided they paid taxes and kept order they could do more or less what they wanted within their own county or city. The nineteenth century reforms were aimed at freeing local initiative rather than promoting centralisation. It was, for example, native Scottish reformers, and not a London government, who tried to replace both Gaelic and Scots with standard English.

In Ireland, however, the British Government – because the island was a potential area of military weakness – acted much more like an imperial power towards a colony, planting settlers and ruling through an alien bureaucracy. Differences were exacerbated by the fact that four-fifths of the population were Roman Catholic in a largely Protestant British state. Doctrines of nationalism thus found fertile ground among the Catholic Irish of the South and West in the nineteenth century. Like many such European nationalist movements, the struggle for independence fused with movements for political emancipation, social advancement and cultural autonomy. These sparked off a century-long series of revolts against British rule (1798, 1848, 1867–68, 1879–83, 1919–22). The last of these succeeded in establishing an independent state, the Republic of Ireland, in the South and West of Ireland.

The Irish example illustrates the ambiguity and interchangeability of the concepts of nation and minority, region and state. Use of these concepts depends on whether a territorially concentrated group has state institutions of its own or whether its area is run by a state in which a larger group dominates. Ireland was a region of Britain and is (mostly) now a separate state. The same could conceivably happen in Scotland and Wales and may well happen in Northern Ireland over the next 20 years.

Northern Ireland illustrates another phenomenon, however, which is equally characteristic of nationalist movements. The nationalist struggles set off reactions not only from the state majority but also from other minorities or from representatives of the state majority within their own region. In the case of Ireland, the Protestants, a local majority in the North, strongly opposed Irish nationalism and upheld the Union with Britain. The Irish War of Independence was also a civil war between largely Catholic nationalists and largely Protestant unionists. When Irish independence was granted, the latter retained their own territory in the North as part of the British state.

Like Chinese boxes, however, nationalist territorial solutions always reveal another minority lurking underneath. Northern Ireland contained a substantial nationalist, Catholic minority who supported a takeover by the Republic. This led to continuing guerrilla warfare and terrorism (1919–23, 1936–41, 1956–63, 1969 onwards) in mainland Britain as well as in Northern Ireland (see Briefing 6.3).

A way in which compromises might be achieved between a minority and the central state is also suggested by Northern Ireland. From 1922 to 1973 it had a provincial parliament and government largely responsible for internal affairs. Its record was marred by discrimination against Catholics, but in other respects the Northern Irish administration modernised the province and vastly improved social conditions.

Key term

Devolution – the delegation of specific powers by a higher level of government to a lower one.

BRIEFINGS

6.3 GUERRILLA WARFARE, TERRORISM AND FREEDOM FIGHTERS

Nationalist groups which feel frustrated with constitutional procedures for expressing their demands may turn to violence, often calling themselves 'freedom fighters' or a 'Liberation Front'. The main example in Britain of such a group is the Irish Republican Army (IRA). The mainstream Welsh and Scottish nationalists are dedicated to nonviolent ways of expressing their claims for self-determination, but fringe groups in both cases have used violence. (The most notable example is the burning of English-owned holiday homes in Wales.) Nationalists may be tempted to follow such tactics because they are minorities within the British state, where the inbuilt English majority can always vote them down. The danger in Conservative Party resistance to all forms of devolution is that nationalists may eventually conclude that there is no other way to independence but violence.

One group's terrorism is another group's liberation struggle. The very definition of the situation is one element in the conflict between the IRA and the British state. The latter has infinitely more soldiers, weapons and resources than the IRA. The 'freedom fighters' or 'terrorists' thus have to adopt hit and run tactics, killing individual members of the armed forces or leaving bombs which will injure or kill civilians indiscriminately. Through these actions they hope to provoke the authorities into indiscriminate action against their group as a whole, thus provoking general resentment and providing recruits to their own movement. Once 'guerrilla warfare' of this kind starts it can therefore become self-perpetuating, as the example of Ireland shows.

The Northern Irish case provides a concrete example of how Welsh and Scottish demands for more autonomy might be met, without breaking up the British state. There is no practical reason why these territories cannot have the 'home' parliament and government dealing with their domestic affairs which the Labour Government is now introducing. Their administration is already devolved to the Welsh and Scottish Offices. A more sweeping form of 'devolution' to Northern Ireland with equal power sharing between Protestants and Catholics may prove to be the only compromise on which the warring sides there might agree.

The Labour Government is committed to devolution ('home rule') in Scotland and Wales, and the last Conservative Government was negotiating similar arrangements in Northern Ireland. Regional autonomy of this kind does not imply the break-up of the United Kingdom. The British state has in the past coexisted happily with a 'devolved' Parliament in Northern Ireland. Certain islands (Man, Jersey, Guernsey) enjoy total self-government over domestic affairs, including taxation, at present.

This is not a curious British anomaly. Most member countries of the EU have such self-governing arrangements within culturally distinctive regions. The argument that any grant of political devolution will break up the United Kingdom is mistaken. Indeed, by compromising with local nationalists before they become totally frustrated, devolution may prevent an Irish situation developing. However, devolution clearly does have constitutional implications, which we shall explore in this chapter and the next.

REGIONAL DISPARITIES IN BRITAIN

Regionalism – regions are geographical areas within a state, and regionalism involves granting special forms of representation within national government to regions, or granting special powers and duties to regional forms of government.

One paradox of the previous discussion is that we have concentrated on Scotland, Wales and Ireland without mentioning the English regions like Merseyside or the North East. In terms of their social and economic profile these regions are almost as distinctive as Scotland and Wales. However, they do not possess the cultural and institutional differences which act as a focus for separatism or nationalism. All these regions have as good a claim to be 'English' as the London area. Social and regional deprivation has fuelled political reactions, but these have taken the form of overwhelming support for the Labour Party in its struggle for power centrally. Discontent has therefore been expressed in support for the opposition at the centre rather than for autonomy and home rule for the region itself.

Labour and, to a lesser extent, the Liberal Democrats have also attracted support in Scotland and Wales for the same reasons. The support of the peripheries in many ways makes Labour a territorially rather than class-based party. The difference is that in Scotland and Wales it has to compete internally with the local nationalist parties, which explains its definite commitment to devolution in these areas compared with its vague rhetoric about greater freedom for local government in the English regions.

The major force behind movements for regional autonomy are feelings of national distinctiveness, but they are also fuelled by feelings of relative deprivation

Plate 6.1 Liverpool Town Hall. In terms of their social and economic profile, regions like Merseyside or the North East are almost as distinctive as Scotland and Wales. Regional civic pride, epitomised in the architecture of grand Victorian Town Halls, diminished under the centralising Conservative governments of 1979–97. The Labour Government has promised to restore regional autonomy

in relation to London and South-East England. Table 6.1 shows a whole series of figures, covering wealth, living conditions and health which illustrate this point. The varying levels of unemployment, a central factor, were shown in Figure 1.2 (p. 12). As Chapter 1 noted, the underlying reason for regional disparities is that nineteenth century industrialisation took place in the North and Midlands. Its attendant problems of rapid and unplanned urban development, slums, badly paid repetitive work, crime and poverty were thus most keenly experienced there and linger on to the present day. Attempted solutions (such as rehousing and reloca-tion in vast uniform housing estates on the outskirts of cities) in turn created fresh social problems.

The area around London, in contrast, always benefited from greater government and consumer spending. When industrialisation came in the 1930s, with light engineering and service industries, it was cleaner and paid better wages. The planning and welfare measures discussed in Chapter 3 ensured that living condi-tions were better.

Apart from modern industrialisation, South-East England has always benefited economically from the overspill of wealth from London. Government employment has always created a disproportionately large middle class which has sustained the largest and most concentrated consumer market in Britain. The end beneficiaries of foreign wars and conquests were the financial interests and markets of the City of London, which reinforced middle-class political and economic dominance of the region.

Foreign wars and Empire did provide markets for industry in the peripheries, particularly for coal, steel and shipbuilding. They also provided jobs, but not at home. Emigration to the new colonies provided an outlet for the restless and

Table 6.1 Disparities between British regions in the 1990s

	South-East England	West Midlands	East Anglia	South-West England	East Midlands	Wales	North-West England	Yorks and Humberside	Northern England	Scotland	Northern Ireland
Percentage of workforce with a degree (1991)	13.6	7.0	8.0	8.2	8.9	7.5	8.3	7.7	6.9	7.3	8.6
Average weekly earnings of men per head (£) (1991)	368.7	299.1	300.2	297.1	292.6	280.1	300.3	286.6	289.3	297.9	272.4
Gross domestic product per head (UK = 100) (1994)	117	93	101	95	96	85	90	89	89	100	82
Mortality rate per 1000 births 1984–86	7.9	10.2	5.9	6.9	8.1	7.4	8.5	8.2	7.9	8.7	7.6
Percentage of households with no car (1990)	28	35	26	25	31	30	37	38	42	42	34

Source: Regional Trends (London: HMSO, various dates)

Map 6.1 The counties of England and Wales

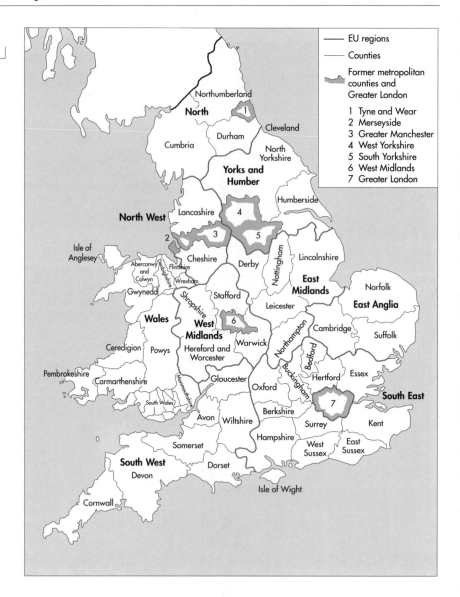

ambitious, supplemented by posts in the colonial administration. The Army and Navy recruited disproportionately in the more deprived areas: between a quarter and two fifths of the nineteenth century Army originated in Scotland and Ireland, far in excess of their share of the British population.

Such outlets for the surplus populations can be seen in two ways. They can be viewed positively, as providing opportunities which would never have been available otherwise. Or they could be judged negatively, as a haemorrhage of the brightest and best who, had they been able to stay at home, would have provided an indigenous regional leadership otherwise lacking.

Whatever one's judgement, 'economic' emigration certainly helped maintain social stability in the peripheries. During the single decade of the 1950s, for example, a third of a million – out of a total population of five and a quarter million – emigrated from Scotland, about 6 per cent of the population, mostly young and disproportionately better educated. Half went to (South-East) England, and half abroad. As a result of emigration the Scottish population remained static while South-East England grew.

The loss of Empire and reduction of military commitments in the 1960s may have contributed to regional discontent by reducing job opportunities. Certainly they helped concentrate attention on domestic rather than foreign problems. Among the more obvious domestic problems were the decline of traditional industries – coal-mining, steel-making, heavy engineering, ship-building and textiles – and the centralisation of the firms that remained on London. Branches in the peripheries, remote from the main consumer markets, tended to be closed first. This applied even to the new industries which found their way to the periphery. Meanwhile, general economic management was focused on the South East. The price of credit and loans was raised when financial markets reacted to 'overheating' in the South at a time when the North had barely warmed up. 'Stop–go' economic policies thus hit particularly hard in the peripheries: from the point of view of peripheral industry it was practically all stop and no go.

Social conditions are poorer and health is worse among the larger numbers of the working class in the outlying regions (Table 6.1). This means that direct government expenditure on social benefits and the Health Service is greater in these areas than in the more prosperous South East. Maintenance of roads and infrastructure in large thinly populated areas, like the Highlands of Scotland, also costs more. Hence the figures for direct government expenditure show more state money being spent per head in Scotland and Wales and Northern Ireland than in England (Table 6.2a and b). (Similar figures for the English regions cannot be obtained.) British 'unionists' (i.e. those who favour retaining the existing United Kingdom) use this to underline the benefits these regions get from being in the British state. Local nationalists say it simply shows that conditions are worse, owing to disparities which can only be eliminated by regional autonomy or independence. They also argue that figures for directly attributed expenditure conceal what happens with other expenditures (research and development, military, administration), which go to South-East England.

Overall comparisons between the constituent countries of the United Kingdom can also be misleading. Within England, some of the most deprived British regions exist in the North and the West. Similarly, inside Wales, there is a great difference between South, East, and North West. And in Scotland, Edinburgh, Aberdeen and their regions are in many ways as prosperous as the London area and contrast greatly with the deprived Glasgow conurbation and the declining industrial city of Dundee.

We shall explore these internal differences further, when we consider Scotland, Wales and Northern Ireland separately. What should be noted here, however, is that regional nationalism is not solely social or economic in character. Its basis, whatever the issues it raises, is primarily cultural and derives from feelings of national or regional distinctiveness. Moreover, even if some peripheral regions

Table 6.2a Identifiable public expenditure per capita as percentage of UK identifiable expenditure per capita (UK = 100)

	1989/1990	**1990/1991**	**1991/1992**
England	95.8	96.1	96.8
Scotland	119.1	118.2	114.6
Wales	107.8	109.0	106.8
Northern Ireland	151.1	141.5	137.0

Table 6.2b 1992 identifiable public expenditure in each British region

	£ million
England	124,585
Scotland	16,638
Wales	8,508
Northern Ireland	6,090

Source: D. Heald, 'Territorial Public Expenditure in the UK', *Public Administration*, Vol. 72 (1994), pp. 147–75

are prosperous, most are not, and it is their situation which fuels the grievance. This emerges more clearly from the individual cases considered below.

Territory and ethnicity

Key term

Ethnicity – a mixture or combination of different social characteristics (which may include race, culture, religion, or some other basis of common origin and social identity), which give different social groups a common consciousness, and which are thought to divide or separate them in some way from other social groups.

There are of course many ethnically and culturally distinctive groups in Britain, as noted in Chapter 1. The most distinctive are recent immigrants from the Caribbean and particularly the Indian subcontinent, who are distinguished racially and, in the case of Sikhs, Hindus and Muslims, by language and religion as well. Accommodating them may raise political problems from time to time, especially when the group suffers from high unemployment, poverty, poor living conditions and social break-up. Riots, crime and delinquency tend to spread under these circumstances.

However, one thing immigrant groups do *not* do is threaten the sovereignty of the British state. This is because they do not constitute a local majority in any city or region where they have settled. Demands for better treatment or recognition therefore are channelled through all-British institutions, through national parties like Labour and the Liberal Democrats, or through London-based pressure groups.

Groups like the Welsh, Scots and Irish are in many ways less culturally distinctive than immigrant groups. Over the last two to three centuries they have evolved within the British context and many of their cultural patterns and institutions mark them out as British. Paradoxically, however, they still pose more of a threat to the integrity of the British state than more obviously 'different' groups, because they occupy a distinct territory within which they constitute a local majority. Their demands, mainly for greater regional autonomy, thus become bound up with their territorial distinctiveness. The British state is nothing if not a territorial unit subject to a central political authority. Thus the territorial demands voiced by the Scots, Welsh and Irish constitute more of a threat to it than the demands of more distinctive groups which can be met without territorial concessions.

WALES: CULTURAL DISTINCTIVENESS AND POLITICAL FRAGMENTATION

Wales is arguably the region of Britain with the most distinctive popular culture. Like the other non-English regions it emerged from Celtic kingdoms which held out against the invading Germanic tribes after the collapse of the Roman Empire. However its rugged geography, with high mountains protecting it against invasion and hindering communications, meant that it was not united under a single political authority before its final incorporation into the English administrative structure in 1536.

This mattered less than its cultural and religious distinctiveness. Almost all the Welsh population spoke a separate Celtic language until the last quarter of the nineteenth century. In common with other 'submerged' European languages, Welsh experienced a cultural renaissance in the nineteenth and twentieth centuries. However, its popular base was concurrently eroded through universal education in English, the English language mass media, and massive immigration of English speakers into industrial South Wales. Although there is a special Welsh language TV channel and schools encourage bilingualism, Welsh is now spoken by only half a million people (20 per cent of the population), mainly located in North and West Wales (Table 6.3).

Another nineteenth century development, however, reinforced Welsh distinctiveness. This was religious revivalism, spearheaded by Methodists and Congregationalists, radical Protestant denominations opposed to the torpor and worldliness (as they saw it) of the Anglican state Church. The Nonconformist Churches used Welsh as their medium and penetrated every village and town of the country. They voiced demands for the 'disestablishment' of the Anglican church, loss of its special privileges especially in education within Wales. This was a uniquely Welsh demand, which was met in 1920. By that time, however, religious passions had started to ebb. While the Nonconformist tradition still gives Welsh life a particular flavour it is not particularly influential in contemporary Wales, where only 12 per cent of the population attend church at all regularly.

Nonconformity and the call for disestablishment did, however, give Welsh voters a push towards radical politics as they were enfranchised in the late nineteenth and early twentieth century. This expressed itself in support for progressive Liberalism and subsequently for Labour and nationalist parties in the North and West.

Table 6.3 Differences between regions inside Wales in the 1990s

	North West (Gwynedd and Dyfed)	North East (Clwyd and Powys)	South (Gwent and Glamorgan)
Percentage of households with no car	27.3	27.0	35.7
Percentage with limiting long-term illness	16.1	15.4	18.0
Percentage unemployed	12.5	9.9	12.2
Percentage with higher educational qualifications	13.2	11.5	12.0
GDP per head (1993)	£7118.5	£8044.5	£8015.5
Percentage Welsh-speaking	50.7	18.5	7.8

'Welsh Wales', the North West, has the highest percentage of Welsh-speaking people and therefore is culturally the most distinctive. It is also the poorest region, with lower GDP per head, in spite of having a higher percentage of the population well qualified. (In rural Wales cars are a necessity which accounts for the greater number of car-owners compared with the South.)

The English-speaking South suffered all the evils of early industrialism: slums, overcrowding, bad health, precarious employment. This too generated votes for reforming Liberals in the nineteenth and early twentieth century. The political party that really gained, however, was Labour, the defender of working class interests against the free market. South Wales became one of the earliest trade union and Labour strongholds, and from there Labour spread out to the rest of Wales. In the 1997 election Labour held 34 out of 40 Welsh seats, the Liberal Democrats 2, Plaid Cymru (the Welsh Nationalist Party) 4, and Conservatives none.

The overall figures mask a very marked regional variation inside Wales. Table 6.4 shows that Labour predominates everywhere but particularly in the industrialised south, traditionally home to a militant working class. 'English Wales' – the border area of the East – provides the highest level of support for the Conservatives. The strongest support for nationalism comes from the North-West territory of Gwynedd, the Welsh kingdom which held out longest against English domination. This is the predominantly Welsh-speaking area where the influence of Nonconformity lingers. Its economic base is mainly farming and tourism, a fragile means of livelihood. The extractive industries, slate and stone, which supported the population from the mid-nineteenth to the mid-twentieth century, have now substantially disappeared. This may explain why the nationalists have not opted for a separate Welsh-speaking entity in this area, leaving the English-speaking regions to themselves.

Attracting support in the rest of Wales is difficult for the nationalists. Unlike the Scottish Nationalist Party, Plaid Cymru is predominantly a cultural defence organisation. The party wants separate political institutions to protect and extend the Welsh language, together with a stronger economic and social base to support the Welsh-speaking population. This gives it a strong appeal in the North. Its problem, however, is how to appeal to the English-speaking borders and South Wales, whose voters are opposed to the extension of the Welsh language, which they themselves do not speak.

Table 6.4 The parties' share of the vote in the Welsh regions, 1997

	North West	**East**	**South**	**Wales as a whole**
Labour	35.9	46.4	62.9	54.7
Conservative	19.5	26.8	17.3	19.6
Liberal Democrat	11.7	18.4	10.6	12.4
Plaid Cymru	28.1	5.1	5.7	10.0
Other	4.9	3.3	3.4	3.4

Regional political differences are heightened by geography. Most of the regions are difficult of access (the reason the Welsh were able to survive in the first place). But each of them is more accessible from the neighbouring part of England than it is from the rest of Wales. This fact of geography has been underpinned by the building of railways and roads from East to West, rather than from North to South. It is easier for all-Welsh bodies to meet in Shrewsbury, an English town – or even in London – than in far southern Cardiff, the official capital.

Rural West Wales (the coastal strip and its hinterland down to Carmarthen on the Bristol Channel) is linked to Gwynedd both historically and politically. Here support for the nationalists is strong. The regions over the mountains to the East, bordering on England (Clywd and Powys), are the most Anglicised, and here nationalism attracts little support. These differences are almost perfectly illustrated in the referendum votes for a separate Welsh Assembly, shown in Map 6.2. The North and West supported devolution and the East was totally opposed. The South was split between the old mining valleys (for) and the coast (against).

South Wales (the triangle of Cardiff, Swansea and Merthyr Tydfil) is the most populous area of the country and the classic heartland of industrial working-class Wales, the country of trade unions and Labour. Labour has controlled all of local government and most of the constituencies of South Wales for generations.

In many ways this consistent support for Labour has defined Welsh politics as a whole better than sporadic upsurges of nationalism. Support for Labour, the national 'opposition party', can be seen as the main political expression of Welsh distinctiveness. Labour, in its turn, can be seen as a representative of peripheral protest against the centre in Britain, as much as a class-based party. In South Wales both fuse because the region itself is defined by its working-class nature.

Welsh Labour MPs may express some political demands for their region but some have been bitter opponents of nationalism inside Wales, denouncing it as a distraction from the real task of improving living standards and getting jobs. The Cardiff area's relative proximity to London (200 miles) makes it a favoured location for new industrial development, provided it remains well integrated into Britain. This is an argument supported by Labour inside Wales as well as by the Conservative Governments of the 1980s and 1990s.

The opposition of many Welsh Labour MPs to a Welsh Assembly ensured the high vote against it in the Welsh referendum of September 1997. The furthest Labour has gone in the past in terms of devolution was the creation of the Welsh

Map 6.2 The three Wales: how the country split on the Devolution Referendum, 18 September 1997

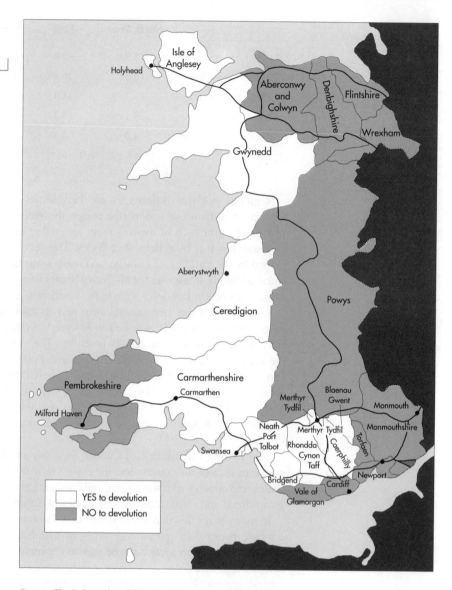

Source: *The Independent*, 20 September 1997

Office in Cardiff in 1965, on the model of the well-established Scottish Office. The Welsh Office is a regional ministry which administers culture, environment, local government, housing, social affairs, agriculture, infrastructure and economic development in Wales (see Briefing 6.4). It thus groups functions which in England (and in Wales until 1970) were handled by separate functional ministries from London.

BRIEFINGS

6.4 THE WELSH OFFICE

Politically and administratively, Wales was much more thoroughly incorporated into the English structure than was Scotland. English law was applied and London-based ministries handled functional responsibilities in Wales as they did in England, with one or two subordinate boards and departments established mainly for dealing with education in Welsh.

However, the fact that Scotland had a special territorial ministry – the Scottish Office – provided an argument for budding Welsh nationalists to use in support of administrative devolution for Wales. This was relatively unthreatening to Welsh opponents of devolution and provided more local jobs. By the 1970s the Welsh Office had acquired practically the full range of powers held by the Scottish Office: education, culture, economic development, health and local government. The Secretary of State for Wales was a member of the Cabinet, even though arguably the least important one.

However, under the Conservative Governments of the 1980s and 1990s the ambiguity of the Welsh Office's position became apparent. It concentrated Welsh administration in Cardiff instead of London, but only in order to impose Conservative policies on an area which had largely rejected them. While some claims were made that Wales was pursuing a separate path from the rest of the country (state intervention rather than free market) the most detailed study of policy making concluded that strong Thatcherite policies were being enforced. The impression of distant, quasi-colonial rule was reinforced by the Conservative Government's transfer of power from elected local government to quangos (see Chapter 10), on which the few Welsh Conservatives could pursue almost a full-time career. This situation stimulated more Labour support for an elected Welsh Assembly which could oversee or abolish quangos and institute more effective local democratic control of Welsh administration. For further reading on Welsh administration, the best and most up to date book is Dylan Griffiths (Gower 1996).

Having a separate administration in these areas does mean that a Welsh Assembly charged with overseeing it can be set up with relatively little difficulty. Such an Assembly has been urged on democratic as well as nationalistic grounds, given that the British Parliament has little time for specifically Welsh business. Its specialist committee on Welsh Affairs has little power, and is dominated by the party which won most British votes, not necessarily by the parties preferred by Welsh voters.

This is the reason given by New Labour for having put the creation of a Welsh Assembly to a referendum in Wales, this time with Labour more united in support for the proposal. From the viewpoint of stimulating local democracy the argument is clearly correct. Labour-dominated councils, particularly in the South where they face little challenge, have often been accused of corruption and nepotism. A Welsh Parliament would be open to wider influences and more party

BRIEFINGS

6.5 CLIENTELISM, CORRUPTION AND PATRONAGE

Whatever happens in British general elections, Labour always dominates the local governments of South Wales, often as the only party. Freed from effective accountability, the ruling group of councillors can in these circumstances favour their own supporters and friends in matters over which they have local control – jobs, minor building contracts, priority on public housing lists, etc. Patronage of this kind can be used to favour party supporters ('clientelism') and can slide over into corruption if money is given in exchange for favours.

Remarkably little overt corruption has been uncovered in British local government, either in Wales or out of it. Rumours of a 'Taffia' in local politics are widely believed, however, and to some extent were used by Conservatives to justify the transfer of powers to non-elected 'quangos'. That this is not the answer was demonstrated by the case of the Chairman of the Welsh Development Agency in the early 1990s, who had to leave hurriedly after incurring colossal personal expenses and appointing nominees to the Board without open competition. Probably the best solution to accusations of local malpractice which cannot exactly be nailed down is more transparency in government (which may be produced by a Welsh Assembly) and challenges to Labour predominance by other parties. It is noteworthy that Plaid Cymru has made most headway in South Wales as a challenger to Labour predominance on local councils.

competition, and would therefore expose the corruption and abuse that often accompany local government dominated by a single party (see Briefing 6.5).

At national level the Welsh Office may act to favour Welsh interests against the rest of the Civil Service. It has also had the task during the last 18 years, however, of enforcing Conservative policy on a hostile population, producing some spectacular examples of incompetence and corruption on the way. More Welsh democracy may well be needed, if British New Labour can impose it on its own Welsh traditionalists. Meanwhile it is pressing ahead with the creation of the Assembly on the basis of its narrow victory in the Referendum of September 1997, where only half the Welsh population voted and the Assembly was approved by a majority of only 50.3 per cent.

SCOTLAND: SOME CULTURAL, BUT MORE INSTITUTIONAL, DISTINCTIVENESS

Scotland covers the northern third of Britain but has a population of only just over five million. Most Scots live in the central lowland area between the two major cities of Glasgow and Edinburgh, and on the Eastern coastal plain stretching through Dundee and Aberdeen. Most of the country consists of mountain massifs

Map 6.3 The regions of Scotland (with cities, island groups and main communication routes)

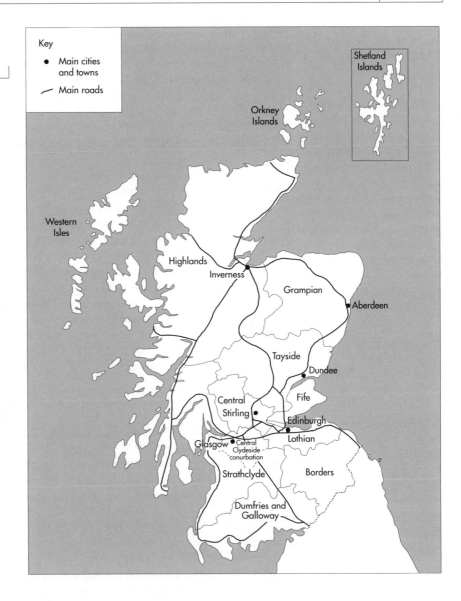

and islands which are very thinly populated. Unlike Wales, however, the various areas of Scotland are more accessible from each other than from England.

Historically, the differences between the Highlands and Lowlands of Scotland were just as great as those between Scotland and England. The Highlands (the Grampian massif, West Coast and Western islands) were a tribal, pastoral society speaking a Celtic language (Gaelic). The Lowlands were a feudal, arable society speaking Scots, a form of Northern English. The assimilation of the Highlands through internal immigration, improved communications and compulsory schooling in English has eliminated the cultural gap. Gaelic remains an important symbol of national distinctiveness but is spoken by just 60 thousand people. It remains a first language only in the remote Outer Hebrides. Scots has also been eroded by universal education in standard English. Like Gaelic, however, it has an important literature and experienced a cultural revival (the 'Scottish Renaissance') in the mid-twentieth century, just as it was ceasing to be widely spoken.

Cultural distinctiveness clearly provides local nationalism with a focus, as in Wales. Unlike the Welsh case, however, the negotiated Union with England in 1707 preserved the distinctive institutions which Scotland had developed as a sixteenth and seventeenth century state. These were first a state church, organised on presbyterian and not episcopalian lines (that is, governed by elders and not bishops), and therefore sharply distinguished from the Church of England. Secondly, the separate body of Scots law, with supporting courts, was retained. Scots law differed from English law in basing itself on Roman Civil Law rather than on precedent. The retention of the supreme courts in Edinburgh meant that Scotland retained a separate legal elite, which provided a high level career outside London.

The Church's responsibility for education and social welfare, and the judiciary's for internal order and policing, passed over to other governmental bodies in the nineteenth century. Their initial organisation on a Scottish basis, however, meant that Scottish bodies based in Edinburgh emerged to handle them (eventually grouped together as the contemporary Scottish Office). The separate legal code made this a logical development. It also fostered the emergence of a Scottish banking system more closely meshed with local commerce and industry than its English counterpart.

These administrative developments also encouraged autonomous institutions in nineteenth-century Ireland but not in Wales, which was integrated administratively with England. In this sense all regions of Scotland focused on Edinburgh in a way that Wales was not focused on Cardiff. The Scottish institutions, however, were emanations of the British state, often more intent on enforcing London's wishes on Scotland than in pushing Scottish interests in the corridors of power.

However, Scottish institutions *do* function separately and they *are* based in Scotland. They thus provide a focus for another Scottish difference: the existence of a distinctive mass media (see Briefing 6.6). Press and radio in Britain are generally very centralised. London-edited papers have a national circulation and there are remarkably few morning newspapers based in the 'provinces' (see Chapters 13 and 14). Scotland is the major exception, with local mass-circulation newspapers dominating readership in the big cities. Regional programming of radio was strong even under the BBC (British Broadcasting Corporation) monopoly and is stronger now. Television in Britain has been regional since the emergence of independent television. Scotland has its own independent television companies, some of which, such as STV, have developed into media conglomerates.

The Scottish media face two ways, like other Scottish institutions. On the one hand, much of their comment and reporting is of British affairs, which differs little in essence from the London-based media. However, their location and particular audience mean that they have a particular interest in Scottish affairs, which then tend to get defined as news. They may have little to do directly with politics but certainly support the idea that Scotland is different. From these it is a short step to thinking of it as a cultural and social entity which ought to have its own political institutions.

BRIEFINGS

6.6 THE SCOTTISH MEDIA

In an age of mass communication, control of the media – particularly of newspapers and television – is often the major factor influencing cultural identities and the political agenda. Generally the centralisation of the British media on London serves to depress regional self-consciousness and focus attention on the glittering scene in the capital.

Scotland and Northern Ireland, in part because of their distance from London, are the major exceptions here. Moreover, Scotland has enough autonomous institutions, both political and cultural, to provide something of an alternative focus to London. This has resulted in Glasgow and Edinburgh each having a quality local paper (the *Herald* and the *Scotsman*), which contain all local as well as national and international news, and hence are almost a necessity for middle-class reading. The mass-circulation *Record* and *Scottish Sun* are based in Glasgow, with 50 per cent Scottish content. Dundee and Aberdeen have local papers which transcend the quality/mass divide (the *Courier*, and *Press and Journal*).

The BBC has always had a strong Scottish regional unit with an autonomous Council. The independent television companies (Borders, Scottish, Grampian) have developed Scottish and local programming over the last 20 years. Scottish Television (STV) has bought the (Glasgow) *Herald* and is looking for more local acquisitions. More Scottish programmes provide more employment for Scottish actors, musicians and artists as well as writers, who in turn contribute to a more distinctive Scottish voice.

Thus developments towards deregulation and competition have in this case strengthened the bases of Scottish identity rather than eroding them. The new Scottish Parliament will provide even more of a focus for, and possibly help to, a distinctively Scottish media.

This sounding board from which to address the whole of the (potential) nation perhaps accounts for the most salient feature of the Scottish National Party (SNP), its tendency to argue the case for independence in economic and material, rather than cultural, terms. The main plank of the SNP platform is that Scotland would do much better economically outside the United Kingdom than by staying inside, for example, by taking over the oil revenues in its sector of the North Sea or securing direct subsidies from the European Union. This position is summarised in its slogans 'It's Scotland's Oil' and 'Scotland in Europe'.

Clearly Scottish cultural distinctiveness offers a focus and a basis for the SNP. Anyone with a strong sense of Scottish identity is likely to be susceptible to its appeals. To gain power in Scotland, however, the party needs to win over a substantial block of Labour supporters. These identify themselves as Scottish but have massive material problems – which they share with the other British peripheries – such as unemployment, poor housing and bad health. To gain their votes

Figure 6.1 Support for
Scottish independence/
devolution in the 1990s

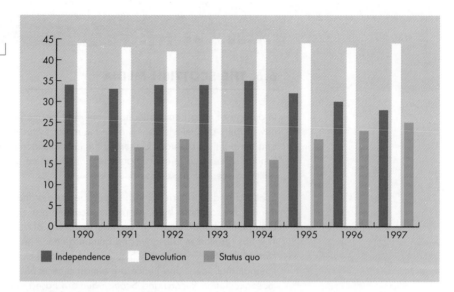

Note: Figure 6.1 data taken from MORI opinion polls. The question wording was 'Do you favour…
1   An independent Scotland which is separate from England and Wales but part of the European
    Community?
2   Scotland remaining part of the UK but with its own devolved Assembly with some taxation and
    spending power?
3   No change from the present system?'
Note that totals are not 100 per cent because 'don't knows' have been excluded.

the SNP has to convince them that they are not just 'Tartan Tories', but committed
to social redistribution and welfare. The SNP has therefore become one of the
most left-wing minority nationalist parties in Europe, lauding political radicalism
as an essential element in the Scots character.

Opinion polls and election results suggest that about a third of Scots consistently support total independence. Opposing them are about one fifth who support
the Union as it is. In between there are 40–45 per cent who want devolution and
greater autonomy within Britain (Figure 6.1). The Scottish Convention of the early
1990s, convened by nonparty figures but supported by the Liberal Democrats and
Labour, represented these people. 'Scotland's Claim of Rights', which it produced, promotes the kind of political reform they wish to see: the creation of the
parliament now being put in place by Labour, with powers over Scottish home
affairs.

The Scottish Referendum of 1979, called to vote on a modest proposal to set
up a Scottish Assembly, approved it by 51.6 per cent. However, Parliament had
required that it be approved by at least 40 per cent of the total Scottish *electorate*,
not a majority of those who actually voted, and as only 32.9 per cent of the
Scottish electorate approved, it failed owing to a high rate of abstention. With a
stronger lead from the new Labour Government, the proposal for a much stronger

Table 6.5 Party votes in the Scottish regions, General Election 1997 (%)

	Grampian	Borders	Dumfries and Galloway	Lothian	Highlands and Islands	Tayside	Central	Fife	Strathclyde	Scotland Total
Labour	25.6	21.2	33.2	46.7	31.6	30.3	51.7	48.5	55.7	45.6
Scottish Nationalist (SNP)	25.2	14.2	26.7	18.2	23.7	36.3	23.8	18.7	20.2	22.1
Conservative	25.0	22.9	29.2	19.3	12.7	24.2	18.9	14.4	13.7	17.5
Liberal Democratic	22.6	38.7	8.9	14.4	29.6	7.5	5.4	17.2	8.4	13.0
Other	2.0	2.0	2.0	1.0	2.0	1.5	1.0	1.0	2.0	2.0

Note: Figures do not always add up to 100 per cent because of rounding. The figures show considerable variation in voting support for the different parties across regions. However, the most populous regions of the Centre Belt (Lothian, Central and Strathclyde) show a clear predominance of Labour voters. The most marked Labour support comes from the single most populous area (Strathclyde) centred on Glasgow. Lothian, centred on Edinburgh, gives less support to Labour and more to the Conservatives and Liberal Democrats. The SNP's areas of strength are Tayside (centred on Dundee) and Grampian (Aberdeen).

Assembly with power to tax was approved by a convincing majority in September 1997 when two-thirds of Scottish voters voted for a parliament with powers of taxation, with a majority in all areas of the country, unlike Wales.

The main political division inside Scotland is between the Glasgow conurbation ('Strathclyde'), which contains about half the population and is overwhelmingly Labour, and the rest of the country where Labour is challenged by Scottish Nationalists, Liberals and Conservatives, in more or less that order. The votes and seats going to different parties in the various regions illustrate this point. Labour obtains most support in the areas around the cities of Glasgow and central Scotland. The 'service' cities of Edinburgh (Lothian) and Aberdeen (Grampian) give less support to Labour and more to other parties. In the Highlands the Liberal Democrats tend to dominate. Table 6.5 shows regional differences in voting in the 1997 General Election. These political differences are based on considerable social disparities, which are not without some cultural reinforcement, as Table 6.6 shows.

Scotland as a whole does not appear to differ significantly from South-East England in terms of most social indicators (Table 6.1). The regional figures show that this is due to the relative wealth of Edinburgh (Lothian) and Aberdeen (Grampian). This prosperity contrasts with severe deprivation in Glasgow and Dundee (Tayside), both of which have had to cope with the social legacy of early industrialisation, followed by later industrial collapse. It is this heritage, shared with other deprived peripheries such as Northern England and South Wales, which pushed them into fervent support for trade unions and the Labour party.

An additional factor fostering such support in Scotland is religion. The core of Labour Party support is the Roman Catholic vote. Catholics in Scotland are

Table 6.6 Regional disparities inside Scotland in the 1990s

	Grampian	Borders	Dumfries and Galloway	Lothian	Highlands and Islands	Tayside	Central	Fife	Strathclyde	Scotland Total
Percentage of workforce with a degree, 1991	6.2	7.6	7.9	5.5	8.9	6.8	7.3	7.6	8.0	7.3
Average weekly earnings per head, 1991 (£)										
Men	363.7	n.a.	268.2	294.6	293.6	277.8	299.8	292.4	293.1	297.9
Women	n.a.	174.5	183.4	214.7	206.7	201.3	189.2	196.5	209.2	206.5
GDP per head, 1994	140.7	82.4	89.2	123.3	83.2	94.2	88.4	82.0	89.3	100
Percentage of unemployed, 1993	8.2	8.4	9.2	9.4	10.2	9.9	10.1	10.2	11.3	9.7
Mortality rate per 1000 births 1995	6.8	6.8	8.5	9.3	6.2	8.2	11.2	7.7	11.2	9.6
Percentage of households with no car, 1991	31	32	32	42	33	41	36	38	48	42

Sources: 1991 Census, Individual Regional Reports, The Scottish Office Central Statistics Unit, Office for National Statistics, *Family Expenditure Survey*, 1995, *The Scottish Economic Bulletin*, No. 53, September 1996, General Registrar's Office of Scotland, the Scottish Office Education and Industry Department

Note: Figures relate to local authority regions which ceased to exist on 1 April 1996. As the data relate to the period when these local authorities were in operation no attempt has been made to rework data into new council areas. The normal threshold used by the European Commission for designation of the most economically deprived regions in the EU is 75 per cent of average GDP levels. While the Highlands and Islands do not strictly meet this criterion, factors such as peripherality and higher cost of living should be considered. The Rural Scotland Price Survey shows that Highlands and Islands price levels are 5–10 per cent above Scottish averages, with the islands being worst affected due to additional transport costs.

descendants of immigrant groups, mostly Irish, who came in the nineteenth and early twentieth century to take the jobs nobody else wanted. Their poverty was compounded by the large families which the Church encouraged. Once the Church accepted that the Labour Party was not hostile to religion, the social circumstances of Catholics pushed them overwhelmingly into voting Labour. At the same time their religious ties made them less susceptible either to Conservative appeals to support the (Protestant) British state or to nationalists harking back to the traditions of a largely Presbyterian Scotland. The concentration of Catholics in the West of Scotland makes the habit of Labour voting hard to break there and Labour is, as a result, the dominant party in Scotland.

Plate 6.2 Bill McArthur cartoon in the (Glasgow) *Herald* 25.7.97. Caption: 'Freedom Son? ... It's the right to vary income tax by 3p in the pound'. The biggest change in Scotland's links to the rest of Britain for nearly 300 years was heralded as the Government published plans for an Edinburgh Parliament that can raise taxes and make many of its own laws

However, Labour in its turn has had to safeguard itself against nationalist appeals by going part-way to meet them, with its proposals for devolution. We have noted at various points that Labour is as much a coalition of British peripheries against the centre as a class party. Nowhere is this aspect of Labour's character more marked than in Scotland, where it tries to state its claim to be the major exponent of Scottish interests against the Scottish Nationalists.

ON THE RECORD

ALEX SALMOND MP NATIONAL CONVENER, SCOTTISH NATIONAL PARTY: WHY I BELIEVE IN SCOTTISH INDEPENDENCE

'Scotland is one of the longest-established countries in Europe; her culture, law and institutions preserve her identity as a modern, outward-looking European nation. Yet Scotland has no effective democratic voice. Westminster appointed a Secretary of State for us without a democratic mandate and misrepresented us with its isolationist attitude to Europe.

ALEX SALMOND MP NATIONAL CONVENER, SCOTTISH NATIONAL PARTY: WHY I BELIEVE IN SCOTTISH INDEPENDENCE (continued)

The House of Commons doesn't have time or enough interest to meet the real political needs of Scotland. Last year the London Parliament spent only one hour discussing the Scottish National Health Service. This will change when we have our own parliament devoted to getting the best deal for Scotland and giving us a real say in the running of our country.

A Scottish Parliament can break free from the sleaze that has corrupted the House of Commons. A new parliament will attract fresh talent, a new generation that will sweep away the tired has-beens.

One of the first positive actions the parliament can take is to introduce fair voting at local government level. With fair voting, no one political party will have absolute control. All politicians will have to co-operate in the best interests of the whole country. This will also sweep away the scandals which have resulted from one party's domination of Scotland's councils, just as one-party domination has corrupted London politics.

While the Parliament that is proposed is not as powerful as I would like, Scotland's parliament would still be able to abolish Skye Bridge tolls, end the feudal system of land ownership, fight the creeping privatisation of the health service and the galloping privatisation of all our universities and colleges.

The independent parliament that I seek would put even more power in Scotland's hands. It would be able to remove Trident from the Clyde, demand Scotland's share of the oil revenues and speak up for Scotland in Europe.'

ON THE RECORD

SIR TEDDY TAYLOR MP: DEVOLUTION

'As regards devolution, I believe it could lead to the break-up of the United Kingdom because the proposed Scottish Parliament will have very limited powers and the funding available to it will only be of the level of finance they have at present less the substantial costs of the new assembly which is estimated at £5 per head. My fear is that the new assembly will simply become a complaints department about alleged inadequate financing and provision of power from London and this will lead to continuing disputes.

'The same problems could arise with devolution in Northern Ireland, without the additional problem of the policies of a devolved Parliament being interpreted as being biased in a particular direction.

SIR TEDDY TAYLOR MP: DEVOLUTION (continued)

'I do believe European integration to be a greater danger to democracy and international integrity than devolution of Scotland and Wales. The devolved parliamentary proposals can of course be changed by a future national Parliament if it is found to be utterly unacceptable. However as far as Europe is concerned all the power we hand over is wholly and permanently without the control of democracy.'

Sir Teddy Taylor was first elected in 1964 to a seat in Glasgow and was appointed as a Junior Minister in the Scottish Office and resigned this position because of opposition to the membership of the European Community. He voted against the Treaty of Rome and against all subsequent treaties. He lost his seat in 1979 and was re-elected for a seat in Southend where he is still the sitting MP.

NORTHERN IRELAND: RIVAL CLAIMS OF NATIONHOOD

Religious differences inside Scotland pale before those of Northern Ireland. This region had no history as a separate political entity before 1922. It was created at that time out of the six counties of Ireland which had a Protestant majority. These were set up with a separate parliament and government as part of the Government of Ireland Act (1922) which effectively recognised the remaining 26 counties as a separate state (see Briefing 6.7).

BRIEFINGS

6.7 NORTHERN IRELAND, ULSTER AND THE 'SIX COUNTIES'

The largest concentration of Protestants in Ireland was in the North-East around the industrial town of Belfast. They thinned out towards the North-West of the island, though there was a concentration in the town of Derry (or Londonderry). In the 'Troubles' of 1919–22 the Protestant paramilitary groups, supported by the British Army, gained the upper hand in this part of Ireland. When the British Government decided on partition between a Catholic-dominated Free State (the future Republic of Ireland) and the Unionist-Protestant North as the only stable solution to the Irish conflict, they carved out the largest area Protestants could dominate from the historic province of Ulster, following county boundaries. They left out the three western and southern counties of the historic Ulster because these had Catholic-Nationalist majorities. The remaining 'Six Counties' had no previous tradition as a political unit and Derry in particular was cut off from its natural hinterland. Because it comprised the bulk of the historic province of Ulster, the region was often referred to, loosely, by that name. However the official term was 'Northern Ireland' (even though the tip of Donegal, in the Republic, lies further north!). This is the entity that had full internal home rule from 1922–72, with its own parliament and government based at Stormont, near Belfast.

Map 6.4 Northern Ireland, showing local government districts shaded according to religious affiliation

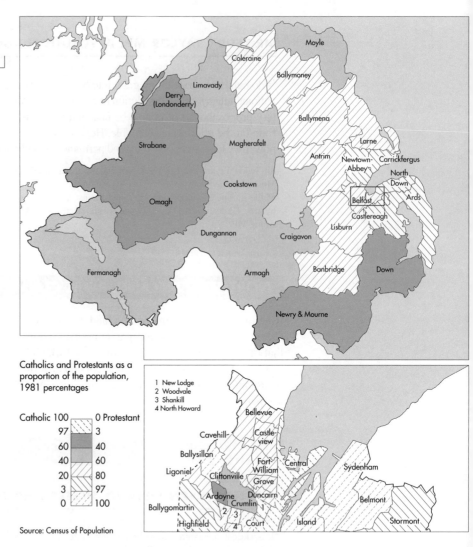

Catholics and Protestants as a proportion of the population, 1981 percentages

Catholic		Protestant
100		0
97		3
60		40
40		60
20		80
3		97
0		100

Source: Census of Population

The British Government believed that the new political entity of 'Northern Ireland' would not be viable without a respectable territory. Hence it included many areas where Protestants were in only a tenuous majority, or were actually a minority. Substantial numbers of Catholic nationalists were thus incorporated against their will in this 'Protestant state for a Protestant people' as Viscount Craigavon, its first prime minister, described it. Thus there is a major division inside Northern Ireland between the Protestant heartland of Down and Antrim – on the East – and Armagh and the counties of Fermanagh, Tyrone and Londonderry in the West. This division is not only a religious one, but a social and economic one too, as Table 6.7 shows.

Table 6.7 Regional disparities within Northern Ireland in the 1990s

	Belfast and District	**Rest of East**	**West and South**
Percentage unemployed (1993)	13.3	14.2	19.0
Infant mortality per 1000 live births (1995)	10.00	7.62	7.73
Relative Deprivation Index (various dates)	29.98	−18.4	12.8

Sources: *Quarterly Economic Report*, Department of Finance and Personnel, Northern Ireland Office, *Relative Deprivation Index,* Centre for Urban Policy Studies, University of Manchester, *Occasional Paper* 28.
Note: The best indication of regional disparity is the composite Index of Relative Deprivation compiled by Manchester University researchers. This combines absence of basic household amenities with unemployment and educational qualifications. A high positive figure shows severe deprivation. On this Belfast has far and away the worst conditions in the Province, followed by the heavily Catholic West and South. The Protestant heartland – the East (Antrim and Down) – is best off. On employment prospects the West and South are clearly worse off than the rest of the Province.

    The Western part of the Province is more rural and less developed than the East, which is centred around the industrial city of Belfast. Such East–West differences exist in the Republic of Ireland too. They have been exacerbated in Northern Ireland, however, by the tendency of the Protestant-dominated 'Stormont' Government (so called from the suburb of Belfast where it is located) to concentrate investment in Antrim and Down.

Plate 6.3 Stormont Castle, Northern Ireland. Seat of the Northern Irish Parliament 1922–72

Practically the whole of the politics of the Province can thus be traced back to the Protestant–Catholic religious division. This extends to voting too, as Table 6.8 illustrates. Nowhere else in the United Kingdom, not even in Scotland, does a person's religious affiliation so emphatically determine their vote. The parties themselves are founded on the basis of such divisions. Sinn Fein is the Irish nationalist party associated with the underground Irish Republican Army, while the Social Democratic and Labour Party (SDLP) is the representative of moderate Catholics. Northern Ireland Labour attempts to bridge the sectarian divide and attract both Protestant and Catholic votes from the working class. The various Unionist groupings represent Protestants of varying degrees of extremism. As their name suggests, they advocate 'no surrender' to Catholic nationalist demands and support continuing union with Britain.

This pervasiveness of religion in politics is not surprising. Northern Ireland was created on the basis of a politico-religious division in Ireland. Its continuing existence perpetuates it unless a way can be found to accommodate the demands of both sides within it. However, such a settlement would have implications for both the territorial integrity and sovereignty of the existing British state, as we shall see.

Outsiders, including the English, cannot understand why religion should be such an explosive force in the Province. In the rest of Britain it is regarded as an individual matter, having nothing to do with politics and certainly not party politics. To understand why religion goes to the root of personal and political identity in Northern Ireland one must go back into Irish history and relations with the rest of the British Isles.

In the course of the seventeenth century the Gaelic-speaking Catholic tribes of Ireland were colonised by Protestants from Great Britain, just as happened to the Algonquian-speaking, pagan tribes of North America. Settlements were planted, the natives converted, massacred or driven out in Ireland just as they were in New England or Virginia. The native Irish managed to survive better than the native Americans but only as an exploited peasantry with no political rights.

Table 6.8 Party votes in the Northern Irish regions, General Election 1997

	Belfast	**Rest of East**	**West and South**
Unionist Parties	50.8	71.4	40.4
Social Democratic and Labour (SDLP)	22.6	16.6	31.7
Sinn Fein	22.8	4.2	23.5
Other	3.8	7.8	4.4

Note: Extreme differences in political loyalties show up between the (heavily Protestant) East outside Belfast, where Unionists take almost three-quarters of the vote, and the (heavily Catholic) West and South where the two Nationalist parties, the SDLP and Sinn Fein, take over half. Belfast is evenly split, but this disguises the fact that its constituencies are divided along sectarian lines, three returning heavily Unionist majorities, and one (Belfast West) the Sinn Fein candidate Gerry Adams.

It was in north-eastern Ireland that colonisation succeeded best in driving the natives out because of the continual flow of poor Protestant settlers from Scotland. The growth of Catholic Irish nationalism in the nineteenth century was seen there as a threat to the very existence of the 'Protestant people'. It provoked a popular resistance to nationalism unparalleled in other parts of Ireland where Protestants were thin on the ground. Semi-underground movements, above all the Orange Order (see Briefing 6.8), were created to oppose it, with violence if necessary.

The local Unionist politicians joined the Conservative Party in Great Britain to scupper any concession to nationalism, such as home rule, up to the First World War. The settlement of 1922 was a defeat for the Northern Unionists, because their object was the preservation of British rule (and support for Protestants) everywhere in Ireland. Instead, they found themselves partitioned off in the North, while a Catholic nationalist republic was built up in the rest of the island.

However, the Protestants did have a secure majority in Northern Ireland. The region had been created expressly to ensure this: Protestants constituted 60 per cent of the population. The Unionist leaders organised their built-in majority to control the Northern Irish Parliament and Government for 50 years (1922–72). The British Parliament and Government were content to turn over the internal running of the province to them, incidentally making nonsense of the claim that

BRIEFINGS

6.8 THE ORANGE ORDER

In the eighteenth century Catholic resistance to the 'Protestant ascendancy' in Ireland often took the form of secret societies (Whiteboys, Defenders) which took reprisals against obnoxious landlords. These continued in the South during the nineteenth century (the Fenian Brotherhood). As Protestants began to feel threatened, they formed their own secret societies, most notably the Orange Order, which took its name from William of Orange (William III) who established the Protestant ascendancy with his victory at the Battle of the Boyne (1690).

Widespread at one time on the British mainland and among Army officers, the Orange Order came to have its main strength in Ireland, particularly the North. Modelling itself upon the Freemasons, with which it had many links, it has a strong local organisation of 'lodges', and an overall hierarchy of Grand Masters, lodgemasters, and so forth. What gave it a unique force was its ability to unite the Protestant governing elite with a strong grass-roots working-class organisation.

The Orange Order does not get directly involved in conflict itself. But it forms a valuable recruiting base and communications network for paramilitary groups. Its elaborate symbolism and annual marches to commemorate Protestant victories are a constant provocation to violence and confrontation with Catholics during the 'marching season' (most of the summer). There are also Orange lodges and marches in Central Scotland and Liverpool. However, their activities are very muted compared with the assertions of Protestant dominance in Northern Ireland.

such a delegation of powers subverts the constitutional sovereignty of the British Parliament. No constitutional difficulties arose during the existence of the 'Stormont' Parliament and Government.

Unionist policy was aimed primarily at ensuring the viability and stability of Northern Ireland as a territorial unit separate from the Republic of Ireland. They could count on British armed support, but they also built up their own paramilitary Protestant militia. This was sufficient to deter open opposition from the minority for most of the time.

No lasting settlement, however, could be built on armed force alone. Politically the Unionist Government had to balance three groups. These were the Protestant working class, anxious to protect their jobs and differentials against Catholic competition; the Protestant middle class with something of the same anxieties, but also a concern with modernisation and development, who would be alienated by too open a display of sectarianism; and the Catholic population who had to have some concessions if they were not to pose a constant threat of disorder.

A major Unionist achievement was to get the British Government to agree in 1936 to parity of social provision between Northern Ireland and the British mainland. Thus the postwar welfare state operated fully in Northern Ireland, providing the unemployed and sick with infinitely better payments and facilities than in the Republic of Ireland. This appealed to all segments of the population, and it was a powerful argument for Catholics to put up with political discrimination in return for better living conditions. The other major concession to Catholics – which conciliated the Church – was state support for Catholic schools, again carrying over the practice on the British mainland.

Both these measures enabled the Protestant middle classes to convince themselves that Northern Ireland was as tolerable a political solution to bigotry and violence as could be found in Irish conditions, and preferable to living under the domination of a repressive and reactionary Catholic Church in the Republic. Throughout its existence the Stormont Government pursued an active policy of modernisation of the traditional agricultural and industrial economy, thus creating more middle-class jobs in management and administration.

These activities also demonstrated to the Protestant working class that the Government was trying to conserve their jobs and improve their living conditions. Where Protestants faced the most severe job competition, in the depressed West of the Province, local councils and government agencies actively discriminated in their favour. The Orange Order, a semisecret society dedicated to maintaining Protestant supremacy, enrolled the working class as the rank and file while keeping control firmly in the Unionist leadership's hands. Anti-Catholic rhetoric and rituals contented the membership while keeping it out of real policy making.

Until 1965 Northern Ireland functioned in this way without major difficulties. Successive British governments, Conservative and Labour, saw no need to intervene in its internal affairs. The Unionist MPs affiliated to the Conservative Party (at that time called the 'Conservative and Unionist Party'). When the Conservative Government of 1951–55 depended on their votes for its majority the Labour Opposition did not object. Nobody saw any anomaly in Northern Ireland MPs voting on domestic English and Scottish legislation when MPs from these regions could not vote on Northern Irish affairs. (This problem is now raised with regard to the position of Welsh and Scottish MPs if Wales and Scotland get their own Parliament.)

The old system collapsed because of the rise of a new educated Catholic middle class which organised a nonviolent civil rights movement inside Northern Ireland to protest against discrimination and sectarianism (1967–69). Their peaceful protests provoked violent Protestant reactions, culminating in armed attacks on the Catholic areas of Belfast and Londonderry in 1969. A new factor was the television reporting of these conflicts, rendering it impossible for the old tactics of repression to be quietly employed.

The riots and publicity forced first a British military intervention to separate the two sides and finally the abolition of the devolved parliament and government, in an attempt to create a new power-sharing settlement. The disorder provided an opening for both extreme Irish nationalism and extreme Protestant loyalism. The first is represented by the Provisional Irish Republican Army (the 'Provos' or IRA), the second by the Ulster Volunteer Force (UVF) and Ulster Defence Force (UDF). Over the last 25 years both have carried out regular attacks on each other, on the British Army and on the Northern Irish police, as well as indiscriminately against anyone of 'the wrong sort'. The IRA has also carried out terrorist attacks on the British mainland, mainly with explosives and bombs.

Our 'Milestones' at the end of the chapter summarise events in Ireland from the creation of Northern Ireland in 1922. Since 1970 its history has been dominated by political violence on the one hand and attempts at political settlement on the other. The most important of these were the arrangements for inter-governmental negotiations with the Irish Republic in the mid-1980s, which recognised that the heirs of the Irish independence struggle had a legitimate interest in the territory.

The Major Government made a determined effort to resolve the situation by negotiations with all sides to the conflict in 1995–96, which produced a cessation of violence for over a year. Major's insistence on the IRA surrendering its weapons before they could join a constitutional conference proved a demand that the political leadership could not get their rank and file to accept. Renewed attempts at negotiation have taken place under the Blair Government, with varying but never complete success.

The problem for the British Government is that it faces not one but two sets of nationalists, Catholic and Protestant. These religious identities have little to do with the Churches but carry a heavily loaded history and a politically charged sense of cultural identity. Anything seen as a concession to one side provokes violence from the other. Thus a simple cession of Northern Ireland to the Republic would spark civil war in the North, uncomfortably close to British shores.

A straight evacuation of the province must be increasingly tempting for British governments. More likely is the restoration of home rule with power-sharing between the Protestant and Catholic communities, and Britain and the Irish Republic as joint guarantors of the settlement. The only other alternative is to stagger on with continuing violence and military counteraction as at present. This is a situation which has already lasted 25 years so it can by no means be ruled out. At some future point, however, a British government may decide that the cost of its presence is too much. In that case an imposed power-sharing arrangement is the one likely to alienate the fewest people.

CONSTITUTIONAL IMPLICATIONS OF REGIONAL AUTONOMY

It is important to recognise Northern Ireland as the continuing manifestation of the Irish territorial question which has affected British politics for a century and a half. The fact that the Irish Republic was once part of the United Kingdom accounts for such anomalies as the right of Irish citizens resident in Britain to vote in British elections, and the simultaneous recognition of residents of Northern Ireland as both British and as Irish citizens by the United Kingdom and Irish Republic respectively.

Now that both the British and Irish are also recognised as European citizens at another level, these anomalies seem less odd. Overlapping citizenship under different jurisdictions further undermines the old idea of the self-defined 'nation-state' as the sole focus of political loyalties within a given territory.

Challenged by the emergence of a federal European Union, the doctrine that exclusive sovereignty rests with parliament and the government it supports is likely to be further eroded by regional devolution. This will shape constitutional developments in several ways:

1. The most central questions affecting individual rights (social and political) are going to be decided at regional rather than British level in Northern Ireland, Scotland and possibly Wales.

2. Voting for regional assemblies is likely to be by some form of proportional representation rather than by the British system of first past the post within small, one-member constituencies. (We shall detail the nature and effects of electoral systems in Chapter 15.) Broadly, proportional-representation systems aim at making the parties' share of legislative seats proportional to their share of popular votes. First-past-the-post systems ignore this consideration in favour of creating a legislative majority for the party with most votes (even if it does not have a popular majority). It thus contributes to the 'elective dictatorship' of the largest party, which has characterised British politics since 1945. If regional assemblies adopt a system which generally gives no party a majority, and if power sharing is written into the constitution of Northern Ireland, this will put pressure on the Westminster Parliament to reform its procedures.

3. If it does not, confrontations are likely to follow in which a broad-based Scottish or Welsh consensus is opposed by a Westminster government without a British majority. Confrontations between regional assemblies and the Westminster Parliament are likely anyway if they are controlled by different parties.

4. The immediate constitutional dilemma is what voting rights Scots and Welsh MPs should have at Westminster, given that domestic affairs in their regions cannot be voted upon by English MPs. (This is sometimes termed the 'West Lothian' question after the MP for West Lothian, Tam Dalyell,

who first raised it in the 1970s.) The present overrepresentation of Scottish MPs in the House of Commons is going to be reduced. At present Scotland has 72 MPs, but this will be made proportional to population at 54.

5. This may well increase the pressure to have assemblies for English regions, which in most cases are comparable to Scotland and Wales in terms of area and population. Once regional assemblies and governments exist in any area there is likely to be increasing pressure to have them elsewhere. Their existence would contribute to making British government much more decentralised than it is at present.

A likely future scenario would thus see political rearrangements at both regional and European level taking over powers formerly concentrated in the Westminster Parliament. It is important to see these regional and European developments as interconnected. Both are linked to the diminishing credibility of the traditional state's capacity, in Britain as elsewhere, to make definitive decisions about all spheres of life. The more control of the economy and defence passes to the European level, the less credibly Westminster can claim that regional devolution threatens national survival.

Paradoxically, by having less to do the British parliamentary system might actually work better. It would have more time to scrutinise and discuss European legislation, and might be better able to hold the British government to account in this area (see Chapter 5). It could control and scrutinise the Civil Service in detail (Chapters 8–10). It might even exert more control, in a nonpartisan way, over the government itself. Problems both of 'government overload' and of the 'democratic deficit' might well be tackled therefore through a territorial rearrangement of the British state. This is an important aspect of the constitutional developments we go on to discuss in Chapter 7.

ESSAYS

1. Distinguish between the British Isles, Great Britain and the United Kingdom. To what extent is the United Kingdom a unitary state?

2. In what ways is the government of Scotland distinct from that of England? How much regional autonomy do the Scots enjoy?

3. Why do separate arrangements for representation in Westminster exist for the Scots, Welsh and the Northern Irish? How democratic are these arrangements?

4. What are the main political groupings in Northern Ireland? What accounts for the differences between them?

SUMMARY

This chapter has shown that:

- Britain, like most European states, was formed out of different territories with divergent histories and cultures.

- The structure of wealth and opportunity differs considerably across these regions.

- This has produced a political coalition of territorial peripheries against the centre. The peripheries tend to support the Labour Party.

- Where an additional cultural focus and identity exists, as in Wales, Scotland and Ireland, regional disparities have fuelled a separatist nationalist party.

- These peripheries are going to be given greater political autonomy by the New Labour government.

- In the long run, this may lead to autonomy for the English regions as well.

- By losing powers both to regions and the European Union, the British Parliament may actually become more effective in those functions it retains.

MILESTONES

MILESTONES IN IRISH HISTORY 1922–97

Northern Ireland
('Six Counties' 'Ulster')

Republic of Ireland
('Irish Free State' 'Eire')

1922 Government of Ireland Act effectively divides Ireland between Northern Ireland in the North East and the Irish Free State (Eire), covering the South and West

1922 Special Powers Act gives Northern Irish Government exceptional powers to maintain order

1923–27 Civil war followed by extensive disorder over whether to accept partition and dominion status within British Empire. Pro-Treaty side (later Fine Gael Party) wins

1926 Fianna Fail founded to contest Treaty by nonviolent means. This splits it off from Sinn Fein and IRA, which remain committed to violence

1929 Abolition of proportional representation in Northern Ireland parliamentary elections

1932 Unemployed in Belfast hold non-sectarian demonstrations and riot

1932 Fianna Fail wins general election and forms government

1933–38 'Economic war' with Britain

1935 Serious sectarian riots in Belfast renew old hostilities

1936 British government agrees to equality of social support between Northern Ireland and (mainland) Great Britain

1937 New constitution whittles away British Treaty rights and entrenches position of Catholic Church

1938 British return Treaty Ports (where it had had naval bases) to Irish Free State

1939–40 IRA bombing campaign in England

1939–45 Irish Free State stays neutral in Second World War

1940–43 German bombing of Belfast and (London) Derry

1940–45 Northern Ireland forms base for Allied Air forces protecting Atlantic convoys

1943–64 Sir Basil Brooke (Lord Brookeborough) prime minister, maintains system of strict Unionist monopoly of power based on inbuilt Protestant majority

1948–51, 1954–57 Fine Gael forms coalition governments with smaller parties

1949 Bitter Northern Irish election reaffirms Unionist domination

1948 Eire becomes Republic of Ireland and leaves Commonwealth

MILESTONES IN IRISH HISTORY 1922–97 (continued)

Northern Ireland ('Six Counties' 'Ulster')	Republic of Ireland ('Irish Free State' 'Eire')
1958–62 IRA border attacks mostly fail	**1959–72** Modernising Fianna Fail prime ministers, Lemass and Lynch
1963–69 O'Neill succeeds Brookeborough as Unionist Prime Minister. Rhetoric favours Catholics but does nothing practical on discrimination	
1967–69 As a result Civil Rights movement formed to press for reform. TV shows nonviolent protests broken up by Protestant militants and police	
1969 Special police and Protestant militants attack Catholic areas of Belfast and Derry. British troops intervene to protect them	
1970–72 IRA provokes Army into indiscriminate internment and massacres of nationalists ('Bloody Sunday' 1972)	
1972–74 British attempts to introduce power-sharing between Protestants and Catholics thwarted by Protestant general strike. Unionist party splits into small, more extreme groupings	
1972 Joins EU as part of UK	**1972** Joins EU along with UK
1974–98 Direct rule: province run by Northern Ireland Office as part of British Government	
1974–95 IRA, UDF, UVF mount terror campaign (extended by IRA to mainland Britain): killings and bombings, often indiscriminate	**1973–77** Coalition government of Fine Gael and Labour
1982 Elections to a new Northern Ireland Assembly. 'Rolling devolution': Assembly can take over whatever powers it agrees on, no agreement between Unionists and nationalists	**1977–81** Fianna Fail government
	1981–92 Various short-lived minority governments or coalitions alternate

1985 Margaret Thatcher and Fine Gael prime minister, Garrett Fitzgerald, sign Anglo-Irish Agreement providing for joint consultation of two governments on Northern Ireland. These continue and intensify up to present

1986 Referendum rejects divorce

1992–98 Stable coalitions of both major parties with Labour

MILESTONES IN IRISH HISTORY 1922–97 (continued)

Northern Ireland
('Six Counties' 'Ulster')

Republic of Ireland
('Irish Free State' 'Eire')

1994 Downing Street Declaration sets out plans for talks between British and Irish governments and all parties in Northern Ireland. In response IRA and Protestant UDF and UVF ceasefires declared

1995–96 Talks stalled and blocked by Unionists upon whom British Conservatives increasingly depend in British Parliament

1995 Referendum legalises divorce by narrow majority

1996 Renewed IRA bombings in mainland Britain. Violent Protestant marches

1997 New Labour Government in Britain announces accelerated talks

1997 New IRA ceasefire

1997 Talks stalled by Unionist opposition Abolition of internment

PROJECTS

1. Write a historical account of the incorporation of Wales, Scotland and Ireland into the United Kingdom. To what extent do the problems related to these territories today have their roots in history?

2. Distinguish between confederal, federal and unitary states. Can the relationship between Scotland and England be categorised in terms of one of these concepts? Answer with reference to three major areas of public policy.

3. Write a new constitution for the United Kingdom providing for the full representation of all the peoples of the UK.

FURTHER READING

The Irish background is reported in T. P. Coogan, *The Troubles: Ireland's Ordeal 1966–1995* (London: Hutchinson, 1995). The Northern Irish dilemma is analysed in J. McGarry and B. O'Leary, *Explaining Northern Ireland* (Oxford: Blackwell, 1995). A comprehensive analysis of Scottish politics is Alice Brown, David McCrone and Lindsay Paterson, *Politics and Society in Scotland* (Edinburgh: Edinburgh University Press, 1997). Welsh politics is analysed in Dylan Griffiths, *Thatcherism and Territorial Politics: A Welsh Case Study* (Aldershot: Avebury, 1996).

http://www.awl-he.com/politics/newbritpol

Internet resources – visit *The New British Politics* Webpage for links to a specially-chosen selection of Internet resources relevant to this Chapter.

http://www.awl-he.com/politics/newbritpol

PART II
Government

CHAPTER 7

A British constitution?

A constitution enshrines in law the rights and duties of citizens and the functions and powers of the state and its major branches, such as the Crown, Parliament, regional assemblies, courts, civil service and local government. The British 'constitution' is almost unique among the world's democracies for its premodern origins, gradual evolution and 'unwritten' status. Until recently most commentators celebrated the 'unwritten' constitution as a unique feature of the strong but flexible and responsive government which had served Britain well over the centuries. Its major features – parliamentary sovereignty, the rule of law, the unitary state and the convention of governmental restraint and responsiveness – were seen as evidence of British pragmatism and political genius. Under the Conservative Governments of the 1980s and 1990s these principles were eroded by government action and by Britain's membership of the European Union. Criticisms of the British 'constitution' have grown louder in the 1990s. There have been calls for reform, some of which are echoed in the Labour Government programme. Sceptics question whether Britain has ever really had a constitution at all, which explains the question mark in the chapter title.

This chapter covers:

- The 'unwritten' character of the British 'constitution'

- The sources of constitutional authority

- The myth and reality of constitutional conventions

- The principal doctrines of the 'British constitution': the unitary state, parliamentary sovereignty, constitutional monarchy and elective dictatorship, governmental self-restraint

- The impact of Europe

- The movement for constitutional reform

BRITAIN'S 'UNWRITTEN' CONSTITUTION: STATUS AND SOURCES

People talk of a country's constitution in two different ways. Sometimes they refer in broad and abstract terms to the general body of laws and rules that encompass the major institutions of the state, their functions and powers, and their relation to the rights and duties of the ordinary citizen. In this sense every country, including Britain, has a constitution.

At other times they refer in narrow and particular terms to a single document, typically written on vellum and solemnly ratified with a grand seal, which incorporates these laws and rules. Examples are the American Constitution of 1787, Germany's 'Basic Law' of 1949 and the constitutions which Britain itself handed down to its former colonies when they became independent. In this second sense, Britain, along with Israel among the world's democracies, is almost unique: there is no such document. One has to visit Lincoln Castle to look at the Magna Carta of 1215 for the last and only example of a written constitution in Britain.

'Unwritten' is a little misleading. Many of the laws and rules that describe and regulate Britain's political system are in fact written down. They appear in Acts of Parliament (statute law), treaties with foreign states, Orders in Council (that is, government directives made in the name of the Crown), judgements handed down through the ages by the courts (common law), European law, and the expert commentaries of independent scholars (Bagehot and Dicey in the nineteenth century, Jennings and Bogdanor in the twentieth). Table 7.1 defines these sources and gives examples.

However, these writings have never been assembled, codified and ratified into a single document which the ordinary citizen can easily obtain and understand. Moreover, there are gaps: important aspects of Britain's political arrangements are not written down at all but instead take the form of widely accepted but unspoken understandings: constitutional 'conventions'. Britain's constitution is more accurately described as partly written and wholly uncodified. It is the unplanned and unsystematic product of the slow evolution in Britain's system of government.

Constitutions are usually drawn up to inaugurate, regulate and symbolise a new state. Most present-day democracies were established in the twentieth century, the majority after the Second World War, and therefore have written constitutions.

The lack of a single constitutional document in Britain reflects the exceptional continuity of the British state. Its boundaries have changed – most recently in 1922 when all but the six northern counties of Ireland broke away – but it has been spared the dictatorships, civil wars, colonisation and foreign invasions which, after liberation, herald a fresh start, a new state and thus a constitution. There has been no historical moment since 1688, when the 'Glorious Revolution' against James II secured the Protestant succession for the throne, when a need or opportunity has arisen for an old constitution to be torn up and replaced with something new.

The 'constitution' of Britain differs from that of most other countries in another and more significant respect: it carries no special legal status. A written constitution necessarily requires a special court, such as the US Supreme Court, to determine whether legislation and executive action comply with it. In Britain, by contrast,

Key term

Statute law – the sum total of laws passed by Parliament.

Key term

Common law – law which is overtly made by judges and which has become part of custom and precedent.

the role of the courts is simply to apply laws passed by Parliament, not to pronounce upon their constitutionality (although the courts may judge the legality of action taken by government ministers, which goes a long way towards making constitutional judgements).

In most other countries constitutional law is 'entrenched': it can only be repealed or amended by special provisions that do not apply to ordinary legislation. For example, an amendment to the US Constitution requires the assent of two thirds of both houses of Congress and ratification by the legislatures of three quarters of the states. In Britain, Parliament can repeal or amend a constitutional law exactly as it would any other law. It has recently done this in the acts setting up the Welsh and Scottish assemblies. In some countries major constitutional changes must be approved by popular referendum, as the Treaty of Maastricht was in France, Ireland and (at a second attempt) in Denmark. In Britain it was just approved by Parliament. Referendums have occasionally been held to *approve* major constitutional changes, notably in 1979 and again in 1997 on the establishment of elected assemblies in Scotland and Wales. But there is no legal requirement or convention that they be held. It is the government, not the law, that decides, and Parliament which passes the crucial legislation.

The differences between Britain and most other democracies in regard to the authority and status of the Constitution is shown graphically in Figure 7.1. This emphasises the diffuse nature of the British constitution compared with most countries and also its susceptibility to changes made in Parliament.

Figure 7.1 Sources of constitutional authority in democratic political systems

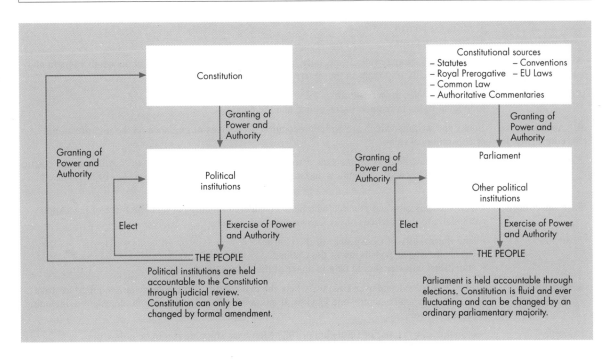

SOURCES OF CONSTITUTIONAL AUTHORITY

Table 7.1 lists the various sources of the British constitution and gives examples. Its plural and untidy origins may at first sight give the impression of a balance in which Parliament, the Crown and the courts (including the European Court) all provide checks against the executive. In reality, with the partial and minor exceptions of common law and European law, the sources of constitutional authority are controlled by the government of the day.

Because the constitution allows for a pronounced concentration of power in the government, and laws and rules making up the constitution do not require special procedures or machinery to be passed, the party in office can reshape the consti-

Table 7.1 Sources of the British 'constitution'

1. Statutes	Acts of Parliament, which override all other British constitutional sources and account for a growing proportion of the 'constitution'. Particularly important for elections, relations between the houses of parliament and local government.
Examples	• Representation of the People Acts, 1832-1969 (extended right to vote) • the Peerage Act, 1963 (created life peers) • European Communities Act 1972 (UK joined the European Community)
2. Royal prerogative	Functions performed by ministers acting on behalf of the monarch; their authority derives from the Crown, not Parliament. Executed by Orders in Council or through proclamations and writs under the Great Seal. A gradually diminishing sphere of the constitution, but still important for the conduct of foreign affairs and security matters.
Examples	The power to: • dissolve parliament • declare war and make treaties • dispense honours • appoint ministers
3. Common law	This means customary rules, especially 'precedents' established by judicial decisions in particular cases. Especially important in the sphere of civil liberties.
Examples	Freedoms of speech and assembly Individual rights in relation to the police and the courts
4. Authoritative commentaries	Books and writings which are widely recognised as sources of guidance on the interpretation of constitutional rules.
Example	T. Erskine May, *Treatise on the Law, Privileges, Proceedings, and Usage of Parliament*, the classic guide to parliamentary procedures and rights ('privileges'), used by the Speaker of the House of Commons.
5. Conventions	Established customs and practice which are considered binding but lack the force of law. Applies particularly to the practices of the Crown and the Cabinet.
Examples	• the impartiality of the Speaker of the House • the collective responsibility of the Cabinet • the prime minister should be a member of the Commons
6. European Union law	EU law has precedence over UK law, where the two conflict. British courts are required to strike down UK laws which contravene EU law. Important for social and economic legislation, including the rights of workers.
Example	Factortame case: House of Lords judge 1988 Merchant Shipping Act to be unlawful.

tution to its own advantage. The single most important influence on the constitution is statute law. So long as the government enjoys a secure majority in the Commons it can push through legislation that shapes the constitution, however controversial and partisan.

Most other countries devise procedures such as referendums or the requirement of large majorities to ensure that constitutional change commands widespread support in the country. Controversial or blatantly partisan constitutional legislation has been rare in Britain since 1918, although the measures taken on party finance by recent Conservative governments are an exception. A 1984 Act required trade unions to organise ballots of their members on their right to hold political funds, which go mainly to the Labour Party. No legislation was introduced (until Blair's Labour Government was elected) requiring companies or wealthy individuals to be more accountable for their political donations, which go mainly to the Conservative Party. The Government's willingness to change the ancient Bill of Rights (1689) at short notice in order to help one of its MPs sue the *Guardian*, shows how easily – and at times recklessly – statute law can be used to change the constitution (see Briefing 7.1).

Key term

Bill of Rights – a formal statement of the rights and privileges that may be actually or theoretically claimed by citizens. Unlike a modern Bill of Rights, however, the one passed by Parliament in 1689 was more concerned to restrict the royal prerogative and assert the powers of parliament.

BRIEFINGS

7.1 THE HAMILTON AFFAIR AND THE AMENDMENT OF THE BILL OF RIGHTS OF 1689

In 1994 the *Guardian* newspaper published allegations that the MP and trade minister, Neil Hamilton, had accepted payments from a millionaire businessman and owner of Harrods, Mohamed al Fayed, without recording the payment in the register of interests, as required by parliamentary rules. Hamilton initiated libel proceedings against the *Guardian*, which successfully applied to the court to have the action struck out on the ground that in order to defend it properly they would need to rely on evidence of Hamilton's conduct in the House of Commons, which was precluded by the terms of Article Nine of the Bill of Rights of 1689 as well as the rules of parliamentary privilege. Many Conservative MPs and peers considered this unfair because it prevented Hamilton from clearing his name of a serious charge through the courts. The government hurriedly inserted a new clause in the Defamation Bill which was then passing through Parliament, which permitted an MP to waive Article Nine of the Bill of Rights in order to bring a libel action. In the event Hamilton abandoned his libel action, was defeated in the May 1997 election and soon after was found by the Parliamentary Commissioner for Standards to have acted improperly.

This is a recent example of how government can exploit its majority in the House of Commons, and the absence of any special status for constitutional law to overturn at short notice and without careful consultation a long-established provision of the constitution. This case may be regarded either as an illustration of the flexibility of the constitution or as an illustration of the government's ability to alter the constitution for short-term partisan advantage.

For more detail see: Dawn Oliver, 'Regulating the Conduct of MPs: The British Experience of Combating Corruption', *Political Studies* 45 (1997), pp. 539–58.

Other sources of constitutional authority are effectively controlled by the government. The royal prerogative is exercised by ministers who derive their authority, not from a sometimes watchful parliament, but from a wholly compliant Crown. Common law and judicial decisions sometimes prove a temporary embarrassment for the government but can be overturned by an act of parliament. And constitutional conventions only bind the executive to the extent that they are recognised as such. The 'constitution' is little different from 'what the government decides to do'.

CONSTITUTIONAL CONVENTIONS: MYTH AND REALITY

British constitutional practice depends in large part on 'conventions', unwritten understandings based on established custom and practice, which are held to be binding on the politicians and officials to whom they apply, but lack the force of law. Defenders of the current constitution emphasise the flexibility that conventions provide. They fill the gaps left by the written parts of the constitution and enable it to adapt to changing circumstances. They are 'the oil in the machinery of the constitution'.[1] Sceptics point out that it is the Government that wields the oil can, lubricating the executive machinery while leaving those parts on which the opposition relies to rust. (See Briefing 7.2 for other comments on the constitution.)

Conventions are the grey area of the constitution. No rules exist to determine what is and is not a convention. When does a customary practice cease to be a convention? When does a new practice become one?

Some are so firmly fixed that it seems unimaginable that they would change. The Crown assents to bills passed by both houses of parliament. The monarch calls upon the leader of the largest party in the Commons to form a government. The prime minister always sits in the Commons. The Speaker is impartial. The Government must resign if it loses a parliamentary vote of confidence. Parliament must meet every year.

None of these fundamental features of the political system is actually part of the law or enforceable by the courts or the presiding officers of Parliament. They endure because to breach the convention would be self-destructive: an obstructive monarch would undermine the Crown's position, a peer as prime minister would lack a parliamentary power base, and so forth.

Many so-called conventions, however, turn out to be more fluid. Change is sometimes a response to changing political realities. For example, the nineteenth century convention that the cabinet as a whole advises the monarch when to dissolve Parliament has yielded to the convention that it is the prime minister alone who so advises, a recognition of the power that present-day prime ministers have over the cabinet. More often, however, the flexibility of a convention reflects the fact that the sanctions for a breach are political, not legal.

---

[1] Philip Norton, *The Constitution in Flux* (London: Martin Robertson, 1982), p. 7

BRIEFINGS

7.2 THE BRITISH CONSTITUTION: COMPLACENCY AND CONCERN

Everybody talks of the constitution, but all sides forget that the constitution is extremely well, and would do very well, if they would let it alone.
(Horace Walpole, letter to Sir Horace Mann, 1770)

Well, it [the political system] works, doesn't it? So I think that's the answer, even if its on the back of an envelope and doesn't have a written constitution with every comma and every semicolon in place. Because sometimes they can make for difficulties common sense can overcome.
James Callaghan, Prime Minister 1976–79, in an interview with
Peter Hennessey

Alone in Europe, the history of the United Kingdom has been one of stability and security. We owe much of that to the strength and stability of our constitution – the institutions, laws and traditions that bind us together as a nation.
Our constitution has been stable but not static. It has been woven over the centuries – the product of hundreds of years of knowledge, experience and history.
Radical changes that alter the whole character of our constitutional balance could unravel what generations of our predecessors have created.
Conservative Party Manifesto, 1997

Time and the development of our society have rendered the checks and balances, such as they are, of the constitution of no avail ... to restrain an oppressively minded executive if it should win control of a majority of the House of Commons. The path to an 'elected dictatorship' is open and must be blocked now before the bad boys realise their opportunity and organise a take-over of the British constitution.
Lord Scarman, 'The Shape of Things to Come', 1989

Governments will bend the accepted rules for short-term advantage if they think they can get away with it. The combination of party discipline, a majority in the Commons and the legal supremacy of Parliament means that they usually can. In 1977 the Labour Prime Minister, James Callaghan, decided to allow a free vote on the rules for regulating European elections. Challenged in Parliament to say whether this breached the convention of collective cabinet responsibility, he nonchalantly replied: 'The convention still applies except in cases I announce that it does not'.

The convention that a government resigns if it loses a vote of confidence is a case in point. The principle is firm but the definition of a 'vote of confidence' is not. In the nineteenth and much of the twentieth century, any financial or legislative measure that was central to a government's programme was regarded as a matter of confidence. This understanding was simply ignored by the 1974–79 Labour Government which was elected on a tiny majority of three and became a minority government in March 1977. It was defeated on a number of major measures but insisted that only a defeat on a censure motion required it to resign, as it did in March 1979.

The 1992–97 Conservative Government, beset by a dwindling majority and backbench rebels, took the same line when it was defeated on the imposition of a second increase in VAT on fuel in the November 1994 budget. On other occasions the Government deliberately described an issue as one of confidence in order to pressure reluctant backbenchers into supporting it and in order to impose discipline on all 120 or so MPs 'on the government payroll' (even as unpaid parliamentary private secretaries). In the same month that John Major denied that VAT on fuel was a confidence issue, he insisted that increased contributions to the EU budget were a matter of confidence, and secured a majority. When is an issue an issue of confidence? When the prime minister says it is.

'Ministerial responsibility' offers a telling example of how changing political circumstances and the self-interest of government have together eroded a once firm constitutional convention. The gist of the convention is that ministers are responsible for what they and their officials do (or omit to do). They are therefore answerable to Parliament for the conduct of their department and are held accountable – that is, expected to resign – if major personal lapses or departmental errors occur.

Lord Carrington and two junior ministers resigned after the Argentine invasion of the Falklands in April 1982, taking responsibility for what turned out to be a major error of foreign policy. In 1986 the Minister for Trade and Industry, Leon Brittan, accepted responsibility for a leaked letter designed to damage Michael Heseltine during the Westland affair, and also left the government. However, in the 1980s and 1990s many other ministers presided over equally serious policy failures and refused to resign. They include:

- James Prior, the Northern Ireland minister, over the breakout of prisoners at the Maze prison in Belfast in 1986;

- Various ministers associated with the introduction of the poll tax, which was abandoned by the government in 1991 because of its electoral unpopularity, widespread avoidance of payments and inefficiency;

- Norman Lamont, the Chancellor of the Exchequer, over Britain's forced exit from the Exchange Rate Mechanism (ERM) in 1992;

- Michael Howard, the Home Secretary, in 1995, over the escape of three prisoners from Parkhurst high security prison, following the escape of five IRA prisoners from Whitemoor prison in 1994;

- William Waldegrave, who held various cabinet posts, and Sir Nicholas Lyall, the Solicitor General, in 1996, following the Scott Report's finding that the former misled the House of Commons over the Government's policy on arms to Iraq and that the latter wrongly instructed ministers to sign certificates of immunity for the Matrix-Churchill trial (which would have withheld evidence showing that the arms exporters being prosecuted were simply following undeclared Government policies);

• Douglas Hogg, the Agriculture minister, over the concealment of 'mad cow' disease and the European Union's banning of British beef exports in 1996, to the enormous cost of British cattle farmers.

The weakening of the convention can be defended on the grounds that it is no longer realistic or reasonable to hold ministers personally responsible for the actions of the thousands of civil servants in their ministry. The huge growth in the size and workload of modern departments, the rapid turnover of ministers, and the delegation of much of the administration to executive agencies at arms-length from the department can be cited as reasons for allowing the convention to fall into disuse.

These arguments might exonerate Prior and Howard, who could not be personally blamed for prison breakouts, but they hardly excuse Lamont, Waldegrave and Lyall who had direct personal responsibility for their errors. They clung on to office to avoid damaging not only their own careers but, more important, their government's reputation. The convention, in reality, is that ministers only resign if they want to or if the prime minister wants them to.

Key term

Unitary state – a state in which there is a single sovereign body, the central government. Unlike a federal state, the central government of a unitary state does not share power with smaller territorial areas within the state (states, regions, or provinces) although it may devolve some powers to them.

THE PRINCIPAL DOCTRINES OF THE BRITISH 'CONSTITUTION'

The British constitution is a puzzle. This is because where it is written it is uncodified and scattered across numerous texts, and where it is not written it must be assumed from the behaviour of politicians and officials. It is therefore a matter of interpretation, although it must be added that the meaning of a formal, written constitution is also open to endless legal disputation, as the United States testifies. Nonetheless, despite its untidiness, there is some order and structure in the British constitution: principal doctrines which, while never planned, have evolved over time and operated until the 1980s. These are: the unitary state, parliamentary sovereignty, constitutional monarchy and elective dictatorship, and governmental self-restraint. In the 1980s, however, these doctrines weakened, and a movement for constitutional reform developed as a result.

The unitary state

The British state is unitary rather than federal or confederal. In this it resembles France and differs from the United States, Canada and Australia. There is only one sovereign body, the central government in London, which derives its authority solely from the Parliament at Westminster.

Local government exists at district, metropolitan and country level, with limited tax-raising and legislative powers, but only with the assent of the Westminster Parliament. It was this that Tony Blair probably meant when in the 1997 election campaign he likened a Scottish parliament to a parish council: it cannot challenge the supremacy of the Westminster Parliament. The central government can create and abolish regional parliaments and councils at will: the Heath government suspended the 50-year old Stormont Parliament in Northern Ireland in 1972, replacing it eventually with direct rule from London; and the Thatcher government abolished the Labour-dominated Greater London Council in 1986, replacing it with cross-borough 'residuary authorities'. (The Channel Isles and Isle of Man have their own parliaments and are self-governing in domestic affairs but are ultimately subject to Westminster's authority.) Similarly, central government can create and abolish county and regional boundaries (and their names), as the appearance and disappearance of the ill-fated Avon, Cleveland and Humberside demonstrate. Imagine the federal government in Washington trying to abolish Texas!

As Chapter 6 explained, Wales, Scotland and Northern Ireland have a considerable degree of *administrative* devolution, with government offices in Cardiff, Edinburgh and Belfast. All three countries are entitled to elect more Westminster MPs per population than England, and there are special committee procedures to deal with legislation on the three countries. None of this, however, undermines the legislative supremacy of Westminster Parliament and the central government. Nor does the creation of a Scottish Parliament in Edinburgh and Welsh Assembly in Cardiff, for it is legally open to a future Westminster Parliament to abolish or modify them, however politically difficult that might prove.

Parliamentary sovereignty

A.V. Dicey, the foremost authority on the British constitution in the late nineteenth century, described parliamentary sovereignty as 'the one fundamental law of the British constitution' and 'the ultimate political fact upon which the whole system of legislation hangs'.[2]

Sovereignty is the power to make law, and 'parliamentary sovereignty' means that no body other than Parliament (strictly speaking 'the Queen, Lords and Commons assembled') can make law. An act of parliament is not subject to or constrained by a higher law, such as a written constitution, or another body such as a regional parliament or international assembly.

Nor are there any types of law, within the territorial jurisdiction of the British Parliament and courts, that Parliament cannot make: it would be within its *legal* rights to abolish elections. The courts cannot declare an act of parliament

---

[2] A. V. Dicey, *Introduction to the Study of the Law of the Constitution* (London: Macmillan, 1952), p. 29

unconstitutional or otherwise invalid; their job is to interpret and apply the law as passed by Parliament. Because Parliament can make or unmake any law, it cannot be bound by its predecessors nor bind its successors: thus *each* Parliament is sovereign.

The doctrine is a useful reminder of the concentration of legal power in Parliament, but can easily be misinterpreted. It does not mean that Parliament has supreme power. Legal power is not the same as practical power or political power. Legislation cannot control the value of sterling, the level of unemployment or the rate of inflation (not even in a totalitarian command economy) nor illness and death rates. Parliament has the legal right to prohibit football, dancing, television and alcohol but not the political capacity to pass or enforce the law. In theory Parliament could repeal the Act giving India independence but it could hardly implement it (in this sense, one parliament *does* bind its successor). Overseas governments, the City, the foreign exchanges, backbench pressures, organised interests, political activists and public opinion make for powerful *political* checks on what Parliament can do. But these are not formal or constitutional checks.

Even as a strictly legal doctrine, however, parliamentary sovereignty has been severely undermined by Britain's membership of the European Community, and the supremacy in certain areas of the law of the European Court of Justice (ECJ) (see Briefing 7.3). We consider this fundamental change in the British constitution below.

BRIEFINGS

7.3 EUROPEAN LAW AND PARLIAMENTARY SOVEREIGNTY

The sovereignty of Parliament is the dominant characteristic of our political institutions ... the principle of Parliamentary sovereignty means neither more or less than this, namely, that Parliament thus defined has, under the English Constitution, the right to make or unmake any law whatever; and further, that no person or body is recognised by the law of England as having the right to override or set aside the legislation of Parliament.

(A.V. Dicey, *Introduction to the Study of the Law of the Constitution* (London: Macmillan, 1952), p. 29

On the basis of the powers thus conferred on them, the Community institutions can enact legal instruments as a Community legislature legally independent of the Member States. Some of these instruments take effect directly as a Community law in the Member States, and thus do not require any transformation into national law in order to be binding, not only on Member States and their organs, but also on the citizen.

European Commission, *ABC of Community Law* (Luxembourg: European Documentation Series, 1991)

Constitutional monarchy and elective dictatorship

In legal theory, Parliament consists of (and thus sovereignty rests with) the Crown, the Houses of Lords and the House of Commons 'assembled'. In reality sovereignty rests with the majority party in the Commons: Britain has party government.

Britain has a hereditary but 'constitutional' monarchy. Media exposure of embarrassing incidents in the private lives of the Royal Family has weakened public respect and affection, although support for the *institution* of the Crown remains widespread. The Crown plays a largely ceremonial role as head of state and symbol of the national community, having gradually ceded its political powers in the eighteenth and nineteenth century (and thus survived).

For the past century the monarch's rights have been 'to be informed, to encourage and to warn' in the famous words of Walter Bagehot, the nineteenth century economist and expert on the constitution. The Crown retains the right to dissolve Parliament, on the prime minister's advice, and to choose the prime minister. These functions are normally uncontroversial but situations could arise in which it would be difficult for the monarch to maintain the appearance of nonpartisanship.

For example, the Crown would face a dilemma if the prime minister advised the dissolution of Parliament before the end of the five-year term but the Crown believed that an alternative leader could command the confidence of Parliament and form a government. It would also be drawn into controversy when choosing a prime minister if no party had a majority in the Commons and no group of parties could agree on who should be prime minister. Such delicate situations are more likely to arise if proportional representation is introduced for elections to the Westminster Parliament.

The 1911 Parliament Act prohibited the House of Lords from blocking a financial measure and limited its delaying powers on a nonfinancial bill. Moreover, the Lords follows a convention (the 'Salisbury Convention') that it will not block measures that were included in the government's election manifesto. Occasionally, Commons bills are defeated in the Lords (for example, the War Crimes Bill) but usually in these cases the Commons approves the Bill again, possibly after minor amendments, and the Lords are then required to accept it.

Power therefore resides in the House of Commons, or, more accurately, the majority party in the Commons. Britain's first-past-the-post electoral system normally provides the winning party with an overall majority in the Commons. So long as the government can impose party discipline (i.e. ensure that MPs on its side vote for the party line), the party leadership, and in particular the prime minister, will get Parliament to approve its measures and initiatives. Party discipline (discussed in Chapter 18) and the electoral system (discussed in Chapter 15) form the basis of Britain's 'elective dictatorship'.

Governmental restraint

'The British Constitution presumes more boldly than any other the good sense and the good faith of those who work it', said W. E. Gladstone, the nineteenth

Plate 7.1 The Queen at the State opening of Parliament. The Crown plays a largely ceremonial role as head of State and symbol of the national community, having gradually ceded its powers in the 18th and 19th centuries. The Crown retains the right to dissolve Parliament, on the prime minister's advice, and to choose the prime minister

century statesman. Because unwritten conventions are so important, because so much power is concentrated in the hands of the Westminster Government – effectively the Cabinet and prime minister – the constitution implicitly assumes that those in high office will exercise their power with self-restraint and reasonableness.

A mixture of self-interest and ingrained values normally inhibits governments from abusing their power. Most ministers want to avoid media criticism, an embarrassing rebuke in the courts and a critical report by the Ombudsman or a select committee. Moreover, they know that after the coming election they and the main opposition party may swap places. These calculations are supplemented

Plate 7.2 Steve Bell cartoon in the *Guardian*, 8 October 1996. Sir Geoffrey Johnson Smith, the Chairman of the Select Committee on Privileges, fiercely denies being influenced by the whip, David Willetts, over the Ian Greer cash-for-questions affair. This was another example of so-called Tory sleaze in the run-up to the 1997 General Election which was seized upon by advocates of constitutional reform

Plate 7.2 Steve Bell cartoon in the *Guardian*, 8 October 1996. Sir Geoffrey Johnson Smith, the Chairman of the Select Committee on Privileges, fiercely denies being influenced by the whip, David Willetts, over the Ian Greer cash-for-questions affair. This was another example of so-called Tory sleaze in the run-up to the 1997 General Election which was seized upon by advocates of constitutional reform

by a sense of proper conduct which develops from social and working contacts with the opposition parties and the procedures of the Houses of Parliament.

However, many commentators observed an erosion of governmental self-restraint during the Thatcher and Major years. The replacement of an old guard of 'gentlemen' by a new generation of professional 'players' among Conservative MPs, who had an ideological mission to break with what they regarded as the old, too cosy, consensus politics, made them more cavalier about observing constitutional conventions. The outbreak of financial 'sleaze' associated with Conservatives in the 1992–97 Parliament, and the Government's (and MPs') reluctance to tackle it, is one example. Another is the increased readiness of the 1992–97 government, especially the Home Office, to engage in brinkmanship with the law and to criticise the judiciary publicly if the courts declared their action unlawful, as increasingly they did.

THE IMPACT OF EUROPE

Britain's membership of the European Union since 1973 has had profound consequences for the British constitution. Some of these consequences arose from the political repercussions of membership and in that sense were avoidable; others are a necessary concomitant of membership.

The debates in the 1970s over whether to join the Union, and their revival in the 1990s over extending integration, deeply divided successive governments and both major parties. Britain's role in Europe is one of the few political issues over which MPs and ministers have shown themselves ready to put personal conviction before party loyalty: for many it is an emotive matter. To avoid party splits over Europe, governments have resorted to constitutional innovation.

In June 1975 the Labour Prime Minister, Harold Wilson, held the first national referendum in Britain's history on the question of whether to accept new terms of membership (which barely differed from the old ones). For the duration of the campaign he suspended the convention of collective ministerial responsibility, allowing cabinet ministers to take different sides in public and join forces with leading politicians from other parties. Handing the final decision over Britain's membership to the electorate was effectively a breach of parliamentary sovereignty and of the formal role of MPs as independent representatives. But it was the only way of keeping the Labour Party united.

In 1977 the Labour Government allowed its MPs a 'free vote' on the question of the system to be adopted for direct elections to the European Parliament, effectively suspending the principle of collective responsibility. Once again the reason was short-term political necessity, not principle: the Labour Government had lost its parliamentary majority and depended on the support of the Liberals, who were strongly in favour of a proportional system. In the 1992–97 Conservative Government, collective cabinet responsibility on the Maastricht Treaty and the related issue of European Monetary Union crumbled: ministers on both sides waged a fierce and semipublic battle through the media.

Even more significant constitutional changes have arisen from the terms of membership themselves. The most profound is the clear breach of the doctrine of parliamentary sovereignty. Signing a foreign treaty or joining an international organisation does not necessarily contravene parliamentary sovereignty. Long before it joined the European Community, Britain was a member of the United Nations, NATO and GATT (the General Agreement on Tariffs and Trade). But although membership imposed obligations on the British Government it did not affect the right of Parliament to make or unmake any law.

Joining Europe was altogether different. The 1972 European Community Act incorporated the Treaty of Rome, secondary legislation and the jurisprudence of the European Court of Justice into British law. Section 2(1) provides for the direct implementation of the Treaty and of European Community legislation in Britain. Section 2(2) stipulated that other EC legislation was to be implemented by subordinate domestic legislation; and, most significantly, Section 2(4) provides for the supremacy of EC law over domestic law.

Membership of the European Community therefore undermined parliamentary sovereignty in four ways. First, it imposed a higher constitutional authority than Parliament – the European Court of Justice (ECJ) – in at least some spheres of law.

Second, the ECJ could – and did – declare some parliamentary statutes (more usually, some of their provisions) as contrary to European law *and therefore illegal*.

Third, Parliament's sphere of legislation is restricted to those areas that fall outside European law. The European Commission, the Council of Ministers and, to a lesser extent, the European Parliament – bodies in which Britain only has a limited vote – make European law. The Westminster Parliament's ability to shape European legislation is minimal, limited to examination by select committees in the Commons and Lords.

Fourth, by passing the European Communities Act and agreeing to the Treaty of Maastricht, Parliament for all practical purposes bound its successors and is bound by its predecessors into accepting all these provisions.

Many constitutional commentators argue that parliamentary sovereignty nonetheless remains intact because it is always open to Parliament to repeal the 1972 Act, and always open to the Crown (on government advice) to annul the 1993 Treaty of Maastricht. Technically and legally this is so. But while the UK belongs to the European Union and has no prospect of quitting it, the courts are obliged to given precedence to European law (formulated and passed by bodies on which the UK has not got a veto). When Parliament passed the 1972 European Communities Act it in effect used its sovereignty to restrict its future sovereignty and the sovereignty of successor parliaments.

The most striking example of a British court judging the constitutionality of parliamentary action is the Factortame case. The case involved a claim by the owners of a Spanish fishing boat that the Merchant Shipping Act 1988 was contrary to EU law and should not be applied. The House of Lords unanimously held (subject to a European Court of Justice ruling in support of the EC rights claimed by the fishermen) that Union law should prevail over the 1988 Act. There are many similar, although less fundamental, cases of the European Court of Justice overturning UK law or the decisions of UK courts, as Briefing 7.4 shows.

BRIEFINGS

7.4 PARLIAMENTARY SOVEREIGNTY? SIX EXAMPLES OF HOW THE EUROPEAN COURT CAN OVERTURN BRITISH LAWS AND BRITISH COURTS

Case C-292/89 R v Immigration Appeal Tribunal ex p. Antonisson *[1991] ECR 1-745*

Mr Antonisson, a Belgian national living in the UK and seeking work, was convicted of a drug offence, and deportation proceedings commenced. The UK Court held that article 48(3) did not include a right to free movement in search of a job. However, the ECJ held that article 48(3) does include the right of freedom of movement to seek work.

Case 30/77 R v Bouchereau *[1977] ECR 1999*

Bouchereau was a French national working in the UK who had two drug convictions. The UK Court recommended deportation. The ECJ held that prior criminal conviction could not justify deportation (Directive 64/221 article 3(2)) unless this was evidence of personal conduct that constituted a present threat to public policy.

Case 170-78 Commission v UK *[1983] ECR 2265*

The UK's excise duty was five times higher on wine than on beer. The EJ held that 'the tax policies of a member state must not ... crystallise given consumer habits so as to consolidate an advantage acquired by national industries concerned to respond to them'. It declared the excise duty to be in breach of Article 95 of the EC Treaty.

7.4 PARLIAMENTARY SOVEREIGNTY? SIX EXAMPLES OF HOW THE EUROPEAN COURT CAN OVERTURN BRITISH LAWS AND BRITISH COURTS (continued)

Case 124/81 Commission v UK *[1983] ECR 203*

UK regulations required UHT (Ultra Heat Treated) milk to be imported only with a licence and marketed by licensed dealers who had packed it at a local dairy. This made imports wholly uneconomic.

The ECJ rejected the public health arguments (Article 36 of the EC Treaty) which were cited to justify a breach of intracommunity free trading rules (Article 30). It argued that:

- all Member States have similar hygiene rules,
- all Member States use similar machines,
- the nature of the UHT milk obviates the need for control of the production cycle if there are sufficient controls at the time of the heat treatment.

The UK was found to be in violation of Article 30.

Case 207/83 Commission v UK *[1985] ECR 1201*

UK law required that all goods were marked with their country of origin. The UK argued that such a measure was nondiscriminatory and benefited the consumer.

The ECJ held that the measure allowed consumers to distinguish, exercise prejudice and discriminate. 'The Treaty seeks to unite national markets in a single market having the characteristics of a domestic market'. Marking the country of origin would slow down the economic interpenetration by handicapping the sale of goods produced as a result of a division of labour between Member States.

Case 121/85 Conegate v Commissioners of Customs and Excise *[1986] ECR 1007*

Inflatable sex dolls were imported into the UK and seized by Customs and Excise. The importers claimed that seizure was contrary to Article 30 of the EC Treaty, which prohibits obstructions to free trade between Member States.

The ECJ held that the fact that the goods cause offence was not enough to justify a ban on their import. Imports could not be banned when there was no corresponding prohibition on their internal domestic distribution.

THE MOVEMENT FOR CONSTITUTIONAL REFORM

In the Victorian and Edwardian eras (1837–1914) issues of constitutional reform dominated the political agenda, pitched the parties into battle and inflamed the passions of politicians and people alike. The Chartist movement (a popular movement of the 1830s and 1840s that pressed for universal suffrage, a secret ballot, the abolition of the property qualification, equal constituencies, payment of MPs and annual elections), the Home Rule movement in Ireland and the Suffragette movement for votes for women all led to mass demonstrations, riots, and loss of life. After 1918 constitutional issues played a much lesser role in British politics. Combined Labour–Liberal attempts to introduce electoral reform in 1918, and again in 1929, were blocked by the House of Lords and killed by the landslide election victory of the National (effectively Conservative) government in 1931. After 1945 the Labour Party ceased to favour electoral reform, as it benefited from the existing system. In the 1960s, disgruntled backbench MPs occasionally complained about the growing dominance of the executive over Parliament; sometimes they secured minor reforms of procedure and structure, such as the establishment of a system of select committees in 1979 (see Chapter 18). Sporadic electoral successes for the Welsh and Scottish nationalist parties in the 1960s and 1970s led to calls for independence or at least greater autonomy for these two countries. Following the success of the Scottish Nationalists in the October 1974 election, when they won 30 per cent of the Scottish vote and 11 seats, the Labour Government attempted to devolve power to elected parliaments in Wales and Scotland. However, the proposals failed to obtain the required level of support (40 per cent of the electorate) in the referendums held in March 1979, and the issue subsided under the newly elected Conservative Government of 1979, which was strongly opposed to any form of devolution.

Since the mid-1980s, constitutional reform has returned to the political agenda. It remains an issue of almost no interest or meaning to most voters in England and of only limited importance in Wales and Scotland where the 'bread and butter' issues of jobs, taxes, pensions and housing take priority. The contrast with American citizens, for whom the US Constitution has considerable emotional and political significance, is often noted. However, among the 'political classes' of the centre and left (MPs, party activists, opinion leaders in the media and universities etc.) there has been a significant resurgence of interest in constitutional reform, focused particularly on the programme of the Charter 88 movement. The core of the programme consists of:

- Scottish and Welsh parliaments with powers to tax, directly elected by some form of proportional representation;

- devolution of power to the English regions, although not necessarily in the Welsh/Scottish form;

- proportional representation for parliamentary (Westminster), local and European elections;

- the reform of the House of Lords, a (mainly) directly elected second chamber and the abolition of hereditary members;

- a Freedom of Information Act to reduce secrecy in government;

- a Bill of Rights, achieved by the incorporation of the European Convention on Human Rights into British law;

- a written constitution and the establishment of a 'constitutionalist' culture.

Not every constitutional reformer favours all these proposals and some favour others, such as directly elected local mayors, greater use of referendums to determine controversial political issues, fixed dates for elections, and the abolition of the monarchy. But among Liberal Democrats, Welsh and Scottish Nationalists and a growing proportion of Labour supporters – especially the new generation of MPs and members – there is a consensus of support for the 'core programme'. Much of this programme, rather watered down, was incorporated in New Labour's 1997 election manifesto. The most significant modification here was on the electoral system for the Westminster Parliament. The Labour government is committed only to a referendum on the issue. Tony Blair's statement that 'he is not personally persuaded' of the merits of proportional representation is a clear indication that he would advise Labour supporters to vote against.

Liberal Democrats and Nationalists have supported this constitutional reform programme for many years, partly out of genuine radicalism, partly out of self-interest as minority opposition parties who would gain more power if the reforms were implemented. The significant shift of opinion has been within sections of the Labour Party. From the mid-1930s to the mid-1980s the Labour Party was traditionalist and complacent about constitutional issues (the left-wing MP Tony Benn is the conspicuous exception, although he has a more radical agenda than Charter 88). Most of the Labour leadership, however, saw no need to change the rules and structures of a political system which, it believed, enabled it periodically to win power and implement its policies. Left-wingers like Michael Foot (Labour Party leader 1980–83) were as likely to take this view as right-wingers.

The Labour Party's shift of position on constitutional reform arose from the frustration of being in impotent opposition for 18 years (1979–97), the unspoken fear that it could not win an election outright, and the perceived need to move closer to the position of the Nationalists and the Liberal Democrats. This move was politically necessary in order to win over their supporters and to form a coalition with the leaders if an inconclusive election result produced a 'hung' parliament without a working majority.

Scottish Labour was converted to the merits of a Scottish Parliament because from 1979 to 1997 Scotland was ruled by a Conservative Government, even though an overwhelming proportion of Scots voted against it and a large majority of seats returned Labour MPs. The Conservative Government even used Scotland as a testing ground for some of its more unpopular policies such as the poll tax and local government reform. The Scottish Nationalists effectively exploited this electoral disjunction to campaign for an independent Scotland, steadily increased their vote over the period, and replaced the Conservatives as the main challengers in Labour areas. For the Labour Party, acceptance of a Scottish Parliament – which Labour would anyway expect to dominate – was a necessary (and not very heavy) price to pay for heading off the SNP. Once the case for a Scottish Parliament was conceded, it followed that the Welsh should have an assembly of their own (with lesser powers) and that the English regions, if they wanted it, should have greater powers.

Labour's change of heart on freedom of information and a bill of rights – to which the last Labour Government, under James Callaghan, was opposed – stemmed from its growing dismay at what it regarded as the Conservative Government's excessive secrecy and disregard for individual and group rights. Examples included: the ban on trade unions at GCHQ (Government Communications Headquarters); the ban on the radio and television broadcasting of the words of members of the IRA or Sinn Fein; the bullying of the BBC over its coverage of Northern Ireland; the prosecution of the civil servants Sarah Tisdall and Clive Ponting for leaking documents which showed the government had lied to Parliament; the modification of the right of a person charged by the police to remain silent; and the whittling away of the rights of political asylum seekers from abroad. What particularly disturbed Labour and other opponents of these measures, all of which touched upon the fundamental rights of individuals, was that no countervailing power existed to question or stop the Government. The existing constitution concentrated too much power in its hands. Basic individual and group rights needed the protection of the law and the courts.

In theory the House of Lords acts as a bulwark against the government exercising overweening power. However, the hereditary elements in the Lords, supplemented by the Conservative majority among (government-appointed) life peers, produces an automatic Conservative majority in the Lords irrespective of which party is in office. The Labour Party was particularly angry when Conservative hereditary peers who rarely attended the House turned up to vote in favour of the poll tax, a measure of considerable personal benefit to them in most cases as the tax ignored the value of people's properties. It feared that the unelected but Conservative-dominated Lords would use its delaying powers to obstruct Labour government measures, especially towards the end of the parliament. The composition (but not the powers) of the Lords had to be reformed.

The part of constitutional reform towards which Labour is understandably lukewarm is electoral reform. A Labour Party commission on electoral reform (the Plant Commission) was deeply divided on the issue. On the one hand, Labour was acutely aware that the Conservatives had formed four successive governments on the basis of a minority popular vote of 42 to 44 per cent. These had sufficient majorities to push through unpopular policies such as the water and railway privatisations, the poll tax and VAT on fuel. On the other hand, a change to a more proportional system has two major drawbacks for the Labour Party. First, in regions in which Labour wins a disproportionate number of seats (e.g. Merseyside, South Wales, the North East) some local Labour MPs would lose under the new system. To ask them to vote for a Commons bill for proportional representation would be to ask them to vote for their own redundancy. Secondly, no party has won more than 50 per cent of the vote since 1935. Thus a proportional system would mean that no single party commanded a majority in the House of Commons and that all governments were coalitions. For Labour the benefit of electoral reform would be the end, for ever, of unalloyed Conservative government. But the cost would be the end, for ever, of unalloyed Labour government. It would always have to share office with the Liberal Democrats or Nationalists.

The case for and against constitutional reform is discussed in more detail at the end of this book. The next chapter examines the real beneficiaries of the existing British constitution, the seat of executive power in Britain, the prime minister and cabinet.

SUMMARY

This chapter has summarised the main features of Britain's 'unwritten constitution', starting from the question of whether it really is a constitution at all. Whether this is the case or not, its informal and diffuse nature leaves it open to manipulation by the government of the day and its parliamentary majority. European Union law, paradoxically, forms a major bulwark against this and empowers British courts to make overtly constitutional judgements, deeming both legislation and government actions illegal where they come into conflict with European precedents. Movements for internal reform have had a major success with the introduction of regional assemblies, which politically (if not in legal theory) breach earlier constitutional emphases upon the unitary state.

The particular constitutional features highlighted by this discussion are:

- the uncodified and unsystematic nature of the legal provisions of the Constitution (in Statute and Common law);

- the extent to which these have to be supplemented by 'conventions', practices or customs which can, however, be radically changed whenever this suits the party in power;

- the principal constitutional doctrines: unitary state, parliamentary sovereignty, 'elective dictatorship' of the government, governmental restraint;

- the extent of change and constitutional modification over the last 20 years.

These have had two conflicting results:

- an increase in governmental power and freedom to take arbitrary action;

- limitations on 'elective dictatorship' imposed by European legislation and movements for reform which have produced regional assemblies and pressure for a written Bill of Rights.

ESSAYS

1. Do you agree or disagree with the proposition that 'The British constitution is whatever the government chooses to do'?

2. Analyse the impact of the United Kingdom's membership of the European Union on the British constitution. In your answer remember to mention those aspects of the constitution that have *not* been affected.

3. Why was constitutional reform rarely on the political agenda between 1945 and 1983? Why has the movement for constitutional reform grown since then?

4. What does 'parliamentary sovereignty' mean? In what sense does the British Parliament still retain sovereignty and in what sense is the British Parliament losing it?

FURTHER READING

R. Brazier, *Constitutional Practice* (Oxford: Clarendon Press, 1988) and, by the same author, *Constitutional Reform* (Oxford: Clarendon Press, 1991) are clear and comprehensive accounts of the constitution as it is, and as it might be. The publications

MILESTONES

MILESTONES IN BRITISH CONSTITUTIONAL DEVELOPMENT

1215 Magna Carta (The Great Charter). English Barons force King John to recognise their personal rights (which extend to all freemen) and right to collective consultation about important matters

1296–1306 Edward I begins to summon representatives of towns and counties, regularly, along with the Lords, to agree to taxation for the Scottish wars. In return, the King makes concessions to meet their requests, a process which continues for the next two hundred years

1532–59 Parliament is used by the Tudor monarchs to ratify the most important royal actions (settling succession, setting up Protestant Church, etc.)

1640–51 Parliament fights Civil War against King and wins. Establishes its supremacy over the Law Courts

1688–89 Bill of Rights. Parliament deposes James II and installs William III as King (the Glorious Revolution). It reaffirms that taxes can only be raised with its consent and affirms specific citizens' rights

1701 Act of Settlement. Parliament establishes (Protestant) succession

1707 Act of Union with Scotland. The English Parliament absorbs the Scottish one, but accepts the separate Scottish legal system and church

1715–1832 The 'Eighteenth Century Constitution'. The government has to be acceptable to the King but must also maintain a majority in the House of Commons. Party organisations ('Whigs' and 'Tories') develop from time to time to secure and organise this majority

1832 Great Reform Act substitutes election for ownership of seats as the basis for representation in the House of Commons. Election is within small constituencies by plurality vote on first-past-the-post system

1838 Accession of the 18-year-old Victoria marks end of active involvement of monarch with the government, which is now effectively nominated by the largest party in the House of Commons

1867 Second Reform Act (Representation of the People Act) extends franchise to most male town dwellers

1868–89 Conservatives and Liberal parties create mass organisations throughout Britain and alternate in government with support of a Commons majority

1884 Third Reform Act (Representation of the People Act) extends franchise to most male country dwellers

1911 Parliament Act. Reforming Liberal Government with support of Commons majority restricts powers of (hereditary) House of Lords (a) over financial bills, (b) to delaying any legislation for only three years

1918 Representation of the People Act enfranchises all remaining males over 21 and women over 30

1922 Government of Ireland Act sets up regional parliament and government in Northern Ireland

1928 Representation of the People Act gives women the vote on the same terms as men

1949 Parliament Act. Reforming Labour Government restricts delaying powers of House of Lords to one year

1963 Peerage Act. Creation of 'life peers' to serve in House of Lords but not to pass on title to children

1969 Representation of the People Act reduces age for voting to 18

1972 European Communities Act. Britain accedes to the EU Parliament and accepts that all previous European legislation and judicial decisions are binding and European legislation superior to British legislation

1973–74 UK Parliament abolishes Northern Irish Government and Parliament

1986 Single European Act extends competence of EU. Qualified majority voting in the Council of Ministers means that UK government cannot veto European provisions it disagrees with, in the areas where they apply

1993 Treaty of Maastricht further extends European Union's area of jurisdiction and use of qualified majority voting

1997 New Labour Government accepts the Social Chapter of the Treaty of Maastricht

1997–98 Creation of Scottish and Welsh assemblies and governments

PROJECTS

1. Why and in what sense does Britain lack a 'written constitution'? If Britain's existing constitution was written as a single document what consequences might follow?

2. Examine the 'independence constitution' of any former British colony. To what extent is it really a codification of the 'unwritten' British constitution?

3. Compile a list of the cabinet and junior ministers who resigned office during the Major Government of 1992–97 and identify the reasons in each case. In how many cases can the reason be attributed to the doctrine of ministerial responsibility? What is the most usual reason? Compile a second list of ministers whose departments presided over a major policy failure and who might have been expected to resign but did not. What reasons did they or the Prime Minister give in Parliament for their not resigning?

4. For groups: debate the proposition 'Britain is better off without a written constitution'.

of the Charter 88 group provide the standard arguments for constitutional reform. For the details of Charter 88 see *Charter 88* (London: New Statesman and Society, 1988) and R. Holme and M. Eliot (eds), *1688–1888 Time for a New Constitution* (London: Macmillan, 1988). Philip Norton, *The Constitution in Flux* (London: Martin Robertson, 1982), although somewhat out of date, states the case against constitutional reform. Ferdinand Mount, *The British Constitution Now* (London: Heinemann, 1992) offers a thoughtful, if fairly conservative, assessment of the state of the constitution, based partly on his experience as head of Margaret Thatcher's Policy Unit from 1982 to 1984. Jeffrey Jowell and Dawn Oliver, *The Changing Constitution* (Oxford: Clarendon Press, 2nd edn 1989) contains useful studies of constitutional change under the Conservative governments since 1979. Geoffrey Marshall, *Constitutional Conventions* (Oxford: Oxford University Press, 1984) is the classic account of these peculiar institutions.

---

http://www.awl-he.com/politics/newbritpol

Internet resources – visit *The New British Politics* Webpage for links to a specially-chosen selection of Internet resources relevant to this Chapter.

http://www.awl-he.com/politics/newbritpol

CHAPTER 8

The core executive:

Prime Minister and Cabinet

The Prime Minister (or Premier) is the most powerful politician in Britain, and the Cabinet is the most powerful group of politicians. The way they work together raises a set of important and controversial questions about the British system of government. What are the constitutional limits to their executive power? Has the office of Prime Minister been transformed from the traditional 'first among equals' in the Cabinet, into a powerful political executive akin, in many ways, to a president? Or is the Cabinet still the collective centre of policy making with the final power over government? How do Thatcher, Major and Blair compare as prime ministers, and what is likely to be the lasting impact of their periods in office? Does the recently developed concept of the 'core executive' help our understanding of the highest level of British government?

The chapter is divided into six main sections. Each describes how the Cabinet and the premiership are organised and supported by the machinery of government, and outlines the controversies surrounding their powers and interactions. It focuses in turn on:

- The Prime Minister
- The Cabinet and its committees
- The eternal political triangle of Departments, Cabinet, and Prime Minister
- Prime ministerial styles: Thatcher, Major and Blair
- Prime ministerial versus Cabinet government
- The core executive.

THE PRIME MINISTER

Key term

Prime Minister – the head of the executive branch of government and chair of the Cabinet.

Like other features of the British constitution, the powers and duties of the Prime Minister are not written down in legal documents. They have evolved over time according to historical circumstances. As a result, it is difficult to state exactly what the job of the Prime Minister is. As one incumbent (Herbert Asquith, Prime Minister 1908–16) remarked, it is 'what the office holder chooses and is able to make of it'. However, it is clear that the Prime Minister is the head of government

Table 8.1 Postwar Prime Ministers

Prime Minister	Dates	Party
Clement Attlee	1945–51	Labour
Sir Winston Churchill	1951–55	Conservative
Sir Anthony Eden	1955–57	Conservative
Harold Macmillan	1957–63	Conservative
Sir Alec Douglas-Home	1963–64	Conservative
Harold Wilson	1964–70	Labour
Edward Heath	1970–74	Conservative
Harold Wilson	1974–76	Labour
James Callaghan	1976–79	Labour
Margaret Thatcher	1979–90	Conservative
John Major	1990–97	Conservative
Tony Blair	1997–present	Labour

at home (the monarch is the head of state), and the political representative of the country abroad. He or she appoints Cabinet members and chairs their meetings, and is effective head of the Civil Service, the armed forces, and the security services. As the leading member of the government and carrying no special departmental responsibilities, the Prime Minister follows through broad policy issues and keeps the Government as a whole on its chosen course. The office therefore carries huge political responsibilities and powers. Table 8.1 lists postwar Prime Ministers and Table 8.2 the responsibilities and powers that are attached to the office.

Table 8.2 Responsibilities and powers of the Prime Minister

- Leading the government at home and representing the country abroad.
- Keeping watch on the broad political agenda and the course of government.
- Deciding the number and nature of Cabinet and government posts and who fills them. Reshuffling government positions.
- Creating and dissolving Cabinet committees, deciding their remit, and appointing chairs and members.
- Chairing the Cabinet and some of its important committees, managing their agendas and discussions, calling on speakers, summing up discussion, directing the writing of minutes.
- Overseeing the security services.
- Managing relations between the Cabinet and the wider world of Parliament, the media, other countries, and international organisations, including the EU.
- Deciding what government information to release to whom and when.
- Answering formal questions in the House of Commons.
- Appointing senior ambassadors and civil servants. Recommending appointments to senior positions in the Church of England, the judiciary, the Privy Council, the BBC, and other quangos and civil positions.
- Recommendations for the Honours list.
- Dissolving Parliament and calling an election.
- Taking the lead in any unexpected crisis that affects the government or majority party.
- Managing the majority party.

A mere listing cannot really capture the staggering range of responsibilities the Prime Minister has or takes on. 'Leading government' involves so many roles ranging from formal representation of the nation (e.g. reading a lesson at the State funeral of Princess Diana) to crisis management whenever an unexpected event seems likely to blow the government off course. At the same time the Prime Minister has to check how well the normal programme of government is proceeding. The Premier appears on television and in the House of Commons to answer weekly questions – often highly critical ones – and to speak for the government in important debates, often long and wearing.

Besides being at the centre of government, the Prime Minister is also the majority party leader, which involves keeping the parliamentary party happy, and in line. With a mass party it also means rallying supporters and appealing to voters, both those who voted for the party last time and those who might vote for it next time. This cumulation of responsibilities is enormous. Performing them all adequately may well be beyond the reach of one person, even though the incumbent has an office to help with government administration, and Whips and other officials to organise the Party.

BRIEFINGS

8.1 WHO BECOMES PRIME MINISTER? TONY BLAIR AND JOHN MAJOR

The New Labour Prime Minister, Tony Blair, and the last Conservative Prime Minister, John Major, offer a piquant contrast of background and style. The paradox is that the Conservative Major comes from the kind of underprivileged background usually associated with Labour, while the former public schoolboy Blair shares an exclusive background with many Conservative MPs.

Blair's father was a Scottish engineer who did well in North-East England, where he moved in search of work. His political career (as a Conservative!) was cut short by illness, but he managed to send his son to Fettes, an English-style public school in Edinburgh. From there Tony followed the route to Oxford and on to a career in law, from which he moved naturally into politics. He was attracted to Labour by his Christian Socialist beliefs developed at university, reinforced by the influence of his wife Cherie, a devout Catholic.

John Major, by contrast, came from a poor South London family. His father was a circus performer and a manufacturer of garden gnomes. Major left school at 16 with almost no qualifications. He rose through banking and entered Parliament in 1979, four years earlier than Blair. He was favoured by Margaret Thatcher during the 1980s precisely because he had no connections with the traditional Conservative grandees. The factors which helped his rise were his obvious competence, especially in the details of administration, and the general uncertainty about where he stood ideologically, other than having general free market views. This helped his election by the Conservative Parliamentary Party to the premiership in 1990 as a compromise candidate, since all factions were able to believe he might favour them.

8.1 WHO BECOMES PRIME MINISTER? TONY BLAIR AND JOHN MAJOR (continued)

Blair, by contrast, has evangelistic views about what Labour should abandon from its past: state ownership of industry, high taxation, financial profligacy. These are made palatable by his social concern. What precipitated his election as Leader of the Labour Party in 1994 was his performance as Shadow Home Secretary. His slogan that Labour would be 'tough on crime, tough on the causes of crime' combined a new Labour sensitivity to victims with traditional priorities targeted on social welfare and unemployment.

These offer only limited support with the more nebulous and probably more important tasks like crisis management. So it is no wonder that most Prime Ministers have political confidants, who may or may not have formal posts in government, to do much of the necessary negotiation and behind the scenes management that the post entails. The close working relationship between Tony Blair and Peter Mandelson is paralleled by that between Margaret Thatcher and William Whitelaw, and later Norman Tebbit. One of John Major's weaknesses was that he did not have a similar high-level 'political friend' to rely on. See Briefings 8.1 and 8.2 on Thatcher, Major and Blair.

Plate 8.1 Peter Brookes cartoon in *The Times*, 6.5.97: Election chief gets key post. Peter Mandelson is appointed Minister without Portfolio with the task of ensuring that Tony Blair's policies and programme are implemented throughout Whitehall. This image mirrored a Tory election poster showing Blair on Chancellor Kohl's knee. Sitting on Mandelson's knee are: Tony Blair, John Prescott, Gordon Brown, Robin Cook with other New Labour senior ministers

BRIEFINGS

8.2 MARGARET THATCHER, STORMBIRD OF BRITISH POLITICS

The third in the trilogy of modern British Prime Ministers is Margaret Thatcher, who headed the Conservative governments from 1979 to 1990. Probably the outstanding Prime Minister of the postwar period, she is unique in many respects. Though no feminist, she is the only woman to have held the post. She was also a woman with a mission – to regenerate Britain – more so even than the evangelistic Blair. As a result she stirred strong feelings, and was either loved or loathed by public and politicians alike.

Coming from lower middle-class origins (her father was a small town shopkeeper) she bettered herself through a university education and married a rich man. This enabled her to pursue a conventionally successful political career which culminated as Secretary for Education under Heath (Prime Minister from 1970 to 1974).

Two events precipitated her break with the 'social democratic consensus' which had prevailed since the war. One was the election defeat of the Conservative Government in early 1974 as the result of a near general strike by trade unions. The other was her conversion to a free market diagnosis of this failure as the Government 'overloading' itself with responsibilities.

Mrs Thatcher was the only prominent Conservative willing to stand in the party leadership election after Heath's second election defeat in 1974. Winning the 1979 general election as the result of a general revulsion against union strikes in the 'Winter of Discontent', she set out on a long-term campaign to break union power and 'get government out of business' through large-scale selling-off of state enterprises. Her three successive general election victories (1979, 1983, 1987) seemed to make her political position impregnable, in spite of an increasingly autocratic style towards Party and Cabinet. When this led her into imposing the unpopular poll tax, practically on her own authority, and into open hostility to the EU and European partners, the Cabinet dumped her in face of a parliamentary party revolt inspired by fear of losing the 1992 General Election.

Hiring and firing

Central to prime ministerial power is the ability to hire and fire, that is, to nominate members of the government and influence the appointment of important committees and even senior civil servants to ministries. Here we will concentrate on the power to hire and fire members of the government, partly because it is so important, and partly because it illustrates the powers and limitations of the office very well.

Prime Ministers do not just decide which individuals will be in the Cabinet; they also decide how big the Cabinet will be and which jobs are to be in it. Ministries and Cabinet positions can be combined, created or abolished, at the same time as the Prime Minister appoints to them. Consequently postwar Cabinets have ranged from 16 to 24 in number. For example, Major created the National Heritage Department with a Cabinet seat in 1992. Harold Wilson created the post of Deputy Prime Minister in 1964 for his Party leadership rival, George Brown; Major did the same for Michael Heseltine in 1995, and Blair for John Prescott in 1997.

Some Prime Ministers have refused Cabinet positions to powerful political figures, while others have not given them the post they most wanted. Harold Macmillan refused R.A.B. Butler the Foreign Secretary's job, and kept another prominent figure, Lord Hailsham (Quintin Hogg), out of a senior position. Heath excluded Enoch Powell, and, in turn, did not sit in either Thatcher's or Major's Cabinets. Callaghan sacked Barbara Castle. Macmillan favoured pro-Europeans in the 1960s, but Thatcher kept them out in the 1980s. She favoured 'dries' (hardline free marketeers) in spending jobs, giving leading 'wets' (moderates), like Peter Walker, junior positions, such as the Welsh Secretaryship. Thus the composition of the Cabinet can very much reflect the Prime Minister's preferences and policy priorities, an important step to getting them accepted in subsequent discussion and debate.

The Prime Minister can also fire government members in reshuffles which occur about every 18 months in the life of a British government. These can bring in new ministerial talent, end the careers of political enemies, or change policy direction. The most famous example is the 'Night of the Long Knives' in 1962 when Macmillan sacked six Cabinet members. Between 1979 and 1990 Thatcher sacked 12 senior ministers. In the reshuffle of 1989 she changed 62 government positions!

In spite of this, the PM does not have a free hand, or even much choice sometimes, in making up a Cabinet and a government. More than one hundred government posts have to be filled, from the 330–400 MPs in the majority party in the Commons, with a few from the House of Lords. Some MPs are unsuited to government posts for personal or political reasons. Besides, forming a government is a balancing act which demands a mix of people and talents: young and old, experience and promise, men and women, and representatives of major factions such as wets and dries, Europhiles and Europhobes and, for Labour, traditionalists and new Blairites. Some posts have to be filled from a very small pool of possibilities. Major's government was short of Welsh and Scottish MPs for the Welsh and Scottish Offices, so short that English MPs had to be appointed Secretary of State for Wales.

In sum, the Prime Minister's powers to hire and fire government members, like many other features of the office, are a mixture of surprising freedom and tight constraints. There is often little choice, and some ministers virtually choose themselves by virtue of their political stature and support of factions within the party. John Major's choices were increasingly constrained by such factors in the mid-1990s. At the same time, some PMs have juggled with the careers of powerful people and have shaped governments to their own taste. Margaret Thatcher increasingly did so in the course of her decade in office. Tony Blair's current Cabinet is a mixture of powerful figures he cannot ignore, such as Gordon Brown and John Prescott, and people he himself has pushed, like Lord Irvine, the Lord Chancellor.

The Prime Minister's Office

The Premiership is not just one individual, however important his or her style may be. It is also an institution with a corporate existence. The Prime Minister is served by a staff of 35–40 people who form the Prime Minister's Office. This is divided into four main sections:

- The Private Office is run by the PM's principal private secretary, a civil servant, and keeps the PM abreast of important matters, manages official engagements and relations between the PM, Parliament, and Whitehall, and handles the documents that flood into 10 Downing Street. The office works 24 hours a day.
- The Political Office links the PM with Parliament and the Party, drafts speeches and policy documents, and advises on tactical political matters.
- The Policy Unit consists of 8-10 advisors who offer policy advice. They are usually on short-term appointments and often drawn from outside government and the Civil Service.
- The Press Office, with about half a dozen staff, handles the PM's relations with the media and the world at large. Some press secretaries have been especially influential: Joe Haines under Wilson, and Bernard Ingham under Thatcher, were virtually policy advisers.

Prime Ministers in fact often gather around them a collection of influential friends and advisors whom they feel they can trust, although they may often be without official positions in Whitehall or Westminster. They are usually resented by regular politicians and ministers because of their access to the top and are referred to disparagingly by such terms as 'the Kitchen Cabinet'. One can, however, appreciate the PM's need for disinterested or at least alternative advice to that of civil servants and party rivals. Thatcher made extensive use of such an informal group, which included her Press Secretary, Bernard Ingham (a civil servant), Sir Charles Powell (a personal advisor), Nicholas Ridley (a Conservative MP), Professor Sir Alan Walters (advisor on economic matters), and businessmen like Sir Robert McAlpine. Major relied much more on the Cabinet itself. Blair's closest associate, Peter Mandelson, is a minister outside the Cabinet but credited with more influence than many ministers within it.

Key term
Kitchen cabinet – the loose and informal policy-advice group which prime ministers may collect around them, and which may include politicians, public officials, and private citizens.

THE CABINET

Key term
Cabinet – the committee of the leading members of the government who are empowered to make decisions on behalf of the government.

The Cabinet should not be confused with the government. There are usually 20–24 Cabinet members but over one hundred government members. Most Cabinet members are drawn from the House of Commons for the simple reason that it is the overwhelmingly dominant chamber of Parliament, but some Cabinet members come from the Lords. The Lord Chancellor, the highest legal officer in the country, is a member of the House of Lords who holds a Cabinet position. Most Cabinet members are ministers who run Whitehall departments, but some (like the Chancellor of the Duchy of Lancaster) do not have such duties and can range over policy issues without the burden of departmental responsibilities. They often chair general committees and referee disputes between departmental ministers.

The Cabinet, like the office of Prime Minister, has changed over time. Churchill had only five to eight members in his war-time Cabinet, and experimented with a Cabinet of 16 'overlords' in 1951. The experiment did not last long and soon the Cabinet returned to its normal size. Table 8.3 shows Blair's First Cabinet. Whatever its size and composition, the Cabinet is the central committee of government which co-ordinates the policies of separate Whitehall departments, and directs the work of government as a whole. As such it is the main collective body of the political executive which either discusses and makes important decisions, or considers and ratifies the decisions of Cabinet committees. Some of the practices and procedures of Cabinet government are defined in Briefing 8.3.

BRIEFINGS

8.3 PRACTICES AND PROCEDURES OF CABINET GOVERNMENT

Kitchen cabinet. The loose and informal policy advice group which Prime Ministers sometimes collect around them, and which may include politicians, public officials, and private citizens.

Collective responsibility. The principle that decisions of the Cabinet are binding on all members of the Government, who must support them in public in order to maintain a united front or resign their government post.

Cabinet government. The theory that the Cabinet forms a collective political executive in British government and thus constrains the power of the Prime Minister. In Cabinet government the principle of collective responsibility means the Cabinet either makes, or is consulted about, important political decisions.

Prime ministerial government. The theory that the office of the Prime Minister is now so powerful that it forms the political executive, the 'efficient secret of government', that effectively makes the decisions, with the Cabinet only a 'dignified' part.

The core executive. The web of institutions, networks, people and practices which operate around the Prime Minister and Cabinet, and which include the most senior civil servants in Whitehall departments, the Cabinet Office, and the Prime Minister's Office. The core executive is the apex of political power which integrates the government.

Department view. The long-term commitments and plans of each ministry and department for developing their functional area of responsibility.

Adversarial decision making. The clash between differing department views at all levels of Government, which extends to the departmental ministers in the Cabinet and conflicts with the need for collegiality and collective responsibility.

Office	Minister	Age
Cabinet Ministers		
Prime Minister	Tony Blair	44
Deputy Prime Minister	John Prescott	58
Chancellor of the Exchequer	Gordon Brown	46
Foreign Secretary	Robin Cook	51
Home Secretary	Jack Straw	50
Lord Chancellor	Lord Irvine	56
President of the Board of Trade	Margaret Beckett	54
Education and Employment	David Blunkett	49
Social Security	Harriet Harman	46
Health	Frank Dobson	57
Defence	George Robertson	51
Agriculture	Jack Cunningham	57
National Heritage	Chris Smith	45
Chief Secretary of the Treasury	Alistair Darling	43
Scotland	Donald Dewar	59
Wales	Ron Davies	50
Northern Ireland	Marjorie (Mo) Mowlem	47
International Development	Clare Short	51
Transport	Gavin Strang	53
Leader of the Commons	Ann Taylor	49
Leader of the Lords	Lord Richard	64
Chancellor of the Duchy of Lancaster	David Clark	57
Important non-Cabinet Ministers		
Minister Without Portfolio	Peter Mandelson	43
Minister for Europe	Doug Henderson	47
Paymaster General	Geoffrey Robinson	58
Ministers of State at the Treasury	Helen Liddell	46
	Dawn Primarolo	42
Chief Whip	Nick Brown	46
Social Security	Frank Field	54
Environment	Michael Meacher	57
Public Service	Derek Foster	59
Education and Employment	Andrew Smith	46

Collective responsibility

Collective responsibility – the principle whereby decisions and policies of the Cabinet are binding on all members of the government who must support them in public, to maintain a united front, or resign their government post.

As a collective decision-making body, the Cabinet is supposedly bound by the principle of 'collective responsibility'. This states that whatever individual Cabinet members feel about a decision, and no matter how hard they fought against it in the secrecy of the Cabinet, they must always defend it publicly, or resign from the government. The Cabinet may be the centre of private controversy, but it must present a united front in public. As the nineteenth century statesman Lord Melbourne said when he was Prime Minister, 'It doesn't matter what we say as long as we all say the same thing'. Cabinet discussion is in secret (members sign the Official Secrets Act), and to preserve the appearance of unanimity, the Prime Minister sums up the mood of the meeting, which adds to the PM's power. In an evenly balanced discussion or sometimes in an uneven one, the Premier can sum up in favour of a preferred line. Votes in Cabinet are rare.

As we saw in the last chapter, the nature of collective responsibility is changing. Originally applied only to the Cabinet, it now covers all government members. Since 1994 the Labour Party seems to have applied it to members of the Shadow Cabinet as well. On the other hand, the government suspended collective responsibility in 1975 and 1977 over the issue of the European Union. In 1994 a sitting Cabinet member, Michael Portillo, made thinly veiled criticisms of the Cabinet's European policy, but was not disciplined in public. Some ministers have also circumvented collective responsibility by leaking documents. The principle of collective responsibility, it seems, is applied more broadly but also more weakly, in a way that suits the government of the day.

Cabinet committees

Established during the crisis years of the Second World War as a way of doing Cabinet work quickly and efficiently in small groups, Cabinet committees are now part of the system and, as government work grows, increasing use is made of them. The Prime Minister decides the number, terms of reference, memberships and the chairs of committees. Most are staffed by Cabinet members, but some include junior ministers and senior civil servants. There are two types of Cabinet committee:

1. Standing Committees. There are normally 25 to 30 of these dealing with the permanent policy areas of government such as Northern Ireland, the EU, local government and nuclear defence. Normally they will be chaired by the Cabinet Minister responsible for the area. The most important is probably the Economic and Domestic Policy (EDP) committee, chaired by the PM, which has come to form an inner cabinet of very senior government members.

2. Ad Hoc Committees. These are set up to deal with specific matters. Thatcher used them extensively for such issues as the coal dispute of 1984, the Falklands War, and the abolition of the Metropolitan Counties

and the GLC. An important one at the moment is the Millennium Committee, as the government has invested a lot of prestige in the celebrations for the year 2000.

The major cabinet committees are shown in Table 8.4.

Ad hoc committees were a device much used by Mrs Thatcher to bypass discussion in the full Cabinet. She could fill them with her own nominees and thus use them to get her own way. John Major's more consensual style made for fewer ad hoc committees, which became more genuinely representative of opinion in the Cabinet. Tony Blair comes between Major and Thatcher: particularly on the Millennium and education he seems intent to push his own initiatives through ad hoc committees. But he is circumscribed by such powerful colleagues as Gordon Brown and Robin Cook whom he cannot bypass in their own areas of finance and foreign affairs. One of the most interesting Blair

Table 8.4 The major Cabinet Committees and their responsibilities

Domestic Affairs	Foreign Affairs
Economic and Domestic Policy Senior Cabinet Ministers chaired by the Prime Minister. Plans government domestic strategy and functions as an inner cabinet for this	**Defence and Overseas Policy** Its subcommittee on European questions is currently considering the single currency and attitudes to further integration
Public Expenditure Settles those disputes over expenditure allocations which cannot be settled at lower levels. Crucial to balancing social needs with financial requirements	**European Security** Related matters of defence and security
Home and Social Affairs Deals with the related questions of social provision and order	**Northern Ireland** Heavily concerned to promote the peace process in Ireland
Local Government General supervision of local government including central grants	**Intelligence Services** General policy on the intelligence services but not detailed supervision
Industrial, Commercial and Consumer Affairs Industrial and economic policy	
Environment	
Science and Technology	
Future Legislation and Legislation Oversees plans for future legislative programme and drafting of current legislation	
Joint Committee on the Constitution A Blair innovation: a joint committee with the (opposition) Liberal Democrats to discuss constitutional reform	

initiatives is the Joint Cabinet Committee on Constitutional Reform, which incorporates leading Liberal Democrats. This is a harbinger of important change for all sorts of reasons. It breaks the constitutional convention of majority party dominance and total confrontation with the Opposition, discussed in the previous chapter. It keeps constitutional reform firmly on the political agenda. And it may provide a political device for the Prime Minister to put pressure on traditionalists within the Cabinet itself who oppose change. He is bound to get support on reform from the Liberals. In this sense the committee may prove to be less of a mere goodwill gesture and 'talking shop' than at first appears.

The Cabinet Secretariat and Office

Just as Prime Ministers have their Office, so the Cabinet has its Secretariat, consisting of about 40 senior civil servants whose job is to timetable meetings, prepare agendas and documents, and draft and circulate minutes. The Secretariat is so important that its head, the Cabinet Secretary, is the country's senior civil servant. The Cabinet Secretary is in daily contact with the Prime Minister and Cabinet members, attends Cabinet meetings (though not party political items) and some Cabinet committees. The Secretariat is assisted by a Cabinet Office of some 1,500 civil servants. Cabinet committees are shadowed by a set of 'official committees' of civil servants who prepare the work for committees, and follow up their decisions.

THE CABINET AND WHITEHALL DEPARTMENTS

The Cabinet committees and Secretariat are necessary because the Cabinet, like the Prime Minister, has a lot of responsibilities and roles to fulfil. Indeed, many of these overlap with those of the Prime Minister (Table 8.2). That is why it is very difficult to say whether, in Britain, the Prime Minister or the Cabinet really leads, since so much of what the Prime Minister does is agreed or ratified in Cabinet.

Most of the everyday functions of the Cabinet are given by the nature of its committees. Wherever possible they formulate policies which the Cabinet will simply pass on the nod. With its committees, the Cabinet:

- decides on what legislation will go through Parliament;

- hears and ratifies important policy initiatives like those on Northern Ireland, even though the actual decisions have been made in committee;

- considers the political consequences of these from a Party point of view and manages the Party (at meetings from which civil servants are absent and political advisers may be present).

By far the most important collective function of the Cabinet however, and the one which gives it its co-ordinating role in government, is its position as the top committee of the whole administrative structure of government, the place where final decisions must be made if they cannot be taken anywhere else.

This role derives from the adversarial nature of relationships between the government departments and ministries among whom administrative functions are divided. Naturally each ministry is deeply concerned to promote the function it has been set up to perform, whether this is getting more subsidies for farmers (Agriculture), building more roads (Transport) or cutting expenditure (Treasury). These 'departmental views' often conflict, but they then have to be reconciled. It is obvious that very few policy decisions can be made by one government department acting on its own. Typically, they are first considered by committees of civil servants from all the affected departments. At such meetings representatives of the Ministry of Agriculture, for example, might press for more subsidies for farmers who have lost money because of mad cow disease, while Treasury civil servants would resist this proposal in order to keep expenditure down.

If a compromise cannot be reached at civil servant level, the matter will then go up to a committee involving non-Cabinet ministers. If this cannot agree, it would normally be settled by the appropriate Cabinet committee. However, if the Cabinet committee cannot agree – and many departmental and personal political rivalries may be involved – it will finally fall to the Cabinet itself to take a final decision.

This means that many very trivial matters, like the precise amount of aid to be paid to the inhabitants of Montserrat (a small island dependency in the Caribbean, afflicted by a volcano), may have to go up to Cabinet to be settled. Conversely, very important decisions involving billions of pounds, like building a new motorway, may not reach the Cabinet, or certainly not be discussed there, because agreement was reached lower down.

Given the enormous volume of government business, some way of sifting out matters to be considered by Cabinet is obviously necessary. This type of decision making by default does ensure that controversial matters get Cabinet attention. In a rough and ready way, the most important decisions involve more people and are therefore likely to stimulate disagreement and get to Cabinet. But there is no guarantee of this. Moreover there is a bias for particular decisions, like building a new road, to be discussed in Cabinet but not the underlying question of whether new roads are needed in relation to other means of transport! The main co-ordinating body in British government thus tends to be overwhelmed by the pressures of immediate business, rather than taking a calm and considered long-term view.

THE ETERNAL POLITICAL TRIANGLE

This short-termism is partly because of the political dynamics of Cabinet government itself. Decision making within the Cabinet rests upon three important principles which often conflict with each other. One is the conflict engendered by departmental autonomy, which we have just discussed. The others are cabinet collegiality and prime ministerial authority.

1. *Departmental autonomy*. Cabinet ministers mostly have a departmental base and important department duties. Whitehall departments are among the largest organisations in the country, and most ministers spend most of their time on the onerous task of running them. This requires departmental autonomy not just because different departments have separate types of work – education, defence, transport, health – but also because they have their own working practices and 'departmental views'. It is the job of ministers to defend their departments and budgets in Cabinet. The more effectively they do so, the higher their political reputation.

2. *Cabinet collegiality*. The Cabinet thus contains many different interests – personal, political and departmental – and is the centre of intense political conflict. At the same time, it must also be an effective conflict-resolving and decision-making body which is able to defend its collective decisions. Whatever their rivalries, Cabinet members must form a united front, especially against the opposition parties. If they are to defend policies collectively, they must have the chance of discussing them beforehand, or at least be consulted. Too little Cabinet discussion and consultation undermines Cabinet collegiality.

3. *Prime ministerial authority*. Prime Ministers are leaders. Even the most powerful and ambitious ministers want the Prime Minister to lead the Cabinet, the party and the country. Besides, ministers are often so overburdened by their departmental duties that they have little time for general policy issues. It is the Prime Minister who must watch the big picture. It is also the PM's job to rise above conflict in Cabinet and settle disputes authoritatively. In this sense the PM is not a colleague, but the boss.

The three principles do not always fit well together. For example, departmental autonomy clashes with collegiality when ministers fight for money or over policies. Similarly, a Prime Minister who is too dominant will undermine collegiality, and one who interferes with departmental affairs too much will erode autonomy. Conversely, a weak Prime Minister who fails to control departmental and personal rivalries will also undermine collegiality and unity. Too much departmental autonomy results in a weak and divided Cabinet. A good Prime Minister must know when to talk and when to listen, when to lead or follow, when to intervene or delegate. In short, a good Prime Minister must somehow balance the demands of autonomy, collegiality and leadership. It is an exceedingly difficult task, and there are recent examples of it going wrong.

PRIME MINISTERIAL STYLES

Prime Ministers play their roles in different ways, if only because their circumstances and personalities differ. In his first premiership, Winston Churchill concentrated on the war effort, delegating daily government business to his Deputy, the Labour leader Clement Attlee. When he became Prime Minister in 1945,

Attlee was an excellent chair of a vigorous and reasonably united Cabinet, but he could be authoritative when necessary. Macmillan (1957–63) was tactful and astute, able to delegate and to lead, but he probably overplayed his hand and lost authority when he sacked a third of his government in 1962. Wilson's Cabinet and Party was more divided, both in 1964–70 and 1974–76. Though he was a clever politician who knew when to delegate, he was less impressive on long-term policy and strategy. However, the most interesting contrast of prime ministerial styles in recent years is that between Thatcher and Major.

Thatcher as Prime Minister

When Thatcher came to power in 1979 she seemed the kind of strong and dynamic leader who could reverse national decline, and the Falklands War strengthened popular belief in her. Yet when she lost power in 1990, as the longest

Plate 8.2 Anti-Poll Tax celebration march. Though lacking support in her own government, Thatcher pushed through a proposal to shift local taxation from property to individuals. This autocratic style eventually led to her downfall

serving Prime Minister of the century, she was widely seen as dogmatic and auto-cratic. For much of her time in Downing Street she dominated government and stretched prime ministerial leadership to its limits. Eventually she failed because she undermined departmental autonomy and Cabinet collegiality.

The poll tax is a case in point. This proposal to shift local taxation from prop-erty to individuals was described at the time as the worst idea in the world. There was little government or even Cabinet support for it, but Thatcher pushed it through Parliament, forcing her colleagues to support it publicly against their own judgement. Its unpopularity was one of the more important factors leading to Cabinet colleagues eventually combining to force her from office. Other examples of her leadership style are listed in Briefing 8.4.

BRIEFINGS

8.4 PRIME MINISTERIAL STYLE: THATCHER

- Ensured that 'dries' (right-wing free marketeers) dominated the Cabinet and its committees.
- Sacked 12 Cabinet ministers, 1979–90.
- Reduced number of Cabinet and standing committee meetings and the flow of documents. Wilson's annual average of Cabinet meetings was 59, Thatcher's was 35.
- Greater use of ad hoc committees and the Kitchen Cabinet. It is said that some Cabinet members were ignorant of the existence of some ad hoc committees and their membership, although they made important decisions about such things as the purchase of Trident missiles, doubling VAT, founding city colleges, extending the Youth Training Scheme, new unemployment schemes, the poll tax, and support for the American bombing of Libya (1986).
- Intervened in departmental affairs.
- Publicly criticised some of her ministers, or used leaks against them, but strictly enforced collective responsibility for other Cabinet members.
- Started Cabinet discussions by stating her own views, rather than listening and summing up.
- Did not consult her cabinet about some major policy announcements such as the decision to exclude trade unions from Government Communications Headquarters (GCHQ) in 1984.
- Appointed weak ministers who could be easily controlled.
- Kept some major issues off the Cabinet agenda. Michael Heseltine claimed this as a reason for his Cabinet resignation in 1986.

BRIEFINGS

8.5 PRIME MINISTERIAL STYLE: MAJOR

- More use made of the Cabinet, less of committees.
- More emphasis on Cabinet collegiality and consensus, less on leadership.
- A greater mix of opinion in the Cabinet, especially wets and dries, Europhiles and Eurosceptics.
- Greater openness in government.
- Less intervention in departmental affairs.
- Less strict application of collective responsibility: Portillo's veiled criticism of the Government in 1994 went publicly unchecked.

Major as Prime Minister

When Major replaced Thatcher in 1990 he adopted a more collegial and consensual style of leadership (see Briefing 8.5). Initially this succeeded in healing political wounds and unifying the Government. He also came out of the Gulf War (1991) with much respect as a political leader. Yet after a while his quiet and more pragmatic style was described as 'grey', weak, and ineffective. The Cabinet was described as a collection of 'political chums', and was accused of being 'in office but not in power'. Soon intense conflicts about economic policy, social policy and the EU surfaced. The Government appeared weak, divided, and directionless. Major's Cabinet was strong on collegiality and department autonomy, weaker on leadership. This contributed to the Government's defeat in 1997.

Blair as Prime Minister

In the first year of his administration Tony Blair seems to combine some of the characteristics of both Thatcher and Major (see Briefing 8.6). He has imposed an unprecedented discipline on the Labour Party as a whole, forcing it to accept reversals of traditional policies (such as spending on welfare) with little debate and a great show of unanimity. He has taken personal initiatives in certain policy areas without much consultation of the Cabinet (notably on the Millennium and on education).

Yet on many of the more controversial policies followed by the Labour Party the most powerful figures in the Cabinet agree with him. This is true both on the question of raising taxes – any appearance of doing so is to be strictly avoided – and on Scottish and Welsh devolution. So in many areas Blair does not need to

BRIEFINGS

8.6 PRIME MINISTERIAL STYLE: BLAIR

- Took on major agenda and policy-setting powers of the Government and made it clear that he would not tolerate dissent either from his Cabinet or from the Parliamentary Labour Party.
- Emphasised collegial or team spirit in pursuit of common goals. Pledged that he would strengthen the Cabinet Office and give key Cabinet ministers special powers over Cabinet committees.
- Was prepared to delegate considerable discretion to strong Cabinet ministers (for example Mo Mowlem at the Northern Irish Office, Robin Cook at the Foreign Office), provided their policies were broadly in line with government policy.
- Supported a much more open style of prime ministerial government, including changes in Prime Minister's Parliamentary Question Time to make it less adversarial and theatrical and more an opportunity for an exchange of information.
- Supported major policy and constitutional reforms, some of which reduced the power of the central Government or of individual Cabinet ministers. Such was the case with the Chancellor of the Exchequer, whose power to determine interest rates was transferred to the Bank of England in May 1997. Devolution to Scotland and Wales *ipso facto* reduced the government's power following the referendums of September 1997.
- Like Margaret Thatcher, Tony Blair tried to project his office and his persona as the 'spirit of the nation'. Such was clearly the case with his pronouncements following the death of the Princess of Wales at the end of August 1997.

bypass the Cabinet, and it is doubtful at the moment if he could. Winning another election, however, could strengthen his hand considerably, particularly if some senior Cabinet ministers dropped out by accident or design. Blair seems to have the *inclination* to act more autocratically but, for the moment at any rate, lacks the *opportunity*.

Key term

Prime ministerial government – the theory that the office of the prime minister has become so powerful that he or she now forms a political executive similar to a President.

WHO GOVERNS? CABINET OR PRIME MINISTER

It is often said that the power of the Prime Minister has increased relative to the Cabinet, and that the Prime Minister is no longer 'first among equals', but a dominant political executive. The result, it is claimed, is not Cabinet but prime ministerial government. The Cabinet, once said to be the 'efficient secret of government' because it, and not the Commons, made decisions, is now a 'dignified' part of government. Effective power is concentrated on the Prime Minister. This assertion dates back at least to the Second World War and Churchill, but it has surfaced every now and then since, particularly in the Thatcher decade. The 'Controversy' summarises the arguments.

CONTROVERSY

PRIME MINISTERIAL OR CABINET GOVERNMENT?

PRIME MINISTERIAL GOVERNMENT

- The formal powers of the Prime Minister are considerable (see Table 8.2).

- There are no constitutional limits to the power of the Prime Minister.

- The fusion of the executive and the legislative branches of government gives the Prime Minister direct influence over both.

- One-party government and strict party discipline ensures the power of the Prime Minister over the majority party in Parliament.

- The apparatus of Whitehall government is hierarchically organised with the Prime Minister at the peak.

- The office accumulates power over time, ratcheting up with each new incumbent. Wartime conditions gave Churchill special powers which were built upon by strong successors: Attlee, Macmillan, Wilson, Thatcher, Blair.

- The Prime Minister's importance is magnified by media attention, and access to the media gives the Prime Minister power over government colleagues.

- The Prime Minister represents the country in widely publicised international meetings.

- The Prime Minister's Office and the Cabinet Office are increasingly linked under the direction of the Prime Minister.

CABINET GOVERNMENT

- Modern government is now so complicated and demanding that one person cannot possibly control even the key decisions.

- Important political factions in the Party need to be represented in the Cabinet if confidence in the Prime Minister is to be maintained.

- The Prime Minister has powerful and ambitious rivals for office. Some may be ignored, but not all.

- Ministers can use the weapon of resignation against the Prime Minister (Nigel Lawson in 1989, Sir Geoffrey Howe in 1990) but it may do the minister more harm than the Prime Minister in the short term.

- Prime Ministers need to listen carefully to many early warning systems: the Party Whips in the House of Commons (the eyes and ears of the Prime Minister in Westminster), the Prime Minister's Office and advisors, commissions and committees of enquiry, Whitehall staff, the media, and friends. Modern leaders are lost if they surround themselves with 'yes men' (and women). They need friends and advisors to speak their mind.

- The media can be a powerful critic of the Prime Minister. Douglas-Home, Wilson, Heath, and Major were weakened by a hostile press.

- Senior Cabinet figures attract political limelight and represent the country abroad.

- The Prime Minister's Office is relatively small – about 35 compared with the American President's 400.

Prime Ministerial Government

Arguments for prime ministerial government are found in John Mackintosh's *The British Cabinet*, and Richard Crossman's introduction to the 1960 edition of Bagehot's *The English Constitution*.[1] Both claim that the Prime Minister is now so powerful that the office is more like that of a president. In prime ministerial government, the PM and close personal friends and allies make most of the important decisions. The key Cabinet committees under prime ministerial control, or the 'kitchen cabinet', are the centres of power, so the Cabinet often acts merely as a rubber stamp, and may not even be consulted about some matters. At the same time, the Prime Minister may intervene in the business of individual ministries while directing the flow of government information and dominating relations between the Cabinet and the wider world.

Cabinet Government

<table>
<tr><td>Key term</td></tr>
<tr><td>Cabinet government – the theory that the cabinet, not the prime minister, forms a collective political executive which constrains the power of the prime minister to the role of 'first among equals'.</td></tr>
</table>

This school of thought argues that, while Prime Ministers are subject to few formal constitutional constraints, the political system limits their power and ensures that the Cabinet forms a collective political executive. In the short run, Prime Ministers may be formidable, but in the long run they depend upon Cabinet and Party support, and most important matters will have to be agreed by Cabinet. Since the power of the Cabinet rests upon the support of the majority party in the House of Commons, it must, to some extent, reflect the political complexion of the Commons. This, in turn, places constraints on the power of both the PM and the Cabinet, and ensures a degree of accountability of the political executive to the majority party in the Commons.

Cabinet or Prime Ministerial Government?

There is no question that the British Prime Minister holds one of the most powerful political offices in the Western world, particularly as it operated with Margaret Thatcher. What is not clear, however, is whether there is a general trend towards prime ministerial government, or whether there is a tendency to swing between Cabinet and prime ministerial government. Strong Prime Ministers, such as Churchill, Macmillan and Thatcher, have often been followed by weaker ones, like Eden, Douglas-Home and Major. It is difficult to discern general trends amid so many changing conditions. In addition, relations between the Prime Minister and

---

[1] J. Mackintosh, *The British Cabinet* (London: Stevens, 1962); R. Crossman, 'Introduction' to W. Bagehot, *The English Constitution* (London: Fontana, 1963)

Cabinet members are largely secret, so that it is difficult to know what has really gone on. Certainly, there is no agreement among Government members, at least in their public pronouncements. Briefing 8.7 presents some views, but perhaps it is an unresolvable controversy. This is one reason why political scientists have turned to a different way of approaching the issue, using the concept of the 'core executive'.

BRIEFINGS

8.7 THE CONTROVERSY ABOUT PRIME MINISTERIAL OR CABINET GOVERNMENT: SOME VIEWS

... it is no exaggeration to declare that the British Premiership has turned not into a British version of the American presidency, but into an authentically British presidency.

M. Foley, 'Presidential Politics in Britain', *Talking Politics* 6(3) (1994), p. 141

Cabinet does not make all the decisions but it does make all the major ones, and it sets the broad framework within which more detailed policies are initiated and developed.

M. Burch, 'Prime Minister and Cabinet: An executive in transition', in R. Pyper and Robins (eds) *Governing the UK in the 1990s* (London: Macmillan, 1995), p. 103

The Prime Minister is the leading figure in the Cabinet whose voice carries most weight. But he is not the all-powerful individual which many have recently claimed him to be. His office has great potentialities, but the use made of them depends on many variables – the personality, the temperament, and the ability of the Prime Minister, what he wants to achieve and the methods he uses. It depends also on his colleagues, their personalities, temperaments and abilities, what they want to do and their methods.

G. W. Jones, 'The Prime Minister's Power, in A. King (ed) *The British Prime Minister* (London: Macmillan 1985), p. 216

...the present centralisation of power in the hands of one person has gone too far and amounts to a system of personal rule in the very heart of our parliamentary democracy.

Tony Benn, 'The Case for a Constitutional Premiership', in A. King (ed) *The British Prime Minister* (London: Macmillan, 1985), p.22

The Prime Minister leads, guides and supports his team, but relies upon their energies and expertise, just as they in turn rely upon his leadership ... The relationship is subtle and variable, but essentially it is one of mutual reliance. A strong Prime Minister needs strong ministers.

S. James, *British Cabinet Government* (London: Routledge, 1992), pp. 133–34

... the way departments engage with the centre can be much more open and fluid than in a strictly hierarchical system of government with a heavy centre and weaker departments. The more I've been here, the clearer it's become to me that cabinet government is a reality; let's say that the power of departments and departmental ministers is strong ... this is a huge plus in the system because it creates a plurality at the centre of government that is vital. I should perhaps add that this is the way this Prime Minister, in particular, likes to work and it very much places weight on the views of his cabinet colleagues. He's a conciliator and therefore goes with the grain of the system of cabinet government, rather than against it.

1993 interview with senior civil servant, quoted in C. Campbell and G. K. Wilson, *The End of Whitehall* (Oxford: Blackwell, 1995)

THE CORE EXECUTIVE

Some political scientists, frustrated by the endless debate about Cabinet versus Prime Ministerial government, point out that both are embedded in a network of relations with other influential bodies and people. This network at the apex of power is called 'the core executive'. It consists of the Prime Minister and the Cabinet and the individuals and organisations that circle closely around them. Specifically, the core executive includes:

- the Prime Minister, senior members and advisors of the PM's Office, and the 'kitchen cabinet';
- the inner Cabinet of most important ministers;
- cabinet committees;
- the Cabinet and senior members of the Cabinet Office;
- the most senior civil servants in some Whitehall departments, notably the Treasury, the Foreign Office, the Home Office and the Lord Chancellor's Department.

The advantage of focusing on the core executive is that it extends analysis beyond the old concerns about PM and Cabinet to a large network of power relations in Westminster and Whitehall.

The core executive is not fixed, but changes according to circumstances. During the Falklands and Gulf Wars it included top military leaders, but in peace time they are probably excluded. The difficulty, therefore, is knowing exactly who it includes in general or at any particular time. Should the Chief Whip and chairs of the backbencher committees of Parliament be included? Are all Cabinet committees 'core', or only the most important ones? How many individuals in the Cabinet Office and the PM's Office are included? If the 'core executive' changes according to circumstances, is there any such thing as the core executive at all, and are we back to identifying the PM and Cabinet as the 'inner core' with a constantly shifting 'outer core' circling around it? These questions perhaps reflect the shifting and ambiguous nature of power relations at the top of British government. But they need to be answered before the new concept can work as anything more than a recognition of this shifting ambiguous nature.

SUMMARY

- There is no question but that the British Prime Minister has considerable power. Absence of formal rules, a centralised political system, and a series of strong Prime Ministers since 1940 (at least) has led to an accumulation of power in the office.
- Nor is there much doubt that the Cabinet can be a powerful body. It reasserted its power over Thatcher in 1990, and it is not a factor which even an authoritative leader like Tony Blair can easily ignore.

- An effective political executive rests upon the three principles of Cabinet collegiality, departmental autonomy, and prime ministerial authority. If these are unbalanced, the system will not work effectively.

- The power of the Prime Minister relative to the Cabinet has swung substantially over time. Thatcher started in a more collegial mode than she ended, as may also happen with Blair. Strong Prime Ministers have quite often been succeeded by weaker ones.

- Consequently, there is much evidence to support both the theory of prime ministerial government and of Cabinet government, and the view that the system seems to shift between them. This is illustrated by the Milestones in postwar relationships between the two.

MILESTONES

MILESTONES IN RELATIONS BETWEEN PRIME MINISTER AND CABINET

1940–45 Wartime emergency gives Churchill great powers as Prime Minister. The modern Cabinet committee system created

1945–51 Attlee (deputy Prime Minister under Churchill) continues as a strong leader

1951 Churchill's short-lived experiment with a Cabinet of 16 'overlords'

1962 Macmillan's 'night of the long knives' in which he sacks a third of his Cabinet

1964 Wilson creates a Political Office in 10 Downing Street. Ministers allowed their own special advisors

1970 Central Policy Review Staff (CPRS) created by Heath to help Cabinet work. Superministries created: the Department of Trade and Industry, and the Department of the Environment

1974 Wilson sets up PM's Policy Unit

1975 Collective responsibility suspended during the EC referendum

1977 Collective responsibility again suspended over the issue of the voting system to be used in EC elections

1983 Thatcher abolishes the CPRS
Cabinet Secretary becomes head of the Civil Service

1986 Heseltine resigns from Cabinet claiming that Thatcher kept the Westland helicopter issue off the agenda

1989 Thatcher shuffles 62 government positions
Lawson (the Chancellor of the Exchequer) resigns

from government, criticising Thatcher's leadership and her use of economic advisors

1990 Sir Geoffrey Howe resigns from the Cabinet, criticising Thatcher's leadership. Thatcher's domination of government contributes to her downfall

1990 Major replaces Thatcher as PM and introduces a more collegial style of Cabinet government

1994 Michael Portillo ignores the principle of collective Cabinet responsibility with criticisms of the government's EU policy

1996 Reports (*The Times*, 11 November 1996) that the Major Government planned to use the Civil Service to promote its policies. Plans withdrawn when Cabinet secretary, Sir Robin Butler, objected. A few days later another *Times* report claims that the government was using the Civil Service to draw attention to Labour spending plans

1994–97 Principle of collective responsibility applied to the Labour Shadow Cabinet

1997 Major's apparent weakness as PM contributes to the Conservatives losing the election

1997 Blair's new Cabinet includes a predominance of strong party notables but marked by consensus on central policies

1997 John Prescott, Labour Deputy Prime Minister, groups Environment, Transport and Regions under his own control

1. Do we have prime ministerial or Cabinet government in Britain?

2. Discuss the claim that Thatcher's period in office offers clear evidence of prime ministerial government while Major's period offers clear evidence of Cabinet government.

3. Is it correct to call the British political system an 'elective dictatorship'?

4. What do you understand by the principles of Cabinet collegiality, departmental autonomy, and prime ministerial authority? Is a balance between them essential for effective government?

PROJECTS

1. Select any three postwar British Prime Ministers and compare their style and effectiveness in office.

2. Read a good daily paper every day for the next two weeks and take notes on what it reveals about Cabinet government in Britain.

- Quite possibly the issue of which dominates will never be decided, if only because Cabinet and governments try to keep their inner relationships secret.

- Some political scientists have stopped contrasting prime ministerial and Cabinet government and developed the concept of the core executive. This is useful because it draws attention to a wider network of power relations in Whitehall and Westminster. Its disadvantage is the difficulty in identifying exactly who is a member of the core executive, either in general or at any particular time.

FURTHER READING

S. James, *British Cabinet Government* (London: Routledge, 1992) has general chapters on the Prime Minister and the Cabinet, while Anthony King (ed.), *The British Prime Minister* (London: Macmillan, 2nd edn 1985) contains a very useful set of readings. The chapter by A. King on 'Cabinet co-ordination or prime ministerial dominance', in I. Budge and D. McKay (eds), *The Developing British Political System: The 1990s* (London: Longman, 1993) lays out the argument about Cabinet collegiality, department autonomy, and prime ministerial authority. A collection of articles on the core executive is contained in R.A.W. Rhodes and Patrick Dunleavy (eds), *Prime Minister, Cabinet and Core Executive* (London: Macmillan, 1995).

For shorter articles see M. Burch, 'Prime Minister and cabinet: An executive in transition', in R. Pyper and L. Robins (eds), *Governing the UK in the 1990s* (London: Macmillan, 1995); P. Dorey, 'Widened, yet Weakened: the changing character of collective responsibility', *Talking Politics*, 7(2), 1994/1995; and M. Foley, 'Presidential Politics in Britain', *Talking Politics*, 6(3), 1994.

http://www.awl-he.com/politics/newbritpol

Internet resources – visit *The New British Politics* Webpage for links to a specially-chosen selection of Internet resources relevant to this Chapter.

http://www.awl-he.com/politics/newbritpol

Ministries, ministers and mandarins: Central

Government in Britain

The top civil servants in Britain are sometimes referred to as 'mandarins', after the civil servants of ancient China, implying perhaps that they too are inscrutable and impermeable! It is this small number of very senior Whitehall civil servants who work closely with Government ministers in setting and implementing public policy. Relations between ministers and mandarins are crucial to the Government of the country. In theory ministers have the political function of making public policy, and mandarins the administrative task of advising on policy matters and implementing whatever ministers decide. In practice, it is impossible to draw such a clear distinction between the two tasks, which are much more tangled and complicated than this.

In fact, the relationship between ministers and mandarins raises all sorts of important issues which are the subject of this chapter: Can we draw a clear distinction between the political and policy-making functions of ministers, and the policy advice and administrative functions of mandarins? Should civil servants be responsible to the public or to Parliament, or should they be responsible only to their ministers? Should ministers be responsible for everything their civil servants do? Do civil servants, not ministers, run the country? Has the Civil Service become politicised?

This chapter examines:

- 'Whitehall': departments and ministries

- The role of ministers, and the nature of ministerial responsibility

- 'Mandarins' and their role in government

- Policy making and administration in the ministries

- The power of the 'mandarinate'

- The alleged politicisation of the Civil Service

BRIEFINGS

9.1 PERSONNEL AND PROCEDURES OF BRITISH CENTRAL ADMINISTRATION

Ministers. The 80 or 90 most senior Government members, consisting of the Prime Minister, Cabinet ministers, ministers of state, and parliamentary undersecretaries.

Ministerial responsibility. The principle that ministers are responsible to Parliament for their own and their department's actions. In theory ministers take responsibility for administrative failure in their department, and for any individual injustice it may cause, whether they are personally responsible or not.

Civil servant. A servant of the Crown (in effect, the Government) who is employed in a civilian capacity (i.e. not members of the armed forces), and who is paid for wholly and directly from central government funds (not by local government, nationalised industries, or quangos).

Mandarins. A term given to the thousand or so top civil servants who have regular, personal contact with ministers and act as policy advisors.

Osmotherly Rules. A set of rules for the guidance of officials appearing before House of Commons select committees and designed to protect the principle of civil service impartiality, anonymity and secrecy.

The Armstrong Memorandum. The official statement on the duties and responsibilities of civil servants, including their role in relationship to ministers.

Mandarin power. The theory that top civil servants exert a powerful influence over government policy making because of their ability, experience, expertise, training, and special knowledge. One version of the theory claims that civil servants, not ministers, run the country.

DEPARTMENTS AND MINISTRIES

The central administration of Britain (see Briefing 9.1), like that of almost all other countries, is organised into separate departments or ministries (there is no real distinction between the two). There are about 70 of these, mostly headed by non-Cabinet ministers. Seventeen of the major ministries are headed by Cabinet ministers (Table 9.1).[1]

---

[1] Environment, transport and the regions have been made a single ministry under John Prescott, the Deputy Prime Minister. It is not clear how far an administrative amalgamation has taken place, however, so they are shown separately in the table.

Plate 9.1 Aerial view of Whitehall looking towards Houses of Parliament

Plate 9.1 Aerial view of Whitehall looking towards Houses of Parliament

Both the number and nature of ministries may change, just as Cabinet posts change, when the government reorganises departments. National Heritage, for example, was created in 1992, and in 1988 the functions of the Department of Employment were split between the then Departments of Education and Science (DES), the Department of Trade and Industry (DTI) and the Department of the Environment (DoE).

The most important department is the Treasury, because it manages the national economy and controls the spending of other government departments. Its annual expenditure surveys and other reviews thus provide an opportunity to co-ordinate departmental activities across the board, and enforce general government policies. Co-ordination is limited, however, because the Treasury regards its role in narrow terms as containing expenditure, rather than concerning itself with the substantive merits of policy. Instead, each department tends to push its own priorities, and final decisions are made through a process of advocacy and pressure through a hierarchy of committees.

Ministries are sometimes conglomerates of responsibility which have grown up rather haphazardly. The most obvious example of this is the Home Office, which

Table 9.1 The major
departments and ministries
of Central Government

Department/Ministry	Functions	Budget (£ billions)	Staff
Treasury	Management of the national economy, budget allocations to departments		2,850
Defence (MoD)	Defence	23.8	139,500
Social Security (DSS)	Welfare, security benefits	61.2	78,000
Transport	Transport	6.8	15,000
Home Office	Justice, police, prisons, law and order, public safety	6.0	50,000
Lord Chancellor's Department	Law, the courts	3.6	11,600
Trade and Industry (DTI)	Trade and industrial policy, technology, research and development	1.7	11,400
Foreign and Commonwealth Office (FCO)	Foreign policy	1.4	10,000
Agriculture	Food, agriculture, fisheries	2.3	9,800
Environment (DoE)	Housing, environment, local government, urban problems, cities	41.2	8,200
Scottish Office	Scotland	12.7	6,200
Health	Health	28.3	4,800
Education and Employment	Education, science policy, employment	7.0	2,700
Welsh Office	Wales	6.0	2,400
Northern Ireland Office	Northern Ireland	6.6	206
Law Officers Department (Attorney General in England and Wales; Lord Advocate in Scotland)	Criminal law enforcement, government legal advice, representation of the Crown in major court cases	2.4	44
Culture, Media and Sport	Heritage, arts, media, sport	1.0	206

has retained all the activities of Government that have not been hived off into specialist ministries. Even the Home Office is primarily concerned with public order, however. More recently created ministries like Transport and Social Security are clearly focused on one policy area.

This focus contributes to the development of the 'departmental view' already noted as contributing to the clash of views and adversarial nature of decision making in British administration. Clearly, having a department narrowly charged with advancing one particular concern – roads, environment, health – does mean that it will want to push particular areas and interests. Moreover, contacts between civil servants, specialists and affected interests will mean it develops strong views over how this is best done.

Advancing one concern means that there will be fewer resources for others. Thus there are often clashes of interest between the 'spending' ministries over which should have priority. These are compounded when one ministry's priorities directly conflict with another: new roads have a negative effect on the environment, for example. As one ministry cannot have total jurisdiction over what is to be done, it has to negotiate or fight with others through a series of Civil Service and ministerial committees, right up to the Cabinet if necessary.

Potential conflicts are not confined to relations between ministries, but may also involve different groups within a ministry. An obvious cleavage is between the ministry itself and the executive agencies to which its work has been increasingly hived off under the 'Next Steps' initiative of the Thatcher governments. We consider this in Chapter 10.

There may also be conflict between the minister(s), the political head of the department, representing the party and Government in power, and the civil servants running the ministry. These civil servants may be nonpartisan and expected to be impartial, but what if government or ministerial priorities run counter to long-standing and deeply held 'departmental views' about policy?

Much of this chapter is concerned with what happens in such a case and in the parallel one of where the 'departmental view' has been taken over by the policies of one government and one party.

Before coming to these questions it is useful to consider:

- the general structure of ministries and departments;

- the enormous dependence created by this structure of politicians on civil servants, a dependence which is perhaps unique to Britain.

The structure of ministries

Each major department is run by a minister or secretary of state, who usually holds a Cabinet seat. To try to keep pace with the huge increase in government work, further layers of ministers and government officials have developed, as follows:

- About 30 ministers of state who are usually responsible for specific aspects of their department's work.

- About 30 parliamentary undersecretaries of state. Ministers of state and parliamentary undersecretaries are known collectively as 'junior ministers'.

- About 45 private parliamentary secretaries (PPSs) who are the general assistants of ministers (not undersecretaries). They hold unpaid parliamentary positions, not department ones.

The more important the department, the more ministers, junior ministers and PPSs it has. The Treasury has two Cabinet seats and more than 15 junior ministers, but the Welsh Office has just one of each. See Figure 9.1 for the structure of a typical department.

These political appointees, ministers and junior ministers, are superimposed on a hierarchy of civil servants. Normally the minister will deal even with the upper civil servants in the ministry through his or her private secretary (a younger, up and coming civil servant appointed to organise the minister's administrative schedule) and the permanent head of the ministry. The Civil Service is now less hierarchical than it was in the 1980s, because of the unresolved and often ambiguous relationships between the executive agencies and their sponsoring ministries, which we discuss below. The importance of the work done by agencies such as the Prisons' Agency in the Home Office means that their chief executive officer may be as important a figure as the permanent secretary.

However, as far as the actual ministry is concerned, the latter is the head who organises and channels contacts between the minister and other civil servants.

Key term

Ministers – the 80 or 90 most senior government members consisting of the prime minister, cabinet ministers (22–26 people), ministers of state (about 28), and parliamentary under-secretaries (about 33).

Key term

Junior ministers – ministers of state and parliamentary under-secretaries.

Figure 9.1 The structure of a typical 'Whitehall' department/ministry

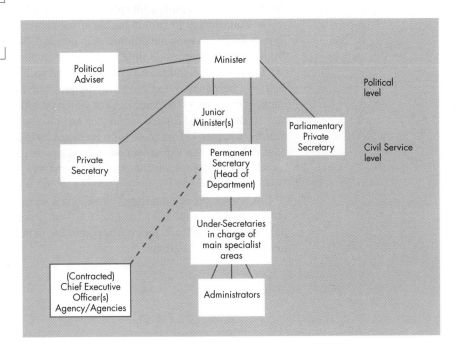

Ministers and civil servants

British ministers are, in fact, dependent on career civil servants to a degree that is unusual in Western democracies, where political heads bring in a whole train of personal advisers with them. Civil servants organise the minister's day as they compile the appointments diary, write letters to be signed by the minister, speeches for the minister to give, draft replies to parliamentary questions, arrange transport and meetings, and meet ministers' more political needs as well as implementing their decisions as the heads of the department. They will even brief the minister on what is politically expedient, going so far, in the case of the Westland Affair (1986), as to leak confidential papers to the press in order to discredit their minister's Cabinet opponent. Only the most overtly partisan activities of the minister, such as giving a speech to a party conference, are outside the responsibilities of career civil servants.

All top politicians rely heavily on their support staff in the Civil Service but in Britain they have almost no control over the selection of their civil servants. The tradition has been that new ministers should try to work with the civil servants they inherit, with a qualified right to choose among unknown candidates for posts in their private office. Only if 'things don't work out' is a minister able to demand a change, and each minister is unlikely to be able to demand more than one change. Of course, new ministers will have one or more political colleagues in the shape of the junior ministers, but these will be as inexpert in the ministry's work as the ministers themselves and equally dependent on civil servants. One private political adviser, if present, is not likely to make much headway against a large number of civil servants with specialised knowledge.

The bureaucracy in Britain has therefore enjoyed something much closer to a monopoly on advising the politicians in power than is the case in other countries. British political parties do little to turn their campaign policies into specific policy. Little has changed since Crossman[2] noted with dismay in 1964 that the file at Labour's headquarters on one of its longest standing commitments was almost empty. 'Think tanks' (outside centres which provide policy advice) are relatively new to Britain, and limited in number and resources. Parliamentary select committees (Chapter 18) are more to be managed and ignored than used as sources of advice. Thus, when British ministers need advice on how to handle the problems for which they are responsible, there is almost nowhere they can get it outside the Civil Service.

This makes the relationship between civil servants and ministers crucial, not only in running a ministry but also for their general role in government, since politicians' dependence on civil servants for policy advice extends far beyond purely departmental affairs.

[2] Richard Crossman, *The Diaries of a Cabinet Minister*, Vol. 1 (London: Hamilton and Cape, 1975)

MINISTERIAL ROLES AND RESPONSIBILITY

Politicians' structural dependence on civil servants is reinforced by their incredibly busy and crowded schedule. There is just not much time to seek out alternative sources of advice. Indeed, time is probably lacking even to assimilate the flow of information that comes from the Civil Service.

In an average day a minister may meet with his or her officials to talk about departmental matters, attend a press meeting, travel to a public function, be briefed about parliamentary business, receive a deputation from the public, attend a political meeting or an evening or late night sitting of the House of Commons, and then work on a dispatch box of papers to be read for an early start the next day. Ministers must also attend Cabinet and Cabinet committee meetings, receive officials from abroad, travel to Brussels and to their parliamentary constituencies, and attend Party meetings. During the year there will be special journeys abroad, the Party conference, and departmental and other emergencies to attend to.

The daily workload of a minister is varied and crushingly heavy because it involves many different activities:

- *Administration.* Ministers are involved in the executive administration of their departments, among the largest organisations in the country.

- *Policy making.* Ministers set the policy of their department and are involved in general government policy making in the Cabinet and its committees. They are involved in many meetings with other ministers whose business overlaps with their own, and they have to fight for their department and its resources in the Cabinet.

- *Politics.* Ministers are accountable to Parliament, and attend its sessions to answer questions, speak in debates, vote, and pilot legislation through Parliament. They have party functions to attend and constituencies to nurse.

- *Public relations.* Ministers meet the media regularly to explain departmental policy and further their own careers. They keep up a demanding schedule of travel around the country to dinners, conferences, meetings, and openings of various kinds. They meet deputations from interest groups, and receive a huge volume of mail.

- *The EU.* Ministers read mountains of documents, attend innumerable meetings, and travel thousands of miles on EU business.

In spite of these back-breaking demands, ministers are amateurs with no special background or training for their jobs. They are very largely drawn from the approximately 350–400 people who happen to get elected to Parliament for the majority party. If their party has been in opposition for some time they may have no experience of government or Whitehall when appointed to their post. None of the current Labour Cabinet, for example, has served in Cabinet or in their departments before.

Moreover, ministers spend little time in one department before being moved in a government reshuffle. On average they spend two years in one job before switching to another. Between 1945 and 1992 there were 24 ministers of education. One of them, Kenneth Clarke, was Chancellor of the Duchy of Lancaster, and Secretary for Health and then Education, and Home Secretary, within a six-year period, before becoming Chancellor of the Exchequer in 1993, a post he then held until 1997. It is said to take over a year to master the work of a department, and at least another to have any sort of impact on it.

Ministerial responsibility

Key term
Ministerial responsibility – the principle whereby ministers are responsible to parliament for their own and all their department's actions. In theory ministers are responsible for administrative failure in their department, and for any injustice it may cause, whether personally responsible or not.

Ministers are responsible to Parliament (see Briefing 9.2), and can be forced to resign if they or their departments perform badly. According to convention they bear responsibility for administrative failure in their departments, for any injustices it may cause, and for general policy failures, whether or not they are personally responsible. In theory, ministers are responsible for everything that goes on in their departments. The classic example is the famous Crichel Down affair of 1954 when the Minister of Agriculture, Sir Thomas Dugdale, resigned because of departmental maladministration about which he knew nothing.

In practice, however, ministerial responsibility does not always work this way. Since the Second World War no minister has resigned because of Civil Service mistakes. Table 9.2 shows that most ministers resign for personal reasons (sex scandals or drunken driving) or because of an error in their ministerial role (the

BRIEFINGS

9.2 MINISTERIAL RESPONSIBILITY

The individual responsibility of ministers for the work of their departments means that they are answerable to Parliament for all their department's activities. They bear the consequences for any failure in administration, any injustice to an individual or any aspect of a policy which may be criticised in Parliament, whether personally or not.

Central Office of Information, *The British System of Government* (HMSO: London, 1994), p. 42

The evidence of this study destroys the Crichel Down Affair as the key example of ministerial responsibility. The true convention regarding ministerial resignations is hang on for as long as you can. How long a minister can hang on depends upon his or her stock of political capital.

Keith Dowding, *The Civil Service* (London: Routledge, 1995), p. 169

Year	Minister	Cause of resignation
1982	Nicholas Fairbairn (Solicitor-General for Scotland)	Personal life and handling of a departmental matter
1982	Lord Carrington (Foreign Secretary) Humphrey Atkins (Lord Privy Seal) Richard Luce (Minister of State, Foreign Office)	Failure to take due note of warnings that Argentina was planning a Falklands invasion
1985	Cecil Parkinson (Transport Secretary)	Personal life, the Sara Keays affair
1986	Leon Brittan (Secretary of Trade and Industry)	Leaking official documents about the sale of Westland helicopters
1986	Michael Heseltine (Defence Secretary)	Disagreement with Cabinet over sale of Westland helicopters
1988	Edwina Currie (Undersecretary of State, Health)	Claimed (correctly) that British eggs are infected with salmonella and forced to resign
1990	Patrick Nicholls (Undersecretary of State, Environment)	Drunken driving
1992	David Mellor (National Heritage Minister)	Personal life and acceptance of hospitality from businessmen lobbying government
1993	Norman Lamont (Chancellor)	Withdrawal of pound from European Monetary System
1993	Michael Mates (Minister of State, Northern Ireland)	Relations with Asil Nadir, business man who jumped bail in a fraud trail
1994	Tim Yeo (Minister of State, Environment)	Personal life and illegitimate child
1994	Lord Caithness (Minister of State, Transport)	Personal life
1994	Tim Smith (Undersecretary of State, Northern Ireland)	Accepted cash for asking parliamentary questions
1994	Neil Hamilton (Undersecretary, Corporate Affairs)	Cash for questions
1995	Allan Stewart (Undersecretary, Scotland)	Waving pickaxe at antiroad demonstrators
1995	Charles Wardle (Undersecretary, Industry and Energy)	Opposition to government's immigration policy
1995	Robert Hughes (Parliamentary Secretary)	Personal life
1996	David Willetts (Parliamentary Secretary)	Secretly directing Conservative members of Privileges Committee when he was a Whip

Table 9.2 Some ministerial resignations and their causes

Falklands in 1982, or salmonella in 1988). Even the much-quoted precedent of Crichel Down can be explained in terms of the minister losing backbench support, rather than taking responsibility for Civil Service errors. There are many more recent examples of ministers hanging on to their posts, in spite of departmental failures. To take just one small policy area as an example – that of prison escapes – we find four recent cases of ministers refusing to take responsibility for departmental failures: in 1983 (Secretary of State for Northern Ireland, James Prior), 1991 (Home Secretary, Kenneth Baker) and 1994 and 1995 (Home Secretary, Michael Howard).

There are four main reasons why the convention of ministerial responsibility is not always followed in practice.

1. Ministers cannot possibly know everything about their huge departments or be held responsible for every one of its actions. It is estimated that they usually know about little more than 1 per cent of departmental matters.

2. While ministers are supposed to resign because of 'failure' or 'injustice', or 'criticism' in Parliament, these are difficult terms to define. Besides, ministers are continuously criticised in Parliament.

3. A minister who should resign may be protected by his or her Cabinet colleagues for political reasons, though in different circumstances the same minister might be sacrificed to public opinion. Sometimes governments make a political gesture and find a scapegoat, and sometimes they close ranks to protect themselves.

4. The creation of Whitehall agencies with a degree of independence from ministers (Chapter 10) makes it more difficult to distinguish between the policy failures of ministers and the bureaucratic failures of agencies. Both sides can blame the other.

As a result, the convention of ministerial responsibility is vague, and mainly results in resignation where ministers have lost the support of their government colleagues and/or their party backbenchers.

THE CIVIL SERVICE ROLE

Key term

Mandarins – the comparatively small number (about a thousand) of very senior civil servants who have close and regular contact with ministers in their capacity as policy advisers.

Ministers and junior ministers are politicians who set public policy and direct the Whitehall departments. Most departmental work, however, is carried out by the army of permanent civil servants who range from porters and filing clerks to a thin layer of exceptionally able and experienced civil servants at the top of the bureaucratic hierarchy. In this chapter we concentrate on the comparatively small number of very senior 'mandarins' who have close and regular personal contact with ministers and act as their policy advisers. There are about a thousand of them, barely 0.2 per cent of all civil servants in the country.

While most ministers are elected politicians who hold their posts for a short time, civil servants are permanent, appointed servants of the Crown. Their role has four main features: impartiality, anonymity, permanence, and secrecy. (See Briefing 9.3 for quotes on Civil Service impartiality and anonymity.)

1. *Impartiality*. Civil servants must serve their political masters – their ministers – and be strictly impartial about party politics and ministerial policies. Therefore, ministers must not ask civil servants to perform political tasks, and civil servants must not enter the political fray. Appointments and promotion in the civil service should not involve political considerations, or be affected by a change of government. According to the Osmotherly Rules (after Edward Osmotherly, the civil servant who wrote them) Commons committees must not ask civil servants 'questions in the field of political controversy'.

Key term

Civil service impartiality – the principle whereby civil servants should be politically neutral and serve their cabinet ministers regardless of which party is in power and of what they may personally feel about their minister's policies.

Key term

Civil service anonymity – civil servants are the confidential advisers of ministers and must not be asked questions about politically controversial matters or the policy advice they give.

Key term

Osmotherly rules – a set of rules, named after their author, Edward Osmotherly of the Civil Service Department, for the guidance of civil servants appearing before Commons Select Committees and designed to protect civil service impartiality, anonymity, and secrecy.

BRIEFINGS

9.3 CIVIL SERVICE IMPARTIALITY AND ANONYMITY

In the determination of policy the civil servant has no constitutional responsibility or role distinct from that of the minister. It is the civil servant's duty ... to give the minister honest and impartial advice, without fear or favour, and whether the advice accords with the minister's views or not ... When, having been given all the relevant information and advice, the minister has taken a decision, it is the duty of civil servants loyally to carry out the decision with precisely the same energy and good will, whether they agree with it or not.
HMSO, *Civil Servants and Ministers: Duties and Responsibilities* (London: HMSO, 1986), pp. 7–8

The civil service as such has no constitutional personality or responsibility separate from the duly constituted Government of the day... The duty of the individual civil servant is first and foremost to the Minister of the Crown who is in charge of the department in which he or she is serving.
The Armstrong Memorandum, *Civil Service Management Code*, Issue 1 (London: HMSO, 1993), paras 3–4.
(Sir Robert Armstrong was Cabinet Secretary 1979–88, and Head of the Civil Service 1981–88)

Although my generation of civil servants has been brought up to regard every act taken by an official as an act in the name of the Minister, our successors may ... have to be prepared to defend in public and possibly without the shield of ministerial protection, the acts they take.
Sir D. Wass, 'The public sector in modern society', *Public Administration*, 61(1) (1983), p. 12
(Sir Douglas Wass was Permanent Secretary at the Treasury 1974–83 and Joint Head of the Civil Service 1981–83)

2. *Anonymity*. Civil servants are anonymous. The Osmotherly Rules state that parliamentary committees must not ask questions about the conduct of particular civil servants or about the advice they give to ministers.

3. *Permanence*. Unlike the system in many other countries, top British civil servants do not change with a change of government. Impartiality and anonymity should mean they can serve whichever party is in power.

4. *Secrecy*. Civil servants sign the Official Secrets Act and their advice to ministers is secret.

Events in the 1980s and 1990s, however, suggest that these principles are under pressure to change.

- *Impartiality and the Tisdall Affair*. In 1983, the civil servant Sarah Tisdall was sentenced at the Old Bailey to six months in prison for leaking information about the arrival of Cruise missiles at Greenham Common. She believed the Defence Secretary was avoiding ministerial accountability. Her case raises the question as to whether the Civil Service should carry out all ministerial directives, even those they feel are morally or legally dubious. Is their first duty to the public interest, or to their minister?

- *The Ponting Affair*. Clive Ponting was a civil servant who was prosecuted in 1985 for releasing secret information suggesting that the battleship Belgrano was sunk during the Falklands War for political reasons and not for military ones, as the government claimed. He argued that civil servants have a duty to the pubic interest which might, under certain circumstances, require them to 'go public'. The judge instructed the jury to find him guilty, on the grounds that ministers should judge what is in the public interest, but the jury acquitted him.

- *The Arms to Iraq Affair*. The Scott inquiry into the 'arms to Iraq' affair (where the Conservative government had secretly relaxed the rules on exporting arms to Iraq) found that ministers had asked civil servants to help them misinform Parliament and the public, and that civil servants seemed to have colluded with them.

- *Anonymity*. An inquiry into the collapse of Vehicle and General Insurance in 1971 placed the blame on named officials. An inquiry following the Westland affair in 1986 criticised five named officials for their role in leaking a letter, and another, Sir Robert Armstrong, the Cabinet Secretary, for failing to take disciplinary action against them. In recent times, the anonymity of civil servants has been increasingly difficult to maintain, as the media, political memoirs, and official inquiries have publicised Civil Service and ministerial conduct.

- *Permanence*. Civil servants are also now less permanent than they used to be. The chief executive officers in charge of executive agencies are on fixed-term contracts.

In sum, the role of the civil servant is becoming decreasingly clear. Like ministerial responsibility, theory and practice are different things, and the practice seems to be changing under the pressures of modern government. The same is true of the theory and practice of policy making and administration.

POLICY-MAKING AND ADMINISTRATION

In theory, ministers are the elected politicians who make public policy; civil servants provide policy advice and carry out ministerial decisions. Civil servants 'are on tap, but not on top', as the saying goes. In practice, it is impossible to draw a clear distinction between policy and administration. First, policy inevitably involves administrative questions. For example, the poll tax, whether or not it was a good idea in principle to change local government taxation from a property to a personal basis, was exceedingly difficult and expensive to implement and might have been rejected on administrative grounds alone. Second, administration often involves important policy issues. A series of administrative decisions about how to run a programme can easily affect the goals it is supposed to achieve. Toughening up security in prisons, for example, can easily subvert their educational and reformative role.

Consequently, the roles of ministers and their Whitehall staff are blurred. It is clear that ministers are the heads of departments, but they depend heavily on their civil servants for both policy and administrative advice and experience. Where the minister's job ends and the permanent secretary's begins is not at all clear. As Sir Humphrey, the caricature of the archetypal mandarin, says in the TV programme 'Yes Minister', with deliberate lack of clarity:

> I do feel that there is a real dilemma here, in that while it has been government policy to regard policy as the responsibility of ministers, and administration as the responsibility of officials, questions of administrative policy can cause confusion between the administration of policy and the policy of administration, especially where the responsibility for the administration of the policy of administration conflicts or overlaps with the responsibility for the policy of the administration of policy.[3]

The overlap of policy and administration is not just of theoretical interest. It has important implications for the power potential of Whitehall mandarins.

According to the German sociologist Max Weber, permanent officials, especially civil servants, hold the reins of power in the modern bureaucratic state. 'For the time being', he wrote, 'the dictatorship of the official, not that of the worker, is on the march'.[4] There are many arguments for and against this startling claim.

Key term

Mandarin power/the dictatorship of the official – the theory that no matter which party forms the government, civil servants will exert a powerful influence over government, or even control it, because of their ability, experience, and expertise.

---

[3] S. Lynn and A. Jay, *Yes Minister* (London: BBC, 1982), p. 176

[4] As quoted in H. H. Gerth and C. Wright-Mills, *From Max Weber* (London: Routledge and Kegan Paul, 1957), p. 50

For every argument in favour of mandarin power, there is another contradicting it (see Controversy). While they do not necessarily cancel each other out, it might be sensible to look for some evidence about the matter. The obvious place to search is the growing body of political memoirs of ministers who have personal experience of Whitehall (see Briefing 9.4). Unfortunately these are also inconclusive. Not only is the evidence anecdotal and patchy, but for every minister – Benn, Castle, Crossman – claiming that civil servants were unhelpful or obstructive, there is another – Wilson, Carrington, Heath, Healey – saying that they are professionals who can be controlled.

CONTROVERSY

MANDARIN OR MINISTERIAL POWER?

Mandarin Power

Numbers
There are about 1,000 civil servants with a direct input into the policy-making process compared with about 60 ministers and junior ministers.

Time
Civil servants are full-time; ministers divide their time between many activities.

Permanence and Experience
Civil servants are permanent; ministers are temporary; civil servants have many years' experience; ministers have few (if any).

Ability and Training
Top civil servants are exceptionally able and usually have excellent educational qualifications. Ministers are untrained and not selected for their educational qualifications.

Monopoly of Advice and Information
Ministers are heavily dependent upon their civil servants for policy advice. This is a uniquely British situation as elsewhere they take independent policy advisers in with them, as a matter of course.

Ministerial Power

The Boss
Numbers may not count for much when ministers can use their legitimate power to overrule civil servants.

Time is Not the Essence
It does not take a good minister long to come to grips with the essentials of policy decisions.

Permanence and Experience
Some ministers take charge of their department quickly: a few have a lot of government experience if their party has been in power for some time.

All Amateurs
Civil servants are generalists, not specialists, and have no more professional training for their job than ministers. Some ministers are exceptionally able.

Outside Advice
Ministers are not totally dependent upon civil servants or advice; they have their own (non-Civil Service) advisors, professionals, the Party, pressure groups, academics, and the media.

MANDARIN OR MINISTERIAL POWER? (continued)

Mandarin Power

Ministerial Power

Tricks of the Trade
Civil servants may use tricks of the trade: putting important documents at the bottom of the dispatch box; concealing major policy issues in long, complex reports; giving ministers little time for decisions; selective use of facts; getting other departments to intervene in matters of mutual interest.

Ministerial Experience
It does not take ministers long to learn these tricks and ways of countering them. They have tricks of their own, and may be able to make life difficult for noncompliant civil servants.

The Departmental View vs Vague Party Platforms
Departments have a comprehensive policy view; ministers have sketchy guidance from their Party manifesto.

Cabinet and Party Backing

Ministers can use the Party election manifesto and the weight of Cabinet opinion to force reluctant civil servants to accept a policy.

Civil Service Ambition
Those at the top of the Civil Service hierarchy are able and ambitious. Some ministers are weak, appointed because they can be controlled by Cabinet colleagues.

Personality
Ministers are not famous for being shy and uncertain; many have great ambition, confidence and force of character to drive their will.

Civil Service Empire Building
Civil servants are ambitious for their departments: they want to build empires.

Professional Ethos
The Civil Service has a strong and well-developed ethos or ethic of serving ministers to their best ability.

BRIEFINGS

9.4 MINISTERIAL VS MANDARIN POWER: INSIDER VIEWS

The trouble with the civil service is that it wants a quiet life. The civil servants want to move slowly along the escalator towards their knighthood and retirement and they have no interest whatsoever in trying to develop new lines of activity.

Tony Benn, *Out of the Wilderness, Diaries 1963–1967* (London: Arrow Books, 1987), p. 195

9.4 MINISTERIAL VS MANDARIN POWER: INSIDER VIEWS (continued)

I believe that civil servants like to be under ministerial control. There is nothing they dislike more than to have a minister whom they feel is weak, who does not know his mind and who wants to leave it all to them ... What they like is to have a minister who knows a policy he wants to pursue, who will take advice on the consequences of it, and how it can be implemented, who will carry sufficient weight in the Cabinet to see it through and who will have sufficient influence with the Chancellor of the Exchequer to get it financed.

Edward Heath, quoted in Peter Barberis (ed.), *The Whitehall Reader* (Buckingham: Open University Press, 1996), p. 83

Even at the ODM [Ministry of Overseas Development] I remember Andy Cohen, the Permanent Secretary, trying to wear me down. He used to come in on policy points and things like appointments. He would be in my office about seven times a day saying 'Minister, I know the ultimate decision is yours but I would be failing in my duty if I didn't tell you how unhappy your decision makes me'. Seven times a day. One person [the Minister] against the vast department.

Barbara Castle, *Mandarin Power*, quoted in Barberis, *op.cit.*, p. 66

I think the minister who complains that his civil servants are too powerful is either a weak minister or an incompetent one.

Denis Healey, quoted in Barberis, *op. cit.*, p. 81

I have always found British civil servants, anywhere in the higher reaches of the profession, to be models of what such men and women should be – intelligent, selfless, knowledgeable and fair minded ... they preserve, from my observation, both integrity and loyalty despite what must frequently be trying circumstances; and every Cabinet owes them a great deal.

Lord Carrington, quoted in Barberis, *op. cit.*, p. 81

Already I realise the tremendous effort it requires not to be taken over by the civil service. My Minister's room is like a padded cell ... there is a constant preoccupation to ensure that the Minister does what is correct.

Richard Crossman, *The Diaries of a Cabinet Minister*, Vol. 1 (London: Hamilton and Cape, 1975), pp. 21–2

If neither abstract argument nor concrete evidence from ministerial memoirs are conclusive, perhaps the most significant evidence is provided by developments under Thatcher and Major. Their governments reformed the Civil Service in fundamental ways and won big battles against determined opposition from some sections of Whitehall. This constitutes clear evidence that British civil servants can be brought under government control. Whatever may have been the case before, Whitehall mandarins were not 'on top' in the 1980s and early 1990s. On the contrary, civil servants of the time were severely criticised for being too compliant, even to the point of compromising their political neutrality.

POLITICISING THE CIVIL SERVICE?

Since the 1980s, indeed, the problem may be not that civil servants use their powers for their own purposes, but, on the contrary, that the Government has used civil servants for its own narrowly political purposes. Critics argue that under Thatcher the Civil Service became politically partial. There is some evidence for this view:

- A civil servant (Bernard Ingham) was used in the political job of the Prime Minister's Press Officer.

- The Cabinet Secretary, Sir Robert Armstrong, was used to defend the government policy of banning the publication of the book *Spycatcher* (which contained relevations about the security services) in an Australian court.

- Civil servants were used to leak a confidential document in the Westland affair.

- The Scott Inquiry into the Arms to Iraq affair suggests that civil servants were used to implement the Government's secret policy, and then to try to cover it up.

- Some civil servants may have been promoted and others blocked on political or ideological grounds rather than professional grounds. Mrs Thatcher was credited with always asking the question, 'Is he (or she) one of us?' in relation to appointments.

- Civil servants in the 1980s and 1990s may not always have given advice that conflicted with government policy, however sound such advice might have been, for fear it would affect their careers.

- Most senior civil servants now in post owe their positions to the Thatcher/Major governments, and may share their views, given Thatcher's preference for 'people like us'. This may be a difficulty for the Blair Government, though no problems materialised at the time of the government changeover in 1997.

Although there are many examples suggesting a certain politicisation of the Civil Service in the 1980s, it is also clear that much of the evidence is circumstantial and inconclusive. How can one tell whether civil servants have been cautious with advice, or told their ministers what they thought they wanted to hear? How can we know that some civil servants were promoted on political and ideological grounds, while others with the 'wrong' views were blocked? Secrecy and confidentiality make it difficult to draw any firm conclusions about the politicisation of the Civil Service, although circumstantial evidence suggests that it may well be a problem.

Concern about the issue built up from the mid-1980s onwards. In 1994, after much pressure, the Government accepted a formal Code of Ethics drafted by the

Treasury and Civil Service Select Committee. An appeals procedure was set up for civil servants who felt under pressure to compromise their political neutrality. It is not yet clear how effective this will be. Probably the smooth adjustment of civil servants to working for the Blair Government will sideline these concerns for the time being.

MILESTONES

MILESTONES IN RELATIONS BETWEEN MINISTERS AND MANDARINS IN THE POSTWAR PERIOD

1954 Crichel Down affair. Secretary of State for Agriculture, Sir Thomas Dugdale, resigns because of maladministration in his department. Later research suggests that he was forced from office because he lost backbench support

1955 Creation of junior minister posts (to fill in for ministers away from London)

1964 Junior ministers given specific departmental responsibilities.
Named Ministry of Aviation officials blamed for excessive profits paid in defence contracts to Ferranti Ltd for Bloodhound missiles

1968 Foreign Office officials named by Commons select committee for failure to pay British victims of the Nazis (the Sachsenhausen case)

1971 Collapse of Vehicle and General Insurance Co. A named civil servant is blamed, but the minister, John Davies, does not resign

1973 Cabinet Office sets up its European Secretariat to co-ordinate departmental policy on the EEC

1976 Publication of Osmotherly Rules for guidance of officials appearing before Commons select committees

1983 Departments of Trade and Industry amalgamated

1983 Sarah Tisdall jailed for leaking documents about the siting of Cruise missiles on Greenham Common

1984–85 Ponting trial. Clive Ponting had leaked documents which showed the political motives for sinking the Argentine cruiser, Belgrano, in the Falklands War with the loss of 700 lives

1985 Publication of the memorandum of Sir Robert Armstrong (the Cabinet Secretary) on the duties and responsibilities of civil servants

1986–87 Westland Helicopter affair. Colette Bowes, a civil servant, publicly identified for leaking a secret letter on the instruction of her minister, Sir Leon Brittan, who then resigned

1987 A revised version of the Armstrong Memorandum

1988 Department of Health split from Department of Health and Social Security. Department of Employment split between Departments of Education, Trade and Industry, and Environment

1992 Creation of National Heritage Department

1995–96 Controversy about Scott Report into the 'Arms for Iraq' affair (also known as the Matrix Churchill affair). The government had tried to suppress embarrassing information at the trial on grounds of 'national security'

1997 Smooth transfer of power from Conservatives to Labour after May general election

ESSAYS

1. Is ministerial responsibility a constitutional myth?

2. Are impartiality, anonymity, permanence and secrecy still the defining features of the civil servant's role?

3. Comment on the view that ministers make policy and mandarins give advice and administer.

4. Why is it important that ministers, not civil servants, have final control over public policy? Do they?

PROJECTS

1. Imagine that you are a permanent secretary in Whitehall and that your minister is about to implement a policy which you think unwise. Would you try to stop the minister and, if so, how?

2. What are the constitutional issues raised by the Tisdall, Ponting, Bowes, and Arms to Iraq cases, so far as the relations between ministers and civil servants are concerned?

3. Compare and contrast the way in which any two central departments work.

SUMMARY

- In British administrative theory, ministers are responsible for policy and civil servants for administration, but in practice no clear line can be drawn between policy and administration.

- In theory ministers are responsible to Parliament for their own actions and those of their departments and civil servants. In practice, the principle of ministerial responsibility is often breached.

- In theory civil servants are impartial, anonymous, permanent, and protected by secrecy. In practice all four features of the civil servant's role have been undermined in recent years.

- As a result, critics of the Whitehall system claim that the doctrines which are supposed to regulate ministerial and Civil Service behaviour are more mythical than real. They argue for clearer and firmer rules and procedures, including a more effective code of conduct for civil servants, a more effective appeals procedure for civil servants who feel misused by ministers, and (more controversially) a right for Commons select committees to question ministers and civil servants more closely about their work.

The old controversy about the extent of Civil Service power is unlikely to be resolved, although it is clear that politicians wielded the power in the 1980s and 1990s when the Thatcher and Major Governments implemented sweeping reforms of Whitehall. We consider these in the next chapter. Meanwhile our 'Milestones' chart relationships between ministers and their departments over the postwar period.

FURTHER READING

A good, short and general treatment of the Civil Service can be found in R. Pyper, *The Evolving Civil Service* (London: Longmans, 1991). A long but very readable book is P. Hennesy, *Whitehall* (London: Fontana, 1990), and a more advanced text is K. Dowding, *The Civil Service* (London: Routledge, 1995). S. James, *British Cabinet Government* (London: Routledge, 1992) has a chapter on 'Ministers and their departments'. For an excellent set of insider views on the relationships between ministers and mandarins see P. Barberis (ed.), *The Whitehall Reader* (Buckingham: Open University Press, 1996). The same book has a section on Civil Service loyalties, responsibilities and ethics. An excellent account of the decline of the Whitehall model based on extensive interviews is Colin Campbell and Graham K. Wilson, *The End of Whitehall: Death of a Paradigm* (Oxford: Blackwell, 1995). Labour's plans for Civil Service reform are outlined in Peter Mandelsen and Roger Liddley, *The Blair Revolution: Can New Labour Deliver?* (London and Boston: Faber, 1996).

Short articles include R. Pyper, 'A new model civil service', *Politics Review*, 2(2) (1992) and 'When they have to go ... why ministers resign', *Talking Politics*, 5(2) (1993); and K. Theakston, 'Ministers and mandarins', *Talking Politics*, 4(2) (1991/92).

The changing state:
administrative reforms

This chapter continues the discussion of the Civil Service in Britain, concentrating on the major reforms which have all but transformed the nature of British public administration over the last 20 years. Alternative models and critiques of the civil service are examined, as are the ways in which the Conservative governments from 1979 to 1997 used some of these ideas as a basis for major reforms. Costs and benefits are discussed, with a particular emphasis placed on public accountability and on the quality and efficiency of public services. A major consequence of the reforms of the 1980s has been the spread of what has been called 'quasi-government', that is, the increasing need, following privatisation and the scaling back of the state, for semi or quasi-autonomous bodies ('quangos') to oversee and regulate devolved and privatised industries, services and programmes. Discussion of quangos also raises crucial questions of accountability and control which are at the heart of modern democratic government.

This chapter therefore discusses:

- Models of British public administration

- Reforming the Civil Service: the Fulton Report

- The 1980s managerial revolution and 'Next Steps'

- The spread of quasi-government and rise of the quango

- Whether quangos can be both efficient and accountable.

MODELS OF BRITISH PUBLIC ADMINISTRATION

As we have seen, the traditional view of how British government *should* operate deviates greatly from how British government *actually* operates. The notion of individual ministerial responsibility has little application in practice; a genuinely impartial Civil Service is very difficult to achieve; civil servants often find them-

Key term

Administration – either (1) the process of co-ordinating and implementing public policy through the machinery of public administration or (2) another word for government – as in 'the Blair administration'.

selves in conflict between their own conceptions of the public interest and that represented by their political masters. These inconsistencies between theory and practice have prompted criticism that traditional ideas give at best an optimistic view of how government works, and at worst are simply false. Three competing conceptions of British public administration were current in the 1970s, one of which was to gain ascendancy over the others during the 1980s.

The traditional model and its critics

Following the Ponting affair in 1985 (when a civil servant leaked documents which showed that his minister was lying), the Cabinet Secretary, Sir Robert Armstrong, issued a 'Note of Guidance of Duties and Responsibilities of Civil Servants in Relation to Ministers'. In this he stated unequivocally that civil servants had no 'constitutional personality' and that their first and only responsibility was to their ministers. In other words they must do as they are told. There was no such thing as a 'departmental view'. Civil servants could not (or at least should not) dominate their ministers.

Most observers – and indeed most senior civil servants – saw this memorandum as a normative statement. It represented what, in an ideal world, the Civil Service should aspire to. In reality, however, bureaucrats always have some independent power. Their access to complex information ensures that they can sift and select for their political masters in a way which must give them some agenda-setting ability. Taken to an extreme this alternative view of Civil Service power portrayed ministers as puppets in the hands of civil servants. The television series 'Yes Minister' and 'Yes Prime Minister' represent the polar opposite of the traditional model: ministers are powerless in relation to highly manipulative mandarins; policy options are presented to the Government in such a way that the preferred ministerial choice is always foreclosed in favour of less radical 'safer' choices. In spite of some ministerial autobiographies in support of this view (notably by the 1960s Labour ministers Richard Crossman and Barbara Castle), it resembles caricature more than reality. Over the last 50 years, British government policies have changed frequently and often in radical directions. Either civil servants consented to these policy changes in line with the traditional model or they shared the same values as ministers and therefore went along with the preferred policy.

The radical critique

The notion of shared values is at the heart of the second model of civil servant power: the idea that, with their public school and Oxbridge backgrounds, civil servants are naturally inclined to support the 'establishment' view of the world and to oppose radical, and in particularly, socialist alternatives. Such critics as Brian Sedgemore in his book *The Secret Constitution* and the Labour MP Tony Benn, in *Arguments for Socialism*, represent this position. However, the evidence in support of this view is scant, to say the least. Few civil servants support the Conservative Party. The role of government was greatly enhanced during Labour's periods in office. Civil servants did not block the nationalisation of basic industries and the creation of the welfare state. Even during the 1960s and 1970s, when Labour governments were accused by the left of betraying their socialist principles, government grew enormously in size. In 1960 government expenditure as a percentage of Gross National Product stood at 32.9 per cent; by 1975 this had increased to 44.4 per cent. What is true is that during the Labour periods in office in the 1960s and, especially, during the 1970s, calls for yet more state intervention and government spending were resisted. But the resistance came from centre and right-wing members of the Government itself, who in turn were pressurised by external events such as strikes in strategic industries, or by falls in the value of the pound on the foreign exchanges. There is little evidence to suggest that civil servants played a major role in these events.

The rational choice critique

Key term

Rational choice – an approach to political science which treats politics as the outcome of the interaction between rational individuals pursuing their own interests.

Both the traditional model and the radical critique are concerned with the distribution of political power. Traditionalists assign all power to the minister; leftist critics see a Tory-dominated establishment as the ultimate source of political authority. Neither perspective is centrally concerned with the *efficiency* of public administration, however. This in spite of the fact that in the 1970s the British Civil Service operated much as it had done at the end of the nineteenth century, when government's role in society was dramatically smaller. Yet it was concern about the efficiency of the public service, rather than questions about where power lay in Whitehall, that drove most of the attempts to reform the Civil Service from 1968 to 1990. There were two related strands to these reform attempts. Initially the main concern was that the Civil Service was insufficiently *professional* in the conduct of public affairs. The tradition of generalists and amateurs running the Civil Service was seen as inappropriate in an increasing managerial and technocratic world. The critique here was not so much that civil servants were seeking power for themselves. Rather it was that the recruitment and management structure of the service rendered them incapable of responding efficiently to rapid technological changes in society.

By the late 1970s, thinking among right-wing intellectuals had evolved a second and much more radical critique relating to the efficiency of the service. Drawing on the increasingly influential *rational choice theory* (see Briefing 10.1), they assumed that what drove politics was the rational self-interest of politicians and officials. From this assumption they argued that the institutional structure of the Civil Service provided officials with a huge incentive to maximise their pay and pensions and to expand government programmes and spending, not in the name of the public interest, but for the aggrandisement of the public service itself and hence their own pay and position. Many of the problems relating to government 'overload' in the 1970s – ever-increasing public expenditure, a growing army of officials, and inefficient public services – were linked to this view of the personal incentives of civil servants. In effect, the public sector lacked the discipline which competition forced on the private sector and which rewarded the employees and shareholders of competent and efficient companies while penalising those associated with badly run companies.

Two possible solutions to this problem existed. First, services that were presently in the public sector could be privatised. Second, when privatisation was not possible or feasible, institutional changes could be introduced to change the incentive structures for civil servants in ways that would combine their self-interest with the public interest. As we will see, the Conservative governments of the 1980s attempted to implement both of these solutions.

BRIEFINGS

10.1 RATIONAL CHOICE THEORY AND POLITICS

Rational choice theory (sometimes known as public choice theory) assumes that all actors in the political process (politicians, voters, officials, interest groups) are self-interested and seek to maximise benefits, whether it be votes, income or power. As far as officials are concerned, if left to their own devices they will seek to maximise their budgets so as to accumulate personal benefits (promotion, salary, kudos). Clearly there are limits to this process, if only because the demand for public services is not infinite and officials must be paid for out of taxation. Nonetheless, in traditionally structured bureaucracies some over- provision will occur and will result in unit costs higher than those that would prevail if the services were provided by the market.

Privatisation should, according to the theory, eliminate this problem. Where full privatisation is not possible, governments can change the institutional rules and procedures in ways which alter officials' incentives to maximise spending. Creating quasi-independent agencies run by managers on fixed contracts, under instructions to meet predetermined cost and performance targets, results in a changed incentive environment and reduces unit costs. In particular, officials will see a common interest between improvements in efficiency and their career and pay prospects.

These ideas were pioneered by a number of American economists, including William Niskanen and Gordon Tullock. They also provide the basis for the influential book by David Osborne and Ted Gaebler, *Reinventing Government: How the Entrepreneurial Spirit is Transforming the Public Sector* (Reading, MA: Addison Wesley, 1992), which has influenced reforming politicians in both the United States and Britain.

REFORMING THE CIVIL SERVICE: THE FULTON REPORT

The first attempt to reform the Civil Service in modern times occurred in 1966 with the commissioning of the Fulton Report, which was eventually published in 1968. Fulton represented the most fundamental review of the service since the Northcote–Trevelyan Report of 1854, which recommended the abolition of patronage and established the principle of a meritocratic and neutral Civil Service. Fulton attacked what it saw as an exclusive and aloof administrative class (top level civil servants) drawn predominantly from a narrow social and educational background. Most of these were Oxbridge-educated generalists whose first concern was the servicing of ministers, rather than seeing to the management of their departments. Put another way, the British Civil Service was run by a largely untrained upper-class elite, mobility between grades was low, technical knowledge limited and outside advice excluded or ignored. This system persisted, Fulton pointed out, in spite of the massive growth of both the Civil Service and of government programmes. The report produced 158 recommendations for change, the most important of which were:

- Less dependence on gifted all-rounders and more on highly trained specialists and graduates from a variety of backgrounds;

- The creation of a single Civil Service career stream to encourage the advancement of the most talented from all grades;

- The creation of a Civil Service Department responsible for all recruitment and a Civil Service College responsible for post-entry training;

- The hiving off of some responsibilities to semiautonomous agencies and departments.

Note that this agenda fits well with the concern in the 1960s that the Civil Service was unprofessional or amateurish. And while a more *efficient* service was clearly an objective, the report was equally concerned that the service should be more *egalitarian*. In spite of the fact that Fulton attracted a great deal of publicity at the time, its recommendations were largely ignored. A Civil Service Department and Civil Service College were created, and the administrative class was nominally merged with the executive and clerical grades. In reality, however, these changes were cosmetic. A *de facto* administrative class remained. With intensifying economic crisis in the late 1960s and the 1970s, governments' attention was diverted elsewhere. In the end it was left to the Civil Service to reform itself, which in practice meant minor changes rather than wholesale reform.

THE 1980s REFORMS: A MANAGERIAL REVOLUTION?

New Right ideas became increasingly influential during the 1970s and, on coming to power in 1979, Margaret Thatcher was determined to apply these ideas to the Civil Service. As part of her campaign against big government, the Prime

Minister immediately set about reducing the size of the Civil Service and curtailing many of their privileges (such as pay rises based on 'fair comparisons' with equivalent employees in the private sector). Instead, pay would be related to a notional 'market-determined' level, which usually meant lower rises. In addition, performance-related pay was introduced and secondments to and from the private sector were encouraged. As can be seen from Figure 10.1, the number of civil servants did drop sharply after 1979, although the largest decreases were among industrial rather than regular civil servants.

In 1981 the service embarked on a strike over pay, but after 21 weeks the Civil Service unions capitulated to the government. Also in 1981 the government banned trade union membership at its General Communications Headquarters (GCHQ) in Cheltenham following a shutdown of this security information-gathering service during the strike. In spite of protestations by Civil Service spokespersons that the ban was a denial of a fundamental right to workplace union representation, it remained. Finally, in 1981 the government abolished the Civil Service Department, which was regarded as too partisan a supporter of Civil Service interests. A Management and Personnel Office was created in its place and this in turn was, via a number of intermediary changes, transformed into the Office of Public Service (OPS) in 1995. (For fuller detail see Briefing 10.2.)

While significant, these changes pale into insignificance compared with a number of further initiatives taken later in the 1980s, which in total were to result in the transformation of government service in Britain. The impetus behind these changes was a conviction that market or market-like arrangements were the only means whereby government services could be rendered both cost-effective and

Figure 10.1 Number of civil servants 1945–94

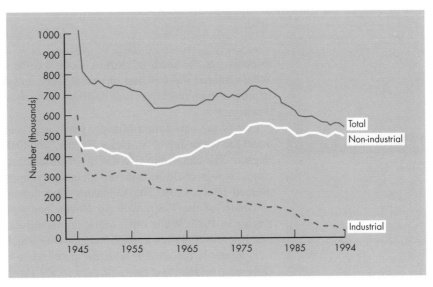

Source: Civil Service Statistics, as reproduced in Peter Barberis (ed.) *The Whitehall Reader* (Buckingham: Open University Press, 1996) Figure 1

BRIEFINGS

10.2 THE MANAGEMENT OF THE CIVIL SERVICE, 1965–98

Until 1968 most of the personnel and training functions of the Civil Service were the responsibility of the Treasury, indeed the Head of the Home Civil Service was also the head of the Treasury. In 1968 the Civil Service Department (CSD), responsible for all personnel matters, was created, along with a Civil Service College (CSC) responsible for training. However, following a brief period of success under its first chief, Sir William Armstrong, the CSD was viewed with increasing hostility by the Thatcher Governments as a change in policy emphasis raised the profile of the Treasury and the Cabinet Office. In 1981 the CSD was abolished. Some of its functions were transferred to the Treasury while a new unit, the Management Personnel Office (MPO), took on most of the personnel functions under the general control of the Cabinet Office.

Further changes occurred in the late 1980s involving first the transformation of the MPO into the Office of the Minister for the Civil Service (OMCS), which in turn became the Office of Public Service and Science (OPSS) in 1992, and finally the Office of Public Service (OPS) in 1995. These new units remained under the wing of the Cabinet Office and its permanent secretary, Sir Robin Butler, throughout. From 1988, Sir Robin served in the dual roles of Cabinet Secretary and Head of the Home Civil Service. Significantly, the OPS is responsible for the overall implementation of the Efficiency Unit, Next Steps and the Citizen's Charter, as well as recruitment and training. Most commentators agree that, in comparison with the old Civil Service Department, the OPS facilitates a greater degree of central control.

responsive to the needs of citizens. Gone was the egalitarian ethos of the 1960s. What mattered was cost and service delivery, and any institutional change which improved these objectives was desirable. Let us examine these changes in more detail.

One of the new Prime Minister's first acts was to create an Efficiency Unit under the leadership of Sir Derek Rayner, who had been Chairman of Marks and Spencer. The unit's objective was to persuade departments to identify areas where major savings could be achieved including, if appropriate, the abolition of tasks deemed unnecessary. The Efficiency Unit quietly continued its work for the remainder of the 1980s with Sir Robin Ibbs replacing Sir Derek (later Lord) Rayner in 1983. While other efficiency initiatives were taken during the 1980s (see Briefing 10.3), it was the Efficiency Unit which was to produce the most radical proposals for change with the publication of *Improving Management in Government: The Next Steps. Report to the Prime Minister* in February 1988. This report (generally known as the Ibbs Report) identified a serious management

Key term

Next Steps – the short title of the Ibbs report (1988) which identified serious management failure in the Civil Service and recommended far-reaching reforms in the shape of executive agencies.

BRIEFINGS

10.3 THE DRIVE FOR EFFICIENCY 1979–92

1979   Prime Minister Margaret Thatcher appoints Sir Derek (now Lord) Rayner as head of a new Efficiency Unit. Based in the Cabinet Office, the Unit's brief was to improve efficiency by reducing costs and eliminating waste. Departments themselves were to identify areas for cost savings. Derek Rayner was replaced by Sir Robin Ibbs in 1983.

1982   As Environmental Secretary, Michael Heseltine introduces Management Information Systems for Ministers (MINIS). Heseltine wanted to know what was going on in his department and MINIS was designed to provide, on a continuous basis, systematic information on the running of the department. Curiously, not only had this not been attempted before, but many in Whitehall believed it was inappropriate for ministers to become 'involved' in the running of their departments. No other department adopted MINIS in full, although some adopted watered-down versions.

1983   The government launches the Financial Management Initiative (FMI) which required departments to identify clear policy objectives, and to test performance in relation to these objectives. Managers within departments were also given more control over their budgets or 'cost centres' and required to operate within cash limits. FMI was not, however, fully implemented, mainly because in many cases it was difficult to identify clear objectives.

1988   The Efficiency Unit publishes *Improving Management in Government: the Next Steps. Report to the Prime Minister*, which proposes the separation of policy from management. The Government would set policy but executive agencies with considerable operational and budgetary autonomy would be responsible for management.

1991   Publication of the White Paper *Competing for Quality* heralds the adoption of market testing throughout government.

1992   The Government launches the Private Finance Initiative (PFI) to encourage the private financing of public facilities. Private consortia raise capital and then, via a contract with the Government, build a facility which generates income for them for a fixed period. The initiative got off to a slow start but by 1997 the Dartford and Skye road crossings, and a few hospital and prison buildings, had been financed in this way. On coming to power in 1997, Labour endorsed the idea by approving the private financing of the Birmingham Northern Relief Road.

deficit in the Civil Service and recommended radical and far-reaching reforms. Its tone was very different from Fulton. As one commentator has put it:

> Next Steps is more like a report from a management consultancy firm than a traditional civil service review. It is glossy, bold and evangelical. The traditional mandarin style of drafting to avoid commitment has been replaced by a fresh passion for revitalisation and change. The style and thrust of the report reflects the views and skills of its relatively youthful authors. The Next Steps report was written by a new breed of civil servant.

It is predicated on the belief that there is an important discipline of 'management' which has been traditionally and mistakenly overlooked by the civil service in favour of traditional 'policy skills'.[1]

The main recommendations of Next Steps were:

- To separate 'steering from rowing' or policy from management. In other words once the government has made policy, the actual management of policy can best be undertaken by decentralised self-management units working to predefined cost and performance targets.

- This decentralised system should be expedited through two main devices: the creation of semi-independent executive agencies devoted to particular functions, and the creation of *contracts* between agencies, and between agencies and the private sector. Contractual arrangements – including limiting the terms of employment of the agencies' chief executives – were designed to mimic the discipline of the private sector (see Briefing 10.4).

The Government accepted these recommendations with enthusiasm and immediately set about the business of setting up executive agencies. Five years later no

---

[1] Patricia Greer, *Transforming Central Government: The Next Steps Initiative* (Buckingham: Open University Press, 1994), p. 6

BRIEFINGS

10.4 PATRICIA GREER ON CONTRACT GOVERNMENT

One of the basic principles of Next Steps is that executive agencies are provided with the freedom and the tools to get on with their 'businesses' and that in return agencies must deliver certain outputs or standards of service within the available resources. This basic principle is enforced through a serious of 'contracts' which essentially specify what freedoms an agency has, how much money it has and what ends the agency must achieve. The documents forming these overall agency 'contracts' are: the agency framework documents which at present must be reviewed around every three years, the annual business plans and the three or five yearly corporate plans.

At a more detailed level agencies contract other agencies through 'service level agreements' to perform particular functions such as computer services, providing contribution record data or accommodation services. In other words, the 'contractor' becomes a 'client' organisation which must manage its dealings with other contract agencies. Individual staff are also contracted to

10.4 PATRICIA GREER ON CONTRACT GOVERNMENT
(continued)

achieve agency aims. Agency chief executives are contracted to meet the agency targets and a proportion of their pay is dependent on them meeting those targets. The chief executives are employed on a short-term basis with the renewal of their contract also being dependent on their performance. Some other senior agency staff are also employed on a short-term basis and some also have their pay linked to the performance of the agency. At a lower level, the general staff of the agency are also in effect contracted to achieve the agency aims and, in recognition of this, may receive pay bonuses when targets are met.

Patricia Greer, *Transforming Central Government: The Next Steps Initiative* (Buckingham: Open University Press, 1994), p. 60

fewer than 97 executive agencies had been created, employing nearly two thirds of all civil servants (see Table 10.1). Most of these are quite small and include such services as the Central Statistical Office, the Public Records Office and the Royal Mint. But some, including the Benefits Agency (responsible for social security benefits) and the Contributions Agency (responsible for collecting social security taxes) involve the most important of all central government functions.

In addition to meeting performance targets on costs (very often a euphemism for reducing the number of civil servants), the executive agencies were given increased discretion on such matters as recruitment and pay levels following the publication of a White Paper in 1994, *The Civil Service: Continuity and Change*.

Table 10.1 The top 10 Next Step agencies, 1993

Agency	Staff
Benefits Agency	64,055
Employment Service	44,490
Her Majesty's Prison Service	39,060
Defence Research Agency	10,110
Social Security Contributions Agency	9,370
Land Registry	9,190
RAF Maintenance	6,180
Northern Ireland Social Security Agency	5,830
Valuations	4,965
Scottish Prison Service	4,625

Source: Treasury and Civil Service Committee, 1993, as reproduced in Robert Pyper and Lynton Robins, *Governing the UK in the 1990s* (London: Macmillan, 1995) Table 3.1

In 1991 the Conservative Government published a White Paper, *Competing for Quality* (Cm 1730) which extended much of the thinking inherent in Next Steps to other areas of government. 'Market testing', or tendering services to outside contractors, could be adopted for a whole range of services including financial, statistical and other services. Depending on the agency or service concerned, in-house bids from those already providing it could be excluded or included, although by 1996 in-house bids had won most of the contracts. One potential problem with 'outsourcing' of this kind is that, once a service is contracted out, it tends to stay contracted out and the expertise relating to it is lost from the government. Predictably, criticisms of outside contractors were common in the early days. Group 4's contract with the prison service to transport prisoners brought public derision following a number of escapes. However, by 1997, the idea of outside contracts was well established in central government (and even more so in local government, see Chapter 19). The New Labour Government made no attempt to reverse this process when elected to power in 1997.

Next steps: an assessment

There can be no doubt that these changes led to a state of permanent revolution in Whitehall. Gone were all the old assumptions of a unitary, hierarchical Civil Service staffed by permanent career officials. Instead the service has effectively been broken up into a number of semi-independent units. Such radical change has naturally produced criticism from a number of quarters.

One criticism is that more flexibility may have reduced accountability. The main purpose of the reforms was to curtail the budget – and personnel-maximising tendency among traditionally organised bureaucracies. Most studies conclude that some improvement in performance (measured in costs and quality of service) has occurred since the introduction of Next Steps. However, these same studies agree that it is very difficult to make meaningful comparisons between the pre-reform and post-reform periods. More serious is the blurring of accountability that occurs when the minister, who remains responsible for the overall operation of his or her department, refers to an agency chief executive when a problem arises. If 'operations' are separated from 'policy', the strong implication is that the agency chief is responsible for errors or maladministration. Yet, constitutionally, the minister is responsible. This problem was graphically illustrated in the case of the Prison Service Agency when, in 1995, the chief executive was obliged to resign following a series of successful prison breakouts. The Home Secretary, Michael Howard, said it was an operational and not a policy problem, even though there was substantial evidence that the Home Secretary had intervened on operational matters. The sacked chief executive retorted that, 'you … invented a new definition of the word "operational" which meant "difficult"'.[2]

---

[2] Derek Lewis, quoted in C. D. Foster and F. J. Plowden, *The State Under Stress* (Buckingham: Open University Press, 1996), p. 167

Another criticism is that the British public service ethos may be under threat. The British Civil Service tradition emphasises impartiality, anonymity and unstinting service to the democratically elected government. Replacing traditional departments with executive agencies may undermine these values. In particular, performance-related pay, short-term contracts and hiving off some functions to the private sector may not be compatible with the sort of loyalty to the public interest that a lifelong career in the service may engender. Of course, this critique takes for granted the traditional model of the Civil Service which may never have been wholly applicable to the way in which officials actually worked.

In spite of these misgivings, most of the early verdicts on the *operational* role of the new agencies were positive. Performance targets have been met around 75 per cent of the time and staff numbers have been reduced without sacrificing the quality of service. This said, some agencies have attracted strong criticism. For example, the Child Support Agency (CSA), which is responsible for ensuring maintenance payments by absent fathers, came under constant attack for the insensitivity with which it dealt with cases.

Criticisms of individual agencies are not as important, however, as are the *constitutional* questions raised by the Next Steps initiative. Undoubtedly the most important of these is the ambiguity surrounding the status of Whitehall departments. What, traditionally, has held departments together has been ministerial control and Treasury directives on public expenditure. But the relationship between ministers and agency chiefs is a complex and difficult one. Also, as agencies are given the freedom to make their own financial bids in the public expenditure round, so the *rationale* of the traditional department is further undermined.

One thing, however, is certain: there will be no going back to the old days of unitary, hierarchical departments. Further reforms may be needed, especially in the area of parliamentary accountability, but the Civil Service is now a very different animal from what it was in the mid-1980s.

THE SPREAD OF QUASI-GOVERNMENT

Key term

Quangos – quasi-autonomous non-governmental organisations financed by the government to perform public service functions but not under direct government control. Examples include the BBC, and the Commission for Racial Equality (CRE).

Another consequence of the reform agenda which swept Whitehall during the 1980s was the spread of what has variously been called quasi-government, nondepartmental public bodies (the Government's own definition), quangos (quasi-autonomous nongovernmental organisations) and extra-Government organisations (EGOs). These organisations are large in number and varied in function (see Briefing 10.5). What they have in common is that their directors or managing committees are usually nominated by the Government. Along with other comparable countries, Britain has long had public or semipublic bodies which are distinct from the traditional central departments and from local government. The National Health Service, for example, has always had a separate management structure. The reforms of the 1980s, however, led to a further and rapid spread of quangos. There are a number of reasons for this:

1. Conservative Governments' opposition to politically independent local governments with control over council housing and other local services led to the creation of a number of organisations with semi-autonomous status, such as housing action trusts, urban development corporations and local enterprise companies. These were designed to bypass traditional local governments and deliver particular services in line with central government policy.

2. Concern with over-bureaucratisation and standards in health and education led to the creation of opted-out schools and colleges, and to hospital trusts and family health authorities. (Opted-out schools, colleges and health facilities are freed from local education or health authority control and are instead funded directly by central government.) Opted-out institutions are quasi-self-governing and have devolved control over the implementation of their budgets.

3. Privatisation of the utilities led to the setting up of regulatory agencies such as Oftel, Ofgas and Ofwat to monitor pricing and the quality of service in the provision of telephone services, gas and water supplies.

BRIEFINGS

10.5 CLASSIFYING QUASI-GOVERNMENT

The government's own classification of quangos identifies four varieties:

- *Executive Non-departmental Public Bodies (NDPBs)*. These include such bodies as the utility regulators, the Arts Council and the Commission for Racial Equality.
- *Advisory NDPBs* such as the Parliamentary Boundary Commission.
- *Tribunals* with judicial functions such as the Supplementary Benefits Appeals Tribunals and Rent Tribunals.
- *NHS bodies.*

To this list must be added a number of other agencies, however, including opted-out schools, colleges, hospitals and family health services, training and education councils (TECs), and housing action trusts. It could be argued that executive agencies (because they have great operational autonomy) resemble quangos more than traditional local or central government departments. According to the Democratic Audit, in 1994 no less than 6,708 quangos existed of which 5,521 had executive powers. The Government's own figure was 1,389 for that year. On coming to power in 1979 the Conservative Government pledged itself to reduce the number of quangos. However, by almost any measure the number has increased rapidly since then.

EFFICIENCY AND ACCOUNTABILITY

In 1994 two academics, Stuart Weir and Wendy Hall, carried out a survey of quangos as part of a project associated with Charter 88 (the constitutional reform group). The idea was to produce a 'democratic audit' of government in Britain. Their findings revealed the existence of nearly 6,700 quangos, spending (in 1992/93) over £46 billion and accounting for around a third of all public expenditure. The report was highly critical of quangos on two main grounds:

1. *Public accountability*. Conservative governments generally appointed Conservative supporters to the most important executive quango positions. Few Labour or Liberal Democrat supporters were appointed. This political patronage might be regarded as a natural tendency that would equally apply to a Labour government. But the authors pointed out that the autonomous nature of many quangos, including NHS hospital trusts, meant that major parts of British public administration were being run, not by professional managers and bureaucrats, but by Conservative notables who had no direct channel of accountability either to voters or to the users of services. In addition, most of the management decisions in the quangos were shrouded in secrecy, thus preventing any objective assessment from outside bodies.

2. *Efficiency*. Devolving the management and the financing of major services to quangos involved considerable additional administrative costs. Clerical and accounting costs had risen rapidly in opted-out schools and trust hospitals. In addition, cost management in some of the new authorities was found wanting.

The Democratic Audit was accused by some members of the Government of anti-Conservative bias. It was difficult to direct the same accusation at the Commons Public Accounts Committee which in 1994 argued that management standards of quangos, rather than rising, as was the intention of the original reforms, had actually fallen during the early 1990s. In some instances cases of corruption and serious maladministration were uncovered. The committee was also concerned that public accountability in the new organisations was very difficult to identify.

The Government's response was that these critics misunderstood the nature of recent administrative changes. As with the executive agencies, recipients of national health, education and other services were now customers or consumers rather than passive citizens. As such, market criteria rather than traditional public accountability standards would test the new organisations' performance.

To this end the Government set up a 'Citizen's Charter' in 1991, aimed at raising the quality of public services (see Briefing 10.6). By the mid-1990s this concept had been institutionalised, and bodies as diverse as the Immigration Service, British Rail and the Benefits Agency had all published 'Charters' declaring a devotion to raising standards and servicing consumers. Note that the Citizen's

Charter was to be applied both to quangos such as hospital trusts and to the executive agencies discussed earlier in this chapter. Also, as with the executive agencies, quango performance would be measured through the use of widely publicised performance indicators such as school examination league tables, hospital waiting lists and train punctuality data.

Few now seriously dispute that the spread of quangos and semigovernment does raise serious problems of public accountability. This was confirmed in the

BRIEFINGS

10.6 THE PRINCIPLES OF THE PUBLIC SECTOR ACCORDING TO THE CITIZEN'S CHARTER

Standards

Setting, monitoring and publication of explicit standards for the services that individual users can reasonably expect. Publication of actual performance against these standards.

Information and openness

Full, accurate information available in plain language about how public services are run, what they cost, how well they perform and who is in charge.

Choice and consultation

The public sector should provide choice wherever practicable. There should be regular and systematic consultation with those who use services. Users' views about services, and their priorities for improving them, to be taken into account in final decisions on standards.

Courtesy and helpfulness

Courteous and helpful service from public servants who will normally wear name badges. Services available equally to all who are entitled to them and run to suit their convenience.

Putting things right

If things go wrong, an apology, a full explanation and a swift and effective remedy. Well publicised and easy to use complaints procedures with independent review wherever possible.

Value for money

Efficient and economical delivery of public services within the resources the nation can afford. Independent validation of performance against standards.

The Citizen's Charter: Raising the Standard, Cm 1599 (London: HMSO, 1991)

first report of the Standing Committee on Standards in Public Life (the Nolan Committee), which made a number of recommendations relating to the appointment and conduct of quango staff. In particular, appointments should be strictly on merit, a Commissioner for Public Appointments should vet all application procedures, and party interests should be declared. In addition a review of the changing nature of accountability in quangos should be undertaken and a code of conduct similar to that operating in the Civil Service introduced.

While these recommendations were accepted by the Government and whole-heartedly embraced by the then Labour Opposition, the accountability problem remains. Put at its simplest, the assumptions of market testing and consumer choice can only work in fully mature commercial markets. In a range of services provided by quangos and the new executive agencies, the service provided is often a natural monopoly, such as social benefits, or can incorporate only very limited consumer choice. It is, for example, impossible to provide every patient and every parent with a full choice of doctors, hospitals and schools in a particular community. An *element* of choice can be provided, but no more.

Even more problematic is the link between such choices and the democratic process. In some countries such as the United States, services which are considered a state-provided public right, such as primary and secondary education, are funded out of local taxation and schools are run by democratically elected officials. In Britain opted-out schools and hospitals are given *managerial* autonomy but no *political* autonomy. In addition, although their budgets are devolved, their income ultimately comes from general taxation over which the individual consumer (the parent or patient) has no direct control.

What the reforms mean in practice, therefore, is a high degree of procedural autonomy, but continuing central government control over general spending levels and, via a host of carefully monitored performance criteria, increased control over the nature and quality of the service provided. Central governments may *wish* reforms to redound to the benefit of the consumer. But, except at general elections, citizens have little direct control over the funding and running of such crucial services as education and health.

It may be, of course, that in their dealings with quangos and executive agencies, members of the public do receive a better service today than that available 10 or 15 years ago. For all their faults, performance indicators do provide a basis for making comparisons and evaluating the quality of service. But in terms of democratic accountability and control, the reforms have been a backward step. In a range of services, including education, the role of local elected officials has been drastically reduced. In addition, the steady erosion of ministerial responsibility has weakened the link between the citizen and nationally elected officials.

In recognition of this, the Blair Government has pledged to implement in full the recommendations of the Nolan Committee and in particular to improve the accountability of quangos. Labour's constitutional reforms involve the return of some responsibilities to local governments, including, of course newly created assemblies in Wales and Scotland and an elected government in London. It is unlikely, however, that the fundamentals of the new system of quasi-government will be attacked. Indeed, Labour's conception of a 'stakeholder society', where those affected by an agency have a say about how it is run, is quite close to the

ESSAYS

ESSAYS

1. What were the main recommendations of the Fulton Report? Why were many of them not implemented?

2. What were the motives behind the Next Steps initiative? Have the resulting reforms been a success?

3. Why has there been so much concern at the lack of accountability of quangos to elected representatives? Which reforms might redress this democratic deficit?

4. Do civil servants operate in their own or in the public interest? Illustrate your answer with reference to reform in the Civil Service since 1968.

Conservative idea of the 'consumer citizen'. Labour argues that, much like consumers in the market place for goods, citizens have a stake in the political market place for government-provided services.

The main reforms over the last 30 years are outlined in the Milestones at the end of the chapter.

SUMMARY

- The traditional Whitehall model of the Civil Service with clear lines of responsibility from ministers through impartial civil servants to the public has never been an accurate portrayal of British public administration.

- An alternative view that Britain is run by a Conservative 'establishment' is difficult to reconcile with the radical changes in public policy which have occurred since 1945.

- Early reforms of Whitehall proposed by the Fulton Report addressed the lack of professionalism of senior civil servants. However, few meaningful changes resulted from the Report's recommendations.

- During the 1980s, Conservative governments implemented a number of major reforms in the Civil Service, the most important of which was the Next Steps initiative which transferred much of the business of Whitehall departments to semi-independent agencies. Most commentators agree that while this change has resulted in important efficiency gains it has also blurred lines of ministerial responsibility.

MILESTONES

MILESTONES TO ADMINISTRATIVE REFORM

1968 The Fulton Report aimed at a more professional Civil Service which recruited more widely

1968 Civil Service Department (CSD) set up

1968 Civil Service College founded

1979 Efficiency Unit set up by Margaret Thatcher to review departmental performance

1981 CSD abolished. Management Personnel Office more closely linked to Cabinet Office

1983 Financial Management Initiative requires policy objectives to be specified and more managerial autonomy

1983 Cabinet Secretary emerges as Head of the Civil Service

1983 Privatisation of state-owned property and industry begins in earnest

1988 Efficiency Unit publishes *Next Steps*, which proposes the separation of management from policy and creation of autonomous executive agencies in central government. Many such agencies created in the following years

1991 Citizen's Charter launched, specifying consumer rights in various areas

1992 Private Finance Initiative (PFI) encourages private finance of government projects

1995 Office of Public Service succeeds Civil Service Department but remains under control of Cabinet Office

1997 New Labour Government accepts use of Private Finance Initiative for Birmingham Northern Relief Road, along with other administrative changes of 1980s and 1990s

1. Assess the performance of a major executive agency in Britain. In your research take account of the following:
(a) cost savings;
(b) quality of service;
(c) public accountability

2. Classify quangos as they operate in Britain today. Given their variety, is it possible to apply one model of accountability to their operations?

3. Write a historical review of the concept of ministerial responsibility. Given recent reforms, how relevant is the concept to British public administration in the late 1990s?

- Conservative initiatives also resulted in the spread of quasi-governmental institutions or quangos during the 1980s and 1990s. Again, while the use of performance indicators has produced some improvements in the quality of services, quangos remain largely unaccountable to elected representatives. It remains to be seen whether further changes promised by the Blair Government will solve the accountability problem.

FURTHER READING

A vast literature exists on the Civil Service in general and recent reforms in particular. The Open University series, *Public Policy and Management*, produces good up-to-date reports. See, in particular, Christopher D. Foster and Francis J Plowden, *The State Under Stress: Can the Hollow State be Good Government?* (Buckingham: Open University Press, 1996) and Patricia Greer, *Transforming Central Government: The Next Steps Initiative* (Buckingham: Open University Press, 1994). A good reader on recent changes is Peter Barberis (ed.) *The Whitehall Reader* (Buckingham: Open University Press, 1996). On accountability, see Colin Pilkington, *Representative Democracy in Britain Today* (Manchester: Manchester University Press, 1997). Radical critiques of the traditional Whitehall model are provided by Tony Benn, *Arguments for Socialism* (Harmondsworth: Penguin, 1979) and Brian Sedgemore, *The Secret Constitution: An Analysis of the Political Establishment* (London: Hodder and Stoughton, 1980). For a careful empirical study of the demise of the Whitehall model, see Colin Campbell and Graham K. Wilson, *The End of Whitehall: Death of a Paradigm* (Oxford: Blackwell, 1995).

CHAPTER 11

Judicial review of administration

The absence of political accountability for many areas of administration, and the frequent failure of 'political markets' to respond to the consumer, make recourse to legal remedies for administrative injustices an increasingly attractive option in modern Britain. This tendency is strengthened by a growing awareness of the possibility of appeals to European law and the European courts. The British courts' willingness to overrule statute law in favour of European law means that appeals need not go as far as Luxembourg to be successful.

Even where European law does not apply, the constitutional doctrine of parliamentary sovereignty need not hinder the Courts from passing judgement on civil servants' or ministers' actions, or even on decisions taken by the Government as a whole. Acts of Parliament are often vague and general, or badly worded. This may give greater scope for the executive to make up rules as they go along. But it also allows, and at times impels, the courts to consider whether administrative action has been taken after 'due consideration' or on 'reasonable grounds', to use the words of many statutes. They may well decide not. Such decisions go some way towards assessing the 'constitutionality' of specific government actions. The frenetic activism of Conservative governments of the 1980s and 1990s, and the widening scope given to administrative initiatives by their reforms, rendered their decisions increasingly subject to judicial review. This resulted in public confrontations between the judiciary and ministers in the mid-1990s, during the last years of the Major Government, giving judicial intervention in politics a prominence it never had before.

The chapter considers:

- The growing importance of the courts in the process of government

- The extent of judicial review of political powers and its recent growth

- The impact of judicial review on politics and administration

- The constitutional justifications for judicial review: 'powers-based', 'impact-based' and 'process-based'

- The future of judicial review under a New Labour Government.

THE GROWING IMPORTANCE OF THE COURTS

The growing importance of courts to the process of government in the United Kingdom has been one of the most significant political developments of the past two decades. In the past it was thought that the role of the court in politics and administration was sporadic and peripheral. It is now claimed that the influence of the judges on the practical exercise of power is constant and central, so much so that the power of judges to review the legality of governmental action has become a new and important stage in the public policy process.

How and why has this change come about and what is its significance? Must we, for example, now assume that the task of governing the country routinely involves unelected judges who have the authority to overthrow governmental decisions? If so, how can this judicial power be justified in a democracy?

As these questions suggest, lawyers and political scientists are being forced to re-evaluate the relationship between the courts and government. This Chapter introduces some of the principal issues involved in this re-evaluation.

THE GROWTH OF JUDICIAL REVIEW

Key term

Judicial review – the process whereby the courts supervise the way in which public officials and bodies carry out their duties. It involves the power to nullify actions the courts believe to be illegal or unconstitutional.

Our starting point is the legal process known as judicial review. In 1987, concerned by the growing number of successful legal challenges to actions of the central Government, government lawyers produced a short booklet for civil servants called *The Judge over your Shoulder*. This explained what judicial review was and how it might be avoided. According to this booklet:

Judicial review is, as the name implies, how the Courts of England and Wales supervise the way in which Ministers, Government departments, agencies, local authorities or other public bodies exercise their powers or carry out their duties. It is therefore merely a means (although a very powerful one) by which improper exercise of power can be remedied ... it is a part of the whole process of good administration.

Judicial review, then, is the means by which courts can be used to challenge action taken by ministers and other public bodies on the grounds that the body has:

- exceeded or abused its legal power;
- failed to follow proper procedures;
- reached a decision that is unreasonable or irrational;
- acted unfairly.

An application to seek judicial review must be made to the High Court (see Briefing 11.1) and will be dealt with in two stages. First a High Court judge will

BRIEFINGS

11.1 THE HIGHER COURTS OF ENGLAND AND WALES

The whole system, from the lowest local courts to the highest, is summarised in Table 20.1. Judicial review has so far only been undertaken by the higher courts sitting in London. These are in the first instance the three divisions of the High Court: the Chancery, Family and Queen's Bench Division. Judges on the Queen's Bench may be appointed to consider applications for judicial review.

Appeals against decisions in the High Court will normally be heard in the Civil Division of the Court of Appeal. Should a further appeal be made against a decision at this level, it will be heard in the House of Lords, acting in its judicial capacity and composed exclusively of Law Lords, the most senior judges usually sitting as a Bench of five. This is the ultimate court so far as domestic law is concerned, although the European Court of Justice is the final arbiter of European Community Law.

decide whether the application should be fully considered on its merits. This is known as the leave (permission) stage. If a judge takes the view that the application is not arguable or that it has been brought too late, leave to proceed will be refused. (Applications must be made promptly and within three months of the taking of the action being challenged.) Approximately 50 per cent of applications fail to obtain leave for these reasons.

If leave is granted the case may be fully considered by the court. In practice only half the cases which are granted leave will be fully considered. The other half are withdrawn by applicants, often because the public body agrees to settle the dispute once the judges have given permission to proceed.

When a case is fully considered by the court, the judge's job is to review the legality of the actions complained about. If they are unlawful for one or more of the reasons mentioned above, the court may quash the decision, force the body to make a new decision, prevent the body from proceeding with its plans, or simply declare what the correct legal position is.

It is important to notice that judges cannot intervene solely on the ground that they believe that the public body has acted wrongly. Their only concern is whether the body has exceeded or abused its legal powers. If judges were to overturn decisions of ministers simply because they disagreed with them, that would clearly transgress the principle that there must be a separation between the powers of the politically accountable Government and the non-elected judiciary.

We shall return to this point below. Suffice it to say here that observance of the distinction does not prevent judges being accused of overstepping their powers and intervening because they do dislike what ministers or other public bodies have done!

The increasing resort to judicial review

Most accounts of the growing importance of judicial review start by pointing to the statistical increase in its use. According to one eminent judge, Lord Justice Woolf, this shows a convincing picture of an increased need to resort to the courts for protection against alleged abuse by public bodies of their public duties. As we shall see, however, the statistics are not as convincing as they first appear.

Between 1981 and 1996 the annual number of applications for leave to seek judicial review increased from 533 to 3,901. The general increase in litigation 1981–94 is indicated in Figure 11.1.

There is no doubt that there has been a marked growth in judicial review. But research has warned us to treat these figures with some caution. There are three main reasons for this. First, the vast bulk of the litigation has been in two main areas of 'mass' use:

- immigration (e.g. challenging decisions of the immigration authorities to refuse permission to enter the country or decisions of the Home Secretary not to grant political asylum to refugees);

- homelessness (challenging decisions to local authorities not to provide housing to people claiming to be homeless).

During 1996 there were 1,748 immigration applications to seek leave and 340 homelessness applications.

Outside these two areas, growth has been far less striking. Indeed, many aspects of governmental activity which affect the vital rights and interests of individuals and groups still attract very few legal challenges. Two examples of this

Figure 11.1 Trends in the use of judicial review 1981–94

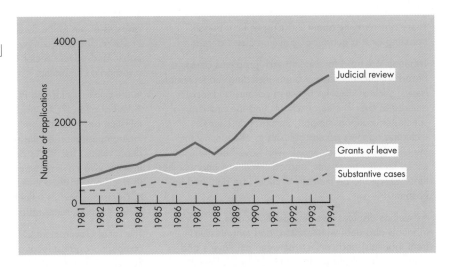

Source: L. Bridges, G. Meszaros and M. Sunkin, *Judicial Review in Perspective* (London: Cavendish, 1995), p. 9

Tribunals – in Britain tribunals are quasi-judicial institutions set up to resolve conflicts between public or private individuals or bodies. They are a way of avoiding the expensive and time-consuming needs of the courts, and of settling a large number of fairly small and simple cases.

involve prisoners and social welfare. In the mid-1980s there were approximately 100 judicial reviews a year brought by prisoners questioning such things as disciplinary decisions of prison authorities. By the end of the decade there were fewer than 20 such cases annually. Each year literally millions of decisions are taken concerning the provision of welfare benefits, yet in the three years 1987 to 1989 there were fewer than 90 applications for judicial review in this field!

These figures may indicate that judicial review is rarely needed in these areas, perhaps because people are generally satisfied with the decisions being taken or because of the existence of other remedies (such as resort to statutory tribunals or ombudsmen, see Briefing 11.2) which render judicial review unnecessary.

On the other hand, the figures might suggest that judicial review is not being used because people cannot afford the cost of going to law, do not have access to lawyers, or simply do not have the energy to pursue litigation against public bodies. Either way it appears that across many areas of government, judicial review has been far less common than the general statistics imply (see Table 11.1).

BRIEFINGS

11.2 TRIBUNALS AND OMBUDSMEN

As well as courts, there are also tribunals and ombudsmen to resolve conflicts between citizens and government and provide a quality check on administrative decision making.

Tribunals

There are currently about 2,000 specific tribunals handling over a quarter of a million cases a year.

Tribunals are used for dealing with problems across a broad spectrum of subject areas including: educational issues, such as disputes between parents and local authorities over choice of schools and the provision of special educational support; immigration issues, including appeals against refusals to allow entry into the UK; appeals by claimants who have been refused social security payments; and adjudications into whether those alleged to be mentally ill should be detained in hospital.

As well as disputes involving public bodies, tribunals also deal with landlord and tenant issues (rent tribunals) and conflicts between employers and employees involving unfair dismissal and unlawful discrimination.

The procedures adopted by tribunal reflects this variety. Some are as formal as courts (e.g. industrial tribunals) whereas others hold very informal hearings.

Ombudsmen

The term ombudsman means 'grievance handler' and owes its origin to the Swedish ombudsman established in 1809. The term is now used to refer to a range of public and private sector bodies established to investigate complaints.

In the public sector, the Parliamentary Commissioner for Administration (PCA) investigates complaints that injustice has been caused as a consequence of maladministration on the part of central government departments. The PCA's department has wide investigative powers but cannot compel compliance with its decisions. Instead it reports its decisions to the House of Commons and its influence is ultimately political. In 1995 the PCA received a record 1,706 complaints.

The Local Government Ombudsman investigates similar complaints against local government and the Health Services Ombudsman does the same in relation in health authorities.

Table 11.1 Applications for
leave to seek judicial review
by subject areas, 1987–89
and 1st quarter 1991

	1987 No.	1987 %	1988 No.	1988 %	1989 No.	1989 %	1991 No.	1991 %
Criminal:	214	14.2	164	13.4	219	14.2	71	15.6
Civil:								
Immigration	671	44.4	356	29.1	430	27.7	103	22.7
Housing	141	9.3	161	13.2	232	15.0	108	23.8
Planning	59	3.9	84	6.9	132	8.5	17	3.7
Family	42	2.8	44	3.6	26	1.7	7	1.5
Discipline	36	2.3	27	2.2	18	1.2	6	1.3
Tax	29	1.9	17	1.4	41			
Education	27	1.8	24	2.0	46	3.0	27	5.9
Legal Process	25	1.7	43	3.5	36	2.3	20	4.4
Local Govt Affairs	25	1.7	37	3.0	38	2.5	17	3.7
Prisoners	17	1.1	25	2.0	16	1.0	5	1.1
Health	17	1.1	24	2.0	34	2.2	3	0.7
Environment	15	1.0	11	0.9	21	1.4	3	0.7
Employment	15	1.0	16	1.3	18	1.2	2	0.4
Rates	14	0.9	9	0.7	13	0.8	2	0.4
Agriculture	12	0.8	7	0.6	7	0.5	–	–
Transport	12	0.8	7	0.6	14	0.9	–	–
Legal Aid	10	0.7	20	1.6	32	2.1	5	1.1
Coroners	10	0.7	9	0.7	15	1.0	3	0.7
Benefits	10	0.7	15	1.2	29	1.9	4	0.9
Trade	9	0.5	7	0.4	19	1.2	4	0.9
Compensation	6	0.4	6	0.8	11	0.9	9	2.0
Travellers	6	0.4	4	0.8	16	1.0	3	0.6
Other	90	6.0	107	8.7	123	7.9	29	6.4

Source: L. Bridges, G. Meszaros and M. Sunkin, *Judicial Review in Perspective* (London: Cavendish, 1995), p. 15

The second reason for caution about the increase in reviews flows from the first. We have just seen that much of the growth in the use of judicial review has focused on particular areas of mass use. A corollary to this is that a few public bodies are being very regularly challenged. But many others are reviewed far less frequently. Since challenges to central government have usually involved immigration, the respondent in many of these cases has been the immigration section of the Home Office. Given this, it is not surprising that the Home Office has been by far the most regularly challenged government department, attracting approximately 75 per cent of all challenges to central decision making. The next most frequently challenged departments were the Department of Environment (7 per cent of the applications against central government) and the Inland Revenue (4 per cent). Only three other central government departments were the subject of 10 or more judicial review challenges during the period 1987–89: the Department of Social Security, the Department of Transport and the Welsh Office.

Despite the huge growth in the overall caseload, therefore, challenge by judicial review still remained a relatively infrequent occurrence in the mid-1990s. For most central government departments it occurred no more than a handful of times a year. In other words, we should not assume from the figures that government in general is becoming more directly accountable to the courts.

The third reason for being cautious in the way we view the increase in judicial review concerns the procedure itself. The statistics are based on the number of *applications* for leave to seek judicial review rather than the number of judicial reviews themselves. In fact, as we now know, only half of all applications are granted leave and only half of these lead to fully fledged reviews. This means that only about a quarter of applicants will have their challenge fully dealt with by the courts.

THE IMPACT OF JUDICIAL REVIEW ON POLITICS AND ADMINISTRATION

As we know, statistics never tell the whole story. The importance of court decisions does not depend just on the number of cases and the frequency of legal challenges alone. Particular decisions can be acutely embarrassing for the Government. For example, when the High Court held that the Foreign Secretary had unlawfully agreed to support the Pergau Dam project in Malaysia, there were calls for his resignation and considerable adverse publicity (see Briefing 11.3). Likewise the Home Secretary in the last Conservative Government, Michael Howard, found himself regularly in the courts, often losing in decisions which were politically damaging to his and the Government's reputation.

Litigation can also have other practical effects. Whether challengers win or lose they can delay the implementation of decisions, help to attract publicity for those campaigning against the policy, and force governments to expend resources defending themselves. Losing a succession of well-publicised cases may also affect the ruling party's general reputation for competence, or create an impression of its bending the law. This effect was certainly apparent in the last two years of the Major Government.

Where public bodies lose in the courts they will have to respond. This may require no more than rephrasing the offending decision in accordance with the court's judgement. Since judicial review is not supposed to be concerned with the merits of decisions, this might mean that the same decision is made, but this time following the proper procedure. For instance in an immigration case, the decision of the court might be that the Secretary of State acted unlawfully in refusing entry to someone without first providing reasons. The Secretary of State's department is then obliged to provide reasons but not necessarily to change its mind and allow the person into the country. In other cases procedures may have to be reformulated or policy changed. In the example just given, the department would be expected to reform its procedures to ensure that reasons are given in future.

BRIEFINGS

11.3 JUDICIAL REVIEW OF THE PERGAU DAM DECISION

In 1991 the then Foreign Secretary, Douglas Hurd, agreed to spend £234m supporting a project to build a dam in Malaysia (the Pergau Dam). The decision was taken to fulfil a pledge earlier made by Margaret Thatcher, when she was Prime Minister, to the Prime Minister of Malaysia. That pledge was widely believed to have been part of an arrangement to secure the export of arms.

The decision to support the money was investigated and criticised by the Comptroller and Auditor General as well as by two House of Commons select committees. During these investigations it was revealed that senior civil servants had questioned the legality of the decision and advised ministers against making the grant. Their concern was that the project was not economically sound and that the expenditure would not further development.

Following these investigations, the World Development Movement (WDM), a body which campaigns to improve the quality of British aid to developing countries, applied for judicial review challenging the legality of the Foreign Secretary's decision.

Rejecting the Government's argument that the WDM ought not to be heard because it was not directly affected (it lacked standing to challenge) the court held that Douglas Hurd had acted unlawfully.

The Overseas Development and Co-operation Act 1990, section 1, provides that financial aid may be given 'for the purpose of promoting the development ... of a country'. This implies that the aid can only be given for projects which are economically sound. In this instance the project was not established to be economically sound and the payment was therefore unlawful. The Government did not appeal against the court's decision.

Sometimes new secondary or even primary legislation will be required to give effect to judgements. If the Government decides that it cannot live with the court decision it could ultimately overturn it by Act of Parliament. Given its dominance of Parliament through control of the majority party, the executive can usually escape the effect of adverse judicial decisions where it feels it needs to.

Litigation may also have more subtle, long-term effects on the way government functions. It has been argued that the:

> most profound and enduring influences of judicial review are not to be found by examining the statute book, or by seeking formalised and public shifts of policy in responses to litigation. Rather they are to be found in the effects of litigation on the less accessible aspects of government: the internal and informal working practices of departments, their management systems and decision-making culture.[1]

For example, in recent years lawyers have come to play a more active part in decision making in local and central government. Officials have been encouraged to think far more carefully about the legal implications of their work and the prospect that they might be legally challenged and forced to explain themselves

---

[1] M. Sunkin and A. Le Sueur, 'Can Government Control Judicial Reviews?', *Current Legal Problems*, 44 (1991), p. 162

to the courts. Whether this leads to better quality decision making or simply to more defensive and cautious approaches remains an open question. However, taken in conjunction with the administrative reforms of 'Next Steps' and the growth of executive agencies, it certainly implies major changes in practice.

Political controversies about judicial review

What goes on within government departments is usually hidden both from the public gaze and the scrutiny of academic researchers. In any case, routine procedures are hardly likely to capture the popular imagination. For most people it is the high profile and very public nature of recent controversial clashes between government and the courts which is significant. Certainly, in recent years, Conservative Government ministers became far more overtly critical of the judges.

During the final years of the Major Government, the relationship became particularly tense. By convention, ministers and MPs use respectful and deferential language about judges and court judgements even when they dislike them. During 1995 this public decorum broke down: ministers and their supporters became robustly critical about what was seen as increasingly inappropriate judicial activism.

This change was largely prompted by a series of high profile legal challenges to decisions taken by the then Home Secretary, Michael Howard. Following these he was held, for example, to have acted unlawfully when he used prerogative powers to alter the Criminal Injuries Compensation Board Scheme; when he excluded the cult leader, the Rev. Moon, from the United Kingdom without first affording him an opportunity to make representations; and when he delayed referring the cases of IRA prisoners to the parole board.

Plate 11.1 Chris Riddell cartoon in the *Observer Review*, 26 May 1996: During the final years of the Major Government, relations between the Government and the judges deteriorated. In particular, the populist law and order instincts of the then Home Secretary, Michael Howard, led him to make several high profile decisions which were held to be unlawful by senior judges

According to *The Times* (3 November 1995) there was 'a potentially alarming hostility between an over-mighty executive and an ambitious judiciary'. The tabloid press was more outspoken. The *Daily Express* denounced what it saw as 'the sickness sweeping through the senior judiciary – galloping arrogance' and a headline in the *Daily Mail* asked rhetorically of Judge Sedley's judgement in the Moon case, 'does this judge think he's above democracy?'. According to one judge there was a 'hate campaign' against the judiciary.

As well as illustrating the way in which judicial decisions can act as an irritant to government, these events also highlight the public interest in the constitutional limits of what judges can legitimately do. This in turn raises a key question: what are the constitutional justifications for judicial review in a modern liberal democracy?

THE CONSTITUTIONAL JUSTIFICATIONS FOR JUDICIAL REVIEW

The current system of judicial review has roots going back centuries. Like those of Parliament itself, these pre-date modern conceptions of democracy. Unlike Parliament, however, the courts have no visible democratic credentials in the sense that judges are not elected and are not accountable to the people for their decisions. They cannot be removed if their decisions are unpopular and there is no obvious way of ensuring that they act in accordance with the wishes of the community. Upon what basis, then, can the courts claim authority to review and invalidate decisions taken by elected and politically accountable ministers, elected local authorities and other official bodies? This question lies at the core of most discussions of the relationship between the courts and government. While many have attempted to reconcile the conflicting tensions between judicial review and democratic theory, others argue that this is impossible.

How is this approached within the British scheme of things? Three main lines of thinking may be used to justify and explain the constitutional justification for judicial review. For convenience these may be labelled the 'powers-based', the 'impact-based', and the 'process-based' approach to judicial review.

The powers-based approach

The powers-based approach assumes that the principal task for the courts is to ensure that public bodies act in accordance with the powers granted to them by Parliament. The main conceptual tool used by the judges in performing this task is the *ultra vires* doctrine (*ultra vires* is Latin for 'beyond the powers'). In essence the *ultra vires* doctrine rests on the theory that public bodies only have those legal powers which have been conferred explicitly or implicitly by Parliament. If they act beyond these powers their actions lack a legal basis and can be struck down by the courts as invalid and of no legal effect.

This view of the judicial role assumes that the constitutional system can be understood as a hierarchy. At the top stands Parliament, the supreme law-maker,

Key term

Powers-based approach – the approach to judicial review which assumes that the principal task of the courts is to, ensure that public bodies act in accordance with the powers granted to them by Parliament.

Key term

Ultra vires – the doctrine that public bodies have only those powers explicitly or implicitly granted by Parliament, and no others.

and below it are the subordinate authorities of the state to which it delegates legal powers. Within this structure, the judicial role is to ensure that these subordinate authorities do not exceed the powers which have been conferred upon them. In this way the courts play a policing role on behalf of Parliament.

This 'top down' conception of a legal system is not inherently democratic. However, since Parliament is assumed to be politically accountable to the electorate, the judges also derive their ultimate authority from this democratic base.

The main practical implications of this line of theory may be summarised as follows:

1. Judges have no power to question the validity of parliamentary legislation itself, unless Parliament has authorised them to do so. This is indeed the orthodox justification for the court's power to review Acts of Parliament to ensure that they comply with European Community law. Parliament gave the judiciary this authority when it enacted the European Community Act in 1972. Likewise, Parliament could enact a Bill of Rights giving power to judges to invalidate primary legislation which conflicts with human rights provisions contained in the Bill.

2. Judicial review is essentially a technical process by which the judges are required to apply Parliament's intention as it is expressed or implied in the words of statutes.

3. Judges are unable to impose upon official bodies obligations derived from principles or values not contained in legislation, since their main task is to ensure that ministers and others act in accordance with the will of Parliament.

This approach sees the system of review as a hierarchy within which the courts are primarily concerned with discerning how much power Parliament intended to give public authorities. As such it contrasts with the approach taken in countries which have constitutional guarantees of individual rights and liberties, like the United States. Here, although issues of powers necessarily arise, judicial attention primarily focuses on the impact that official action has on the rights and liberties of citizens. As we shall see, this approach is becoming more important here as well.

CRITICISMS OF THE POWERS-BASED APPROACH

In recent years writers have questioned the adequacy of both the powers-based image of judicial review and of the *ultra vires* doctrine. Oliver[2], for example, argues that the doctrine no longer provides an adequate basis for the courts' jurisdiction, and that much judicial practice simply cannot be explained by *ultra vires*. For example, judges often adopt a fairly liberal approach to the interpretation of statutes and are inclined to give effect to the spirit of the legislation rather than the literal meaning of the words used. Also, it is now well established that courts will intervene to invalidate *abuse* of power and unfairness, as well as *excess* of power. When they do so they apply principles which are made by judges and rarely, if ever, specifically referred to in statutes. Moreover, it is difficult to see

---

[2] D. Oliver, 'Is the *Ultra Vires* the Basis of Judicial Review?', *Public Law* (1987), p. 567

how the doctrine can justify judicial review where powers are not granted by Parliament. Such cases arise when ministers claim to exercise powers granted by royal prerogative or when courts are called upon to review bodies which have not been established by Parliament.

More fundamental criticisms may be levelled at the democratic credentials of the doctrine itself. These credentials rest on a theory of parliamentary democracy which is now widely criticised for failing to provide an effective system of accountability (elections are too sporadic and the executive is usually able to control the House of Commons), or adequate protection for minority interests.

The impact-based approach

Impact-based approach – the approach to judicial review which assumes that the principal task of the courts is to protect the rights and interests of citizens, rather than to ensure that public bodies act in accordance with the powers granted to them by Parliament.

Unlike the powers-based approach which concentrates on the legal powers possessed by public bodies, the impact-based approach to judicial review focuses on the impact that governmental decisions have on the rights and interests of citizens. From this perspective its function is to protect these rights rather than to police the will of Parliament. This way of thinking can be traced back several centuries. However, as the concept of parliamentary supremacy took hold and the *ultra vires* doctrine grew to dominate judicial thinking, the impact-based approach declined in importance. Its recent revival owes much to the renewed interest in securing greater protection for human rights, both internationally and within the United Kingdom. The influence of the European Convention on Human Rights on European Community Law (see Briefing 11.4), as well as the legal consensus that a Bill of Rights should be introduced in the UK, has given the approach particular momentum. It is now very influential within the judiciary.

Typical of the impact-based approach is the argument that judges should ensure not only that public bodies have the appropriate legal powers, but also that they can justify decisions which interfere with the rights and interests of citizens, by showing that they have acted fairly and reasonably. The more important the rights infringed, the higher the level of justification required. Where decisions impinge upon rights which are regarded as being fundamental, judges will subject decisions to very intense scrutiny, including scrutiny of the merits of the action taken. One judge, Sir John Laws, for example, has said that:

> The greater the intrusion proposed by the body possessing public power
> over the citizen into an area where his fundamental rights are at stake, the
> greater must be the justification which the public authority must demonstrate.

He went on to say that ministers will be left largely to their own devices when dealing with matters which are not for the judges to become involved with, such as national economic policy. However, courts 'will scrutinise the *merits*' of decisions much more closely when they concern refugees or free speech.[3]

---

[3] Sir J. Laws, 'Is the High Court the Guardian of Fundamental Constitutional Rights?', *Public Law* (1993), p. 69

BRIEFINGS

11.4 THE EUROPEAN CONVENTION FOR THE PROTECTION OF HUMAN RIGHTS

The European Convention of Human Rights and Fundamental Freedoms (ECHR) came into force in 1953. The Convention is an international treaty to which the UK is a party. The main provisions of the ECHR are as follows:

- the right to life (Art. 2);
- freedom from torture or inhuman or degrading treatment or punishment (Art. 3);
- freedom from slavery, servitude or forced or compulsory labour (Art. 4);
- the right to liberty and security of the person (Art. 5);
- the right to a fair trial (Art. 6);
- freedom from retroactive criminal offences and punishment (Art. 7);
- the right to respect for private and family life, home and correspondence (Art. 8);
- freedom of thought, conscience and religion (Art. 9);
- freedom of expression (Art. 10);
- freedom of assembly and association (Art. 11);
- the right to marry and to found a family (Art. 12);
- the right to an effective national remedy (Art. 13);
- freedom from discrimination in respect of the rights protected by the Convention (Art. 14);
- the right to property (Art. 1 of the First Protocol);
- the right to education (Art. 2 of the First Protocol);
- the right to free elections (Art. 3 of the First Protocol).

Most of the rights set out in the European Convention are qualified by expressions allowing interference with the right 'in accordance with the law [of the state]' or in circumstances where interference with the right is 'necessary in a democratic society'. Article 15 also allows states to interfere with rights 'In times of war or other public emergency threatening the life of the nation'.

In order to secure the protection of these rights the ECHR established the European Commission of Human Rights and the European Court of Human Rights, both based in Strasbourg. (These institutions must not be confused with the institutions of the European Community and in particular the European Commission and the European Court of Justice.)

Those claiming that the UK has breached the provisions of the ECHR may petition the European Commission on Human Rights, which is a body of independent experts. The Commission decides whether the complaint should be considered on its merits. If the complaint is considered and a friendly settlement is not reached, the Commission issues a report containing its opinion as to whether a breach has occurred. The report has no binding legal effect, but the matter may be referred by the Commission or by a State to the European Court of Human Rights for final adjudication. If the case is not referred to the Court, it will be dealt with by the Committee of Ministers of the Council of Europe, which is composed of representatives of the Members States of the Council of Europe.

Because the ECHR is a treaty, it is not part of UK internal law. Since the ECHR has yet to be incorporated into UK law its provisions cannot confer rights upon individuals which can be relied on in UK courts. Note that the ECHR differs from the European Union and European Community law. European Community Law is also based on treaty provisions, but, unlike the ECHR, European Community Law has been incorporated into UK law by the European Community Act 1972.

The current Government has agreed to enact a Bill of Rights, which is most likely to incorporate relevant provisions of the ECHR into English and Scottish law so that they can be relied upon before domestic courts.

While it may be self-evident that judges should be able to protect fundamental rights, it is not self-evident that in a democracy they should be able to upset decisions of elected ministers. How then can this be justified? It seems that two types of justification are possible.

One is to argue that courts must have the power to protect fundamental rights and liberties because such rights are basic to the very dignity of individuals. No other justification is needed, because in seeking to protect such rights against government interference judges are furthering values which form the very basis of our democratic system.

The other possible justification looks beyond the dignity of individuals. It argues that when judges claim the authority to protect fundamental rights they are giving effect to principles and values which are central to our society and culture, even though Parliament has not embodied these rights in specific legislation. In other words such rights must be protected by judges even where Parliament does not say so (and may say the reverse). After all Parliament may be more influenced by the political goals of the executive than it is by respect for human rights. For this reason judicial review provides a vital counterbalance to the power of an executive-dominated Parliament. It helps to ensure that public bodies act in accordance with principles which cannot be manipulated by the whims of passing majorities.

In developing human rights principles, the courts are able to play a more proactive role in society than is contemplated by the *ultra vires* doctrine. They can positively help to secure values that make democracy a worthwhile system for all citizens, and not only for those whose interests are directly promoted by those in power.

Far from viewing judicial intervention as being antidemocratic, this approach sees the role of judges as being central to democracy and the promulgation of democratic values.

CRITICISMS OF THE IMPACT-BASED APPROACH

The impact-based approach to judicial review could be criticised at various levels. The first practical problem is one of uncertainty. Of course we should protect fundamental rights, such as free speech and liberty. But in what sense are these rights fundamental and what other rights and interests could individuals and groups claim to be fundamental? Would rights to privacy, to family life, to a clean and healthy environment qualify? What about rights to housing or education?

Is the decision about what is or is not fundamental to be left to the judges? If so, will citizens, ministers and other officials be able to predict what judges will decide? Suppose, which is likely, that the views of judges are controversial. This question raises other constitutional problems. Given that the nature of fundamental rights may be controversial, why should a judge's view on what is appropriate in the circumstances be constitutionally sounder than that of a minister?

In practice judges decide for themselves what principles such as reasonableness and fairness mean and what they require in specific cases. This being so, what is to stop judges using these principles to strike down decisions of public bodies because they disagree with the decision made or action taken? In the words of R. Cotterrell[4], the 'invocation of values in judicial review appears [to be] a cloak for the exercise of judicial discretion, the activity of judges as essentially political actors'. He argues that when judges interfere with the decisions of ministers and other official agencies by employing principles and values: 'they

---

[4] R. Cotterrell, 'Judicial Review and Legal Theory', in G. Richardson and H. Genn (eds), *Administrative Law and Government Action* (Oxford: Oxford University Press, 1994), p. 28

appear, more often than not, to be putting forward their own discretion alongside or in competition' with those of governmental decision makers. Even if these appearances are misleading, for some they are sufficient to cast serious doubts about the democratic legitimacy of judicial review.

A further concern follows from the way judges exercise their discretion. While some judges advocate the protection of rights and liberties, the record of the courts in providing such protection is at best mixed. Even in recent years, the courts have consistently held that they will not intervene to protect individual rights where government has acted in the interests of national security (e.g. the famous GCHQ case, see Briefing 11.5).

BRIEFINGS

11.5 JUDICIAL REVIEW OF THE GCHQ CASE

Relying on prerogative powers, the then Minister for the Civil Service (who was also the Prime Minister) Margaret Thatcher gave an oral instruction banning union membership at the Government Communication Headquarters (GCHQ). Employees who refused to relinquish their membership would no longer be able to work at GCHQ. There was no prior consultation with the unions or with the employees affected. The decision to impose the ban was later announced in the House of Commons by the Foreign Secretary, Sir Geoffrey Howe.

The Council for Civil Service Unions, together with five individuals affected, applied for judicial review of the banning order on the ground that the failure to consult was unfair. The Government claimed that the matter could not be reviewed by the courts because (a) the ban was imposed under prerogative powers, and (b) the decision was taken in the interests of national security. The House of Lords held that the courts can review the exercise of certain prerogative powers and that in this case the Government had acted unfairly. However, the ban was not held to be unlawful because there was evidence to show that the Government had acted in the interests of national security. It appeared that the Government feared that if it had consulted prior to imposing the ban this might lead to industrial action and threaten the work of GCHQ.

The saga is significant for a variety of reasons. It illustrates a situation in which the executive can make decisions with minimal parliamentary scrutiny. Because the decision was taken under prerogative powers, the Commons only learnt of it after it had been announced. As soon as it could, the Commons' Select Committee on Employment investigated the events leading up to the ban and issued a report heavily critical of Government.

The court decision is important, first because it decided that judges can review the exercise of prerogative powers and a failure to consult. On the other hand, the case also illustrates the reluctance of the courts to intervene to protect individual interests where the government claims to act in the interests of national security. For a full discussion of the case see Andrew Le Sueur and Maurice Sunkin, *Public Law* (Harlow: Longman, 1997), especially Chapter 1.

To summarise, the impact-based approach claims to be justified by reference to community or society values, but it can be criticised on the grounds:

- that it is impossible to know for sure what these values are;

- that it is unclear upon what authority judges can decide what they are;

- in any case the past record of the judges in the protection of human rights raises questions about their ability to protect such rights in the future.

Process-based approaches

Some of these problems may be avoided by adopting a third, process-based, approach to judicial review. While there are several lines of thinking, they are connected by the general idea that citizen participation in government is central to democracy. This being so, courts have a legitimate role in ensuring that citizens can participate as fully and as effectively as possible. At its narrowest, this means that the decision-making procedures adopted by public bodies must enable participation and, in this sense, be fair.

The implications of process-based approaches, however, extend beyond the procedures which must be followed by ministers and official bodies in specific situations. If citizens are to participate effectively in government then they must have access to information and to other resources. Participation, in this sense, therefore implies not only procedural rights, but effective systems of accountability including a culture of openness and real opportunities to influence governmental decision making. This form of participation implies continuous involvement of citizens in government and is therefore not satisfied by the ability to vote at periodical elections.

Arguably, the courts have a key role in ensuring that this involvement is possible. Judicial review is in these terms an important way of imposing accountability on government. It can ensure that official bodies adopt procedures which reflect principles of openness. Judicial review also enables those wanting to challenge official actions to participate in decision making. Seen from this perspective, it may be argued that judges are justified in using their discretion to further accountability and participation. Some have even argued that judges might also be justified in reviewing Parliament itself in order to impose 'quality controls' on primary legislation and to ensure that Parliament fully complies with democracy and the rule of law.

CRITICISMS OF PROCESS-BASED APPROACHES

Process-based theories of judicial review have many attractions. Ultimately, however, they depend on an acceptance of the underlying theory that democracy justifies the use of judicially created principles to promote participation in government. Some may doubt, however, that judges are willing and/or able to develop principles which promote participation. Again, why should their opinions be valued more than those of politicians who owe their place to popular participation in elections?

In addition there are problems associated with access to the courts. Given the cost of litigation, only certain organisations and individuals have the resources to make regular use of judicial review. These are thus able to exercise a disproportionate influence on judicial attitudes. While process-based theories present the courts as democratic institutions, in practice the courts are likely to be of greatest use to those already well placed to exert pressure through the parliamentary system.

THE FUTURE OF JUDICIAL REVIEW IN A NEW LABOUR GOVERNMENT

Whichever of these justifications is adopted, everything indicates that the role of the courts will become even more important and controversial in the future. The New Labour Government's advocacy of constitutional reform, including the introduction of a Bill of Rights and greater devolution, will almost certainly increase the range of problems that come to be handled by judges. In any case, the influence of European law and the example of the European Court of Justice will also strengthen this trend. It will be particularly reinforced if the EU extends its areas of operation in Britain, and thus multiplies the number of possible points of conflict between European and domestic legislation.

We need not assume, however, that judicial involvement in these cases will necessarily involve the same level of controversy and hostility as became evident under the Major administration. A Labour government introducing the Convention on Human Rights into Britain and agreeing to enhance European jurisdiction can hardly object when these are taken up by the judges. A government which wills judicial review must also accept it when it occurs in practice. Future Conservative governments will have to adapt themselves to a changed situation. In the encounters of the mid-1990s, a somewhat discredited government lost more than it gained by taking on the judges. This lesson will not be lost in the future. We may expect therefore that judicial reviews of administrative actions will not only increase as a matter of practice in the future but also become more generally accepted as a regular feature of the Constitution.

SUMMARY

This chapter has:

- Traced the growth in judicial review of administration since the early 1980s (see Milestones for developments from 1964 to 1993);
- Pointed out, however, that it has occurred more in fields such as immigration and housing policy than on individual rights, taxation, and so forth;
- Commented on the great political impact of individual cases (Pergau Dam, arms to Iraq, etc.) where the Government has been held to be wrong and political controversy has ensued;
- Examined the various constitutional justifications for review. None are entirely conclusive but in combination they make a powerful case for an active judicial role;

ESSAYS

1. How significant are the statistics on the trends in use of judicial review since the early 1980s?

2. On what grounds should the judges be able to review the decisions of ministers? Why is this question important?

3. There can be no justification for unelected judges to interfere with decisions of government in a modern democracy such as the UK.'

'Judicial review is a key component of the British system of democracy.'

Which of these views is the more accurate and why?

PROJECTS

1. Law in the News: The task is to study newspapers, radio and television for reports on and articles covering legal proceedings against public bodies.

The work can be undertaken over any period, from say a week to three months. Researchers will be expected to record the subject matter of the litigation (what's the case about?), the parties (who is bringing the case and against which public body: is the case being brought by a pressure group: if so, which and

PROJECTS (continued)

why?) and the court procedure being used (is this a judicial review case or is some other proceeding being used?). What are the main arguments being used? How is the public body responding to the case? What impact is the case having on the news?

The information collected should be quantified. If the work is being shared among a group who have studied different media or different newspapers, compare the quality of information obtained. Do some papers, for example, provide better and more accurate coverage of litigation than others?

Finally, students can be asked to write an assessment of the importance of particular cases and/or the relevance and impact of litigation in general over the period.

2. Rights: The task is to draft a 'Bill of Rights'.

This should be done in small groups. First, consider what rights to include. Second, consider whether the rights are 'fundamental' or whether they can be infringed in certain circumstances and, if so, by whom and in what circumstances?

When your 'Bill of Rights' has been drafted compare it with the European Convention on Human Rights and with the UK's Bill of Rights. How does your Bill differ and why?

• Observed that judicial review may, therefore, be expected both to grow in quantitative terms and become more politically important in the future, particularly in the context of the constitutional changes going on in the British regions and in Europe at the present time.

MILESTONES

MILESTONES IN JUDICIAL REVIEW

1964 Courts emphasise that governmental decisions which affect rights of individuals must be fairly taken: Ridge v. Baldwin [1964] AC 40

1968 Courts decide that they can review decisions of ministers to ensure that they comply with the 'policy and objectives' of legislation: Padfield v. Minister of Agriculture, Fisheries and Food [1968] AC 997

1969 Courts decide that they can intervene even when Parliament has said in statute that decisions 'shall not be called into question in any court of law'. If the decision is *ultra vires* it is not a 'decision' but only a 'purported decision': Anisminic Ltd v. Foreign Compensation Commission [1969] 2 AC 147

1977 Modern procedure for seeking judicial review introduced. This specialist procedure differs from other procedures. In particular, it requires applicants to obtain the leave (permission) of a judge in order to apply for judicial review

1983 Courts decide that the judicial review procedure must be used whenever litigants are seeking to enforce their public law rights against governmental bodies. This means that litigants can no longer avoid obtaining permission from the court before challenging public bodies: O'Reilly v. Mackman [1983] 2 AC 237

1985 Courts decide that they can review the exercise of prerogative powers by the executive on the same grounds as they can review statutory powers. These grounds were summarised by Lord Diplock as being to detect 'illegality, irrationality or procedural impropriety'. Council for Civil Service Union v. Minister for the Civil Service [1985] AC 374

1991 The UK courts, following the guidance of the European Court of Justice, decide that they can review Acts of Parliament to ensure compliance with Community Law: R v. Secretary of State for Transport ex p Factortame Ltd (No.2) [1991] AC 603 (ECJ) and 658 (HL)

1993 Courts hold the Home Secretary to be in contempt of court for deporting a person contrary to an order of the court: M v. Home Office [1994] 1 AC 377

FURTHER READING

Lee Bridges, George Meszaros and Maurice Sunkin, *Judicial Review in Perspective* (London: Cavendish, 1995) and Andrew Le Sueur and Maurice Sunkin, *Public Law* (Harlow: Longman, 1997), puts judicial review in the context of public law as a whole. J. Jowell and D. Oliver (eds), *The Changing Constitution*, (Oxford: Oxford University Press, 3rd edn 1994) relate judicial review to the overall constitutional debate.

PART III

Participation

CHAPTER 12

Pressure groups

Legal appeals and administrative processes do not drive themselves. Civil servants may spontaneously develop their own policies which promote their special departmental views. But these do not usually emerge autonomously within the administration itself. More often than not they respond to demands articulated by sectors of society outside administration – business, trade unions, churches, charities and so on – which may have close contacts with 'their' ministry. Along with political parties, 'pressure groups' are the major agents that articulate interests and causes and inject them into politics.

This chapter looks at the role and influence of pressure groups in the government of Britain and the European Union. It is divided into seven main sections which cover:

- Pressure groups and 'civil society'

- The variety of groups and interests in modern British society

- The differences between pressure groups, political parties, and new social movements

- The many different types of pressure group which exist in Britain, and their main characteristics

- How groups operate: tactics and targets

- Group impact: what factors determine success or failure?

- Pressure groups and democracy: do such groups sustain or threaten democracy?

PRESSURE GROUPS AND 'CIVIL SOCIETY'

Like political parties, pressure groups face two ways. Their leaders interact with and influence administrators and governments. But at the same time groups have their roots deep in society, spreading out to mobilise otherwise isolated individuals and define their political concerns (see Briefing 12.1).

BRIEFINGS

12.1 POLITICAL PARTICIPATION IN BRITAIN

The most authoritative study of the extent to which people undertake political action shows that, apart from voting (75–80 per cent in general elections, about 40 per cent in local elections), most action is stimulated by social groups. About 14 per cent of adults take part in informal group activity and 11 per cent in organised group activity to do with politics (like writing letters or distributing leaflets to express concerns). Twenty-one per cent had contacted a local councillor and almost 15 per cent had attended meetings to protest against some policy. Sixty-three per cent had signed a petition.

Most people do not do these things very often: three or four of them are undertaken in a five-year period. When they do, however, it is generally at the prompting of some group which organises the action. The percentages are from Geraint Parry, George Moser and Neil Day, *Political Participation and Democracy in Britain* (Cambridge: Cambridge University Press, 1992).

Such activities are more than just political. Indeed the strength of many groups is that they are not primarily political at all. Football clubs do not attract their fans by talking politics. But safety at stadiums has been a major concern since the Hillsborough disaster of 1981, when panic broke out among supporters and 81 were killed. Implementing safety measures is expensive and clubs want to have a say in what regulations will be enforced, creating a need to talk with sympathetic MPs and to influence public inspectors.

No matter how remote its concerns seem from politics, a group can quickly be affected by them and so have to act politically. The great strength of most groups is precisely, however, that they have social, economic or welfare concerns at their core. They thus have a major role in mass societies like Britain in reaching out to ordinary members of the population and drawing them into communal life and civic affairs. That is why groups have often been regarded as a major component of a strong 'civil society', which operates autonomously of politics but may from time to time inform and correct politicians and administrators, and promotes general civic engagement (see Briefing 12.2).

Watching television news or reading a good newspaper will quickly show how important and potentially powerful such groups are. An average day's news will report the views and activities of many groups with a wide variety of interests, from business organisations, trade unions, and consumer groups to churches, community associations, arts and leisure organisations, protest groups and charities, among many others.

For theorists of 'civil society', such groups are an essential part of democracy and the natural product of freedom of speech and association. Because of the unequal distribution of resources, however, groups with economic advantages like business and trade unions often seem to succeed in placing their own narrow

Key term

Civil society – the aspects of social and economic life (primarily voluntary associations and private organisations) which are outside the immediate control of the state. A strong civil society based upon a large number and wide variety of private associations and organisations is thought to be the basis for democracy.

BRIEFINGS

12.2 CIVIL SOCIETY, MASS SOCIETY AND SOCIAL GROUPS

The idea of 'civil society' was very important in the classical political theory of the seventeenth and eighteenth centuries. It implied that there was a society which could exist independently of the state and, if necessary, organise itself to overturn a corrupt state and reconstitute it on better lines. The term has come back into fashion recently, particularly to describe the social requirements necessary to sustain democracy in Central and Eastern Europe. A strong civil society would have active and diverse voluntary groups, which need have nothing directly to do with politics. However, they provide a basis on which individuals can relate to other individuals in a spontaneous and unforced way. They give people experience in managing their own affairs, and an organisational basis for political discussion and action if they want to take it. Social groups are absent from a mass society (as contrasted to a civil society). A mass society is composed of isolated individuals who have few links with their neighbours. They have, therefore, no independent social basis on which to evaluate media or political propaganda and can thus be manipulated by leaders and the state.

Key term

Mass society – a society composed of isolated individuals who, because they have no deep roots in community and social life (civil society is weak), are liable to manipulation by political elites.

self-interests above the public good, and so to threaten democracy. Which view of groups is right and why? Do some groups threaten democracy while others strengthen it?

SOCIAL GROUPS AND VOLUNTARY ASSOCIATIONS IN BRITAIN

If a thriving group life is one of the preconditions of a healthy society and vibrant democracy, Britain certainly has it. Table 12.1 shows the percentage of the population over 16 who belong to various types of groups or voluntary associations. To get an idea of how the British situation compares with that of other partners in the European Union the table also lists percentages for Germany, France and Italy.

The main differences which emerge between Britain and the other countries is that Britain has a higher level of group membership and participation than Italy and even France: more than half the population participate in some kind of group in Britain. The situation resembles that of Germany fairly closely, except that sports in Germany attract about double the number they do in Britain.

A majority of the British population is nonetheless mobilised, and into a range of activities which extends right across the spectrum from the altruistic and charitable to economic and self-interested, taking in cultural and overtly political activities along the way.

Does this mean Britain has a sound civil society, with a high level of participation and social engagement? Or does high membership show the potential to split society apart between class-based groups pursuing their own self-aggrandisement? Probably a bit of both, although the table emphasises social pursuits and charities more than economic self-interest as a basis for social groupings.

Table 12.1 Percentage of population over 16 belonging to different types of groups 1989/90

Type of group	UK	Germany	France	Italy
Social welfare services for elderly, handicapped or deprived people	7.1	7.2	6.6	4.1
Religious or church organisations	16.6	15.9	6.2	8.0
Education, arts, music or cultural activities	9.3	12.0	8.8	4.9
Trade unions	14.4	15.7	5.2	5.9
Political parties or groups	4.9	7.5	2.7	5.0
Local community action on issues like poverty, employment, housing, racial equality	2.7	1.7	3.3	1.6
Third world development or human rights	2.0	2.2	2.6	1.1
Conservation, the environment, ecology	5.0	4.6	2.3	3.3
Professional associations	9.8	8.9	5.0	3.9
Youth work (e.g. scouts, guides, youth clubs, etc.)	4.6	3.6	3.2	3.6
Sports or recreation	16.9	32.3	15.7	11.3
Women's groups	4.8	5.6	1.0	0.4
Peace movement	1.1	2.0	0.5	1.2
Animal rights	1.9	4.8	2.3	1.7
Voluntary organisations concerned with health	3.5	4.4	2.8	2.6
Other groups	7.1	8.9	5.3	2.1
None	0.0	0.0	0.0	0.0
Don't know/No answer	1.3	0.2	0.4	0.1

Source: S. Ashford and N. Timms, *What Europe Thinks: A Study of Western European Values* (Aldershot: Dartmouth, 1992), p. 142
Note: The data are based on responses to the question: 'Please look carefully at the following list of voluntary organisations and activities and say which, if any, do you belong to'

However, business groups, while small in membership terms and lumped under 'other' in Table 12.1, may still have a lot of power from being better financed and organised and having strategic economic importance (Chapter 2). So this brief survey of membership is far from telling us everything about pressure groups in Britain. To know more we need to analyse their characteristics and activities much more closely.

PRESSURE GROUPS, POLITICAL PARTIES AND SOCIAL MOVEMENTS

'Pressure groups' is the term generally applied to social groups when they get involved in politics. Pressure groups of course, being primarily social and economic in nature, are mostly not dedicated to such activity. They can be defined as

Key term

Pressure groups –
private, voluntary
organisations which wish
to influence or control
particular public policies
without actually becoming
the government or
controlling all public
policy.

private, voluntary organisations which want to influence or control particular public policies, but do not want to take over the government or control all policy making.

Four main features distinguish pressure groups from political parties:

- Parties want to become the government, pressure groups only want to influence government. Action on Smoking and Health (ASH), for example, wants to influence a small part of government policy, but does not want control.

- Parties have broad policy interests, pressure groups have narrow policy interests. The British Field Sports Society is concerned with the issue of hunting and counters attempts to stop it, but nothing else.

- Parties are primarily political, pressure groups are not. Many try to avoid politics as much as possible. The Rambler's Association becomes involved in politics only when access, walking and the countryside are involved.

- Parties fight elections, most pressure groups do not. The British Medical Association (BMA) is a powerful pressure group in the health sector, but it does not run candidates for political office.

At the same time, there is no *very* clear distinction between political parties and pressure groups. Some pressure groups have a very broad range of policy interests, for example, the Trades Union Congress (TUC) and the Confederation of British Industries (CBI). Some groups (e.g. Friends of the Earth) are inextricably bound up with politics: to save the environment you need to change everything.

Plate 12.1 Single issue politics: 'tree people' protesting at the site of the Newbury By-pass demonstration

Certain groups do fight elections, although some seem more interested in getting publicity than winning. One thing is clear, however: while there are few political parties, the range, diversity, and number of groups are enormous.

Pressure groups and new social movements

A distinction between pressure groups and new social movements is even harder to draw. The term 'new social movements' was introduced to describe the organisations that emerged in the 1970s and concerned themselves with the environment, nuclear energy and weapons, peace, women and minorities. They have a wider range of policy interests than most pressure groups, but are more loosely knit than political parties. In some ways the new social movements form a subset of pressure groups which want to influence not only government policy, but also public opinion on a broad range of issues. It is significant that, while political party membership has generally declined in recent years, new social movement and group membership have increased. Perhaps this indicates a shift from party to group politics in modern society.

Some people dislike the term 'pressure group' because they think it implies the use of sanctions, coercion, or illegitimate pressure. They prefer the term 'lobby' or 'interest groups'. 'Pressure groups' is used here as the collective term, partly because it does not necessarily connote illegitimate pressures or sanction, and partly because the term 'lobby' is also misleading. Not all – not even the majority of – pressure groups congregate in the lobby of the House of Commons to whisper in the ears of MPs. The term 'interest groups' is also reserved for a particular kind of pressure group. See Briefing 12.3.

Key term

New social movements – are organisations which emerged in the 1970s in order to influence public policy about such issues as the environment, nuclear energy and weapons, peace, women, and minorities. They have wider policy interests than most pressure groups, but are more loosely knit than political parties.

Key term

'Fire brigade' groups – are formed to fight a specific issue and dissolved when it is over (e.g. the Anti-Poll Tax Federation).

Plate 12.2 Nuclear demonstrators gather outside the French Embassy in London, September 6, 1995, to protest against nuclear tests at the Muroroa Atoll in the South Pacific

BRIEFINGS

12.3 DIFFERENT TYPES OF PRESSURE GROUPS

Interest groups

Interest (or sectional) groups represent the interests of occupational groups. The three main types are business organisations, professional associations and trade unions. Major examples include the Institute of Directors, the British Medical Association, and the Transport and General Workers Union. The National Union of Students (NUS) is an interest group. Such organisations are mainly (not exclusively) concerned with material (mainly economic) interests.

Cause groups

Cause groups (promotional or attitude groups) promote a general cause or idea. Membership is not limited to particular occupations, and can cover a very broad range of people and activities: religion, education, culture, leisure, sport, charity and welfare, community, social, youth, and scientific. Major examples include the Royal Society for the Protection of Birds (RSPB), Shelter (a housing action group), the Consumers' Association, and Amnesty International.

New social movements

These are new political organisations broader than the average interest or cause group but more loosely knit than political parties. The most obvious ones like Greenpeace are concerned with saving the environment.

Episodic groups

These groups are not normally political, but may become so when circumstances require (e.g. football clubs).

Fire brigade groups

Such groups are formed to fight a specific issue, and dissolve when it is over (e.g. the Anti-Poll Tax Federation).

Peak associations

Peak associations are 'umbrella' organisations that co-ordinate the activities of different pressure groups in the same area of interest. Examples include the Confederation of British Industry (CBI) and the Trades Union Congress (TUC), but equivalents exist for education, the arts, sports, churches, charities, and community associations. There are international peak associations, globally and in Brussels.

Insider groups

Insider groups (sometimes called established groups) are recognised as speaking for legitimate interests and have access to decision makers. Some are incorporated into official consultative bodies or consulted regularly. Most professional associations have an official status within policy-making bodies and some groups are legally entitled to be consulted, for example, the National Farmers' Union in the annual farm prices review. Insider groups have a privileged status, but pay for this by playing by the rules of the Whitehall and Westminster game, which means not being too critical of ministers and behaving 'responsibly'.

12.3 DIFFERENT TYPES OF PRESSURE GROUPS (continued)

Outsider groups

These groups do not have easy or official access to decision makers. They are kept at arm's length because of who they are or what they represent. Examples include the Campaign for Nuclear Disarmament (CND) and the Animal Liberation Front. Not all groups want greater insider status, because they fear that they might become 'domesticated' by being too closely involved with government. Sometimes groups move from an outsider to more of an insider status, like environmental groups in the late 1980s.

Cross-bench groups

Some groups are inevitably aligned with a particular party, but others try to maintain party neutrality, knowing that they must deal with whichever party is in power. They are called cross-bench groups after cross-bench (non-party) members of the House of Lords. In recent years some trade unions have sought cross-bench independence from the Labour Party.

THE WORLD OF PRESSURE GROUPS

The group world has three main features already hinted at: its huge numbers, its great diversity and the density of its networks.

Numbers

> **Key term**
>
> **Episodic groups** – groups which are not normally political, but become so when circumstances require. For example, football clubs are politically involved only when issues such as football ground safety or hooliganism become a political issue.

There are hundreds of thousands of organised groups in the country, so many that it is virtually impossible to count them. A few are continuously active in politics, but others (episodic groups) are only sporadically involved. The Fabian Society and Charter 88 are political pressure groups, but the Rum Importers' Association is only political when it needs to be. It is therefore important to distinguish between the group world, which covers all voluntary associations, and the pressure group world which includes the organisations which are politically active. Government now affects so many people and interests that tens of thousands of groups are likely to be politically active in national and local politics at any given time.

Diversity

There is a huge variety and diversity of groups; they cover almost every conceivable interest, and come in many forms. Some groups are loose-knit and informal; others are highly structured. Some are old and established; some are ad hoc and short-lived (e.g. the Anti-Poll Tax Federation). Some are local, others large and national or international. Some are small, others are impressively large and wealthy. The Confederation of British Industry (CBI) employs 400 people, has an annual budget of six million pounds, and specialist research and public relations departments. The size and diversity of the group world means that the political arena is crowded with groups, and there are often rival groups on a given issue: Sunday trading, abortion, drinking hours, capital punishment, blood sports, road building, economic matters, and so on.

Networks

> **Key term**
>
> **Peak (umbrella) associations** – co-ordinate the activities of different organisations with the same general interests (e.g. The Trades Union Congress or the Council of Churches).

Many groups are part of a complex and elaborate structure which rises from local branches to area and regional organisations, to national organisations with head-quarters in London (and international ones based in Brussels). A trade union such as the Transport and General Worker's Union (TGWU) is organised vertically in this way from its local branches to the national office. Many local groups are also linked horizontally with a number of other similar local organisations. For example, TGWU branches are members of their local Trade Union Council, an 'umbrella' organisation or 'peak association' which co-ordinates all trade unions in a locality. Local Trade Union Councils are, in their turn, vertically organised into a national network with the Trade Union Congress (TUC) at its peak. This complicated horizontal and vertical linkage is repeated in many areas of group activity such as charities, churches, business, the professions, sport, education, arts, and leisure. Often national associations and national peak associations are themselves integrated into international organisations such as the European Trade Union Confederation (ETUC), the Olympic movement, and the World Council of Churches.

> **Key term**
>
> **Interest groups (sectional groups)** – are pressure groups which represent the interests of particular economic or occupational groups, especially business organisations, professional associations, and trade unions.

Classification of pressure groups

Pressure groups come in so many forms that attempts to classify them run into difficulties. But some helpful distinctions can be made. Interest groups are generally regarded as organisations or associations linked to one's job or occupation, which give individuals in them a set of common interests to pursue. Good examples are trade unions and professional associations. Such groups have a variety of other objectives than political ones, such as maintaining wage levels and standards in their own area.

> **Key term**
>
> **Cross-bench (non-aligned) groups** – groups which are not aligned with a party and try to maintain party political neutrality (like cross-bench groups in Parliament).

On the other hand, legislation and policy making will be important to them as they affect the way members earn their livelihood. Interest groups may be aligned with a particular party, like trade unions and the Labour Party for example. Most business groups normally make their sympathy and support for the Conservative Party very clear. Professional associations, on the other hand, generally try to stay nonaligned.

Key term

**Cause groups
(promotional groups)** –
promote a general cause
or idea. Unlike interest
groups, their members are
not drawn from particular
occupations but may come
from a wide variety of
social backgrounds.

'Cause' and promotional groups, by way of contrast, usually come together on the basis of some principle or activity that individuals are committed to. Often this is a political cause which focuses attention on Parliament and the Government (Greenpeace and other environmental groups, for example).

The difficulty is that most of the activities of pressure groups overlap at least a little. Hence, the distinction between interest and cause groups is not always clear. The National Union of Teachers is an interest group but it often expresses the same concern for educational quality as some cause groups. Equally, some cause groups promote the interests of those who find it difficult to form their own interest groups, such as children or the mentally or physically handicapped (NSPCC, MIND). Nor is the distinction between nonaligned and party-aligned groups watertight, since many party-aligned groups (the TUC and CBI, for example) try to establish working relations with other organisations in the same sector, whatever their politics. Nevertheless, such categories do give an insight into how groups work politically and how successful they are likely to be.

HOW GROUPS OPERATE

Pressure groups adapt themselves to the institutions they try to influence. In Britain, this means that national pressure groups are usually headquartered in London, because of the concentration of political power in the capital city. They also rather centralised in structure, reflecting the hierarchical nature of the political system.

There are two general rules for pressure group operations. First, get into the policy-making cycle as early as possible, when options are being considered, before government takes a position and the political parties draw public battle lines. Second, work at the highest possible level of the political system to which you have access, because that is where the least effort can have the greatest influence. There is a hierarchy of *pressure points*, starting with the most favoured option, as shown below.

Civil servants

Key term

**Insider groups
(established groups)** –
are pressure groups which
are able to work closely
with elected and appointed
officials in central or local
government.

Efficient and effective groups usually start with top civil servants. First, much pressure group activity does not concern great policy issues, as many assume, but detailed and technical matters which are usually handled by Whitehall departments. Second, the policy cycle often starts and ends with senior civil servants, who draft the early documents and implement policy decisions, so it is sensible to concentrate early efforts on them. Third, groups try to get their views established before the issue is politicised by Government and Opposition parties. 'Insider' groups have the advantage of close working relations with Whitehall because both need and use the other: groups provide civil servants with technical information and practical advice; civil servants provide groups with inside political information, and are channels of communication to ministers. Early consultation between the two may avoid much trouble later on.

Ministers and the Cabinet

Top civil servants cannot 'deliver' their ministers, any more than ministers can guarantee their proposals being accepted by the Cabinet. If an issue is already politicised, then groups may have to go to Westminster to press their case. They will start with ministers and members of the Government, if they can, because this is where the power lies. Insider groups may have access to this high level, where much may be accomplished by small, private meetings. Outsider groups, however, have to work through public campaigns which are more expensive, time-consuming, and uncertain.

Westminster

Groups which fail to convince the Cabinet or the Government, or which have no access to them, may turn to the House of Commons, although it is a larger and more uncertain arena than the Cabinet or top Whitehall offices. Nevertheless, many pressure groups approach Parliament, and most MPs could fill their days several times over just reading mountains of pressure group mail, or receiving delegations. Some groups employ professional lobbyists with contacts and experience, but this is expensive and used mainly by the wealthier interest groups. Groups with a sympathetic MP have been able to take advantage of private members' bills in the Commons (with pressure group assistance the laws on abortion and homosexuality have been changed this way). Some groups have the chance to air their views before select committees, while others have been able to influence party backbench committees. Groups which fail to do so, or which do not have the necessary resources even to try, may use tactics aimed at parties, the general public, or the mass media. See Briefing 12.4 for an example of a pressure group influencing the detail of legislation.

Political parties

Groups with strong links to a political party will use them to try to influence party policy. The League Against Cruel Sports and the Howard League for Penal Reform have sympathisers in the Labour Party, for example, and the Electoral Reform Society among the Liberal Democrats. However, most groups try to maintain a cross-bench status so they can work with whichever party is in power.

BRIEFINGS

12.4 AFFECTING THE DETAIL OF LEGISLATION

In 1996 a very detailed measure requiring water to be supplied to caravan sites was being considered in a Parliamentary standing committee (Chapter 18). It was uncontroversial and the need was not disputed between the parties. The Country Landowners' Association, however, was extremely active in the Committee, using both professional lobbyists and interested MPs (some of them members of the Association). The point with which the CLA was concerned was who would be obliged to install the water-point at the caravan site, the proprietor or the water company. As installation was expensive, members of the CLA would gain financially if responsibility was put on water companies by the legislation. The water companies had, of course, spotted this possibility as they were well able to employ political consultants and lobbyists too. However, more MPs were landowners than shareholders in water companies and were able to be more discreet about declaring their interest. So the CLA had the advantage.

This case illustrates several points:

- even very technical legislation or administration will have positive or negative consequences for groups;

- groups benefiting will often be opposed by groups which might lose, thus promoting more debate and pluralism in the political process;

- however, the group with more resources will usually win;

- 'lobbying' for support may slide over into near corruption where MPs are able to avoid declaring their interest. Given the nexus of connections between politicians and social groups this may often happen, and this situation provoked a series of scandals under the Major Government.

Local councils

Many pressure groups have purely local objectives which simply involve their town or neighbourhood: opposition to a new road, support for parking restrictions or traffic quietening schemes, better local schools. In such cases a natural target is the local council since such matters fall into its immediate remit. Even where pressure is being exerted on a national issue, however, it pays to get the local council on your side. As a popularly elected body it has a legitimate claim to represent local opinion and the resources and expertise to defy or challenge central policy. Councils took an increasing number of cases to the courts in the 1980s, even as far as the European Court.

Public campaigns and the mass media

Public campaigns are often the last resort of pressure groups, but less so than they were, given the ability of groups like Greenpeace to stir up national and even international feeling. In spite of modern mailshot, advertising and marketing techniques, public campaigns tend to be expensive, time consuming, and unpredictable. Some groups use advertising firms, but this can be expensive, and most have to use personal contacts with journalists. If this is not possible, and because there is fierce competition for news space, some groups try to force themselves into the news by organising a demonstration, protest, petition, or some eye-catching event. In extreme cases, illegal or violent means are used to gain public attention.

Courts

Some groups have achieved their goals (equal pay, the abolition of corporal punishment in Scottish schools) by taking cases to judicial review, including the EU's Court of Justice in Luxembourg, and the Council of Europe's Court of Human Rights in Strasbourg. Most groups avoid legal action, however, because it is often costly and the outcome is uncertain.

The European Union

In general, pressure group operations in Brussels are even more expensive and uncertain than those in London. But because the EU is so important, many groups have turned their attention to it, paying special attention to the Commission, as the main executive body of the EU. Groups can operate in Europe in one of four different ways. The simplest is to set up an office to lobby in Brussels, but this is expensive and often groups look around for partners to share the cost. Second, they can combine with similar interests in all other EU states to form a Eurogroup. The EU encourages and officially recognises over a thousand such groups at present, but they tend to be rather weak and fragmented. Third, British groups can form a European pressure group drawing support from some, but not necessarily all, EU Member States. There are thousands of such groups in Brussels. Fourth, groups can try to work through the British government, which takes us back into the kinds of action outlined above.

Policy communities

Groups often use a combination of targets. But the most prestigious insider groups normally work smoothly and quietly by using their high level contacts. Outside groups have to use the noisier methods of public campaigns. Paradoxically, the quieter the group, the greater its influence; the more noisy and obstructive its tactics, the less influential it is likely to be.

Plate 12.3 National Union of Mineworkers rally: Outside groups have to use noisier methods of public campaigns. The miners were a very vocal and ultimately unsuccessful interest group under the Conservative governments

In some cases contacts between pressure groups and government are so tight that they form what is known as a policy community. These are small, stable groups of pressure group representatives and public officials who are in close contact, and who agree on many of the main issues in their particular policy arena. Policy communities have been formed around food and drink policy, technical education and water privatisation. Policy networks, in contrast, are larger, more loosely knit, and have more conflictual sets of interests formed around particular policy areas.

The biggest and most powerful policy community in Britain centres on the financial interests of the City of London (see Chapter 2), which extend into government through the Treasury and the Bank of England. The need to protect the currency and consolidate London's position as the leading international centre is so obvious to policy makers that financial pressure groups need do very little to ensure that their case is heard and heeded. Thus financial interests opposed to inflation, for example, have usually been able to win out over manufacturing interests when it came to raising the price of money. Their supporters in government are much better placed in the Treasury, perhaps the most important government department, than manufacturers at the Department of Trade and Industry, which is much less important.

This also raises the question of 'institutionalised pressure groups', when a government department itself becomes an advocate for a particular interest rather than regulating it. Another example would be the Department of Defence, with regard to arms manufacturers. Britain is one of the largest arms exporters in the world and arms manufacture employs a sizeable proportion of the British workforce. Thus, when Robin Cook, the New Labour Foreign Secretary, began to talk after the election of May 1997 about ethical limits on what kinds of arms could be exported, quiet pressure was exercised through the Defence department to ensure that no real restrictions were imposed, and that Cook moderated his rhetoric.

As noted above, action through the Civil Service is the most effective a pressure group can take. When the Civil Service itself acts on your behalf, an interest is even more powerful. Questions may well be raised as to how far pluralist democracy operates in this case and how far such business and financial interests should even be discussed within the same frame of reference as social groups in general. We will take up this question later, since it does bear very directly on the question of whether pressure group activities are good for democracy or not.

THE IMPACT OF PRESSURE GROUPS

So many factors affect ordinary pressure group campaigns that it is difficult to unravel the part played by any particular group or set of groups. For example, the death penalty was abolished in 1965 after a long campaign by many groups. But the change was also accompanied by a change of government and the arrival of many new MPs, by a series of widely publicised miscarriages of justice, and by a shift in public opinion. Similarly, various environmental groups claim recent successes for their cause, but these have also been helped by media coverage of environmental incidents (nuclear accidents, petrol tanker disasters, burning rain forests), a shift in public opinion, and by pressure from the EU and other international bodies.

While it is impossible to pin down the exact influence of any particular group, a set of general considerations influence their likely impact. These may be grouped under two headings, the first relating to internal features of the groups, and the second to features of their external political environment.

Group features

Some of the internal features of groups that might influence their impact are:

- *Membership size and type*. Groups with a large membership can raise money through subscriptions and contributions. With about 800,000 members the Royal Society for the Protection of Birds (RSPB) has an annual income of about 30 million pounds and a full-time staff of some 600 people.

- *Money.* Some groups are wealthy because of the people and interests they represent. The National Farmers Union (NFU) has 150,000 members and an income of 20 million pounds, compared with Friends of the Earth's 200,000 members and annual income of less than two million. This contrast in resources is typical of that between 'interest groups' of producers (NFU) and 'cause groups' (in this case environmentalists).

- *Organisational advantages.* Some groups are easier to organise than others. Interest group members can be organised at work, but cause group sympathisers are often scattered, and difficult to identify and contact. For this reason producer groups are easier to organise than consumer groups.

- *Membership density.* A group representing practically all its possible members (e.g. the British Medical Association with 100 per cent density) is in a stronger position than a trade union with 50 per cent density.

- *Divided membership.* The BMA speaks for almost all doctors; miners are divided between competing unions.

- *Internal structure.* Interest groups are often centralised, making political action easier. Cause groups are often more decentralised and participatory, making it difficult to respond quickly and effectively to events.

- *Sanctions.* Some groups have powerful sanctions: businesses may move capital or jobs; professional bodies may withdraw co-operation; some organisations can call upon public sympathy. Other groups have few sanctions: the homeless cannot strike, withdraw co-operation, or move their investments.

- *Leadership.* A charismatic leader is an asset. Examples go back to William Wilberforce and the Abolition Society (for the abolition of slavery, one of the first pressure groups) in the late eighteenth century. Recent examples include Frank Field (Child Poverty Action Group), Des Wilson (Shelter) and Jonathan Porritt (Friends of the Earth).

The political environment

Features of the political environment that might affect the impact of pressure groups include:

- *Public opinion.* A group with public support, such as the British Medical Association, is more likely to get a sympathetic hearing from the Government. Conversely, the poor image of students hinders the negotiating power of the National Union of Students (NUS). Public opinion may also change (on environmental issues, for example), and it is not always important. Nurses seem to get a more sympathetic hearing in public than around negotiating tables.

- *Legitimacy.* A group which is thought to speak for legitimate interests – doctors, lawyers, teachers, business – is likely to get a better reception than one which does not, such as groups representing drug addicts or ex-criminals.

- *Insider status.* Insider groups are more likely to be successful than outsider groups.

- *Politicisation.* Much group activity concerns policy detail and technicality. On big political issues, in contrast, groups usually have less room for manoeuvre, since they often compete with parties or other groups.

- *Opposing groups.* Some groups operate alone in their field of interest, especially on technical matters. Others face organised opposition, especially on moral matters such as blood sports, smoking, Sunday shopping and abortion. Groups involved in the same issue are not necessarily equally matched, however. The BMA is powerful, the Patient's Association much weaker.

The Thatcher governments of the 1980s created a difficult environment for pressure groups. In the earlier postwar era of consensus politics, both Conservative and Labour governments co-operated with business and labour organisations to solve economic problems. The most visible expression of this consensus style of policy formulation was the National Economic Development Council (NEDC), created in 1961 to take joint action on economic policy. A good number of similar organisations were subsequently created (as our Milestones at the end of the chapter show) in the 1960s and 1970s. Some writers describe this period as 'corporatist', though others argue that Britain never had sufficiently cohesive interest groups to be a corporatist state like Austria or Switzerland. They prefer the term 'tripartite' to refer to consultation between government, business organisations and trade unions (often described pejoratively as 'beer and sand-wiches at No. 10').

The 'Winter of Discontent' of 1979 effectively brought an end to this period of British politics. When Margaret Thatcher came to power she dismantled or weak-ened many tripartite practices and institutions. According to her, close co-opera-tion between government and pressure groups was neither democratic nor functional, giving too much political power to private, narrow interests, and inter-fering with the efficient operations of the market. It thus caused the very economic problems it was supposed to solve.

Thatcher confronted trade unions and many other groups on these grounds, including businesses, teachers, lawyers, civil servants, doctors, local government associations and the churches. Official advisory bodies were cut by one third, and those remaining were weakened. Many groups were excluded from the early stages of policy formulation, though less often from the final implementation

> **Key term**
>
> **Corporatism** – a system of policy making in which major economic interests work closely together within formal structures of government to formulate and implement public policies. Corporatism requires a formal government apparatus capable of concerting the main economic groups so that they can jointly formulate and implement binding policies.

> **Key term**
>
> **Tripartism** – compared with corporatism, tripartism is a looser, less centralised and co-ordinated system which brings together three main interests (government, business, unions) in economic policy-making. It is a consultative rather than a corporatist method of reaching and implementing decisions.

stages, where group co-operation is often essential to get the membership to accept the measures. The Major Government of the 1990s was less confrontational. It remains to be seen whether the Blair Government will move back towards the consultation of the tripartite era. Even if it does not, we can expect warmer relationships to develop with the trade unions. New Labour is also anxious to keep business and the City on board, and that means consultation.

PRESSURE GROUPS AND DEMOCRACY

Thatcher's policy towards pressure groups was based on the view that they are dangerous for parliamentary democracy. Are they?

In theory, groups play an important part in democracy. They are an important means of political participation and influence, especially for minorities. They collect and sort out group opinions to produce an agreed position (interest aggregation), and defend these opinions in the political arena (interest articulation). Groups inform and educate their members about political issues, and act as channels of communication between citizens, and between citizens and political elites. They mobilise citizens politically, and act as centres of influence outside government. They serve as pools of talent for political recruitment: many politicians start their careers as group activists. Finally, groups help governments by providing them with aggregated opinions, technical expertise, and practical advice. For their part, governments obviously have a democratic duty to consult with all interests affected, including organised groups, and may depend upon them for policy information and implementation.

In practice, the role of pressure groups has been hotly disputed by the competing schools of pluralism, elitism, and the New Right (see Controversy).

Pluralists believe that groups on the whole do not conspire against the general interest in a democracy but rather conflict, because they have different ideas about what the common interest is. This does not rule out the possibility that some groups may be better resourced and altogether more powerful than others, and therefore win out in most situations. Elitists emphasise this last point to the extent of believing that one powerful group may totally dominate decision making to its own advantage, as seems to happen in the case of financial interests in Britain. Adherents of the New Right, like Margaret Thatcher, cut across this argument by regarding all groups, no matter how powerful, as narrow and sectional. It is up to the elected Government to judge on its own what is the national interest and to act on it without consultation.

The main issue between these schools of thought involves the delicate balance between groups having too much and too little power. Certainly, groups have a democratic right to be heard and to try to influence public policy through their arguments. But, as sectional and often narrowly self-interested actors, they do not have the right to make public policy. Too much group power results either in domination by one 'sinister interest' or in fragmented, confused, and unaccountable

Key term

Pluralism – according to pluralist theory political decisions are the outcome of competition between many different groups representing many different interests.

CONTROVERSY

ARE PRESSURE GROUPS A GOOD THING FOR DEMOCRACY?

The Pluralist Case

The greater number and diversity of groups ensures political struggle and competition.

As a result (nearly) all issues are contested by competing groups. Groups rarely get their own way by default.

Groups look for allies in the political struggle which forces them to compromise.

All groups have some resources to fight battles: money, members, leadership skills, public sympathy, or access.

Group resources are not distributed equally, but the inequalities are not cumulative. No group is powerless, none all-powerful.

Power is distributed between many different groups. There is no fixed 'power structure'; it depends on circumstances.

Groups which fail in one arena (Parliament) may succeed in another (the courts, local government, the EU).

Groups do not get everything they want. They compromise to get something.

Some groups cannot always get something positive, but often they can at least veto new proposals.

Pluralist democracy is not perfect, but it works reasonably well, 'warts and all'.

The Elitist Case

The distribution of power in society reflects inequalities of wealth. Some groups have few resources, others many.

Some interests are unorganised, some rely on others to protect them, some are poorly organised, such as minority groups, children, the mentally ill, the homeless, the poor.

The group world is dominated by educated, wealthy, middle and upper class 'joiners'.

Group resources are distributed with cumulative inequalities; some groups have many resources, some have very few.

Groups fight their battles within a political structure and according to rules of the game which are systematically loaded in favour of middle and upper class interests or even a particular sector, like the financial interests of the City of London.

Organisations are internally oligarchic. A few leaders wield power, and are often unelected and unaccountable to members.

A small national elite controls all important decisions, but leaves smaller issues to pluralist competition.

The group world reflects and reinforces the power structure in which the wealthy dominate the political system.

The New Right Case

Groups represent narrow sectional interests; governments are elected by citizens to represent the public good.

Groups distort market operations, especially trade unions, but also professional bodies and some business groups. Their power should be reduced to ensure market competition.

Groups fragment policy making and prevent government developing a coherent programme.

In protecting their sectional interests groups slow economic growth, and cause unemployment, inflation, and high public expenditure.

Groups create 'hyper-pluralism': too many economic and political demands on government.

This undermines good economic policy and democracy and creates 'ungovernability' and 'democratic overload'.

Group leaders are often unelected and unaccountable to their members.

Government may consult and groups may advise, but government should hold the reins of power.

decision making, what is sometimes called 'hyperpluralism'. Too little group power means that government is too autocratic. The difficulty, of course, is knowing what is 'too much' and 'too little' power, because this is a personal political judgement. The balance will presumably be adjusted through the choice of one political party over another at elections, the particular interests favoured by each party being one element which enters into the electoral choice.

ESSAYS

1. Do pressure groups sustain or threaten democracy?

2. Is pluralist theory a more accurate account of the pressure group world than elitist theory?

3. Why are some pressure groups more powerful than others? How can you tell which are more powerful?

PROJECTS

1. What sort of pressure group campaign would you propose to the National Union of Students to improve student grants?

2. Classify all the groups mentioned in this chapter into their different types. What do you learn from this exercise?

3. Make a 'diary' of pressure group activity mentioned in a week's issues of a 'quality' newspaper.

SUMMARY

- Pressure groups are the politically active organisations among the huge number of voluntary and social groups in Britain. Some pressure groups are continuously active, but others (the episodic groups) are only occasionally involved in politics.

- The distinction between pressure groups and parties is not clear-cut, but generally groups have a narrower range of policy interests than parties, and want to influence the Government, not replace it.

- The main features of pressure groups are their huge numbers, great diversity, and density of organisational networks.

- The main targets (pressure points) for groups are: top civil servants, ministers and the Cabinet, Westminster, political parties, the mass media and the public, local councils, the courts and the European Union.

- Insider groups are able to work through civil servants and ministers; outsider groups have to use less certain, more time-consuming methods aimed at the public and the mass media.

- Group influence is impossible to measure but depends upon characteristics such as membership size, type and density; income; ability to recruit members; ability to respond quickly to political change; ability to use sanctions; group unity, and outside factors such as public opinion, legitimacy, insider status, whether their issue is politicised and the power of opposing pressure groups.

- The period of tripartite co-operation in the 1960s and 1970s was brought to an end by Mrs Thatcher who was more inclined to confront and exclude certain groups on the grounds that they represented their own narrow interests and not the national interest.

- Theorists of pluralism (and 'civil society') place great emphasis on the role of groups in democracy. Elite theorists claim that group politics reinforce elite or class power. The New Right argues that group politics in Britain has produced hyperpluralism, ungovernability, and overload.

FURTHER READING

A recent comprehensive book is R. Baggott, *Pressure Groups Today* (Manchester: Manchester University Press, 1995). **On business groups see** W. Grant, *Business and Politics in Britain* (London: Macmillan, 2nd edn 1993) **and on trade unions**, D. Marsh,

MILESTONES

MILESTONES IN THE DEVELOPMENT OF BRITISH PRESSURE GROUPS

1950s British pressure groups 'discovered' by British and American political scientists.

1961 National Economic Development Council (NEDC) set up.

1965 Confederation of British Industry (CBI) formed.

1966 Devaluation of the pound postponed for a year by the Labour Government because of financial pressures from the 'City'.

1969 Trade union pressure forces the Labour Government to abandon plans for trade union reform ('In place of strife').

1970s Rise of the new social movements.

1971 The Conservative Industrial Relations Act reduces trade union powers.

1974 The Prime Minister (Heath) calls an election, as a result of the miners' strike, and loses.
The Labour Government's 'Social Contract' with the trade unions agrees to social legislation and repeal of the Industrial Relations Act in return for a 'prices and incomes policy' but no agreement is struck with business or professional organisations about prices, salaries, or profits.
Manpower Services Commission (a tripartite agency for jobs and training) created, followed by

1975 Health and Safety Commission, and

1976 Advisory, Conciliation, and Arbitration Service (ACAS) to deal with industrial relations disputes.

1979 Thatcher begins to dismantle the machinery of 'tripartism'.

1982 CBI Director-general, Sir Terence Beckett, threatens to 'get the gloves off' with the Thatcher Government over its financially orthodox economic policy.

1984–85 Miners' strike, the most bitter and prolonged industrial dispute since 1926, lost by miners.

1980, 1982, Employment and Trade Union Acts
1984, 1988 reducing powers and rights of trade
1989, 1990 unions

1988 Edwina Currie, junior health minister, resigns after her (true) claim that eggs are widely infected by salmonella angers egg producers and the NFU.

1992 NEDC abolished.

1994–96 Payment to MPs and other incidents of sleaze involving pressure groups and lobbyists prompt Nolan Committee to investigate MPs' interests.

1997-98 Stronger regulation of MPs' interests by House of Commons.

The New Politics of British Trade Unions and the Thatcher Legacy (London: Macmillan, 1992). A good account of European pressure groups is found in S. Mazey and J. J. Richardson, in *Lobbying in the European Community* (Oxford: Oxford University Press, 1993). Slightly older, but concise accounts of British pressure groups can be found in W. Grant, *Pressure Groups, Politics and Democracy in Britain* (London: Philip Allan, 1989), and M. Rush, *Parliament and Pressure Politics* (Oxford: Oxford University Press, 1990).

Useful shorter articles include R. Baggott, 'Pressure Groups and the British Political System: Change and Decline?', in B. Jones and L. Robins (eds.), *Two Decades in British Politics* (Manchester: Manchester University Press, 1992); W. Grant, 'Pressure Groups', *Politics Review*, 1 (1), (1991); and R. Baggott, 'The measurement of Change in Pressure Group Politics', *Talking Politics*, 5 (1), (1992); S. Mazey and R. Richardson, 'Pressure Groups and the EC', *Politics Review*, September 1993: 20–24.

CHAPTER 13

The nature and impact of the mass media

Like pressure groups, newspapers, television and radio influence decision makers and reach out to the populace. Indeed, their scope and influence is greater than that of all but the richest and largest pressure groups.

This is partly because they are also the means ('media') by which pressure groups, along with parties and all other political actors, communicate with each other, with their members and with the public. Newspaper and television groups may act in some ways like pressure groups: pushing certain ideas, pursuing their proprietors' economic interests, supporting particular political parties. But in order to retain their audience and keep up revenues they also have to be more than that, reporting major events and showing themselves open to general ideas. The question is how far they manage to balance the particular points of view of proprietors, managers and staff with the objectivity enforced by regulators and expected by readers and viewers.

This chapter examines the impact of the modern mass media on British politics.

- It compares the state of affairs in 1945, before the media age, with that in the late 1990s, showing how the media system has been transformed out of all recognition. Then it considers three important and interconnected questions:

- What sorts of citizens make what sorts of use of what sorts of political media for what sorts of purposes?

- Do the modern media have an impact of their own on modern politics? Are they just messengers, or do they actively mould and influence political life and public opinion? Four theories of how the media operate help us to answer this question. These are: reinforcement theory, agenda-setting theory, framing theory, and direct effects theory

- Are the British media biased? Do they report the news in a balanced and neutral way, or do they incorporate a systematic political bias into the news, perhaps even a party political bias?

THE POLITICAL MEDIA: 1945 AND 1998

We take the modern media for granted in many ways, and yet their main features are barely a generation old: a choice of five TV channels, colour TV, cable and satellite channels, commercial radio, fat newspapers with supplements, extensive election campaign coverage, election night TV, the broadcasting of Parliament, round the clock broadcasting. A look at the 'Milestones' at the end of this chapter will show how recent are many of the things we take for granted.

A good way of understanding how far we have come in the last 50 years is to compare the postwar situation with the present. In 1945 there was no television, and politicians in the 1945 election communicated with the electors mainly through newspapers and public meetings. Newspapers were under wartime controls (finally lifted in 1955) and were very slim. News of the election was cursory by modern standards, and offered little in-depth analysis or commentary on either the campaign or the results. There were no opinion polls.

In 1945 about 10 million households had a 'wireless' which received the two national BBC channels. Broadcasting hours were limited, and there was little coverage of the 1945 election campaign, apart from party election broadcasts. Other than the formal news, there was no political commentary or analysis on the radio. Postwar television resumed in 1946 when approximately 25,000 people in the country could watch one BBC channel in black and white for a few hours in the evening.

The situation is transformed today! Virtually every household in the country has at least one colour TV set which receives five channels, and increasing numbers have cable or satellite TV. There are five national BBC radio stations, more than 30 local ones, and most people have a choice of commercial radio. TV stations broadcast most of the day and some radio goes on round the clock. Although there are about the same number of national daily papers as in 1945, they are nothing like the flimsy, dull news sheets of wartime. They are fat, in colour, and the broadsheets (the serious papers) have all sorts of special supplements. They carry far more political news and commentary, and they are often more overtly party political than they were.

On average we now spend more than 25 hours a week watching TV, more than any activity other than working and sleeping. Few of us spend many hours watching political TV, but nevertheless the audience for the main evening news runs into millions. Collectively the print and electronic media now pour out a vast amount of political news and commentary, especially during election campaigns. Almost everything the country's leading politicians do and say is scrutinised, and parties and their leaders think long and hard about their image and campaigns. Media advisors ('spin doctors' like Peter Mandelson and Alastair Campbell in the Labour Party) have become key figures in politics, and parties spend millions on advertising. Public meetings in town halls and squares have been replaced by carefully stage-managed media events which provide 'photo opportunities' and 'soundbites'. This is the age of media politics. But exactly what this means, and exactly how the media affect British government and politics, is a complex matter which is open to dispute.

WHO MAKES WHAT USE OF WHICH MEDIUM FOR WHAT PURPOSE?

Most generalisations about 'the media' are wrong. Apart from anything else there are different kinds of media. Among the political media it is important to distinguish between electronic communications (radio and TV) and print media (newspapers and magazines). As we will see in the next chapter, TV news is required by law to be balanced and impartial whereas the papers can be as party political as they like. There is also a world of difference between the tabloids (popular daily papers like the *Sun* and *Daily Mirror*) and broadsheets (serious papers like *The Times*, *Guardian*, and *Independent*). As Table 13.1 shows, the tabloids outsell the broadsheets by more than three to one, but the tabloids have less political news and analysis than the

Table 13.1 National newspaper sales, 1997 (millions)

Daily Broadsheets		Sunday Broadsheets	
Daily Telegraph	1.13	*Sunday Times*	1.45
The Times	0.82	*Sunday Telegraph*	0.94
Guardian	0.43	*Observer*	0.50
Independent	0.33	*Independent on Sunday*	0.31
Financial Times	0.29		
Total sales	3.00	Total sales	3.20
Number of titles	5	Number of titles	4
Average sales	0.60	Average sales	0.80

Daily Tabloids		Sunday Tabloids	
Sun	3.89	*News of the World*	4.62
Daily Mirror	2.44	*Sunday Mirror*	2.42
Daily Express	2.34	*Mail on Sunday*	2.32
Daily Mail	1.24	*People*	2.00
Daily Star	0.73	*Express on Sunday*	1.26
Daily Record	0.70		
Total sales	11.34	Total sales	12.62
Number of titles	6	Number of titles	5
Average sales	1.89	Average sales	1.76

All National Dailies		All National Sundays	
Total sales	14.34	Total sales	15.82
Number of titles	11	Number of titles	9
Average sales	1.31	Average sales	1.76

Source: Audit Bureau of Circulations

Key term

Tabloids – less serious national and Sunday papers, so called because of their smaller format than broadsheets. Daily tabloids are the *Sun*, *Daily Mirror*, *Daily Express*, *Daily Star*, and *Daily Record*.

broadsheets and they tend to be more party political. Some media analysts argue that newspapers are better at conveying information and an understanding of politics than TV, which by its very nature tends to be superficial and entertaining. Those who spend time with a good newspaper are usually better informed than those who watch TV news. But it is not always clear whether this is due to the inherent properties of different media, or to the education of those who use them.

There are different types of media because there are different types of media users. Not surprisingly, broadsheet readers are usually better educated, spend more time with their paper than tabloid readers, trust their paper more than TV as a source of news, and know more about politics. Conversely tabloid readers spend less time with their paper, but much more time with the TV. They even watch more TV news than broadsheet readers, and they trust TV news more than their paper (see Tables 13.2 and 13.3). But they are less interested in politics, and know less about them.

Table 13.2 Different media, different uses, 1996

| | Educational Qualifications | | |
	O-level/GCSE or less	A-level (percentages)	Further or Higher
Newspapers	%	%	%
Irregular readers	43	47	43
Regular tabloid	54	41	31
Regular broadsheet	4	13	27
(Total)	(101)	(101)	(101)
Television hours per week			
Up to 3	28	46	58
3–4	41	39	32
5 or more	30	15	9
(Total)	(99)	(100)	(99)
TV news per week			
3 or less	27	32	28
4–6	14	24	22
every day	59	44	50
(Total)	(100)	(100)	(100)

Source: British Social Attitudes Survey, 1996 as reported in R. Jowell *et al.* (eds) *British Social Attitudes: the 14th Report* (Aldershot: Dartmouth, 1997), p. 156
Note: Columns total more than 100 per cent because respondents mention more than one source. Broadsheet readers mention more than tabloid readers.

Table 13.3 Main sources of political information

Main Source of Political information	Broadsheet Readers	Tabloid Readers
	(percentages)	
TV	32	62
Papers	57	28
Radio	25	14
(total)	(114)	(104)

Source: Calculated from R. Negrine, *Politics and the Mass Media in Britain* (London: Routledge, 1994), p.2

Key term

Knowledge gap – the result of the process whereby those with a good education and high status acquire knowledge faster than those with a poorer education and lower status.

Social scientists refer to this growing division between tabloid and broadsheet readers as the 'knowledge gap', a process in which educated and higher status people acquire information more quickly than less well-educated and lower status people. Educated people and those interested in politics read quality newspapers and magazines, listen to serious radio and watch serious TV, thereby accumulating a broader and deeper understanding of politics. Poorly educated people, who read the tabloids and watch a lot of entertainment TV, are likely to know less and understand less about politics. In other words, there is a tendency for the information rich to become information richer.

THE IMPACT OF THE MEDIA

Many people have strong views on the impact of the media. Some believe that their impact is self-evident and strong, but others argue, with equal conviction, that the media have no direct effects of their own. In spite of these strong views, it turns out to be remarkably difficult to demonstrate media effects, or measure them. There are four main problems:

1. It is difficult to untangle the effects of the media from other influences, such as family life, education, work, or the community. The media are only one set of influences among many, and sorting out their distinctive impact is a tricky matter.

2. It is difficult to generalise about 'the impact of the media'. If different people use different media for different purposes, it is likely that the media will have different effects on different people. Moreover, the different media may well push or pull in different directions: Labour and Conservative papers, for example, or partisan papers and neutral TV. Some of these may cancel each other out.

3. There is an acute problem of establishing causes and effects. People pick the sorts of media which suit their tastes and opinions. They self-select themselves so what appear to be media effects may be self-selection effects. At the same time, the media shape themselves to appeal to particular sorts of people and markets, so that what seems to be a media

effect may simply be the media reflecting the views of the consumers they want to attract. The cause-and-effect relationships almost certainly flow in both directions from media to audiences, and vice versa.

4. Individuals watching the same TV programme may come away with very different impressions. People not only attend to the messages which suit their tastes and opinions, but they also have a well-developed capacity to turn whatever they see and hear to suit their tastes and preferences. They can suppress, forget, distort or misinterpret messages to fit their view of the world.

Consider the simple figures in Table 13.4. They show that people who read Conservative papers generally identify with the Conservative Party, compared with those who read Labour papers who generally identify with Labour. This is scarcely surprising, but which causes what? Do papers create the party sympathies, or do people usually select a paper to suit their politics? Or is it a bit of both?

Given these great difficulties, it is only to be expected that experts fail to agree about the impact of the mass media on politics. There are four main schools of thought on the subject: reinforcement theory claims minimal effects; agenda-setting theory and framing theory claim indirect effects; and media impact theory claims direct, though not necessarily strong, effects.

Reinforcement theory

Key term

Reinforcement theory (media effects) – argues that the media do not create or mould public opinion so much as reinforce pre-existing opinion.

Reinforcement theory argues that the media do not create or mould public opinion so much as reinforce pre-existing opinion. First, in a free market the media are forced by competition to give consumers what they want, rather than telling them what they want. They seek out tastes and preferences, as other businesses do, and try to satisfy them or reflect them, rather than create or change them. The modern media are bound by the golden chains of the market. Moreover, in a

Table 13.4 Party identification and newspaper readership

Party Identification of Reader	Politics of newspaper		
	Conservative	Labour	Other
	(percentages)		
	%	%	%
Conservative	55	13	28
Labour	30	74	46
Other	15	13	26
(Total)	(100)	(100)	(100)

Source: MORI Polls

pluralist system the media present such a diversity of political opinion that there is no dominant voice, just a wide variety of opinions, each clamouring for attention, and sometimes cancelling each other out.

Second, individuals show a strong capacity to preserve their beliefs by passing everything through their own ideological filters. They start by picking the media which best suit them, and within those media they pay attention selectively according to tastes and predispositions. Then, if they are still presented with unwelcome messages, they show a capacity to protect their beliefs and values by misinterpreting, forgetting, distorting, or simply refusing to believe the evidence of their own eyes and ears. If, after 70 years of concerted government propaganda the Soviet Union could not undermine strong religious convictions, how much weaker are the media in more pluralist societies such as Britain in regard to political opinions?

In sum, reinforcement theory argues that individual psychology, on the one hand, and consumer sovereignty in a competitive market, on the other, renders the media all but powerless to influence mass political opinion. Media effects are minimal.

Reinforcement theory does not fit all the facts about the British media, however. First, the British media do not operate in a free competitive market. As we will see, radio and TV are controlled in nonmarket ways by public regulation, and the print media form an oligopoly rather than a free and competitive market. Second, individuals may adhere strongly to their core values – religion and morality – and to attitudes based upon their own experience, but politics are fairly remote for most. Few have first-hand experience of political matters (the Gulf War, the European Monetary System, Parliamentary practice, defence policy), and they may be more open to media influence as a result. Third, the potential power of the media, especially TV, has grown enormously since reinforcement theory was first accepted in the 1950s and 1960s, and there is an accumulation of evidence showing that the media have far more than minimal effects.

Agenda-setting theory

Key term

Agenda-setting theory – argues that the media cannot determine what people think, but can have a strong influence over what people think about.

Agenda-setting theory claims that the media cannot determine what we think, but they can strongly influence what we think *about*. Not all political matters are equally important, and their importance often changes over time. By concentrating on some issues rather than others the media can push these issues up the political agenda. Examples are the way Conservative papers concentrated on Labour's tax plans during the 1992 election campaign, and on the issue of political sleaze in the 1997 campaign. Another is the media attention focused on the Social Democratic Party at its foundation, which helped it in its early years.

Early agenda-setting theory tended to assume a pliant and passive public which responded to the media's agenda. Some even claimed that the business tycoons or politicians controlling the media could keep some issues out of the public spotlight, what political scientists call 'nondecision making'. The concentration of ownership and control in the hands of a few multimillionaires or multinational corporations was said to ensure that the public is presented with an agenda that was safe for business interests. Some claimed that the media manage to keep

Plate 13.1 Sun cover on the day of the 1992 election: Would the last person to leave please turn out the lights. Repeated attention focused on the Labour Party's tax plans led the *Sun* to claim they had won the election for the Tories

politics largely out of the public mind by providing the popular distractions of soap operas, sport and gossip. Others argued against this, claiming that most issues will get a hearing in a pluralist system. At any rate, later agenda-setting theory accepts the view that the public has its own agenda, while claiming that the media can still influence its priorities, especially on matters about which the public knows little.

Key term

Framing effects (of the media) – the argument that the media can exercise a subtle but strong effect on how public opinion thinks about politics in a general way, and how it reacts to particular events.

Framing theory

Framing theory goes one step further than agenda-setting theory and argues that the way in which the modern mass media treat politics affects political life itself, and the way people see and understand it. The 'media' may frame politics in different ways:

1. *Interpretation.* The same event may be presented in different ways to give it a completely different meaning: were those who tried to prevent road building across Twyford Down holding up progress, or protecting the

environment? Are urban guerrillas terrorists, or freedom fighters? Are strikers holding the country to ransom, or exercising their rights? The media may influence our view of an event in all sorts of subtle and indirect ways, and the effects may be both unintentional and unconscious.

2. *Bad news*. The mass media concentrate on bad news, conflict and violence, because these sell papers and hold TV audiences. The news tends to be an endless account of wars, deaths, disasters, conflicts, incompetence and corruption. Negative news may leave a bad taste in the mouth of the public, creating 'videomalaise', that is, cynicism and disillusionment with politics, distrust of politicians and political apathy.

3. *The 'fast-forward' syndrome*. In Victorian times, news spread slowly, especially foreign news. Politicians had time to think, deliberate and try out ideas. Now news and reaction to it spread so fast that policies can be launched in the morning news, criticised at lunch time, and virtually buried by the evening. Moreover, news breaks around the globe so rapidly that the public is increasingly bewildered by a fast-moving, ever-changing flow of unconnected events which it cannot understand.

4. *Personalisation and trivialisation*. The mass media concentrate not on policies or issues, but personalities and appearances. They treat election campaigns not as a struggle between parties and policies, but as a horse-race between two party leaders. The soundbites and the photo-opportunities of political publicity machines are not conducive to serious discussion, but encourage parties to concentrate on packaging, presentation and appearance. Rather than offering clear policy options, politicians are inclined to make bland statements, but take care that they look and sound right. Many politicians now go to TV charm schools which train them to speak, smile and dress correctly.

> **Key term**
>
> **Videomalaise** – the attitudes of political cynicism, despair, apathy, and disillusionment (among others) which some social scientists claim are caused by the modern mass media, especially television.

Direct effects theory

The fourth and most recent school of thought argues that the mass media do not only influence the agenda or frame the news, but also directly influence attitudes and behaviour, including voting behaviour. First, a large minority of citizens read a paper which does not suit their own politics (see Table 13.4 and Figure 13.2). For many years before the 1997 election campaign, the shortage of Labour papers meant that many Labour sympathisers and voters read a Conservative paper (mainly the *Sun*). In part this is because some, mainly tabloid, readers do not know what party their paper supports, or misunderstand its position. About 13 million readers of four tabloids (*Sun, Mirror, Mail* and *Express*) fail to perceive correctly the politics of their paper. This undermines one important part of reinforcement theory which assumes that people pick their paper for its politics. People with a political interest may well behave this way, but many others probably choose their daily paper for its sport, gossip columns, agony aunt, page 3, women's page, TV news, horoscopes or because it is the paper their partner or parents take.

Statistical analysis suggests that newspapers do influence the voting behaviour of readers.[2] After taking account of such things as class, education, party identification and attitudes towards key election issues, there is still a statistically significant association between reading a paper which supports a given party and voting for that party. In other words, comparing people with the same sort of social background, political attitudes and party identification, the figures show that readers of Conservative papers are more likely to vote Conservative than readers of Labour papers. Conversely, given the same social background, attitudes and party support, readers of Labour papers are more likely to vote Labour than readers of Conservative papers. The evidence suggests that the papers have a big enough effect to influence election outcomes, particularly when parties and candidates are evenly matched and voters are inclined to take voting cues from their paper.

This leads to the question of media bias, especially party political bias.

CONTROVERSY

CONFLICTING THEORIES OF MEDIA EFFECTS

Reinforcement Theory

- The media do not create opinions, they reinforce existing opinions.
- Market competition between the media ensures that they adapt to their audiences and give them what they want.
- In a pluralist system all views have a voice, and ways of making it heard.
- Different media with different messages compete. There is no single or dominant voice.
- Individuals select their media to suit their opinions and tastes. They tend to suppress, distort, forget or misinterpret what does not suit them.
- The effects of the modern mass media are therefore minimal, they confirm what people already believe rather than creating, moulding or influencing political life and attitudes.

Agenda-setting Theory

- The media cannot exercise much influence over what people think, but they can influence what they think about.
- Only a few issues can be important at any one time and the media play an important role in sifting and sorting issues for public attention.
- Different media often focus on the same events or phenomenon. They indulge in 'feeding frenzies' about issues such as the monarchy, football hooligans, road rage, political sleaze.
- Concentrated media attention highlights these issues in the public mind, and can push them up the political agenda.
- Examples of agenda setting are the intense publicity given to the Social Democratic Party at its foundation, Labour's tax plans in the 1992 election, political sleaze in the 1997 election, Princess Diana's death and sanctification, 1997.

[2] For details of the research see W. Miller, *Media and Voters* (Oxford: Clarendon Press, 1991); P. Dunleavy and C. Husbands, *Democracy at the Crossroads* (Cambridge: Cambridge University Press, 1985); K. Newton, 'Do People Read Everything They Believe in the Papers', in I. Crewe *et al.* (eds) *British Elections and Party Yearbook 1991* (Hemel Hempstead: Simon and Schuster, 1992).

CONFLICTING THEORIES OF MEDIA EFFECTS (continued)

Framing Politics

- The way in which the modern mass media treat politics subtly affects political life, and how people view it.

- By concentrating on bad news, conflict and disagreement, the media give politics a bad name. The modern media tend to create alienation, political cynicism and distrust.

- The 'fast-forward' syndrome speeds up political life, and makes it difficult to understand.

- In order to provide human interest the media tend to trivialise and personalise politics. They emphasise style and appearance, soundbites and photo-opportunities, rather than policies and programmes.

- By focusing on particular issues the media favour the politicians and parties which 'own' those issues ('priming' effects).

- Reports which concentrate on episodes, particularly individual stories, tend to emphasise individual causes. News which deals with themes tends to emphasise 'the system'.

Direct Effects

- Reinforcement theory was mainly a product of 1950s social science before the creation of the powerful modern media, especially TV, so it underestimates media impacts.

- Many people now spend a large proportion of their leisure time in front of the TV, and newspapers are cheaper and larger than they were.

- TV has powerful effects: it encourages audience passivity, it entertains rather than explains or informs, it isolates people socially, but it is not good at passing on information.

- Media effects go beyond agenda setting and framing. They directly influence not just what people think about, nor even attitudes about particular political issues, but the very way in which people think about politics, in general.

- There is some evidence that newspapers influence the voting patterns of their readers. Allowing for the effects of background characteristics and political attitudes, readers of Conservative papers are more likely to vote Conservative than readers of Labour papers, and vice versa.

MEDIA BIAS?

Many people are convinced that the media are biased. The problem is that right-wingers are convinced that the bias is left-wing, and left-wingers are equally convinced that it is right-wing! British governments of all persuasions usually feel that the press is unfair to them. We are unlikely to get far in this debate unless we go back to basics.

Bias in the mass media is most likely to originate in two sources: political authorities, especially the Government, and the media themselves.

Government bias?

Government is only one source of political information, but it is a particularly important one which provides a large proportion of the daily news through its press releases and tries to shape the news ('give it a spin') in its own interests. Government efforts to market itself increased substantially in the 1980s, and Whitehall and Downing Street now employ 1,200 press officers with a combined budget estimated to approach two hundred million pounds. The marketing of government policies is a major aspect of modern statecraft. The Labour Government reorganised government information services in September 1997 in order to present itself more effectively.

But British government has more powerful ways of shaping the news than just using its press and public relations departments. This topic is discussed at greater length in Chapter 22, and we will only outline the basic issues here. On the one hand, Britain has no written constitution, bill or rights, or freedom of information act which guarantee citizens the right to information. On the other, the government has many powers (notably the Official Secrets Act) to restrict the flow of information. The governments of the 1980s were also strongly critical of both the BBC and ITV for their treatment of some political issues, and there were whispers that this might affect both the renewal of the BBC Charter in 1994, and the price of the TV licence (the BBC's main source of income), which the government controls. In short, British governments have many legal and political powers to control news and influence its presentation, and have not been shy about using them.

Media bias? Newspapers

When dealing with media bias, it is essential to distinguish between print and electronic media. The electronic media are required to be balanced and impartial, while newspapers can be as partial and party political as they like. We will deal first with the easier case of the print media. Their are four main reasons why British newspapers usually have a particular ideological leaning.

1. The press is mostly controlled by multimillionaires and multinational companies which often (but not always) have the same economic and political interests.

2. Generations of British press barons have pursued not money, but power. They have frequently controlled the editorial policy of their newspapers, even written the editorials themselves: Northcliffe, Rothermere, Astor, Beaverbrook, Thompson, King, Matthews, Maxwell, Rowland and Murdoch have all followed the practice.

3. At the same time, newspapers and commercial TV rely heavily on advertising income, and are unwilling to bite the hand of the business interests that feed them.

4. Since the late 1950s, the British press has tried to carve out a media market which is distinct from television's. TV is required to be balanced and impartial, so the tabloid press has increased its party political bias, and the quality press has increasingly presented in-depth commentary and analysis of the news.

The result is that the British press as a whole is party political compared with that in most other Western countries. If there were strong party competition between papers this might not matter. But the press weighs heavily on the side of Conservative economic interests and Conservative politics. As Figure 13.1 shows, the circulation of Conservative newspapers has outnumbered that of Labour or Liberal papers ever since 1951, and from the 1970s to mid-1990s Conservative papers dominated. During these decades, a large majority of people read a Conservative paper, including about 70 per cent of the working-class people who traditionally provide Labour with most of its support. Three of the largest circulation mass tabloids (*Sun, Mail,* and *Express*) were strongly Conservative, and the fourth *(The Daily Mirror)* sometimes offered Labour only lukewarm support. The result is that Conservative papers often have more Conservative and fewer Labour voters than expected, given the social class of their readers (Figure 13.2). Given what we know about self-selection, and how papers adapt to markets, Figure 13.1 proves nothing. But it is circumstantial evidence that the Conservative nature of the national press may have helped the Party in the war of words.

Figure 13.1 Party politics of the press: percentages of national circulation

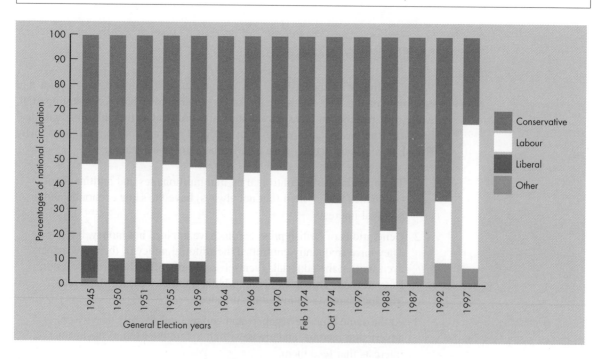

Sources: Calculated from C. Seymour-Ure, *The British Press and Broadcasting since 1945* (Oxford: Blackwell, 1991), pp. 196–97; D. McKie, 'Fact is Free but Comment is Sacred', in I. Crewe and B. Gosschalk (eds), *Political Communications The General Election Campaign of 1992* (Cambridge: Cambridge University Press, 1995), p. 133; *Guardian*, 5 May 1997
Note: Papers with divided support are split equally between the parties they support

Figure 13.2

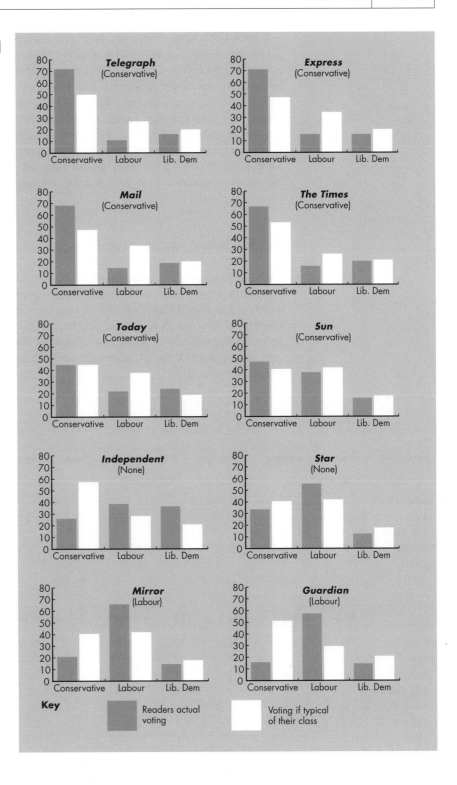

For the 1997 election, however, there were dramatic changes. The *Sun*, a strongly Conservative paper in the 1980 and early 1990s, switched support to Blair and Labour. For the first time in the postwar period, Labour had a news-paper advantage. In addition, the *Times, Telegraph* and *Financial Times* were not as staunchly Conservative as usual (see Table 13.5). Did this contribute to Labour's mammoth victory? We cannot be sure. Labour scored a remarkable win in 1945 with minority newspaper support, and won in 1964, 1966 and 1974 with most papers against it. Besides, it has been estimated that about 60 per cent of *Sun* readers would have voted Labour in 1997, even if the paper had not switched. So many people had clear voting intentions of their own in 1997 that the newspaper effect may have been small.

Media bias? Radio and TV

The electronic media are an entirely different matter. Radio and TV news is required to be impartial and balanced, and most people feel that they are, so far as this is possible. A large majority of viewers trust both BBC and ITV news. A minority of between 15 and 20 per cent believe the BBC has a Conservative bias, and a smaller minority of about 5 per cent think it has a Labour bias. About 5 per cent believe that ITV has a Labour bias, while about the same proportion perceive Conservative leanings.

Table 13.5 Party positions of newspapers and TV during the 1997 election campaign (percentages of material favouring one party or another over the campaign)

Favouring	Times	Guardian	Telegraph	Independent	Financial Times	Sun	Mirror	Star
	%	%	%	%	%	%	%	%
Con.	23	18	23	17	20	38	14	31
Lab.	21	19	19	23	24	34	48	31
Lib. Dem.	6	6	4	9	1	0	1	3
Neutral	40	50	47	41	48	22	34	30
Other	10	7	7	10	7	6	3	5
(Total)	(100)	(100)	(100)	(100)	(100)	(100)	(100)	(100)

	Mail	Express	BBC1	ITV	Channel 4	Radio 4 Today
	%	%	%	%	%	%
Con.	35	32	14	11	12	16
Lab.	21	14	10	12	9	2
Lib. Dem.	1	4	9	10	5	2
Neutral	38	46	55	59	70	60
Other	5	4	12	8	4	20
(Total)	(100)	(100)	(100)	(100)	(100)	(100)

Source: Guardian, 5 May 1997, p. 4

Nevertheless, some research argues that TV news is systematically prejudiced. Most notably, the Glasgow Media Group (GMG) has published a series of books (the main ones are *Bad News, More Bad News, Really Bad News,* and *War and Peace News*) which claims there is a pervasive elitist and conservative bias in the BBC's news. *Bad News* concludes that BBC TV is inclined towards 'laying the blame for society's industrial and economic problems at the door of the work-force'.[3] The Glasgow team has been criticised, in its turn, by those who argue that their work is sometimes wrong or exaggerated, and ignores contradictory evidence. The controversy about broadcasting bias continues and is likely to generate more heat than light for some time to come.

ESSAYS

1. 'Most generalisations about the media are likely to be wrong'. Discuss.

2. Explain how education and different media might interact to produce a British 'information gap'.

3. What are the reasons, if any, for believing that 'reinforcement theory' underestimates the influence of the mass media on British politics?

4. Are the political media in Britain biased?

SUMMARY

- The mass media have been transformed out of all recognition since 1945 (see Milestones). They now play a hugely important role in British politics, although they are often taken for granted. We are in the 'media age', but exactly what this means is a controversial matter.

- Different people use different media for different purposes. Well-educated people tend to read a broadsheet, and watch comparatively little TV. Poorly educated people tends to read a tabloid and watch a lot of TV, including TV news.

- This results in a 'knowledge gap' in which those with high education and status acquire information faster than those with lower status and education.

- It is extremely difficult to demonstrate the impact of the media. They are so pervasive in modern society, and their relationships with their audiences and readers so complex and interdependent, that it is exceedingly difficulty to pin down what sort of medium has what sort of impact on what sorts of people.

- There are four main schools of thought on media impacts: reinforcement theory, which claims minimal effects; agenda-setting theory, which claims indirect effects; framing theory, which claims indirect and direct effects; and direct effects theory.

- Evidence of indirect and direct effects is increasing (including direct effects on voting), but the topic remains a highly controversial one.

- National newspaper circulation has been dominated by Conservative papers since 1945, but this changed dramatically in 1997 when the *Sun* switched to Labour, and Conservative support was lukewarm among some other papers.

- Most people believe that TV news is relatively unbiased, but there is also an unresolved dispute about this among social science researchers.

- In general, it is clear that there is no such thing as *the* media, or *a* media effect, only different media with different effects on different types of people. On the whole, TV seems to affect what people think is important. Newspapers have more direct effects and probably increased Conservative support from 1979–92.

---

[3] Glasgow Media Group, *Bad News* (London: Routledge, 1976), p. 267.

MILESTONES

MILESTONES IN BRITISH MEDIA HISTORY

1945–46 BBC Radio resumes normal peacetime broadcasting with the Light Programme, the Home Service, and in 1946 the Third Progamme

1946 BBC TV resumes with about 25,000 viewers clustered around the only broadcasting station at Alexandra Palace, London

1950 First TV coverage of general election results First political programme on TV (*In the News*)

1951 Beveridge Committee on broadcasting recommends public service TV similar to radio

1953 First edition of BBC *Panorama* programme Press council set up

1954 Television Act establishes commercial TV (ITV)

1955 ITV goes on the air

1956 Anthony Eden makes first prime ministerial TV broadcast (about Suez). Labour Opposition insists on a reply

1959 First TV election campaign coverage

1962 Pilkington report recommends second BBC TV channel. Advertising Standards Authority established. First Telstar TV satellite broadcast

1964 BBC 2 goes on the air. Radio Caroline (illegal offshore pop music station) goes on the air

1967 First colour TV (BBC 2). First BBC local radio station

1969 Rupert Murdoch (News International) buys the *Sun* and *News of the World*

1970s Investigative journalism spreads as a feature of all newspapers and television

1971 Commercial local radio authorised

1972 First cable TV

1974 First election phone-in on radio

1975 Trial radio broadcasts from the House of Commons

1979 Independent Broadcasting Authority Act gives Channel 4 to IBA

1981 Rupert Murdoch (News International) buys *The Times* and *Sunday Times*

1982 First Channel 4 broadcasts

1983 Breakfast TV on BBC and ITV

1984 Robert Maxwell buys Mirror group

1985 Lord Stevens (United Newspapers) acquires Express group

1986 Peacock Report on Financing the BBC recommends only fairly minor changes. BSB wins contract for direct satellite broadcasting. Eddie Shah launches *Today*, but then sells to Lonrho ('Tiny' Rowland). *Independent* launched

1987 *Daily* and *Sunday Telegraph* bought by Conrad Black

1988 Broadcasting Standards Council established to regulate radio, TV and video standards. Rupert Murdoch announces Sky TV (satellite TV)

1989 House of Commons televised

1990 Commercial TV franchises auctioned amid much criticism. Murdoch's Sky TV merged with BSB to form B Sky B. BBC Radio 5 launched

1991 BBC launches World TV. Press Council transformed into Newspaper Press Complaints Commission with stronger powers

1992 Classic FM goes on the air. Mirror Group passes to creditor bank when Robert Maxwell dies. The *Sun* claims it won the election for the Conservatives

1993 Channel 4 sells airtime. TV ownership rules relaxed to make multiple ownership possible

1994 BBC charter renewed until 2006

1995 Increasing concern about press invasion of privacy and 'cheque book' journalism

1996 Rupert Murdoch (News International) establishes monopoly over digital TV, but under strict regulation to provide access to other broadcasters

1997 Channel 5 TV goes on the air

PROJECTS

1. The figures in Figure 13.2 show an association between newspaper reading and voting, but do they show a causal relationship of any kind? Outline different theories which might explain the pattern of the figures.

2. Define political bias. How could you establish beyond reasonable doubt that a news report was politically biased? Give reasons for believing that the British media are, or are not, politically biased.

FURTHER READING

There is a large and growing literature on the British media. Among the best general books are C. Seymour-Ure, *The British Press and Broadcasting Since 1945* (Oxford: Blackwell, 1991); R. Negrine, *Politics and the Mass Media in Britain* (London: Routledge, 2nd edn 1994), and B. Franklin, *Packaging Politics* (London: Edward Arnold, 1994).

On the way in which different people use the media, and its effects on them, see K. Newton, 'Politics and the Mass Media: mobilisation or videomalaise?', in R. Jowell *et al.* (eds), *British Social Attitudes: the 14th Report* (Aldershot: Dartmouth, 1998).

Studies of the political impact of the media, especially newspapers on voting, include W. Miller, *Media and Voters* (Oxford: Clarendon Press, 1991); P. Dunleavy and C. Husbands, *Democracy at the Crossroads* (Cambridge: Cambridge University Press, 1985); and K. Newton, 'Do People Read Everything they Believe in the Papers?', in I. Crewe *et al.* (eds), *British Elections and Parties Yearbook 1991* (Hemel Hempstead: Simon and Schuster, 1992). On press bias and its effects on the 1992 election see D. McKie, 'Fact is Free but Comment is Scared: or was it the *Sun* wot won it?', in I. Crewe and Brian Gosschalk (eds), *Political Communications: The General Election Campaign of 1992* (Cambridge: Cambridge University Press, 1995).

The most quoted research on bias in the TV news is the books of the Glasgow Media Group (GMG). See the trenchant critique of the GMG research in M. Harrison, *TV News: Whose Bias?* (Hermitage, Berks: Policy Journals, 1985). On bias in the newspapers see M. Hollingsworth, *The Press and Political Dissent* (London: Pluto Press, 1986), and R. Snoddy, *The Good, the Bad, and the Unacceptable: The Hard News about the British Press* (London: Faber and Faber, 1992).

http://www.awl-he.com/politics/newbritpol

Internet resources – visit *The New British Politics* Webpage for links to a specially-chosen selection of Internet resources relevant to this Chapter.

http://www.awl-he.com/politics/newbritpol

CHAPTER 14

The mass media and pluralist democracy in Britain

As newspapers and TV grow more important in British politics, so they cause more controversy. How should the media be organised? Should they be as independent as possible of state regulation, in the interests of freedom of speech, or should the state oblige them to inform and educate citizens with news programmes that are accurate and impartial, and election coverage that is fair and balanced? Can we rely on market competition to ensure democratic pluralism in the media, or is the BBC's 'public service model' preferable? What are the implications of technological change for the British media and their role in democracy?

These difficult questions are considered by the chapter, which starts with a general account of the role of the media in pluralist democracy. It then considers the nature and role of the print and electronic media, as follows:

- The commercial nature of the national press, and the difficulties this has created

- The ways in which the electronic media – radio and TV – differ fundamentally from the print media, especially in terms of market regulation, content regulation, and the public service model of broadcasting

- The implications of technological change for the organisation of the electronic media and the controversy about increasing commercialisation

- The problems which the growing concentration of ownership and control of the mass media are creating for the pluralist model

- The smaller media and investigative journalism as counter-trends to media consolidation

PLURALIST DEMOCRACY AND ROLE OF THE MASS MEDIA

The mass media are an essential part of modern democracy (see Briefing 14.1). The reasons are easy to understand. Democracy requires, at a minimum, informed and politically educated citizens who can make decisions for themselves. In turn, they need reliable news and access to a wide variety of opinion about it in order to make informed choices rather than being manipulated.

BRIEFINGS

14.1 PLURALIST DEMOCRACY

This is the idea, referred to a lot in discussions of pressure groups and of the mass media, that modern societies contain all sorts of competing groups, interests, ideologies and ideas. These are equally legitimate so long as they do not advocate violence against the others. In this context, democracy is seen as a struggle by interests and ideas to predominate, often by inspiring the formation of political parties or pressure groups, or of newspapers or radio/TV stations. This will stimulate debate and create a 'free market place of ideas' (J.S. Mill) where the best ideas and arguments will win.

This is an attractive ideal. Unfortunately Britain, along with other modern societies, may fall far short of providing a free market of ideas. Powerful groups and interests – including the party in power – may censor news and manipulate comment so that only certain ideas and arguments get heard. This then causes controversy between those who feel a free market can only (paradoxically) be preserved by strong public regulation and those who prefer a commercial market, even if it is highly imperfect.

At the same time, few of us have much first-hand experience of politics. We do not know national politicians personally, and we rarely hear their speeches for ourselves, or witness political events with our own eyes. Most of us do not have a deep understanding of political issues. We rely upon the media to keep us informed, primarily through TV news, but also in newspapers and on the radio (see Figure 14.1). Indeed, the great merit of television is that it brings political leaders and events from around the world into our own living rooms where we see and hear them for ourselves, and form our own judgements.

Figure 14.1 Sources of world news

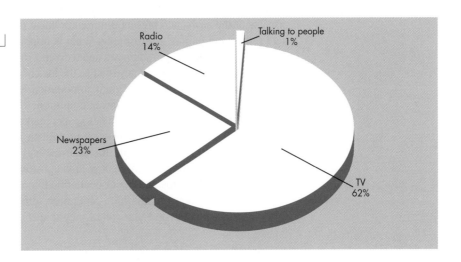

The news media are sometimes described as 'the fourth estate of the realm', or 'the watchdog of the constitution'. This role is a demanding and complex one, which requires them to perform a number of tasks, some difficult to achieve, and others not easily combined:

- The news must be accurate, but it is often difficult to get facts right in the rushed world of news deadlines.

- The media must present a full account of the news, but they cannot possibly report all the news. There is too much of it, and the media must select and impose their subjective judgement about what is important.

- The news must be fair and impartial. But it is impossible to be completely neutral about politics. Facts depend upon interpretation, and the language we use is sometimes loaded. It is difficult to be objective about emotional or dramatic political events.

- The news should be objective and detached, and also critical and engaged. We require our news media to be fair and balanced, but we also want them to dig beneath the surface, to engage in investigative journalism, and to be critical.

- The news media should present a wide variety of opinion, not just the views of government leaders. But official views are greatly overrepresented in news reports because it is quicker and easier to rely upon neatly packaged government press releases than hunt for alternative views and information.

- Lastly the news media must resist the pressures of political leaders and governments who often feel badly treated by the media and attack them for unfair reporting.

Pluralist theory and the media

It is clear that no single newspaper or TV news programme can possibly cover all news and opinion. On the contrary, the news media often specialise in different aspects of the news, and present different political positions. There are left, centre, and right-wing papers, for example. What is important is that the news media as a whole present the important news and a diverse range of opinion. For this reason the pluralist theory of democracy (that is, the idea of democracy as the 'free market' of ideas and opinions) places great importance in a diversity of news sources which cover a wide range of issues and opinion.

In the late nineteenth century, the newspaper market roughly met these conditions. It was relatively easy and inexpensive to publish a paper or newssheet to serve small, local markets. As a result, the industry was fragmented and run by many different people with many different political positions, many of them independent of large political parties and major economic interests.

Nowadays the news media have an entirely different appearance and market. They stretch far beyond the small newspapers and political pamphlets of

Plate 14.1 The Internet is an increasingly important source of news and information. During the May 1997 General Election campaign all the major parties used the Internet to publicise their policies and recruit members. The most striking use of the medium was seen on the Labour Party's special election website, created by The Wire Station

Victorian times to include radio, TV, films, tapes, CDs, videos, the Internet and, of course, the mass circulation newspapers which are quite different from their Victorian counterparts. Tabloid newspapers and TV news are read and watched by millions every day, and there are relatively few of them. The question, then, is whether the modern mass media play their proper role in democracy.

In the rest of the chapter we will examine the role of the mass electronic and print media in British democracy. In the previous chapter we drew an important distinction between the print and the electronic media. Here we will take up the distinction again, and show how important it is for the functioning of democracy.

THE PRINT MEDIA

In theory anyone can set up a newspaper or a magazine, especially in the age of desktop publishing. For example, the student body of almost every British university and institution of further education produces its own newspaper. In theory there is no limit to the number of producers who can compete in this market. As a result, there is no more theoretical need for state regulation of the print media than there is, say, for soap powder. Moreover, some people argue that the requirements of freedom of speech and of media independence from government mean that the less regulation of publishing there is the better. Therefore, newspapers should not be subject to any political controls: they should print the news as they see fit, and publish whatever editorials and political advertisements they wish.

Since 1945, and the lifting of wartime restrictions, the state has intervened in the newspaper industry only in exceptional circumstances. The first of these is supposed to be in cases of market failure which result in oligopoly (the situation in which a market is dominated by a small number of producers). The British newspaper industry, however, has long shown strong oligopolistic tendencies toward concentration of ownership (although never total ownership by one person). Attempts to prevent concentration have been notably unsuccessful.

In recent years this problem has caused less concern than the content and standards of tabloid journalism: bias, inaccuracy, sensationalism, cheque-book journalism, and invasion of privacy. Press standards have been a long-standing issue. But tabloid journalism in the 1970s and 1980s raised the issues in acute form and it was clear that the old forms of regulation were too weak and inadequate. Unwilling to impose direct state regulation on the press, the Government has experimented with self-regulation.

The Press Council was set up in 1953. Initially funded by the press industry, and composed entirely of its representatives, it acted as a complaints tribunal, but it had little authority and no formal powers. A lay chair and some lay members (i.e. people outside the industry) were introduced in 1963, but the Council continued to be ineffective and without authority.

Following the Calcutt Report (1990) on the press, and amid growing concern about tabloid standards, in 1991 the Press Council was converted into the Press Complaints Commission, with the warning that this would be last chance for the press to get its own house in order. It did not do so, and the Calcutt review of the Commission (1993) recommended stronger action, which was rejected by the Government.

Tabloid press standards remain a difficult and unresolved issue. Few outside the newspaper industry believe that self-regulation has worked. But state regulation is a minefield of political problems.

THE ELECTRONIC MEDIA: MARKET REGULATION, CONTENT REGULATION AND THE PUBLIC SERVICE MODEL

Key term

Spectrum scarcity – the shortage of broadcasting frequencies for radio and TV caused by the fact that the wavelengths available for public broadcasting on the spectrum are limited.

Until quite recently the number of radio and television wavelengths available for broadcasting has been strictly limited and only one broadcaster can use any single wavelength. Some of these wavelengths had to be set aside for special purposes such as shipping, air traffic control, police, fire, ambulances and radio taxis. Consequently, the electronic media did not form an open market as the print media do; they were natural monopolies. The limit on the number of broadcasting frequencies is known as 'spectrum scarcity', and its consequence is that the air waves were regarded as a public good, and closely regulated by the state in the public interest.

Spectrum scarcity results in two forms of state regulation of the electronic media which do not apply to newspapers. The first is known as market regulation, in which the state controls the allocation of broadcasting licences and divides them between public and private (commercial) organisations. In the second, known as content regulation, the state lays down regulations requiring the electronic news media to use their broadcasting powers in the national interest. Among other things this means maintaining 'balance ... accuracy and impartiality' in the reporting of the news and election campaigns. Independent TV was obliged to follow these rules from the very start and the BBC, which had tried to follow the same standards from its creation, voluntarily observes the regulations and restrictions. For example, unlike in the USA, paid political advertising is not permitted on radio or television in Britain, except under the carefully controlled conditions of party political broadcasts and party election broadcasts. Nor may radio or TV broadcast political editorials of the kind that newspapers print every day. (See Briefing 14.2.)

BRIEFINGS

14.2 MARKET AND CONTENT REGULATION OF THE ELECTRONIC MEDIA

Market regulation

Because broadcasting wavelengths are limited in number (spectrum scarcity) and chaos would result from different broadcasters using the same wavelengths, the state controls the electronic media. Initially it gave the British Broadcasting Corporation (BBC) a monopoly over radio and TV, and required it to broadcast in the public interest. As technology developed it became possible to introduce commercial TV and radio stations, but because there are still only a few broadcasting wavelengths, the state continued to control broadcasting licences.

In order to prevent monopoly or oligopoly emerging in the limited market, the state also regulates cross-media ownership of TV, radio and newspapers. Given the importance of a pluralist media for democracy, the intention is to ensure that ownership and control of different media does not become concentrated, and that financial interests spanning radio, TV and papers should be limited in their influence on the market. Market regulation is found mainly in electronic media, but some is supposed to apply to the print media as well. In Britain market regulation of the print media has not been conspicuously successful.

Content regulation

Because the air waves are public property, it is argued that they should be used in the public interest. The amount and content of commercials is controlled, and programmes unsuitable for children are not broadcast until the late evening. News and election programmes are closely regulated by the Television Act of 1954 which established Independent (commercial) TV, and which was amended by the Broadcasting Act of 1981:

- Political and religious advertising and editorialising are banned.
- Political programmes are required to maintain 'proper balance ... accuracy and impartiality'.
- Election candidates and parties must be treated fairly and impartially.
- Party political programmes and election broadcasts, made and financed by the parties, are broadcast free of charge, with time allotted to parties in accordance with a set of generally accepted rules based upon their voting support.

The BBC is not legally bound by the 1954 or 1981 Acts, but it voluntarily observes their codes of practice.

14.2 MARKET AND CONTENT REGULATION OF THE ELECTRONIC MEDIA (continued)

Content Regulation by the European Union

The European Union has also begun to regulate the media and advertising. It has banned cigarette advertisements on TV, and regulates the amount and timing of advertisements. The advertising of alcohol and products aimed at children are also controlled. Further EC regulations concerning the press, advertising and broadcasting are being considered, and in the next decade the EU is likely to play a much bigger role in the regulation of broadcast content.

As a result, most people believe that BBC and ITN news are reliable and impartial sources of news. In fact, the great majority of tabloid readers, who make up 80 per cent of all regular newspaper readers, place much greater faith in TV news than the paper they read. Whereas about two out of three people trust BBC and ITN 'a great deal', and about half say the same of their broadsheet newspaper, fewer than a third trust their tabloid.

Initially, market regulation of the electronic media in Britain meant that the BBC (British Broadcasting Corporation) had a monopoly of broadcasting which is used according to what is termed 'the public service model' (see Briefing 14.3).

BRIEFINGS

14.3 THE PUBLIC SERVICE MODEL

The main aim of the public service model of broadcasting is not to use the media to make money in a commercial market, but to use radio and television as a national resource for the public good. Lord Reith, the founding father of the BBC, saw it as 'the voice of the nation' with a duty to 'educate, inform and entertain', in that order of priority. The main features of the British public service model are:

- *Market regulation.* Since the electronic media form natural monopolies it is thought they should be regulated by the state, which issues broadcasting licences or gives a monopoly to a public body.

- *Content regulation.* If broadcasting wavelengths are public property, then they should be used for the public good. Programmes should appeal to a wide range of tastes, both majority and minority. News and election programmes of the BBC and ITN are required to be balanced, accurate and impartial.

Political advertising and editorialising are not allowed.

- *Accountability.* The electronic media should be accountable to the public, not to the market or to the Government.

- *Self-regulation or regulation by quango.* To avoid the dangers of state or political interference, the media should be controlled and regulated by their own bodies or quangos which are independent of government.

- *National broadcasting.* Broadcasting should serve the entire nation, including remote areas, not a particular territory or section of the population.

- *Public funding.* Broadcasting should be financed mainly from public funds, not commercial sources. Public funds may take the form of general subsidies from the Government, or licence fees, or some combination of the two.

Distanced from the profit-making demands of the market by its state-granted monopoly, and financed by licence fees, which all users had to pay, it followed a policy of providing high-quality education, information and entertainment for the nation as a whole. The public service model of television operated from 1946 (when the BBC resumed its postwar broadcasting) until 1955 when commercial TV went on the air. In radio the BBC's monopoly lasted from 1926, when the BBC was founded, until commercial radio was legalised in 1971. British radio and TV are still publicly regulated, but the ITC (Independent Television Commission) has joined the BBC as a controlling body (see Briefing 14.4).

The advantages of BBC public service broadcasting are said to be high quality programmes for a wide range of the population, avoiding the worst forms of commercialisation. The disadvantages are elitist or paternalistic programming which gave people not what they wanted but what the BBC thought they should have. Since commercialisation, however, the BBC has had to pay more careful attention to its audience ratings, and 'back-door commercialisation' is the result. The

BRIEFINGS

14.4 THE BBC, THE ITC, THE BCC AND THE BSC

BBC (British Broadcasting Corporation)

Established in 1926 as a public radio monopoly, the BBC now runs two national TV channels, five national radio stations, and 48 local radio stations. The Home Secretary appoints its Board of Governors, which appoints the Director General, who has day-to-day authority. Its charter is periodically renewed, the last time in 1994 until 2006. It is funded from the TV licence fee which is set by the Government.

ITC (Independent Television Commission)

The Broadcasting Act of 1990 created the ITC in place of the previous controlling body (the Independent Broadcasting Authority). The ITC has three TV channels, and two national and 132 local radio stations. Like the BBC, its Board of Governors is appointed by the Home Secretary. Unlike the BBC, daily business is conducted by the private broadcasting companies which are granted licences, which, since 1990, have been auctioned. Commercial broadcasting is funded by advertising revenues.

BCC (Broadcasting Complaints Commission)

Established by the Broadcasting Act of 1990, the BCC is a complaints tribunal for individuals who feel unfairly treated by broadcasting bodies.

BSC (Broadcasting Standards Council)

Also created by the 1990 Act, the BSC is responsible for drafting a broadcasting code of conduct.

public service model of political reporting – 'balance, accuracy and impartiality' – still applies to radio and TV. But other aspects of the model have been diluted or have disappeared as commercial companies have taken a larger share of audiences. Commercialisation of the media has been a fiercely controversial issue in British politics and it is likely to remain so for some time to come (see Controversy).

CONTROVERSY

PUBLIC SERVICE VERSUS FREE MEDIA MARKETS

Public service model

- There is no market for ideas or for political news as there is for soap powder or motor cars. Ideas are not goods for which supply and demand curves can be drawn. News programmes cannot be put to the same tests as consumer durables, nor can political ideas be subject to the same sort of tests as soap powder.

- The market does not ensure that truth will prevail, or even that the best ideas will survive, only that popular demands are satisfied. If people want soundbites, gossip, trivia, racism, sexism, prejudice, chauvinism, that is what the market will deliver.

- The news is far too important to be left to commercial forces which are only interested in profits. Only public regulation can ensure balance, accuracy, truth, or impartiality.

- There is not yet a competitive market in the electronic media as there is, in theory, in the print media, and state control should remain at least until there is.

- There are dangers in the state regulation of the media, but these have been avoided in some Western countries where there is no state control or influence over the political content of the media.

- In the commercial media the bad drives out the good, and in a competitive system, the best are forced to adopt the standards of the worst.

- The state will still have to regulate in cases of market failure, and the media market shows clear signs of oligopoly, not healthy competition.

Free market model

- There is no difference in principle between the market for goods and services and the market for news and ideas, and we should turn ideas over to the market just as we do for goods and services.

- The market ensures that people get what they want, which is more democratic than BBC directors broadcasting what they think people need.

- The news is far too important to be under the control of the state or government, and regulation of the media is inconsistent with free speech. The media should be completely independent of government and left to do 'investigative journalism' unhampered.

- Already cable and satellite TV and local radio have reduced spectrum scarcity, and in the near future there will be no difference between the markets for electronic and print media. State control in the public interest is no longer necessary.

- No matter how good arms-length control by quango, the only way of avoiding government influence of the media is by turning them over to the market.

- Some claim that market competition between ideas will ensure that the 'truth will out', others that truth is relative, and only media competition will deliver a multiplicity of truths.

- The state can regulate cases of media market failure as it does other cases of market failure, but this only means intervention is sometimes necessary, not total control.

PUBLIC SERVICE VERSUS FREE MEDIA MARKET (continued)

Public service model

- Media oligopolies are increasingly driven by conservative ideologies, which renders their content politically biased and conservative.

- The state will have to continue its regulation of such things as pornography, racism and incitement to violence.

- Self-regulation of the newspapers has produced low journalistic standards, cheque book journalism, sensationalism and the invasion of privacy.

Free market model

- As the media market develops it will be driven by commercialism, not ideology.

- Content regulation of the media should go no further than dealing with the conditions for public order and the protection of those unable to protect themselves, especially children. Some libertarians even argue that the state has no role in the regulation of such things as pornography.

- Low journalistic standards are better than repression or manipulation by governments.

COMMERCIALISATION OF THE ELECTRONIC MEDIA

Broadcasting technology is changing fast. The development of satellite and cable television, and of community radio and TV, makes it possible to generate a much larger number and diversity of broadcasting stations. Spectrum scarcity, and the natural monopoly it creates, is quickly being supplanted by commercial competition in the form of an abundance of radio and TV channels. In the future, the huge potential of the 'wired nation', with information superhighways and digital broadcasting, is expected to introduce more competition and variety, in which case a media market may well emerge little different, in principle, from the print media. As the Peacock report on funding the BBC stated in 1986, technological developments promise the end of spectrum scarcity and the creation of a consumer market in broadcasting. Although the report opposed advertising by the BBC, it anticipated that there will soon be no need for state regulation; almost everything can be safely left to the 'free market'.[1]

Postwar Conservative governments were persuaded by these technical changes to introduce more and more commercial elements into radio and TV, so ending the BBC monopoly and progressively diluting the public service model. The Television Act of 1954 authorised commercial (Independent) TV which went on the air a year later, the first in Western Europe. Then, pressured by pirate radio (illegal commercial radio broadcast from ships outside territorial waters), commercial radio was authorised in 1971. A second commercial TV Channel (Channel 4) was set up by the Independent Broadcasting Authority Act of

---

[1] *Report of the Committee on Financing the BBC* (London: HMSO, 1986), p. 126

1979, and it went on the air in 1982. Meanwhile, cable TV was introduced in 1972, and satellite TV (first broadcast in 1962 from Telstar) expanded rapidly in the late 1980s.

The arguments for commercial radio and TV, as against the public service model, are complex and many-sided, and ultimately they are ideological and political rather than technical or economic. Advocates of the market claim that only full commercialisation can guarantee pluralist competition, and the absence of state regulation which freedom of speech demands. Defenders of the public service model fear that commercialisation will produce the worst kind of 'tabloid TV', just as the print market has produced the worst kind of newspaper journalism. They claim that Britain should avoid the American model which is widely and strongly criticised in the USA, partly because of its poor quality news and current affairs programmes.

The BBC's monopoly has long since ended, and with it the pure public service model of broadcasting. But although there may be greater commercialisation in future, state regulation of the media is not likely to end altogether.

- The European Union wants to impose greater regulation on the media market and its content.

- Those who most strongly advocate a media market are often most strongly opposed to some of its products: pornography on satellite TV and the computer net, for example.

- Local and community TV and radio could potentially fall into the hands of political extremists, which would be likely to raise difficult issues of free speech.

- Hate radio, if its spreads from America, will provoke demands for regulation.

- The requirements of balance, accuracy and impartiality for TV and radio news are still in place, as are the restrictions on election campaigning and reporting. There has been no discussion of lifting these requirements.

In other words, the deregulation of the electronic media in some respects is likely to result in regulation and re-regulation in others, as in other areas of public policy. At the same time, there is cause for concern about the democratic role of the mass media (print and electronic) which derives not from its content, but its structure of ownership and control.

OWNERSHIP AND CONTROL OF THE BRITISH MEDIA

The history of the British mass media in the twentieth century is marked by five separate but related features:

- consolidation and centralisation;

- a declining number of newspaper titles;

- concentration of ownership and control;

- the growth of multimedia conglomerates;

- internationalisation.

Consolidation and centralisation

Britain is geographically a small, densely populated, and politically centralised country, so it is not surprising that the media have developed large, national, centralised markets. In 1920 the total circulation of regional and provincial morning and evening papers was about one third larger than national dailies. By 1945 national sales were twice as large, by the 1990s over three times as large. There are still many local and regional daily and Sunday papers, but two thirds of the adult population regularly see a national daily paper, and 70 per cent a national Sunday paper. In other Western countries the newspaper business tends to be more fragmented and local.

As a result, the national newspaper market in Britain is very large by most standards. In round figures, 185 million newspapers a week are sold in Britain, of which 102 million are national dailies or Sundays. Of the 11 daily and Sunday papers with the largest circulation in Western Europe, nine are British. The national dailies have a circulation of 14.5 million copies a day, and the national Sundays sell 15.5 million. Since each paper is read by between two and three people, the readership of the dailies is around 35 million, and of the Sundays around 40 million. National newspaper sales have dropped substantially since their peak in the late 1950s because of competition from TV, and more recently because of high unemployment. But the two best sellers – the *Sun* and the *Daily Mirror* – sell over six million daily between them. The great majority of newspaper sales are national papers, and all national newspapers have their headquarters in London, even if they print regional editions in Manchester, for example, or in Scotland.

Radio and TV are also highly centralised, with a few national organisations dominating the market. ITV is based upon regions, and there has been a rapid expansion of local and community radio stations, but most viewers and listeners still tune to national stations and watch national programmes.

Declining number of newspaper titles

In the same way that the market for cars has produced an ever decreasing number of mass manufacturers who require ever increasing capital investment, so the newspaper market has less and less room for competing titles. Between 1900 and 1921 the number of national daily titles fell from 21 to 12, although from then until 1997 the number fell by only one. In 70 years after 1920 the number of provincial morning papers declined from 41 to 18, of provincial evening papers from 89 to 76, and of national and provincial Sunday papers from 21 to nine. There were about 1,400 local and regional daily and Sunday titles in 1947, but only 550 in the early 1990s. In 1975 only 18 per cent of British towns had competing papers run by different owners, half the percentage of 1921. In 1900 London had 11 evening papers; now it has one.

Concentration of ownership and control

Concentrated ownership and control of the British newspaper business is by no means new. In 1910 the biggest press magnate of the day, Lord Northcliffe, controlled 39 per cent of national daily circulation. In 1987 his modern equivalent, Rupert Murdoch, had only 35 per cent of the market. However, in 1910 the three best selling national dailies accounted for two thirds of total circulation. In 1983 the biggest three (Murdoch, Maxwell and Matthews) took 75 per cent. In that year, the five biggest companies accounted for 84 per cent of national daily and 96 per cent of national Sunday sales.

The big five (see Briefing 14.5) have also increased their control of the local and provincial press. In 1947 they had 44 and 65 per cent of provincial evening and morning circulation. In 1983 the figures had risen to 54 and 72 per cent

Plate 14.2 A meeting of moguls: Rupert Murdoch (centre) with the late Robert Maxwell (right) and Lord Rothermere

BRIEFINGS

14.5 THE MEDIA MOGULS

Robert Maxwell

When Maxwell died in mysterious circumstances in 1991, his newspapers (*Mirror/Daily Record, Sunday Mirror, Sunday People,* and *Sporting Life*) sold close to 12 million copies a week, accounting for a quarter of the daily tabloid market. Maxwell also had financial interests in TV (Central, Border, SelecTV, MTV, and Rediffusion Cable), books (EJ Arnold and Pergamon Press), magazines and journals, computer software, transport and plastics.

Rupert Murdoch

Rupert Murdoch, an Australian who has taken American citizenship, owns newspaper and TV stations on three continents. In Britain his companies own the *Sun, News of the World, The Times, The Sunday Times, Today,* and *The Times* supplements with sales of over 10 million copies, including a third of the daily and Sunday tabloid market and almost half of Sunday broadsheets. His financial interests include London Weekend TV, BSkyB (the largest satellite company in Britain), cable TV, films (Metromedia and Twentieth Century Fox), recording, magazines and journals, general publishing (Collins, Fontana and Granada Books), the Reuters News Agency, and property, land and air transport (TNT trucking),computer software, gas and oil.

Lord Matthews

The main Matthews company, Trafalgar House, ran the Express Group (sold to United Newspapers in 1985), which published, among others, the *Daily Express, Sunday Express, Star,* and *Standard,* and 11 local papers (a circulation of over seven million). At various times his companies have had interests in TV-AM, Capital Radio, publishing houses in Britain and abroad, Cunard shipping and hotels, and in property and insurance.

Lord Rothermere

Rothermere's Associated Newspapers publishes the *Daily Mail, Mail on Sunday,* and *Weekend* which have a circulation of around five million. It also has financial ties with Northcliffe Newspapers in companies on three continents which cover publishing, broadcasting, theatre, oil, transport and investment finance.

United Newspapers

When United Newspapers (Lord Stevens) absorbed the *Express* group it controlled a quarter of daily tabloid and 10 per cent of Sunday tabloid circulation. In the 1990s it published eight regional dailies, over a hundred weeklies, and controlled two large publishers of magazines and directories, as well as the Extel news agency.

respectively. Over the same period they increased their share of the local weekly market from 8 per cent to almost a third.

The policy of regulating the market to preserve competition has not been effective in Britain. The Royal Commissions on the Press of 1949, 1962, and 1977 all expressed concern about increasing concentration of ownership and control. As a result of a recommendation of the 1962 Commission, it was decided in 1965 that large companies should get the consent of the Secretary of State for the Department of Trade and Industry before acquiring more newspaper holdings. Between 1965 and 1977 50 such applications were made, and none were refused. In 1981 Rupert Murdoch bought *The Times* and *The Sunday Times*, increasing his share of national daily sales to 30 per cent, and of national Sunday sales to 36 per cent.

In 1990, Murdoch's Sky company merged with its main rival, British Satellite Broadcasting (BSB) to form a satellite monopoly, BSkyB, although this was inconsistent with the 1990 Broadcasting Act. The companies did not consult the Independent Broadcasting Authority before the merger, but the IBA approved it after the event. In 1992 there was a moratorium on mergers of commercial TV stations, following the first franchise auction of the previous year. Nonetheless, Yorkshire Television absorbed Tyne Tees Television and the Independent Television Commission agreed to the merger.

The concentration of ownership and control is likely to continue, even to speed up, over the next decades, because of economic pressures and because controls were loosened in 1993 by allowing companies to hold two licences. Carlton then took over Central, Granada absorbed London Weekend, and Meridian gained Anglia TV. In 1995, controls of cross-media ownership were loosened even more, although large newspaper groups have only restricted rights in TV.

> **Key term**
>
> **Cross-media ownership** – when the same person or company has financial interests in different types of mass media – radio, TV, newspapers, magazines, films, recording, etc.

> **Key term**
>
> **Multi-media conglomeration** – when the same company has financial interests in different media and (usually) in a range of other economic activities as well.

Multimedia conglomeration

What makes the current situation different from the earlier times of press barons, such as Lords Northcliffe and Rothermere, is that the concentration of ownership and control now extends far beyond the press to publishing and other media forms. The largest multimedia conglomerates now include newspapers, journals, books, films, recording, radio, TV and entertainment. They also extend into commerce and finance of other kinds, such as property, banking, insurance, oil, transport and computers. As the Press Commission of 1977 wrote: 'Rather than saying that the press has other business interests, it would be truer to argue that the press has become a subsidiary of other interests'.[2] In short, the media have been absorbed into the general world of business and finance.

Internationalisation – the borderless world

In the last decades multimedia moguls and corporations have emerged that span not just countries but continents. The most conspicuous examples include Ted Turner in the USA, Berlusconi in Italy, the Bertelsmann and Springer groups of Germany, and Rupert Murdoch whose companies operate in Australia, Europe and the USA. While newspapers usually cater for national (that is, specific language) markets, they are increasingly controlled by multinational companies. Some journals and magazines are also increasing their international circulation (the *Financial Times*, the *Economist*, *Time*, *Newsweek*). The inherently international nature of films and TV is being strengthened by the spread of cable and satellite which is creating a

---

[2] *Royal Commission on the Press 1974–79*, Cmnd 6810 (London: HMSO, 1977), p. 149

global, or borderless, television network. The American news channel CNN International is available to over 65 million people in more than 200 countries, and BBC World TV is chasing the international market hard.

There are two dangers in increasing ownership and control, and of growing multi-media, multinational conglomerates. First, such companies are increasingly beyond public regulation, and represent growing power without accountability or responsibility. Second, by controlling large market shares they weaken media competition which pluralist theory says is essential for democracy. There are, however, some counter-trends to the consolidation of media markets.

THE COUNTER-TRENDS

The smaller media: specialisation and diversity

As ownership and control of the mass media becomes increasingly consolidated and centralised, so the mass media become progressively homogeneous. At the same time, modern technology also makes it possible for the smaller media to become increasingly specialised, fragmented and pluralist. For example, there is an ever increasing number and variety of broadsheets, newsletters, leaflets, magazines, journals and other publications. A visit to any high street newsagent will reveal this pluralist magazine heaven. Nevertheless, many of the larger circulation magazines in Britain are published by a few of the largest companies. Between 1966 and 1974 over half the new consumer magazines with sales of 30,000 or more were launched by four major publishing groups. The largest, the International Publishing Corporation, has over 200 titles.

For a time it was felt that new, computerised methods of production would weaken the Fleet Street publishing empires. Between 1960 and 1985 only two new national papers were launched, but eight were created between 1986 and 1992. Few survive. The most notable was *Today*, Eddie Shah's attempt in 1986 to use the latest, colour printing technology to break into the national newspaper market. He was widely hailed as a giant-killer who would beat the entrenched forces of Fleet Street (newspaper barons and trade unions alike) at their own game. Within weeks of the first issue, *Today* was in financial trouble and a few months later Shah sold it to Tiny Rowland's Lonrho group, a multi-media, multi-national company. Ironically, the person who benefited most from Shah's venture was Rupert Murdoch. He used new technology to break union agreements and moved News International from Fleet Street to Wapping, where he exploited computer-driven production. Far from undermining the old media moguls, the new publishing technology seems to have strengthened them.

One major exception is the successful launch of the *Independent* in 1986, and the *Independent on Sunday* in 1990 with the remarkably small capital investment of £18 million. The *Independent* was the first successful new national daily since 1873, but nevertheless with daily sales of less than 300,000 (less than 3% of the national total), it has barely disturbed the mass circulation papers.

Another example of growing diversity and pluralism is local and community radio. The BBC launched its first local radio station in 1967 and there were over 30 of them by the early 1990s. The first local commercial radio went on air in London in 1973 and now almost everyone in Britain has a choice of at least two commercial stations. At the same time, ownership and control of the new mass audience cable and satellite channels show signs of increasing consolidation.

Investigative journalism

Key term

Investigative journalism – in-depth and often critical journalism which involves research which is usually time-consuming and expensive.

When we look at the content rather than the control of the biggest newspapers and TV companies, however, we also see trends which go against the standardisation of news and opinion associated with concentration of ownership. Media moguls and multinationals alike want to appeal to the market and increase their audience share. Commercialisation and the need to boost dividends for shareholders become an overriding imperative even in a semicompetitive or oligopolistic market. This can override the proprietors' political opinions if they sense they are losing out because of them.

Plate 14.3 Guardian cover of Neil Hamilton: A liar and a cheat. Their investigative journalism is a rarity, partly because of British libel laws

A clear example of this is the way all newspapers, even strongly Conservative ones like *The Times* and *Telegraph*, were drawn into reporting government scandals and sleaze in the run-up to the 1997 election. Such stories allowed the broadsheets to compete with the tabloids in terms of their lurid coverage, even if they damaged the party they supported.

The breakdown in inhibitions about what constitutes legitimate coverage was associated with the tabloids' fight-back against television from the 1950s. Cheque book journalism covering sex and crime extended to areas which had previously been taboo to journalism, including government incompetence and the personal lives – and business dealings – of ministers.

Such coverage spread into the 'serious' print media in the 1970s under the name of investigative journalism. This was a broad title for in-depth reporting of particular decisions or events, mostly political. Straight reporting was supplemented by detailed analysis and comment. Many of the case studies reported in this book and other textbooks on British politics use the fruits of investigative journalism.

In some ways television programmes like *Panorama*, *Newsweek* and *Today* pioneered and certainly extended such no-holds-barred investigations. The tabloid press joyfully took them up when sex or corruption was involved, as they usually were.

Stories like these were highly embarrassing to the Government, whose attempts to suppress them also became news. Thus the attempt by the Conservatives to get a legal injunction against the publication of extracts from the book *Spycatcher* in Britain (it contained revelations about the security services) was itself reported, defeating the object of the intervention.

In this area several developments already commented on have helped the media fulfil its 'watchdog' role:

- the increasing tendency for civil servants to 'leak' embarrassing details they disapprove of;

- politicians' own bending of constitutional provisions like 'collective responsibility', which means leaking stories that favour themselves or embarrass rivals within their own party;

- increasing use of legal appeals and judicial review, which allow the press to comment on cases without fear of libel suits;

- activities of parliamentary select committees, which often uncover and publish details of maladministration;

- the very diversity and pluralism of the 'little magazine' world, which means that some publication somewhere is investigating and publishing a newsworthy story that will then be taken up generally.

In spite of proprietors' personal sympathies and the arsenal of devices British government has to suppress and manipulate news, market forces have therefore driven a much wider coverage of political affairs than when reporting could be managed by private contacts among the elite in the 1940s and 1950s. This is a hopeful development which goes against some of the negative trends otherwise associated with commercialisation and the breakdown of the public service model in Britain.

ESSAYS

1. Do the British media sustain or undermine pluralist democracy?

2. Why is it important to distinguish between the electronic and the print media in any discussion of the political media in Britain?

3. Should the process of commercialisation of the British media be followed to its logical conclusion?

PROJECTS

1. Collect and organise figures about the increasing concentration of ownership and control of the British media. Cover the print and the electronic media, and consider the counter-trends.

2. Debate the cases for and against the public service and commercial models of the mass media.

SUMMARY

- There can be no doubt that the mass news media play an increasingly important role in the government and politics of Britain, but their role is the subject of heated disagreement.

- The print and electronic media have been fundamentally different until recently. The print market is, in theory, an open and competitive one, and the state has imposed minimum regulation upon it.

- Spectrum scarcity required public market and content regulation of the electronic media, and the resulting BBC monopoly allowed it to develop the public service model, an example which many other nations followed.

- New technology (cable, satellite, new terrestrial channels, and local radio and TV) is rapidly bringing spectrum scarcity to an end, and commercialisation of the media has followed.

- This has had conflicting effects so far as media coverage of politics is concerned: (a) concentration of control of the major outlets; (b) diversity of the 'little media', such as magazines, newsletters, local radio; (c) the growth of investigative journalism and 'muckraking'.

FURTHER READING

The issues of ownership and control and public accountability are fully covered in J. Curran and J. Seaton, *Power Without Responsibility: The Press and Broadcasting in Britain* (London: Routledge, 4th edn 1991). Particularly good on the public service model is D. McQuail, *Media Performance: Mass Communications and the Public Interest* (Beverly Hills, CA: Sage, 1992). Recent, concise, and useful accounts of the development of the mass media in Britain since 1945 can be found in K. Newton, 'The Mass Media and Politics' in L. Robins (ed.), *Fifty Years of British Politics* (Manchester: Manchester University Press, 1997), and A. Weymouth, 'The Media in Britain', in A. Weymouth and B. Lamizet (eds), *Markets and Myths: Forces for Change in the European Media* (Harlow: Longman, 1996).

http://www.awl-he.com/politics/newbritpol

Internet resources – visit *The New British Politics* Webpage for links to a specially-chosen selection of Internet resources relevant to this Chapter.

http://www.awl-he.com/politics/newbritpol

Elections and voting

Newspapers and television derive their power from the influence they have over political opinions, which ultimately get translated into votes. As British governments have to face elections every four or five years, everything that might affect their chances of winning or losing is important and that gives them a strong motivation to control coverage or to seek the support of newspaper proprietors.

However, many other factors shape election results than the nature of media coverage. Voters' opinions are not wholly dependent on the media. Group endorsements may be important in influencing some voters towards particular parties. Other electors may find themselves in social situations which push them towards a vote for one party or another regardless of the particular issues in an election.

The exact number of votes a party receives may be less important than how these get translated by the electoral system into seats in Parliament. British governments depend on controlling a majority of Commons' seats, not on getting a majority popular vote. Labour's 1997 landslide victory, which netted the party 418 out of 659 seats in Parliament, was achieved with only 43.3 per cent of the vote, a similar percentage to that won by the Conservatives from 1979 to 1992.

This chapter will review all the factors affecting election results. Accordingly it will:

- Give an overview of elections and parties since 1945

- Examine the effects of the current 'first past the post' system and alternative forms of electoral system currently being contemplated

- Analyse the factors which give electoral victory to one or other of the main parties

- Review the characteristics which make some electors always vote for the same party, giving Conservatives and Labour a 'core support' of around 27 per cent, which contributes greatly to their enduring electoral strength

ELECTIONS AND PARTIES SINCE 1945

The first thing to say about British elections is that they are primarily a register of party strengths, which results in the plurality party (the one with the largest vote) forming a government.

The next chapter will discuss how the parties came to dominate elections. It is clear, however, that in Britain, as in practically all other democracies, elections are a choice between party alternatives. In Britain, where one or other of the main parties can normally count on getting a majority of seats, elections are unusually focused on the question of whether the country is going to have Conservative or Labour government. Generally, Conservatives favour less and Labour more government intervention in society, so the party choice carries with it a general policy choice: do we want free markets or more state provision? This is the main ground on which the postwar elections listed in Table 15.1 have been fought and won.

Three major points emerge from the table. First, the percentage of parliamentary seats the winning party gets is generally larger than its vote. From 1979 to 1992 the Conservative Party got a remarkably consistent vote of 42 to 44 per cent. With this it always obtained a parliamentary majority, which was of varying size but of course was always enough to give them control of government, the real electoral prize.

The second point is important, however, for appreciating the workings of the electoral system. That is, with roughly the same overall vote, the Conservative majority fluctuated from 51.6 per cent of Commons seats to 61.1 per cent. This demonstrates that under the current electoral system of small constituencies awarded to the party candidate with the largest vote, a party's parliamentary strength depends very much not only on how many votes it gets, but also on where they are and how they are distributed over constituencies. Shifts in the distribution produced the fluctuating parliamentary majorities.

The extreme example of this is of course the Liberal Democrats, who with 25.4 per cent of the vote got only 3.5 per cent of seats in 1983 and even worse ratios at other times. This occurred because Liberals were spread relatively evenly over the country and so won only a few constituencies. In contrast, the big parties dominate certain regions, as we have seen, and so win more constituencies, but are also vulnerable to shifts in the territorial distribution of their votes.

In spite of such distortions in party representation a third point is also clear. That is that the leading party in terms of vote generally gets the majority of seats. In this respect the electoral system dispenses a kind of rough justice by rewarding the largest party. (The two exceptions are 1951 and February 1974, when Conservatives and Labour respectively got more seats for slightly fewer votes than their rival. However, the voting discrepancy was not great and both parties were rising in popularity at the time.)

COUNTING VOTES INTO SEATS: ELECTORAL SYSTEMS

This discussion shows that the method of counting votes into seats is very important in determining election results and affecting the performance of political

Table 15.1 Election results, 1945–97

Elections	Conservative			Labour			Liberals			Others			Total number of MPs
	Seat No	Seat %	Vote %	Seat No	Seat %	Vote %	Seat No	Seat %	Vote %	Seat No	Seat %	Vote %	
1945	213	32.7	39.8	393	61.2	47.8	12	1.9	9.0	22	4.1	3.4	640
1950	298	47.7	43.5	315	50.4	46.1	9	1.4	9.1	3	0.5	0.7	625
1951	321	51.4	48.0	295	47.2	48.8	6	1.0	2.5	3	0.5	0.7	625
1955	344	54.8	49.7	277	44.0	46.4	6	1.0	2.7	3	0.4	1.2	630
1959	365	57.9	49.4	258	41.0	43.8	6	1.0	5.9	1	0.2	0.9	630
1964	304	48.3	43.4	317	50.3	44.1	9	1.4	11.2	0	0.0	1.3	630
1966	253	40.2	41.9	363	57.8	47.9	12	1.9	8.5	2	0.2	1.7	630
1970	330	52.4	46.4	287	45.7	43.0	6	1.0	7.5	7	0.9	3.1	630
1974 (Feb.)	297	46.8	37.9	301	47.4	37.1	14	2.2	19.3	23[a]	3.6	5.7	635
1974 (Oct.)	277	43.6	35.8	319	50.2	39.2	13	2.0	18.3	26	4.1	6.7	635
1979	339	53.4	43.9	269	42.4	36.9	11	1.7	13.8	16	2.5	5.4	635
1983	397	61.1	42.4	209	32.2	27.6	23[b]	3.5	25.4	21	3.2	4.6	650
1987	375	57.8	42.3	229	35.2	30.8	22[b]	3.4	22.6	24	3.5	4.3	650
1992	336	51.6	41.9	271	41.6	34.4	20	3.1	17.8	24	3.7	5.8	651
1997	165	25.0	31.5	418	63.4	43.3	46	7.0	17.0	30	4.5	8.2	659

Notes: [a] Northern Irish MPs are counted as 'others' from 1974
[b] In 1983 and 1987 'Liberal' includes the SDP/Liberal Alliance

Key term

Proportional representation (PR) – a voting system which uses an allocation formula (there are many of them) which distributes seats among parties in proportion to their vote.

Key term

Coalition government – where two or more parties combine to form the government, in contrast to single party government where all the offices of government are held by members of the same party.

parties. In the case of Liberal Democrats the 'first past the post' method may have even greater effects. Since the party has been able to win only a few seats and was therefore permanently excluded from government, many potential supporters have been put off, so the party's *voting strength* is not what it might be under an alternative system.

This is clearly unfair. However, supporters of the present system claim that the unfairness to Liberal Democrats is more than counterbalanced by the fact that it allows one of the two main parties to form a majority government, offering electors a real focused choice between two alternative governments and programmes. If Britain adopted a system, such as some form of proportional representation, which gave seats in a strict ratio to votes, no party would have a majority. Two of them would always have to join to form a coalition government, but it would never be clear in advance what combination would form or what programme it would have. In spite of its unfairness, therefore, the present electoral system at least offers electors a clear choice. See Briefing 15.1 on main types of electoral systems.

BRIEFINGS

15.1 THE MAIN ELECTORAL SYSTEMS: PLURALITY AND PROPORTIONAL REPRESENTATION

Free elections are the backbone of modern democracy, and although at first sight they may appear to be a simple matter – expressing a preference for one party over others – they turn out to be very complex affairs. There are two main types of electoral systems in modern democracies: simple plurality voting and proportional representation (PR).

Simple plurality

Sometimes called the 'first past the post' system, this only requires the winning candidate to get more votes than any other candidate, no matter how many candidates there may be, and no matter how small the winning percentage of the vote may be. In a three-way contest the winner may get little more than a third of the total, and in a four-way contest, little more than a quarter. Simple plurality voting is usually linked with single-member constituencies, and the whole package is called the single-member, simple plurality system (or SMSP). In Europe it is used at present in the UK, and outside Europe in the USA and Canada. The advantage of the system is simplicity. The disadvantage is that it is likely to produce disproportionate election results in that the distribution of votes between parties does not closely match their proportion of seats in the legislature. The simple plurality system also means that minor party supporters, even large minorities like the Liberal Democrats, may 'waste' their vote.

Second ballot and alternative vote

The second ballot system tries to avoid the worst disadvantages of the simple plurality system, by requiring a winning candidate to get an absolute majority (50 per cent + 1) of the votes cast in the first round. Failing this a second (run-off) ballot is held for the strongest of the first round candidates. This is the system that will probably be used to elect the Mayor of London.

15.1 THE MAIN ELECTORAL SYSTEMS: PLURALITY AND PROPORTIONAL REPRESENTATION (continued)

Alternative vote

Another variation on simple plurality voting is to allow voters to indicate their first and subsequent preferences among candidates, so that if no candidate receives a majority of first preferences in the first count, second (and subsequent) preferences may be brought into play in second and subsequent counts. This is Labour's preferred reform.

Proportional representation (PR)

Proportional representation is an allocation formula which tries to distribute seats among parties in proportion to the votes. In other words, PR tries to ensure that minorities as well as majorities are represented in proportion to their voting strength. The three main ways of doing this are the party list system, the single transferable vote and the additional member system.

Party list system

One of the simplest ways of ensuring that seats are proportional to votes is to distribute the seats on a national basis (as in the Netherlands) or in large regions (Italy). Parties draw up a list of candidates in order of preference, and they are elected in proportion to the number of votes their party receives, starting from the top of party lists. This gives a lot of power to the party leaders who decide where candidates are ranked in the list. The system is used in European elections.

Single transferable vote (STV)

This voting system is used in Ireland, and is preferred by the Liberal Democrats. Voters may rank order their preferences for candidates, so that their second, third, or subsequent preferences can be taken into account. If their first-choice candidate achieves the desired quota before other seats are filled, then their lower preference(s) may come into play. Or if their first-choice candidate is eliminated, then their second or subsequent preference can be taken into account. In this way, those casting a first choice for a minor party can choose to cast a second choice for another party, thereby reducing the chances of a 'wasted' vote and making electoral alliances important. There are many different variations on STV, and many different ways of calculating the final result. In Ireland, voters can order their preferences within and across parties, so ensuring the closest possible relationship between voter preferences and candidates elected. STV must be used in conjunction with multimember districts.

Additional member systems

These are ways of trying to keep personal links between elected representatives and voters, while making the end result more proportional. Two election systems are used: single-member districts elect representatives by simple plurality, second ballot, or the alternative vote, and additional seats are allocated in such a way as to achieve overall proportionality.

One important element in the current 'single-member simple plurality constituency system' in Britain is how the constituency boundaries are drawn. Changing the boundaries – which is necessary to keep up with shifts of

Key term

Single member, simple plurality (SMSP) – the electoral system used in British general elections in which the country is divided into constituencies, each returning one Member of Parliament who only needs more votes than any other candidate in that constituency to win the election.

population – may give victory to one party or another by excluding a bloc of previous supporters or including a new bloc. That is why decisions are left to an independent commission rather than to the parties or the Government.

Even so, changes can materially favour one party. The new constituencies drawn up between the 1992 and 1997 general elections affected Labour's particular distribution of regional support. The average electorate of Labour-won seats in 1997 was 65,236 while for seats held by the Conservatives it was 70,497. So Labour could win more seats with fewer votes. Labour's majority of seats was 179 with 43 per cent of the vote. Had their voting percentages been reversed, with the same distribution of support, the Conservatives would only have secured a majority of 45 seats! Labour's large majority was the reflection of a major bias of the electoral system in its favour, which will endure over the next couple of elections at least.

This advantage derives from the precise way constituencies are drawn up, and party voters distributed, which makes the detailed effects of any change in the electoral system rather unpredictable. Only the broader effects are obvious, in that any move towards a more proportional system would benefit Liberal Democrats and the minor parties. How they would affect the balance between Conservatives and Labour is not obvious.

Given this, the major parties would probably prefer to stick with the present system. However, pressure for change comes from the fact that other methods of translating votes into seats are being employed in other elections in Britain, notably those for the regional assemblies and the European Parliament.

Both Scotland and Wales are to have an additional member system. Basically this involves electing representatives as at present from the existing constituencies. Additional members will then be elected in proportion to the national distribution of preferences indicated by electors at the same time as they vote for their constituency member. The additional members will be added to the constituency members to make up the final Assembly. The overall membership of the Assembly will be far from proportional (though more so than under a simple constituency-based system) since the proportionally elected members will simply be added to the constituency members. This will dilute the biases of the first past the post system but not eliminate it.

Another way of keeping the link between MPs and constituencies is the alternative vote. This retains single member constituencies but asks voters to indicate multiple preferences between candidates (numbering candidates 1, 2, 3, etc. on the ballot paper). If no candidate has a majority of first preferences, the second preferences of low-ranked candidates will be redistributed until one of the survivors secures over 50 per cent of the vote.

Because it keeps the present constituencies and does not radically change the system of voting, this reform is the one that finds most support in the two main parties. Calculations on the basis of the 1992 election results indicate, however, that it would change the outcome very little, though giving a little more representation to Liberal Democrats. The new system would retain almost all the biases of the present one.

Proposals are in hand, however, to change the basis of election to the European Parliament to a party list system of proportional representation. This would require several candidates to stand for election in a reasonably large area (as has been done for Northern Ireland for European elections since the 1980s). Parties then draw up a list of candidates in order of preference and they are elected in proportion to the number of votes received by the party, starting from the top of the list. As chances of election vary very much with being at the top, this puts a lot of power in the hands of party leaders.

This might make a change to such a system acceptable to those in control of parties. A sticking point, however, remains in the attachment of both electors and MPs to small constituencies, where it is felt that MPs are able to service their constituents better.

A breach could be made in this by the electoral arrangements for the new Greater London Authority. In this area the Executive Mayor will be elected directly by seven million electors, hardly a constituency in the conventional sense. To give the Mayor greater authority, a second ballot system will probably be instituted. Either the winning candidate will get over 50 per cent of votes on the first ballot, or a second (run-off) ballot will be held between the two most successful candidates on the first ballot where the winner must get over 50 per cent of votes and can thus claim to represent a majority. The controlling 24-member London Assembly will also be elected on a London-wide basis or in very large electoral divisions. In neither case will traditional constituencies be preserved.

However, both electors and long-serving MPs value constituencies for the contacts and services they provide between representatives and constituents. So it is unlikely that the new London model will be followed either in the rest of local government or in general elections. The most likely change is towards an alternative member system which will retain small constituencies for the foreseeable future.

Tactical voting in 1997

Key term
Tactical voting – the practice of voting for a candidate who is not the first preference in order to keep out a less preferred candidate.

Such constituencies encourage the behaviour known as tactical voting among electors, which was in growing evidence in 1997 and may increase in future elections.

Tactical voting is the practice of voting for a candidate other than your first preference, with a view to keeping the least preferred candidate out. The 1997 General Election saw such behaviour increasingly contributing to the parliamentary strengths of both Labour and Liberal Democrats. It was particularly important to the latter, for whom it may have helped double the number of seats they had in Parliament.

The best estimate is that 25–35 seats were lost to the Conservatives through tactical voting in 1997.[1] Given the size of the Labour majority this did not determine the election result. But it might well swing a future election where the contenders are more evenly balanced.

---

[1] J. Curtice and P. M. Steed, Appendix 2 in D. Butler and D. Kavanagh, *The British General Election of 1997* (London: Macmillan, 1997)

Table 15.2 shows how tactical voting worked in accordance with the party balance in the constituencies. Obviously switching votes between Labour and Liberals would have no effect where the Labour or Conservative lead was very large; one might just as well vote for one's preferred party. Thus in Labour-held constituencies where Conservatives were second, there was little reason for Liberals to switch votes, given that Labour was far ahead nationally. In such

Table 15.2 Evidence for tactical voting in the constituencies, 1997 General Election

Tactical situation in constituency	Change from 1992 in per cent voting		
	CON	**LAB**	**LIB DEM**
Labour held with a 1992 Conservative vote over 33.3%	−12.6	+9.6	−0.3
Conservative held with Labour in second place	−12.6	+13.0	−3.0
Lib Dem held with a 1992 Conservative vote over 33.3%	−10.6	+9.6	+1.6
Conservative held with a lead of less than 30% over Lib Dem	−11.8	+6.5	+1.9
Safe Conservative lead over Lib Dem (over 30%)	−13.5	+10.0	−0.8
Three-way marginal seats	−11.6	+10.9	−2.3

Source: J. Curtice and P. M. Steed, Appendix 2 of D. Butler and D. Kavanagh, *The British General Election of 1997* (London: Macmillan, 1997)

constituencies the Labour lead was up by nearly 10 per cent on 1992, which was about average.

However, where Conservatives held the seat but Labour might take it (the second row of the table) the increase in Labour vote was higher on average – 13 per cent – while the Liberal Democratic vote decreased by 3 per cent, almost exactly matching the exceptional boost to Labour. Similarly where Conservatives held the seat but Liberal Democrats had a chance of taking it (fourth row of the table) the Labour increase was only 6.5 per cent but the Liberal vote went up by an exceptional 1.9 per cent, indicating that some Labour voters at any rate were crossing to the Liberals.

Tactical voting is encouraged in an electoral system based on small constituencies like the British. But it will only take place where supporters of two of the parties feel much closer to each other than they do to the third. This now seems true of Labour and Liberals with their joint Cabinet Committee on constitutional reform (Chapter 8) and their increasing ideological convergence (Figure 17.2). Such a convergence could have major effects in future general elections:

- It could boost Labour and Liberal-held seats at the expense of the Conservatives, reversing the advantage the latter had from a split opposition in the 1980s.

- In the event of no one party holding a majority after the next election it could promote a Liberal–Labour coalition, with major consequences for constitutional change and the party balance.

Targeting seats in 1997

Another consequence of a small-constituency electoral system is the temptation for parties to concentrate money, volunteers and resources on those constituencies they think they have a good chance of winning. Such 'targeting' of seats was very prevalent – again among both Labour and Liberal Democrats – in 1997. It was, indeed, a long-standing Liberal tactic to 'target' constituencies where they had done well in local government. In 1997 this tactic worked well for them in South-West England, their area of traditional strength, and to a lesser extent in South-East England. These were the areas where they picked up most of their new seats. Labour, however, seemed to pick up only a few seats, possibly four to six, through this strategy, not worthwhile given the massive concentration of resources involved. So Labour will possibly spread its resources more widely next time.

EXPLAINING ELECTORAL SUCCESS

Up to this point we have been exploring the effects of the electoral system on the election result. It does not determine the results, but in conjunction with the territorial distribution of votes it can have a strong influence both on who wins and how the parties act, as the examples of tactical voting and targeting showed.

However, whatever its other effects, the first past the post system does reflect the major result of the election quite clearly, that is, it gives a parliamentary majority to the party that gains most votes nationally. To win a British general election therefore a party must get a voting plurality. How does it do that? What factors explain the change from a Conservative plurality of just over 42 per cent in 1992 to a Labour plurality of just over 43 per cent in 1997?

So many factors could potentially affect voting that the task of selecting the most important and using them to explain the overall result seems almost impossible. As pointed out earlier, electors vote differently in different regions of the country; according to class, religion and other social characteristics; in terms of their own opinions and what they see the parties as standing for; or even because of tactical considerations produced by the particular constituency situation they find themselves in. How can one sift through this nexus of influences to come up with the more important ones? How do we know anyway that the same influences are important for everyone and not just for some British electors while others vote on different grounds?

The vast amount of research that has been done on the relationship between social, economic and political factors and the actual election result has nevertheless sorted many of these voting relationships out. Research has now got to the point of identifying the central processes which explain the overall election result and is even capable of predicting it accurately beforehand.

A first simplifying step is to recognise that what we want to explain first of all is the *change* in the result from one election to another. Ultimately, of course, we also want to know why some electors always vote for the same party, since they are also contributing to the overall result. But clearly change between one election and the next will not be caused by them, even if their support for a party gradually erodes over the long term. We shall examine this possibility below.

Alteration in the result over a five-year term is much more likely to be caused by changing opinions and attitudes to the parties rather than underlying social factors, as these are unlikely to shift so quickly. Which out of the vast range of potential issues might be the most relevant to voting decisions?

Here it is useful to think about the factors which historically have influenced the policies and ideology of the political parties. It is, after all, the parties which electors are choosing between when they cast their votes, particularly between Conservatives and Labour. The great historical dividing line between these parties, which became increasingly evident in the twentieth century, has been the extent to which the state should intervene directly in economic and social relationships, or how far these should be left to the free market (Chapter 2). Margaret Thatcher completed the move of the Conservatives to being a totally free market party. Labour, while taking over many of her ideas, has remained much more favourable to direct government action where it felt it was needed. Even New Labour has embarked on a massive 'welfare to work' programme financed by a tax on the privatised utility companies. (As we shall see, differences about the nature and extent of government action are at the heart of the left–right differences we discuss in Chapter 17.)

It is likely, therefore, that the central concerns electors have in mind when voting are economic in nature. It would be natural to think of one's own and one's family well-being and ask whether that would be served best by direct government action or by the government standing aside and letting things take their course. When more electors feel insecure about job security they may well feel the need for direct government action. When they feel more secure and are more concerned with maintaining the value of their wages and savings, they might well want fewer taxes and less intervention.

Direct evidence about British electors' main concerns comes from studies of public opinion. From 1960, the Gallup organisation has asked a regular question of British electors: 'What do you think is the most important problem facing the country at the present time?' The three highest-ranking answers to this question, averaged for each year from 1960 to 1995, are shown in Figure 15.1. No other domestic issues had a significant number of mentions, and foreign affairs ceased to concern people very much as the Cold War faded in intensity in the late 1960s. Round about 1970 electors became increasingly concerned about inflation and unemployment. This is not surprising when we remember the very high inflation recorded in the 1970s and early 1980s, and sharply rising unemployment associated with rises in the oil price during those years (Chapter 3).

Some people do worry about other issues such as welfare, law and order and the environment. But the major issues are economic in nature and related to very immediate concerns about jobs and money: personal economic well-being in short.

As economic conditions can change quite rapidly, particularly over the four or five years separating elections, such worries could well provide a dynamic for voting change. Of course, economic factors are unlikely to be the only circumstances influencing votes, that would be too Marxist and deterministic! Dramatic political events like the Falklands War in 1983, and changes in party style and leadership (like the Labour selection of Tony Blair in 1994) are also likely to have had an effect.

Figure 15.1 Electors' perceptions of important problems facing the country

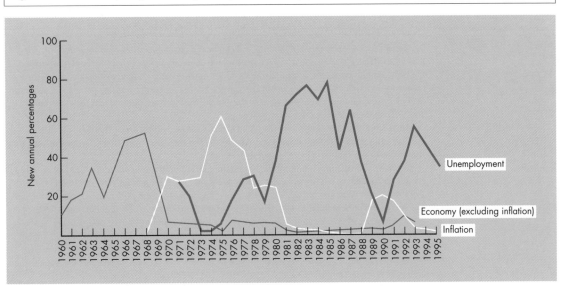

Source: Gallup Political Index. Responses to question: 'What is the most important problem facing the country?' aggregated for each year

Key term

The Essex Model – a method of explaining past election results and predicting future ones based on a statistical analysis of the changing economic basis of previous election results.

All these influences are incorporated in an explanation of the election results from 1979–1997 which was also used successfully to predict the results of the 1992 and 1997 elections in advance, quite a hard test of its truth and relevance! We can therefore take it as the best available explanation of the British election results of the last decade and a half.

This explanation is known as the Essex Model of Voting, after the Department of Government at the University of Essex where it has been developed over the last decade. It is summarised in Figure 15.2, and incorporates a lot of the influences on voting which we have discussed above.[2]

Figure 15.2 The 'Essex Model' of the factors shaping British Election results, 1979–97

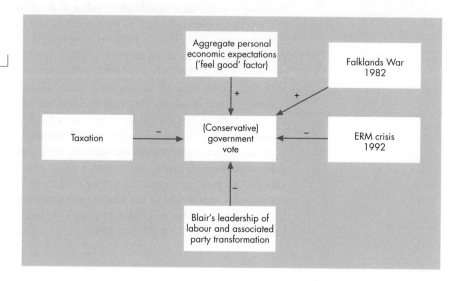

<hr />

[2] A 'model' is a concise representation of a theoretical explanation, often statistical in form. What the 'Essex Model' shows is that, as electors become generally more optimistic about how well off they are going to be in the months ahead, the Government vote goes up (presumably because it is credited with producing more prosperity). Conversely, if more people become pessimistic about this they blame the Government and withdraw their vote. Raising taxes also reduces the Government vote as it takes money directly away from people.

These economic considerations affect the Government vote all the time. But there are also political influences, although these are shorter lived. The Falklands War, Black Wednesday and Tony Blair's election as Labour leader all had their effects.

The 'vote' which is explained by all these factors includes voting intentions which Gallup asked about every month over this period, as well as the actual votes in the four elections of 1983, 1987, 1992 and 1997. What the 'model' does is to relate fluctuations in the explanatory factors to the ups and downs in voting intentions and actual vote for the Conservatives. The Labour vote can be explained in the same way simply by reversing the 'plus' and 'minus' effects in the figure.

Of course, the explanation leaves out many influences which might be thought to have had an effect on the vote. Why should the 'Gulf War' of 1990 not have had an effect on votes when the Falklands War' did (if only for a short time)? Why did the poll tax or Mrs Thatcher's leadership not have effects when Tony Blair's did?

Various arguments can be made about this. From a statistical point of view, however, none of them improves the performance of this model in predicting the vote if they are added to it, and therefore are not strictly needed to explain the results.

The permanent underlying influences on the vote are:

- personal economic expectations about the family economic situation in the months ahead. This summarises the worries about inflation and unemployment which we saw were at the forefront of electors' minds after 1970 (Figure 15.1);
- taxation, which directly affects family income and hence well-being.

We would be very suspicious if dramatic political events and issues had no effect on voting. The explanation in Figure 15.2 shows that they do but they are less long-lasting than economic considerations. We might expect this from the saying 'a week is a long time in politics'. But, as we will show, some political effects are more lasting than this. The transformation of Labour into New Labour is still affecting votes!

The political effects are:

- the Falklands War. This is a short-term effect, felt only as a temporary boost in Conservative support in 1982. But it has to be taken into account in looking at Conservative support over the 18-year period which includes it;
- the speculation against the pound culminating in 'Black Wednesday' 1992 (described in Chapter 4). This seems to have destroyed many people's belief in the Government's competence and produced a sharp fall in voting support which was never made up;
- the Labour Party's transformation of itself into an attractive alternative for government. When Labour was tearing itself to bits internally, or seemed too extreme, the Conservatives naturally gained support. When it seemed united and competent under Tony Blair, Conservative votes slumped. This process continued over two years, as more and more people came to appreciate New Labour. The 'Blair effect' therefore produced a steady erosion in Conservative support rather than one dramatic fall, unlike the 1992 currency crisis or the Falklands War earlier on.

All these influences, as well as levels of Conservative support, can be measured statistically. We can therefore relate them to each other through the equation shown in Table 15.3.

The Table shows how effects can be estimated for each of the factors which influences the Conservative vote.[3] Thus each one per cent increase in the overall

---

[3] The equation should be read as saying that Conservative support in the present month is:

- a base figure of 6.82 per cent,
- plus 0.83 multiplied by the percentage of Conservative support there was last month,
- plus 0.09 multiplied by the difference between the percentage of poll respondents with positive financial expectations and the percentage with negative ones,
- minus 0.33 multiplied by the increase in the taxation index,
- plus 9.21 per cent in May 1982 ('Falklands effect'),
- plus 5.40 per cent in June 1982 ('Falklands effect'),
- minus 4.91 per cent in September 1992 (Black Wednesday),
- minus 1.44 per cent for each month from June 1995 (delayed effects of election of Blair as Labour leader).

Table 15.3 The statistical relationship between economic conditions, political issues and the Conservative vote, 1979

Overall regression equation

$$\text{Convote}_t = 6.82 + 0.83 \text{ Convote}_{t-1}\ 0.09 \text{ Aggeconexp}_t - 0.33 \text{ Tax}_t$$
$$+ 9.2 \text{ Falklands May82} + 5.40 \text{ Falklands June82}$$
$$- 4.91 \text{ Currency92} - 1.44 \text{ Blair}$$

A tabular presentation of the regression equation

Abbreviation	Full description	Numerical value attached to each factor given by full equation
Convote_t	Conservative voting support in the current month	
Constant	Base figure for Conservative support	6.82
Convote_{t-1}	Conservative voting support in the previous month	0.83
Aggeconexp_t	Balance of positive over negative household financial expectations	0.09
Tax_t	Change in taxation index	−0.33
FalklandsMay82	Increase in Conservative support owing to the Falklands War May 1982	9.21
FalklandsJune82	Increase in Conservative support owing to the Falklands War June 1982	5.40
Currency	Decrease in Conservative support owing to speculation against pound Sept. 1992	−4.91
Blair	Blair leadership effect	−1.44

Source: David Sanders, 'Conservative Incompetence, Labour Responsibility, and the Feelgood Factor: Why the economy failed to save the Conservatives in 1997', Paper presented to Political Studies Conference on Elections, Public Opinion and Parties, University of Essex, September 26–28, 1997.

balance of positive over negative financial expectations will produce an increase of 0.09 per cent in the percentage declaring their intention to vote Conservative. This can be added to the increases or decreases in the vote produced by other factors in the equation to produce a numerical prediction of what the Conservative vote will be, given specified changes in the factors affecting it. In April 1997 that vote was predicted as 32.3 per cent, acceptably close to the actual 31.5 per cent which the party actually obtained on 1 May.

The Labour vote can be explained and predicted by the same equation (with the signs of course reversed). Over the period from 1979–97 it has been the reverse image of the Conservative vote, so the same factors must influence it. (See Briefing 15.2 for more on regression equations.)

The story of the 1997 election told by the Essex Model is thus set against a background of belated economic recovery from the severe recession of the early 1990s. By the time of the election this was gently boosting Conservative support. This had fallen to such a low ebb owing to the previous recession, mishandling of the currency (Black Wednesday) and tax increases, that the recovery was not nearly enough to regain their voting plurality. A final blow was given by the selection of

BRIEFINGS

15.2 REGRESSION EQUATIONS

A regression equation is a numerical description of the relationship between the phenomenon you wish to describe (like votes) and the factor(s) used to explain it (like taxation). You start from a graph of the type with which everyone is familiar, relating these two variables:

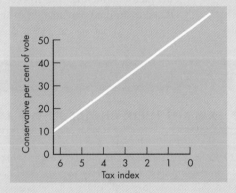

The line starts from a base of 6.82 percentage vote. It shows that for each one unit reduction in the tax index the Conservative vote goes up 10 per cent over the base. This can be expressed numerically as a 'regression equation' as follows:

$$CONVOTE_t = 6.82 + 10.0\ DTAX_t$$

that is, the Conservative vote equals 6.82 plus 10 times the decrease in tax. Each regression equation is thus a summary of a corresponding graph. The one in the example is a 'bivariate' equation because it relates two 'variables', percentage of vote and taxation.

It is possible to think of (but not picture) a graph of four, five or higher dimensions, relating a number of factors simultaneously to the Conservative vote. This can be described by a *multivariate* regression equation just as the two-dimensional graph above was described by a *bivariate* regression equation. The multivariate regression equation in Table 15.3 describes a seven-dimensional graph. This cannot be pictured here directly but it can be described by the equation just as the two-dimensional one was.

Tony Blair as the new Labour leader, and the publicity this gave to all the changes and reforms that had been proceeding in the party. This reduced Conservative support again, pushing them to an almost unprecedented low of 31.5 per cent in the election.

<table>
<tr><td>

Key term

Core party support – the minimum voting support it is estimated a party can gain in a given election.

</td></tr>
</table>

ESTIMATING CORE PARTY SUPPORT

The 'Essex Model' not only answers the question of why Labour won in 1997, and the Conservatives won previously. It also lets us ask 'what if?' questions. We can ask for example what *would* the Conservative vote in 1997 have been if they had not succeeded in improving personal economic expectations by creating a mini boom just before the election? This boom was the only thing that saved the party from an even worse defeat in 1997 than it actually had.

Leaving all other factors unchanged, but assuming that the balance of economic expectations remained highly pessimistic up to the election, the model would give the Conservatives an estimated 26.2 per cent of the popular vote. This is the worst possible figure the Conservatives could have possibly obtained. It assumes that all the factors affecting vote worked against them and nothing for them, a possibility that a quantified explanation of this kind allows us to investigate.

BRIEFINGS

15.3 VOTERS EXPLAIN THEIR CHOICE IN THE 1997 ELECTION

General analyses of voting and elections can get too abstract and statistical, dealing as they do with mass movements of opinion. It is easy to lose sight of the electors' own individual reasoning about how to vote, though it is this which lies at the basis of their choice. Here are some examples of the reasons voters gave for their decision to switch to another party:

Switchers From Conservative to Labour:

'Give young people a chance.'

'The Tories had a poor election campaign.'

'Because of John Major – he let the party fall into disarray and did not take disciplinary action when it was called for.'

'Just decided at the last minute – we needed a change.'

'Because I thought that the Tories had been in power for long enough and it was time for a change.'

'I work in social housing and the Conservative Party had changed its policy on social housing and Labour were offering a better alternative. Education and health, particularly the health service.'

'I followed the majority.'

'The Labour Party offered more policies to help education.'

Switchers from Liberal Democrats to Labour:

'I didn't think the Liberal Democrats had much chance of getting in.'

'Wasn't interested, then heard Tony Blair on ITV 500 and that swayed me.'

Switchers from Scottish/Welsh Nationalist to Labour

'The damage the Tory party has done to so many people – house repossessions and neglect for those in need and the general misery the Tories caused.'

15.3 VOTERS EXPLAIN THEIR CHOICE IN THE 1997 ELECTION (continued)

'I used to vote for Labour but I thought their policies were going out the window but I voted for them to get the Tories out.'

Switchers from Conservative to Liberal Democrats

'The policies generally, they seemed more trustworthy than the rest – the best of a bad lot.'

'I voted Lib-Dem for tactical reasons – the Tory candidate didn't stand a chance and I did not want Labour.'

'Time for a change – didn't want Labour to win. It's a strong Lib-Dem area – it didn't really relate to the government, it was more at a local level.'

'I wasn't happy with what the Conservatives or Labour had to offer and I felt I had to vote for someone.'

Switchers from Labour to Liberal Democrat

'Because they seemed the most likely party to beat the Tories in the constituency.'

'The Labour candidate around here didn't stand a chance anyway – I changed my mind because of tactical voting.'

'On principle, they were an honest party, it was wrong to waste a vote.'

'It was a tactical vote to get rid of the Tories.'

'I thought Liberals had more of a chance in my local constituency.'

'I always have voted Liberal Democrat but I had thought that I might vote Labour tactically in order to get rid of the Conservatives, however not even the local newspaper could advise me on this so I went back to where my heart is.'

'The Tories seem to have lost touch with the ordinary people'.

Switcher from Scottish/Welsh Nationalist to Liberal Democrats

'I preferred the Liberal Democrats' policies. Labour and the Conservatives were very negative throughout the campaign. Blair is going to do so much but where is he going to get the money from?'

Switcher from Other to Liberal Democrats

'I did not want the Tory party back in because of raised taxes. I thought the Liberal Democratic party would take the area – it was a tactical vote plus Liberal Democrats are in line with my political views particularly on the issues of health and education.'

Switchers from Labour to Conservative

'Better the devil you know.'

'I am a Labour supporter, however I voted Conservative as I do not like the local Labour candidate.'

Switcher from Conservative to Plaid Cymru

'Because I live with the Welsh people and I didn't want them to throw me off a cliff or shoot me.'

Switcher from Labour to SNP

'I believe in their policies. Tony Blair said in the national dailies that he was going to control Scotland from England and I don't think that that is feasible.'

Switcher from Liberal Democrats to SNP

'I felt we had more chance of getting the Tories out by voting SNP.'

Switcher from Referendum Party to SNP

'No particular policy reason. I voted SNP because it was obvious the Conservatives were not going to win.'

Switcher from Conservative to the Referendum Party

'All that happened in the last 24–48 hours. I knew that the Tories didn't have a chance in hell and I didn't want Labour to win, so I just went for the people's party which is the Referendum Party.'

Source: MORI On-Line Poll of 7–8 May 1997

This figure of 26.2 per cent which the Conservatives would have obtained under the worst possible circumstances is interestingly close to the 27.6 per cent of the vote actually obtained by Labour in the 1983 election, when they encountered *their* worst possible scenario, being internally divided, with unpopular policies and an unpopular leader, so nothing worked for them. The closeness of the two voting percentages suggests that the two major parties can count on getting around 27 per cent of the vote no matter how badly they have done, with all the issues and other factors accounting for short-term change stacked against them.

These percentages are very substantial. They account for a majority of the vote which Conservatives and Labour receive even under favourable circumstances. Together they add up to a good half of all British voters.

The fact that these electors vote for the parties even when there is very little to commend them suggests that these are people relatively unaffected by election issues or changing economic conditions. Whatever the political situation they are going to go on voting for the same party. Their vote is very important since it provides the stable basis for the fluctuations in party support discussed in the last section. It ensures that the main parties will not disappear even when they do badly, and gives them the ability to 'wait out' the situation until circumstances change in their favour, just as happened with Labour between their resounding defeat in 1983 and their resounding victory in 1997. The following discussion asks why these voters remain so loyal to 'their' party, and whether the characteristics that make them so may be slowly eroding.

Characteristics of core supporters

As we have seen, core support is by definition not affected by issues or changing economic circumstance. This suggests that the explanation for voter loyalty is to be found in factors that do not change, or at most which change quite slowly. These are most likely to be the social characteristics which loom large in traditional 'voting studies' of the electorate: factors like class, region, race which are substantially, though not totally, unchanging.

To see why this might be so, consider the circumstances of a pensioner who lives in council-owned housing in a Northern inner city, who had a manual job and belonged to a trade union. Such a person is very likely to be pushed by all the circumstances of his or her life into voting Labour. Labour supports public expenditure, services and welfare, on all of which the voter is highly dependent. Whether it is boom or bust, therefore, and whatever the political circumstances, this person is likely to vote Labour and not change his or her vote from election to election.

The same thing in reverse is likely to be true of the wealthy stockbroker living in Surrey, all of whose social circumstances push him or her into voting Conservative whatever happens to the general economy. To explain the considerable degree of stability in voting, therefore, we need to turn from the Essex Model of fluctuations in the vote to the social characteristics which insulate certain groups from most of what happens in the surrounding environment and pushes them towards enduring party support.

Table 15.4 Social class and the vote, 1945–97

	1945–1970 (mean)		1979		1983		1987		1992		1997	
	Nonmanual	Manual	Nonmanual	Manual	Nonmanual	Manual	Nonmanual	Manual	Nonmanual	Manual	Nonmanual	Manual
Conservative	65	30	55	36	51	35	49	37	49	35	34	23
Liberal/Other	10	8	19	17	31	28	31	23	25	20	27	19
Labour	24	62	26	46	18	37	20	40	26	45	39	58
Nonmanual Con + manual Lab as % of total vote	63%		51%		45%		44%		47%		45%	

Source: Harris/ITN exit polls 3 May 1979, 9 June 1983, 11 June 1987, 9 April 1992, 1 May 1997

Class – among the many and varied definitions of class, the most useful ranks the social and economic status of individuals according to their occupation, most notably into manual (working class) and non-manual (middle class) groups, and then into sub-groups or strata of these categories.

The social factor most emphasised in studies in British politics is class, which has been described as the 'basis' of British voting behaviour, 'all else is embellishment and detail'.[4] This is an exaggeration, as we shall see, but there is no doubt that class is an important factor in influencing and stabilising voting choices.

The relationship between class and vote is shown in Table 15.4. In the period before 1970 it is quite strong: practically two thirds of nonmanual workers voted Conservative and the same proportion of manual workers voted for Labour. However, this relationship erodes over time. By 1997 more of the nonmanual group voted Labour rather than Conservative (39 to 34 per cent). Almost as many manual workers voted Labour as before 1970 (58 per cent compared with 62 per cent). But this was more a reflection of the general appeal of Labour rather than of its particular appeal to manual workers.

However, what we are doing here is putting all voters in a general class category (manual versus nonmanual) and comparing their behaviour. It is those voters who are in a much more intense and pure class situation, where all the social influences reinforce each other, who are likely to be the unchanging party loyalists. Thus it is not manual workers but manual workers in council houses on low incomes who are also trade unionists, who are likely to have retained their Labour loyalties unchanged.

Class, as we have seen, also interpenetrates with region as an influence on voting: people in the peripheries are more likely to vote Labour than those in the central South East. Table 15.5 demonstrates this for the last two elections. The very strong regional differences in support are partly accounted for by class structure; more of the classic manual working class live in the North, and the regions are in most cases more socially deprived than the centre (Table 6.1).

However, there are also regional effects independent of class composition. Some of these can be indirectly attributed to class. Having a larger concentration of the middle class means that the whole culture and way of life of a region is tilted towards middle-class values, with some influence on manual workers living there too. The famous 'Essex man' of the late 1980s – a manual worker with a lower middle-class lifestyle and Thatcherite values – is an example of this diffuse influence.

But, as we have seen, there are other regional influences – minority nationalism, language differences and so on – not attributable to class, which exist independent of short-term effects. A Welsh speaker in rural Gwynedd is not likely to vote Conservative.

Ethnicity as opposed to regional location also influences votes. Indians, Pakistanis and Afro-Caribbeans show a very strong tendency to favour Labour. This is due in part to the fact that many are poor city dwellers in badly paid jobs. These groups favour Labour also for historical reasons, however, as it was the party most supportive of them during the period of massive immigration in the 1960s and early 1970s. At that time certain Conservative MPs used racialist appeals in their constituencies, while a well-known Conservative personality, Enoch Powell, made a speech in which he predicted 'rivers of blood' flowing from racial tensions in a mixed society.

---

[4] Peter Pulzer, *Political Representation and Elections in Britain* (London: Allen and Unwin, 1967), p. 98

Table 15.5 Regional variations in the party votes, 1992 and 1997 general elections

	Conservative		Labour		Liberal Democrat		SNP/PC	
	1992	1997	1992	1997	1992	1997	1992	1997
Strathclyde	20	13	51	58	8	7	20	20
East Central Scotland	25	17	43	51	11	10	20	20
Rural Scotland	31	22	21	28	22	22	25	26
Rural Wales	32	22	34	42	17	15	16	18
South Wales	25	17	60	64	10	11	5	5
Rural North	46	34	33	43	21	20		
Industrial North East	29	18	56	67	14	11		
Merseyside	28	19	52	63	17	14		
Gtr Manchester	35	24	47	56	16	16		
Rest of North West	41	31	43	54	14	12		
W. Yorkshire	37	28	46	55	15	13		
S. Yorkshire	26	16	58	63	15	16		
W. Midlands Conurbation	42	30	44	54	12	11		
Rest W. Midlands	47	37	34	43	18	16		
E. Midlands	46	34	38	48	15	14		
East Anglia	51	39	28	39	19	18		
Southwest	46	35	18	23	34	35		
Wessex	48	37	20	28	30	29		
Outer Southeast	53	40	20	32	25	23		
Outer Metropolitan	56	42	22	33	21	20		
Outer London	49	34	33	47	16	15		
Inner London	35	24	47	58	15	13		

Source: R. J. Johnston *et al*. 'New Labour Landslide – Same Old Electoral Geography?' Paper presented to Political Studies Conference on Elections, Public Opinion and Parties, University of Essex, September 26–28 1997, Table 1

Ethnic support for Labour is perhaps the strongest among all the groups we have discussed (Table 15.7); it was obvious among both Asians and Blacks in 1997 (Figure 15.3). Here we have a prime example of one of the 'pure' social groups which show strong and stable support for one of the parties. Simply knowing that an elector is a minority group member enables one to predict a Labour vote with a 0.8 probability of being right. These are electors who contribute a stable voting support to Labour, unaffected on the whole by the particular circumstances of the election. As Table 15.6 shows, the overwhelming majority were part of the overall 27.6 per cent of voters who chose Labour in 1983.

Table 15.6 Percentage voting Labour and Conservative among ethnic minorities 1974–92

	1974 (Oct.)	1979	1983	1987	1992
Lab	81	86	83	72	81
Con	9	8	7	18	10

Source: Shamit Saggar, 'Racial Politics', *Parliamentary Affairs*, 50 (1997), p. 696

A combination of such social characteristics, all of which reinforce the push towards one or other party, is thus the probable explanation of why so many voters go on voting for the same party regardless of the economy or political issues. There are many different combinations of such characteristics, even when a vote for the same party is concerned. We can illustrate the general point here with a simplified 'Index of Social Predisposition' (Table 15.7)[5]. This indicates how the pure combinations of characteristics at the extremes of the table push electors towards a vote for Labour or Conservatives respectively, leaving the electors with 'mixed' social characteristics in the middle to respond to situational influences like those in the Essex Model, since they do not get a clear message about what to do from their own social situation. It is likely that many in the mixed groups might vote Liberal or Nationalist for the same reason.

Figure 15.3 Per cent intending to vote for given parties among Asians and Blacks who decided to vote, 1996–97

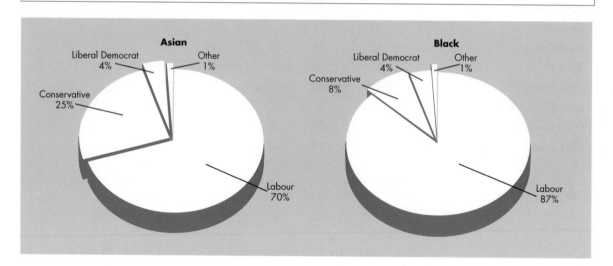

---

[5] L indicates a high 'social predisposition' to keep on voting Labour, C one to keep on voting Conservative; M are the electors in a social situation which gives them a 'mixed' message and renders them liable to change votes in response to economic conditions and political issues.

With the characteristics shown here we end up with more groups predisposed to Labour than to the Conservatives, but of course Conservative groups could have more people in them. If other social characteristics were added the number of Conservative groups would increase.

Table 15.7 An index of social predispositions towards voting Labour or Conservative

| | | Manual Factory Worker | | Other Manual | | Professional Public Employee | | Other Nonmanual | |
		Trade Unionist	Not TU	TU	Not TU	TU	Not TU	TU	Not TU
Public Housing									
Periphery	Ethnic minority	L	L	L	L	L	L	L	M
	White	L	L	L	L	L	M	L	M
Centre	Ethnic minority	L	L	L	L	L	M	L	M
	White	L	M	L	M	L	M	L	M
Private Housing									
Periphery	Ethnic minority	L	L	L	L	L	M	L	M
	White	L	L	L	L	L	C	L	C
Centre	Ethnic minority	L	L	L	M	L	C	L	C
	White	L	C	L	C	M	C	M	C

Key term

Electoral volatility –
large and rapid changes in
voting behaviour from one
election to another.

Electoral volatility

With modernisation and globalisation, social and geographical mobility and political change, it is however likely that 'pure' social groups are being increasingly broken up and their members exposed to 'mixed' political influences. Such developments have already been discussed in Chapters 1 and 2 and are illustrated in terms of social class in Table 15.4. The relation between class location, broadly defined, and vote is being increasingly broken down. The 'purer' social groups defined in Table 15.7 are more resistant to this process. Even Asians and Blacks, however, are going to move out and mix with the general British population over the years, becoming less politically distinctive in the process.

This means that fewer and fewer people are going to be insulated from the economic and political influences which produce changes in the vote. So there is going to be more switching of votes among electors generally and a decline in the 'core support' that parties can rely on.

Some of these effects can be caught by looking at the average votes cast for the parties in the earlier postwar period compared with the later (Table 15.8). The average vote went down markedly for Labour and (less) for the Conservatives. The Liberals, whose recovery after 1974 was partly responsible for destabilising the other two parties, saw their mean vote go up quite spectacularly of course. Nevertheless, their vote fluctuated more from election to election in the later period, like that of the two main parties.

	1945–1970	**February 1974–1992**
Conservative		
Mean %	45.3	39.4
Range	39.8–49.7	31.5 – 43.9
Fluctuation	44.8 +/– 5.0	37.7 +/– 6.2
Labour		
Mean %	46.1	35.6
Range	43.1–48.8	27.6–43.3
Fluctuation	46.0 +/– 2.9	35.4 +/– 7.8
Liberal[a]		
Mean %	7.2	19.2
Range	2.6–11.4	13.8 – 25.4
Fluctuation	7.0 /– 4.4	19.6 +/– 5.8

Note: [a] Liberal/SDP Alliance in 1983 and 1987; Liberal Democrat in 1992

Another indicator of decreasing stability, at least for Labour and Liberals, comes in the declining percentages of electors identifying with the three main parties (Table 15.9). Liberal identifiers fluctuate widely, indicating a fundamental instability in their support. Labour identifiers decline drastically, although the Conservatives recovered in the 1980s. We may expect that identification fell off with their disastrous record in government after 1992, while Labour identification increased (exact figures for 1997 are not yet available).

Electoral turnout

One way in which diminished attachments to the main parties, and increasing volatility from one election to another, may make themselves felt is in fluctuating and diminished turnout. Figure 15.4 shows a general decline in turnout from the early 1950s to the 1990s.

Table 15.9 The party identification of voters, 1964–92

Election	Con	Lab	Lib[a]	Other/None
1964	41	44	12	3
1966	38	49	10	3
1970	43	45	8	4
1974 (Feb.+Oct.)	38	43	15	4
1979	43	40	13	4
1983	41	33	20	3
1987	42	33	18	7
1992	46	34	14	6

Note: [a] Liberal/SDP Alliance in 1983 and 1987; Liberal Democrat in 1992
Source: British election studies 1964 to 1992

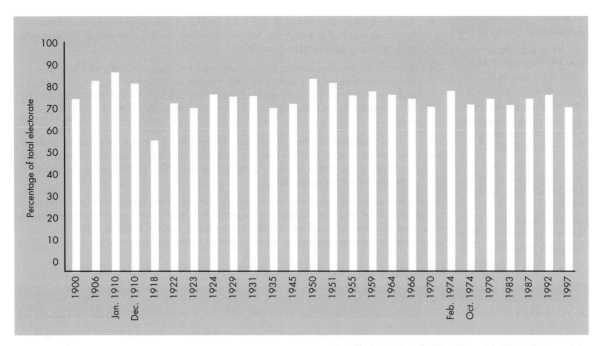

Figure 15.4 Turnout in British general elections

From almost 84 per cent in 1950 the percentage voting decreased to just above 70 per cent in the decisive election of 1997, when the prospect of change made it a more exciting contest than many earlier ones, particularly the later elections of the 1950s. Turnout fluctuates but the underlying trend is for fewer people to vote. As elections are the central political processes of a democracy, abstention from them is a worrying sign of popular apathy and of alienation from democracy itself. It will be a challenge for New Labour to re-energise these electors in future elections.

SUMMARY

This chapter has looked at the results of recent British elections. These raise the following questions:

* What are the effects of the electoral system? We have seen that the first-past-the-post system has penalised Liberal Democrats and generally given the plurality party a parliamentary majority.

* This may encourage strong government but usually means that a popular majority has voted for other parties, perhaps encouraging cynicism and withdrawal on the part of many voters. We shall consider the consequences of this for British democracy in Chapter 28.

ESSAYS

1. Why did Labour win the 1997 election? And why did it win by a landslide?

2. How far did the 1997 election result support the Essex Model of voting behaviour in Britain?

3. Is Britain's single-member, simple plurality (SMSP) electoral system fair?

4. How much do election campaigns affect an election result?

- Are there alternative systems? We have looked at how other electoral systems might work and also examined the way in which small constituencies encouraged tactical voting and targeting in 1997.

- To explain changing electoral results we used the 'Essex Model', which relates party vote to aggregate economic expectations and taxation on the one hand, and contemporary political issues on the other. The 1997 result was explained by the economic factors plus Conservative incompetence and the appeal of Tony Blair.

- To explain stability in the Labour and Conservative 'core vote' we looked at social characteristics such as class, region, and race, and explained how they could be combined in an 'Index of Social Predispositions' which pushed some electors to vote always for the same party.

The whole discussion of elections and voting focuses on the question of which party wins most votes and why. Some of the explanation must lie in the parties themselves. In the next two chapters we look directly at the parties and the ways they seek to organise and define themselves, so as to attract voters and supporters.

MILESTONES

MILESTONES IN POSTWAR ELECTIONS

1945 Labour wins landslide, helped by Army votes, on the basis of an ambitious programme of social reconstruction.

1950, 1951 Conservatives accept Welfare State and most of Labour's social and economic reforms. With this they get a small parliamentary majority in 1951.

1955 Conservatives consolidate their majority on the slogan 'Conservative freedom works'.

1959 The Conservative leader and Prime Minister Macmillan gets an increased majority with the slogan 'You've never had it so good'. The Liberals reorganise and put forward a programme of social reform, doubling their vote. Labour tries to abandon nationalisation as a policy.

1964, 1966 Labour wins a small majority in 1964 which it increases substantially in 1966, with promises of planning for the 'white heat of technology'.

1970 The Conservatives win the election unexpectedly with promises of regulating trade unions and letting the 'lame ducks' of industry go.

1974 Conservatives fight February election in midst of a wave of strikes (the three-day week) on the slogan 'Who rules Britain?'. Labour win by narrow margin on promise of restoring situation through a 'social contract' with unions. Unprecedented levels of

support for Liberals and Nationalists. Pattern repeated in October election.

1979 'Winter of Discontent' – strikes and industrial unrest – lose election for Labour. Mrs Thatcher becomes Conservative Prime Minister.

1983 Labour support descends to just over a quarter of the electorate with a full-blooded socialist alternative economic plan. Alliance of Liberals and Social Democrats almost equals this. Helped by the Labour split and recovery of the economy, Conservatives win election.

1987 Labour reforms and its new leader Kinnock push up this vote only marginally. Alliance vote holds. Conservatives retain their vote on the basis of having seen off the unions and freed the economy.

1992 Conservatives present themselves as a totally new government under John Major, and attack Labour as a high tax party. Labour's attempt to concentrate election campaign on welfare cuts fails. They do increase vote to 34.4 per cent and Liberal Democratic support falls.

1997 New Labour wins a massive parliamentary majority with 43.3 per cent of vote and all the minor parties do well. Conservatives get their lowest vote in postwar elections (31.5 per cent).

PROJECTS

1. What advice would you offer the new leader of the Conservative party on how to win the next general election?

2. The *alternative vote*, the *additional member system* and the *single transferable vote* are considered possible alternatives to Britain's existing SMSP electoral system. Explain how each would work, and which party would benefit most from its adoption.

3. Design a research project for finding out the impact of party bias in the press on the way people vote.

FURTHER READING

The last election is covered in D. Butler and D. Kavanagh, *The British General Election of 1997* (London: Macmillan, 1997). *Parliamentary Affairs*, 50(4) (1997) and Anthony King (ed.), *New Labour Triumphs: Britain at the Polls*, (Chatham, NJ: Chatham House, 1997).

On the Essex Model of Voting, see Simon Price and David Sanders, 'Modelling Government Popularity in Post-War Britain', *American Journal of Political Science*, 37 (1993), pp. 317–34 and David Sanders, 'Economic Performance, Management Competence and the Outcome of the Next General Election', *Political Studies*, 64 (1996), pp. 201–31. On constant voting see Ian McAllister and Richard Rose, *The Nationwide Competition for Votes* (London: Pinter, 1984). On electoral systems see the useful review by Matthew Shugart, Chapter 10 of Ian Budge, Ken Newton *et al.*, *The Politics of The New Europe*, (Harlow: Addison Wesley Longman, 1997).

http://www.awl-he.com/politics/newbritpol

Internet resources – visit *The New British Politics* Webpage for links to a specially-chosen selection of Internet resources relevant to this Chapter.

http://www.awl-he.com/politics/newbritpol

Political parties and party factions

The parties, particularly the Conservatives and Labour, link practically all the political processes and organisations we have examined up to this point. Their influence is obvious in elections, where they provide the alternatives for voting and stimulate popular participation. But they also form a central focus for the media, which they continuously try to manipulate in their own interest. The ultimate aim of vote seeking is to control government, so as to inject party policies and personalities into the decision process. There parties interact with civil servants, business and pressure groups in the ways already described.

External relationships between parties and other political participants are thus the subject of almost every chapter of this book. Here we concentrate on the parties' internal structures and relationships, leaving the core of party identity, their ideologies, to Chapter 17.

We look at internal relationships because we cannot take party unity and discipline for granted. Parties have to unite to win elections and run government (although as we have pointed out, collegiality competes with ministerial autonomy in the Cabinet). But as the deep Conservative splits on Europe show, there can be virulent internal disputes, giving rise to more or less institutionalised factions within the party. Most of the time, party factions can work together, otherwise they could not form a party. But if disagreements become too extreme they may split off to form a new party, as the Social Democrats did from Labour in 1981, and as the 'pro-Europeans' may possibly do from the Conservatives in the near future. We consider the history of party factionalism in this chapter, along with the ways in which party organisations and structures have adapted to counter it and put overall control in the hands of the leadership.

This chapter therefore covers:

- The function of British political parties
- The evolution of the modern parties and the various groups and interests attracted to them over time
- Factions and factionalism within the parties
- How they are organised
- What the parties stand for
- Who are they?

THE FUNCTIONS OF PARTIES

The evolution of the modern British parties cannot be understood without an appreciation of the general role they are called upon to play. Democratic parties are associations of (generally!) like-minded people who, by means of popular election, compete for state power to further their common goals. A unique characteristic of parties is that they serve the dual function of government and representation. As instruments of government they form an executive that seeks to steer the state. They recruit and groom politicians, they implement policies and they mobilise popular support. As instruments of representation they promote the interests and values of sections of the electorate, translate their demands into state policies and give them a sense of place within the wider society. Most important of all, they form the Government or the Opposition, the 'ins' or the 'outs', thereby rendering the Government of the day ultimately accountable to the electorate. Parties offer the public a scapegoat for government failure (or, more rarely, a totem of government success) enabling it to 'throw the rascals out' or 'keep the winning team'.

As instruments of government and representation, the major parties therefore perform a third function: political integration. To win elections, parties must attract support from many different groups. By aggregating their separate interests, parties identify and create consensus across large segments of the population. They must also respond to expectations or persuade electors to modify them, magnifying or minimising ideas about what government can do. Horizontally, parties act as a bridge across groups; vertically, as a ladder between citizen and state.

In their governmental and electoral activities, parties therefore have to concern themselves with interests and needs beyond those of their core supporters, because they need to legitimise themselves and attract other votes. They also aim to form governments which will make policy for the country as a whole. They cannot just pursue a narrowly sectional programme but have to reach out to as many groups as possible by varying their appeals. It is this feature of parties which makes factionalism and internal disputes an ever-present possibility. To be national and representative, British parties have to be coalitions of interests. But such interests often come into conflict, particularly if there is no strong leadership. We can see concretely how this has worked out by looking at the growth of British parties from the mid-nineteenth century onwards.

PARTY UNITY AND INTERNAL DISSENT: CONSERVATIVES, LIBERALS AND LABOUR 1868–1979

The emergence of modern parties: Whig and Tory, Conservative and Liberal

Like most other political institutions in Britain, parties took on their modern form in the mid-nineteenth century. The shift produced by the Second Reform Act of 1867–68 from a small, restricted electorate to a large one numbered in millions meant that local 'notables' could no longer rely on their own resources and efforts to secure election (see Briefing 16.1). These had to be supplemented, and were quite soon replaced, by a central party organisation which fostered local clubs and associations in every constituency, which provided funds and supporters for local campaigns. But members were drawn into them not by personal ties to the candidate but by support for the national party's principles and policies, which local MPs were pledged to support in Parliament. Soon it became immaterial whether the candidate was a local person or not. Anyone pledged to the national leadership and policy was acceptable because essentially the job of an MP was to support and serve the party. MPs thus owed their election to their endorsement by the central organisation and were therefore dependent on leadership approval for (re)election, a powerful factor enforcing party discipline in Parliament and ensuring that MPs there voted as party blocs.

In theory this arrangement should have ensured internal agreement within the parties, in place of bickering personalities. So, up to a point, it did. But because national principles and policy were now the focus of party cohesion, splits involving them would carry more widespread party disruption than continual but diffuse bickering. Thus the history of modern British parties alternates between tremendous unity and enthusiasm round some cause at certain points in time, which attracts new support, followed by splits and ebbing morale as the different groups

---

Key term

Cadre parties – parties of like-minded and wealthy 'notables' who use their own money to fight political campaigns and rely upon their own personal supporters.

Key term

Mass parties – are financed and organised with the help of a mass membership which both pays membership subscriptions and provides the manpower to conduct political campaigns.

BRIEFINGS

16.1 CADRE AND MASS POLITICAL PARTIES

The first recognisable political parties were 'cadre' parties, based primarily on Parliament. They grouped like-minded 'notables' who had organised their own election as MPs, using their own money and supporters. Such men could take a critical independent line if they wanted. They owed little to the party, having secured election by their own efforts, and could secure election again even if they crossed to another party.

The Conservative and Liberal parties in Britain between 1833 and 1867 were examples of cadre parties, whose MPs frequently split off from one side and joined the other. But the Second Reform Act (1867) widened the franchise beyond its narrow middle-class base, so MPs could no longer be personally known to all electors. Consequently their views and policies were identified by most electors with those of the party. If MPs lost their party affiliation their former supporters would cease to vote for them. At the same time financing mass campaigns became more expensive, so individual MPs became more dependent on, and hence obedient to, the central leadership. Mass parties, as the name implies, financed themselves by recruiting a large membership, up to a million or more, and collecting dues from them. In contrast, cadre parties were simply composed of MPs with their personal followers.

within the party quarrel over implementation and emphasis or even attempt to redefine the basic principles themselves. One can see this process at work in both the Conservative and Liberal parties, which emerged from the old Tories and Whigs at the end of the 1860s.

The Conservatives redefined themselves as defenders of traditional institutions like the monarchy, and supporters of Empire and imperial expansion, but at the same time as social reformers concerned about bad living conditions, all in the general name of national unity but with the practical aim of attracting new working-class votes.

Liberals emphasised free trade at home and abroad, and hence were not much interested in the Empire. They pushed political reforms, particularly ones opening careers to the lower middle class, Nonconformists and Roman Catholics. Most Catholics originated in Ireland. Both for electoral and tactical reasons, the Liberals sought an alliance with the Irish Nationalist Party in Parliament, which led them to advocate home rule (a very mild form of devolution) for Ireland in 1886. This was a measure which split the party, driving out self-made manufacturers who saw this as a first step to dissolving the Empire and its markets, and old Whig aristocrats who saw home rule as the latest of a series of attacks on Irish property rights.

The early twentieth century: Conservative, Liberal and Labour

The Conservatives suffered a similar split in 1905 when the new influx of Unionist businessmen supported tariffs to protect British markets in the Empire. The Liberal Party meanwhile united around the home rule project and a programme of social reform, with an eye both to Catholic working-class voters and their political representatives, the Irish Nationalist and the Labour parties. With their parliamentary support, legislation was passed from 1908–11 setting up a rudimentary welfare state; the House of Lords was limited to a three-year delaying power over legislation, and Irish home rule was projected for 1914. Both this and the party were overtaken by the First World War, which split the Liberals over military strategies and foreign policy. A section of the party formed a coalition government with the Conservatives (1916–22), but the breach between the two factions was not really healed during the interwar period.

This provided an opening for the Labour Party. Unlike the other two leading parties, this was not formed by parliamentarians seeking a mass base, but by mass movements, primarily the trade unions, seeking parliamentary representation to get greater recognition of their rights and limited social reforms. They allied with existing socialist parties with a constituency-based organisation to form a party in 1900. From its beginnings Labour existed as an uneasy coalition of committed socialists and pragmatic reformers. It rapidly attracted its 'natural' working-class constituency, eroding the Liberals' electoral basis. The weakening of both Liberal and Conservative parties between 'coalitionists' and 'anticoalitionists' helped Labour form a minority government from 1923–24 and 1929–31.

Key term

Party factions – the sections or tendencies within parties which emphasise different features of party policy while subscribing to the overall aims of the party and its organisation.

The last of these coincided with the financial crisis of 1931 caused by the world depression. Labour split over the question of cutting unemployment benefit as part of a package of financially orthodox measures to restore banking confidence. Most of the Cabinet, including the Labour leader and Prime Minister Ramsay McDonald, joined national governments dominated by the Conservatives and supported also by a Liberal faction, the 'National Liberals'. These dissensions weakened the parent parties and reduced the mainstream Liberals to political impotence up to 1959.

The national governments' conversion to protectionism, government intervention and limited social reform as ways of dealing with economic crisis (Chapter 3) gave Labour a chance to adopt their recommendations, along with Keynesian economic policies, as its own during the wartime Coalition Government (1940–45). These gave Labour a comprehensive package of reforms round which it could unite and obtain a sweeping electoral victory in 1945.

Postwar developments: Conservative, Labour, Liberal and Liberal Democrats

Key term

Unilateralists – people who hold that Britain should renounce nuclear weapons on its own (unilaterally), without waiting for multi-national agreement to do so.

While it remained reasonably united on its social reforms, the Labour Party split on two issues during the 1950s. One was on attitudes to the British nuclear bomb, where a powerful section recommended 'unilateral' renunciation on the grounds that the British bomb added nothing to the NATO deterrent and that British nuclear disarmament would set a moral example to the rest of the world. The other was on 'Clause 4' of the party constitution: whether Labour should retain a commitment to taking industry into state ownership (nationalisation) or not. Both attitudes tended to go together, the traditional 'left' advocating both unilateralism and nationalisation, the reformist right avoiding both positions.

The Labour splits of the 1950s were exacerbated by Conservative electoral successes. The evident popularity of the postwar Labour Government's reforms gave the upper hand within the Conservative Party to the 'one-nation' social reformers led by R.A. Butler and Harold Macmillan who took up the 1870s idea that national unity and stability depended on reasonable living conditions for the lower classes, through government intervention if necessary. This pointed to Conservative acceptance and indeed extension of the welfare state but not to nationalisation, which was reversed in some industries during the 1950s.

This was not enough to challenge the 'social democratic consensus' between the dominant factions in both major parties, and among the 1960s Liberals (see Briefing 16.2). Harold Wilson, Labour Prime Minister 1964–70 and 1974–76, in fact fudged his internal party differences by promising to extend the Government economic planning introduced by the Conservatives. As chronicled in Chapter 3, planning rapidly broke down and the Wilson Governments, followed by the Callaghan administration (1976–79), simply lapsed into pragmatic crisis management. This powered the growth of an 'alternative economic programme' supported by the 'hard left' of the party, for full-blooded nationalisation and protectionism (including withdrawal from the EU) 'to save British industry'.

BRIEFINGS

16.2 THE SOCIAL DEMOCRACTIC CONSENSUS 1950–79

This is the label given to the broad set of ideas which all parties shared in the period 1950–79. They disagreed on details and emphases, of course, but did not query fundamentals. The consensus consisted in:

- acceptance of the welfare state and the National Health Service, which included a commitment to financing a gentle expansion in these services as national prosperity grew;

- acceptance of a 'mixed economy' consisting both of private companies and of nationalised industries, particularly where there was a 'natural monopoly' of supply (coal, electricity, telephones, etc.);

- acceptance of the powers and roles of the main pressure groups (particularly finance, business and trade unions);

- a Keynesian economic policy aimed at balancing inflation against unemployment;

- a managed withdrawal from colonies and overseas territories, retaining links with Britain where possible;

- support for NATO in the Cold War with Russia, at the same time seeking to calm confrontations down (detente).

The Conservative 'New Right' under Mrs Thatcher broke dramatically with these ideas in the 1980s. Their success in doing so has possibly created a new, neo-liberal consensus in the 1990s with the acceptance of many Conservative policies by 'New Labour'.

The Conservatives in the meantime were in hardly better shape. The defeat of the 'one-nation'-dominated party in the election of 1964 prompted a rethinking of its ideas and policies. This produced a more radical right-wing policy in the late 1960s, which involved ending government intervention in industry but imposing it on the trade unions. As Prime Minister (1970–74) however, Edward Heath proved to be almost as pragmatic as Harold Wilson. Even so, a near general strike sparked off by the miners brought him down in the election of February 1974. Convinced that his mistake had been to abandon the free market

Plate 16.1 For many years Europe has been the most common cause of factions within British political parties, as illustrated here in this Michael Cummings cartoon in the *Daily Express*, 4 August 1961: Harold Macmillan tells Charles de Gaulle: 'Already, mon General, we've discarded our two-party system and got lots of extra *new* parties … like France!'

" Already, mon general, we've discarded our two-party system and got lots of extra *new* parties ... like France ! "

programme and to yield too easily to the unions, the 'New Right' won the party leadership election with Margaret Thatcher in 1975. Strict adherents of the new doctrines – the 'dries' – were however still in a minority compared with the 'wets'. The latter had no very clear beliefs beyond a general feeling that the 'social democratic consensus' should be modified only as and when necessary. They confidently expected a return to compromise and pragmatism once the Conservatives returned to power, which they did in 1979.

FACTIONS AND FACTIONALISM SINCE 1979

What they got instead was Margaret Thatcher, a self-described 'conviction politician' and New Right ideologue who set about enforcing strict financial and fiscal orthodoxy, sales of state industry, rigid controls on trade unions, cuts in local government and in central government personnel and administrative reform. Both at home and abroad she followed policies of confrontation with opposing groups, from the Falklands War with Argentina (1982) to the miners strike of 1984–85, both of which she won.

Although Mrs Thatcher and her supporters were in a minority in both Cabinet and Party, she was able to get her way, basically by committing the Government to contentious policies which left it no choice but to back her publicly, whatever the private murmurings among colleagues and backbenchers. Her unparalleled run of election victories and the prestige and authority this gave her in the Party enabled her to get rid of the best-known 'wets' from the Cabinet and parliamentary Party and to win over the survivors to most of her own policies. Thus by the end of the 1980s the 'wet–dry' opposition had been superseded. Most Conservatives accepted the 'free market, strong (but slimmed-down) state' which Thatcher aimed at.

The election victories on which this acceptance rested were, however, due as much to splits within their main rival, Labour, as to the positive attractions of New Right policies. The Conservatives won only around 42 per cent of the vote in the elections of the 1980s. But with a divided opposition the 'first past the post' electoral system gave them a parliamentary majority. The left of the Labour Party diagnosed their electoral defeat of 1979 as due to the failure of Wilson and Callaghan to implement full-blooded socialist policies. These were incorporated into the 'alternative economic programme' supported by the new leader of the Party, Michael Foot. Internal attempts to make MPs more responsive to left-wing pressure included the possibility of deselection of constituency MPs by local meetings dominated by left-wing activists.

The social democratic right of the Labour Party felt generally threatened by these developments. This provoked a major secession of some of the most prominent party figures: Roy Jenkins, a former Chancellor of the Exchequer, Shirley Williams and David Owen, both possible leadership contenders and ex-Cabinet Ministers. This 'Gang of Four' (with another former Labour Cabinet Minister, Bill Rodgers) founded an alternative party, the SDP (Social Democratic Party) which aroused great enthusiasm in 1982–83 with its general commitment to a reformed social democratic consensus.

The Social Democrats were natural allies of the Liberals who, after 20 years of drift, had made a gradual comeback from 1959 onwards with a nondoctrinaire but radical reform programme. The 'Alliance' formed between the two parties gained a quarter of the vote in 1983, driving Labour down to an unprecedented 27.6 per cent.

The Alliance held its ground well in the election of 1987, winning 22.6 per cent of the vote to Labour's 30.8 per cent. By that time, however, bitter clashes between the leaders, provoked by the abrasive Owen, and the low return of seats to votes under first past the post voting, destroyed the morale of the SDP and produced a merger with the Liberals in 1988. The new 'Liberal Democratic Party' has been surprisingly cohesive. Tensions exist between a radical environmentalist wing, committed also to sweeping social reforms, and the mainstream. But such tensions have not crystallised into permanent factions within the party. Helped by strategic voting which more than doubled their parliamentary seats in 1997 (from 20 to 46), the Liberal Democrats are likely to maintain their cohesion for the foreseeable future.

The Social Democratic secession, and the miserable performance of the party in the 1983 election, produced immediate internal effects in Labour. A 'soft left' co-operated with the surviving 'Campaign for Social Democracy' to elect a compromise leader, Neil Kinnock (1983–92). Convinced that the only way to get back their vote was to offer moderate policies and assert strong leadership, the party dumped the alternative economic policy and gradually moved to accepting many Thatcherite reforms. Even so votes returned only gradually (30.8 per cent in 1987 and 34.4 per cent in 1992).

After Labour's election defeat in 1992 Neil Kinnock resigned as party leader to be replaced by John Smith, who followed the Kinnock policy of moderation and appeal to the centre voter. Smith died suddenly of a heart attack in 1994, and Tony Blair was elected to replace him.

The disappointing results were, however, interpreted as pointing towards even further moderation in terms of accepting financial and above all fiscal orthodoxy, with restraints on government spending and low direct taxation. Strong internal leadership was also seen as a necessary element in Labour's appeal. This both produced and was buttressed by internal reforms aimed at purging local parties of Leftist 'entrists' and traditional, mildly corrupt, municipal bosses. It also produced changes in the balance of power between trade unions, individual party members and MPs, giving more power to the latter two groups (see below).

Tony Blair, from the time of his election as party leader in 1994, has benefited and built on these changes, largely by utilising them to impose strong discipline on MPs and constituency parties. His 'New Labour' has put its policy emphasis on building 'community' rather than promoting equality, thus neatly avoiding many of the more contentious issues associated with government intervention in favour of a focus most people, including Labour Party members, can agree with. His overwhelming electoral success in 1997 (43 per cent of the vote and almost two-thirds of Commons seats) gives him great authority in enforcing party unity such as accrued to Mrs Thatcher in her time.

However, Thatcher's legacy to the Conservative Party in the 1990s has been two-edged. The potential ambiguity of her support for a strong state, on the one

Key term

Europhiles – those who are generally well disposed to the further integration of Europe within the framework of the European Union.

Key term

Europhobes – those who are not generally well disposed to the further integration of Europe, at least within the framework of the European Union.

hand, and a free market on the other, has been cruelly exposed on the European issue. As we have noted (Chapter 4), Thatcher accepted the Single European Act of 1986 because of its promotion of a complete single market in the EU. The political institutions necessary to promote and support the single market were, however, also very important in boosting integration and limiting national sovereignty, a tension then exacerbated by the Treaty of Maastricht.

From 1993 these tensions between the sovereignty of the British state and the free European Market came out into the open and produced overt confrontation inside the Conservative Party between 'Eurosceptics' and 'Pro-Europeans'. Essentially, the Eurosceptics believe in defending British sovereignty, by limiting the powers of the EU to what they were in the early 1980s, before either Maastricht or the SEA, or even by withdrawing altogether. They certainly oppose monetary union (EMU) or adoption of a single currency, and have effectively carried the postelection Conservative leader, William Hague, with them.

The 'Pro-Europeans', led by Kenneth Clarke, ex-Chancellor of the Exchequer in the Major Government, believe that Britain cannot stand aside from currency union as it is so heavily involved in the single market anyway. In this they agree with most of the business and financial interests which have traditionally supported the Conservative Party.

The fact that EMU will commence in 1999 means that the Conservatives can hardly avoid the issue till it goes away. It seems likely to split the party, unless New Labour itself fudges the position and leaves the door open to an internal Conservative compromise. Labour, however, is free to decide in terms of all-British rather than partisan interests. It lacks the same depth of internal feeling on the issue and can recommend joining in its promised referendum if it feels there is a strong case which it can carry. The prospect of driving a wedge through the Conservatives and possibly provoking a secession of the 'Pro-Europeans' near the time of the next election is obviously an attractive one for the Government.

Plate 16.2 Matthew Pritchett cartoon from the *Daily Telegraph* of 21 April 1997. From 1993 the Conservative Party split between 'Eurosceptics', who believed in defending British sovereignty, and 'Pro-Europeans', led by Kenneth Clarke.

'Scientists think they might one day be able to produce two Conservatives who agree about Europe'

Key term

Iron law of oligarchy – the 'law' propounded by Robert Michels in 1911 whereby mass organisations cannot, by their very nature, be democratic, and will always and of necessity be controlled by a small elite – the oligarchy.

PARTY STRUCTURE AND ORGANISATION

Factional disputes are thus capable of destroying political parties, or of blasting their hopes of re-election for many years. They are obviously situations leaders would like to avoid. One way of controlling or dampening likely confrontations is through organisation (see Briefing 16.3). We have already seen how Kinnock, Smith and Blair rooted out dissenting tendencies in constituency Labour parties by tightening central control. In this section we look at British party organisations, both in terms of how they enable the party to function generally and in terms of how they allow leaders to exercise control.

The organisational ladder contains four main rungs. At the top is the party leadership, a group of no more than 20 to 30 MPs occupying, or hoping to occupy,

BRIEFINGS

16.3 MICHELS' IRON LAW OF OLIGARCHY AND THE BRITISH PARTIES

In 1911 the German sociologist Robert Michels published *Political Parties*, in which he formulated the famous 'iron law of oligarchy'. This states that mass organisations, by their very nature, cannot be democratic, but will always be controlled by a small elite. The modern world, he said, was faced with an insoluble dilemma. On the one hand, modern life requires large scale institutions and organisations: parties, interest groups, churches, trade unions. On the other hand, large organisations will always be in the hands of a few leaders, no matter how strongly they aspire to internal democracy. There are two sets of reasons for this. First, leaders know all the business of their organisation, control the means of internal communication, and usually have greater political skills than ordinary members. Second, the 'incompetence of the masses': few know much about policy matters, or turn up to meetings, while most feel the need for 'direction and guidance' provided by leaders.

According to Michels, leaders develop their own particular interests and goals which differ from those of members. They control organisations, and use them for their own purposes, not those of the members. Thus leaders of mass movements inevitably become members of the power elite. Leaders of revolutionary movements always betray their cause.

The political scientist Robert McKenzie applied Michels' analysis to the Conservative and Labour parties in the 1950s. He detailed the various devices used by the leaders of both parties to make sure that the party conference, for example, always passed supportive resolutions and that their general control of party policy and activities was left undisturbed. In spite of Labour's claims to internal democracy, with the elected conference having ultimate control, an alliance of moderates made sure the trade union block vote was always used to support the parliamentary leadership and to keep the more left-wing constituency parties in check.

Things changed, however, after McKenzie's book was written, when left-wingers came to power in some unions. Internal reforms have reduced union voting power in the 1980s and 1990s. However, leaders seek other means of obtaining support, by using 'policy forums' and referendums of members to bypass conference. On the other hand, if leaders were seriously out of step with the majority of their party they would clearly have to go.

senior government positions as Cabinet ministers. Their primary interest is in their party winning the next election. A little further down is the parliamentary party of elected MPs and active peers in the House of Lords, from whom the party leadership is drawn. They too place enormous importance on electoral success, but their priorities are subtly different from those of the leadership. Most MPs represent safe seats and have more to fear from deselection by their local parties or from an unfavourable redrawing of their constituency boundaries than from an adverse national swing against the party. Much further down the ladder is the Party in the country – the unpaid officers and active members of local associations – many of them elected councillors on the local authority. For most activists the reward is not career advancement but furtherance of the Party's broad goals, on which they tend to take a more principled stand than the Party's leaders and MPs. On the bottom rung is the Party in the electorate: stalwart supporters who, while not formally members, can be relied upon to vote for the party in elections and to accept the party line on most political issues. See Figure 16.1.

Superficially, all British parties are organised in much the same way. A branch of the party exists in each parliamentary constituency and, where support is strong enough, in each local ward making up the constituency. Its main function is to contest elections by raising campaign funds, engaging in electioneering and, most important of all, selecting the candidate who, in the 500-plus safe seats, will become the MP. Political education and policy debates are intermittent and secondary: in most parties political agreement is taken for granted and politics is not discussed much!

The local parties send delegates to the national Party's annual conference, whose role is ostensibly to discuss Party policy but whose real purpose nowadays is to display the Party, in particular its leadership, to best effect on television. The conference elects a national executive which oversees the day-to-day running of the national Party. Policy is formulated by specialist groups recruited from the Party headquarters, MPs, sympathetic research institutes, and the leaders' personal contacts. The leader of the parliamentary Party is the effective Party leader in the sense of being the Party's spokesperson, its chief campaigner at elections and the prime minister if the Party wins. The Conservative leader is now elected by MPs and Party members; the Labour leader by Labour MPs and the annual conference (on behalf of the wider Labour movement); the Liberal Democrat leader by the Party members.

Despite these superficial similarities, the Conservative and Labour parties differ significantly in their constitutions and ethos. The contrasts owe something to the two parties' very different historical origins. The Conservative Party began in the nineteenth century as a parliamentary faction which gradually built up a party in the country. The Labour movement existed outside Parliament before it put up parliamentary candidates of its own. The Conservative Party has a unitary and hierarchical structure and a deferential culture; the Labour Party a federal and democratic structure and a dissenting culture.

The first structural difference to note is that the Conservatives (and Liberal Democrats) are a party of individual members whereas Labour is a party of 'affiliated organisations' as well as of individual members. These organisations – overwhelmingly trade unions – are entrenched in the party's decision-making bodies and they exercise a vote at the annual conference and in local parties roughly

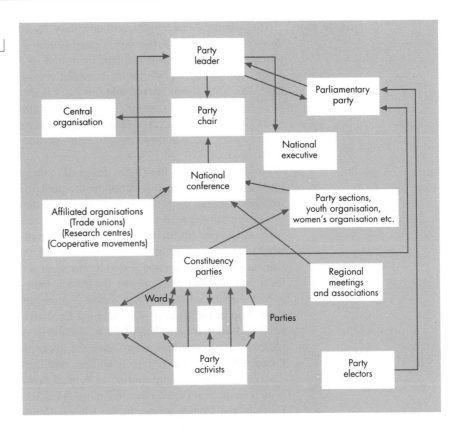

Figure 16.1 British party
structure – a general picture

proportionate to their membership (strictly speaking, to the number of Labour-dues paying members they claim to have when they contribute to Labour Party funds). In the 1980s, affiliated trade unions accounted for 89 per cent of the vote at the annual conference and the five largest unions commanded a majority (55 per cent of the vote) among them. Because of the way the vote is exercised, the leaderships of the big unions wield enormous power in the Labour Party. Their members naturally tend to follow the leadership advice on how to vote. Moreover, the trade union vote dominates the election of 18 of the 28 places on the national executive.

Trade union influence in the Labour Party was less obvious before 1970 and has been declining from the early 1980s. It was not obvious before 1970 since the parliamentary leadership of the Party generally agreed on policy with union leaders, so their block votes were cast to support them. Such support enabled the Party leadership to ignore often critical opinion in the constituencies. It was this alliance which Robert McKenzie[1] used to support his point that both major Britain parties operated in roughly the same way, under leadership control, in spite of the greater appearance of democracy in the Labour case.

[1] Robert T. McKenzie, *British Political Parties* (London: Mercury, 1964)

The alliance between the parliamentary leadership and trade unions broke down in the 1970s as left-wingers gained more ground in the unions. However, they never really controlled all of them and so instituted reforms in the early 1980s, putting more power in the hands of constituency parties, where their real base was. Thus it was agreed that the Party leader would be elected by an electoral college, in which unions, constituency parties and MPs would all have a share (in the 1990s an equal share). The block vote was also eroded in 1990 by providing for union votes to be split in proportion to the distribution of opinions in the union.

A further reform of the 1980s, designed to make MPs more responsive to their local activists, was for reselection of the parliamentary candidate or sitting MP for each election, instead of letting them stand automatically.

The centralising leaderships of the 1990s paradoxically built on these left-wing reforms to open up the party to the influence of rank and file members, from whom the centre feels it can get more support than from either unions or constituency parties (often dominated by the most active, left-wing members). Thus local and national referendums have been held on the abolition of Clause 4 (which committed the party to nationalisation) and on the 1997 election manifesto. Annual elections for the National Executive Committee on a one member one vote basis have also helped the leadership to get rid of opponents. One example of increasing central control was the imposition of all-woman shortlists for the selection of parliamentary candidates (until struck down by judicial review!).

All these changes empowering individual members on the one hand, and the central leadership on the other, have brought Labour closer in its structure to the Liberals and Conservatives. In the Liberal Democratic Party, for example, the leader is elected by the vote of all party members, and there is agitation for a similar system among Conservatives. After his election in 1997, Hague actively sought endorsements from ordinary Party members and pledged reforms giving them a voice in the next leadership election.

Important constitutional differences still distinguish the Conservative Party, however. Much greater power is given to the Conservative leader. In the Conservative Party, the shadow Cabinet, the party chair and vice-chairs, the Chief Whip and deputy Whips are all in the leader's gift. In the Labour Party the shadow Cabinet and Chief Whip are elected by Labour MPs and on becoming prime minister Labour leaders must include the 16-member shadow Cabinet in their full Cabinet (although it is the PM who determines their ministerial responsibilities). The general secretary of the Labour Party (the closest counterpart to the Conservative chairperson) is appointed by the national executive while the treasurer is elected by the annual conference.

The Conservative leader's policy-making powers are equally extensive. The Leader is solely responsible for the Party's election manifesto (the Party programme published during each election campaign) and can incorporate or veto specific proposals without consulting the rest of the Party, as Margaret Thatcher's 1983 manifesto commitment to abolish the Greater London Council testifies. The Labour manifesto is drafted by a joint subcommittee of the national executive committee (NEC) and the shadow Cabinet (themselves elected bodies) and must incorporate any policy passed by a two-thirds majority of the annual conference.

A second, related, difference lies in the formal powers accorded to the Party in the country. The annual Labour conference is the electoral college for the Party leader and deputy leader (with trade unions and the constituency parties and parliamentary Labour Party allocated 33.3 per cent each). It is also the sovereign policy-making body with the right to determine party policy and incorporate provisions in the manifesto. The annual Conservative conferences have no such rights. They can pass policy motions or resolutions critical of the leadership (though they rarely do) but these have no constitutional power. Labour conferences decide; Conservative conferences confer.

A parallel difference exists at the constituency level. Local Labour parties can instruct their delegates to the annual conference on how to vote in elections for the national executive or the leadership and increasingly do so on the basis of ballots of local individual members. They not only choose the local parliamentary candidate but, if their constituency has a Labour MP, require the MP to submit to a formal process of annual reselection. Conservative associations do not mandate those attending the conference and Conservative MPs are automatically reselected unless their relationship with the local party has badly deteriorated.

These constitutional differences are reinforced by quite distinct party cultures. Conservatives have traditionally valued party unity and loyalty above all else, and their conferences are rallies rather than debates. Most resolutions from the constituencies are paeans of praise for the Party leadership or, if critical, expressed in muted and deferential terms. The Labour Party takes ideological principles ('socialism') more seriously and most activists have accorded them priority over party unity, loyalty to the leadership or even electoral success. For most Conservative activists, conservatism has been an instrument for winning elections; for most Labour activists elections have been an instrument for implementing socialism. This is now changing. The Conservative Party is now riven by ideological debate over Europe and grumbles about the lack of internal democracy in the party. In contrast the 'New Labour' leadership has succeeded in muffling ideological debate and uniting the party round a new will to win.

Ironically, 'democratisation' of the election of the Labour leader has made it more difficult for a challenger to succeed. Selection by an electoral college requires three months' notice, the convening of a special conference, and a campaign by the challenger, not only among MPs but among trade unions and local parties. Moreover, Neil Kinnock's leadership between 1983 and 1992 and Tony Blair's record so far demonstrates how powerful a determined leader can be. In the early 1980s, the fundamentalist left was in the ascendant, internal conflict was rife and the Party was unelectable. In the space of nine years, Kinnock and his personal allies expelled the Militant faction, marginalised the socialist left, jettisoned the party's long-standing (but unpopular) policies of nationalisation, trade union legal immunities, withdrawal from Europe and unilateral nuclear disarmament, and reunited the party behind a pragmatic, mild, social-democratic programme. Blair abandoned the hallowed Clause Four. The other constitutional reform of the early 1980s, mandatory re-election, has not led to its intended democratic consequences either. Very few Labour MPs have been deselected, and an increasing number of constituency parties in Labour-held seats have re-elected their MP from a shortlist of one.

However, to dismiss the Labour Party's democratic reforms as inconsequential would be premature. Kinnock, Smith and Blair could not have transformed the Labour Party without the support of sympathetic trade union leaders who, desperate to see the return of a Labour government, turned a blind eye to the auto- cratic practices of the leader's personal office and used their influence to ensure a pliable national executive and an acquiescent annual conference. But such support would not long survive a period of Labour government that presided over a recession or serious inflation. Without economic success the Labour leader, and individual Labour MPs, would be threatened by an alliance of left-wing activists and dissatisfied trade unions exploiting the democratic reforms.

WHAT THE PARTIES STAND FOR

We have seen how different factions struggle for ideological and policy control of British parties. This does not mean, however, that the party does not speak with a clear voice, particularly at elections, but also over long periods of time when it is enjoying reasonable electoral success under a strong leadership. The organisational

Plate 16.3 Conservative and Labour Party manifestos for 1997 election

Key term

Social democratic consensus – the agreement, which was strongest in the 1950–79 period, whereby governments of all parties should accept the broad principles of the welfare state, the mixed economy, Keynesian economic policies and a NATO-based alliance against the USSR.

Key term

Neo-liberal consensus – agreement among different political groups and parties about neo-liberal politics, that is political belief that individual rights should be protected by maximising freedom of choice, limiting the powers of government, and promoting market economics.

structures we have just examined enable all factions in the party to endorse a general public statement about party priorities and commitments, the party manifesto. We shall look at manifestos in more detail in the next chapter. Here we need only note that they give a general programme for government after the election and constitute an agreed statement about what the party stands for, on which, except in extreme cases, all factions concur.

As we have noted, both major parties underwent ideological reconstruction in the 1980s and have emerged sharing a 'neo-liberal' consensus which has replaced the earlier 'social democratic' one. The key elements of the new consensus are:

- acceptance of a privately owned economy in which the government role is limited to ensuring fair competition and protecting consumers;
- acceptance of the present powers of the main pressure groups (and maintaining the limitations imposed on unions);
- an orthodox economic policy aimed more at low inflation than high employment;
- ceilings on state expenditure on welfare and other public services;
- support for NATO as the main defensive alliance and hence for American leadership in the new world order.

A point at issue between the parties remains the degree of integration in Europe (also within the Conservative Party, as we have seen). Whether or not the Labour Government goes into the currency union it will remain much more favourable to the EU for the foreseeable future.

The other major point dividing the parties is political reform. This extends from territorial devolution from the Westminster Parliament and government (Scotland, Wales, London) to entrenchment of individual civil and political rights and freedom of information.

These developments have moved the Liberal and Labour positions much more closely together, which may have implications for future electoral and parliamentary alliances against a rump, Eurosceptic and nationalist Conservative party (if the expected split materialises). However, the New Labour strategy has dangers for the Liberal Democrats too, as Labour has taken over the position of non-doctrinaire, moderate, reforming party held by them since 1959, appealing to moderate voters over most of the political spectrum.

CHARACTERISTICS OF MPs AND PARTY MEMBERS

Many of these tendencies are reflected in the social composition of Party MPs, members and voters. As Table 16.1 shows, the parliamentary Conservative and Labour parties are unrepresentative of both their members and voters. The MPs of both parties at the end of the 1980s were overwhelmingly middle-class, university-educated and male. MPs of both parties in fact resembled each other much more than they did their party supporters.

Table 16.1 Social
composition of MPs,
members and voters of the
Conservative and Labour
parties, 1987

	Conservative Party			Labour Party		
	MPs %	Members %	Voters %	MPs %	Members %	Voters %
Social Class						
Employers, managers, professional (upper middle class)	90	46	31	66	56	14
Intermediate and junior nonmanual (middle and lower-middle class)	9	41	39	15	18	23
Working class	1	12	31	19	26	63
Education						
Independent Schools	68	n.a.	9	14	n.a.	3
Further Education	82	14	13	79	32	10
University	70	n.a.	11	56	n.a.	6
Oxbridge	44	n.a.	n.a.	15	n.a.	n.a.
Women	5	58	52	9	41	52
Ethnic Minorities	0	n.a.	2	2	n.a.	9

Sources: Butler and Kavanagh, *The British General Election of 1987* (London: Macmillan, 1988), pp. 202, 204; Rose and McAllister, *The Loyalties of Voters* (London: Sage, 1990)

This resemblance was due above all to the fact that the parliamentary Labour Party has ceased to be working-class. The proportion of manual workers on the Labour benches steadily fell from 72 per cent between the wars to 36 per cent in the 1950s to 29 per cent in the 1980s. Over the same period the proportion of graduates rose from 17 per cent between the wars to 40 per cent in the 1950s and 56 per cent now. In 1987 twice as many Labour MPs were teachers as miners. The Conservative Party has also lost some of its patrician element, although only very gradually. In the 1950s 75 per cent went to public schools and 22 per cent to Eton alone; in the 1980s the figures were 68 per cent and 11 per cent.

Thus the two parliamentary parties do not so much comprise two social classes, as two strata within the middle classes. Most Labour MPs come from the less privileged and moneyed middle classes: compared with their Conservative counterparts they are more likely to be first rather than second generation middle-class, educated at state rather than private schools, at polytechnics rather than universities, 'red brick' rather than Oxbridge, and to have worked in the public sector and the new professions rather than the private sector and the traditional professions. At a lower level the Labour Party is more middle-class than the Conservatives: a development of the past two decades is the steady replacement of working-class members by white-collar and professional, well-educated middle class.

Most of these tendencies were simply confirmed by the results of the 1997 election. Sixty-one per cent of Labour MPs in the new Parliament, and no less than three-quarters of the Conservatives and Liberals were university educated. Thus the dominance of the middle class among Labour MPs continued to grow.

This may have reinforced their appeal to 'Middle England', but of course the bulk of voters continued to come from the peripheries and Northern and Western England. Most Conservative voters came from Outer London and South-East England.

One difference which has opened up between the parties in Parliament is in proportions of women MPs, who now constitute 35 per cent of Labour MPs, 101 in number, possibly a critical mass. Women constitute only 12 per cent of Conservative MPs and 7 per cent of Liberal MPs. These parties must now be under pressure to increase their female representation, particularly given their numbers of female activists and voters. Minority ethnic groups – Indo-Pakistani and Afro-Caribbean – remain substantially underrepresented, just over 1 per cent of the membership of the House of Commons. The more conspicuous figures are on the Labour side, however.

The social gap which has opened between the parties in Parliament and the parties in the country perhaps accounts for the sharp decline in Conservative and Labour Party membership over the years since the war. In the 1950s the Conservatives claimed to have about three million members and Labour one million. This slumped to a half and a quarter million respectively by 1992.

The decline was due not only to social trends but also to leaders' lack of interest in a mass membership, which was seen as a potential source of trouble in that members might try to impose their own policy views on the Party or support dissent. Moreover, having masses of members to canvass and campaign seemed less necessary in an age of universal television, when parties could appeal over the heads of members directly to electors.

In the 1990s, leaders began to realise that it was still members who mobilised votes on the ground. As part of its renovation and modernisation the Labour Party aimed at recruiting new, younger members. By the election of 1997 it had got back to 400,000 members. The Conservative Party claimed still more but informed estimates put the real figure at around 300,000 (many of them quite old). The party proved unable to mobilise itself on the ground in the Scottish and Welsh referendums of September 1997, which was an ominous sign for the future.

Declining memberships have been interpreted as a symptom of general party decay. Counterbalancing this impression is the fact that the Liberal Democrats have built up their membership to 100,000. Another countervailing consideration is the fact that the nature of local political activity itself has changed. The politicisation of local government has meant that the most active members are now local councillors, sometimes controlling a municipal budget greater than that of some central ministries. Of the new MPs elected in 1997, two-thirds on the Labour and Liberal side had previously been elected at local level. This was true of only a quarter of newly elected Conservatives, but we may expect that figure to grow as more Conservatives get elected locally to counterbalance Labour success in central government.

At the moment these changes in the social base of its representatives strengthen the claim of the Labour Party to be broadening its appeal beyond the traditional working-class base to all voters, particularly to those in the political centre. Our discussion of New Labour's policy changes supports this idea. In Chapter 17 we shall examine these, and the corresponding policy adjustments made by the other parties, in more detail.

ESSAYS

1. How far are British political parties 'umbrella' organisations covering a loose alliance of factions and tendencies, and how far are they basically united?

2. Does Michels' 'Iron Law of Oligarchy' still hold for British political parties?

3. Are party activists inevitably more extreme than party leaders? Why or why not?

4. Does the fact that MPs are socially different from their supporters make them unfit to represent them?

SUMMARY

Textbooks conventionally depict political parties as disciplined armies moving in perfect order on the political battleground. Reality could hardly be more different. As with all voluntary organisations, people join with dissimilar objectives and protest or quit if these are not met. Parties have an inner life, marked by ideological divisions, personal rivalries, and tensions between the leadership and the rank and file. All parties are uneasy coalitions.

This is clearly evident in the recent struggles within both Conservative and Labour parties and goes back a long way, as shown by our earlier discussion and by the 'Milestones' of party development shown below. We have emphasised not only party divisions, however, but also the way in which strong leaders can use their organisational advantages to pull the party together and stake out an advantageous and electorally winning position which often endures over a considerable period of time. Besides covering internal disputes, this chapter has also charted the overall development of the parties, their internal structure and the social sectors from which leaders and members come. Specifically it has discussed:

- inner tensions and ideological developments from 1868 to 1979,

- factional and leadership initiatives of the 1980s and 1990s,

- the way in which parties link grass roots and leadership through their organisational structures,

- the leverage this gives to party leaders in attempts to pull the party together,

- changes in social representation in Parliament, particularly the increasingly middle-class nature of Labour and the new influx of woman MPs, which surely points to a modification of the overall style of party politics in the future.

MILESTONES

MILESTONES IN THE DEVELOPMENT OF BRITISH POLITICAL PARTIES

	Conservatives	*Liberals*	*Labour*
1867–68	Second Reform Act transforms franchise from a small, property basis to a mass electorate		
1870s	Primrose League promotes mass organisation of party, with a branch in every constituency. Party promotes Empire, monarchy and social reform	Joseph Chamberlain and the 'Birmingham Caucus' pioneer a mass party organisation emulated in other parts of Britain	
1868–86	Alternation of Conservatives and Liberals in Government		
1886	Accession of Liberal Unionists initiates 20-year dominance of Conservative Party in national politics	Gladstone's First Home Rule Bill for Ireland splits Liberal Party	

MILESTONES IN THE DEVELOPMENT OF BRITISH POLITICAL PARTIES (continued)

	Conservatives		*Liberals*		*Labour*
				1900	Labour Representation Committee brings together socialist parties and trade unions
1905	Under influence of Liberal Unionists, party advocates imperial preference and protection, is defeated in the general election, and remains divided	**1905–14**	Liberal governments introduce social reforms and push Irish Home Rule, Parliament Act 1911, National Health Insurance Act 1911, Irish Home Rule Bills 1912, 1913, 1914	**1905–14**	Labour supports reforming Liberal Government
				1914–18	Labour internally divided over whether Britain should fight First World War
1922	Break-up of coalition Conservatives propels to office under Borier Law	**1922–29**	Liberals split between 'Lloyd George' and 'Asquith' Liberals	**1923–24**	First minority Labour Government legislates for public housing programmes
1926	General Strike broken by Conservative Government with implicit support of Liberals and Labour				
				1929–31	Second minority Labour Government
1931	Financial crisis related to world slump leads to split in Labour and Liberal parties, and formation of Conservative-dominated 'National Government'				
1932	Government intervenes to impose protection, tariffs, industrial mergers and rudimentary planning		Split between mainstream Opposition and 'National Liberals' who are absorbed by Conservatives	**1932**	Split between mainstream Labour and 'National Labour' who are absorbed by Conservatives
1940–45	Wartime coalition government, in which Labour basically runs home affairs				
				1945–51	Reforming Labour governments establish 'Welfare State', nationalise basic industries and decolonise India
1946–51	Conservatives accept welfare state and most nationalisations. They win elections of 1951, 1955 and 1959 on basis of abolishing controls and freeing economy		Liberals drift without clear leadership		

MILESTONES IN THE DEVELOPMENT OF BRITISH POLITICAL PARTIES (continued)

	Conservatives		*Liberals*		*Labour*
				1951–64	Party divides increasingly between left and right
1962–64	Government shifts to idea of indicative economic planning	**1964**	Gain votes with advocacy of electoral reform, civil rights and European integration	**1964–66**	Wins 1964 and 1966 elections on basis of 'making planning work'. Devaluation of sterling leads to financially orthodox policies. Trade union reform fails. Strengthening of the left
1965–70	Shift to the right – support for free market and trade union reform				
1970–74	Heath Government imposes legal framework on trade unions and joins European Union				
1973–74	'Three-day week' Wave of strikes precipitates election which brings Government down	**1974**	Elections see vote increase to 18–19%	**1974**	Wins elections but with reduced vote. Wage and price controls lead to trade union revolt in 1979 ('Winter of Discontent'). Loses 1979 election
1975	Margaret Thatcher wins party leadership election on a 'New Right' programme				
1979–90	Margaret Thatcher wins a series of elections on a programme of financial orthodoxy, privatisation of state industry, strict regulation of trade unions, cuts in public expenditure, a cautious attitude to EU, and full support of NATO	**1983–87**	Alliance with Social Democrats nets a quarter of the vote in general elections of 1983 and 1987	**1979–83**	Ascendancy of 'hard left'. Alternative economic programme and internal reforms lead to party split with what becomes Social Democrat Party and to disastrous election defeat in 1983
				1983	Election of Neil Kinnock as leader. Centralising reforms and adoption of 'neo-liberal consensus' fails to avert election defeats of 1987 and 1992

MILESTONES IN THE DEVELOPMENT OF BRITISH POLITICAL PARTIES (continued)

	Conservatives		*Liberals*		*Labour*
				1992	Kinnock resigns as party leader. John Smith elected
1990	Thatcher ejected as leader to avert election defeat.			**1994**	Smith dies. Tony Blair elected party leader, imposes strong central discipline, abolishes Clause 4 and evolves image of 'New Labour' which wins 1997 election
1992	Major wins General Election				
1992–97	Split between 'Eurosceptics' and 'Pro-Europeans' weakens party by continual controversy.				
	Series of financial and sexual scandals. Go down to record defeat in 1997	**1997**	Liberals win 46 seats in Parliament which could make them the pivotal party in a future coalition	**1997**	Government initiates programme of political reform starting with devolution

PROJECTS

1. Document with examples the major ways in which *either* Tony Blair *or* Paddy Ashdown can control their respective parties.

2. Update Robert McKenzie's analysis of power relationships within the Conservative and Labour parties.

3. What influence do *either* Euro MPs (MEPs) *or* local councillors have within the Conservative and Labour parties? Base the project on actual newspaper accounts of how they have exerted influence.

FURTHER READING

Much historical material is contained in R. T. McKenzie, *British Political Parties* (London: Mercury, 1964). A graphic account of 'New Labour's management and electioneering, and of Conservative divisions, is found as background in D. Butler and D. Kavanagh, *The British General Election of 1997* (London: Macmillan, 1997). Earlier books in this series chart fluctuating party fortunes. On party membership, activists, and organisational structure, see Paul Whiteley, Patrick Seyd and Jeremy Richardson, *True Blues* (Oxford: OUP, 1994) and Patrick Seyd and Paul Whiteley, *Labour's Grass Roots* (Oxford: Clarendon Press, 1992).

http://www.awl-he.com/politics/newbritpol

Internet resources – visit *The New British Politics* Webpage for links to a specially-chosen selection of Internet resources relevant to this Chapter.

http://www.awl-he.com/politics/newbritpol

PART IV

Representation

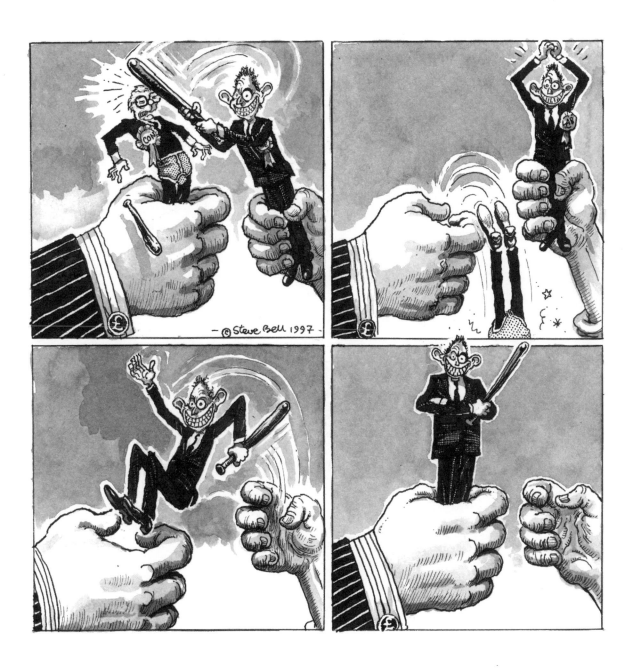

CHAPTER 17

Party ideologies and political representation

Parties are at the heart of British politics not only because of what they are but because of what they do. The last chapter showed how their organisations span the various levels of British society, linking members and electors to a set of leaders who form the government or government-in-waiting.

Parties not only seek to run the country, however. They also seek to run it along certain lines, either as a free-market economy or as a 'mixed' system, in which market competition is regulated and the state intervenes to protect losers. This is only one of the issues which divide the two parties, but it has been a central one over the last 20 years, and has deep historical roots (Chapter 2).

Other policy differences exist over the European Union, respect for individual rights and devolution of power to regional governments. However, parties tend to shift positions on these issues from time to time. Labour was split on the EU in the 1970s but is much more supportive today while the Conservatives have totally changed from support to opposition.

On central questions like the management of the economy and provision for the weaker elements in society, the parties are more consistent in the policies they adopt. This is partly because their stances are embedded in their very identity and ideology, as well as in the expectations of core supporters and members. The Conservatives would not be the Conservatives, for example, if they were not sceptical about the extent to which governments can directly help people.

This chapter will accordingly:

- Examine the concept of 'party families' and the development of party ideologies

- Explore the idea of 'left' and 'right' in British politics and in the ideologies of British political parties

- Examine election manifestos and how these reflect left–right ideologies

- Ask whether ideology is still as important as it was in the past and whether differing party ideologies give voters a real choice

- Question the importance of political parties in Britain and ask whether there is any alternative way of running the country

PARTY FAMILIES

The British mass parties are the second oldest in the world (the Americans had them first). But they are not wholly unique. Labour falls into the general 'family' of socialist and social democratic parties, the most numerous of all party families. The Liberals belong to the rather small family of radical liberal parties. In recent years the Conservatives have joined the conservative-liberal, free-market grouping.

Even the smaller British parties have counterparts in other countries with whom they form a broad ideological grouping (see Briefing 17.1). The Greens, for example, resemble ecologically minded parties elsewhere. And parties like Plaid Cymru (the Welsh Party) and the Scottish Nationalist Party (SNP) belong in a broad spectrum of minority nationalist groupings. The Northern Irish Social Democratic and Labour Party (SDLP) can be classified with Christian party families, given their Catholic basis. Ulster Unionists are in the rather unusual position of being a regional party upholding the central state. Their belief in the indissolubility of the Union groups them with majority conservative parties elsewhere in Europe.

Table 17.1 shows the general 'family' to which each British party belongs. More than that it summarises which groups their supporters come from, what their core values and policies are and where they stand on the extent of government intervention in economy and society: the central issue in the left–right differences we discuss below. 'Families' are in fact roughly ordered in left–right terms (the left-right continuum), from radical environmental groupings through socialists and radical liberals to conservative liberals devoted to the free market and as little governmental intervention as possible.

BRIEFINGS

17.1 IDEOLOGY AND THE CONCEPT OF 'PARTY FAMILIES'

'Ideology' is a system of ideas and assumptions which help us understand and interpret the political world. It is a set of values and beliefs, factual assumptions and ideas, which point towards the appropriate political action to take in given circumstances. The term is often restricted to a fairly explicit, coherent and elaborate set of ideas: a theory of politics. In this sense few people have real ideologies, not even political leaders. But many do subscribe to looser and less explicit ideologies such as socialism, liberalism or conservatism. Parties are built round these conflicting political principles ('political principles' is a positive name for 'ideology', in its broader sense). Parties in different countries which share a similar ideology are usually grouped together as a 'party family', because they share the same beliefs, principles, policies and, often, support groups.

Table 17.1 European 'party families' and their British members

'Family' Ideology	Support Groups	Core Values	Characteristic Policies	Attitudes to Government Intervention	British 'Family Member'
Ecological and communitarian	Young, educated supporters of 'new social movements'	Environment, participation, peace	Encourage sense of community, protect environment, help minorities, disarmament	Supports more intervention to achieve objectives	The Green Party
Socialism	Workers, public employees in social and service sectors, intellectuals	Equality of wealth and opportunity	Extend welfare protection (health and pensions), regulation of capitalism, peace	Government provision in all areas where market does not provide	(old) Labour Party
Minority nationalist parties	Minority groups, especially those with different languages and cultures	Cultural diversity, subsidiarity	Decentralisation, devolution and autonomy	Intervention necessary to uphold minority cultures in the modern world	Scottish Nationalist Party, Plaid Cymru
Radical liberalism	Anti-authoritarian elements of middle class, religious minorities, some peripheral regions	Liberty and a minimum standard of living to enjoy it	Safeguards for political and social rights	Against 'big' government but for enough intervention to safeguard weaker sectors	Liberal Democrats
Christian democracy	Churches, especially Catholic Church, Catholic middle class, country and small towns	Fraternity, community, human dignity, subsidiarity	Strengthen traditional morality and family, extend welfare, mixed economy	Intervention where necessary to ensure welfare and family stability	Social Democratic and Labour Party (SDLP) (Northern Ireland)
Conservative	Traditionalists of the state Church, upper and middle-class, 'loyal' members of working class, country and small town areas	Order, security, social hierarchy	Uphold established state structures and national boundaries, maintain armed forces	Intervention as and when necessary to ensure stability	Ulster Unionist Parties, British Conservatives 1868–1964
Conservative (neo) liberalism	Middle class and business	Liberty, individualism	Freedom from controls, free markets, efficient limited government	Government limited to upholding free market	Conservative Party (post 1964)

Of course a summary table like this inevitably simplifies. The British parties have already been described in much greater detail in Chapter 16. Nevertheless, the comparison shows what a lot in common they have with European parties, not just in the EU but in Eastern Europe where the same party groupings appear.

PARTY IDEOLOGIES

The three major British parties clearly differ in terms of all the factors listed in Table 17.1. Labour draws its members and most faithful supporters from the working class and public employees, is dedicated to equality as a core value and wants extensive government-supported welfare to ensure this. This was played down in the 'New Labour' manifesto of 1997 but was stressed in many government pronouncements after the election.

The Liberal Democrats, who are quite radical and reformist by general European standards, come close to Labour on these matters but are more inclined to set limits on what governments do than Labour, traditionally anyway. As we shall see, the two parties have crossed paths recently.

The legacy of Margaret Thatcher, Conservative leader from 1975 to 1990, was to turn the Conservatives decisively from putting order and stability at the top of their priorities to substituting freedom and individualism, as seen above all in the free market. Traditional Conservatives had often been inclined to trade welfare and intervention for stability (as in the 'social democratic consensus' over policy from 1950 to 1979, when they largely accepted the welfare state). Mrs Thatcher, however, would have none of this and seriously set about reducing 'welfare dependence' during her years as prime minister (1979–1990).

Recent years have thus seen political and ideological shifts on the part of both the New Right and New Labour. One could also say this of the Liberal Democrats, which have transformed themselves into a radical alternative to Labour. How significant are these changes? Are they likely to last? And do they mean that the parties are coming together? Are we seeing both convergence and an end of distinguishing ideologies?

Ideologies and political cleavages

To answer these questions we need to put today's ideologies in historical perspective. All parties date to the beginning of the twentieth century or earlier and many of the traditional differences between them also date to that time, as with other British institutions. Parties adapted their ideology to the needs of particular supporters, both building on and emphasising certain lines of political 'cleavage' in the country (see Briefing 17.2). Seeing how they did this helps us appreciate how enduring ideology can be. Briefings 17.3–17.5 outline the ideological bases of liberalism and conservatism.

The Conservative and Liberal parties trace their origins to the 'cadre' parties operating under the very restricted middle-class franchise from 1832 to 1867

BRIEFINGS

17.2 SOCIAL AND POLITICAL CLEAVAGES

A political cleavage has two elements:

1. A social division in the population (as between working class and middle class), that is, a cumulation of differences in lifestyle, social characteristics and material advantages which differentiates one group of people from another.

2. A political emphasis on one side of that division, usually by political parties, who aim to take up and advance the interests of 'workers' or the 'middle class' or whatever group is involved. By doing so they aim to mobilise them politically, recruit them as members, and get them to vote for them. A first step historically was thus to enfranchise the relevant group so that they could cast votes.

Political parties are thus as important in the creation of cleavages as objective social divisions are. An illustration is that the division between towns and country never turned into a cleavage in Britain, because all parties lined up with urban interests in accepting free trade after 1850. The divisions that did become cleavages were religion, region and class (in that order).

For more on the relationship between cleavages and parties in Western Europe read the classic account, Martin Lipset and Stein Rokkan (eds) *Party Systems and Voter Alignments* (New York: Free Press, 1967).

BRIEFINGS

17.3 CLASSICAL LIBERALISM

The essence of liberalism (with a small 'l') is the belief that individual rights should be protected by maximising freedom of choice and by limiting the powers of government. Historically, liberalism represents a rejection of the absolute powers of a monarch, or other ruler, and seeks to establish limited government, freedom and tolerance under the law. In Britain classical liberalism is built on the writings of John Locke (1632–1704) and John Stuart Mill (1806–1873). In *Two Treatises on Government* (1690) Locke defended the Glorious Revolution of 1688 which established the dependence of the monarch upon parliament and was thus a first important step towards limited, constitutional government. In his *Letter Concerning Toleration* (1693) Locke makes the case for freedom of religious conscience, and so lays out the case for freedom of thought and belief in general, which is a fundamental tenet of liberal theory. In *On Liberty* (1859), Mill argues that the only justification for government interference with the liberty of individual citizens is to prevent them doing harm to others. His great fear is the tyranny of popular opinion (tyranny of the majority) which can threaten individual freedom no less than paternalistic or authoritarian government. In this sense classical liberalism is opposed both to the absolute powers of the monarchy, and to the broad-ranging powers and functions of a socialist state.

Classical economic liberalism is expounded by Adam Smith (1723–90) in his book *The Wealth of Nations* (1776) which argues that the 'invisible hand of the market' succeeds in making individual economic self interest work for the common good. In this way Smith lays out the arguments for capitalism, individualism, and free trade.

BRIEFINGS

17.4 NEO-LIBERALISM

In the twentieth century some of the ideas of classical liberalism have emerged in neo-liberal, or new right, form. Neo-liberals also place supreme importance on the freedom of the individual and on rolling back the frontiers of the state, and argue that market competition is the best way of guaranteeing both political freedom and economic growth. In *The Road to Serfdom* (1944), for example, F.A. von Hayek (1899–1992) argues that socialism and the welfare state inevitably lead to loss of individual freedom. In a similar way, the Chicago school of economics, led by Milton Friedman in the 1970s and 1980s, rejects Keynesian theory in favour of a form of classical economics which strongly favours competitive markets and low public expenditure. The main economic function of government is to regulate the money supply (monetarism) in order to control inflation. The ideas of Hayek and Friedman strongly influenced Margaret Thatcher. The right-wing think tank, The Adam Smith Institute, was established in London in 1978 to promote and develop neo-liberal policies in British government.

BRIEFINGS

17.5 CONSERVATISM

Conservatism (with a small 'c') is a general tendency in politics rather than a clearly worked out ideology like Marxism or socialism. It believes in preserving what is thought best in traditional society and opposes radical change. Conservatives often believe that society is naturally hierarchically organised and should be regulated by a strong state. The classical British work of conservative theory is Edmund Burke's *Reflections on the Revolution in France* (1790) which doubts the capacity of people and governments to plan an ideal society and which, therefore, argues for slow change rather than radical transformation. Old institutions and practices, he said, often have great, though hidden, virtues, and should be allowed to adapt slowly to changing circumstances. The ideas of conservatives have usually been strongly represented in the policies of the Conservative Party.

British conservative thought has changed and varied over the years. Strongly opposed to socialist ideas in the first half of the twentieth century, conservatism and Conservatism moved towards a social democratic consensus in the 1950–1975 period when they were inclined to accept the broad principles of the welfare state, the mixed economy, Keynesian economic policies and a NATO-based alliance against the USSR. The consensus was also known as 'Butskellism' after the left-wing Conservative Chancellor of the Exchequer R.A.B. Butler, and the right-wing Labour counterpart Hugh Gaitskell, who agreed on broad policy issues, though not necessarily the details. The social democratic consensus was broken by Margaret Thatcher in the 1980s, whose politics were closer to the neo-liberal ideas of the New Right than to traditional conservativism.

(when the Second Reform Act transformed the situation). From today's perspective the differences between the notables of these two parties does not seem very great. Many (including Gladstone, the dominating figure of nineteenth century Liberalism) switched between them. Starting from the effective introduction of free trade in 1846–47, however, the Liberals gradually developed a more progressive policy stand, pressing for political reforms and the extension of the franchise. Because of this they attracted the support of minority groups who felt disadvantaged by the old set-up: Scots, Welsh and religious nonconformists (both Protestant and Irish Catholic).

With the actual achievement of a mass franchise it became even more important for the Liberals to attract the votes of these groups to gain power. To do so they took up the causes dear to them: removal of state support from the Church of England in Ireland and Wales; and wider political reforms, particularly of the patronage system in Government appointments and of the Church hold on education. Representing above all the nonconformist middle classes of Northern Wales, Scotland, Northern and Western England, the Liberals could not, however, appear as effective defenders of the working-class interest. This left an opening for Conservatives and the newly formed Labour Party, which they both took.

In the mid-nineteenth century the Conservatives, like other such parties in Europe, defended the traditional state structures – monarchy, Army and Church – against the increasingly reformist Liberals. With the advent of the mass franchise in 1867–68 they developed an appeal to the new working and lower middle class which built on these themes, stressing national unity, British strength and the Empire. Particularly after the Liberals backed devolution for Ireland (1886), the Conservatives consolidated their new support, above all in the South East and Midlands of England. The crisis over Irish Home Rule, which the Conservatives opposed, also shook out traditionalist elements from the Liberals (the Whigs) rendering it more than ever a party of nonconformists on the peripheries.

The peripheries were based economically on manufacturing and so were dominated demographically by the urban working class (Chapters 1 and 2). This left the Liberals vulnerable to a class-based party which could unequivocally put the interests of industrial workers first. The rise of Labour, which did just that from the beginning of the twentieth century, eroded Liberal support. The Liberals suffered from a double haemorrhage, losing working-class support to Labour, while the business classes fled to the Conservatives, who offered stronger opposition to welfarist and protectionist demands.

The consequences were:

- a steady decline in Liberal importance. From one of two major parties they became one of three in the 1920s and dropped to below 10 per cent of the national vote in the 1950s;

- as a result Labour became the main party of opposition to the Conservatives;

- the Conservatives themselves became divided between the traditionalists, still disposed to concede welfare demands for the sale of unity, security, hierarchy and order, and the newly acquired exliberal supporters of free trade and the free market.

> **Key term**
>
> **Patronage** – the giving of favours – office, contracts, or honours – to supporters of the government.

This group progressively took over the party, a process finally completed in the 1980s under Mrs Thatcher. Of course, free markets depend on the state maintaining order and security. The two sides could compromise on the need for both. But in terms of political priorities, order and security began to take second place to economic freedom, both at home and abroad.

While not disputing the need for international free trade, Labour has always wanted protection for workers and weaker elements at home, secured by government intervention, and they parted company with the increasingly radical Liberals (now Liberal Democrats) on this latter point. The Liberals developed the argument that to take advantage of economic freedom you had to have enough resources to back up your choice. It is no advantage having a choice of medical services, for example, if you cannot afford to buy any of them. However, unlike 'old' Labour, they did not see state intervention as a good in itself but as a means to giving individuals economic freedom. As in the case of the other two parties, these ideas spring out of older concerns, modified to fit modern conditions. The question we will confront below is, how far have they been modified?

First, however, we should comment on the relationship between cleavages and ideologies. Just how does the social base of a party relate to its political ideas?

As our historical account implies, the two intermesh because parties aim their appeals at certain social groups in order to gain their votes and support. It is easier to target social groups with identities and interests in common. Trying to appeal to electors at large on the basis of their common interests is more difficult because of a large degree of uncertainty about what their common interests actually are and how they are responding. With a distinctive social group, one can talk with their leaders and communicate more easily.

BRIEFINGS

17.6 MARXISM AND SOCIALISM

Developed by Karl Marx in the mid-nineteenth century, Marxism is probably still the best known and best worked out political ideology. Although it has developed many different branches, Marxism basically states that economic relations, particularly those between the classes created by the system of production, determine all forms of political and social life. In the late capitalist system there are only two classes: the capitalists (or property owners or bourgeoisie), who are increasingly rich; and the workers (or proletariat), who are exploited, and become increasingly poor. As a result, the workers develop a revolutionary class consciousness, overthrow the system and, after a period of state socialism, eventually establish a society without state or property.

According to Marx, history can only be understood in terms of class, and capitalist politics can only be understood as a constant class struggle between the bourgeoisie and the proletariat. Other ideas, such as religion or nationalism, might seem important, but are simply different manifestations of class interests, which are used by the ruling class to mystify politics and create the false consciousness which conceals the real class struggle. A Marxist, therefore, reacts to events by asking whose class interests are being served. Foreign wars, for example, may appear unconnected with the class struggle but, according to Marxist theory, they are actually a means of promoting capitalist interests.

Of course, this is a two-way process because, by appealing to group interests, the party is helping to define them. The working class was much more conscious of itself as a sector over and against the rest of society once the Labour Party was launched than it was before. The Labour Party also helped develop other organisations to represent them (e.g. by strengthening trade unions).

In the books, articles and pamphlets which set out the Labour and working-class case, a systematic analysis of the position of workers in contemporary society appeared, linking together the appeals for more welfare, housing, minimum wages and equality which Labour made at elections. Labour, like other European socialist parties, had the advantage of being able to draw on the immensely influential and comprehensive work of Karl Marx, who wrote in the mid-nineteenth century.

As Briefing 17.6 explains, Marxist theory sees all events in terms of the class struggle, and ideas of nationalism and religion as bourgeois weapons to delude the workers about where their real interests lie. These are in essence to struggle against their bourgeois employers, and eventually to overthrow the capitalist system which allows the latter to control the means of production such as factories

Key term

False consciousness – the state of mind induced in the working class by the ruling class in order to conceal the real nature of capitalism.

BRIEFINGS

17.7 SOCIALISM AND SOCIAL DEMOCRACY

Socialism takes from Marxism the ideas of class interest, equality, and the welfare state. It differs from Marxism, however, in stating that political and social change can and should be achieved by means of peaceful reform and democratic action, rather than revolutionary violence. The British Labour Party is a social democratic party, as are the mainstream labour movements in Scandinavia and Germany. Like most ideological schools of thought – including Marxism and liberalism – socialism has many variations, including anarcho-socialism, Christian socialism, Fabianism, guild socialism, and market socialism. Fundamentally, socialist theory argues for the collective ownership or control of key parts of the economy, for state economic planning, and state provision of basic services such as health care, education and social welfare. But it opposes the complete state control of the economy (the command economy) of communist systems, and favours the retention of large areas of social, political and economic life which are outside the state and independent of it. It is therefore opposed to liberalism, on the one hand, and to communism, on the other.

British socialism has not been strongly influenced by west European socialist thought, and has drawn heavily upon the work of British writers such as R. H. Tawney (1880–1962), John Maynard Keynes (1883–1946) and C.A.R. (Tony) Crosland (1918–77). Tawney's book *Equality* (1931) argues for state action and progressive taxation in the interests of economic stability and growth, and political equality and democracy. But it was Keynes who had a particularly strong influence on political thought and government policy in Britain and throughout the western world. In his book *General Theory of Employment, Interest, and Money* (1936), Keynes advocated some government economic intervention and planning in order to achieve economic stability, growth and full employment. Keynesian demand management and a mixed economy replaced classical, liberal (market) economics as the orthodoxy of economic theory and practice between 1945 and about 1975.

In the 1960s British socialist thought went through a period of change under the influence of Tony Crosland's book *The Future of Socialism* (1956). This argued that socialist goals of freedom and equality require some government economic planning but a large measure of private economic activity. State control and regulation of key sectors of the economy was necessary, but not further nationalisation.

and land. Their monopoly on these enables them to exploit workers by forcing them to sell their labour (their only resource) very cheaply and thus creates gross inequalities of wealth and social conditions in society.

After the fall of the old Communist regimes, few parties in contemporary Europe would support the whole of the Marxist argument. Democratic socialists like British Labour (see Briefing 17.7) could, however, agree that class relationships are the most important ones and that the central issues in politics are those concerned with the distribution of resources between classes. But they would argue that the working class – like all others in society – has an interest in preserving peace and stability and that redistribution achieved through negotiation and argument is much better than imposed solutions supported by force, since these can always be reversed by greater force.

A similar acceptance of nonviolence and democracy occurs among the adherents of the other party ideologies. In practice this means accepting the policies chosen by the elected government, no matter how much one may criticise them as unfair or unjust. Indeed, if an opposition party can persuade enough electors that Government policies are unfair, it can hope to reverse the electoral decision next time and thus modify government policies. Because of this possibility, most governments will tend to compromise with the parties out of government so that the projects they initiate will have some chance of permanency and do not get repealed once there is a change of power.

Within this broad acceptance of democracy, party ideologies differ from each other in terms of which groups are considered to be the important ones in society and how their interests should be served. Are classes so pervasive and central that the interests of the workers should always come first? Or are workers' interests only part of a more general, societal interest, as 'bourgeois' parties tend to argue, and hence better served by strengthening the free market which will create more wealth for all? Or, on the contrary, is economic growth the force which is destroying the natural world in which we all have a common interest, so should it be opposed? Also perhaps, economic growth should be opposed because through uncontrolled development it ravages the countryside and threatens the culture of minority groups, which need to be defended by setting up their own state or sub-state institutions, as in Scotland and Ireland.

It can be seen that there is rich ground for controversy and argument among the adherents of different ideologies. This is particularly so because no-one can say scientifically or objectively which ideology is right. Assertions that class is the most important of social relationships, or that the world would suffer an irreparable loss if Welsh ceased to be spoken, are not subject to 'scientific' or 'objective' proof. They spring out of an identification with or immersion in a particular group in society. One function of an ideology, indeed, is to buttress that identity, as most people belong actually or potentially to many different overlapping groups. Is someone from north-east England who works in a steel factory primarily a worker, British, English, European, Roman Catholic, Polish immigrant or woman? In a situation of multiple individual identities, parties struggle to make one identity predominant and thus to mobilise support for their policies and general point of view.

Ideologies are thus important not only in telling leaders what to do but in telling voters who they *are* and so making them receptive to leaders' diagnoses of the political situation. Ideology is particularly important for political parties, which have to operate across different levels of society. It helps to link up often complex governmental decisions with the broadly defined interests of their supporters and voters.

'LEFT' AND 'RIGHT' IN BRITISH POLITICS

Specific party ideologies can also be distinguished in terms of how far they are to the 'right' or to the 'left' (see Briefing 17.8). This is because differences over the extent of government intervention in society – whether to leave things to the free market or to limit its often disruptive workings – are a central and permanent political issue in modern societies. Intervention is sought by all sorts of groups* which feel themselves weak in social and economic terms: not just the working

BRIEFINGS

17.8 LEFT–RIGHT DIFFERENCES IN BRITISH POLITICS

The terms 'left' and 'right' originated from the location of supporters and opponents of political change in France at the end of the eighteenth century. Supporters of reform sat on the left of the legislative chamber while supporters of the king and established institutions sat on the right. The terms have kept their connection with those who urge change on the one hand, and those who oppose it on the other. However, this connection is often more rhetorical than real, as right-wing parties often in practice introduce greater changes than left-wing ones (an example would be the Thatcherite reforms in Britain in the 1980s).

In the twentieth century the core distinction is defined in terms of support for more government intervention, on the left, and opposition to it, on the right. Left-wing parties want more government intervention to extend the welfare state and more regulation and planning in the economy. Right-wing parties want government to get out of society and the economy so far as possible, in order to extend individual freedom of choice. But they do support strong government measures to guarantee law and order internally, and national security externally. Thus they support a strong, but limited, state. In contrast left-wing parties want peace through international co-operation. Left-wing positions have generally developed out of some variant of Marxist ideology.

Centre parties tend to mix these positions and support limited government intervention in most policy areas, but specifically oppose Marxist analyses of society.

The fact that parties consistently take up these positions means that their election programmes and manifestos can be statistically analysed to see how they 'move' in left–right terms from election to election, as in Figure 17.2.

For more detail, see Ian Budge, David Robertson and D.J. Hearl, *Ideology, Strategy and Party Change* (Cambridge: Cambridge University Press, 1987).

class but also ethnic minorities, women and environmentalists. They want the government to restrict the power of the purely economic interests privileged by the market.

These differences appear in attitudes to foreign affairs as well as inside Britain. The left-wing parties (Greens, Labour, Liberals) all want supranational bodies such as the EU and UN to regulate what states and multinational corporations do. They are 'idealists' in international terms, with a strong belief in the possibility of peaceful co-operation at international level and a commitment to building institutions to encourage this.

In contrast the 'right' adopts more 'realist' views, seeing the international arena as like the free market, a place where states and firms pursue their own interests, and often maximise the general well-being by doing so. To prevent the pursuit of national interests getting out of hand, however, strong military alliances are necessary to create a 'balance of power' where no one side can dominate. The 'Cold War' of 1948–89, when the American and Russian alliances confronted each other, was an example of such a balance where each side deterred the other from taking over the world. Now that the Russians have voluntarily accepted capitalism and free markets, new threats may arise, such as Islamic fundamentalism, which make continuing military preparations necessary. 'Idealists' would be much happier seeing the old alliances dismantled and substituted by world or regional development bodies. The fact that all parties take a position on these questions allows us to place them on a single line running from left to right, as shown in Figure 17.1.

To be sure, left–right differences are not the only ones which exist between parties, and probably not the most important ones for minority nationalists, for example. They are very central to national politics, however, so it is interesting to look at them across the whole political spectrum.

The point that leaps out from Figure 17.1 is that the three main British parties are not, on average, so very distant from each other in terms of the full range of ideological difference (at least in left–right terms) that could exist. Labour is far

Figure 17.1

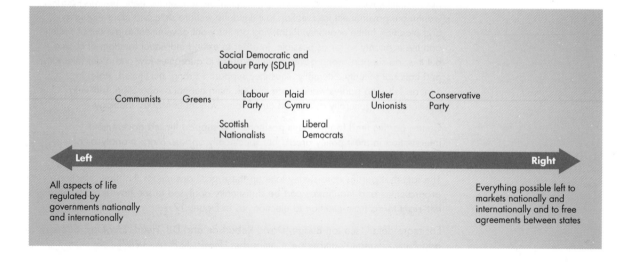

from wanting to have everything regulated and the Conservatives do not want to leave everything to the free market nor (internationally) to only what can be agreed through interstate negotiations. (They, after all, formed the government which joined the EU in 1972.) The Liberals are the most centrist of all, seeking to balance the general efficiency of the free market with necessary government intervention in favour of weaker groups.

Of course, these positions summarise what the parties have said and done over the whole postwar period from 1945–98. A more interesting question is how they have changed *recently*: have they moved closer together or drifted further apart? The next section tries to analyse more precisely what has happened recently and whether these left–right differences still remain.

Meanwhile it is worthwhile looking at the smaller parties' position in these terms. Often smaller parties are thought to be more extreme because they are more 'pure' ideologically than the big parties can afford to be (in case they put off voters). However, none of the regional parties take positions very far (in left–right terms) from those of the main parties. The Scottish Nationalists are somewhat to the left of Labour, a strategic position in left-leaning Scotland. Plaid Cymru is less radical, partly because it is the Welsh-speaking middle class who are its backbone. The Northern Irish SDLP are even more centrist and (in left–right terms) not far from their local opponents, the Ulster Unionists. The latter are traditional conservatives who believe above all in order, security, and the integrity of the British state. But they are not averse to financial aid and government-directed development in Northern Ireland.

The most extreme left-wing parties are those which have a 'cause' and no regional base, the Communists and the Greens (the party that wants government intervention to save the environment). Both are small parties with little political support, and split internally between hostile factions, so they have little practical effect on the British political scene.

With the collapse of communism in Russia and Eastern Europe, and its dilution in China, the British communists are unlikely ever to win much support and are probably on their way out politically. The steady deterioration of the environment, both in Britain and the rest of the world, may well provoke a crisis which will give the Greens more votes and influence. At the moment, however, they are weak and divided.

Left–right differences in the major parties' ideologies

At the national, British level, therefore, it is the three traditional parties which are the real contenders for power. The next sections examine how they have changed their policies and ideologies over the postwar period. Have they moved closer together recently or moved further apart? Seeing how the main parties have changed from election to election, in terms of the left–right differences illustrated in Figure 17.1, provides a way of answering this question.

It is true, of course, that such a 'single line' representation gives only a very summary idea of the full range of party policies. There is more to political life, and ideology, than just left and right. As Table 17.1 showed, parties on the left have important differences of opinion among themselves, on the importance of devolution for example, or the primacy of environmental issues. These do not show up in simple left–right terms.

Left–right differences thus do not cover *all* of British politics. But they are *central* to them for the following reasons:

- Political discussion – in the press, on television, in Parliament – is structured in terms of left and right. An important question for commentators is always whether a party is moving towards the centre or the extremes, particularly in the context of elections. A party that has 'seized the centre ground' is usually considered to have a better chance of winning the election, as most electors are thought to be in the 'middle' (i.e. somewhere between the left and right positions).

- The question of how far governments should intervene – in welfare and the economy above all – is and always has been central to British politics at the national level. Chapter 2 discussed how it defined politics in the late nineteenth century and it has remained the crucial dividing line between the major parties ever since.

- Because of their centrality, the positions parties take in their election programmes on this range of issues are more likely to carry through into actual government policy than others. This is important because the measure we use to trace left–right ideological shifts in party positions is derived from the party election programmes (manifestos), as explained in the next section.

<table>
<tr><td>

Key term

Party manifesto – the document which parties publish at the start of election campaigns outlining the programme of policies they intend to implement if elected to government.

</td></tr>
</table>

ELECTIONS, MANIFESTOS AND PROGRAMMES

A major feature of each general election in Britain is the programme published by each party at the beginning of its campaign (a month or five weeks before the election). This is termed the Party Manifesto. In it the leaders set out their views on how the society should develop and the country should be run for the next five years. Setting out a reasonably detailed overall plan for national development is something only the parties do, and it distinguishes them from all other social organisations in Britain.

Its practical use is that it gives electors an indication of what would be done by different parties if they got into government, and thus enables them to choose between them (if they want to do so on grounds of policy). The parties' commitment to particular programmes thus gives electors a handle which they can use to vote for the party whose policies they endorse. It enables ordinary voters to exert some influence over which policies the incoming government will pursue. The ability of electors to influence government in this way is, however, dependent on the existence of parties with alternative programmes.

If elections simply involved selecting individuals who came together in Parliament after the election in order to form a government, nobody would know in advance what their policy would be and electors would lose their opportunity to influence government policy. It is no coincidence, therefore, that the slow extension of democracy in Britain over the last century and a half has been bound up with the consolidation and growth of parties and the intensification of national competition between them for office. Democracy in Britain is indissolubly linked to the political parties; and electoral influence over national policy is linked to the programmes the parties offer.

Manifestos are prepared under the direction of party leaders. But many of the documents on which they are based have been approved by party conferences and other official bodies. They thus constitute a unique and authoritative policy programme to which the party as a whole is publicly committed.

Despite their importance in setting out a national five-year plan, and offering a choice, party manifestos are not widely read by electors. Their contents are, however, extensively reported in the newspapers and on the television and radio so their contents are widely disseminated, although at second hand. Electors who want to choose between parties in terms of their policies will, in the course of the campaign, be able to acquaint themselves with the main policies they lay out.

What do the manifestos actually say? On first reading they seem rather woolly and far from offering a precise programme for government. New Labour was exceptional in 1997 in making relatively precise pledges about Scottish and Welsh devolution and on limiting tax increases. Usually the manifesto makes precise commitments in only a few areas, often peripheral ones, like building the Humber bridge, which are relatively easy to keep. About 70 per cent of these pledges are carried through if the party gets into government. But this is less impressive than it seems if the promises do not cover central areas of policy.

A lot of the document consists of rambling discussions of various topics like 'youth', 'unemployment', 'the economy', and so on. Topics like these constitute its main sections. Typically, the sections state how important the problem is and give an analysis of past developments and of the present situation, stressing party concerns and achievements in the area, but not committing it to very much. This vagueness is due to a well-founded fear by party leaders that tying themselves down to specific actions while in government might give too many hostages to fortune. Changed circumstances or a financial crisis might result in their not being able to do what they had said they would do, and thus to loss of credibility and accusations of bad faith.

It is better from the viewpoint of parties to emphasise the importance of a particular policy area rather than state what exactly one is going to do about it. This does not render the manifesto valueless as a statement of future policy. One simply has to realise that its main purpose is to set priorities for government action rather than tying the government in advance to specific things it must do. Talking a lot about a particular area like 'youth' implies that the party would do more and spend more in the area, but not exactly what it would do or how much it would spend. Setting priorities in this way actually makes it easier for electors to choose between the parties on broad general grounds relating to what they would want to see done, rather than having to decide on the feasibility of particular courses of action in areas where they have no expert knowledge.

There is often scepticism about the extent to which parties *do* carry through their programmes in government. Many feel that promises made at the election are simply not kept once the party has got in and ceases to need votes. Recent research, however, has shown that not only are the majority of pledges carried through by the winning party but also that the priorities stressed in the manifesto are strongly related to subsequent government expenditure in the different policy areas.

Electors choosing between parties on the basis of their policy priorities can thus have some confidence that they will try to put them into effect in government.

Party manifestos and party ideology

How do election programmes relate to ideology? As we have seen, ideology is a particular way of viewing the political world which makes it understandable from the viewpoint of doing something about the situation. The manifestos are programmes for government action so it follows that they are strongly influenced by party ideology.

This shows when you read manifestos issued by different parties at the same election. These often give such dramatically opposed accounts of the situation that if you did not read the title page you would think they were talking about two quite different countries or times! Thus in 1997 the Conservative manifesto painted a glowing picture of a Britain with an expanding economy and prosperity trickling down to all, while the Labour document talked of the country's crisis in education and welfare and of the growth of poverty.

Such differences occur in part because ideologies lead parties to focus on different groups and developments as important. The Conservative reference point is the South-Eastern middle class and their concerns with financial markets, order and opportunity. Labour is more focused on the peripheries and their problems of economic stagnation, bad housing and health.

Differences in the party programmes also occur because the parties' ideologies and history make them 'proprietors' of different issues. If you want free markets and an emphasis on individual opportunity and law and order, you know from what the Conservative Party has done – and even from what it is – that it is more likely to provide these than any other party. If these issues are the ones people think important in an election, more are likely to vote Conservative. If, on the other hand, more people are concerned about education and welfare, these are Labour issues which will promote support for that party.

Issues like these become important partly because of societal developments outside the political arena. But the parties can also try to focus on them by emphasising 'their' issues in the manifesto and in their campaign. Differences in emphasis thus arise partly from the imperatives of competition, building however on the pre-existing ideological differences between the parties and their reputation for competence in different, ideologically defined, issue areas.

Measuring left–right ideology in manifestos

The fact that party programmes stress different kinds of issues according to their ideology gives us an opportunity to measure the ideological distance between them at each election, by estimating the amount of attention each document pays to the characteristic issues of the left and right. As noted above, its position between left and right is not the whole of a party's ideology but it is a major part of it. It covers the most central issues in British politics and the ones on which electors are most likely to assess parties, and governments to take action.

Table 17.2 The 'top ten' issues in Conservative, Liberal Democratic and Labour manifestos, 1997 General Election

	Conservative % of Sentences in Manifesto	Liberal Democrat % of Sentences in Manifesto	Labour % of Sentences in Manifesto
Government effectiveness and authority	13.4		11.3
Law and order	9.9	5.8	6.9
Economic goals	8.0	5.5	5.8
Regulation of capitalism	5.4		
Technology and infrastructure	5.1	4.5	6.5
Social services expansion	5.1	9.0	6.4
Incentives	4.7		
Noneconomic groups	4.0	4.8	4.0
Decentralisation: positive	4.0	4.5	5.4
European Union: negative	3.9		
Social justice		6.5	5.4
Education expansion		5.8	3.9
European Union: positive			3.4
Environmental protection		8.0	
Internationalism: positive		4.0	

Note: The entries in the table are the percentages of sentences in each party manifesto devoted to the campaign issues listed down the side. Percentages are given only for the leading ten issues in each manifesto. Where these do not coincide, no entry is given for the party(ies) for which they do not come in the top ten. The table shows that the 'big issue' for both Labour and Conservatives was government effectiveness. Conservatives put more emphasis than the other parties on their (reasonable) economic record and law and order. New Labour did not have a very distinctive profile, putting somewhat less emphasis than the Conservatives on government effectiveness and law and order, less than the Liberals on social matters and uniquely supporting the EU. The Liberal Democrats clearly moved to the left of Labour (Figure 17.2) with their greater stress on social matters and the environment.

The emphases parties give to different issue areas can be measured very simply and directly, by counting the number of sentences in each manifesto devoted to each issue area. This assumes, of course, that we are able to distinguish and list the separate issue areas. The best way to produce a comprehensive and plausible list is to read through manifestos informally and group the related policy references together under a more general heading. The writers of manifestos help in this task by dividing their text into sections under such headings as Economy, Agriculture, Women and so on.

Table 17.2 shows how the parties differed on the 'Top Ten' of these topics in the 1997 election. The 'top ten' are the ten most often mentioned categories in each party manifesto, that is, those to which most sentences were devoted. From this it can be seen that Labour stressed education and social justice more and the Conservatives topics like law and order and (free-market) incentives. In many ways the Liberals were the most distinctive of the parties with a heavy emphasis on environmental protection and international co-operation.

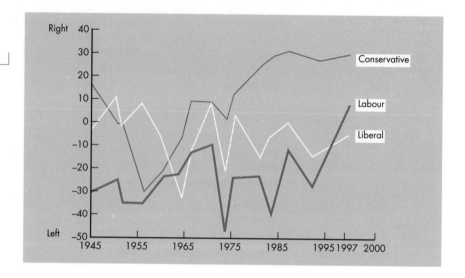

Unusually, in the 1997 election, Labour and Conservatives did converge on some of the same topics, like government effectiveness and authority, traditionally a Conservative issue. Here Labour felt it could attack the government record of division and scandal, while the Conservatives felt they had to defend it. In Figure 17.2, which traces the ideological progression of the British parties over the postwar period, we can see how this affects their ideological positions in relation to each other. To do this we can look at left–right differences more directly (see Table 17.3). All we need do is group 'left-wing' issues together and add up percentage references to them. Then we group 'right-wing' issues together and add up their percentage score. Finally we can take the combined percentage for

Table 17.3 Creating a left–right scale from party manifestos

Negative Items	Positive Items
Nationalisation	Free enterprise
Controlled economy	Economic orthodoxy
Welfare: positive	Social services expansion: negative
Regulation of capitalism	Incentives
Economic planning	Freedom
Protectionism: positive	Protectionism: negative
Military: negative	Military: positive
Peace	Effective authority
Education expansion: positive	Constitutionalism: positive
Internationalism: positive	National way of life: positive
Decolonisation	Traditional morality: positive
Labour groups: positive	Law and order
Democracy	Social harmony

left-wing issues and subtract this from the combined percentage for right-wing issues. That gives us a 'scale' running from + 100% (all references in a manifesto are to right-wing issues) to – 100% (all references in a manifesto are to left-wing issues). In practice, of course, each manifesto will contain references both to left and right-wing issues, so they will never be totally right-wing nor totally left-wing. Nor will all the topics mentioned by parties fit into this particular ideological distinction. This means that the main British parties fall near the middle of the left–right space, as we already saw from Figure 17.1. The positions they take in specific elections vary more, of course, but only within a range of +30 towards the right and –50 towards the left.

Table 17.3 lists left and right-wing issues. As the essence of the left-wing position is support for government regulation and intervention domestically and the creation of governmental bodies to do the same internationally, the topics picked out as leftist all have a bearing on these questions. They include nationalisation (takeover of businesses by government), regulation and control of the economy, provision of welfare and education (again by governments) and peace and international co-operation. The right opposes these emphases with its stress on freedom. The free market needs some government support to keep it going, which is provided by law and order at home and military alliances abroad. All these elements can be seen in Thatcher's policies of the 1980s, which have been characterised as 'free market, strong state'.

Measuring left–right differences in this way enables us to trace the ideological progression of the three main British parties over the whole of the postwar period. In Figure 17.2 left–right positionings are measured on the upright dimension (from +40 – relatively right-wing – to –50, relatively left-wing). The horizontal dimension is time. Each election can be identified by its particular date: 1945, 1950, 1951...1997.

Left and right – convergence or divergence?

Differences between the parties started by being very large in 1945, with the post-Second World War election in which Labour won a large majority and started a programme of intervention and reform in all areas. The Conservatives realised that the reforms, particularly the creation of the welfare state, were popular and that to win elections they had to accept them. By emphasising such left-wing positions they came very close to Labour from 1955 to 1964, the heyday of the so-called social democratic consensus between the main parties. This meant that both parties accepted the welfare state and a mixed economy, in which the government owned large sectors of industry. However, the two-party convergence was due partly to Labour's own move to the right as it tried to tone down the unpopular emphasis on nationalisation in its proposals. Meanwhile the Liberals wandered about between the other two parties with no very fixed principles or positions.

All this changed after the 1966 election as the Conservatives, with some minor deviations, moved far rightwards; up to 1997, in fact, they remained relatively far to the right. The gap between the two main parties widened as Labour moved dramatically left in 1974. In both 1983 and 1992 it also maintained fairly left-wing

Plate 17.1 Dave Brown
cartoon in *The Independent*,
19 November 1996:
'Dammit! He's wearing my
clothes again!' Tony Blair led
the Labour Party towards the
right of the political spectrum
in an attempt to become
electable

positions. Only in 1997 with New Labour did it make a dramatic shift to the right, largely by playing down economic intervention in its programme while continuing to support welfare and education. This move to the right perhaps paralleled that of the Conservatives leftwards in 1955: 'if you can't beat em, join em!'. Unlike the earlier Conservative change, the move did not bring Labour close to its main rival as the Conservatives still remained much further to the right. So the 1997 election saw ideological convergence only up to a point. Much depends on what happens in the next election. If Labour feels it has a winning position and stays where it is, while the Conservatives move leftwards as a result of election defeat, convergence may well occur. But if the right wins within the Conservative Party and Labour moves left to head off the Liberal challenge, a widening gap could well reappear.

From 1964 to 1992 the Liberals occupied the middle ground between the main parties. Labour's rightward move put them more to the left in relative terms in 1997, but without radically altering the slightly left of centre position they have held since 1964.

THE END OF IDEOLOGY?

Ideology is a term with highly negative connotations for many people. It has associations with Marxism and thus with sterile debates among fanatics and extremists about abstract principles. Either that or it is associated with totalitarian regimes which murdered millions in the name of 'racial purity' or 'the victory of the proletariat'. Even when manifested in democratic politics, ideology is seen as preventing agreement and maintaining artificial party differences, which get in the way of national unity and successful problem solving.

BRIEFINGS

17.9 THE CONDITIONS FOR ELECTORAL CONTROL OVER PUBLIC POLICY

Summing up what we have been saying about party representation and electoral choice, we can specify four conditions for electoral control over future government policy:

1. The parties must offer voters a choice.

2. Voters need to be aware of the choice.

3. People vote on the basis of the choice.

4. The party in control of the government follows policies consistent with the options it placed before the electorate (party accountability).

All of these conditions require that the parties have different ideologies to generate policy choices for voters, and to give them an incentive to carry through their programme in government.

No wonder then that many commentators have eagerly predicted an 'end of ideology' at various times in Britain's postwar history. 'Ideology' has been particularly associated with the left. Thus the electoral defeat of Labour and its modification of socialist principles have been seen by many as necessary to creating a more rational and balanced society in Britain.

In reality, however, the positions taken up by the parties, even in 1997, are still quite sharply divided in ideological terms. If any of the parties are close they are Labour and Liberal Democrats, who may well come together at some point in a centre-left coalition against the Conservatives.

Moreover, even if all the parties do converge in 2001, all past experience shows this will be a temporary phenomenon. Convergence is normally followed by divergence. There is no 'inevitable' trend towards general agreement. If this did come to pass the parties would lose their identity and with it their separate existence, and would cease to offer alternative choices to electors (see Briefing 17.9). For all these reasons, drawing together is always likely to be followed by a drawing apart to traditional policy positions. So no 'end of ideology' seems in view, no matter how much party squabbles irritate the public.

The positive contribution of party ideology to electoral choice

Is this necessarily a bad thing however? While 'ideology' has bad connotations it is as well to remember that it is really the same thing as holding to firm political principles. Having principled politicians rather than self-servers and office seekers is generally regarded as good. If the 'death of principle' is involved in the 'end of ideology', the latter appears in rather a different light.

As the discussion at the beginning of the chapter also indicates, it is impossible to operate in politics without an ideology. We need to have a set of beliefs and assumptions about the way the world works in order to react to it at all. Socialism could only be abandoned by replacing it with another ideology. Neoliberalism and free market beliefs are in this general sense just as much ideologies as Marxism. Indeed, far and away the most ideological politician in recent British politics has been Margaret Thatcher, the right-wing Conservative Prime Minister from 1979 to 1990.

We cannot get away from having ideological parties, so the only question is whether they should have different ideologies or all share the same one. The general conclusion we can draw from our examinations of party programmes is that they are likely to remain different.

This has positive advantages for the role parties play in representing the views of the British electorate. To see that this is the case, only consider what would happen if parties did all share the same ideology and offer electors the same policies in their programmes. This would mean that whichever party electors voted into government the same policy would be pursued. Electors would then have no opportunity to choose between policies appropriate to the current situation. Differences in ideology guarantee that different solutions will be offered by different parties and that electors can weigh them up and decide between them with some probability of determining which will actually be pursued.

The constitutional doctrine of the party mandate actually rests on the idea that electors are able to choose between programmes in this way (see Briefing 17.10). Basically the argument runs that a majority or plurality vote for a party in the general election can also be seen as an endorsement of that party's policy programme. This then gives it the authority to put its policies into effect when in

BRIEFINGS

17.10 THE PARTY MANDATE

The idea of a party mandate assumes that the party winning most votes in an election will form a government which will carry through its electoral programme, because this has been supported by a majority or plurality of electors. The details of the argument are:

- Electors choose between parties at least in part on the basis of their programme.
- Such programmes are distinguishable from each other, so they offer electors a basis for choice.

- The party or parties which form the next government have a responsibility to carry out their programme in government, because this is a major basis on which they were elected.
- They also have the authority to carry out their programme in government, as it has been selected by the largest number of electors as the best.
- Parties do carry through their programmatic priorities in government.

government. If all parties offered the same programme governments would lack the authority of a mandate, because no-one would know whether electors had really endorsed their programme or had simply been deprived of the opportunity to express an opinion.

Incidentally, ideology has another positive contribution to make in a party democracy like Britain. It gives parties an incentive for carrying through their programme when they get into government. There is a lot of cynicism about whether they actually do carry through election promises, or whether they ignore their commitments when they get into office, using them only to attract votes in the election. The Wilson governments (1964–70, 1974–76) were felt to be especially bad about this, gaining office with the promise of economic expansion through state planning and ending by restricting economic activity and creating high unemployment.

In contrast, no-one could say that the highly ideological Margaret Thatcher did not rigorously carry through her programme of restricting government and promoting the free market. Thatcher did this because, as well as promising such measures to the electorate, she actually believed in them very strongly!

In theory, governments could be punished retrospectively for breaking earlier election pledges. Some analysts argue that electors would not vote for such a government because they could not trust it to carry through policies they otherwise find attractive. In practice. however, this seems a rather weak sanction because of the lapse of time involved and the many circumstances which will have intervened to make earlier pledges irrelevant or incapable of fulfilment.

While external sanctions or election penalties may be weak, ideological imperatives to carry through the programme may be quite strong, as the case of Thatcher shows. Ideology can thus play a very important role in promoting party accountability. We would surely prefer to have 'conviction politicians' saying and then doing what they believe than opportunists doing the minimum they feel they can get away with.

ALTERNATIVES TO PARTY DEMOCRACY

On the threshold of the third millennium, parties seem to be exerting a more pervasive influence on general debate than ever. Thanks to the media, they totally dominate government and politics. Our evidence shows that they are still divided in ideological terms, and that this situation is likely to continue. It clearly has many advantages in presenting electors with sharp policy choices and guaranteeing that most governments will carry them through.

Many, however, find the constant squabbling between parties deeply distressing. It is epitomised by televised debates from Parliament, where Labour and Conservatives shout each other down, with no attempt to debate the merits of the case or to find agreement. Surely things would be better if the good people on all sides came to a problem without party prejudices and found the best solution which generally served the national interest?

The problem lies in discovering what *is* in the national interest and how best to achieve it? Does it exist at all or is it simply a projection of the interests of one

Key term

Party democracy – either (1) the widespread distribution of power within a political party and/or (2) a system of national democracy resting upon competitive parties.

group, for example the City of London or the South-East 'Establishment', at the expense of others? The national interest is perhaps most easily identified in foreign affairs, keeping Britain strong and influential in the world. Even here, however, there has been much criticism of the costs an overextended world role has imposed on manufacturing industry and internal welfare.

The best people coming together outside their parties would still, therefore, face policy dilemmas, and divide and argue over them. There are just no easy or obviously 'best' solutions to political problems. That is why parties and their ideologies have evolved, to ensure that no major interest or grouping in society lacks an advocate to promote its views on any problem about which it is concerned. As Winston Churchill remarked of democracy in general: it seems unattractive until you look at the alternatives. The same can be said of parties and their ideologies. If they did not exist today they would rapidly re-emerge, as they are so essential to democratic debate and choice and to the control of electors over government. In that sense, British democracy cannot do without them, whatever their incidental defects.

ESSAYS

1. What is ideology?

2. What is a party family? What different 'families' are represented in Britain?

3. What does it mean to say that a party is to the 'left' in politics?

4. What does it mean to say that a party is to the 'right' in politics?

5. Why is it important that British electors should be presented with different party programmes in an election?

6. What are the essential characteristics of 'party democracy' in Britain?

PROJECTS

1. Read three party manifestos without their identifying labels and try to guess:
(a) which party they belong to
(b) whether they were published at the same election.

2. Analyse the reasons for ideological change on the part of the British parties with reference to Figure 17.2.

SUMMARY

This chapter has examined the different party ideologies which exist in Britain today and how they help maintain party identity and distinctiveness. In particular it has looked at:

- the different 'families' to which British parties belong and how they have evolved over time;

- the way in which party families can be 'placed' in terms of an underlying left–right ideology, centred on differences about the nature and extent of government intervention in society;

- how the left–right positions of the main parties can actually be measured from their election manifestos and used to track changes in their ideological positions over time (Figure 17.2);

- the boost this gives to electoral choice between alternative programmes for society and to electoral control over government actions, and hence to the general functioning of representative democracy in Britain.

FURTHER READING

The nature of political ideologies in general is discussed in A. Heywood, *Political Ideologies* (London: Macmillan, 1992) and A. Dobson, 'Ideology', *Politics Review*, 1(4), April (1992). Applications to British election manifestos are made in Ian Budge, David Robertson, Derek J. Hearl *et al.*, *Ideology, Strategy and Party Change* (Cambridge: CUP, 1987). A review of party families and ideologies, as well as of other aspects of parties, can be found in Alan Ware, *Political Parties and Party Systems* (Oxford: OUP, 1996). For a comparison of the British party system with other European parties see Ian Budge, Kenneth Newton *et al.*, *The Politics of the New Europe* (Harlow: Addison Wesley Longman, 1997).

CHAPTER 18

Parties and Parliament

The last two chapters have emphasised the fact that Britain is a *party democracy* rather than a *parliamentary democracy*. That is, elections decide which *party* is to form the government rather than what *individual* is going to represent a constituency in Parliament. MPs get elected because of their commitment to a particular party rather than on their own merits. Once elected they are expected to vote with the Government or Opposition except on the rare occasions when their party does not take a position on an issue, or they dissent on a matter of conscience.

All this leaves limited scope for MPs to act collectively, independently of parties. This raises in acute form the question of whether Parliament can or should be anything more than a forum for the Government to mobilise public opinion in favour of their policies, and for the Opposition to mobilise opinion against them. Such confrontations are designed to influence the result of the next election rather than make any immediate change to policy. This chapter therefore discusses whether Parliament can have a useful role independent of party. Would this improve the quality of democracy in Britain?

The chapter covers the following:

- The structure and procedures of the two Houses of Parliament. Reform of the Lords and party unity in the Commons

- Parliamentary scrutiny of administration (as compared with legislation) and the work of select committees

- MPs' interests and business links. 'Leaks' in government

- Bankbench rebellions in Parliament since the 1970s

- Third parties, coalition government, and ritual 'shadow boxing' between Government and Opposition

GOVERNMENT AND PARLIAMENT

British governments are formed by the party which wins most seats in the House of Commons. Usually, but not invariably, this is the party which also controls the majority of seats. The growth of third parties (Liberal Democrats, Welsh and Scottish Nationalists, Ulster Unionists and Social Democrats) means that a 'hung' parliament, where no clear Conservative or Labour majority exists, is always a possibility. The more usual situation is that of the 1980s and early 1990s, however, where Conservative governments with majorities respectively of 44, 144, 100 and 21, dominated the proceedings. Currently Labour has a majority of 177 overall.

Clearly these different situations have different consequences for relations between Government and Parliament, and within Parliament itself, which we shall explore below. Besides supporting governments, however, and providing their members (all members of a government have to be MPs or peers), Parliament has the equally important role – at least in constitutional theory – of scrutiny, discussion and, if necessary, criticism of executive actions. It is this aspect we shall concentrate on here. There are grounds for believing that the obsessive secrecy of British governments, and their desire to manipulate information to their own advantage, undermine Parliament's role as a forum for informed criticism and constructive debate. Together with the majority party's (i.e. the Government's) control over procedures and legislation, they may deprive ordinary MPs of any real political influence at all. In order to investigate these points we have to look at the structure of Parliament and the nature of its business, before examining the pressures for reform which may come to the fore at the Millennium.

THE STRUCTURE OF PARLIAMENT: THE LORDS

Although we generally equate 'Parliament' with the elected House of Commons, it also comprises the nominated and hereditary House of Lords. Britain is the only country in the world to contain such a chamber within a democratically elected parliament. Its inappropriateness in this context has been clear since 1911, when the Parliament Act (restricting its previous power of veto to one of delay over legislation) promised fundamental reform later. At the end of the century, however, it still exists, with much of its old composition and its delaying powers substantially intact.

Labour made noises before the last election about changing this anomalous situation. It is not at all clear, however, whether in government it will do anything about it. Reform would provoke a political battle, consume much energy and might put in place a more powerful second chamber less subservient to the Government than the Commons. In any case what might be substituted for the existing House of Lords has not been clearly thought through, so it may well continue as it is unless it directly challenges Labour by rejecting central legislative proposals (see Briefing 18.1).

BRIEFINGS

18.1 POSSIBLE REFORMS OF THE HOUSE OF LORDS

As it stands today the House of Lords has four different kinds of member. The bulk, roughly two thirds, are hereditary peers who have inherited the right to be members along with their titles. About a quarter are life peers: ex-politicians and persons of distinction nominated by governments to serve for life. The rest is made up of 26 Church of England bishops and 12 law lords, judges nominated to make up the judicial House of Lords, which functions as the supreme court of appeal.

The least radical proposal for reform is to drop the hereditary element. As the life peers are by far the most politically active element in the House, this would enable it to continue its functions as a scrutinising, revising and debating chamber without much disruption, while removing a major part of its anti-Labour bias. If New Labour does decide to reform the Lords, this is the most likely reform they will undertake.

The most radical reform would be to abolish the House altogether. If the Commons were allowed more latitude for debate and scrutiny, the Lords would probably not be much missed in the overall scheme of things. Such an action would, however, be seen symbolically as very radical and for that reason the Labour Government is likely to avoid it.

With devolution in Scotland, Northern Ireland and Wales, and possibly the English regions, another reform might be to make the House the (nominated or elected) representative of the regions, in a federalised Britain. However, such a move would give it additional weight and authority, which might enable it to challenge the Commons majority supporting the government of the day. No government is likely to create future trouble for itself in this way, so such a reform is unlikely, at any rate in the foreseeable future. Devolution itself will take long enough.

The most likely possibility therefore is that the House will be left as it is, essentially a talking shop for the life peers. A government which wants to give the impression of doing something without actually changing very much could very well phase out hereditary peers, perhaps by letting the present ones stay but legislating to extinguish the rights of their heirs.

Yet the rushed nature of legislation at the present time certainly renders a 'revising' chamber necessary to consider bills more carefully than the House of Commons (which under 'guideline' procedures often passes 'framework' legislation without properly considering the details). It must also be said that, although the Lords is dominated by hereditary peers, most of its active members are distinguished figures nominated by the government to a 'life peerage'. In addition, an active role is played on certain issues by judges and bishops who have attained their position by merit. While hereditary peers still attend (some of course being distinguished in their own right) they do not dominate discussion. The right of all hereditary peers to vote may, however, crucially influence decisions in favour of a Conservative government.

The House, being composed of generally elderly and privileged people, *does* incline towards the Conservatives. It grew increasingly out of sympathy with the minority Labour governments of the 1970s, obstructing much of their legislation. (Its delaying power of one year gives it an effective veto if a government is approaching the end of its term or fears defeat from a reintroduction of the bill in the House of Commons to override the Lords.)

However, it must be said that the House also fell out of sympathy with Thatcherite policies in the 1980s, particularly as they involved a torrent of badly conceived and drafted bills which markedly increased its pressure of work. On technical bills in which members took a personal interest the government suffered notable defeats which they could not reverse in the Commons: for example, the Wildlife and Countryside Bill (1981) and the Sunday Trading Bill (1986). This was also the fate of some of the Major Government's legislation affecting civil rights, such as the bill to give police increased rights of covert surveillance, defeated in early 1997.

Despite these and other notable stands against the New Right, the Lords' major influence is through persuasion and the correction of detail rather than direct defiance of the government. It is still worthwhile to get the support of its members because of their personal influence and weight, and the publicity this attracts for views promulgated in the House. In the last analysis, however, the role of the Lords is peripheral, and it is in the House of Commons that governments are formed and major debates take place.

THE STRUCTURE OF PARLIAMENT: THE COMMONS

The House of Commons (now 659 members) meets for about 200–250 days of the year, on a reasonably continuous basis from late October to July or August. General debates, questions to and statements from ministers, and certain stages of legislation take up full meetings of the House, generally from mid-afternoon to around midnight. Much work is done in specialised committees which meet both in the mornings and later in the day, in tandem with meetings of the whole House.

Such committees are of two general kinds: standing committees and select committees. Standing committees consider the technical details of legislation. Each Government bill put before Parliament receives a formal first reading and then a second reading on its general principles. This involves the whole House of Commons.

Since a government normally has majority support in the Commons and can count on party discipline, Government bills are almost always approved. After the second reading the bill goes to a standing committee for a clause-by-clause review of its details. Occasionally the whole House of Commons may constitute itself as a committee for this purpose, but generally standing committees consist of 40–90 members. A few of these are specialised (for example, the Scottish and Welsh Standing Committees, to which Scottish and Welsh legislation is referred)

Key term

Standing committees – committees of the House of Commons which examine bills after their second reading in order to make them more acceptable for their third reading.

and have a relatively permanent membership. Generally, however, the question of which standing committee a bill goes to is arbitrary, and membership shifts, sometimes because MPs have a direct or indirect interest in the details (see Chapter 12). Each committee is selected to reflect the balance of parties in the House of Commons so that the Government party normally has a majority.

After the technical parts are approved the bill goes back to the full House of Commons for its report stage and subsequently its third reading. All bills pass through the Commons; bills can be introduced first in the Lords but this is not usual. If the Lords amend the bill, then it returns to the Commons which considers those amendments but can override them, unless the Lords go to extremes and throw out the legislation altogether.

Private members' bills introduced by MPs without Government backing, and private bills sponsored by an outside body (normally some local authority) also go through these general stages. Without Government support, however, it is unlikely that they will survive to become law.

Since the Government so strongly dominates legislative proceedings, the process of passing legislation does not provide much of an opportunity for Parliament to affect executive action. By and large, legislative bills pass as originally drafted by the Government. The considerable amount of time given to legislation could indeed be regarded as a device whereby the two major parties' leaderships keep their restive followers occupied and concentrated on the main party battle.

The major instrument through which the legislature independently scrutinises the executive is the other main type of committee, the select committees. These are bodies whose membership is selected to serve for a parliamentary session. They are sometimes chaired by an opposition MP, and are expected to produce nonpartisan reports on detailed aspects of government administration. They may concentrate on the financial side (as with the Public Accounts Committee) or on a particular region (Scottish or Welsh affairs). Mostly, however, they are organised so as to cover the functions and responsibilities of the major ministries on a departmental basis. Committees examine documents and witnesses and issue reports on aspects of policy, which can attract widespread newspaper and television comment.

The role of committees in scrutinising administration is supplemented by questions which individual MPs can put to ministers, including the prime minister, in meetings of the full House. However, answers to these may be evasive or downright misleading. From 1987–89 the Government said it was stopping the export of arms to Iraq when instead it was actually encouraging it! Verbal questions put in the House are supplemented by written questions and answers which are reported in *Hansard* (the transcript of parliamentary procedures published each week). On certain days back-bench MPs can also raise questions for a short adjournment debate at the end of the day's proceedings. See Briefing 18.2 for an example of a Commons question and answer.

The opposition parties also debate broad aspects of government policy on the 'supply' days allotted to them on the parliamentary timetable. These are used to criticise selected aspects of policy, and to promote the opposition party's alternatives, although at a very broad level. Given the secretiveness of both government

Key term

Private members' bills
– are introduced in Parliament by backbench MPs or peers without government backing.

Key term

Select Committees –
committees of the House of Commons and the House of Lords which consider general political issues which are wider than a particular piece of legislation. The Public Accounts Committee of the House of Commons, which considers all accounts of money appropriated by Parliament, is a major example.

BRIEFINGS

18.2 EXAMPLE OF A COMMONS QUESTION AND REPLY

Mr Ian Pearson (Labour: Dudley West): Is the Secretary of State aware that Severn Trent's profits have virtually trebled since privatisation, and customer bills have rocketed by 44 per cent more than inflation, but investment has been cut every year since 1991–92? Is he also aware that since privatisation Severn Trent has paid absolutely no corporation tax on its mainstream sewage and water businesses? Does that not amount to a double whammy on consumers and taxpayers in the West Midlands?

Mr John Gummer (Secretary of State for the Environment): I am aware that, when the water companies were nationalised, they spent an average of £1.6 billion on investment: in comparable terms, they now spend an average of more than £3 billion. The Hon. Gentleman should recognise that the mess that was left behind because of public ownership of the water industry has now been cleared up and that people are coming from all over the world to ask British water companies to do their water improvements.

Source: *Hansard*, (London: HMSO, Vol. 283, 1996/7, Nov. 11–21), p. 827

and Civil Service and the influence of party rivalries, it is difficult for these set debates to be really effective or informed.

Government and Party

The presence of both the actual Government and of the alternative Government (the official Opposition) in the House of Commons has both advantages and disadvantages. It means the chief policy makers directly face elected representatives for most of the year, which makes for close and intimate communication. On the other hand, it also means that proceedings are dominated by ritual quarrels between Government and Opposition which makes it difficult for the House of Commons to organise itself as a distinct entity, or to express an independent point of view.

All one hundred or so ministers in a British government have to be Members of Parliament or peers. In practice a large majority are MPs. The Government continues so long as it is supported by a majority of MPs, normally all members of the majority party. Indeed party cohesion is central to the functioning of parliamentary democracy as it exists at the present time in Britain. It is secured by various devices, such as a special office and officials (Whips) to maintain agreement and discipline, weekly party meetings to discuss policy, and distribution of Party and Government patronage. We consider these along with evidence of some weakening of cohesion below. Of course the emergence of some 76 MPs belonging to minority parties whose support governments may need to get in a close parliamentary situation also undermines the major parties' dominance of proceedings (see Table 18.1). The basic reality, however, is tight control by the majority party leadership (see Briefing 18.3).

Table 18.1 Party strengths
in the 1992 and 1997
Parliaments

	1992	**1997**
Conservative	336	165
Labour	271	418
Liberal Democrat	20	46
Plaid Cymru	4	4
Scottish Nationalist	3	6
Social Democratic and Labour	4	3
Sinn Feìn	0	2
Ulster Unionist Party	10	10
Democratic Unionist Party	3	2
UK Unionist Party	0	1

Party unity in the Commons

Party unity, and the need to keep 'their' government in office, implies that even if a minority disagree with their leaders they will still normally vote for them against the other party or parties. The presence of most ministers in the Commons means that, out of the 350-odd members in a typical majority, a proportion approaching a third actually form the Government. The presence of so many ministers actually in the House of Commons clearly encourages party unity. Conversely it acts against the House developing views independent of the Government in office. Although the leaders of the other main party (recognised as the official Opposition) are more in the position of ordinary MPs, their enforcement of a united front against their rivals also inhibits the House from developing a 'Commons' view of most matters.

Within the Government there is a hierarchy, from parliamentary private secretaries who act as factotums for the more important ministers, through ministers of state who are normally second in command in a large department, and non-Cabinet ministers heading their own departments, to Cabinet ministers who normally take responsibility for running important departments or ministries and also participate in discussions of overall government policy.

Whatever their status or role in the Government, all its members are formally bound by the doctrine of collective ministerial responsibility. This means that ministers defend any government policy as if it were their own, even if they privately disagree with it. Internal party disputes, with occasional spectacular exceptions, are generally fought out in Cabinet committees, rather than provoking debates in Parliament. The last thing major parties want is to have internal clashes aired in a general debate. Collective responsibility and party cohesion operate to maintain at least the semblance of a united effective Government and Opposition and, in doing so, reduce the possibility of MPs expressing autonomous points of view in Parliament.

BRIEFINGS

18.3 THE ORGANISATION OF THE PARLIAMENTARY PARTIES

There are two aspects to the way MPs are organised in Parliament. One is the methods by which the party leadership keeps control over its followers. This is particularly important for the party in government: with a disciplined party majority the Government can do anything. Dissent produces humiliating defeats and an impression of weakness. The same consideration holds, less forcibly, for the opposition parties, particularly the Conservatives.

The second aspect is the question of how backbench MPs (i.e. those who do not hold office in the Government or the 'Shadow Cabinet') organise themselves to take action autonomously of the leadership, so making the Commons more of an independent forum and less of an automatic register of party decisions. The major body here is the Conservative 1922 Committee (named after a famous party revolt against continuing in the Coalition Government with the Lloyd George Liberals). The membership is confined to backbench MPs who elect their own executive committee and chair. Meetings are an obvious focus for party discontent. There is no real equivalent in the Labour Party. The Labour Reform Group of over 100 MPs was not formed until 1996 and extends to only part of the parliamentary party.

Both major parties also have large numbers of policy committees, and 8–10 regional groupings, all for backbench MPs. Cross-party policy committees could provide a 'Commons voice' on policy issues but are usually rather muted and confine themselves to shaping opinion.

The party leadership controls its party in two ways:

1. The meeting of the full parliamentary party to agree policy. Members of the leadership and the Government attend. As the latter consists of over 100 MPs anyway, all of whom are bound to support official policy, the leaders need to get only 100 extra votes to decide party policy, which all members of the parliamentary Party are bound by party rules to support. With the support of less than a third of all MPs, therefore, the Government can dominate the full Commons.

2. The Whips (the name comes from whippers-in of foxhounds at a hunt, hardly flattering for backbench MPs!). There is a Whips' Office in each of the major parties, with a Chief Whip, Deputy and four or five others, each assigned to a regional grouping of backbench MPs. The Conservative leader nominates the Chief Whip while Labour MPs elect theirs.

The Whips' job is complex. They have to ensure that all MPs turn up for important votes (their summonses are also confusingly called whips: a three-line whip is underlined thrice to indicate its importance). Primarily, however, they have to keep up party loyalty and discipline. They do this in three ways:

1. By passing up information about morale and party feelings to the leadership and passing on reassuring messages to backbenchers.

2. By rewarding loyalty, nominating favoured MPs for good committee assignments, trips abroad, and other 'treats'. Most importantly, they advise leaders on promotion to Junior Minister when the party is in government.

3. By punishing disloyalty. Whips prefer rewards to sanctions but they can punish dissenters by withholding nominations and, in serious cases, by 'withdrawing' the whip, that is, suspending or expelling dissenting MPs from the party. If suspension becomes permanent, MPs will lose their party endorsement at the election and thus their seat. But this sanction is like the atomic bomb, hurting the user as well as the target and rarely used.

Labour has supplemented these parliamentary arrangements by having a general Party Disciplinary Committee which can suspend MPs, as it has recently done in Paisley.

Sanctions and rewards only work, of course, because MPs stand or fall together as a party and are strongly motivated to support 'their' Opposition or 'their' Government. Discipline is therefore ineffective where a serious ideological revolt takes place, as with the Eurosceptics under the Major Government.

PARLIAMENTARY SCRUTINY OF GOVERNMENT

Parliamentary scrutiny of government actions, in the sense of critically reviewing what ministers and civil servants do or intend to do, is important for two reasons. First the wider discussion, sometimes by experts, may improve the quality of the policies being pursued. And second, Parliament is, in constitutional theory, the

ON THE RECORD

MARTIN BELL MP

I am the least intentional MP ever elected (though not the least determined). My candidature came about entirely by accident. Since the Government was sitting on the Downey Report, the Labour and Liberal Democrat parties decided that they themselves would have to do something to unseat Mr Neil Hamilton. Separately they could not achieve it, since Tatton was the fourth safest seat in the country. They looked for an outside candidate to stand as an Independent, while both their own candidates stood down. After a week they had not come up with a name acceptable to both of them. Then they thought of mine. I accepted, reluctantly, because I felt that I might achieve something worthwhile, and I would regret not having made the attempt. 'There is a tide in the affairs of men'.

As a foreign correspondent I had taken a layman's interest in the allegations of corruption in British political life. But the publication, by the *Guardian*, of transcripts of the evidence given in the Downey Commission was a shock and an eye-opener, especially in its revelations about Mr Hamilton: that he misled the Deputy Prime Minister, Mr Heseltine, about his relationship with a lobbyist, Mr Ian Greer. And that he received £10,000 from a lobbyist without declaring it, either to the Commons or to the Inland Revenue. To me it was scandalous that he took money from a lobbyist at all. I used an Army term to describe it. It was 'conduct unbecoming'.

The most worrying trend in public life – and for that matter in my former profession, journalism – is the

extent to which its ethos and values are money-driven. We are invited to admire a man because he is rich. There had been a decline of principle and honour as driving forces.

Standards in public life have declined, though not catastrophically. There is, by American standards, a small amount of corruption. We do not sell ambassadorships nor do we buy seats in the House of Commons. But even a small amount of corruption is too much.

I think it is necessary that the enforcement of appropriate standards be taken outside Parliament itself. Sir Gordon Downey remains an officer of the House and his reports can be – and have been – suppressed by the Government (to its own disadvantage, as it turned out). My own role as Independent will depend on the opportunities that arise. I shall serve my constituents, of course. I shall also bring to bear my experience in the war zones: the land mines issue, for example. And I shall do what I can to advance the cause of an honest and accountable Parliament, a cause already strengthened by the result in Tatton.

I have no quarrel with press coverage of my campaign. I doubt whether the tabloids' obsession with the private life of politicians serves any other purpose than to boost their circulation. We have some of the best newspapers in the world – and some of the worst. As for TV, the limitations imposed or self-imposed on it during an election campaign make most of its coverage – to my mind – a waste of air time. The public took the same view and switched off.

main national institution representing the views of the population. Potentially at least it is able to express them more freely than press and television, not being constrained by censorship and libel laws. In other words, the Government is *accountable* to the people through Parliament.

The leader of the party with the largest number of elected members in the House of Commons is assumed to have had his or her policies approved by voters, and is therefore said to have a 'mandate' to carry them through in government. However, many problems unforeseen at the time of the election campaign emerge in the three to five years separating most elections. Many of these could be raised and examined in Parliament. But there is an ongoing tension between the electoral mandate and continuing parliamentary scrutiny, which we look at here.

Electoral mandate versus continuing parliamentary scrutiny

We should start by noting the major obstacles to informed parliamentary debate on policy alternatives. The first is the way in which parliamentary processes and procedures are designed to facilitate Conservative–Labour battles. The domination of business first by the Government, and second by the official leadership of the next largest party, constitutes the major obstacle to independent initiatives by the House of Commons as such.

This institutional monopoly is buttressed both by constitutional doctrine and the entrenched attitudes of many MPs. They consider that the Government's ultimate responsibility to serve popular wishes is guaranteed by exposure to a general election at the end of its term. In the interim, decision making will only be disrupted by undue parliamentary interference. The task of the parties in Parliament is, therefore, to support their government or, if out of office, to keep up opposition morale by attacking the office holders. As Parliament is simply an arena for partisan encounters it can have no collective and independent role *vis-à-vis* the Government. Nor *should* it, since that would blur the responsibility of the majority party for government policy in which it will be judged at the next election.

This belief is in turn linked to a broader idea, also embedded in constitutional theory, that the Government knows best what to do in the public interest, and should be left (at least between elections) to get on with it unhindered. This colours opinion on a wide range of practical questions other than the nature of parliamentary debate:

- government secrecy (desirable, because it prevents too much outside intrusion into government business);

- reform of the relationship between party votes and seats in the House of Commons (undesirable, because the present system, though grossly unfair to third parties, generally allows one major party to take clear responsibility for forming governments and framing policy);

- accountability of the leadership to party members (undesirable, because it renders leaders, who may become ministers, less able to act decisively on their own initiative).

Support of strong, unfettered government thus tells against effective day-to-day scrutiny in Parliament. The justification is that 'the public interest' (a term often used to justify government action) can only be served this way. Governments must not be put under pressure to meet immediate demands, for to do so might result in an inability to plan for the future. In turn the Opposition should set out an alternative government programme for the next election, supported by its MPs. Nobody in the major parties should engage in independent action outside the party line.

These views were very characteristic of Thatcherite thinking in the 1980s. Conservative backbench opposition to government measures was regarded as disloyal. There is no evidence that New Labour is any more relaxed.

The case for MPs adopting a more independent and critical attitude to what the Government is doing is that most of what gets done during its term of office is only tenuously related to the broad lines of policy presented at the election. Implementation of these demands requires many intermediate decisions, some of which may be debatable. Moreover, much of the business of government is unrelated to electorally endorsed party policies and carried on by unelected civil servants. Wider and more informed discussion might improve rather than hamper the business of government. A growing belief that this is so has spurred MPs to develop procedures for discussing the justification, and likely outcomes, of Government policy, on a broadly nonparty basis. We discuss these below.

Government and journalists

The obstacles to establishing even simple facts about what the Government is doing can hardly be exaggerated, given the administrative secrecy already discussed. The selective management of information by government is best illustrated in the parliamentary context by the 'lobby system' of specialist journalists attached to Parliament. (Incidentally it is significant that British political reporters, almost without exception, are concentrated within Parliament rather than in the executive offices, where they have no official place assigned to them. This means that news about government comes second-hand through Parliament rather than directly from within the Civil Service itself.)

The parliamentary 'lobby' is a name given to specially privileged parliamentary correspondents of the main newspapers and television and radio channels who spend most of their time in the 'lobbies' of Parliament. They are given confidential information and have ready access to ministers (rarely to civil servants). It is understood that in return they will reveal only what they are expressly authorised to publish. Failure to observe the understanding leads to exclusion from their privileges. In this way the information that gets published is divulged at the initiative of the Government, and therefore consists of what the Government wants to reveal rather than what it wants to keep hidden.

> **Key term**
>
> **The lobby system** – the name given to specially selected correspondents of the main newspapers, TV, and radio stations who are given confidential information by the government on a non-attributable basis. Not to be confused with 'the lobby', or pressure group system in Parliament.

Two developments have undermined this traditional way of managing news. One is the increasing practice by ministers and administrators of 'briefing' selected journalists, usually in order to resist or push policy proposals within the administration. This is an especially common tactic when resisting budget cuts, even on the part of such figures as the Joint Chiefs of Staff, the supreme military commanders. The briefing shades into the 'leak' of unauthorised news in the case of nominally subordinate administrators opposed to policies backed by their superiors. There have been a lot of these leaks as civil servants became disaffected under the Conservative governments (Chapter 9).

Briefings still represent selective management of information in someone's own interest. The other process undermining the lobby system is the development of a more independent stance on the part of political journalists. This is linked to the spread of 'investigative journalism' where stories are pursued at the initiative of the newspapers or television editors (Chapter 14). In line with this trend, journalists and newspapers have also been prepared to risk prosecution either under the Official Secrets Act, or under the D notices circulated by governments to prevent discussion of topics relating to national security, or under the severe British libel laws, while refusing to reveal the sources of their information. The editors of some newspapers have withdrawn from the lobby (notably, the *Independent* and the *Guardian*) and now explicitly quote their official sources.

In spite of this, however, the ethos of the lobby system still predominates in British government. Information is for insiders rather than outsiders and the Government (or at least its constituent ministers and administrators) determines who shall be insiders. MPs depend heavily on published material for their own information, to supplement erratic personal contacts and the selective confidences of party leaders. So government management of news deprives them of a major source of information just as much as it deprives the general public.

Live radio or television coverage of parliamentary proceedings has not changed this situation, as what is broadcast tends to be set debates which are covered by the quality newspapers anyway. Only if Parliament itself develops procedures for uncovering and evaluating important information will broadcasts be more illuminating.

This accepted, the set-piece exchanges typical of debates or of Prime Minister's Question Time do perform a democratic function. They oblige prime ministers and ministers to state their positions clearly and to make some defence of them. In so doing they have to be convincing to their own supporters and to put up a good defence against Opposition attacks and taunts. For most of the time these exchanges are simply theatre. On some occasions however, such as the attack by Geoffrey Howe on Margaret Thatcher following his resignation as Foreign Secretary in 1990, they can contribute to major political changes.

Scrutiny through select committees

One way to make information more widely available is to use parliamentary privileges to force investigation of important policy areas and publish the findings, in a way in which press and television themselves cannot. Attempts to do this in the last 20 years have concentrated on extending the remit, and strengthening the organisation, of an old parliamentary institution, the select committees. As mentioned earlier, these are bodies with a relatively permanent all-party membership

BRIEFINGS

18.4 THE SELECT COMMITTEE ON EUROPEAN LEGISLATION

We have already discussed the difficulties of this committee – part of the general 'democratic deficit' of the EU – and their dependence on government goodwill. The best that Parliament can hope for in controlling EU legislation is to influence the British Government's negotiating position within the European bodies. In practice, this has been difficult. All the Committee can do is recommend that a matter be referred for debate to a standing committee or, in certain important cases, to the House as a whole. With 30 to 40 documents arriving at the Committee every day, there are few that can be given further consideration.

Once an issue is earmarked for debate, there remains the problem of how Parliament is to influence the Government's negotiating position at the European Council. No specific amendments are allowed to be made to the Commission proposals, and the House or Standing Committee may only debate on a 'take note' motion (see Chapter 5). Additional problems arise from the fact that a maximum of 90 minutes is allowed for a debate, and even this small amount of time is not made available until two hours before midnight.

In 1976, Michael Foot, then Leader of the House, stated on behalf of the Government:

> Ministers will not give agreement to any legislative proposal recommended by the Scrutiny Committee for further consideration by the House before the House has given it that consideration, unless the Committee has indicated that agreement need not be withheld, or *the Minister concerned is satisfied that agreement should not be withheld for reasons which he will at the first opportunity explain to the House.*

The italic type emphasises the considerable freedom of action which the British Government has reserved for itself. The Committee faces further scrutiny problems when the Commons are in recess. No debate can be called and the Committee cannot even meet. The fact that the parliamentary timetable is not co-ordinated with the timetable of the Council of Ministers means that the Committee is often in a position where it cannot carry out its functions. When an instrument is adopted in Council before it reached the Committee, the limit of the Government's obligation is 'that the Committee should be informed, by deposit of the relevant document and by submission of an explanatory memorandum, of instances where fast-moving documents go for adoption before scrutiny can take place'.

Parliamentary approval is not required for European legislation. The Government *may* take it into account but can also ignore it if it wants.

often chaired by an opposition MP and traditionally nonpartisan, which are designed to investigate detailed policy areas and to produce agreed reports. In these, if anywhere, a parliamentary view can be expressed, and the facts discovered.

In the second half of the 1990s there are 26 select committees, the majority covering a particular department of government. These include Agriculture, Defence, Education and employment, Environment and transport, Foreign affairs, Home affairs, Social security, Trade and industry, Treasury and cabinet services and the Scottish and Welsh Offices. Other committees include: European legislation (see Briefing 18.4), Administration, Privileges, standards and procedures, Public accounts and Statutory instruments. Table 18.2 gives an indication of what they are, who chairs them (a Government or Opposition MP) and what inquiries they undertake.

Despite this impressive coverage their role is limited. Committees derive their power from the House of Commons, and governments try to ensure that select committee membership reflects the balance between parties. Indeed, where this cannot be ensured the committee is not formed, as happened with Scottish Affairs in 1987 (when there were few backbench Conservative MPs from Scotland to participate).

However, government must at least seem to co-operate with the select committees. By refusing to allow civil servants to appear before a committee, it appears to be covering up mistakes. Furthermore, committees not only have general powers to choose their area of inquiry but they also have a right to see the relevant documents and to summon persons to appear before them, and to make them answer all questions which the committee puts. Witnesses cannot constitutionally excuse themselves by claiming that this may subject them to civil (legal) actions.

This is the theory but the practice is different. When seeking to elicit information in the early 1990s from Ian and Kevin Maxwell (newspaper proprietors and sons of the late Robert Maxwell, suspected of massive embezzlement of company pension funds to prop up their own business), the Social Security Committee divided across party lines on how hard to push. At least one Labour member was worried that, if they insisted on the brothers answering their questions, it would strengthen the hand of Conservatives who want more general restrictions on the right to silence. However, precedents had already been set by at least two Conservative Government ministers – Lord Young over the privatisation of Rover cars and Sir Leon Brittan over the sale of Westland Helicopters – who successfully refused to answer select committee questions.

The ability of committees to elicit information from civil servants was also limited by the Armstrong Memorandum, which was adopted by the Head of the Civil Service, Sir Robin Butler. When Sir Robin appeared before the Treasury and Civil Service Committee in 1988 he explained that the duty of civil servants to their ministers was similar to that owed by military personnel to their commanding officer. Thus civil servants could only respond to committees (or indeed appear before them) if this had been approved by the minister.

The question of how far civil servants can appear, or give evidence, to committees, is crucial because members mostly lack any professional or research backing of their own and depend on witnesses or expert evidence for their

Committee	Chair	Notable Past Inquiries
Agriculture	Peter Luff (C)	'Mad cow' disease
Defence	Bruce George (Lab)	Gulf War Syndrome
Education and Employment	Candy Atherton (Lab)	'Top people's pay', Urban education
Environment, Transport and Regional Affairs	Andrew Bennett (Lab)	Computer reservation systems for airlines
European Legislation	Jimmy Hood (Lab)	All aspects of EU legislation
Foreign Affairs	Diane Abbott (Lab)	Weapons proliferation in the Third World, Pergau Dam
Health	David Hinchliffe (Lab)	London Ambulance Service
Home Affairs	Chris Mullin (Lab)	Appointment of judiciary
International Development	Bowen Wells (C)	Aid programmes
National Heritage	Gerald Kaufman (Lab)	National Lottery provisions
Public Administration	Peter Bradley (Lab)	'Next Steps' reforms
Public Accounts	Robert Sheldon (Lab)	Sale of County Hall (Former LCC HQ)
Science and Technology	David Atkinson (C)	Scientific education
Scottish Affairs	David Marshall (Lab)	Food poisoning in Scotland (e-coli epidemics)
Social Security	Archy Kirkwood (LD)	Pensions funds
Standards and Privileges	Robert Sheldon (Lab)	'Cash for Questions', MPs' interests
Trade and Industry	Martin O'Neill (Lab)	Export credits
Treasury	Giles Radice (Lab)	Barings Bank collapse
Welsh Affairs	(To be nominated)	Welsh colliery closures

Source: *House of Commons Weekly Information Bulletin*, 19 July 1997, pp. 18–24

information. The exception is the oldest committee, the Public Accounts Committee, with a large and well-qualified staff and back-up from auditors and accountants. However, the PAC can only pass judgement on whether money has been spent as authorised by Parliament and cannot comment on policy as such. Much of the work of select committees is like this, necessary but dull, although many MPs suspect them of being a 'gravy train' for a few individuals favoured by parties and Whips. Only certain MPs are regarded as suitable for particular committees. Thus Foreign Affairs appointees come from backbenchers who can be trusted not to leak information to the media and who endorse current defence policy. This ensures that important committees enjoy a strong sense of cohesion, but perhaps only on condition that they are not controversial and challenging. In contrast, less favoured committees – for example, Environment, Education and

Social Security – are less cohesive. They have fewer secrets, commitment is less robust and there is a higher turnover of members. They are also the committees where established policy has been challenged more.

The method of selection to the more exclusive committees is nicely illustrated by the Defence Select Committee. Prior to 1987 this enjoyed a close relationship with the Ministry of Defence. The three Labour MPs were considered 'sound'. The appointment of a left-winger opposed to the British nuclear deterrent (a 'unilateralist') would have jeopardised that relationship. Following the 1987 election, the Labour Whip removed Dr John Gilbert (Labour MP for Dudley, East) because of his criticisms of the Party's defence policy. The two other Labour members threatened to resign if he was replaced by a unilateralist.

This is not the only problem which has occurred following elections. Critics of current procedures point to the length of time necessary to reconstitute select committees for the new parliamentary term. Following the 1983 general election, it took nearly six months to set up the various committees, owing to party objections. First, the Labour leadership refused to nominate members until after the Shadow Cabinet (the parliamentary leadership in opposition) was elected. Second, the minority parties claimed to be underrepresented. Third, a problem arose with the 13-person Scottish Affairs Committee. Because of the limited number of Scottish Conservative MPs there were too few to allow the Government to form a majority, so it was not formed at all! All the complaints about delays in the setting up of committees, reluctance of witnesses to appear, provision of documents and information, are echoed again in the report of the Liaison Committee on the work of Select Committees for 1996–97 (HC.323–1). So things do not seem to have improved in the meantime.

In part the manoeuvres surrounding select committees reflect party jostling for position. The Government party loses nothing from committees not functioning; indeed, this relieves departments from immediate scrutiny. Increased representation of the Opposition would increase scrutiny and provide opportunities to embarrass the Government. If the Government majority on a committee is only one, the willingness of some backbenchers to criticise the Government means that a favourable majority is never certain.

Parties also interfere with other aspects of committees. We have already mentioned the bias towards picking members with 'sound' views. Party Whips also influence the choice of convenor. In 1995 a concerted attempt was made by Conservatives to oust the Labour MP Greville Janner because of an alleged conflict of interest between his consultancy activities and the inquiry into top people's salaries. (In reality the Government was embarrassed by the publicity given to newly enriched chairmen of privatised industries.) Nicholas Winterton was ejected by his own Conservative Whips in 1992 because he caused too much trouble as chair of the Health Committee.

The Whips' interference with the appointment of committees can go even further, as far as attempts to influence the course of their investigations. In late 1996 David Willetts, a Whip who had become a junior minister in the Conservative Government, was forced to resign because he had tried to direct Conservative members of the Privileges Committee away from the investigation of corruption on the part of Neil Hamilton, a Conservative exminister. This was an unusually strong assertion of party power. Probably, however, a lot of such interference goes on all the time. Willetts was simply exceptional, and unlucky, in making a note of what he had done and being punished for it.

Party influences also make themselves felt in internal divisions on the committees. For example, the Foreign Affairs Committee divided along party lines in a report on the sinking of the Argentine cruiser *General Belgrano* in the Falklands War, with the loss of over 700 lives. This was attacked on the grounds that the sinking was unnecessary. In the committee seven Conservatives argued there had been no cover-up while four Labour members believed there was evidence of ministerial deception of Parliament. (This was the committee to whose Conservative chairman a civil servant, Clive Ponting, leaked papers through a committee member showing that the government was lying. The chairman immediately reported the leak back to the Ministry of Defence so that they could plug it!)

In similar cases the Home Affairs Committee divided on party lines in a report on the Police Special Branch; and the Employment Committee on whether or not British Coal should reinstate miners sacked during the 1984–85 strike, with one Conservative MP siding with Labour on this issue.

The major parties thus use committees as places to carry on their controversies just as they use Parliament as a whole. This threatens the committees' ability to express a cohesive and independent 'parliamentary' view.

Nevertheless, select committees do provide an opportunity for backbenchers to participate, even in a limited way, in government. Inexperienced newcomers have an ideal opening to learn about policy making and administration and, perhaps, to start making a name. Those who might be considered 'has-beens' or 'never-will-bes' are able to participate actively and are more likely to take independent positions (this applies also to members of third parties). And all backbenchers have the potential to put forward the views of particular interests. Thus committees offer a forum for various groups whose views might otherwise not get a hearing, even if action after that is problematical.

INTERESTS: PROPER AND IMPROPER REPRESENTATION

This question of representing interests lies at the heart both of constitutional theory and of the actual practice of parliamentary and party politics. As we saw in Chapter 12, an immense variety of groups and organisations are affected by government policy and want to bend it to favour themselves. The most common and effective way to do this is through contacts with government ministers and civil servants. This illustrates the general predominance of the Executive over Parliament in Britain.

However, legislation can also have very important consequences for particular groups. For example, even such a seemingly boring and technical provision as regulation of hygiene on caravan sites could gain or lose site owners and landowners millions of pounds, depending on what facilities they had to provide themselves or what the water companies were obliged to provide for them. Water companies will also be drawn in to this debate in self-defence (see Briefing 12.5 in Chapter 12).

Mid-nineteenth century institution builders thoroughly approved of the idea that MPs should be linked to outside interests, particularly to business and commerce. They did not approve of MPs being full-time politicians anyway, and thought they could gain both money and experience from being active outside Parliament. Even members with inherited wealth would be linked with the landed interest through their estates or with business through the management of their money.

This generally relaxed attitude towards MPs' links with business and commerce is one of the institutional practices inherited from the mid-nineteenth century which may have become counter-productive for modern democracy. This is due to a series of social and economic changes which have transformed the nature of outside interests and of their representation in Parliament. These include the fact that most MPs are now full-time political professionals, rather than independently wealthy amateurs. This is truer of the parliamentary Labour Party, drawn mainly from the 'talking professions' of teaching, law and journalism, than of the Conservatives. In the case of Conservative MPs with business directorships and consultancies, it is unclear whether they have secured these posts because of their political position rather than having gone on to politics after achieving business success. The former seems true in many cases, so one has to ask why companies and firms find it useful to have MPs on their payroll. Could it be that this favours their business interests?

One reason for this may be that the scope of political and parliamentary action has broadened immensely in the course of the twentieth century. When governments regulated only a few aspects of the economy, and firms could act freely and independently, the business interests involved in Parliament were few and clearly defined. Now that politics is co-terminous with social life, and everything the Government does has economic effects, political influence is much more important and pervasive. How far should MPs have links with firms which stand to gain or lose billions by parliamentary decisions which they can affect?

Some attempt has been made to deal with the problem by requiring MPs to register their interests and financial links in writing (the Parliamentary Register of Interests) and to declare their interest before participating in a debate or committee. However, this has not prevented their lobbying colleagues on behalf of particular provisions which they have been paid to promote. It also transpired in the last Parliament that members were being directly paid to ask parliamentary questions on topics where firms were interested (at £1000 per question!).

Individual MPs' links with big business are to some extent legitimised by the fact that the parties to which they belong have institutionalised links with business as well. Companies have made no bones about the fact that they give millions of pounds to the Conservative Party (which has also had more dubious donations from overseas, mainly from Chinese businessmen). Are they only seeking a better climate for business as a whole, or more particular favours? Labour MPs have often been sponsored and paid for by trade unions, though the practice is declining. However, wealthy Labour supporters have paid directly for research support, particularly for the Leader's Office. In both the Conservative and Labour cases, donations have been left anonymous.

All this led to allegations of generalised 'sleaze' in the last Parliament. These hit the Conservatives harder than Labour, because of their more extensive business links and ability while in government to do more for their sponsors.

Key term

Sleaze – a popular term, much used in the mid-1990s, referring to the corrupt and improper behaviour of public officials, initially mainly members of the Conservative government.

Key term

Committee of Inquiry – a committee appointed by the government, but composed of members outside Parliament, and charged with the job of inquiring into and reporting on a particular matter.

In response to widespread disquiet about individual MPs' interests, John Major as Prime Minister took the unprecedented step of setting up an extra-parliamentary Committee under a judge, Lord Nolan, to investigate. Its recommendations for greater disclosure of interests were reluctantly accepted by the Select Committee on Standards and Privileges in 1996. Under the Labour Government, the Nolan Committee has gone on to investigate party financing, which may in the end force parties into greater transparency about whom they are beholden to.

Information gathering and 'leaks'

Lessening the secret dependence of MPs on particular interests should leave more space to debate and probe them. A prerequisite for informed investigation is, however, the availability of accurate information. The Government and Civil Service have a near monopoly on this but no incentive to disclose it. On the contrary, revealing what is going on might embarrass them or force them to change a dubious or unpopular policy to which they are committed (see Briefing 18.5).

BRIEFINGS

18.5 THE ARMS TO IRAQ SCANDAL

One example of the lengths governments can take to conceal facts from Parliament is the Arms to Iraq scandal. In the 1980s Iraq and Iran fought an eight-year war. To avoid exacerbating the situation most Western governments, including the British, agreed not to export arms to either side. Parliament was assured by government ministers at several points in the late 1980s that the policy had not changed. But in fact the relevant Cabinet committee had decided to supply Iraq with arms from 1987 onwards. Ministers simply lied to Parliament. To compound the scandal, executives of one of the companies encouraged to export arms by the Government were then charged with illegal export in the early 1990s. Their trial could have led to heavy prison sentences. The defence claim that the action was officially authorised rested on documents which the Solicitor-General and other ministers tried to withhold from the court by signing a 'public interest immunity certificate' which stated that their disclosure would endanger national security. In fact disclosure to the court would not have endangered security at all, just embarrassed the Government. To save themselves, the Ministers again lied, as well as being prepared to see innocent men go to jail. Only disclosure of the facts by an eccentric ex-minister, Alan Clark, prevented this outcome. The disclosure provoked a judicial enquiry, the Scott Commission, whose report condemned the Government but was accepted as absolving them by the Conservative majority in the House of Commons.

As this is the case, very little is in fact divulged by Government to Parliament – or to select committees – of its own free will. It is in this context that the practice of 'leaking' information should be viewed.

One controversial factor associated with the working of select committees has been the prevalence of leaks (the passing on of confidential information, usually to the newspapers for publication). This has taken place both from Government and Civil Service to select committees and from these to press or television. Typical examples are *The Times*'s reports in 1990 (on the basis of internal discussion in the Social Services Committee) on errors in government statistics which affected social security payments, and the *Independent*'s reports from the Home Affairs Committee on the weaknesses of the Crown Prosecution Service.

Of course, given the use of secrecy by Government and Civil Service to stifle independent discussion, the occurrence of such leaks from select committees may not be a bad thing. It counteracts selective official leaks to justify government policy, which reached their apex in the later Thatcher years. Nevertheless, leaks can undermine mutual confidence between members of the committees and so undermine their effectiveness. Reforms of the Official Secrets Act in the current Parliament may ease this problem by vastly extending the amount of information publicly available.

Probably the major problem of select committees however – as with Parliament itself and the Cabinet – is the lack of any real administrative or research support. Operating with the minimal assistance of a Clerk of Parliament and a couple of secretaries, possibly with a seconded part-time researcher, they rely heavily on published reports and the evidence which witnesses are willing to give (and as we have seen, witnesses cannot in practice be effectively compelled to reveal information).

This makes the select committees, like the Government itself, heavily dependent on what civil servants provide. As these will not wish to embarrass either their department or their minister, it is clear that whatever information they volunteer will be limited. Without independent resources of their own, select committees are bound to be severely restricted in what they do. The only exception is the Public Accounts Committee with its large staff. However, its remit is confined to cases of maladministration of funds, not evaluating policy.

As their activities cut across the major parties' partisan battles in the House of Commons, and have the potential for unexpectedly undermining one side or the other's positions, the Conservative and Labour leaderships have wanted to keep select committees weak and dependent. This is particularly true when they have a weak parliamentary position and are straining every nerve either to keep themselves in or get the other side out. So perhaps New Labour, with its massive majority, can afford to be more tolerant of their activities.

In spite of their weaknesses, select committees have provided an independent standpoint within Parliament from which to evaluate government activities critically. Without them much necessary information would simply not be available. Over the two parliamentary sessions of 1987–89, for example, the Social Security Committee published a detailed report about resourcing the National Health Service, while the Energy Committee criticised the proposals to privatise electricity. In the meantime, the Defence Committee pursued mismanagement in defence procurement, while the Transport Committee uncovered the complex and hidden world surrounding the computer reservation system for airlines.

However, select committees, like the House of Lords, are only operating at the margins of power. Without more resources – above all to extract information – the parliamentary scrutiny of executive action will remain ineffective and largely ignored by the very people who are supposed to respond to it. The typical ministry reaction to an unfavourable committee report is to ignore it for a year or two in the hope that it will be simply buried by events such as an election or change of government. The committees have no power to demand an immediate response, still less to obtain remedial action for the abuses or weaknesses they have uncovered.

BACKBENCH REBELLIONS SINCE THE 1970s

The major reason for committee and parliamentary weakness in the face of the executive is the loyalty owed by MPs to their party, particularly to the party in power. Much of the preceding discussion has emphasised the key role of party cohesion and loyalty in maintaining the authority of the Government. This raises two crucial and related questions. What mechanisms are available to enforce loyalty? And under what circumstances can loyalty break down? Both relate closely to problems of democratic theory. Tight party discipline is the prerequisite for strong and effective executive action. As a result, the electorate can make a rational choice on the record of an incumbent government at the general election, without having to consider whether it was unable to do as promised owing to circumstances beyond its control.

Members may break with party discipline, however, in order to vote with their conscience or their select committee, or to reflect the interests and preferences of their constituencies. This tension between electoral mandate and individual members' duty to conscience and constituency has increased in recent years.

Enforcing party cohesion

Parties enforce cohesion through a variety of strategies and mechanisms. Within the majority party, the party leader is also Prime Minister and can therefore appoint MPs to government office as a reward for loyalty (and oust them for disloyalty). The Prime Minister can also award honours and make appointments, as can to a lesser extent the leader of the Opposition. The Prime Minister has the power to dissolve Parliament and call a general election through a formal request to the Queen. The uncertainty of the result prevents this threat being made very often but it can promote cohesion on a particular issue. Edward Heath, Conservative Prime Minister from 1970 to 1974 – widely unpopular among backbenchers for his technocratic approach, lack of personal warmth, and failure to distribute honours more widely – still secured a majority of 309 to 301 on the second reading of his much opposed bill to join the European Community (February 1972). He made the issue a vote of confidence, and thus indicated his willingness to hold an election if defeated. Similarly, Mrs Thatcher's uncompromising

Whips – officials appointed by parliamentary parties in the Lords and the Commons to promote party discipline.

attachment to her measures usually brought Conservative rebels into line. Blairite discipline has had similar effects on parliamentary Labour in recent years.

Supporting the leadership are party officials known as Whips, selected from MPs not in the Government (or alternative government, in the case of the Opposition party). One of the Whips' powers is withdrawal of the 'whip' from a dissident, with resulting loss of access to parliamentary order papers and backbench party committees. The ultimate sanction is expulsion from the parliamentary party, involving loss of the party endorsement at the next election and near-certain electoral defeat.

The Whips allocate members to standing committees on government bills, recommend members for standing committees on private members' bills, interfere with select committee appointments and choose members for parliamentary and party delegations abroad. Such incentives can be used to improve the atmosphere on the back benches and thus encourage cohesion. Prime Ministers rely on Whips for advice about appointments to junior government posts, which are the stepping stones to more senior positions. Margaret Thatcher's failure to select ideologically 'sound' Whips contributed to the emergence by 1990 of a Cabinet which was out of tune with many of her own policy positions, and helped to undermine her at the crucial point.

'Ideology' (adherence to a particular doctrine or a programme) was traditionally associated more with Labour than the Conservatives. However, Conservative MPs have become noticeably more right-wing in recent years. Ideology promotes cohesion but may also lead to splits, as the true believers quarrel with those disposed to compromise.

Factionalism has been more evident in the past in the Labour party than among Conservatives, a situation that the Blairite leadership is determined to avoid. However, the experience of the 1990s clearly shows dissent spreading to the Conservative Party. In part this is due to the influx of new style Tories in the 1980s who, like Mrs Thatcher herself, did not fit the traditional male, public school, business stereotype. Many of these populist, self-made men and women were stridently free-trade and patriotic, and thus slid easily into Eurosceptic attitudes in the 1990s. As new converts they were much more ideological than established members and much more prepared to split the party over a principle, in their case, the preservation of 'British sovereignty' against 'Europe'. Meanwhile Labour, desperate to avoid a fifth election defeat in 1997, preserved an uncharacteristic unity despite the reservations of many on the left about Tony Blair's abandonment of traditional positions. This uncharacteristic display of unity seems to be continuing now they are in government, aided by the Party organisational reforms we have described (Chapter 16).

Dissent within parliamentary parties

Even so, governments no longer can rely on unquestioning support if they go against the wishes of substantial numbers of their backbenchers. Along with a decline of deference towards government has come a decay of other forces making for party cohesion. For example, constituency parties will be less inclined to blame rebels when they themselves feel critical of the leadership. And if their own leaders are not achieving what MPs want, the prospect of voting to weaken the Government and allowing another party to gain power is less alarming than it used to be for ideologues who adopt an 'all or nothing' approach. The secession of the Social Democrats in 1981–82 was the culmination of increasing factional tensions among Labour MPs in the 1970s, the last time they were in government (1974–79). Dissent became almost epidemic in the 1974–79 Parliament. No less than 45 per cent of all whipped divisions in the 1978–79 session saw some Labour MPs voting against the Government. (Whipped divisions are those where the leadership requires MPs to vote in a certain way.) What is more, only 62 Labour MPs (19 per cent of the total) cast no dissenting votes, while 40 cast more than 50, and 9 more than 100.

Internal tensions also rose among the Conservatives during that period. Under the aloof Prime Minister Edward Heath (1970–74) an identifiable body of Conservative MPs emerged with a hard line on monetary policy and social issues. They actually took over the leadership with the victory and premiership of Mrs Thatcher. Semipublic dissent by the 'wets' from the prevailing monetarist orthodoxy then became common, and increased in extent after 1980.

The watering down of Thatcherite policies under John Major (1990–97) left the more die-hard members of the party disgruntled. They found a cause to rally round in opposition to 'Europe'. The Government's progressive loss of its majority meant that even small groups of determined opponents within the party could force its hand. An overreaction by the Government, in withdrawing the whip from six 'Eurosceptics' who had voted against it, demonstrated its weakness. It was forced to readmit them without guarantees of their future compliance. In the last Parliament, Conservative dissent did not so much provoke open votes against the Government on legislative measures, as constant trimming and withdrawals by the Government itself in the face of strong internal opposition.

From Heath to Major, internal Conservative dissension markedly increased. Indeed it now seems to have the potential to tear the party apart. The dissensions have been exacerbated by electoral defeat, to which they undoubtedly contributed in the first place. Labour unity may be reinforced for the moment by its electoral victory. But the party has a long history of dissent and it is hard to believe that this will not show as hard decisions need to be taken.

THE ROLE OF THIRD PARTIES

The House of Commons is so dominated by the struggles of Conservatives and Labour that we have not given much attention to third parties. Yet if Parliament is to find a useful role apart from sustaining the Government and official Opposition, their part is crucial. Only they are structurally placed outside the main struggle between Government and Opposition. Thus they can make criticisms which are not simply directed at doing the Government down or which may have been overlooked by the main parties.

Third party representation in Parliament has grown, as Figure 18.1 shows. In the Parliament elected in 1997 there are 30 regionalist MPs particularly concerned with issues affecting their own part of Britain. The Ulster Unionists, the largest single group, are also a 'single issue' regional group in this sense, overwhelmingly concerned with Government policy on Northern Ireland.

Figure 18.1 Percentage of minor party MPs and percentage of Liberal MPs – 1945–97

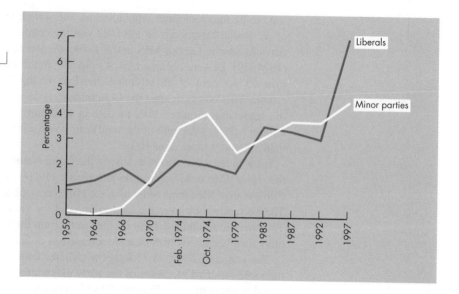

Such MPs are not going to be strongly interested in general British issues, or at any rate they will be willing to trade support on these for regional concessions, if the government is in a tight corner. The Liberals are the party most likely to act as a genuinely independent voice on questions of general concern. It is for this reason that their Parliamentary growth is shown separately in Figure 18.1.

Liberal strength in Parliament has grown fairly consistently, after their initial recovery in the early 1960s. The electoral system, however, prevents them really translating their substantial share of votes into parliamentary seats. This creates a vicious circle. The limited number of Liberal MPs has not been strong enough to break the hold of Conservatives and Labour over parliamentary procedures. This means that House of Commons' debates and questions are always dominated by the clash between the main parties. The clash also spreads into select committee proceedings and appointments. For example, only one Liberal chairs a committee in the present Parliament although in many ways Liberals would be ideal in forging a 'Commons view' outside the main party battle. The parliamentary weakness of the Liberals means that they cannot force through the electoral reforms which would end it. Thus the 'third force' which might help to develop a genuinely autonomous role for Parliament is permanently disadvantaged by the latter's institutional bias towards the two main parties, inherited like so many other British practices and procedures, from the mid-nineteenth century.

POSSIBLE REFORMS OF PARLIAMENT?

Political reform is not impossible in Britain, as Scottish and Welsh devolution shows. However, it has to be in some government's interest to carry it through. No majority party will want to transfer some of its power to others if this risks undermining its own position. The unique electoral importance of Scotland and Wales to Labour, and the ability of regional nationalism to threaten this, accounts for devolution. Only if the Liberals are in a similarly powerful position to threaten or reward Labour will the Government or its successor carry through the crucial change to a more proportional election system. This change would produce a strong bloc of 50–100 Liberal MPs, sufficient to deprive both major parties of an absolute parliamentary majority in most situations. At one stroke this would turn the Liberals into the most powerful party in Parliament because they could always decide whether Conservatives or Labour would govern, by joining with one or the other in a government coalition.

This would also make individual MPs more important, as their immediate voting decisions could affect the survival of finely balanced governments. In turn this would make parliamentary and committee proceedings more crucial, as the fate of governments could be decided by them. MPs would have a more independent standing in regard both to ministers and civil servants, so they could beef up their inquiries and investigations and compel more attention to them.

Precisely because such changes would make life more difficult for governments and the major parties, they are likely to be strongly resisted. The key reform of the election system will only come with a 'hung' Parliament where Liberals can bargain with Conservatives and Labour, and give support for a government only in return for electoral reform. In the meantime the only significant political changes are likely to be external to Parliament, such as Scottish and Welsh devolution. Even reform of the House of Lords may be delayed. However, some strengthening of civil rights and removal of the more excessive restrictions on information could usefully extend the work being done by select committees even if it would take more fundamental changes to really empower them. See Briefing 18.6.

BRIEFINGS

18.6 A USEFUL REFORM OF PARLIAMENT

Usually the idea that Parliament might be reformed is opposed on the grounds that its main function is to support the Government. Mandate theory (Briefing 17.5 in Chapter 17) assumes that a party is elected on the basis of its programme and is accountable to voters at the next election for its success or failure. From this perspective any exercise of autonomous power by Parliament simply blurs government and party accountability.

If one accepts that central policies are subject to 'party democracy' rather than 'parliamentary democracy', one could still see a role for both Commons and Lords outside the central election issues. A convention could be adopted that independent parliamentary action should not be taken in regard to these (rather as the House of Lords currently accepts that it must pass legislation embodying election pledges, no matter how distasteful). However, there could be no objection to Parliament:

- getting and publishing *information* about central election policies, how they are being implemented, whether they have been changed, and what their cost is;
- making recommendations and even taking action about policies and decisions *not* covered in the manifestos.

A prerequisite to both of these activities is to compel witnesses to attend and give evidence. The House of Lords could concentrate more on an information-gathering and evaluation role and the Commons on action, as is appropriate given their different constitutional status.

ESSAYS

1. Could we still have a democracy in Britain without Parliament? If yes, how would it function? If no, what is the irreplaceable contribution that Parliament makes?

2. What does the House of Lords do? Is it really useful? Why or why not?

3. What can a parliamentary select committee do that an investigative journalist cannot?

4. Outline the reforms which you think are necessary for the Commons to operate better.

SUMMARY

This chapter shows that:

- Parliament at the present time is dominated by the two major political parties. The mass of MPs owe their election to party support and thus tend to support their party and shield it from criticism, however much it is justified.

- This means that Parliament's main role at the moment is sustaining the Government and providing a forum for the Opposition to criticise it.

- However, some weakening of major party cohesion and increased Liberal representation have allowed backbench MPs to assume more of an independent role in questioning aspects of government policy.

- This has been expressed by voting against some government legislation, and has also shown in more vigorous questioning and investigation by select committees.

- Scrutiny and questioning of the administration is probably a more important and justifiable activity for Parliament than querying legislation. Important legislation has been given a 'mandate' through the government party's electoral success. The details of implementation, however, have not, nor have the many major administrative decisions made internally at the moment by the Civil Service. A useful role of committees is simply to provide more information about the workings of secretive British governments.

- Parliament has a useful role to play in scrutinising administration, but could be much better organised to do it. Most reform will have to wait until third parties or dissident MPs are in a position to force change out of the leadership of one of the major parties. In spite of rhetoric, New Labour is no more anxious to diminish its present or prospective power than any other government. Thus major parliamentary reform is unlikely to come until the Millennium, at least.

MILESTONES

MILESTONES IN PARLIAMENTARY DEVELOPMENT

1295–1306 Edward I summons representatives of boroughs and countries, as well as Lords, to consent to taxation. In return he redresses grievances they complain about

1306–1532 This practice continues and the Parliament clearly divides into two Houses (Lords and Commons). The Commons establishes itself as the more active House, with power to grant taxation

1532–59 Parliament confirms the Royal Succession and sanctions the major religious changes

1640–51 Parliament fights Civil War against the King and wins. It establishes its supremacy over the Law Courts

1688–89 The Glorious Revolution. Parliament transfers Crown from James II to William and Mary and establishes exclusive power to raise money and sanction military forces. Members given personal immunities

1701 Parliament settles Protestant Succession

1715–1832 'Eighteenth century constitution'. Government has to be acceptable both to King and Commons majority. From time to time party caucuses ('Whigs', 'Tories') form to manage the majority

1832 Great Reform Act. Election clearly becomes basis of Commons membership. Government is now totally dependent on a Commons majority. Monarch withdraws from active politics

MILESTONES IN PARLIAMENTARY DEVELOPMENT (continued)

1867–68 Second Reform Act institutes mass franchise. Mass parties impose strict discipline on MPs in return for sponsoring their election. 'Elective dictatorship' of Government commences

1874–86 Imposition of procedural devices to ensure Government legislation passes in spite of filibustering of Irish nationalists ('guillotine' to curtail debate on clauses, etc.)

1911 Parliament Act confirms convention that Lords cannot oppose financial legislation and can only delay legislation for three years

1922 Government of Ireland Act sets up Northern Irish Government and Parliament

1949 Parliament Act limits delaying power of House of Lords to one year

1972 European Communities Act significantly limits parliamentary sovereignty

1970 onwards Growth of dissent from the party line among backbench MPs

1979 Creation of present system of largely departmental select committees

1994–96 Scott Committee reveals extent to which governments may mislead the Commons

1994 Government sets up a committee of inquiry into standards of public life, under Lord Justice Nolan

1995 Nolan Report recommends public disclosure of Party and MPs' interests and donors

1996 MPs obliged to register all details of outside contracts with a new Parliamentary Commission

PROJECTS

1. On the basis of the 1997 Labour Party Manifesto and the Queen's speeches made in the present Parliament, estimate the extent to which the Government has fulfilled its election pledges up to this point.

2. On the basis of newspaper accounts and *Hansard* (the report of parliamentary proceedings) calculate the amount of dissent within the parliamentary Labour Party and the parliamentary Conservative Party in this Parliament.

2. 'Shadow' two select committees in this Parliament on the basis of newspaper reports. Do you feel one is more effective than the other? Why?

FURTHER READING

For recent and general works on Parliament see P. Norton, *Does Parliament Matter?* (Brighton: Harvester Wheatsheaf, 1993), especially Chapter 10, 'The Role of Party'. For a longer study of parties in Parliament see J. Brand, *British Parliamentary Parties* (Oxford: Oxford University Press, 1992), and for the work of party whips, K. Alderman, 'The Government Whips', *Politics Review*, 4 (4), April (1995). Select and standing committees of the Commons are discussed in P. Norton, 'Select Committees in the House of Commons: Watchdogs or Poodles?', *Politics Review*, 4 (2), November (1994) and 'Standing Committees in the House of Commons', *Politics Review*, 4 (4), April (1995). For recent discussions of the reform of the House of Commons see The Hansard Society, *Making the Law: Report of the Commission on the Legislative Process* (London: Hansard Society, 1993) and The Constitution Unit, *Delivering Constitutional Reform* (London: The Constitution Unit, 1996).

http://www.awl-he.com/politics/newbritpol

Internet resources – visit *The New British Politics* Webpage for links to a specially-chosen selection of Internet resources relevant to this Chapter.

http://www.awl-he.com/politics/newbritpol

CHAPTER 19

Local democracy?

For at least the last one hundred years, local government has had a dual function: it is responsible for implementing policy decisions of national Government; it is also the only layer of democratically elected government in Britain besides central Government itself. This has created an ambiguity at the heart of the local government system. On the other hand, local authorities are accountable to their local citizens, and are often in the hands of a different party from national Government. On the other, local government is the creature of central Government and must comply with its decisions. This ambiguity has been increased by the transfer of some local government functions to quangos (see Chapter 10).

As a result the stage has been set for conflict, and there has been plenty of this over the past two decades and more, especially during the Thatcher era. Indeed, after trade unions, local authorities were the main objects and opponents of Thatcherite reforms during the 1979–97 period. Almost every recent discussion of local government states that it was transformed in the 1980s, and issues health warnings about it being 'in turmoil', subject to 'massive upheaval', and enmeshed in 'endless reform'. Under New Labour, local government in Britain seems set for further change.

To understand what is happening we must look closely at the structure of local government, before dealing with the broader issue of its overall place in British politics, and how it may evolve in the next century.

This chapter accordingly covers:

- The unusual institutional setting of British local government

- Territorial and functional reorganisations

- Local councils and how they function

- Parties and political control

- Money and power in local government, and financial reforms

- Local democracy and local government

- The changing world of local democracy

- New Labour: democracy revived?

LOCAL POLITICS IN CONTEXT

To know about local government we also need to know about the British state. For all the power concentrated at the centre by constitutional doctrines, which enable it to abolish one local authority and create another through ordinary legislation, the central Government does not have its own local agents to execute its orders. There is nothing in Britain which remotely resembles the French Prefect, a civil servant posted in a locality to implement national legislation directly. Central departments in Britain mostly lack this kind of 'field administration', as it is called, and therefore rely on local governments or quangos to execute their policies. These responsibilities are laid on local authorities either by legislation (requiring them to carry out its provisions) or by central 'circulars' or 'directives' from government departments.

Examples of functions run administratively by local governments include education, public works like road building, housing and police. In other European countries these are responsibilities of the central administration. Their delegation to local governments in Britain accounts for the fact that they spend about a quarter of all public money. It also explains why the major part of their revenue comes from central Government and less than 20 per cent comes from local taxes.

This situation also means that most of their administrative activities are not initiated locally nor are they accounted for locally. Indeed the professional administrators employed by local authorities may feel more responsible (both legally and in terms of their own conceptions) to a central department than to their own elected council. They may belong more in a national 'policy community' or 'policy network' (Chapter 12) rather than in their own locality.

However, local officials are clearly also responsible to their local council. Where the council agrees with government policy this need not create conflict, but there is a tendency for opposition parties to win control locally to protest against what the party in power at the centre is doing. In such a situation the majority party may try to subvert or change what central Government wants done, particularly in politically sensitive fields like education or social services.

In such a situation the central Government cannot simply bypass local government, since it has no local administrator whom it could use to do this. Either it has to force the locality to comply, abolish it or transfer its powers, or set up nominated 'quangos' to do what it wants. All these strategies have been pursued by Conservative governments in the last 20 years.

Controversy and tension in local politics are thus paradoxically associated with:

- the close mutual dependency of local and central government: local government depending on the centre for revenues, central government depending on the locality for administrative action;

- their shared democratic status, the fact that both are elected and have a 'mandate' from their respective electorates to pursue their policies, which have often conflicted;

- the constitutional latitude which central Government has to bludgeon local governments into submission – by abolition, legal action, 'capping' and other means – combined with the 'blocking' ability of the locality.

None of this makes for happy relationships. It is probable, now there is a Labour Government centrally, that the Labour or Liberal councils now in power practically everywhere will work better with it. The Conservatives, however, are building up their local organisations and will probably win back control in many areas by the end of the 1990s. So the potential for conflict will continue, because it is built into the structure of central–local relationships. The restraint on both sides, on which the workings of the unwritten Constitution so crucially depended, has been broken. At the very least it will take a long time to repair them, however consensual New Labour tries to be. The system may, however, now depend on the same party (or parties) being in power both locally and centrally, and also regionally, now that intermediary elected bodies are also coming into the relationship.

TERRITORIAL AND FUNCTIONAL REORGANISATIONS

Nowhere is the centre's legal power over local authorities shown better than in their abolition and creation, which has taken place with increasing frequency since the 1960s.

Parliamentary sovereignty and the constitutional traditions of a unitary state (Chapter 7) have meant that local areas and functions can be set up and changed by British governments without effective legal challenges. Thus territorial boundaries have been freely revised and functions added and taken away at various dates. Nevertheless a core of tasks and responsibilities have remained with the localities throughout. Similarly the territorial units of today, at least in England, mostly have roots that go back into the nineteenth century.

As described in Chapter 2, the most pressing needs at that period (drainage and sewers, public health, housing, street lighting, law enforcement, education) were experienced in the rapidly expanding industrial cities. So it was those cities which first enjoyed local democracy and self-government. The 1835 Municipal Corporations Act instituted town councils elected by property holders. The 1888 Local Government Act extended the franchise for local elections and established county councils for the rural areas on the same pattern. It thus brought in the *two-tier system* to local government, whereby county councils ran general services such as planning, education and police, affecting broader territorial areas; and the lower units ran more personal services like housing, health and local amenities better tailored to a small area. Lower units in the counties were set up as either urban or district councils, also with elected councils and an administration. London was organised like a county but other large cities were 'unitary', that is, the city council covered both general and personal services. Outside England and Wales, Scotland and Ireland were organised on broadly similar lines but with differences in detail. Briefings 19.1 and 19.2 outline the reorganisations in English, Welsh and Scottish local government since the nineteenth century.

Key term

Two-tier local government – where the functions of local government are divided between an upper level (counties, for example) and a lower level (boroughs or districts, for example).

Key term

Unitary system – where local functions are controlled by only one layer of local government.

BRIEFINGS

19.1 LOCAL GOVERNMENT TERRITORIAL REORGANISATONS IN ENGLAND AND WALES, 1800–1997

1800 and before

Unelected borough councils (or corporations) were gradually established by Royal Charter for some cities. Benches of magistrates and parish councils appointed by local notables provided rudimentary government in other areas.

1835 Municipal Corporations Act

Established elections (with limited suffrage) to town (borough) councils. The City of London retained its medieval corporate privileges.

1888 Local Government Act

Established the principle of a two-tier local government system with the creation of county boroughs with elected councils. Also created the London County Council (LCC) responsible for education and transport. By 1899, 28 metropolitan boroughs became the lower tier of government within the London area.

1894 Local Government Act

Two-tier principle extended to all of England and Wales with the creation of urban and district councils for cities and small towns. Parish councils retained residual responsibilities in small villages.

1963

The Greater London Council was created to accommodate the continuing growth of London. The two-tier principle remained with Greater London embracing 32 London boroughs. The GLC was responsible for transport and planning, while the Inner London Education Authority (ILEA) was retained with jurisdiction over the old LCC area.

1972 Local Government Act

The major change was the creation of six metropolitan counties and 36 metropolitan districts for major urban areas. In addition, the number of counties was reduced to 39 and urban and district councils replaced with 296 district councils. The two-tier principle was retained and strengthened.

1984–87

The Conservative Government abolished the GLC and the metropolitan counties. Responsibilities were devolved to London boroughs, district councils (outside London) and to a variety of quangos. Two-tier principle was abandoned for large urban areas.

1995–96 Local government reforms

Following extensive consultation by a local government commission, a number of unitary authorities were created, but the old two-tier structure remained in many areas. In Wales the two-tier structure was abolished and replaced with 22 county and county borough councils.

Subsequent reforms were all designed to achieve the best possible balance between a sensible allocation of *policy functions* to local governments and suitable *territorial* units for carrying out these functions. From the end of the nineteenth century until the 1980s almost all Westminster politicians accepted the recommendations of royal commissions on local government reform that the system is best organised on a two-tier basis. Hence the recommendations of the Redcliffe-Maud Report *Local Government in England* (1969), which led to the 1972 Local Government Act, rationalised the existing two-tier system as outlined in Figure

BRIEFINGS

19.2 LOCAL GOVERNMENT TERRITORIAL REORGANISATION IN SCOTLAND, 1833–1997

1800 and before

Royal burghs, membership of which was often linked to guild associations, performed most local government functions. Magistrates performed a minor role compared with England.

Royal Burghs (Scotland Act) 1833, 1889 and 1894 Local Government (Scotland) Acts

Elective principle extended first to the burghs and then to the counties and parishes.

1929 Local Government (Scotland) Act

Created 33 counties, four counties of cities (Edinburgh, Glasgow, Dundee and Aberdeen), 21 large burghs and 176 small burghs. The counties of cities were unitary authorities performing all local government tasks within their jurisdictions. Otherwise the system was two-tier and resembled the English model.

1973 Local Government (Scotland) Act

Created a completely new system consisting of nine regional councils, three island authorities and 53 district councils. The island authorities were unitary in nature, while the regional governments took on most traditional local government functions.

1996 Local Government (Scotland) Act

Further wholesale changes involved the abolition of the regional councils and the creation of 29 unitary councils.

19.1. Even this seemingly straightforward allocation of responsibilities has to be qualified. Arrangements for London were different, as they were for Scotland and Northern Ireland. In addition a number of other locally provided services remained in the hands of ad hoc bodies, and several health services previously provided by local governments were transferred to the National Health Service.

Driving these reforms was the belief that major functions were best carried out by larger political units while others were best performed at the level of the local community. Few now believe that the particular division of responsibilities enshrined in the 1970s legislation was entirely rational; much was a result of political expediency. The reforms simply tinkered with the haphazard pattern of local government which had evolved over many centuries.

Figure 19.1 The local government structure in England following the 1972 reforms

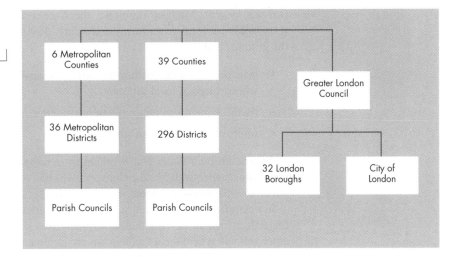

Two further changes in territorial organisation occurred in the 1980s and the 1990s. Between 1984 and 1987 the Conservatives abolished the Greater London Council and the six metropolitan counties. All were Labour-controlled at the time and there is no doubt that abolition was designed to cut local government expenditure by what were regarded as high-spending leftist councils. But it was also an attack on Labour power bases. The powers of the abolished counties were devolved to existing district and borough councils and to a number of nonelected quangos.

These changes set precedents both for the transfer of (elected) councils' powers to (centrally nominated) quangos, and for the creation of unitary local governments. We shall look at the transfer of functions below. The second change, to unitary authorities, helped undermine the previous consensus on a

Plate 19.1 County Hall, London. The Greater London Council was seen as a high-spending Labour power base and was abolished by the Conservative government in 1984

two-tier system. Michael Heseltine, the Conservative technocrat who became responsible for local government in the early 1990s, advocated them strongly on the grounds that they:

- promoted local democracy by fixing responsibility on one council for the whole range of local services;
- by the same token reduced administrative costs;
- improved the quality of services.

As a result both Wales and Scotland were reorganised into 21 and 28 unitary authorities respectively. As the Conservatives had little to lose politically, the new structure was imposed without much consultation and ignored local objections.

It was different in England where the Conservatives had their electoral base. Objections had to be entertained seriously and the 46 new unitary authorities emerged only where local feelings ran predominantly in favour of them. In so far as there was a consistent logic other than a political and electoral one, it was that certain areas on the fringes of existing counties which were strong local communities needed all-purpose local governments. Some of this comes through from the new territorial distribution of the authorities (Map 19.1).

As well as the new unitary authorities there were the urban ones originally created in the mid-1980s when the metropolitan counties were abolished. Over most of the country, however, the old two-tier system created in 1972 (Figure 19.1) was substantially retained. The two-tier system has been strengthened by the proposal, supported by a local referendum in May 1998, to recreate an all-London author-

Plate 19.2 Peter Brooke's cartoon in *The Times*, 30 July 1997. Simon Jenkins commented in the same issue of *The Times*, 'The Government is set to deliver the British constitution its biggest shock since the war. Direct election of a London mayor will overturn the whole cabalistic tradition of party politics.'

Map 19.1 The new
territorial organisation of
local government in England
1995

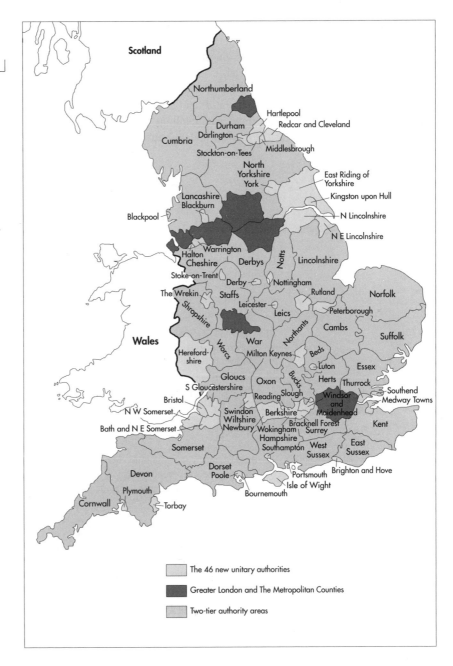

Map 19.1 The new territorial organisation of local government in England 1995

Source: *Local Government Commission for England* (London: HMSO, 1995), Map 2

ity with a directly elected Mayor and Council responsible for overall strategy in the conurbation. This could touch off demands from areas like Birmingham and Manchester for similarly elected executive mayors.

As matters stand, therefore, Figure 19.1 still gives a pretty good idea of the territorial structure and division of functions over most of England in the late 1990s. The intrusion of unitary authorities here and there, and the horizontal division of local powers with ad hoc bodies and quangos, still support the comment made by an MP in 1871: 'The truth, sir, is that we have a chaos as regards authorities, a chaos as regards rates, and a worse chaos than all as regards areas'. None of this helps democratic accountability and representation in the localities, dramatically shown by the confusing distribution of functions between the two tiers (Table 19.1).

Table 19.1 Services and responsibilities of county and district councils at January 1995

County Councils	District Councils
EDUCATION • Most schools • Special education • Nursery, adult and community • Planning and quality assurance • Resource management	ELECTORAL REGISTRATION COUNCIL TAX AND UNIFORM BUSINESS RATE COLLECTION
PERSONAL SOCIAL SERVICES • Securing provision for the elderly, children and those with disabilities (including care in the community) • Policy planning and quality assurance	HOUSING • Management and maintenance of housing stock, policy and co-ordination, homelessness
POLICE FIRE PLANNING • Strategic planning • Mineral and waste planning • Highway development control • Historic buildings	PLANNING • Local plans • Planning applications (including listed buildings)
TRANSPORT • Public transport • Highways and parking • Traffic management • Footpaths and bridleways • Transport planning	TRANSPORT • Unclassified roads • Offstreet car parking • Footpaths and bridleways • Street lighting
EMERGENCY PLANNING ENVIRONMENTAL SERVICES • Refuse disposal	EMERGENCY PLANNING ENVIRONMENTAL SERVICES • Refuse collection • Building regulations • General environmental services • Street cleaning
RECREATION AND ART • Parks and open spaces • Support for the arts • Museums • Encouraging tourism	RECREATION AND ART • Parks and open spaces • Leisure centres and swimming pools • Support for the arts • Museums and art galleries • Encouraging tourism

Table 19.1 Continued

County Councils	District Councils
ECONOMIC DEVELOPMENT SMALL HOLDINGS REGISTRATION • Births, deaths and marriages CONSUMER PROTECTION • Trading standards etc. • Public analysis LIBRARIES COUNTY AND DISTRICT EMPLOYERS' PENSIONS (administering authority)	ECONOMIC DEVELOPMENT ALLOTMENTS CEMETERIES AND CREMATORIA

Source: *Local Government Commission for England* (London: HMSO, 1995)

In retrospect, the territorial reforms of the 1970s through to the 1990s were more important for what they did *not* change than for what they did change. In particular the legislation really failed to address two vital areas which dominate most of the debate on the shortcomings of local government in Britain today:

• the nature of local democracy, and

• the arrangements for local government finance.

We look at these questions in more detail below.

LOCAL COUNCILS AND HOW THEY FUNCTION

Before we can really assess the quality of local democracy, however, we need to examine the way it functions and how it organises itself. Unlike Parliament, local councils are executive bodies as well as legislative ones. Of necessity they have to delegate detailed supervision of each policy area, but they delegate to committees rather than to individuals. Council committees, in contrast to Parliamentary ones, are therefore executive rather than simply supervisory bodies. Table 19.2 shows a typical set of committees for Colchester, an urban council within the administrative county of Essex. In contrast with the first part of the postwar period, the committees focus less on managing various departments of the authority (housing, parks social services, etc.) and more on performance and service delivery. This is in keeping with the central reforms which have taken away much of the property and enterprises previously managed by the authority and substituted a role as facilitator and service provider.

In many ways these changes have cleared the way for a more political role to be taken by the council in responding to and participating in local demands as compared with a routine administrative one, where it confronted many local electors as clients rather than constituents.

Committees	Functional responsibilities
Policy and Resources	Corporate strategy including annual budgets
Arts and Leisure	Includes tourism, town twinning, sports, museums, culture and recreation
Housing and Community Services	Council and private sector housing and services for elderly people, welfare rights
Planning and Transportation	Policy matters including High Street, harbour and market
Public Protection	Environmental health, pollution, food safety, building regulations, street cleaning, refuse collection, cemetery and crematorium
Human and Financial Resources	All personnel policy issues, budgets and council tax
Land Resources	Council land and buildings
Development Control	Planning applications

In theory the committees act on behalf of the full council, which collectively endorses or (more occasionally) changes their decisions. As with Parliament, however, the reality is quite different. Local democracy too is *party* democracy. If there is a majority of one party on the council, policy will be decided at the party meeting. Party discipline will generally ensure that party decisions are voted in as council policy, even if individuals disagree with them. The convenors of all important committees will be members of the majority party and will implement its policy in their committee. Thus what seems to be a somewhat rambling and disarticulated structure of separate committees will actually be quite tightly co-ordinated through parties and the party executive committee.

This is, of course, what happens in central government too. The difference at local level is that three-party competition has often resulted in coalitions (Labour and Liberals) running councils, or in the plurality party taking over but relying on voting support from another party. Table 19.3 shows the distribution of party

Table 19.3 Party control of English local councils 1997–98

Control by:	Number of Councils	Percentage of Councils
CONSERVATIVE	26	6.8
LIBERAL DEMOCRAT	42	11.1
LABOUR	173	45.5
NO OVERALL CONTROL (Minority administration or coalition)	127	33.4
INDEPENDENT	12	3.2
TOTAL	380	100.0

control across England and illustrates the extent to which coalition or minority government has become a normal state of affairs locally, again contrasting with Westminster.

Where there is a coalition, committee convenorships are distributed between the parties. In some cases they are also given out to minority parties to get their support, and in such cases the party meetings are necessarily less effective in determining policy. It then tends to be decided by interparty negotiations on central co-ordinating committees such as Policy and Resources. The failure of any one party to dominate thus renders the council itself, and its committees, more important, as coalition arrangements nationally would probably do with Parliament (Chapter 18).

Corresponding to each council committee there is an administrative department with a chief officer, who attends committee meetings and takes instructions from them. Depending on their area of responsibility, local officials are often professionally trained with specialised degrees. Public Health requires a medical doctor and Public Works architects and engineers, for example. Because of the way that councils have been compelled by Conservative governments to contract out services and simply buy them from completing suppliers, this is, however, less true today.

Traditionally, administrative co-ordination was handled by the town clerk, a solicitor. Most councils today have replaced the clerk by a chief executive officer or manager with business experience and a degree in administration. This reflects general tendencies in the society towards greater professionalisation, but it also reflects a need for a more sophisticated approach to administration than was called for when the major task for the local authority was routine delivery of services. We now turn to the reasons for this change in local functions, which are driven mainly by the nationalisation of local politics.

PARTIES, POLITICAL CONTROL AND LOCAL POLITICS

Most discussions of local government concentrate on its administrative tasks and delivery of services rather than on its political dimension. This is because it was less politicised in many places before the reorganisations of the 1970s. Moreover, the routine delivery of fairly concrete services in the context of a growing national provision for them tended to mute party conflict. The 'social democratic consensus' from 1950 to 1976 largely removed issues of principle from the localities and left them to effect fairly agreed national decisions.

Two things changed the situation:

1. The Conservative Governments from 1979 to 1997 cut down support for services, forcing local councils to decide on highly political priorities about what they should support, or whether indeed they should resist central cuts.

2. The parties excluded from power at the centre organised and radicalised themselves locally. A natural corollary, where they took power, was to choose the second option of resistance, which then sparked off an unprecedented series of confrontations and crises.

It was the Liberals who first built themselves up locally by espousing 'community politics', a concentration on highly local issues and grievances which often sparked confrontations with bureaucratic and unresponsive Labour councils. This Liberal tactic gained them widespread local support. With the defection of the Social Democrats from Labour groups in 1982 it often gave them local control or at least an influential place in local coalition politics. Local success was then used to build up support and credibility for their parliamentary campaign, which paid off in tactical voting in the 1997 General Election (Chapter 15).

The Liberal example stimulated Labour to base their national recovery on local politics. In part this was connected with the new leadership (Kinnock, Smith and then Blair) putting in new people to regain control of ward and constituency parties from the 'hard left' of the early 1980s. New Labour was also hampered by the survival of traditional local politicians, whom it was unable to oust, in many of the large cities. All the Labour factions were, however, able to unite against Thatcherite cuts in financial support and social services and other locally hostile policies (see below).

Labour and Liberal successes were also helped by the fact that local elections were held annually. The results thus reflected popular discontent with the Government which was more muted at general elections. Thus councils became increasingly Labour and Liberal-dominated from 1979 to 1997 to the extent that only 6 per cent were left in Conservative hands. The result was that national political divisions between the parties were mirrored in the confrontation between localities and centre, whose results we shall examine below.

Party penetration has thus revolutionised local democracy by making it more than ever *party* democracy. It is worthwhile noting also the difference this has made to the national parties themselves (Chapter 16). Balancing the decline in their general membership has been the emergence of a large body of active politicians who control large local organisations and resources on their own account. Party activists have often been thought of as idealists and ideologues who press the top leadership into more extreme policies and constitute a constant threat to them which they have to keep under control by organisational means.

This is quite unlike the reality of the new activists, well-versed in pragmatic local politics and the realm of the possible. They are at the same time more powerful and authoritative than the old-style activist, and more realistic. They now constitute an important group both among Labour and Liberal Democrats: two thirds of new Labour MPs and 70 per cent of Liberal Democrats in the 1997 Parliament have been local councillors. We may also expect the Conservatives to try to rebuild from the localities after their electoral defeat. Thus inside all the national parties local politicians are likely to extend their influence.

The conversion of local government into party democracy revitalised grass roots democracy and the parties themselves. However, it increased the potential for confrontation with the centre. In the 1980s this was first fought out in the field of finance, where local revenues and expenditures were closely bound up with national ones because of the interdependency of central and local administrative functions.

MONEY AND POWER IN LOCAL GOVERNMENT

Up to the 1980s, local revenues were traditionally based on the 'rates', a tax based on the value of residential and commercial property and which dated back to when property ownership was linked to voting. For many years the rating system worked moderately well. Only a minority of citizens – property owners – paid rates directly, and shortfalls in local government income were made up by central government subventions, the Rate Support Grant (RSG).

However, during the 1960s and 1970s, home ownership grew rapidly to become the dominant form of housing tenure. As this happened, so the mildly regressive nature of the rates became more apparent (the tax was based on property values rather than on income or ability to pay). At the same time, legislation expanding the role of local government proceeded apace and so, therefore, did the size of the RSG. In the late 1930s, the RSG stood at around 30 per cent of total local spending, but by 1977 it had risen to over 65 per cent. Adjusting the rates to pay for a larger proportion of local services was politically difficult. With inflation and house prices rising rapidly, adjustments resulted in apparently sharp increases, which seemed to affect household budgets. As a result, governments began to search for alternative means of financing local government.

In its 1974 election manifesto, the Conservatives pledged that they would reform the system. Labour was less enthusiastic about reform, in part because fewer of its supporters were homeowners, and in part because it was less hostile to ever-increasing rises in the RSG. In the event it presided over the largest ever increases during the first three years of its tenure in government from 1974 to 1976. In 1976, it experienced one of the most momentous and humiliating events of postwar history. With the pound sterling collapsing on the foreign exchanges and the national finances in disarray, the International Monetary Fund (IMF) was called in to bail the country out. One of the stipulations of the IMF loan was that taxes be raised and public expenditure cut (Chapter 3). Local expenditure was a quarter of the total. As a result the RSG was reduced (proportionately, at least) for the first time since the 1930s.

These events added further impetus to Conservative determination to reform local finance. Once in office (1980) they replaced the RSG with a new system called Grant Related Expenditure, which enabled the central Government to set spending targets and to cut the grant if local authorities exceeded them. The Conservatives hoped both to shame and to punish overspending authorities by publishing a list of noncomplying local governments, and by 'clawing back' the grant by 3 per cent for every 1 per cent that local governments overspent.

In response, many authorities simply increased their rates. This was especially true of Labour-controlled authorities in the larger cities which were increasingly hostile to the Conservative Government. Indeed, the overt politicisation of local government stems from this period. This is a point we will return to later.

New legislation took central control further by granting to central Government the power to set individual authority rates. If a local government overspent then it would be formally required to keep its rate income to a certain level. In the parlance of the time it would be 'rate capped'. Rate capping proved a highly controversial device. If properly implemented it would affect overspending Conservative as well as Labour-controlled councils (for example, Portsmouth

Council in 1983). Thereafter – and following a Social Democrat election victory in a Portsmouth by-election – the Government introduced a complex new formula which made it very difficult to penalise Conservative authorities and very easy to punish inner city Labour-controlled councils. (In fact not one Conservative authority was rate capped following this change in the rules.)

CONTROVERSY

WHAT IS THE BEST SYSTEM OF LOCAL GOVERNMENT FINANCE?

TYPE OF TAX SYSTEM	*FOR*	*AGAINST*
Rates	Well established (until abolition) and easy and cheap to collect. As a tax on the use or rentable value of property a progressive element exists.	Subject to apparently large increases during periods of inflation. Falls only on residential and commercial property owners. Difficult for central Government to control. Abolished in Scotland in 1989 and in England and Wales in 1990.
Community Charge (Poll Tax)	As a flat rate tax everybody has to pay. Is very simple and highly visible so should provide an electoral check on high-spending – and therefore high community charge – local authorities.	Falls on millions of people unused to paying a large annual local tax. Proved very difficult and expensive to collect. Very regressive. Politically highly unpopular. Introduced 1989–90, abolished 1993.
Council Tax	Relatively simple and easy to collect. It is levied on households, but the amount paid is determined by the value of the properties which are placed in seven value bands. It assumes a two-person household, but rebates are available for single people, the poor and disadvantaged.	Banding can be arbitrary. May prove as unpopular as the rates during periods of inflation. Progressive element is linked to property values rather than income or ability to pay. Effective since 1992–93.
Uniform Business Rate	Easy to collect and to understand. Linked to property values as with the old rating system.	Not really a local tax at all as the revenue goes to the central Government which then redistributes to localities. Unpopular with small business. Can be regressive as it is unrelated to the profit or turnover of business. Effective since 1990–91.
Local Income Tax	Easy to collect and to adjust. Strongly progressive and linked to the ability to pay. Highly visible so may force councils to curb spending.	Could be inflationary and encourage inner city Labour authorities to go on spending sprees. Not amenable to control by central governments and therefore unlikely to be adopted in Britain outside Scotland where the Scottish assembly will be given limited power to raise income tax for the whole of the Scottish jurisdiction.

WHAT IS THE BEST SYSTEM OF LOCAL GOVERNMENT FINANCE? (continued)

TYPE OF TAX SYSTEM	FOR	AGAINST
Local Sales Tax	Could be 'hidden' in prices (like VAT) and therefore be acceptable to voters. Easy to collect.	Highly regressive and unrelated to ability to pay. Could – as with a local income tax – cause migration of people or businesses from high to low tax areas. Also, as with income tax, is highly unlikely to be adopted because central government could not control spending levels.

Key term

Community Charge or Poll Tax – the local tax which replaced the rates (or property tax) in which every adult resident of a local authority paid the same amount. It came into operation in 1990 and was replaced by the Council Tax in 1993.

By 1985 this issue had become a source of major conflict between the two parties. Local authority spending continued to increase at a pace faster than the Government desired. Sixteen Labour councils declared that they would not meet the Government's rate target and would either not set a rate or would indulge in deficit spending. Although they won the support of the parliamentary Labour Party, it was clear that they were acting illegally. In a unitary system like Britain, national government has complete authority over local government matters. In the event, and following a change of heart by the Labour leadership who urged compliance with government policy, all but one of the rebel councils set a rate. The exception was Liverpool City Council. There a group of far left activists, led by Deputy Leader Derek Hatton, decided that they would close local services down rather than comply. They eventually kept services running by borrowing from Swiss banks. But their actions, which were clearly illegal, led to several council members being charged for the losses. Hatton and several of his colleagues were made personally bankrupt and were subsequently expelled from the Labour Party.

These events strengthened the Government's conviction that a wholesale reform was needed of the local government finance system. From a number of alternatives the Government chose the one that was likely to arouse the most hostility: the community charge or poll tax. The idea behind the poll tax was simple: every individual adult living in a particular area would pay a flat charge to the local council. And although the charge would be reduced for the poor and disadvantaged, the vast majority of people would pay the same amount. In effect some 17 million people who had never paid rates (at least not directly) would now pay a sizeable new tax. Occupants of stately homes who previously had paid large rates bills would pay the same as occupants of tiny council flats who previously had paid nothing.

Margaret Thatcher, who was one of the most enthusiastic supporters of the idea, argued that the tax would be highly visible. It would make the fiscal effect of local policies very clear, thus strengthening the local accountability of councils and parties and forcing spending down. As for its regressive nature (a flat rate tax unrelated to individuals' income or wealth), she argued that it was no more regressive than value-added tax which was a well-established and successful source of government revenue. Critics, who included many senior Cabinet ministers and civil servants, said that collecting the tax would be extremely difficult and the whole idea was political dynamite.

The detractors proved to be right. Without exaggeration, the introduction of the Community Charge represents one of the most important policy mistakes in British government in the twentieth century. The tax proved very expensive to collect (in some poorer areas the cost of collection exceeded poll tax revenue) and cost the Government further losses in local and by-elections. It was deeply unpopular, so much so that it caused major rioting in some cities and helped contribute to the downfall of Thatcher. Indeed when Michael Heseltine challenged the Prime Minister for the leadership of the Conservative Party in November 1990, he made the abolition of the poll tax part of his manifesto. On John Major becoming leader, Heseltine was given the job of devising an immediate replacement.

What emerged were the council tax and the uniform business rate. The former is a hybrid of the old rating system and the poll tax. Every property is rated according to value in seven (later eight) bands (A to H), but the tax falls on the current occupant of the property. Rebates are available for the poor and the disadvantaged.

As of 1998, the tax has worked moderately well. It has proved easy to collect and an element of fairness was incorporated into the banding system by weighting the tax towards the occupants of more expensive properties. In other words, occupiers of Band A, B and C properties only pay a proportion of the tax, Band D pays the full tax, while Bands E to H pay progressively more than the full tax. The uniform business rate is much like the old rating system. But it has been the subject of more criticism mainly because it falls on a large number of small businesses and because it has been increased substantially over the years. So much so, in fact, that the Government has periodically introduced centrally funded 'transitional relief' to ease the burden on a vocal and electorally important small business sector.

By the end of the 1990s the whole subject of local government finance had declined in political importance. This was partly because of the relative success of the council tax reform, but mainly because successive Conservative governments had gradually stripped local governments of many of their functions. New management controls, privatisation and the removal of a number of traditional functions from local government control had reduced the proportion of public spending accounted for by local authorities. These changes have important implications for the nature of local democracy, to which we now turn.

> **Key term**
>
> **Council Tax** – the local tax, which replaced the Community Charge in 1993, in which, like the rates, payment is related to property values and levied on all occupants of property.

LOCAL DEMOCRACY AND LOCAL GOVERNMENT

Local councillors in Britain are unpaid elected officials (although they do receive expenses in the form of attendance allowances). A complicated electoral system exists whereby county councillors are elected every four years, but the timing of district council elections can be varied. So districts can hold elections concurrently with county council elections, or at the mid term of county elections, or by thirds, that is, one third of district councillors elected every year that there is no county council election. All elections are held on the first Thursday in May. Few voters are familiar with this system which may help account for the low turnout in local elections, usually below 40 per cent. Eligibility is different from national elections: Commonwealth citizens can vote, as can citizens of the EU.

Generally county councillors have higher status – and more power – than district councillors do, although in the London boroughs and big city districts local councillors can achieve a higher political profile.

Council members are not typical of the population. By definition they have to have the time to do the job, which may explain the relatively large number of women elected to local office. At around 20 per cent, it was significantly higher than female representation in Parliament until the 1997 General Election. Councillors also tend to be middle class and to come from professional or self-employed backgrounds. The unrepresentative nature of the councillor class has led to calls for the institution of full-time paid elected officials like the new Mayor of London.

As noted above, there has been a professionalisation and politicisation of councillors' roles. At one time council membership was regarded as a casual part-time job which (usually Conservative) members performed on behalf of the less advantaged mass of the working population. Today, in contrast, councillors spend around an average of 30 hours per week on the job, with Labour and Liberal Democrat councillors more committed than Conservatives. Power in individual councils depends on the balance of local parties, exercised through the committee chairs and vicechairs (committees being the key policy-making units in local authorities).

In 1986 the Widdecombe Report into the conduct of local authority business directly addressed the question of politicisation and made a number of recommendations, including pay for councillors and a formalisation of the role of political parties on committees. In the event the Government rejected most of the report. Instead it legislated to prohibit council publicity of a party political nature.

The day-to-day work, as we have noted, is carried out by full-time officers. The local bureaucracy is not unlike the civil service, but there are some significant differences. Each authority decides on its own management arrangements, although it must appoint a chief executive. Expertise is more important than in the past.

Most importantly the officers are appointed by the council, not by the executive as in central Government. As a result they tend to be more politicised than national civil servants. This does not mean that they overtly wear a party label. But it does mean that their values and those of the dominant political grouping in the council are likely to coincide. Hence a council dominated by councillors intent on rapid commercial and residential expansion is likely to employ planning officers who are sympathetic to development. Such values are more associated with the Conservative than the Labour and Liberal Democrat parties, although many rural Conservatives are also hostile to development.

More publicity has been attracted to the shared left-wing values of councillors and officers in inner city Labour strongholds. So-called 'loony left' policies favouring sexual and ethnic minorities have been attacked by the Conservatives as evidence of the politicisation of council officers.

Paradoxically, a further criticism of local officers is that they are running the show independently of elected councillors. This critique stems from the fact that council members are both part-time and temporary. Moreover, the highly technical nature of many local government functions – planning, sanitation, transport – puts a premium on expert opinion, which many councillors lack.

DEMOCRACY AND THE CHANGING STRUCTURE OF LOCAL GOVERNMENT

One of the most enduring debates in democratic theory concerns the proper division of powers between different levels of government (see Briefing 19.3). All democratic theorists accept that some governmental functions are best carried out by central Governments and some by local (or regional or provincial) governments. Advocates of a minimal governmental role usually ascribe very few functions to central Government, in effect only the provision of *public goods* or those services which benefit all citizens equally such as defence, foreign policy and macroeconomic management. In reality most central Governments do a great deal more than this, especially since the creation of modern welfare programmes requires national action and national standards.

In Britain, democratic accountability for centrally provided services, such as unemployment benefit and most income support programmes, has been enforced through periodic general elections which put a party and its programme in power (Chapter 17). When, however, programmes are required to respond to local conditions and local needs, central Governments have delegated responsibility for the implementation and sometimes for the design of services to local governments.

So, typically in the period down to the 1980s, the management, location and quality of council (public) housing was left to local district and borough authorities even if the housing programme was largely funded by central Government. Similarly, education, law enforcement and many other services were provided by county council governments. Again, they depended in part on central subventions via the Rate Support Grant (RSG).

Crucially, however, local people had a direct say in the management of these services through the election of local councillors. Sometimes this involved crucial choices in matters dear to the electorate's hearts. For example, in October 1965 the Labour Government recommended that all county councils abandon grammar schools and opt for comprehensive education. Most Conservative-controlled councils refused to comply, however, at least until the directive was made compulsory in 1976. With the return of the Conservatives in 1979, local authorities were once again given freedom of choice over the status of selective schools, a freedom which the Labour Government retained after 1997.

At the district level, Labour-controlled councils provided many more public housing units than Conservative councils, again reflecting the wishes of the local electorate. Admittedly this system of local representation was flawed: the role of

BRIEFINGS

19.3 THE DIVISION OF FUNCTIONS AMONG DIFFERENT LEVELS OF GOVERNMENT

With the growth of powers of the European Union, and the devolution of power by central governments to regional and local governments in such countries as Spain, Italy and indeed Britain, the debate about which level of government should do what has received fresh impetus. Within the EU, the issue is referred to as subsidiarity: the principle that lower level governments should carry out public policies unless they are more efficiently and fairly carried out by central or federal governments. Unfortunately, which level is best at doing what is usually a matter of custom, tradition or political expediency rather than efficiency or fairness. As long ago as 1861 the political philosopher John Stuart Mill argued that there are three levels of responsibility: the purely local where such tasks as street cleaning, lighting and refuse collection should be performed; those where because of 'spillovers' to other areas, such as with education or policing, the central Government should administer policy; finally those areas such as sanitation and welfare where the central Government should set minimum standards, but localities should administer and pay for the services.

Mill was, of course, writing in the context of nineteenth century England, and since then central Governments have taken on vast new responsibilities. Public choice theorists (or 'rational choice' theorists, see Chapter 10) have argued that this rapid expansion in government has led to a great overprovision of public services. The solution, they argue, is to confine central Government responsibilities to foreign and defence policy and macro economic management. All other services should be provided either by the market or by lower level governments. As earlier chapters have shown, a significant move towards market provision has occurred in Britain, but even right-wing Governments have been reluctant to devolve major programmes to local governments.

Writing in the American context, the political scientist Paul Peterson has argued that federal (or central) governments should continue to play a major role in *redistributive* policies such as income support (welfare), pensions, health and housing, but that what he calls *developmental* policies or such things as sanitation, transport, education and utilities should be left to lower level governments. In fact this division is not so very different from that which prevails in Britain today, except that successive Conservative governments have privatised or centralised a number of developmental policies. One thing is for sure: debate over the proper division of responsibility, including which level of government should pay for what, will continue for many years, and will probably intensify following Scottish and Welsh devolution and the possible creation of regional governments in England.

the central Government was always ambiguous and blurred accountability, the quality of local councillors was often low, as was interest in local elections. But it did provide for the rudiments of local democracy. Beginning with the election of a

Conservative Government in 1979, this system was slowly but surely undermined, so that by the late 1990s relatively few direct links exist between the local provision of services and the local democratic process. The major changes have been:

1. *Privatisation and deregulation.* Many services previously provided by local governments have been privatised or opened up to private competition. Bus and rapid transit systems which used to be local monopolies are now unsubsidised and competitive. Street cleaning and refuse collection are provided by private companies. Compulsory competitive tendering, or the requirement that competitive bids from the private sector have to be obtained before contracts are given, was introduced for a limited range of services in 1988. This provision was extended to almost all services including accounting, computer equipment and professional services in 1992.

2. *Council house sales.* Between 1980 and 1996 2.2 million dwellings previously owned by local authorities were sold to sitting tenants or housing associations. This massive transfer of housing units has greatly reduced the role of local authorities in the provision of housing.

3. *Educational reform.* One of the most important local government functions both in terms of expenditure and in public perception is education. Since 1979 local government's role in education has been transformed. The former polytechnics (now universities) have been totally removed from local control, the management of schools (including decisions over hiring and firing and resource allocation) has been devolved to school governors, and schools have been given the opportunity to 'opt out' of local government funding altogether and instead receive finance direct from the central Government. The opt-out rate has been low, but has tended to involve higher status secondary schools. In addition the introduction of the National Curriculum, and of testing for standards among both teachers and pupils, has increased central control.

Implications for local democracy

These changes imposed by central Government are not, of course, necessarily bad in themselves. Indeed some, such as the sale of council houses, have been popular and successful. There is no doubt, however, that they have changed the nature of what local government does. Instead of administering national programmes and tempering them to the needs of the locality they have become purchasers of local services and thus constrained by the guidelines laid down by central Government (cheapest bids) and the alternatives offered by the market. Large areas of responsibility have been transferred away from them.

There are two opposing views about the effect this transformation has had on the nature of local democracy.

The enabling or facilitating role of local democracy

The first view is that it has changed the role of local governments from originators of policies reflecting the wishes of local electorates, to *enablers* or *facilitators* of a range of policies decided on by the central Government or by the market. This represents a further erosion of the link between citizens and locally provided services.

Some commentators have argued – and to some effect – that this link was always weak in Britain owing to the role of local government as a national service. Thus the changes have few implications for democracy. The recent politicisation of local elections in Britain, rather than strengthening the citizen– representative link, may simply have had had the effect of transforming local elections into mini versions of national elections. In other words, the trend may constitute more evidence of the centralisation of political life in Britain (see Briefing 19.4).

Local democracy has, according to this argument, simply merged into national democracy, in the sense that two country-wide parties compete to form the national government, and localities are simply another forum (like Parliament) for their vote-seeking endeavours.

Many on the right go even further and claim that market provision of services is the best guarantee of quality and value for money, so there is little need for elected local government. Such a perspective is difficult to reconcile with the fact that the vast majority of the public do regard a range of services as best provided

BRIEFINGS

19.4 THE POLITICISATION OF LOCAL GOVERNMENT IN BRITAIN

Until the spread of local responsibilities under national legislation during the 1940s to 1970s, local government in Britain (see Chapter 6) was relatively free of party politics. Many local councillors were labelled independents, or members of rate-payers' associations. From the 1960s onwards, however, candidates increasingly stood as party representatives. In many councils, party groupings emerged and majority parties (or sometimes coalitions) took control of committees and the leadership of the council. The polarisation of national politics which occurred following the economic traumas of the 1970s and the election of the Thatcher Government in 1979, led to sometimes fierce battles between opposing party groups over such contentious issues as council house sales, secondary school education and rates levels. Left-wing inner city councils also became associated with a variety of issues such as gay rights and opposition to Britain's independent nuclear deterrent, which greatly angered the

Conservative Government. These developments led to the abolition of the Greater London Council and the six metropolitan authorities in the mid-1980s. At the 1984 Conservative Conference the Government announced that it was setting up a committee (the Widdecombe Committee) to look into the conduct of local councils. Although it eventually recommended a number of reforms, including the strengthening of local democracy, the major legislation stemming from the committee involved a ban on the use of local authority resources for politically motivated publicity and advertising.

Increasingly, local elections became reflections of changes in the national mood, and in particular the electorate's perception of the performance of the Conservative Government. By the time of the 1997 General Election, Labour, the Liberal Democratic and the nationalist parties represented the overwhelming majority of seats at all levels of local government.

by government, and that local provision is the best guarantee that public account-ability will be maintained at a high level. Such is certainly the case with primary and secondary education and arguably with a range of transport services.

In many political systems accountability is maintained by a close link between locally raised taxes voted for by the public and which go directly to pay for local services. In Britain this has been eroded by ever increasing central control over local government finance. As a White Paper on local government finance con-cluded in 1986: 'Local accountability depends crucially on the relationship between paying for local services and voting in local elections. As this link has been evaded so local democracy has been weakened'.

An expanding role for local democracy

Accepting this last point, one can argue however that these pessimistic assessments see local democracy as essentially service-driven in nature rather than having a wider representative role in the locality. After all, many saw local autonomy being crucially undermined when municipal gas works and water undertakings, health clinics and electricity were nationalised in 1946. Retrospectively we can see that local councils then went on to take a vastly expanded role in other service provision.

Similarly, in the year 2000, other responsibilities of local authorities – notably planning and development, amenities and environment – will take on a vastly expanded role as they move up the political agenda. The role of enabler and facil-itator, as well as regulator, may not be such a trivial one for local government after all. Who needs to provide a local service if one can decide from whom to purchase it and how it is to be delivered?

The political and representative role of local councils may also become more important, now that the European dimension is opening up and there is a precedent for standing up to national Government on local concerns.

With regard to the nationalisation of local democracy, this thesis rather ignores the success of the Liberals, followed by Labour, with community politics, fight-ing on local concerns. Local parties, as branches of the national parties, do fight out the left–right conflict at their level. But this is because the question of how far local government should intervene in its community is just as relevant and vital locally as whether central Government should intervene in the nation as a whole.

NEW LABOUR AND LOCAL DEMOCRACY

Whichever of these assessments is valid, it is clear that New Labour's policies will closely affect the future of local democracy. Here one thing is for sure: Labour will not 'return' education to local authority control. Instead its 1997 elec-tion manifesto promised a commitment to self-management and independence. Even if this involves more democracy in school management, it clearly will not mean a transfer of taxing powers to the local level. Instead, education looks set to become ever more dependent on central Government resources. As far as other local services are concerned, Labour is likely to strengthen local democracy, partly because of the influx of excouncillors in 1997 among New Labour MPs, who are naturally sympathetic to the localities. For this reason alone, the draconian policies of the Conservatives are unlikely to be repeated.

By late 1997 plans had been drawn up for the creation of a new London authority with an elected executive Mayor, and further changes are likely in other jurisdictions involving directly elected mayors. And devolution to new Scottish and Welsh assemblies and possibly to the English regions is now firmly on the agenda (Chapter 6).

However, with the exception of the new Scottish assembly, it is highly unlikely that the Labour Government will grant new taxing powers to any local or regional government. In this sense, the moves towards local accountability will be quite limited. Some increase in the proportion of local spending that is financed locally is likely to occur, however.

As far as more directly political reforms are concerned the Government may also accept a move to annual council elections and even to local referendums about public works projects. But all of these changes will apply to a policy universe that is significantly smaller than that prevailing 20 years ago. In other words, few of the dramatic changes wrought by the Conservatives, most of which involved a reduction of local responsibilities, are likely to be reversed. Briefing 19.5 discusses possible reforms for improving local democracy.

BRIEFINGS

19.5 WHAT REFORMS WOULD IMPROVE LOCAL DEMOCRACY?

At present the proportion of electors voting in council elections is 40 per cent or below. This could be taken as a sign of satisfaction about what is being done locally but hardly shows great enthusiasm or involvement!

One reason for the lack of interest is the feeling that it is general elections which are important, even in the local sphere, and that local elections (like European ones) do not make much difference. The solution here would be to buck the trend by giving local councils more, not less, responsibility, perhaps particularly for taxation. It is unlikely that all local services could be paid for by local taxation, however, because of the fact that so many are created or demanded by national Government.

Another way of making local decisions more significant would be to allow local councils to do whatever they want provided it is not illegal. This would permit much more local innovation and experimentation. At the moment councils labour under the dead hand of the *ultra vires* doctrine, according to which local authorities can do only what they are expressly allowed to do by

law. The Scottish Constitutional Convention (1988–92) recommended such a reversal, which may be taken up by the new Scottish government. As it does not cost money, the reform might appeal to New Labour as part of their package of constitutional reforms.

At the moment the diffusion of power and responsibility between two tiers of local government confuses people and diminishes interest. The answer would be to have unitary authorities everywhere. Concentrating elections for the whole council on one day every three or four years would also make them more visible and encourage turnout.

Concentrating power and responsibility on a highly visible elected Mayor is just what Labour has done in London. This may have consequences for national as well as local politics, as the Mayor will have had more votes cast directly for him or her than any other politician in the country, and may thus be a prime candidate for the national leadership of the party. On the other hand it may depress voting in the (second-tier) boroughs.

ESSAYS

1. Outline the main changes in the territorial and functional division of powers in local government since 1970. Have the changes produced a more efficient system?

2. Why was local government progressively politicised during the 1970s and 1980s? What are the criticisms of a politicised local government system?

3. Should education be a local responsibility run by local councils or should the central government play some role?

4. What reforms would make local government more democratic?

SUMMARY

More perhaps than any other sphere of British life, local politics have reflected the heightened ideological confrontations and clashes of the 1980s, but may now be moving into quieter waters. This chapter has highlighted:

- the mutual dependency of central and local government in Britain, which produces conflict when political control is divided;

- the repeated reorganisations, both territorial and functional;

- politicisation, privatisation and deregulation which transformed local government into a buyer or 'facilitator' rather than a provider of local services;

- finance, especially the poll tax, a local issue which for the first time brought down a prime minister;

- the precarious constitutional and political position of sub-national government in Britain (in many democracies state, provincial or local governments have constitutionally protected status or their position is secured by long-established traditions);

- the limited renewal of local democracy with the election of a Labour Government in 1997, not least in Scotland and Wales. Elected mayors and regional government may also be introduced elsewhere. It is highly unlikely, however, that Labour will give new taxing powers to local governments. In this sense the close linkage between local voters, local taxation and local policies, which is the essence of local democracy in many countries, is unlikely to develop in Britain.

MILESTONES

MILESTONES IN LOCAL GOVERNMENT IN BRITAIN

1888 and 1894 Local Government Acts create the local government structure that prevails until the 1970s

1966 Creation of the Greater London Council

1967 Redcliffe-Maud Commission on Local Government

1972 Local Government Act rationalises the system of local government and creates metropolitan counties and districts

1975 Local government reorganised in Scotland

1976 Local Government and Planning Act: overspending curbed, sale of council houses compulsory

1984–86 GLC and metropolitan counties abolished. Local transport subsidies curbed

1986 Widdecombe Report recommends major changes in role of political parties in local government. Only minor changes made in the ensuing legislation

1987 Central Government grants are fixed to expenditure

1988 Government announces abolition of rates, creation of community charge and uniform business rate, plus other measures including the opting out of schools

1989 Poll tax (community charge) introduced in Scotland

1990 Poll tax introduced in England and Wales

1991 Government announces phasing out of poll tax and introduction of a replacement council tax

1994–96 Two-tier local government systems abolished in Scotland and Wales. Some unitary authorities created in England

1997 Referendum in Scotland produces a four to one majority for the creation of a Scottish assembly and three to one majority for the assembly to have tax-raising powers. Referendum in Wales produces a very small majority for a Welsh assembly. Plans for devolution to English regions in doubt

1998 May referendum on directly elected executive Mayor for London

PROJECTS

1. Attempt to devise a rational and efficient distribution of power between local, regional and national governments in Britain. Illustrate your answer with reference to arrangements in other countries.

2. What are the pros and cons of different systems of local government finance? Illustrate your answer with reference to how different systems may facilitate:
(a) local democracy and accountability and
(b) financial responsibility.

3. On balance, were the numerous reforms introduced by the Conservatives in the 1980s and 1990s a good thing or a bad thing for local government in Britain ? Use a case study of one local authority with which you are familiar to illustrate your answer.

FURTHER READING

An up-to-date textbook treatment is provided by J.A. Chandler, *Local Government Today* (Manchester: Manchester University Press, 1996). A stimulating collection of essays on local democracy is Desmond King and Gerry Stoker (eds), *Rethinking Local Democracy* (Basingstoke: Macmillan/ESRC, 1996). The definitive study of central–local relations in the 1980s is R.A.W. Rhodes, *The National World of Local Government* (London: Allen and Unwin, 1986). Recent organisational changes are covered by Steve Leach, John Stewart and Kieron Walsh, *The Changing Organization and Management of Local Government* (Basingstoke: Macmillan 1994). For information on quangos and local government, see Howard Davis (ed.), *Quangos and Local Government: A Changing World* (London: Frank Cass, 1996). Comparative perspectives are provided by Margaret Bowman and William Hampton (eds), *Local Democracies: A Study in Comparative Local Government* (Melbourne: Longman Cheshire, 1983), and David McKay, 'Urban Development and Civic Community: A comparative analysis, *British Journal of Political Science*, 26 (1996), pp. 1–23.

PART V
Order

Courts and judges

Central and local administration in Britain are complemented by the legal system. This not only scrutinises and reviews their decisions (Chapter 11) but in many ways also functions as a parallel line of administration on its own, processing and deciding a variety of matters that would otherwise need to be handled directly by the political authorities. As it is, governments can express their general intentions through parliamentary legislation, which judges then apply to specific cases in the courts.

Unfortunately, governments do not always express their wishes clearly, and are even deliberately ambiguous on certain matters for political reasons. This gives considerable scope for judges to interpret or even to modify law, even where they are not explicitly reviewing it. Some consequences of this have already been touched upon in Chapter 11. Their powers make the question of who the judges are, and how the courts operate, of considerable political relevance.

This chapter accordingly:

- Describes the court systems of England and Wales, Scotland and Northern Ireland

- Comments on the way law is interpreted in the courts and the consequences this has for their political role

- Examines the appointment, background and outlook of the judges

- Describes the nature of legal procedures and the way in which they require political judgements to be made in some cases

COURT SYSTEMS

The court structure of England and Wales (it differs in Scotland and Northern Ireland) has not changed since a major reorganisation in 1972. Its main components are summarised in Table 20.1. In the localities are the magistrates' courts, which outside the main conurbations are staffed by part-time, unpaid laypersons.

BRIEFINGS

20.1 LAW AND DIFFERENT KINDS OF LAW

The essence of law is that it is a general rule backed by sanctions against those who break it. Who decides and applies such sanctions (international bodies, state or sub-state governments) may vary. There is debate about whether law could take the form of customs and conventions backed by public opinion in societies without government. However, in the modern world law is generally defined by having the backing of some authority which issues the rule in written form.

The *general* nature of law consists in the fact that it specifies appropriate behaviour for everyone under a particular set of circumstances. These circumstances are likely to arise, however, only for particular groups or types of people. Thus laws will have more relevance for some groups and individuals than others, which is why these are more involved in lobbying the executive and legislature and in court actions designed to change existing rules.

The body of law is divided up according to the area of life it regulates. Thus there is a body of criminal law, commercial law, private law, family law, public, constitutional and administrative law, and so on. The borders between these are fluid and often depend on rather arbitrary definitions: for example, whether sharp practice in business comes under commercial law or criminal law depends on whether it can be classed as a fraud (illicit deception). Legal cases are often defended on the grounds that an inappropriate charge has been brought.

Some practices, like making contracts, cut across a number of fields, so that the law of contract has a general applicability, as does the law of evidence. Law about procedures (such as how valid laws must be made) thus have a more general impact than most substantive law, since they affect the whole process of law making. This is why constitutional courts generally have a higher status than ordinary courts. Very often the outcome of a particular case depends on whether the relevant laws under which it is brought are valid or not. Ultimately, therefore, decisions about political and legal procedures will affect us all.

Key term

Law – a body of rules enforced by the power of the state.

These are local worthies, appointed by secret committees nominated by the Lord Chancellor. There are over 30,000 magistrates, known as Justices of the Peace (JPs). In 1995 53 per cent were men and 47 per cent women. Though magistrates courts are sometimes described as 'the people's courts', JPs are in no sense representative of the populations in their areas, and no direct public participation in their selection occurs. On the other hand, JPs may have more contact with local communities than professional full-time judges. They deal with most minor crime and also decide whether more serious cases should be sent for trial by judge and jury in the Crown Court. Though the crimes are minor, they have, and very often use, the power to imprison for up to six months. Though they are aided by legally trained clerks, the biggest problem about the magistrates' courts is the enormous variation from area to area in their sentencing practices.

England and Wales are the only jurisdictions in the world to rely on this fourteenth century relic, which has enormous power because it handles so much of the work. Magistrates only handle minor crime, but the huge bulk of crime *is* minor. Two million cases a year – 98 per cent of all criminal cases – start and end with magistrates.

A peculiar anomaly of English law makes the fact that one can appeal from the magistrates' decision almost irrelevant. This is because convicted people sentenced to prison start their sentence immediately, even if they are appealing. The slowness of appeal means that anyone serving a sentence of a month or six weeks, the most common sentence, will have served at least half before the appeal is heard. And as Crown Court judges often increase the magistrates' sentence, it is seldom rational to appeal, however innocent one feels.

As well as the magistrates' courts, there are two sorts of professionally staffed local courts: the crown courts for criminal law and the county courts for civil law. There are 90 crown court centres in England and Wales, and about 260 county courts. Crown courts are staffed, for most trials, by the most junior rank of judge, the circuit judges or by part-time recorders. There are about 500 circuit judges drawn from the legal profession, most being barristers. Though solicitors can be appointed, no more than 10 per cent of circuit judges come from that branch of the profession, though solicitors outnumber barristers by ten to one. (Barristers are lawyers, mostly concentrated in London, who specialise in court appearances, and have more prestige than solicitors, who do the bulk of legal work. Although the situation is changing, historically the barrister side of the profession has been seen as both socially and intellectually the superior, and until 1977 it was officially known as 'the senior branch'.) In the county courts most of the work is done by circuit judges and district judges.

Crown and county courts are the workhorse courts respectively for more serious crime, and for the overwhelming bulk of civil cases. In 1994 over 2.5 million cases were started in the county courts, most for the recovery of money. Very few of these were actually tried, most disputes being settled out of court. The crown courts try all serious criminal offences; the more serious the crime, the more senior the judge, but almost all crime will end at that level. Of the criminal cases dealt with in the crown courts, about 120,000 per annum, in only 34,000 do defendants fail to plead guilty thus requiring the case to be fully tried. Only 8,000 of those found guilty appeal, and the bulk of appeals are about the severity of sentence, not the verdict itself.

Above these courts we enter the world of the real legal elite. The first step is the High Court. This is a very complex institution which handles more substantial and difficult cases. The High Court is divided into three divisions, the Queen's Bench Division (QBD), Chancery Division and the Family Division. The QBD handles the most complex tort and contract cases. It is headed by the Lord Chief Justice and staffed by approximately 63 High Court judges. As well as dealing with civil cases in the QBD these judges also spend some of their time on circuit hearing the most serious criminal cases in Crown Courts.

The principal business of the Chancery Division is insolvency disputes, trade and industry disputes, disputes over intellectual property and trusts. It is staffed by approximately 17 High Court judges. Family disputes of various types are

Table 20.1 The modern English court system in outline

Court	Functions Criminal	Civil	Number of Courts	Annual Case Load	Composition	Additional Comments
Magistrates' Courts	Minor crime	Very limited	Several hundred	Vast	Part-time lay JPs, except in major conurbations	Apart from trying minor crime, these courts vet all prosecutions to check whether there is a case to be heard before judge and jury in the Crown Court
County Courts	None	Extensive case load for all civil law cases subject to financial limits	260	Approximately two million cases started each year; less than 5% come to trial	Circuit judges and (more than 500) district judges	Most civil cases start and finish here, and much of the work is small claims business
Crown Courts	All	Some limited areas	Technically one court, with 90 centres	Approximately 100,000 cases put down for hearing[1]	High Court (QBD) and circuit judges and recorders	This is the main criminal court. It has three tiers; in the first High Court judges sit to try the most serious crimes, in others circuit judges try more minor offences. It also hears appeals from magistrates' courts and passes sentences on certain cases where conviction has taken place before magistrates
The High Court[2] A: Chancery Division	None	Trusts, wills, tax law, company law, property, etc.		Approximately 700 trials	17 High Court judges under the Vice-Chancellor	
B: Family Division	None	Family law in general		2–3,000 defended cases	15, under the President	All divorce cases start in the county courts but defended ones may come here, as with adoption procedures

Table 20.1 Continued

Court	Functions Criminal	Civil	Number of Courts	Annual Case Load	Composition	Additional Comments
C: Queen's Bench (including its Divisional Court)	Some appeals, mainly in public law from tribunals and magistrates courts	All civil law not dealt with elsewhere, especially contract and tort		1,500–2,000 full trials	63 judges under the Lord Chief Justice	
Court of Appeal					Lord Chief Justice, Master of Rolls and 17 Lord Justices	
A: Criminal Division	Most criminal appeals	None		6–7,000	It sits in benches usually of one or two judges from the Court of Appeal sitting with judges from Queen's Bench Division	
B: Civil Division	None	Appeals from High Court, County Court and certain tribunals		c. 1,500	Usually sits in three-person benches.	
The House of Lords		Appeals from any court in England and Wales on any matter, and from Scotland and Northern Ireland in many cases. Most of the work consists of civil appeals from the Court of Appeal.		50–60	Between 10 and 12 Lords of Appeal, under the Lord Chancellor (who will very rarely sit). Usually works in five-person benches	

Notes:
[1] Case loads are very difficult to estimate because the bulk of civil cases are resolved either before coming to trial at all, or before the trial is over. The figures given are rough estimates of the number of cases that actually do come to trial, whether they are brought to judgement or not.
[2] The various divisions of the High Court all play some role in appeals over cases in their areas from lower courts and from tribunals. This is particularly so for the QBD which has an overall responsibility to supervise all inferior courts and tribunals.

dealt with in the county courts, the magistrates courts and the Family Division of the High Court. The Family Division can hear all cases involving children and is the only court which has jurisdiction in wardship matters. It is staffed by approximately 15 High Court judges.

Confusingly, each of these divisions has its own divisional court. The most important of these is the Divisional Court of the Queen's Bench Division which deals with applications for judicial review of decisions of public bodies (see Chapter 11).

The Court of Appeal is divided into the Criminal Division and the Civil Division. It is staffed by the Lord Chief Justice who heads its criminal division, the Master of the Rolls who heads its civil division, and by 27 lord justices of appeal (lord justices are not law lords. Law lords sit in the Judicial Committee of the House of Lords (see below)). The Criminal Division hears appeals from the Crown Courts and handles in the region of 7,000 appeals a year, most of which are appeals against the sentence imposed rather than the verdict itself. The Civil Division hears approximately 1,000 appeals a year from decisions of the High Court, county courts and certain tribunals.

Most jurisdictions have only one court of appeal, but Britain has two. Above the Court of Appeal itself is the (Judicial Committee of) the House of Lords, a different entity from the Parliamentary House of Lords. The Judicial Committee of the House of Lords consists of 12 specially created life peers – the law lords (technically, Lords of Appeal in Ordinary) who have reached the summit of the legal profession. By convention, two of the law lords will be Scots lawyers. The House is also the ultimate Court of Appeal from Scotland but only on civil matters. On criminal ones the High Court of Justiciary in Edinburgh gives the final rulings.

The judicial Committee of the House of Lords is very senior indeed. It handles less than 200 cases a year and there is no automatic right of appeal to it; this has to be granted either by the Lords themselves or by the Court of Appeal. The doctrine is that it will only handle cases which have far-reaching implications for the impact of law on the whole society.

There are, in addition, two other legal structures which have a potential impact on politics. At a level lower than the High Court are innumerable tribunals and appeal tribunals, which handle a massive and diverse range of disputes (see Chapter 11). There is also the Judicial Committee of the Privy Council, which is essentially the Law Lords under another name. This committee acts as a final court of appeal from certain commonwealth and colonial countries. As such it often acts as a fully fledged supreme court interpreting a written constitution. The Privy Council has, for example, decided on the constitutionality of the death penalty in Singapore.

Courts in Northern Ireland, though separate, closely resemble the English, with less of an emphasis upon lay magistrates and juries. The law administered there derives largely from English common law, modified for Irish conditions and shaped to some extent by Acts of the former Northern Irish Parliament between 1922 and 1972. There is an Appeal Court in Belfast, but the judicial House of Lords has ultimate jurisdiction.

The Scottish system is more distinctive. While there are district courts with lay magistrates, the major court is the Sheriff Court, with jurisdiction over a considerable population and area, and powers to try all but major criminal and civil cases. The sheriff is a professional lawyer, like the judges in the Crown Courts in England. At the centre of the system are the 18 senators of the College of Justice in Edinburgh, who staff both the chief civil court, the Court of Session, and the chief Criminal Court, the High Court of Justiciary. Other senators than those who tried the original case sit as a Court of Criminal Appeal, which is the final authority in criminal cases. There are also appeals in civil cases from the Outer to the Inner House of the Session, but the final authority here is the Judicial Committee of the House of Lords, sitting with two Scottish Lords of Appeal.

These institutional differences are reflected in the different nature of the law administered in Scottish courts. This diverges from the English system in two principal ways. The actual law, in the sense of the legal rules applied by courts, is often different from equivalent rules in England. Property law, for example, retains much more of the feudal inheritance than does the English law of real estate. Secondly, the sources of law, and the general theory of law is different. Although this difference can easily be exaggerated, Scots lawyers operate under a system heavily influenced by Roman law, as is true in continental Europe. There is no room here to discuss Scotland separately. Much of what is said below will still be true of Scottish courts and judges, but not all. It will certainly be the case, however, that any conclusions about the autonomy and political importance of English judges will apply equally, if not more, to Scottish judges (and for that matter to Northern Irish judges).

A last general point about all the legal systems is the exceptional degree of autonomy which lawyers as a profession enjoy. With regard to the practice of their profession and its ethics, they are totally self-regulating under their elected councils. Since legal ethics determine the conduct of business in court, and much of the interpretation of law, the self-government of lawyers is even more important politically than the self-government of other professions like doctors.

It reaches out to the substance of law in the proceedings of the (separate) Law Commissions for England and Scotland. These are quangos charged with revision of law, and composed wholly of lawyers. Formally they deal with technical revisions – cleaning up obscure language, consolidating and codifying branches of law, repealing obsolete statutes – and everything they recommend has to be approved by Parliament. In practice, the matters being technical and noncontroversial, their recommendations may be accepted with little debate. Although technical, such revisions can have enormous importance for individuals, as when they changed the basis of Scottish landholding to absolute freehold from a form of tenure where the superior still retained certain rights (such as mineral rights) and could prohibit development, for example. In some areas the Law Commissions act like a mini-legislature, except that they are nominated, not elected bodies, and are responsive to legal opinion much more than to any other influence. One very good example of the influence of the English Law Commission is the 1986 Public Order Act. This was the cause of much parliamentary furore and lobbying by such bodies as the Police Federation and the NCCL. Looked at closely, however, the Act hardly deviates at all from the draft bill published by the Law Commission in 1983.

BRIEFINGS

20.2 THE ATTEMPTED REFORM OF THE ENGLISH LEGAL PROFESSION IN THE EARLY 1990S

In 1989–90 Mrs Thatcher and her reformist Lord Chancellor, Lord Mackay (significantly a Scottish lawyer) put forward proposals for the most far-reaching reform of the English legal profession since the nineteenth century. This involved effectively abolishing the distinction between barristers and solicitors, simplifying court procedures and throwing open the selection of judges to the whole of the legal profession.

The proposals, though they had the support of solicitors representing the vast majority of lawyers, were fought tooth and nail by judges and the barristers' associations. They were diluted more and more until only minor changes remain. Legal reform changed direction, in sympathy with the Government's value-for-money concerns, by cutting down on legal aid (which

assists persons of up to middling incomes with the high legal costs of any court action) and expanding administrative discretion in such areas as appeals by immigrants against deportation. Sentencing, which involves enormous prison costs, remained unaffected.

The changes the Government made in the end thus adversely affected solicitors rather than barristers and made no difference to judges.

It is a sign of its entrenched power that the Bar managed to fight off nearly all proposed legal reform during the 1980s and seems well able to continue its successful resistance over the next decade. Given the autonomy of the legal profession and its influence over the substance of the law, this is of great political significance.

THE POLITICAL ROLE OF THE COURTS

Key term

Constitutional review – the process by which laws and other acts of the legislature can be overruled by a court if the court holds them to conflict with constitutional rules, human rights, or other laws treated as superior to legislation.

Key term

Natural law – the universal moral rules to which, it is claimed, human laws should conform.

It is clear from what has been said earlier about a growing recourse to legal action to resolve political disputes, that the higher courts have an important mediating role between central and local government on the one hand; and between both of these and European Community institutions on the other. Conservative legislation of the 1980s, particularly the laws regulating industrial relations and trade union activities, has also extended the supervisory and decision-making powers of the courts into new areas, where they have found themselves in conflict with powerful political interests.

All this has happened in a system where the courts lack what has often been taken as the distinguishing mark of a 'political' jurisdiction, that is, the power of 'constitutional review'. 'Constitutional review' in its layperson's sense means a system in which laws and other acts of the legislature can be overruled by a court if they are held to conflict with constitutional rules, basic human rights, or any other laws treated as superior to ordinary legislation. In the United States the Supreme Court can invalidate acts of the Federal Congress or the state legislatures if they contradict the Constitution. Courts with similar powers exist in Canada, Australia and West Germany among other countries and, as we have seen, the European Court has similar powers in countries of the Community.

When this sort of power belongs to a court, its judges are clearly of political importance. Until recently most experts would have agreed that no such power belonged to English courts: no act of Parliament could be brought before a court and challenged as to its basic lawfulness (Scottish courts have asserted vague claims to do this on occasion, but have never actually done so). This is part of the general doctrine that Parliament is supreme and knows no constraint at all (Chapter 7).

This formal supremacy of Parliament also applies, of course, to governments, quangos, local government, and all other public bodies. Nonetheless these can by their actions render parliamentary or even governmental action ineffective, and sometimes a dead letter. Thus it does not follow that, because the courts cannot overrule state law, they therefore lose their political relevance. It is useful in this regard to note a seldom-mentioned fact about other national courts that do have the power of judicial review, which is that they seldom use it! Only a handful of congressional acts have been overruled in America since the 1930s, and in Canada, Australia and West Germany the use of a court to veto legislation is even rarer. But no one will try to argue that these supreme courts have stopped being politically important.

Moreover, in recent years there has been a significant growth in the political importance of the courts. As we saw in Chapter 11, the judges have developed the principles of judicial review to a point where they are now prepared to scrutinise the actions of all public bodies to ensure that their decisions are legal, fair and reasonable. Where fundamental rights or other important interests are at stake, this scrutiny may extend to examining the substance of decisions taken by ministers and other governmental bodies, even where it is claimed that Parliament has conferred complete discretion on the minister or body concerned. Moreover, where EC law is involved judicial review may even extend to acts of Parliament. This is not constitutional review in the strict sense of the term because the courts will not declare acts of Parliament unlawful as contrary to the Constitution. But they may declare provisions of an act to be unlawful in so far as they deprive individuals of rights created by EC law (e.g. Factortame, see Chapters 5 and 7). In this sense it can no longer be assumed that primary legislation is legally unassailable. If the Human Rights Bill is enacted, the courts will have the power to declare primary legislation to be incompatible with the provisions of the European Convention on Human Rights.

Whether or not the courts possess a potential power to review acts of Parliament, the reality is that much of the exercise of power and control by the state in Britain does not involve the application to a citizen of statutes passed by Parliament. For one thing, local authority by-laws are controllable by the courts, who may overrule them if they do not fit with the parliamentary legislation authorising them.

One example is the series of important cases in England during the 1960s which involved the 1961 Caravan Sites Act. Under this, local authorities were given great powers to plan and control the development of caravan sites. But their effective power to do so was severely limited by the Judicial Committee of the House of Lords, who used the empowering legislation, the parliamentary act, to curtail and alter what the local authorities wanted to do.

Next we should note that many parliamentary acts do little more than empower ministers to reach decisions in conformity with often vague and general parliamentary intentions. This discretionary power is entirely subject to control by the

> **Key term**
>
> **EC law** – the treaties, legislation, and case law of the European Court of Justice, which are the legal basis of the European Union.

> **Key term**
>
> **Statute law** – law passed by Parliament (in contrast to European law or common law).

courts, with the effect that, though an act may not be overruled, most of the steps necessary to make the act *do* anything can be. One case to hit the headlines in the late 1970s illustrates this. This was the Tameside case, where the (Labour) Secretary of State for Education tried to stop a local authority changing from an original plan to go comprehensive, in order to retain its grammar schools. The act certainly gave him, in general, the power to intervene in such situations. But when the minister tried to intervene, the courts held that he lacked the power to do so.

Next, although courts cannot overrule an act of Parliament, that does not mean acts do not come before the courts. The vast majority of legal cases, whether they are between private citizens or between a citizen and the state (either as criminal cases or otherwise) involve statutes. No one asks a judge to say a law is not a law at all in Britain, as they sometimes do in America. What they ask is what the law actually means. This process is called interpretation, or 'construction'. It is in interpreting the meaning of the act, often a matter of dealing with very vague or general phrases, that judges have most of their power. The whole thrust of a piece of parliamentary legislation can be changed or bent or reduced or increased in impact in this way, and all entirely legally. In Chapter 11 Milestones we saw the example of the Anisminic case where the courts effectively nullified an act by doing precisely what it appeared to prevent: namely, judicial intervention in the affairs of the Foreign Compensation Commission. Another example is when the 1971 Race Relations Act was very considerably reduced in its ability to prevent discrimination between citizens of different racial backgrounds by two decisions of the House of Lords which were presented as simply matters of 'interpreting' what the words in the act actually meant. In one case a local authority was allowed to refuse to give a council house to a man who had the legal right to live permanently in Britain, and who had done so for 20 years, and who was otherwise entitled to a house, simply because he was, in origin, a Pole. The court 'interpreted' the word 'race' to mean only colour, not nationality, so it was acceptable to discriminate between whites from different countries.

In another case a political club was allowed to refuse membership to a card-carrying member of the relevant party because he was black. They 'interpreted' a clause that forbade discrimination by anyone 'providing services to the public or a section of the public' in such a way as to allow this discrimination, though no one could possibly have thought Parliament wanted to let political clubs off the duty to be unprejudiced.

Finally, our courts have enormous influence over the rules we all have to obey in our relations with each other, because much of criminal law and most of civil law does not come from parliamentary acts at all, but from what is known as 'common law'. Common law is overtly made by the judges. It was the original law of the country before Parliament existed or bothered much about regulating private activities. It is a matter of tradition, a slow developing of rules based on previous cases known as 'precedents'. Most of the law of contract, for example, which regulates business activities, is still common law; what rule shall govern a contract drawn up between two private parties is essentially up to the judges and their ability to understand or to change the rulings in previous similar cases.

The principles of judicial review are all judge-made. What is a fair procedure? When will a minister be held to have acted unreasonably? The answers to questions like these cannot be found in any statute. Parliament has never legislated on

> **Key term**
>
> **Construction** – the practice whereby the courts define and interpret the meaning of Acts of parliament, especially where they are vague or general.

> **Key term**
>
> **Precedent** – a decision or practice of the past which is accepted as a guide for the present. In the law, precedents are past decisions of the courts which are thought to apply to similar legal problems or situations of the present.

BRIEFINGS

20.3 JUDICIAL AUTONOMY: SENTENCING AND DEALING WITH CRIMINALS

The biggest problem, intellectual and practical, about crime, is what should be done after the sentencing of criminals. In the last 20 years it has become ever more clear that orthodox penalties imposed by courts have an entirely negligible impact on crime, either by deterring criminal behaviour or by reforming those convicted and imprisoned. This worldwide criminological finding is often known as the 'Nothing Works' thesis. Research in many countries has shown that recidivism (the probability that someone once convicted will offend again) is completely uncorrelated with the sentences imposed. If there is any pattern, it is a social-psychological pattern related to the offenders' age and sex: most crime is committed by males aged between 18 and 30. 'Nothing Works' is a very strong finding, and it rubs against the 'common sense' assumptions of many people, and of most Conservative politicians.

In particular, research shows that lengthy prison sentences have only one effect: to increase the probability that prisoners will reoffend, because they will have been further socialised into a criminal lifestyle. This general idea has been accepted by the Home Office for some years, and for a decade or more efforts have been made to reduce the rate of imprisonment and substitute other sentences. Community service orders, for example, have been operative in Britain since the mid-1970s, and have been copied in most other common law countries. Probation services have been expanded and encouraged to find more sophisticated ways of dealing with criminals.

Though community service is doubtless preferable on humanitarian grounds to prison, research again suggests no real impact. Community service recidivism is simply neither better nor worse than recidivism from any other sentence.

All of this has long been accepted by professional criminologists, including those in the Home Office.

Combined with their concerns about prison overpopulation, it has led to increased efforts to reduce the use of prison sentences. These have all come to nothing, with prison populations rising inexorably year after year, and the recidivism rate staying constant.

The first effort was the idea of a suspended prison sentence. This simply increased the imprisonment rate, because so many reoffended that they ended up serving both the new sentence and the suspended sentence. Community service was introduced to replace prison at the 'lower end' of imprisonable crimes. However, the courts used such orders for people who would not have gone to prison anyway, and happily continued sending down everyone they would have sentenced to prison before.

Britain continues to have the highest *per capita* prison population of any major Western democracy except the United States. Why do these reforms fail to reduce the number imprisoned in the face of indubitable evidence that prison does not work? Because the criminal justice system, once it gets to the courts, is completely out of the Governments' control; the judges simply *will not* take on board the Government's, or anybody's, belief that imprisonment is useless in the vast majority of cases.

To the judiciary, sentences must follow, and only follow, the seriousness of the crime, and not the utility of the sentence. The most recent attempt by the Government to restrict prison sentences and replace them with 'community correction', the 1991 Criminal Justice Act, is ineffective because it plays into the judges' hands by making 'seriousness' the test of what sentence is appropriate. It is drafted so loosely that no judge who wants to send someone to prison could possibly be prevented from doing so.

the matter. But hundreds of judges over the centuries have made decisions which can be seen as containing rough and changeable rules.

All these powers go together to suggest that courts and judges in England are very important indeed. If the judges can create rules that we have to obey, or can alter rules created by Parliament, or can control the exercise of powers given to ministers and authorities by parliamentary acts, are they not actually governing us, or at least influencing the way we are governed? Who then are the judges?

APPOINTMENT AND IDEOLOGY OF JUDGES

According to John Griffith, 'The most remarkable fact about the appointment of judges is that it is wholly in the hands of politicians'.[1] High Court and Circuit judges and magistrates are appointed by the Lord Chancellor who is a member of the Government and the most senior judges are appointed by the Prime Minister after consultation with the Lord Chancellor. Almost all High Court judges are appointed from the ranks of QCs (Queen's Council) who are senior barristers (the Lord Chancellor decides which barristers are to become QCs). By 1990, all but one of the law lords and all the lord justices of appeal had been appointed by Margaret Thatcher when she was Prime Minister.

It is now unlikely that senior judges will be appointed because of their political allegiance to the Prime Minister of the day. Certainly, since Lord Haldane was Lord Chancellor (1912–15) appointments are believed to have been based on legal and professional qualities rather than political affiliation, as was the case in earlier years. Today 'being a known supporter of a political party seems to be neither a qualification nor a disqualification for appointment'.[2] Senior appointments may nonetheless be politically controversial. For example, it is known that in 1996 the right wing of the Conservative Party 'strongly resisted' the appointment of Lord Bingham as Lord Chief Justice and Lord Woolf as Master of Rolls following the retirement of Lord Chief Justice Taylor.

Because senior judicial appointments tend to be made from the most experienced barristers, the choice of candidate at any one time is extremely limited, possibly not extending beyond five or six suitable people. Officially no regard is had to gender, race, religion, secular orientation or political affiliation. But the fact that the potential number of candidates is so small inevitably means that the vast majority of judges are white middle-aged or elderly males. Since they have spent their professional lives working as barristers they are overwhelmingy likely to have come from privileged backgrounds. There have been many studies of the social background of the senior judges over the years. Overall these show that 80 per cent of the senior judiciary are the products of public schools and of Oxford or Cambridge; that they have an average age of about 60; that 95 per cent are men; and 100 per cent are white.[3]

---

[1] J. Griffith, *The Politics of the Judiciary* (London: Fontana, 5th edn 1997), p. 8
[2] J. Griffith, *The Politics of the Judiciary* (London: Fontana, 1997), p. 16
[3] *Ibid*, p. 21

Clearly, such a socially restricted group are likely to share particular attitudes and social and political orientations. How far does this affect their interpretation of the law?

The ideology of English judges

The autonomy and political power of the courts render specially important the nature of the legal culture, the criteria according to which judicial decisions are made. Specifically, how far does it reflect general attitudes and interests, or how far act against them?

Judges themselves conceive the courts as neutral appliers of law, thinking of their function as 'deciding disputes in accordance with law and with impartiality'. The law is thought of as an established body of principles which prejudges rights and duties. Impartiality means not merely an absence of personal bias or prejudice in judges but also the exclusion of 'irrelevant' considerations such as their religious or political views. In contrast it has been claimed that judges in the United Kingdom:

> ...cannot be politically neutral because... their interpretation of what is in
> the public interest and therefore politically desirable is determined by the
> kind of people they are and the position they hold in our society; [and
> because] this position is part of established authority and so is necessarily
> conservative, not liberal.[4]

This assertion is buttressed by the demonstration that the family and social background of judges is extremely privileged and atypical of the population: they come from wealthy professional, upper-middle-class families; were predominantly educated at exclusive schools and Oxbridge; are 40 or 50 when first appointed and in their sixties before they attain a really powerful position in the House of Lords or Court of Appeal. With a more formal training system for barristers, and with adequate incomes to be earned soon after admission to the Bar, the system of recruitment should be less exclusive in the future, but most barristers, and hence most judges, will even then be far from being ordinary citizens.

The same can be said of the personnel of all the key institutions in Britain, including the Labour Party. So a more exclusive background is not necessarily associated with Conservative opinions. However, Griffith's main thesis is not that judges are conservative because of their upbringing and training. Judges are conservative because they are judges. The judiciary as an institution in every society, whatever the background of its individual members is bound to be conservative (with a small 'c'), since its task is to maintain order and the stability of the state. This implies respect for precedents, history and the established way of doing things.

---

[4] Griffith, *op. cit.*, p. 336

Judges themselves do not see themselves as free, and often give decisions that go against the grain. Hark to Lord Hailsham who, as a member of several Conservative Cabinets, can be categorised unambiguously politically. He was giving judgement in a case where a woman was being prosecuted for breaking regulations governing overcrowding in boarding houses, though actually she was running a refuge for battered wives:

> At the beginning of this opinion, I said that my conclusion, though without doubt, was arrived at with reluctance ... This appellant ... is providing a service for people in urgent and tragic need. It is a service which in fact is provided by no other organ of our much vaunted system of public welfare ... When people come to her door, not seldom accompanied by young children in desperate states and at all hours, because, being in danger, they cannot go home ... the appellant does not turn them away ... but takes them in and gives them shelter and comfort. And what happens when she does? She finds herself the defendant in criminal proceedings at the suit of the local authority because she has allowed the inmates of her house to exceed the permitted maximum, and to that charge, I believe, she has no defence in law. My Lords, this is not a situation that can be regarded with complacency by any member of your Lordships' House, least of all by those who are compelled to do justice according to the law as it is, and not according to the state of affairs as they would wish it to be.[5]

He then cast his vote against the side he undoubtedly favoured.

Similar examples are too numerous to mention. The extent to which judges believe that they are restricted by precedent and by a duty to follow Parliament is something that could not be exaggerated were it not that the orthodox view in English law unfortunately has exaggerated it. Perhaps there is no better example of this role belief than the voting in one case in 1972, *Jones v. Secretary of State for Social Services*, which, as far as facts went, was a nearly identical replay of a case in 1967. In the Jones case at least two Law Lords voted for Jones, in order not to overrule the earlier case, *even though* they felt that both Jones and the earlier plaintiff were not entitled to win, and *even though* they acknowledged that the House has the right to reverse itself; so strong was their adherence to the principles of certainty and *stare decisis* (letting previous decisions stand).

The law, however, is often not clear, and judges have wide areas of discretion. What legal values guide them in this case, and are they systematically biased towards one political side rather than another? It is certainly the case that judges (and lawyers generally) are professionally trained into notions of restraint, caution, restriction, respect for property and family, and obedience for law. Probably they also have a leaning towards conventional moral values. These are attitudes congenial to Conservatives in Britain but they are also values cherished by most Labour supporters. In other words, to equate generally conservative attitudes with

---

[5] Lord Hailsham [1997] 2 All ER 432, p. 443

politically Conservative attitudes on the part of judges also implies categorising the British population as a whole as Conservatives, which is obviously not correct. The striking similarity between legal attitudes and those of the population suggests on the contrary that the courts may reflect rather well the underlying preferences of most citizens.

One can put the idea of a politically Conservative bias on the part of judges to a partial test by examining their actual decisions on a number of cases. Judges who regularly vote in a way that, for example, protects individuals against state intervention by ruling against tax inspectors and planning bodies and so forth, but who very frequently vote to uphold criminal law convictions, might be seen as revealing pro-Conservative sympathies. If most judges voted in this way the bench collectively might be seen as Conservative. In fact even a partial check on decisions of a few leading judges reveals considerable differences between them. It is hard to explain why these should exist if we have a consistently pro-Conservative bench. If judges divide among themselves (or incline to different sympathies on different issues) they are doing no more than reflecting general tendencies among the population and can hardly be singled out as politically biased on that ground.

Moreover, the great expansion of judicial review occurred during a period of Conservative government. As we saw in Chapter 11, in recent years the most controversial legal situations have involved conflicts between judges and Conservative ministers. Michael Howard, Douglas Hurd, Kenneth Baker and Margaret Thatcher all found themselves criticised by the courts. The experience of the last Conservative Government does little to suggest that the courts are prejudiced towards the Conservative Party and much to suggest otherwise. But here again it may well be, as Griffith has argued, that seeking party political prejudice is beside the point.

More often judges decide on the basis of their own values and these are generally conservative. However, rather than seeing this as a deliberate attempt to impose their own views on the rest of us, it can more usefully be seen as evidence of weakness in the structure of our laws. When a judicial decision is not strictly determined by the legal/factual material before a judge, the judge is not only free, but forced, to give a decision that will have ideological undertones. There is no such thing as a 'neutral' decision in these circumstances.

Consider, for example, the decision mentioned earlier in which the Law Lords allowed discriminating practices on the part of political clubs. The judgement was criticised for using a restrictive definition that curtailed the reach of the Act. It has often been asserted that they should instead have extended the scope of the legislation. Perhaps they should. But had they done so, they would not have been acting neutrally, but demonstrating another ideological bias. Wherever choice exists, the choice made will be representative of some set of values. Neutrality in any absolute sense is hardly to be obtained.

JUDGES' VALUES AND COURT DECISIONS

From what has been said it is clear that judicial political values, often conservative in a general sense, slip into the system via structural weaknesses in the law.

The following are the most important situations in which judges are forced to exercise choice or discretion and in which judicial 'values' will play a part:

- the interpretation of statutes where they are unclear;

- the inclusion within statutes of concepts which call for judges to decide an essentially unknowable thing, such as what a reasonable person would do, or whether a minister 'is satisfied that', or whether (more rarely) something is 'in the public interest';

- statutes that require judges themselves to use discretion with little in the way of guidelines, for instance, family law cases where judges must decide themselves what is in the interest of a child.

Statutory construction

This is the most important, because the most frequently found, of these situations. When a statute is unclear on what it requires a court to decide, the judge must find some way of removing what is unclear. Although there exist a host of rules for statutory interpretation, they provide little real help. Like 'interpretation acts', they are best seen not as telling judges how to decide, but how to express what they have decided.

Basically what judges have to do in such a situation is to try to work out what Parliament really intended when it passed an act. Until recently they were supposed to work only from the text of the act itself and, in theory, not supposed to take account of what was said in the relevant debate.

Although some of the difficulties of discovering parliamentary intent are pragmatic, in that it is probable that Parliament had some intention relevant to the case and expressed itself badly, most cases are not like this. The worst problems of statutory construction arise because no one ever thought of a particular problem at all during the legislative phase, and so there is no intention there to be discovered! And, of course, the whole idea of Parliament's intention is often metaphysical; who is Parliament? The best approximation is probably that 'Parliament' means the people who actually composed the text and the secretary of state responsible for the bill's progress through Parliament.

These combined pragmatic and logical difficulties mean that, where lack of clarity exists in a statute, judges may resolve it only by setting themselves in Parliament's place and deciding what they would themselves have intended to do about a problem had they been legislators. Indeed, this is precisely what judges are told to do by the Swiss rules for interpretation, which gain at least in honesty in that respect.

Other rules of interpretation, notably the 'plain words' rule, help to point out a further essential weakness in the structure of statute law. One must follow the literal meaning of a statute unless to do so would either be clearly unjust or lead to a situation that Parliament would not have intended. This is tantamount to saying that not only must judges use their own initiative where there exists a lack of clarity, but also that it is up to them to decide whether there is a lack of clarity. Remembering, of course, that the judge's task is to decide between two sides of an argument, both sides will often have plausible but very different views of which the legislation means. Statutory lack of clarity is not a practical problem that can, hypothetically, be got round. The judgement of when a statute requires interpretation is itself a political judgement. The law reports are full of cases where a statute that is the very model of linguistic clarity is deemed to require interpretation, not because it is hard to see what Parliament *said it intended* but because a judge was unable to believe that it *could have intended* that thing.

It is in the decision to use such interpretative powers that political ideology can most often be seen to invade judicial impartiality. Consider the two following examples of statutory interpretation. The first demonstrates a conflict between judges where there does appear to be genuine uncertainty about the meaning of a phrase. In the second the conflict is really not about verbal confusion but about whether Parliament could possibly have meant what it said.

In the *Suthendran v. Immigration Appeal Tribunal* the Lords had to decide the meaning of a clause of the 1971 Immigration Act, Section 14(1), which allows an immigrant 'who has a limited leave' to stay in the country to appeal against a decision of the Home Office not to extend that leave. Mr Suthendran, having entered as a student with a 'limited leave to stay' while he underwent a training course, defied the terms of his leave, took a job, and overstayed his permit. Various efforts were made, by him and by his employers, to get his leave extended and to get him a work permit, though none of these actions were taken until his original one-year permit had expired. He appealed against the Home Office's refusal to let him stay. Originally his appeal was upheld but later was rejected by the Immigration Appeal Tribunal on the ground that the act clearly only granted the right of appeal to those who *have*, not to those who *no longer have*, 'a leave to stay'. Suthendran's appeal had not been lodged until some time after his permit had expired.

Is the act unclear here? Can one say that 'has a leave to stay' automatically includes those who 'have had' but do not now have a leave to stay? The Lords were divided three to two on the issue, the majority denying Suthendran's appeal and upholding the Home Office's right to deport him. Divorced of context it might seem that the debate is trivial, but the political context introduced on both sides of the case important reasons for finding one way or another. The minority were worried at the potential injustice of the 'literal reading', for it would allow the Home Office to win dubious cases by delaying their decision on a request to remain until the original leave had expired and thus save themselves from a potentially embarrassing appeal. The majority felt it necessary to stick to the literal words of the act. Although they did not say so, there was a political reason here too, in all probability. The reason is demonstrated by a case going on in the Court of Appeal at almost the same time: if immigrants manage to remain in Britain for five years, they win an automatic right to permanent residence. The court clearly feared that, by indefinite delay and by using up all the various rights of appeal given in the act, immigrants could prevent themselves ever being deported.

The majority in this case were what Americans term 'strict constructionists' (i.e. those who interpret constitutional law strictly). Lord Simon, one of the majority, said, for example:

> Parliament is *prima facie* to be credited with meaning what it says in an Act of Parliament ... The drafting of statutes, so important to people who hope to live under the rule of law, will never be satisfactory unless the courts seek ... to read the statutory language ... in the ordinary and primary sense which it bears in its context without omission or addition.

He goes on to admit that this must not be done were it to produce injustice but that 'it would be wrong to proceed on the assumption that the Secretary of State would act oppressively'.

The minority simply invert this last argument. Lord Kilbrandon said: '... faced with two interpretations of this somewhat perplexing statute ... neither of them altogether convincing, I prefer that which ... at least avoids giving a statutory sanction to a possible injustice which I do not believe Parliament would knowingly have countenanced'. One thing is certain: no decision in this case would have been neutral, and nothing, other than a private feeling about what one would have done as a legislator oneself, can solve the problem presented.

Although in the American context one is used to the idea that strict constructionists are conservative, no simple lining up like that is possible in Britain because strict construction may, on occasion, require the more liberal of two possible readings. The next case demonstrates this, for three of the judges – Wilberforce, Dilhorne and Kilbrandon – heard both cases. Whereas Dilhorne was a strict constructionist and conservative in the Suthendran case, in *Davmond v. SW Water Authority* he insisted that the words of the act could *not mean* what they said and again produced a conservative judgement. Wilberforce, in the minority on Suthendran, now turns into a strict constructionist so as to render a liberal judgement.

Mr Davmond complained that he ought not to be required to pay a sewerage charge in his water rates because he was not connected to mains drainage. The statutory clause in question provides that water authorities can fix such charges 'as they think fit' and Dilhorne said: 'This section is silent as to the persons from whom water authorities can obtain payment of their charges. I find this most astonishing'. After insinuating that the Government deliberately left this section unclear so as to avoid controversy in Parliament, Dilhorne went on to say that it was unthinkable that the intention was to allow water authorities to tax anyone in the UK, and proceeded to demonstrate that Parliament could only have intended to make those pay who actually benefit from a service. In so doing he rejected the argument, persuasive to Wilberforce and Diplock in the minority, that as local authorities had *always* had the right to pay for sewerage from a general rate, Parliament could not be seen as intending to remove this vital public health power from the new authorities, unless they said so. This second case, like the first, demonstrates that statutory interpretation necessarily involves private belief. How else could a judge first decide whether a clause was in need of interpretation and then go on to interpret it?

Inconclusive concepts

A second structural feature of the law is that statutes often require judges to interpret such notions as 'reasonable care'. In some other cases, laws which appear to be 'hard' are, in fact, quite empty. A good example is the task set by the law on negligence when the courts have to decide whether people have exercised reasonable care. In public law the vital questions refer to a minister's judgement of a factual situation. Courts may hold ministers to be acting *ultra vires* where a statute empowers them to act 'if they are satisfied that' something is the case. Judges have to decide whether ministers considered anything they ought not to have considered, or failed to consider what they ought to have done. By their own testament, judges *may not* replace the minister's judgement with their own; they are entitled only to decide whether or not the minister *could* be satisfied of something.

These examples are even more pernicious than statutory interpretation because they pose problems only soluble by judges in fact doing what they are supposed not to do, that is, replacing a minister's judgement with their own. The Tameside case, mentioned earlier, is one of the best known examples. The 1944 Education Act authorises the Secretary of State for Education, where he or she is satisfied that an education authority is acting unreasonably, to instruct them to desist. When a minister had been to court to enforce a decision that an education authority was acting unreasonably the House of Lords had a double inference problem: what constitutes 'unreasonable behaviour' by an LEA, and could the minister be satisfied in this case that these constituent elements existed?

The case centred round the cancellation, by a newly elected Conservative education authority, of plans to introduce comprehensive education due to go into effect in September 1976, the authority not being elected until the spring of that year. In particular the controversial point was whether the hastily reintroduced selection procedures would be fair, given the shortage of time to implement them, and a strike on the part of teachers who were angry at the abandonment of the comprehensive plans.

The Lords unanimously argued that 'unreasonable' must be taken not to refer to mistaken behaviour but only behaviour so guaranteed to create chaos that no reasonable education authority could possibly undertake it. On these grounds it was further argued that the Secretary of State, who only had 'to be satisfied' that the authority was acting unreasonably, could *not* have been considering the situation correctly, because there were no grounds on which he could possibly believe Tameside's new plan to be literally unreasonable in this way. It had to be borne in mind that the council had recently been elected with a mandate to maintain selection, despite the fact that the authority in the end had to plan on doing the assessment of several hundred children, for only 200-odd grammar school places, in a few weeks, with a team of only a few teachers not joining the strike; and where, though there was testimony by some experts that it was possible, there was testimony by others that it was not.

Here the Lords had no choice but to put themselves in the minister's place. The only way they could possibly come to the conclusion that he was misdirecting himself in law was by considering the evidence available to him (and, actually, evidence *not* then available to him) and deciding that *they* did not think the authority was acting unreasonably.

This, naturally, is not the only case raising similar problems. In the past the courts' tendency has been to treat ministers' statements that they were satisfied with something as sacrosanct except when there was objective evidence that they had cheated. So in the classic case of *Padfield v. Minister of Agriculture*, in the mid-1960s, a minister required to use his discretion in allowing or refusing a special investigation into the Milk Marketing Board was held to be acting *ultra vires* in refusing an investigation only because he had stupidly written a letter admitting that his action was dictated by party political motives. However, over the last decade, courts have increasingly felt able to say that a minister *could not* be satisfied, while at the same time insisting that they were not applying their own reasoning but objectively testing the minister's process of reasoning.

Often statutes as well as common law rules involve the idea of 'reasonable behaviour', or rest on what a 'reasonable person' would do in some situation. For example, one branch of family law entitles a court to dispense with the consent of a parent to the adoption of a child where that consent is 'unreasonably' withheld. On this criterion the Lords, in a case in 1976 concerning a homosexual father, felt entitled to ignore the father's objection to the adoption of his son. Though he wished only to be allowed to visit the boy for a few hours a week, in the mother and stepfather's home, they argued that no *reasonable* person could fail to agree that a homosexual has nothing to offer his son. Certainly a conservative judgement by much modern opinion.

Discretionary judgements

In a vein generally similar to the case considered above, one must separately add those cases where the courts are not so much called upon to vet another's decision as to make their own first-order decision. The second example discussed below is again taken from family law because it is an area where cases most richly demonstrate the inevitability of judicial ideology having a role. But the first example is more directly political.

It is no dramatic case of the overthrow of a parliamentary statute by a powerful and independent judiciary, merely the 'automatic' application of a written law in a civil case against a local authority. In 1979, elections to the former Greater London Council were won by the Labour Party which campaigned on one issue above all others: it would introduce cheaper fares on London Transport. It was, therefore, a manifesto commitment. As soon as possible after their election they introduced an extensive flat-rate policy of cheaper fares under the general label of 'Fare's Fair', but in order to cut the fares they had to increase the property tax on London residents. The GLC did this by telling the London borough councils to apply a supplementary rate. Most obeyed without question, and public transport fares in London dropped dramatically, though rates did go up. One Conservative borough council rebelled and appealed to the courts. The case did not come up until the London Transport Executive, under the instructions of the GLC, had completely restructured its transport plans and fare structures to fit the Labour Party manifesto.

When the borough council's case came to the High Court it failed, but they went on to the Court of Appeal under the presidency of Lord Denning. This upheld the appeal on an interpretation (ultimately accepted by the law lords) of one word in the governing act, the 1969 London Transport Act. This had a phrase which said that the LTE, under conditions set by the GLC, must organise the capital transport 'economically'. Nobody in the country knows what, if anything, that was really supposed to mean. Most probably it was there as a caution against rampant inefficiencies. However, the courts saw it as very simple. It meant that London Transport must be run on a break-even basis. It could not adopt any policy known ahead of time to be sure to incur a deficit, even if the relevant political elected authority asked it to do so and guaranteed to make up the deficit by a grant, financed from local taxation, which they had every right to levy. Whether or not such a policy is just, sane, politically admirable or whatever is no decision for us to make. But no more is it a decision for eight senior lawyers to make. This one decision had immediate and direct effects on a travelling population of nearly 10 million people, involving, in the estimate of the transport experts, an average fare rise of 150 per cent, in a world where almost no mass public transport system breaks even and during a period when it would throw a large number of newly employed transport workers out of a job in a city which already had more than 300,000 on the dole. Right or wrong, this was an enormous power to be exercised by an odd interpretation of one word.

But cases of less public importance can also reveal the extent of the power wielded by judges through their interpretations. In one typical family law dispute a father wanted custody of his daughter as his former wife, her mother, had died. He could offer a home with a perfectly adequate income, a wife (the daughter's stepmother) and a stepsister for the daughter, with a generally suitable background in terms of parental and sibling age. But he was challenged by his wife's mother, the girl's grandmother, known to the social services as bitterly opposed to the father and determined to make the child hate him. The father, on the other hand,

Plate 20.1 MAC (Stan McMurty) cartoon in the *Daily Mail*, 10 September 1996: A 12-year old boy, beaten by his step-father with a cane after he tried to stab another child with a kitchen knife, takes his case to the European Court of Human Rights

'Before you decide what action to take over my smashing up your car, father, I'd like you to meet my lawyer, my social worker and a bloke from the European Commission of Human Rights . . .'

was accepted by social services as doing his best to help the daughter continue loving her other relatives. The job of a judge in such a case is to choose whatever is in the child's best interest. The High Court and the Court of Appeal both decided that the grandmother should have custody because the stepmother, now in her late twenties, admitted having been promiscuous as a teenager. Although most readers will agree with the social services report in this case, firmly on the side of the father and stepmother's right to custody, no one can complain that the judges unfairly exercised a biased opinion. Yet again they were given no choice but to rule as their private attitudes required because there *is* no other solution.

Instead of this harrowing family law case we might have quoted a more traditionally 'political' example from, say, the Restrictive Practices Court, where judges are required, off their own bat, to decide whether some complicated trade arrangement is or is not in the public interest. We chose the family case only because it has an immediate subjective meaning for most of us. The problem remains the same in that judges are required to decide what is or is not in X's interest, in a political system that supposedly decides 'interest' questions through a pluralist electoral representative system. It is hardly surprising that they consult their private views and decide, in the family case, that the grandmother should have custody, and in restrictive practices cases readily accept high unemployment rates. Still, if Parliament insists on judges answering problems that legislatures and executives fight shy of, they can only blame themselves if the answers are not always to their taste.

JUDGES' ATTITUDES AND THEIR POLITICAL ROLE

The political importance of the judges grew tremendously during the 1980s as they become involved in many facets of central–local relations as well as industrial relations. Conservative legislation created a whole corpus of new law in this area. It was no accident that the restrictions on trade unions, such as the prohibition of secondary picketing and the obligations to ballot their membership through a secret vote before undertaking strike action, were imposed as laws and given to the courts to enforce. By so doing the Government intended to distance itself from actual enforcement of its constitutional victories over the trade unions, and give the provisions the aura of nonpolitical technical expertise which judges enjoy. The current Labour Government, with its policy of constitutional reform including the introduction of a bill of rights, is likely to increase the political role of the courts further.

In enforcing the new labour relations restrictions in the 1980s, the courts certainly did not act to reduce their impact. In imposing financial penalties on SOGAT 82, a print workers' union in dispute with Rupert Murdoch, owner of *The Times*, over his dismissal of many of their members, the Court of Appeal did not take into account, for example, that Murdoch had deliberately split up his newspaper's holdings into separate companies. By picketing his distribution company (engaged exclusively in distributing *The Times* and its companion newspapers), SOGAT 82 were only technically engaged in illegal secondary picketing. They were actually carrying on their primary dispute against *The Times* by one of the few means at their disposal. Courts have emerged as strict constructionists on the union legislation. If they have not sought to mitigate their consequences they have not sought to extend them either. This rather passive interpretation of their role paid off in terms of avoiding the overt hostility of trade unions. These concentrated on political support for the Labour Party, in hopes of getting the legislation modified, rather than on the tactic (counterproductive electorally) of attacking the courts which apply it.

In the less constrained field of local–central relations, the courts' record was more mixed, sometimes upholding Conservative governments and sometimes Labour authorities. In the 1990s, however, the extension of judicial review increasingly involved them in conflict with the Conservatives, to the extent that they were openly criticised by leading members of the Major Government (Chapter 11). Such overt conflicts seem unlikely under New Labour, where the Government itself is acceding to majority judicial opinion by incorporating the European Convention on Human Rights into English (and Scots) Law.

While this will enhance the political role of courts and judiciary it will hardly create it from new. If this chapter shows nothing else it demonstrates that the courts must take a political stance because:

- it is inherent in many decisions they have to make;
- it is thrust upon them by politicians, in most pieces of ordinary legislation, let alone through the Human Rights Convention or the accession to the EU.

In the absence of any other guidance, judges are prone to making judgements in line with their own class and career socialisation. The best way of improving this situation is not to remove their need to make political judgements – probably impossible – but to open up recruitment to wider groups, particularly minorities and women. Lord Irvine, the New Labour Chancellor, has taken a cautious step in this direction by making appointment criteria more transparent, but has shrunk from radically reforming the system. Thus it is likely that judges will continue to be drawn from a relatively narrow group, and continue to make conservative judgements (but with a small 'c').

ESSAYS

1. To what extent do judges want to make political judgements and to what extent are they forced into making them?

2. How far would judges' decisions be different if they came from different social groups?

3. What is meant by the 'political role of the judiciary'? Why is it increasing?

4. To what extent is the court system in England and Wales efficiently organised for the work it must do?

PROJECTS

1. Determine the extent to which the different legal systems of Scotland and of England and Wales produce different results, by studying the Law Reports for the two countries.

2. Analyse the reform of the English legal profession attempted by Lord McKay of Clashfern under the Major Government. Examine the reasons for its failure. State whether these would have applied to any attempt to reform the system or were peculiar to this attempt.

SUMMARY

This chapter has discussed the workings of courts and the thinking of judges, mainly with reference to the situation in England and Wales, but with applications elsewhere in the United Kingdom. It has concluded that:

- Courts handle an enormous volume of work which would otherwise need political decisions. They thus substantially ease the general task of administering Britain.

- The general political role of the courts has been growing. This is not just due to constitutional changes like the superiority of EU law over British, and the adoption of the Convention on Human Rights. It also stems from the volume of politically related legislation (like the Trade Union laws) passed in the last 30 years.

- In interpreting this and other legislation, judges are often thrown back on their own reasoning because laws are ambiguous or unclear. Hence they have to use their own personal opinions as a guide.

- Since judges are drawn from a narrow and exclusive social and professional group, the criteria they apply are likely to be cautious and rooted in respect for precedents, property and established rights.

- Recruitment patterns are not likely to be changed in the foreseeable future so we may expect judgements to continue along the same lines into the next millennium.

MILESTONES

MILESTONES IN LEGAL DEVELOPMENT, 1846–1997

1846 County Courts established for small civil disputes

1873–75 High Court established for major civil disputes. Court of Appeal established

1876 House of Lords becomes highest court of appeal

1949 Civil legal aid established

1953 UK becomes party to European Convention for Human Rights but the treaty is not incorporated into UK law

1966 Law Lords decide that House of Lords is no longer bound by previous decisions

1972 Crown Courts replace Assizes and Quarter Sessions

1972 European Community Act incorporates Community law into UK law

1974 Jury Act abolishes property qualifications for jurors who are to be drawn from the electoral register

1981 Supreme Court Act lays down current jurisdiction of the High Court and its three Divisions

1985 Solicitors lose their monopoly over conveyancing

1990 Courts and Legal Services Act: barristers lose their monopoly of arguing cases in court; cases involving less than £25,000 to go to County Courts; cases involving more than £50,000 to the High Court Factortame case – European Court of Justice rules that UK courts can suspend the provisions of Acts of Parliament which appear to contravene European law until a definitive ruling can be made

1994 Barristers' monopoly to appear in High Court abolished

Woolf Report, *Access to Justice*, recommends radical streamlining of civil litigation

1997 Substantial reforms of civil legal aid scheme proposed by government, cutting public aid

Human Rights Bill to incorporate the European Convention for the protection of Human Rights into UK law

FURTHER READING

The classic work on the subject matter of this chapter is J.A.G. Griffith, *The Politics of the Judiciary* (London: Fontana, 5th edn 1997). Other recent and useful books are R. Stevens, *The Independence of the Judiciary* (Oxford: Oxford University Press, 1993), and P. Madgwick and P. Woodhouse, *The Law and Politics of the Constitution* (Hemel Hempstead: Harvester Wheatsheaf, 1995). L. Blom-Cooper and G. Drewry, *Final Appeal* (Oxford: Clarendon Press, 1972) deals in depth with the House of Lords.

The police and policing

The police in Britain link with both local government and courts. Officially they are under the supervision of police authorities, composed in part of local councillors and in part of other local people and magistrates. Britain is almost unique in Europe in not having a national police force directly under the Ministry of the Interior (the Home Office). Instead it has many different, mainly local, police forces. The question of who actually controls them is ambiguous, as we shall see. But there is no doubt that control of the police is more dispersed than it is on the Continent.

The relationship of the police to courts and judges is more straightforward. The police uphold the law and bring criminals to court for trial. However, since there is much legislation and only limited power to enforce it, the police are forced to set priorities about what laws they will act on, just as judges are forced to fall back on their own opinions in the absence of clear guidance from Parliament. The police are not therefore just executors of policy made by local or central government or judges. They also make day-to-day policy decisions themselves, not necessarily because they want to but because they are forced to do so by the absence of clear guidance from elsewhere.

This chapter focuses on police in England and Wales and considers:

- The principles, pressures and politics underlying and shaping modern policing

- The history of the British police and how this influences the way they operate today

- Police accountability: for what are they responsible and to whom?

- Police procedures and the individual citizen

- The politicising of policing

- Law and order legislation

- EU legislation and policing

WHAT ARE 'THE POLICE' AND WHAT DO THEY DO?

'The police' have been variously regarded as a key *social and political institution*, as a *law enforcement agency*, as a *social service* and as a symbolic *site of power*. They can be regarded as homogeneous and treated as a complex organisation of hierarchical command, or as pluralist and as harbouring many conflicting goals and interests. Our own encounters with the police are primarily as individuals or groups. This chapter focuses on the organisational aspects and their relationships with other organisations. The chapter also focuses on policing in England and Wales, because the system in Scotland (described briefly in Briefing 21.1) is rather different.

It is important to distinguish between 'police' and 'policing'. 'Police' refers to a particular, established organisation found in some but not all types of society. 'Policing' is about the creation of arrangements for maintaining social order. All societies have to maintain order, so policing is an activity they all engage in, but not necessarily through 'the police'.

There are three major influences shaping modern 'policing' in Britain:

1. *Function*. The police have to maintain order and prevent and detect crime. Doing this makes them highly visible participants in the community through their characteristic activities of patrol and surveillance. Their duties here also include control of crowds, gatherings and other potential sources of disruption.

BRIEFINGS

21.1 THE POLICE IN SCOTLAND

The development of policing in Scotland illustrates the original breadth of the term 'police'. Thus, from 1833, various nineteenth century statutes authorised 'burghs' to adopt a 'code of "police", covering watching, lighting, paving, cleansing and water supply, and thereby to become "police burghs"' (Walker, 1992, p. 131). Authority was given to police magistrates and police commissioners. In the counties, paid police were established under Acts of 1839 and 1857.

The Home and Health Department of the Scottish Office oversees the eight police forces of Scotland. Walker (1992; p. 367) summarises the function of the police in Scotland as being to 'preserve law and order, to enforce a great volume of legislation, to search out and apprehend criminals and to report crimes detected to the appropriate procurator-fiscal'. In Scotland, the latter takes on the process of prosecution under the Lord Advocate. Hence the function of the police in Scotland does not differ greatly from that in England and Wales; however, the legal system within which it works is significantly different (Walker, 1992).

Source: D.M. Walker, *The Scottish Legal System: An Introduction to the Study of Scots Law* (Edinburgh: Grein/Sweet and Maxwell, 6th edn, 1992)

Key term

Legitimation – the process of making something morally acceptable in the view of the population.

2. *Legitimation*. The police have a great need to keep what they do acceptable to the public. Prevention of crime is difficult and the detection of offenders even more so. Both rely heavily upon the goodwill and assistance of the public. Detection, in particular, relies on witnesses, confessions, informants, the general gathering of intelligence and, increasingly, the use of technology (e.g. matching databases, DNA testing and so on). These order-maintaining and investigative activities have to be seen to be legitimate and agreed to reflect the exercise of power on behalf of an elected body. The legitimated use of force by the police must be seen to be used on behalf of the community and at the behest of its elected representatives. It must not be seen to favour particular social or political interests above others.

3. *Autonomy*. The policy themselves seek to influence their own development. As a key institution of the state and as a large-scale organisation, the police seek to maximise their resources, power and status. This is not to say that 'the police' are a wholly unified body: there are conflicts and contradictions within the police service overall, between the 43 different forces, between ranks, between officers and so on.

These three underlying influences can be seen at work in all the aspects of police activity we examine below.

A BRIEF HISTORY OF BRITISH POLICING

Historically, up to the Middle Ages, policing was regarded as a communal responsibility and every adult male had an obligation to play his part. During the eighteenth century a wide variety of private and voluntary forms of policing flourished and initiatives to establish a formally administered system were rather piecemeal. By the mid-eighteenth century the system of watchmen was being criticised by many as inadequate, and in 1750 two magistrates, Henry Fielding (the author of *Tom Jones*) and his brother John, sought improvements by creating a small force of their own, the Bow Street Runners. In 1798, another magistrate, Patrick Colquhoun, established a police force for the Port of London and in 1800 this became a statutory force, recognised and part-funded by the Government. The Fieldings and Colquhoun were prolific social commentators on the problem of crime and the need for a police force, and their views were greatly influenced by the work of the Italian legal philosopher Cesare Beccaria and his 1764 *Essay on Crime and Punishment*. Beccaria's ideas were influential within the 'vigorous branch of political economy known as the "science of police"'.[1] This 'science' embraced broader concerns about the governing and good order of the community than are conveyed by our modern and narrow notion of policing, and was promoted by political philosophers of the day of such stature as Jeremy Bentham and Adam Smith.

---

[1] R. Reiner, 'Policing and the police', in M. Maguire, R. Morgan and R. Reiner (eds), *The Oxford Handbook of Criminology* (Oxford: Oxford University Press, 1994), p. 705

Parliament was less enthusiastic, indeed hostile, toward such proposals, and parliamentary committees considered and rejected the idea of a police for the capital in 1770, 1793, 1812, 1818 and 1822. Opposition to the proposal reflected a mix of concerns, including those of the landed and merchant classes wary about what a police force might do and the need for higher taxes to pay for it. There was also a general mistrust of the continental model of state-controlled police and their association with spies and informers. The 1822 Committee thus argued that 'it is difficult to reconcile an effective police force with that perfect freedom of action and exemption from interference which are the great privileges and blessings of society in this country'.[2] Nonetheless, the Home Secretary of the day, Sir Robert Peel, finally saw his Policing Bill for the creation of a Metropolitan Police Force succeed in 1829. The foundations of modern British policing were laid by that bill and its provisions.

Among these were guiding principles which remain pertinent today. They emphasised the independence of the police from direct political control or interference, and strict internal disciplinary systems to prevent the unconstitutional abuse of authority. The police were also encouraged to develop friendly relations with the public, to be 'civil and obliging to all people of every rank and class', though never so far as to compromise their authority. The important legacy of this mix of the 'helping hand' and 'figure of authority' was the image of the 'benign British bobby'. A further consequence of earlier mistrust was the local nature of the forces set up outside London. These were created by local authorities to police their own area and were under the supervision of a local 'watch committee'. Despite amalgamations, the tradition of local forces with supervision by local representatives still survives and accounts for the patchwork of local forces which we have in Britain today.

From 1945 to the 1970s: consensus and controversy

As Reiner[3] observes:

> The 1950s were the heyday of cross-party consensus on law and order, as on other social issues. The police were generally regarded as national mascots, totems of patriotic pride, routinely referred to as role models for the world. The pedestal on which the police stood is illustrated by the popularity of the TV series *Dixon of Dock Green*, in which the central character was a kindly, avuncular PC who captured the cosy stereotype of the British bobby which then prevailed in the public imagination.

As the decade came to a close this cosy image was challenged by a series of scandals involving officers of high and low rank. Although by today's standards these incidents seem unremarkable, it was felt that public confidence in the police had been damaged. The Home Secretary established a Royal Commission in 1960

---

[2] P. Evans, *The Police Revolution* (London: Allen and Unwin, 1974), p. 46
[3] Reiner, *op.cit.*, p. 710

and its report in 1962 provided an overdue review of the role, organisation and accountability of the police. The result was a major piece of legislation, the 1964 Police Act. With regard to the question of accountability and restoration of public confidence, the most enduring contribution of the 1964 act proved to be the tripartite mechanism for supervision of the police, involving the Local Authority Police Committee, Chief Constable and Home Secretary. For some time, this seemed a reasonably effective structure and it was only as society and policing changed that the inherent weaknesses of the model became abundantly apparent. Calling the police to account is far from being a straightforward matter; this stems from the distinctive basis of their constabulary powers which have been defined by the courts as inherent to the police themselves and not subject to scrutiny by outside bodies (see Briefing 21.2).

Perhaps more stringent requirements concerning accountability and appropriate conduct were seen as unnecessary while consensus reigned and the 'British bobby' was still a folk hero in the national consciousness. In fact, we now know from autobiographies and archive research that, even in the 'golden age' of the 1950s, some members of the police service were rather flawed heroes. However, it was the exposure of corruption within the Metropolitan Police in the late 1960s

BRIEFINGS

21.2 POLICE POWERS

The legal status of police powers has developed in a peculiar way. It is derived less from Parliament than from two typically British oddities of legal judgement: a 1930 High Court case concerning mistaken identity (*Fisher* v. *Oldham Corporation*), and a controversial decision by Lord Denning in 1968. Under the former, it was held that a police officer is not the servant of the Watch Committee (i.e. of the representatives of the local council) but that police officers act on their own 'original' authority and are answerable only to the law. In the latter case, Lord Denning made a judgement regarding the Metropolitan Commissioner, which he clearly implied was equally applicable to all chief constables, defining their principal duty as being to 'enforce the law of the land' and arguing that the Commissioner:

> ... is not the servant of anyone, save of the law itself. No Minister of the Crown can tell him that he must, or must not, keep observation on this place or that; or that he must, or must not, prosecute this

man or that one. Nor can any police authority tell him so. The responsibility for law enforcement lies on him. He is answerable to the law and the law alone. (*R* v. *Metropolitan Police Commissioner, ex parte Blackurn* [1968]; All ER, 769).

This is regarded as a notoriously unsound judgement, with the legal commentator Lustgarten (1986, p. 64) remarking that 'seldom have so many errors of law and logic been compressed into one paragraph'. Nonetheless, this is where the law stands, and the outcome is that police officers wield great powers of discretionary decision making. These powers are facilitated by vague and ambiguous rules which have frequently been inadequate to specify appropriate conduct properly (Reiner, 1994, p. 725).

Sources: L. Lustgarten, *The Governance of Police* (London: Sweet and Maxwell, 1986); R. Reiner, 'Policing and the police', in M. Maguire, R. Morgan and R. Reiner (eds), *The Oxford Handbook of Criminology* (Oxford: Oxford University Press, 1994)

Plate 21.1 Peter Schrank cartoon in the *Independent* on Sunday, 23 February 1997: Three men jailed 18 years ago for the murder of Carl Bridgewater were freed amid allegations of 'serious, substantial and widespread police malpractice' after new methods proved that the confession used to condemn the three had been obtained under false premises

and 1970s that truly tarnished the image, with members of specialist squads being charged with receiving bribes and corrupting the course of justice. 'Dixon' was laid to rest as journalists charted, in the title of a famous book on this period, *The Fall of Scotland Yard*.[4]

New structures

The first moves at postwar reform were not, however, procedural but organisational in nature, and were more related to the concurrent restructuring of local government than to burgeoning scandals. They stemmed from the report in 1962 of the Royal Commission mentioned above, the first since 1919. Their recommendations were effected through the 1964 Police Act, which, as a first step, combined many of the smaller forces.

Before the amalgamation consequent on the 1964 act, Britain had a very large number of local police forces, over 170. Apart from the Metropolitan Police covering London, and a few forces in the other larger cities, most forces were small by today's standards, some tiny. Their average size was probably around 600, and some were as small as 150. The small size and small area they policed made these forces very local, and local politicians had, one way or another, a good deal of influence over them.

---

[4] B. Cox, J. Shirley and M. Short, *The Fall of Scotland Yard* (Harmondsworth: Penguin, 1977)

There was, in fact, a sharp distinction historically between two sorts of police forces: those in towns and cities, called the 'borough forces', and those covering nonurban areas, the 'county forces'. The borough forces were ultimately governed by local watch committees, essentially committees of the town or city council, while the county forces were controlled, much more loosely, by the county's magistrates. In fact, because there was a tendency to appoint upper-class ex-army officers as the chief constables in the county forces, there was little need for direct control. The concerns and attitudes of the magistracy and the chief constables coincided to a very large degree, and county force policy represented these interests.

The borough forces were nearly all commanded by professional police chiefs who had come up through the ranks, and there were occasional tensions between them and the watch committees, with the police wanting to take a more independent line. London has always been policed in a different way, with the Metropolitan Police and the City of London Police being commanded by commissioners directly appointed and controlled by the Home Secretary.

By the early 1960s, the sheer inefficiency of having many small forces, combined with a growing concern about lack of uniformity, led to the appointment of the Royal Commission. This immediately became the focus for an often impassioned debate about whether the entire structure should be thrown away and replaced by one national police force, accountable to Parliament, as is the model throughout the rest of Europe. The debate was often confusing because the key issue, which was accountability to political control, could be argued in several ways. Opponents of a national police force feared political intervention and the thought of a highly partisan police under government control. At the same time, many of the proponents of a single national force argued that there was far too little democratic control in the current system, and a single force would be more democratic because of its accountability to Parliament. The Metropolitan Police, it was argued, had never been politicised, even though controlled by the Home Secretary.

The legislation that followed in 1964 was a compromise, picking up ideas from both the majority and minority reports. The number of forces was to be cut enormously by amalgamations that ran across the old county–borough distinction. This happened in several stages, and there are now only 43 police forces in England and Wales. The smallest forces have at least 1,500 officers, and the average is around 3,000. A few, like the West Midlands Police, are much bigger than anything that existed before; one of its Chief Constables is on public record as saying he could not control it. Similarly the Thames Valley Police, with nearly 5,000 officers, covers three entire counties.

Key term

Accountability – to have to answer for one's conduct, or be subject to review or evaluation by a higher body.

POLICE ACCOUNTABILITY AND CONTROL

The question of control of these forces immediately became a serious problem, and has remained so. The 1964 act envisaged a three-cornered control system, with political authority (and budgetary obligations) shared between the Home Office, chief constables and new bodies, called 'police authorities', consisting of both local magistrates and local councillors. However, the old question of how far either of these authorities could extend their control to details of police policy was left essentially as it had been in the county, rather than the borough, forces. The basic doctrine is that no one can give chief constables any orders about how to carry out their job. They can be sacked for incompetence, but not directed. Even the courts have held in subsequent case law that they cannot intervene to order a police force to do anything particular in their carrying out of their functions.

In fact the police authorities have almost no powers. They need Home Office approval to appoint a chief constable; they can be ordered by the Home Office to dismiss their chief constable; and, because so much of the finance comes from the Government, directly or otherwise, they hardly even have financial power over the police. (In fact it is also the Home Office which sets minimum and maximum staff levels, equipment tables and so on.) This situation finally became clear in 1988 in a major case where the Northumbria Police Authority tried to get the courts to forbid the Home Office from interfering with their own preferred policy. The case in question (*R v. Home Secretary, ex parte Northumbria Police Authority* [1988] 2 WLR) is probably the most significant legal ruling on police and politics in the twentieth century.

The Home Office decided that it would authorise the acquisition of plastic bullets (technically 'baton rounds') for use by police forces, and hold these centrally for distribution to any force who had convinced the Home Office Inspectors of Constabulary that they might need them. The Chief Constable of Northumbria decided that he might have a need for such weapons, but his police authority took the policy decision that he should not have them, and refused to authorise his purchase of plastic bullets out of funds he was granted. The Home Office authorised him to have them. The police authority, outraged that their view of what was acceptable in Northumbria had been flouted, went to court, asking for an order to quash the Home Office decision. The court held that the Home Office did have the power to provide weapons to a police force against the wish of that force's own police authority. Even more, they held that the Home Office had this power, not because of the 1964 Police Act, but under the 'royal prerogative'.

What this means is that the central Government has an automatic right to fix local police policy, whether or not Parliament has specifically given it this right! The only control on weaponry, and probably on any policy question where a chief constable wants something is, therefore, the central Government. The powers of the police authority are simple: they are entitled to one yearly report by the chief constable on the activities of the force. They are also entitled to ask for other reports on specific matters, *but chief constables can refuse to make these reports if they feel they should not give them*! In contrast, the Home Office can demand any report or investigation it likes, and the chief constable must then report.

So the situation is that police forces are entirely under the control of the chief constables, subject to the Home Office. There are only 41 chief constables of English and Welsh forces. There are about a dozen inspectors of constabulary, and perhaps 50 policy level civil servants controlling the use of police throughout the UK. This is a significant level of elite power.

The question is also whether this constitutes a move towards a national police force. The debate on a national force has never been properly resolved. Most chief constables themselves do not wish for one, and no government has ever suggested its creation. But it is often suggested that a *de facto* national force already exists. Some critics have even argued that the Government prefers to have a system which operates effectively as one force but with the formal trappings of a series of separate forces. This way, it is argued, parliamentary control is avoided, making the police force even more independent of democratic control than it would otherwise be.

The basic argument behind the thesis that Britain has a *de facto* national force involves the fact that there is a small national police elite from whom all senior police officers are recruited. Apart from chief constables themselves, there are two other ranks – deputy chief constables and assistant chief constables – who make up the membership of an extremely powerful pressure group, the Association of Chief Police Officers, usually known as 'ACPO'. These people, and more junior officers aspiring to membership, share a closely integrated set of experiences. They have all been on senior officers' courses at the Police College in Bramshill; they all have some sort of national experience, for example, being a staff officer to an inspector of constabulary or being seconded to the Home Office; and they have all served in several forces, almost certainly including a stint in 'the Met'. Their career patterns are interesting. Although they have all started as constables, and will usually have taken seven or eight years to become sergeants, they will have gone through the next five ranks, to assistant chief constable, at the rate of about two years per rank. They are high flyers, and the need to move from force to force in order to fly so fast leads to a much more national outlook. As with any small elite, these officers know each other well, have attended endless courses and seminars together, and have formed their ideas and attitudes in concert. Most important of all, they are members of ACPO. (ACPO membership is open to those of assistant chief constable rank upwards and equivalent rank in the Metropolitan Police.)

As is typical in Britain, ACPO is not an official governmental organisation, and technically is simply the professional organisation of senior police officers, part trade union, part club, part official representative for professional views, something like, say, the British Medical Association. However, it is funded by the Home Office, and it is ACPO who selects delegates to Home Office conferences and committees. The importance of ACPO became completely clear during the 1984–85 miners' strike. The problems of policing the picket lines were beyond the capacity of any one force so ACPO set up the National Reporting Centre (NRC) to co-ordinate demands for support from heavily embattled forces and the supply of such support. Although technically chief constables could refuse to co-operate with other forces, the Home Office made it quite clear that they would use legal powers to enforce co-operation if the NRC did not work. The felt need to co-operate was intense, and at least in terms of staff supply the British police became effectively a national force, under ACPO control, for over a year.

Nor was it merely a matter of delivering officers to the right spot. A nationally co-ordinated policy of putting up road blocks, to stop convoys of pickets rushing to particular mines from all over the country, was put in place. Effectively this meant that operational decisions in some areas far from the crisis points were being made in the light of operational needs hundreds of miles away. (The policy was, incidentally, of very dubious legality.) The chief constables themselves deny that ACPO and the NRC constituted a national force. But significantly, what they argued was that if they had not organised themselves unofficially the Government would have created an official national force. It is unclear that saying there is no *de jure* national force because there is a *de facto* one means very much. This combination of independence from local control, dependence on the Home Office, a small national elite of common-minded professionals, and ACPO's co-ordinating role, adds up effectively to a national force. Other factors, like the increasing importance of specialised units, nearly all run by the Metropolitan Police, and a serious concern for a uniform position to be taken in Europe after the frontiers go down, encourage this move to centralisation.

POLICE PROCEDURES AND THE INDIVIDUAL CITIZEN

There have been two crucial changes enforced by recent legislation that have materially affected police work. The most important was the passing of the 1984 Police and Criminal Evidence Act, known universally as 'PACE', which was partially based on the report of the Royal Commission on Criminal Procedure published in 1981. This act is hard to assess objectively because it managed to offend both civil libertarians and the police. Civil libertarians object, for example, to the general power the act gave to stop and search people or vehicles where an officer has reasonable grounds for suspecting stolen or prohibited objects. In fact, to a large extent, this part of the act just generalised and tidied up a mass of separate stop and search powers and has probably not changed police procedure very much. Civil libertarians are in part suspicious of the act because ACPO's evidence to the Royal Commission stressed the need for new legal powers for the police, but now very few officers think they need them as they got what they wanted in PACE. However, they also got a lot they did not want.

> **Key term**
>
> **Civil liberties** – the freedoms which should not normally be constrained by others, whether private individuals or the state.

PACE enormously changed procedures for questioning suspects and for taking down what they say and any statements they make. Police are unanimous that they are seriously hampered by the need to tape record all interviews, and to have a complete *and contemporaneous* account of the entire interview process. Second, a suspect's rights to have a solicitor present, and to say absolutely nothing to the police, mean that police cannot risk detaining and interrogating anyone until they already have enough evidence to win a committal in a magistrates' court. In other words, they have had to abandon the practice of relying on getting a confession because they do not have enough evidence otherwise. (There is still pressure to make a conviction impossible merely on the basis of a confession, which is already the law in Scotland.)

In fact PACE has merely formalised rights that existed in judges' rules before, but putting them in a formal statute has made them very much more effective. In the words of one expert, 'the old informal procedures for crime control, based on fabricating evidence, have had to go'. It is interesting to note that the recent rash of acquittals in the Court of Appeal of people wrongfully convicted years earlier all stem from the days before PACE.

PACE has had an interesting side-effect on statistical measures of police effectiveness. The 'clear-up rate' for crime has declined substantially. In part this is because, before PACE, detectives could often persuade offenders to confess to a series of other crimes which they would ask to be 'taken into consideration' (TIC) in court. Criminals are very much less willing to co-operate with police in this way now, and 'TIC' clear-up has dropped considerably. The fact that police were so dependent on these admissions, and the question of just how people were persuaded to co-operate in this way (against their interest, because a court was likely to increase the sentence if there were a number of TICs) suggest PACE was very much needed.

The secondary statutory restriction on the police to come out of the 1981 Royal Commission was the creation of the Crown Prosecution Service (CPS) by the Prosecution of Offences Act 1986. This is, constitutionally, a more radical change than PACE, which (at least in theory) simply gave statutory recognition to received practice. Before the setting up of the CPS, England and Wales had a system quite unlike that of any other Western democracy. Everywhere else in the world there was a sharp distinction between the job of detecting crime and the task of deciding whether or not to prosecute and handling the prosecution. In continental Europe the decision to prosecute (as well as the supervision of much of the investigation) is in the hands of a member of the judiciary called an examining magistrate. In Scotland an official rather like the examining magistrate, the Procurator Fiscal, played this role. In the USA these decisions are taken by an elected district attorney (or a politically appointed one in the case of federal jurisdiction).

But in England and Wales the police themselves decided whether or not to prosecute. In the magistrates' court they themselves handled the prosecution and in higher courts they instructed counsel themselves. Now all such decisions are made by solicitors who are full-time salaried officers of an independent service, organised regionally but under the ultimate control of the Director of Public Prosecutions, a central Government officer who had always had this power for certain very serious crimes.

The previous fusion of responsibilities mattered principally because there is always a considerable element of discretion involved in the decision to prosecute, and in what evidence will be used by the prosecution. Discretion covered both which crimes to prosecute, and when to prosecute any particular offender. There may be some value in discretion in the first sense, because community standards on, say, pornography, do vary. In fact the police can still exercise some discretion in this area by simply refusing to investigate crimes they do not want prosecuted, given that the police authority cannot order them to act. The police also used their discretion not to prosecute cases which were simply not worth taking to court.

This use of discretion was effectively using court appearances as a method of social control, as a policing activity, rather than as a legal consequence of clear guilt. For example, police very often merely cautioned, or simply talked to, young offenders guilty of minor affrays or disturbances of the peace. But if there were complaints about behaviour on a certain housing estate they would suddenly start to prosecute instead. It was an inappropriate use of the discretion to prosecute. The CPS is much more likely to use objective, nationally determined guidelines in this sort of case.

Discretion on when to prosecute really depends on how high a probability of conviction there should be before a prosecution is launched. The rate of conviction in a jury trial where there is no plea of guilty often surprises people, because it is only around 70 per cent. As the cost and suffering of going to trial can be devastating, even for those acquitted, no prosecution should be launched lightly, however certain the police may be in their own minds that they have the right person. There is no doubt that the Crown Prosecution Service demands a significantly higher probability of conviction before they will prosecute than the police used to expect. Finally, the CPS will inevitably be much keener to check that evidence is reliable and all police procedures watertight, thus further enforcing civil rights against police enthusiasm. The CPS has not yet won widespread approval in any sector, because it has been seriously underfunded and understaffed, and there are doubts about its administrative competence. But the change in constitutional control over the police may ultimately be more important than any other likely or previous reform.

THE POLITICISATION OF POLICING

During the 1970s, the police and their role became increasingly politicised, reflecting a broader social context of tension and conflict. Political and industrial protest, and the anxieties provoked by rising crime rates, led to a new strategy put forward in the Conservative 1979 election campaign. Suddenly, providing more policing was given equal (if potentially contradictory) priority with the promise of reducing taxation. As Mrs Thatcher declared (28 March 1979), 'the demand in the country will be for two things: less tax and more law and order'. The support of the 'rank and file' Police Federation was immensely valuable in making 'law and order' a vote-winning issue for the Conservatives. Deeply hostile toward Labour after a pay dispute in 1977, the Federation provided a well-publicised, openly political endorsement of Tory policy.

Once elected to Government, the Conservatives delivered what they had promised to the police: greatly enhanced pay awards and increased budgets for recruitment and resources. In turn the police were supposed to deliver their part of this bargain. They had been given the rewards in advance; now there could be no excuses for losing the 'fight against crime'. Of course, once mutual admiration and rhetoric were put aside, it became apparent that the practical problem of crime control could not be reduced to a simple formula of 'more police equals less crime'. Crime rose and, with fluctuations here and there, it continued to do so throughout the 1980s, though the statistics improved somewhat in the early 1990s.

While this suggested that 'more policing' was not working, two key and symbolic episodes of the first half of the 1980s kept the police high on the Thatcher Government's list of 'favourites'. These were, first, the inner-city riots of 1981, and second, the miners' strike of 1984–85 (see Briefing 21.3).

In urban riots then and since, the police have first contained disorder and then moved in to enforce order. Their efforts at 'community policing' after rioting, in

BRIEFINGS

21.3 POLITICAL ASPECTS OF POLICING

Discrimination, minorities and the police

Prejudicial treatment of minority groups has long been a key issue for critics of the police. Considerable evidence suggests that, whilst police policy has belatedly but increasingly sought to stamp out sexual and racial discrimination and increase recruitment of ethnic minority officers (Holdaway, 1991), prejudice nonetheless remains part of what is known as the 'canteen culture'. In everyday policing, the disproportionate 'stop and search' of black youths has been one expression of this.

Tensions between black youths and the police were the volatile background against which the inner-city riots of 1980–81 flared, first in Brixton, south London, and then in Toxteth, Merseyside; Mossside, Manchester and Handsworth, Birmingham. The first event was investigated by a senior judge, Lord Scarman, whose *Report on The Brixton Disorder* (1981) made recommendations concerning the need for police and community consultation. The Government expressed gratitude to the police for their efforts in containing such outbreaks of inner-city disorder.

The miners' strike: the police in a political dispute

The miners' strike is significant for what many saw as the *political* use of the police by the Government and for the operation of a national command and control strategy through the National Reporting Centre (NRC). The NRC has no statutory basis but arises out of agreements within the Association of Chief Police Officers (ACPO) and can co-ordinate all the 43 forces of England and Wales in combined operations. This agreement was in place before the miners' strike but it was its employment in this context that suggested to some that it provides a *de facto* national riot police. Home Office ministers and chief constables have traditionally argued that Britain does not and should not have a national police force but should be responsive and accountable to local interests; that this renders them less susceptible to central and politically inspired direction by national government. The legacy of the miners' strike was to expose the emptiness of such an argument, given a government which was prepared to use the police in pursuit of its political objectives.

Source: S. Holdaway, *Recruiting a Multi-ethnic Police Force* (London: HMSO, 1991)

line with the Scarman Report of 1981, have also helped prevent further outbreaks of protest.

In the case of the miners' strike of 1984–85, the most widespread challenge ever to the Conservative Governments, the police acted as very effective agents in beating the strike, deployed and controlled by central Government (in spite of their nominal local status).

Financial scrutiny and the push for reorganisation

Inevitably however, regardless of such service, the police came under financial scrutiny. As crime rose, despite high investment in police pay and resources, the yardstick of 'value for money' was introduced (see Briefing 21.4). The first step in this direction was the 1983 Financial Management Initiative requiring the setting of objectives and priorities, efficient allocation of resources, and the planning

BRIEFINGS

21.4 POLICE EFFECTIVENESS AND 'VALUE FOR MONEY'

Just how effective are the police? In recent years the adequacy of government policy concerning law and order has become more and more politically sensitive. The increase in the importance of the issue has come about largely because the Conservative Party has always presented itself as much more concerned about law and order than Labour, and the governments since 1979 have considerably increased resources for crime control. This is just as true for New Labour as the Conservatives, since they are anxious to take over this issue. It is necessary first to get some sense of scale on the problem. The British police force has a total of 128,000 officers (20,000 in the Metropolitan Police) with perhaps 40,000 civilian employees. This makes it roughly half the size of the French police, and not much more than a third of the size of the Italian forces; that is, Britain has roughly one police officer for every 450 inhabitants, France one for every 250.

Second, unlike European counterparts, the British police are a general duty and entirely civilian force, handling every aspect of policing. Elsewhere in Europe the police are more functionally specialised, usually with a paramilitary organisation like the French Gendarmerie or the Italian Caribinieri who are primarily responsible for public order. It is a predominantly (though decreasingly) unarmed force, and one which has always tried to police consensually.

In this latter respect the British police have probably improved since the severe criticisms of heavy-handed tactics in the 1981 Scarman Report. Usually senior officers will avoid using serious force to contain rioting in case it exacerbates the situation, although this has

not been the policy in industrial disputes like the miners' strike and the one at the News International plant at Wapping in the period 1986–88. On the whole this policy has paid off, and public order policing is fairly effective without being too oppressive. In the other sense of use of force, the use of deadly force with firearms, there has been a clear rise in the number of criminals, or simply disturbed people, shot to death by the police in recent years. But the total numbers are too small to constitute a significant rise.

Assessing how effective the police are in detecting and 'clearing up' crime other than public order offences is a methodological nightmare. Crime statistics are widely regarded as the most unreliable social indicators published by any government in any policy area. Taking an entirely uncritical view, there has apparently been a major increase in crime in Britain over the last two decades. The total of all reported crimes hit 5.3 million in 1991, an increase of 16 per cent over the previous year, almost double the rate for the early 1980s. From 1981 to the mid-1980s crime increased at around 8 per cent per year. It levelled off for two or three years, and then started a very sharp increase from 1988, at about 15–17 per cent per year. However, it fell by 8 per cent from 1993 to 1995, and Britain is still substantially safer than Germany and most other developed countries.

Over this period police staff levels increased by an average of 8 per cent in most forces and by much more in the Metropolitan Police. The cost of the police force increased even more sharply because of major pay rises in the early 1980s. The detection rate, however,

21.4 POLICE EFFECTIVENESS AND 'VALUE FOR MONEY' (continued)

remains very low: roughly one third of crimes are cleared up, with the rate dropping marginally every year.

It should immediately be noted that, even were these figures reliable, they do not represent quite the epidemic of horror some politicians use them to indicate. Ninety-six per cent of all crime is crime against property, and the overwhelming bulk of that is very minor, where the cost of the stolen or damaged property is less than £200, and often very much lower. For example, although the overall change for 1990–91 was 16 per cent, the rate of increase in sexual offences was only 1 per cent, and in violence against the person it was only 3 per cent. In fact 'violent crime' accounts for only 5 per cent of all crimes, and annual increases fluctuate randomly.

But these data cannot be taken at face value. For example, criminal damage is only recorded if the property is worth more than a set figure. In 1972 this figure was set at £20 and the figure remains set at £20, although to avoid a spurious increase in crime, it should now only be recorded for property worth around £200. Another example is that the greatest increase in crime in recent years has been in car-related crime. These crimes are always reported, because they cover insured objects, and the insurers will not recompense unless the theft is reported. Rape has increased, but so have efforts to make it easier and less 'shaming' to report rape, and the concept of 'date rape' has become legally recognised.

More than all of this, crime is reported, in part, according to how easy it is to report it, and what the police do to encourage the reporting of particular

crimes. There almost certainly has been some increase in property crimes, especially opportunistic minor property crimes, roughly along the lines one would expect from increased unemployment and a rising debt burden on the less well-off. How exactly the police are supposed to prevent a rise in such crime is unclear, but it is certainly not a matter of increasing the detection rate.

One example of the arbitrariness of the detection rate was reported in March 1991. One single criminal, in prison, confessed to a prison visitor that he was responsible for 3,000 unsolved shoplifting cases. This accounted for 25 per cent of the clearing up of crime in his county in 1991! Yet most of these crimes would never have been reported in the first place, as undetected shop-lifting never is. None the less, the force in question was able statistically to demonstrate an increase in crime detection over the previous year.

Concentration on the detection rate, as opposed to crime prevention and deterrence measures, has always been misplaced. Roughly 30 per cent of police staffing is in the CID, yet the huge bulk of crime is not detectable. It is of some interest that the clear-up rate has varied very little for several decades; the obvious point is that dealing with crime after it has happened, except for a few major crimes against the person, is neither easy nor cost effective. However, the Government and Opposition are equally unhappy with the police: the Conservatives want better value for money, and Labour wants local accountability. Plans are afoot which will almost certainly mean a decrease in the autonomy of the police in future years.

of policing. After a period of relative immunity from public expenditure cuts, the police now experienced the push toward centralisation and privatisation already applied to most other public services. The language of accountancy became paramount, with HM Inspectorate of Constabulary (HMIC) being given a more substantial and critical remit to monitor efficiency (as measured by a 'Matrix of Performance Indicators'), and the Audit Commission and National Audit Office also evaluating aspects of policing. The police responded with hesitant and small-scale reforms but not to the satisfaction of the Government. By the 1990s, more far-reaching changes were envisaged, first, through the 1993 Sheehy Report on

BRIEFINGS

21.5 SHOULD POLICING BE PRIVATISED?

The 1996 Home Office Review was widely expected to take the privatisation agenda pursued elsewhere and push it firmly and radically into the province of policing. With relative ease the Government had already accomplished the previously unthinkable feat of (partially) unhitching the state from the administration and delivery of punishment. It had done this by contracting out the building and/or the management of some prisons to the private sector and turning the prison service into an 'agency' with a director appointed from outside the sector (Chapter 10). On this basis, the idea of privatising criminal justice still further seemed a highly likely reality. Indeed the police had always seemed a *more* likely candidate for the privatisation agenda than prisons. There was little twentieth century precedent for the latter. Yet a key feature of the provision of police services in Western societies since the 1960s has been the phenomenal growth in private security companies (South, 1988). Policing is now provided by a mixed market but the question remains: how much further can the privatisation of policing go?

Sources: N. South, *Policing for Profit: The Private Security Sector* (London: Sage, 1988)

pay, conditions and rank structure, and then through a 1996 Home Office Review of Police Core and Ancillary Tasks. This raised the question of how far 'public' policing could be privatised.

Both initiatives were embarrassing failures for the Government. The Sheehy Report attracted derision in the press, criticism from a significant alliance of Labour and police, and faced a highly organised and high profile opposition from the united police ranks. The result was serious dilution of Sheehy's recommendations (see Briefing 21.5).

The second initiative, the Review of Core and Ancillary Tasks, was supposed to fit in with the Government's drive to push services into the market sector wherever possible. However, the promise of a 'big bang' actually resulted in little more than the 'whimper' of transferring various minor tasks to local authorities and private companies. In hindsight, the fate of these two attempts to reshape policing in Britain were signals that the Tory law and order engine was running out of steam.

As relations between the police and the Conservatives deteriorated, so they warmed with Labour. The culturally conservative character of the police might have reacted strongly and adversely against the 'loony left' of the old Metropolitan administrations but the soundbites of emerging 'new realism' in the Labour party were rather more palatable.

Across the floor

Views of the police from Labour and the left have varied over time. In the 1960s there was some feeling on the left that changes in the strategy of policing, with moves to patrol cars and 'fire-brigade policing' (i.e. responding to calls rather than being on the beat), meant that the police were increasingly remote from the communities they served. The corruption cases of the 1970s, followed by revelations about the number of deaths in police custody (274 between 1970 and 1979), sparked further distrust (even though most – though not all – deaths arose from natural causes). Police confrontations with demonstrators and strikers created 'a suspicion in the Labour Party and the trade union movement that the real function of the police is to maintain the inferior and subordinate status of the working classes'.[5] The local elections of May 1981 were particularly significant, with the councils of all of the (then) Metropolitan areas now being dominated by radical Labour. These provided critical power bases for the questioning of police policy, generating acrimonious but important debates about the actual nature of police accountability and leading to several high-profile clashes between police authorities and chief constables. Given this history of Labour antipathy towards the police, post-1979 Conservative administrations had good reason to think that their stance on the police and 'law and order' was far more appealing to the voters. There were some in the Labour party who took note.

In terms of the recent realignment of British politics, it is interesting (though unsurprising given who was involved) that it was the issues of crime and policing which provided an early indication of new Labour thinking on social policy. In early 1993, the Home Secretary, Kenneth Clarke, was in debate with his 'shadow', Tony Blair, on *The World This Weekend*. An apparently 'off-the-cuff' (but actually well-rehearsed and polished) proposition from Blair encapsulated a new Labour approach to policing and crime control. The phrase 'We need to be tough on crime and tough on the causes of crime' surprised Clarke, and immediately passed into the 'newspeak' of New Labour.

POLICE, PUBLIC AND THE LAW

In reviewing the law relating to the police in the 1980s, the first point to make is that there was a great deal of it! This is partly related to the stamp which successive home secretaries wished to make on policy, but was also driven by electoral strategy, the need to be constantly producing 'new ideas'. The key piece of legislation is undoubtedly the Police and Criminal Evidence Act 1984 (PACE), discussed above, which brought various existing 'informal' police practices within the law, provided some wider powers, but also introduced certain checks on police behaviour (e.g. the tape recording of interviews in police stations). Subsequently, legislation on police powers was produced at a furious pace, from

[5] H. Elcock, 'Law, Order and the Labour Party', in P. Norton (ed.) *Law and Order and British Politics* (Aldershot: Gower, 1984), p. 157

Figure 21.1 The new police authorities of April 1995

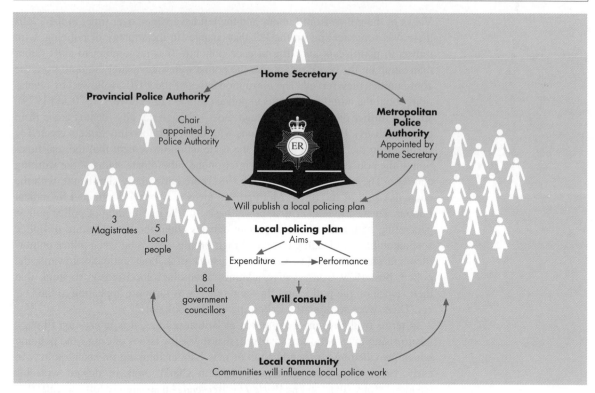

Source: E. McLaughlin, 'Police, policing and policework' in E. McLaughlin and J. Muncie (eds), *Controlling Crime* (London: Sage, 1996), p. 99

the Public Order Act 1986 to the Police and Magistrates Courts Act 1994. This 1994 act has reshaped the tripartite structure of police accountability noted earlier, reducing membership of the police authorities, giving them wider powers within a 'business-oriented' brief, and making them accountable to the Home Secretary. Critics have argued that these committees are now little more than mini-quangos and are far from being democratically representative of local people. Figure 21.1 shows the structure of the new police authorities.

Clearly the strengthening of police powers was one of the dominant motifs of 'law and order' legislation of the 1980s and early 1990s. Some may feel that the wisdom of this trend was highly questionable as another and darker theme emerged in parallel. This concerned the misuse of police powers and the miscarriage of justice. A dramatic sequence of appeal cases, from the early 1980s through to the mid-1990s, revealed serious police malpractice (e.g. suppression or falsification of evidence, and wrongful arrest) resulting in appalling miscarriages of justice. Earlier disclosures of corruption had, it seemed, produced few enduring lessons for the police. As Rose[6] remarks, 'If police detectives could steal

[6] D. Rose, *In the Name of the Law* (London: Jonathan Cape, 1996), p. 43

BRIEFINGS

21.6 RECENT CASES OF WRONGFUL IMPRISONMENT

The *Birmingham 6* were imprisoned for causing explosions in Birmingham pubs in 1974 in which 21 people were killed and 162 injured. The six were freed from jail in 1991 and cleared of charges.

The *Bridgewater 4* were found guilty of murdering 13-year-old Carl Bridgewater in 1978. The four were later released and cleared because police evidence against them was found to be wrong.

The *Guildford 4* were found guilty in 1975 of causing an explosion in a Guildford pub frequented by British soldiers. They were freed in 1989.

Stephen Kiszko was found guilty of murdering a young girl and imprisoned in 1976 but was released in 1992 when it was found that evidence of his innocence had been withheld.

or take bribes, it did not take a vast leap of the imagination to consider that they might also present evidence produced by fabrication or duress'. The cases exposed presented a dismaying picture of dishonesty, impropriety and callousness on the part of some police officers. Notable among these cases were those of the Birmingham Six, the Guildford Four, Stephan Kiszko and, most recently, the Bridgewater Four, all judged to have been wrongly imprisoned (see Briefing 21.6).

Unsurprisingly, a recurrent concern for reformers and critics of the police has become the question of how to detect and prevent police deviance, corruption and prejudicial mishandling of cases (see Briefing 21.7). It was hoped that the calling of an inquiry into the criminal justice system under Lord Runciman would offer a programme for sweeping reforms. In the event, the report of the Royal Commission on Criminal Justice (1993) suggested very few.

BRIEFINGS

21.7 THE 'WAYS AND MEANS ACT': THE CANTEEN CULTURE AND POLICE DEVIANCE

Police accountability always faces the problem of balancing strict application of rules with the need to allow operational flexibility. This is generally accepted within reasonable limits. However, such limits may be *unacceptably* stretched by the informal police culture (often called the 'canteen culture'), and invocation of the fictitious 'Ways and Means Act' as a form of justification. An important investigation of police culture and police perceptions of the public was a study commissioned by the Metropolitan Police and undertaken by the Policy Studies Institute in the early 1980s (Smith and Gray, 1983). The research found evidence of disturbing levels of racism and sexual discrimination (still a problem according to the latest report from the HMI, 1996, pp. 103–6),

21.7 THE 'WAYS AND MEANS ACT': THE CANTEEN CULTURE AND POLICE DEVIANCE (continued)

and also distinguished between three types of 'rule' within police culture: the 'working', the 'inhibitory' and the 'presentational' (*ibid*, pp. 169–72). The first type represents the 'accepted' way of working but is by no means always in line with formal regulations. Inhibitory rules are *formal* rules which carry organisational weight and must therefore be followed, even if seen as unnecessary by officers. Presentational rules highlight the disparity between how the police are supposed to act and how they actually act. As Reiner (1996, p. 730) summarises, 'Presentational rules are those official rules which have no bearing on police practice, but which none the less provide the terms in which accounts after the event must be couched'. The continued existence of such organisational sources of resistance to management supervision and public accountability is a strong reminder that the internal politics of the police are far from transparent.

Sources: D. J. Smith and J. Gray, *The Police in Action* (London: Policy Studies Institute/Gower, 1983; *Report of Her Majesty's Inspector of Constabulary* (*HMI*) (London: HMSO, 1996)

THE POLICE AND EUROPE

The so-called 'Third Pillar' of the Maastricht Treaty on European Union (1991) is concerned with justice and home affairs, including provisions for co-operation between police and customs services of the EU Member States. Such co-operation obviously has a long history but is an accelerating trend. Forms of organised crime, smuggling, drug trafficking, terrorism and international fraud have all stimulated mutual assistance through treaties, secondments, intelligence sharing, joint training and so on. However, the representatives at the Maastricht Summit accepted a proposal which takes co-operation a stage further with the creation of a European Police Office, or 'Europol'. At least initially, this is to be an agency for the collation, analysis and exchanging of information. Some states, notably Germany, support the idea of making Europol an *operational* police force, but most others are unenthusiastic. Anderson *et al.*[7] make several important points here:

> The absence of a federal structure in Europe, a common criminal justice system, and a supranational accountability mechanism, makes operational powers for Europol extremely unlikely. However, even a Europol without operational powers may grow into a powerful institution, a prospect which may strengthen the argument against such powers.

> Successful and acceptable progress toward a 'borderless Europe' is highly dependent upon the ability of the police and customs services to ensure that

[7] M. Anderson, M. den Boer, P. Cullen, W. Gilmore, C. Raab and N. Walker, *Policing the European Union* (Oxford: Clarendon Press, 1995), pp. 282–23

BRIEFINGS

21.8 EUROPE AND HARMONISATION: TWO SUBJECTS OF CONTROVERSY

One question that the 'Europeanisation' of policing will raise is 'will Britain adopt practices common in other European states but controversial here?' Two topics for discussion suggest themselves.

The first is the case of identity cards. Of all EU members, currently only Britain, Ireland and Denmark do not have ID card systems. One argument for mandatory carrying of ID cards is the suggestion that this would help prevent terrorism and smuggling. The idea of a national scheme for Britain was endorsed by the then Home Secretary at the 1994 Conservative Party Conference. Such a system is not without precedent within living memory: National Registration cards were introduced during the Second World War and only abolished in 1952. Two possible public reactions are well (if inconsistently) provided by the *Sun*

Why not? No law-abiding citizen should object to carrying them. ID cards will be a big weapon against crooks, illegal immigrants and terrorists. (*Sun*, 10 August 1994)

If we ever get identity cards they will be used to bully, nanny, and harass us. We are being suffocated by the State, treated as imbeciles, to be herded and prodded and controlled. (*Sun*, 11 August, 1994)

This subject obviously invites debate!

The second concern relates to firearms. Other European police forces are routinely armed. In Britain there has traditionally been a great reluctance on the part of government and senior police officers even to contemplate (at least in public) moving toward arming the police beyond the minimal arrangements currently in place (Waddington, 1991). Since the Dunblane tragedy, when a class of five-year-old children were shot by a gunman in Scotland, public opinion has swung against firearms. At present, Britain is unlikely to 'harmonise' in this respect. Will it ever do so?

Source: P. J. Waddington, *The Strong Arm of the Law* (Oxford: Oxford University Press, 1991)

transnational crime and the movement of illegal immigrants are not advantaged by the removal of frontier controls. The Schengen Agreement started this process among some partners from 1985 onward. It is clear from this experience that the lifting of borders will confirm and push further the shift in national and now pan-European policing toward intelligence-led methods relying on surveillance, informants, and exchange of information. While there are serious and convincing arguments about the desirability of such developments if policing is to keep pace with the threats of transnational crime, nonetheless the accompanying threats to civil liberties and the need for systems of accountability are also very real (see Briefing 21.8).

CURRENT AND FUTURE ISSUES

Whether because they have been placed on a pedestal, or because of the importance of their powers, the police attract a great deal of attention and criticism. It should, of course, be emphasised that the police also receive a great deal of deserved praise, and public and political support, and that they perform an unenviable and difficult task. However, there are areas for future development and reform.

The police have faced recurrent criticism for being predominantly male and white. Forces have sought to improve recruitment of women and ethnic minority officers (see Figures 21.2 and 21.3), but the issue will remain important, raising

Figure 21.2 Percentage of female police officers, England and Wales

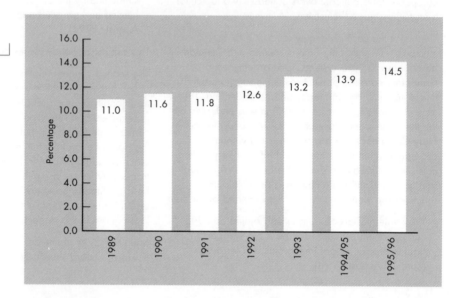

Figure 21.3 Percentage of ethnic minority police officers, England and Wales

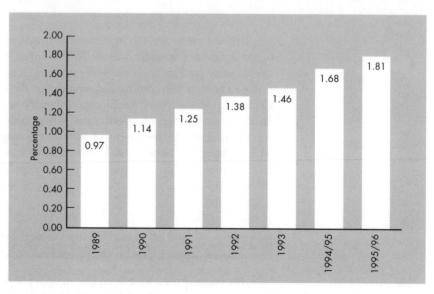

Source: Report of Her Majesty's Chief Inspector of Constabulary for 1995–96, House of Commons, 10 (London: The Stationery Office, 1996) p. 104

the question of the representativeness of the police. A related question is, who actually 'polices' society? In fact, 'the police' make only a particular kind of contribution to this. The general public do a great deal of 'police work', regulating young people, providing surveillance and intelligence (Neighbourhood Watch, Crimestoppers). Various public and private bodies employ inspectors, investigators, wardens and guards. The 'boundaries of policing' are increasingly blurred, most significantly because of the unrelenting growth of the private security sector. A mixed market now flourishes and readers might note some interesting echoes of eighteenth and nineteenth century arrangements for policing society.

The future of policing is likely to raise (once again) the issues of centralisation of control and amalgamation of forces. The run-up to the European 'single market' of 1992 concentrated some police and policy minds on the idea of centralised policing and the creation of around six 'super-forces' created by amalgamation.[9] The different views of successive home secretaries, as well as the radical changes and costs that would be involved, eroded enthusiasm for this proposal. However, it will almost certainly reappear at some point. The recently created NCIS (National Criminal Intelligence Service) incorporates several formerly distinct databases. Does this represent an Orwellian vision of data centralisation, or is it simply a practical response to the increasing diversity and incidence of serious organised crime?

In the post-Cold War era, the involvement of the Security Service, first in operations against domestic terrorism, and now in relation to organised crime and drug trafficking, has also been a development to note. This represents the involvement in criminal investigation of a highly centralised yet largely invisible and unaccountable agency. Another centralised agency has also been promised, with John Major announcing to the Conservative Party Conference in 1995 that a national crime squad would be formed. The Police Act 1997, passed just before the general election, paves the way for the creation of such a squad. In the future, co-operation between NCIS, the Security Service and the new agency will create a very powerful, intelligence-led but also operational, centrally directed police establishment. How such power is perceived will, without doubt, generate many questions, some of which we pursue in the next chapter.

ESSAYS

1. Are 'the police' a police 'force' or a police 'service'? What are the implications of these different terms?

2. One conclusion of the Scarman Report was that: 'public tranquillity should have a greater priority than law enforcement if the two conflicted' (Reiner, 1996, p. 725). Discuss in relation to the policing of (a) minority communities or (b) environmental protests.

3. 'The fact that the British police are answerable to the law, that we act on behalf of the community and not under the mantle of government, makes us the least powerful, the most accountable and therefore the most acceptable police in the world' (Sir Robert Mark, Metropolitan Commissioner, *Policing a Perplexed Society* (London: Allen and Unwin, 1977), p.56. Debate this argument.

4. Is the idea of the 'public' police an anomaly? What issues does the privatisation of policing raise?

SUMMARY

The new Home Secretary, Jack Straw, enjoyed a warm reception on his first visit to the Police Federation annual conference (Blackpool, 21 May 1997) but has yet to say how Labour policy on policing is going to develop. A reasonable prediction, however, would be that the Labour Government will express three principal political concerns about the police. These are likely to be probity, accountability and effectiveness.

Key decision makers in the police service have high hopes of a Labour agenda. On the other hand, Government ministers and students of politics alike would do well to remember that the police are not 'apolitical' and that the politics of policing are a complex business. This has been amply demonstrated by the questions and problems raised in this chapter, chief among them:

- the scope of 'policing' as distinct from 'police',
- police organisation and accountability: who is really in control?
- moves from a local to a national organisation,
- procedural reforms and individual rights in relation to the police,
- the politicisation of policing,
- the privatisation of police functions,
- Europeanisation,
- the police and New Labour.

MILESTONES

MILESTONES IN THE DEVELOPMENT OF BRITISH POLICING

1829 Sir Robert Peel's Metropolitan Police Act

1830–60 Establishment of county and borough forces under local control

1856 County and Borough Police Act establishes Home Office inspection of, and grants for, local police authorities

1960 Establishment of the Royal Commission on the Police

1962 Report of the above

1964 Police Act amalgamates 117 police authorities into 43. Tripartite control by chief constables, police authorities and Home Secretary

1972 Bains Committee recommendation that chief constables should be as accountable as local authority chief executives is defeated

1976 Police Complaints Board (PCB) established

1979 Central government controls over local government expenditures also mean central control over police expenditure

1981 The Brixton disorders (10–12 April) and the Scarman Report, which criticised aggressive tactics

used by Police Authority, Chief Constable and Home Secretary

1984 Police and Criminal Evidence Act (PACE) consolidates police powers but introduces better safeguards for suspects

1984 Police Complaints Board replaced by Police Complaints Authority (PCA)

1984–85 Miners strike. National co-ordination and control of local police forces

1986 Creation of Crown Prosecution Service (CPS)

1988 Court of Appeal gives the Home Secretary powers to override the police authorities on matters of equipment and expenditure

1993 Royal Commission on Criminal Justice (Runciman Report)

1994 Police and Magistrates' Courts Act reduces police authorities to agents of Home Secretary

1995 First woman chief constable appointed. Metropolitan Police Commissioner states that some police routinely carry firearms

FURTHER READING

R. Reiner *The Politics of the Police* (Hemel Hempstead: Harvester Wheatsheaf, 1992) is generally regarded as the best introduction to the study of the police and policing, and R. Reiner (ed.), *Policing* (Aldershot: Dartmouth, 1996) contains a collection of classic articles on the subject. For more specialised studies see: M. Anderson, M. den Boer, P. Cullen, W. Gilmore, C. Raab, and N. Walker, *Policing the European Union* (Oxford: Clarendon Press, 1995) on European police co-operation; C. Elmsley, *The English Police: A Political and Social History* (Hemel Hempstead: Harvester Wheatsheaf, 1991) on the history of the police; L. Lustgarten, *The Governance of the Police* (London: Sweet and Maxwell, 1986), the classic study of the police and the constitution; N. South, *Policing for a Profit: The Private Security Sector* (London: Sage, 1988) on private policing; and B. Fine and R. Millar (eds), *Policing the Miner's Strike*, (London: Lawrence and Wishart, 1985).

G. Drewry, 'Judges and Politics in Britain', *Social Studies Review*, November (1986) is a concise treatment of the subject, and D. Woodhouse, 'Politicians and the Judges: a conflict of interest', *Parliamentary Affairs*, 49 (3) (1996) is more recent but advanced.

PROJECTS

1. Using newspaper reports, contrast the priorities of any two local police forces in enforcing specific laws.

2. Is the idea of a 'private' police an anomaly? Write a discussion document on the issues raised by the privatisation of the police.

http://www.awl-he.com/politics/newbritpol

Internet resources – visit *The New British Politics* Webpage for links to a specially-chosen selection of Internet resources relevant to this Chapter.

http://www.awl-he.com/politics/newbritpol

CHAPTER 22

Security and secrecy

As noted in the last chapter, police efforts to maintain order have been increasingly supplemented over the postwar period, most spectacularly by private security firms. Related groups like Customs and Excise and various bodies of inspectors also operate to detect crime in their specialised areas. Ordinary citizens have been drafted in, notably through Neighbourhood Watch schemes, and have been encouraged to use designated 'hotlines' to denounce social security frauds. In the summer of 1997 travel agents were being co-opted to relay information about suspicious clients who made a booking.

Wherever we go and whatever we do in Britain therefore we may be under surveillance and scrutiny by someone, even our neighbours. Much of this activity is initiated and co-ordinated by the secret services, who have increasingly been brought in by successive governments to combat Irish terrorism and international drugs trafficking.

All modern states have security services to protect themselves against terrorism, subversion, and violence, but such services present democracies with dilemmas. First, one of the most important principles of democratic government is that no person or organisation is above the law. Yet the British security services are constitutionally outside, if not above, the law. Second, all branches of a democratic state should be publicly accountable, but the security services are under a blanket of secrecy. Third, to be effective the security services must have powers necessary to operate secretly and effectively against the enemies of the state; they must not be used by the Government against its own citizens. Governments should use the security services for the public interest, not for their own political purposes. Nor, protected by secrecy, must the security services be able to take the law into its own hands and act against either the Government, or its citizens, or both.

Every modern state faces these dilemmas and none has an easy solution for them. And yet the British state appears to be unusually secretive, by Western standards, and gives its security and intelligence organisations broad and unaccountable powers. How and why this is the case is discussed in this chapter. It is divided into six parts, as follows:

- The rise of security and secrecy as a political issue over the past 30 years

- Security organisations and their accountability

- Laws and conventions about secrecy, especially the Official Secrets Acts of 1911 and 1989

- Motives and opportunities for state secrecy

- Open government: pressures for more information

- Prospects for the security services under New Labour

Throughout the chapter it must be kept in mind that the security services are secretive, and therefore not much is known about them. This makes it difficult to say much with confidence about them, or to draw clear and firm conclusions.

THE RISE OF SECURITY AND SECRECY AS POLITICAL ISSUES

In the 1950s and 1960s, national security was not a major issue. On the contrary, the importance and success of wartime intelligence, and then fear of communism during the Cold War, helped to sustain the security services and their secrecy. The issue grew, however, as a result of a sequence of events in the 1970s and 1980s, including:

- IRA action in Northern Ireland and the mainland;

- International terrorism;

- Rising crime, including large-scale international drug and crime rings;

- Most importantly, a long series of revelations about high-level failures of the security system involving, among others, the double agents Guy Burgess, Donald MacLean, and Kim Philby. Later spy scandals included (Sir) Anthony Blunt, Sir Maurice Oldfield (former head of MI6), and Michael Bettaney who was sentenced for 23 years in 1984 for spying for the USSR. Sir Roger Hollis, former head of MI5, and John Cairncross of MI6, are believed by some experts to have been Soviet double agents.

These events all contributed to a sense of threat about both personal and state security. On the other side of the coin there was also mounting concern about growing government power, and threats to individual rights and civil liberties. Fears were fuelled by:

- The growing power and centralisation of the police force, and its apparent lack of accountability (Chapter 21);

- The growing power of central Government, especially the PM and Cabinet, and the apparent weakening of the legislature (the Commons) and local government;

- The growing power of the security services and the police;

- New technology for surveillance and the centralisation of computer records;

- An increasing awareness of the secretive nature of the British state, and of the ways in which the Official Secrets Act had been used;

- Increasing use of the Official Secrets Act. In the 29 years between 1945 and 1974, 34 people were prosecuted under the Official Secrets Act, and between 1978 and 1986 the number was 29;

- A ruling by the European Court of Human Rights in 1985 stating that Britain's laws on phone tapping were insufficiently clear;

- A series of events involving the security forces and government secrecy, such as prosecutions of various journalists for reporting on government activities, censorship of TV programmes and surveillance and harassment of politicians by the security services (see Briefing 22.1).

BRIEFINGS

22.1 OPERATIONS OF THE SECRET STATE

Arms Sales to Nigeria, Jonathan Aitken, 1971

Aitken (then writing for the *Sunday Telegraph*) and a retired general were prosecuted under the Official Secrets Act for reporting that arms sales to Nigeria were much larger than the Government claimed. Both were acquitted, and the judge said that the Official Secrets Act was in urgent need of reform.

ABC Trial, 1977

Two journalists, Crispin Aubrey and Duncan Campbell, were tried with John Berry, a former member of Signals Intelligence, for disclosing defence information. Although this information was in the public domain already, they were found guilty, but given only light sentences.

Tisdall and Cruise Missiles, 1984

Sarah Tisdall, a clerk at the Foreign Office, believed her minister, Michael Heseltine, was deceiving the public about the arrival of Cruise missiles at Greenham Common in order to minimise public opposition. She released information to the *Guardian*, was prosecuted, and received a six-month prison sentence.

Ponting and the Belgrano Affair, 1985

Clive Ponting was a high-flying civil servant who released information suggesting that the Government had concealed the true circumstances of the sinking of the Argentine battleship *General Belgrano* in the Falklands War. Ponting defended himself in court on the grounds that he was acting in the public interest, and was acquitted by the jury.

Political Vetting in the BBC, 1985

It was revealed that MI5 had an office in the BBC in order to vet job applicants. It was promised that the practice would stop.

Phone Tapping, 1985

A former member of MI5, Cathy Massiter, claimed in a TV documentary that MI5 routinely tapped the phones

22.1 OPERATIONS OF THE SECRET STATE (continued)

of trade union officials and CND (Campaign for Nuclear Disarmament) leaders.

Spycatcher, 1987–88

The Government tried to ban the book by Peter Wright, formerly of MI5, even though it was easily available abroad. The Government sent the Cabinet Secretary, Sir Robert Armstrong, to an Australian court to try to ban publication there. This was itself a controversial political use of a civil servant, and Sir Robert Armstrong caused more criticism by admitting that the Government had been 'economical with the truth'. Among other things Wright claimed that some members of MI5 tried to destabilise the Wilson Labour Government, and that MI5 'bugged and burgled its way across London'.

Zircon, 1987

A film about the British spy satellite, Zircon, made by the journalist Duncan Campbell (also of the ABC case), was seized by the Special Branch from the Edinburgh offices of the BBC, together with five other programmes in the same series. The Government claimed that the film was a danger to state security, but critics argued that the Government wanted to conceal the fact that the Zircon project was behind schedule.

Defending the Realm, 1991

Evidence from an ex-security services official, Robin Robison, was presented in a Guardian/ITN World in

Action inquiry, claiming that the security services regularly engage in unauthorised spying on, among others, Britain's EU partners, to discover their negotiating positions, on commercial companies both at home and abroad, and on trade union leaders. Robison claimed that the security services keep some of this activity from their ministers.

Surveillance of MPs and Ministers

The memoirs of ex-minister Alan Clark suggested that MPs and ministers are under MI5 surveillance. Before him, MPs Jonathan Aitken and Sir Richard Body made the same claim.

The Scott Inquiry (1996)

The official inquiry into Arms to Iraq revealed how secretive British Government is at the highest levels, and how little is known even by MPs.

State Censorship

Examples of government censorship of TV include among others, Yesterday's Men (1971), Real Lives (1985, about politicians in Northern Ireland), The War Game (1965), A Question of Ulster (1972) and the Zircon affair (see above). The Government also strongly criticised the BBC for its reporting of the Suez War, the Falklands War, and the American bombing of Libya, and the Independent Broadcasting Authority for showing Death of a Princess (1980) and Death on the Rock (1988).

As a result of such events the security services have been drawn into the political limelight, and the problems they pose for democracy have become a political issue. While the need for effective security is more urgent than ever, there is strong suspicion (it cannot be proved because of secrecy) that governments have sometimes enforced secrecy, not in the public interest but to protect their own political reputations. There are also fears that the powers of the security services may have been used by governments to spy on citizens. It is also claimed that the security services themselves have engaged in covert operations against citizens and the Government itself. To understand how this might be so, it is necessary to understand the nature of the security services and the laws and conventions under which they operate. These are the subjects of the next two sections of the chapter.

SECURITY ORGANISATIONS AND THEIR ACCOUNTABILITY

Little is officially known about British security services, although some information about MI5 was released in 1993. It is known that there are five main branches of the service: MI5, the Special Branch, MI6, the Defence Intelligence Staff (DIS) and Government Communication Headquarters (GCHQ) (see Briefing 22.2). Overseas operations are carried out mainly by MI6, and the Defence Intelligence Staff. Domestic operations are mainly the responsibility of the Special Branch and MI5. MI5 was made a statutory authority (i.e. given a basis in statute law) for the first time by the 1989 Security Service Act which refers to it as the Security Service. The Act defines its role as:

> ... the protection of national security and, in particular, its protection
> against threats of espionage, terrorism, and sabotage, from the activities of
> foreign powers and from actions intended to overthrow or undermine
> parliamentary democracy by political, industrial or violent means ... to
> safeguard the economic well-being of the United Kingdom against threats
> posed by the actions or intentions of persons outside the British Isles.

Plate 22.1 MI5 Headquarters on the River Thames

BRIEFINGS

22.2 THE SECURITY SERVICES

MI5

The domestic intelligence service concerned with subversive and terrorist activity within the UK. In 1993 some facts about MI5 were made public: it employs 2,000 people; its budget is spent on counter-terrorism (70%), counter-espionage (25%) and counter-political subversion (5%). In 1992 it took over from the police the responsibility on the British mainland for gathering intelligence about the IRA. MI5 is also engaged in political vetting, and with 'the preventing and detection of serious crime, and for connected purposes'. Its annual budget is not public information but is estimated at about 150 to 200 million pounds. It has newly built headquarters at Millbank in London, and is under the control of the Home Secretary.

Special Branch

This branch of the police is concerned with terrorism and subversion within the UK. Under the direction of a senior officer of the Metropolitan Police, and therefore under the political control of the Home Secretary, the Special Branch works closely with MI5. Its responsibilities include intelligence work, enforcing official secrets laws, the security of VIPs, watching ports and airports, and making arrests for MI5. It employs about 2,000 people in its central and local offices. The Metropolitan office of the Special Branch has a budget of over 20 million pounds.

MI6

This is the international equivalent of MI5. Its main purpose is to gather political and military intelligence abroad. It works closely with DIS (see below) on military matters, and is under the control of the Foreign Secretary. MI6's budget is not known but estimated at about 150 million pounds.

Defence Intelligence Staff (DIS)

Mainly concerned with foreign military threat assessment, but also with the internal security of the armed forces, the DIS employs 600 people who work closely with MI6 and with offices abroad.

Government Communications Headquarters (GCHQ)

The existence of GCHQ was acknowledged in 1983 as the result of a spy scandal. It is mainly concerned with government coding and decoding, and with the use of satellites and listening posts to monitor world communications. It works closely with its equivalents in the USA, Canada, Australia and New Zealand. Its British headquarters in Cheltenham employs 7,000 people and its estimated annual budget is 500 million pounds. It was the subject of political controversy in 1984 when the government banned its workers from trade union membership (allegedly under pressure from the Americans after a spy scandal). Trade union rights were restored by the new Labour Government in 1997.

The exact constitutional position of the security services is not clear. They operate under the vaguely defined royal prerogative powers (Chapter 7), and clearly they are not accountable to Parliament. MI5 and the Special Branch report direct to the Home Secretary, MI6 and GCHQ (the communications-monitoring and code-breaking agency) direct to the Foreign Secretary. Ultimately the Prime Minister is responsible for all security services and operations, and chairs the Cabinet committee which deals with their business, the Security and Intelligence Services Committee, or IS. The heads of MI5, MI6, and GCHQ have direct access to the PM, and sit on the important Joint Intelligence Committee (JIC) of Whitehall which supplies the Cabinet and the PM with most of their information about security matters. An official of the Cabinet Office known as the Co-ordinator of Intelligence and Security also sits on the JIC, and has direct access to the PM. In all, no more than about a dozen people have first-hand information about the security services and their activities, and half of these are unelected and unaccountable.

Ministers can refuse to answer any parliamentary question related to national security, and MI5 is not accountable to Parliament for its budget. Only the Prime Minister sees the total budget for all services. Select committees of the Commons have not been successful in recent attempts to interview security officials, or in their claims to exercise some scrutiny of security policy and its effectiveness. Instead, a Security Commission, chaired by a senior judge, issues public reports which say very little. The security services are not subject to a public complaints procedure, as are the police with the Police Complaints Authority, but are monitored by a security service tribunal which works entirely in secret. Between 1989 (when it was set up) and 1996, the tribunal considered 187 complaints against MI5, rejecting them all. MI5 documents are protected from scrutiny by the courts and when MI5 officers have appeared to give evidence in court they have always been unidentified and hidden. MI5 is not required to tell the police about its operations.

In short, the security services are 'self-tasking': they set their own goals, choose their own means, and monitor their own activity. They are beyond the scrutiny of all but a few of the most overworked politicians in the land, and perhaps even beyond this. According to Peter Wright in *Spycatcher*, and Robin Robison in the TV programme *Defending the Realm*, the PM and the Cabinet do not know half of what goes on.

Some hoped that the role and size of MI5 would be reduced after the collapse of the Soviet Union, but instead its activities were expanded to include 'the prevention and detection of serious crime, and for connected purposes'. Thus, MI5 is no longer exclusively concerned with national security but now has duties which were previously reserved for the police. At the same time MI5 is charged with vague duties – serious crime and connected purposes – but unlike the police is not subject to democratic accountability.

LAWS AND CONVENTIONS ABOUT SECRECY

The security services work within a framework of laws and conventions which gives them substantial powers and protects them from public scrutiny (see Briefing 22.3). The centrepiece of the legal system is the Official Secrets Act of 1989 which replaced the 1911 Act after many years of pressure and debate. Section 1 of the 1911 Official Secrets Act made it an offence to engage in conduct contrary to the safety or interests of the state, including the disclosure of information of use to enemies. In most cases this section has been uncontroversial. It was Section 2 which caused trouble. This made it a crime for anyone employed by the state to pass on official information to those not authorised to have it. The section was so broadly and vaguely worded that it included almost any information: the number of paper clips used by a government department, or the number of cups of tea it drinks.

BRIEFINGS

22.3 INSTRUMENTS OF THE SECRET STATE

Privy Councillor's Oath

Since the year 1250 members of the Privy Council are required to swear, in the presence of the monarch, an oath dealing with secrecy, among other things. Only senior Government and Opposition members are privy councillors, but membership is for life.

Royal Prerogative

Powers inherited by governments from the Crown which are held constitutionally to be independent of parliamentary approval or scrutiny. They are, like the rest of the 'unwritten constitution', vague and undefined, so give governments and their security advisers great scope to do what they want (Chapter 7).

'D' Notices

Introduced in 1912, Defence Notices are confidential letters sent by the D Notice Committee to newspaper and television journalists to prevent the disclosure of information harmful to national defence and security. The system is informal, voluntary and confidential. It was used to prevent the publication of information about the spies George Blake and Kim Philby, but may well have fallen into disuse in recent years.

Government Directive, 1952

This directive stated the convention that ministers 'do not concern themselves with the detailed information which may be obtained by the Security Service in particular cases but are furnished with such information as may be necessary for the determination of any issue on which guidance is sought'.

Public Records Act, 1958

Under the Public Records Act certain government papers are not publicly available until they are 30 years old, or longer if the Lord Chancellor decides. The Act covers about 40 categories of documents including those with distressing or embarrassing information about living people, confidential government information, matters of state security, and state papers on Ireland. Papers covered by the 30-year rule amount to about 5 per cent of all government documents, not including those which are permanently secret, such as Cabinet papers.

The Interception of Communications Act, 1985

This act made it possible to issue warrants to bug, phone tap, or open mail in the interests of national security, the prevention and detection of serious crime, and to protect the economic well-being of the UK.

The Official Secrets Act, 1989

- The Act covers the following subjects: security, defence and international relations; crime and its investigation; warrants issued under the Interception of Communications Act (1985) and the Security Services Act (1989) and information which these warrants produce; secret information provided by foreign governments and international agencies.

- Release of information which is deemed 'harmful' to the public interest is a criminal offence. It is no defence to argue that public disclosure of the information is in the public interest, or that the information is publicly available abroad.

- Disclosure of information covered by the act is harmful in itself; the prosecution is not required to prove that disclosure has probable or actual harmful effects.

- The Act covers Crown servants, members of the security services, government contractors, and journalists. Editors who encourage journalists to disclose such information are liable to prosecution.

Security Service Act, 1989

The 1989 act gave MI5 (not MI6) a statutory basis, and a broad range of rather vaguely defined functions.These were expanded in 1997 to include the prevention and detection of serious crime and connected purposes. It also provided for a security services commissioner to review phone tapping warrants, and a tribunal to revoke improper warrants. Critics argue that the commissioner and the tribunal are weak and ineffective.

It was widely believed that Section 2 suppressed legitimate discussion about British Government, a belief supported by a series of incidents. The judge who tried the journalists who revealed that the Government was supplying large quantities of arms to Nigeria (1971) said that the section should be pensioned off. The 1972 Franks Committee on Official Secrecy recommended repeal. A string of events in the 1970s and the 1980s brought the issue to the surface again, but nothing was done until 1988 when a private members bill to reform the act was defeated by the Government, which then passed its own Official Secrets Act of 1989.

Section 1 of the 1911 act remained unchanged in the 1989 act, which concentrated on Section 2. The Government claimed to have liberalised the law by dropping many of the items covered by the 1911 act. Critics claim that the new act simply excludes harmless information which has not been a problem in the past, while at the same time increasing secrecy in other areas, including those raised by the *Spycatcher*, Tisdall, and Ponting cases, all involving civil servants who leaked information about government activities that they thought harmed the public interest. They also argue that the definitions of what is 'harmful' are both broad and vague: it is estimated that the act creates about 2,300 offences. In short it was said that the 1989 Act increased rather than decreased state secrecy by tightening the Government's grip on a range of broadly and vaguely defined matters, by expanding the range of people to whom they applied, and by eliminating the most important grounds which might be used in defence by those prosecuted under the Act.

STATE SECRECY: MOTIVES AND OPPORTUNITIES

Enough has been said to suggest that Britain well deserves its reputation as one of the more secretive states in the Western world. Secrecy is tightest around the security services, but it extends into all areas of central Government. Why is British Government so secretive? One way of answering the question is similar to the procedure in murder mysteries. To solve the case one must first examine motive and opportunity. British Government has both in abundance.

Some of the motives for secrecy are:

- Government accountability. One of the great strengths of the British system of government is the clear chain of responsibility which runs directly from the electorate through the majority party in Parliament to the Cabinet and Prime Minister. Because it is not easy for the PM to escape this, there is a motive for suppressing information which might cause problems, as noted in many previous chapters.

- The broadening scope of government activities. The more a government spends and does, the greater the chances that something will go wrong, and the bigger the incentive for secrecy.

- Geopolitical role. Britain continues to play an important political role in the world – the United Nations Security Council, NATO, the G-7 group of nations, the EU, and the Commonwealth – and has state secrets of corresponding importance.

The UK has opportunities for secrecy through:

- The unitary state. The more powerful the central Government, the greater its ability to maintain secrecy. In Britain it is difficult for any branch of government or any other body to challenge central Government.

- Partial fusion of executive, legislative and judiciary gives central Government substantial powers to protect itself with secrecy (we have noted how party control of the Commons operates to stifle inquiry and debate).

- No written constitution which places clear legal limits on the powers of government.

- No Bill of Rights as yet which clearly states the rights of citizens.

- No freedom of information act to guarantee open government.

- Some claim that Britain has an elitist political culture which gives governments a good deal of independence.

By Western standards, this is a rather unusual combination of factors which creates an unusually strong and centralised form of government with both the motives and the opportunities to maintain government secrecy, and security services to match these.

OPEN GOVERNMENT

> **Key term**
>
> **Open government** – the relatively unconstrained flow of information about government to the general public, the media, and representative bodies.

> **Key term**
>
> **Freedom of information** – free public access to government information and records. Freedom of information is a necessary condition of open government.

Critics of the British security system do not deny the need for some secrecy, especially where defence against foreign and internal enemies of the state is concerned. What they argue is that Britain is unnecessarily secretive compared with most other Western states. The argument frequently comes down to the case for freedom of information.

Many Western democracies have freedom of information acts which guarantee citizens the right to see a wide variety of documents, both state and personal. State secrets in these countries are exempt, of course, but they are more narrowly and precisely defined than in Britain. Although there are many practical difficulties with freedom of information acts (documents can be lost, destroyed, or suppressed), countries such as the United States and Sweden have operated them with some success for many years. Britain has no equivalent.

The Campaign for Freedom of Information was created in 1984 with the backing of many leading, all-party politicians and senior ex-civil servants. Some progress was made with the Data Protection Act (1984), the Local Government (Access to Information) Act (1986), and the Access to Health Records Act (1990), but these measures left secrecy in central Government largely intact.

The Major Government of 1990 promised more open government and followed this up by releasing information about Cabinet committees, rules of ministerial conduct, some Public Record Office documents, and even some information about MI5. The Citizens Charter of 1991 then promised, among other things, more open government and more information. A code of practice was also introduced in 1994 which promised:

- secrecy only where there is good reason for it;
- increasing amounts of information to promote policy discussion and good decision making;
- more information about government policies and actions.

Critics argued that the Citizens Charter and the code of practice were only a small step forward, with more promises than firm action, because:

- The code of practice is a weak and vaguely worded document;
- It leaves great areas of government secrecy untouched, including information about what policy advice has been given to ministers and by whom;
- Citizens are only given the right to information, not access to government documents or records;
- The government ultimately controls what sorts of information will be released.

In addition, events cast doubt over the Major Government's real intentions for more open government:

- A broad freedom of information act was rejected;
- Two private members' bills to introduce freedom of information were defeated (1992,1993);
- The powers of MI5 were expanded by the Security Services Act of 1996;
- The Scott Inquiry of 1996 (into the Arms to Iraq affair) shows how little is known about some government operations at the highest levels;
- In 1994 the European Union published an information code calling for public access to a wide range of government documents. The British Government did not respond;
- In the 'cash for questions' issue some evidence suggests that the Government may not have divulged crucial information until forced to by the courts.

PROSPECTS FOR THE SECURITY SERVICES UNDER NEW LABOUR

Our discussion has made it clear that secrecy and the use of security to protect themselves rather than the country are temptations for all British governments of whatever political persuasion, under the existing set-up. On the other hand New Labour did promise a reform of the Official Secrets Act when it was in opposition. It is also true that Labour has been a victim of security service surveillance and spoiling operations even when it was in power from 1974 to 1979. Allegations have been made that even the then Prime Minister's (Harold Wilson's) telephone was tapped and associates put under surveillance. Certainly two Blairite Labour ministers Jack Straw (now Home Secretary) and Peter Mandelson (the Prime Minister's closest adviser) were under surveillance as suspected radicals in the 1970s. It is unclear when surveillance was lifted, assuming it has not continued.

These facts were made public in August 1997 by Peter Shaylor, an ex-MI5 agent. The response of the authorities at that time was instructive. Did they investigate the use of surveillance in regard to radical (but not subversive) student leaders? No. Instead they issued a warrant for Shaylor's arrest! This has a familiar echo of the prosecutions of Ponting and Wright in the 1980s. In cases of whistleblowing, catch the whistleblowers and shut them up, rather than investigate the allegations.

The impression that New Labour was at one with its predecessor in using security and secrecy in its own interests, was buttressed by two other actions of the new Government:

1. The promised Freedom of Information Bill was removed from the agenda of the first session of the new Parliament because of 'technical difficulties of drafting'. It was widely felt that the proposals had been defeated by the Defence bureaucrats and that any new bill would be substantially watered down, if it ever emerged.

2. Robin Cook, the Foreign Secretary, announced a greater use of MI6 in the international 'war against drugs'. The improbability of this war ever being won means that MI6 may have found a permanent and expanded role, just as MI5 has found it in combatting IRA terrorism. Both 'wars' justify continued secrecy, surveillance and absence of guaranteed rights in regard to the security services.

Labour has subjected the intelligence services to a comprehensive spending review. An interdepartmental committee is currently tying them to zero-based budgeting, a procedure which would require justifying all of their expenditures and programmes. However, a similar attempt was made in the 1980s, which the security services resisted (probably with Margaret Thatcher's backing).

Modest steps towards transparency have been made in the 1990s, therefore, but the odds are that New Labour will not carry them much further, certainly not to the extent of opening security up to parliamentary scrutiny, which might be a first step to real reform.

SUMMARY

- It is difficult to write about the security services, or to draw any hard and fast conclusions about them, because they are so secretive.

- The security services present democracy with an acute dilemma: they must be effective enough to combat terrorism and the subversion of democracy, and this requires secrecy; but they must not be so powerful, so secretive, or so

ESSAYS

1. Is Britain moving towards more open or more secretive government?

2. Should Britain have a freedom of information Act?

3. Britain has a reputation for being one of the most secretive states among the democracies of the Western world. What features of British government and politics best explain this secrecy?

unaccountable that they resemble a secret police which could be used against ordinary citizens or the Government. There are no simple solutions to these dilemmas.

- The main agencies of state security and intelligence in Britain are MI5, MI6, the Special Branch, the Defence Intelligence Staff (DIS), and Government Communications Headquarters (GCHQ).

- The main laws and conventions governing state secrecy are the Privy Councillor's Oath, the 'D' notices system, the Public Records Act (1958), the Interception of Communications Act (1985), the Security Services Acts (1989, 1996) and, most important, the Official Secrets Act (1989).

- The high level of secrecy in the British state, particularly in its security services, is best explained in terms of central Government having an unusual combination of motives to exercise secrecy, and opportunities to do so.

- Some argue for a general freedom of information Act to open up government to more public scrutiny. Government has responded with some information, and with Citizens' Charters and codes of practice, but critics claim these are small steps forward, and that the Official Secrets Act of 1989 extends secrecy and the real power of the security services.

MILESTONES

MILESTONES IN BRITISH SECURITY AND SECRECY

1958 Public Records Act. Designated documents not available for 30 years after the event, or longer if the Lord Chancellor decides

1968 The Fulton Committee on the Civil Service argues that it is too secret and recommends more openness

1972 The Franks Report on Section 2 of the Official Secrets Act recommends its repeal and replacement with a new and narrower official information Act

1977 ABC trial: journalist tried and sentenced for disclosing defence information

1984 MI5 officer Michael Bettaney sentenced to 23 years' imprisonment for spying

1984 The Tisdall case about disclosing arrival of US Cruise missiles. Data Protection Act

1985 The Ponting case about the sinking of the Argentinian battleship *General Belgrano*

1985 PM states that security service members will not appear before select committees of the House of Commons. The European Court for Human Rights states that British law about phone tapping is insufficiently clear. This results in the Interception of Communications Act

1986 Local Government (Access to Information) Act

1986–87 The Spycatcher affair

1987 The 'Zircon' affair: TV film impounded by security services

1989 Security Services Act. Official Secrets Act

1990 Access to Health Records Act. MPs Jonathan Aitken and Sir Richard Body claim that MPs are under MI5 surveillance

1991 A TV programme, *Defending the Realm*, claims that MI5 routinely spies on EU partners, commercial organisations and trade union leaders, and keeps much of this secret from ministers

1991 Citizens Charter promises more open government

1993 Home Secretary states that the Head of MI5 will not appear before the Home Affairs Select Committee of the Commons. Ex-minister Alan Clark claims that ministers are under MI5 surveillance. Limited official information released about MI5

1996 Scott Inquiry shows how secretive British government is at the top levels, and how little Parliament knows. Security Services Act.

PROJECTS

1. Prepare a case for and against the amount of secrecy in British government.

2. Analyse the sequence of events culminating *either* in the Ponting trial *or* in the attempt to ban Peter Wright's book *Spycatcher*.

FURTHER READING

Not much is written about the security services in Britain, no doubt because little is known. Some textbooks barely even mention the matter. Books on the subject include P. Birkinshaw, *Reforming the Secret State* (Milton Keynes: Open University Press, 1991), S. Dorril, *The Silent Conspiracy: Inside the Intelligence Services in the 1990s* (London: Heinemann, 1992), and R. Norton-Taylor, *In Defence of the Realm? The Case for Accountable Security Services* (London: Civil Liberties Trust, 1990). Two useful short articles on state secrecy in general are S. Hunt, 'State Secrecy in the UK', *Politics Review*, 1 (4) (1992), and K. Jones, F. Millard, and L. Twigg, 'Government Information Policy in the 1980s', *Talking Politics*, 1 (3).

http://www.awl-he.com/politics/newbritpol

Internet resources – visit *The New British Politics* Webpage for links to a specially-chosen selection of Internet resources relevant to this Chapter.

http://www.awl-he.com/politics/newbritpol

PART VI
Policy

Foreign and defence policy

A main justification for keeping the extensive, and expensive, security apparatus described in the last chapter emphasises Britain's position in world affairs. Its role as a major power means that it is vital for hostile states to know about government intentions and policies. By the same token it is important for Britain to know about theirs. This justifies large investments in decoding and intelligence gathering (spying) abroad, and restricting freedom of discussion at home to prevent foreign spies doing the same things here.

This rather chilling picture of Britain being unable to trust its allies and of countries constantly surveilling and undermining each other rests on a particular view of states. This defines them by their possession of a particular territory which they have to control and defend against the efforts of neighbouring states to overrun it. States are thus always in potential conflict with each other, no matter how united and friendly they seem.

This chapter will:

- Outline the 'realist' and 'idealist' views of foreign policy

- Briefly review the major events and developments in British foreign policy since mid-century and examine the way in which these have been influenced by Britain's structural and geographical position half-way between Europe and overseas

- Trace the changes in the world that have influenced Britain's postwar foreign policy

- Analyse the motivations and assumptions governing Britain's foreign policy and the consequences of these on its military role and capabilities

- Ask how successful Britain has been in achieving a world order to her government's liking and assess whether Britain really does remain a 'big player' in international affairs. Are the massive investments in security and military capabilities still justified or should they be reined back in favour of other priorities?

REALISM AND IDEALISM

The view that states need to be on perpetual guard against each other is the so-called 'realist' view of international relations. It is termed 'realist' because its proponents claim to be able to see beyond governments' protestations of good intent and desire for the common good to their 'real' motives, which on this view are always selfish and aimed at material and territorial gain at the expense of their neighbours.

As most other states are too small and weak to hurt Britain this analysis mostly concerns the 'big players', that is, France, Germany, Russia, the USA, Japan and China. 'Realist' assessments of the world are most influential in regard to military affairs, where decision makers are usually obliged to adopt a 'worst case' view in order to know what their capabilities should be to ward off the worst threats. Of course, it also dominated assessments during the so-called 'Cold War' (1948–89)

BRIEFINGS

23.1 THE SOVIET UNION (USSR) AND THE WARSAW PACT

The collapse of the Russian Empire in the First World War (1917) led to a political takeover by the Communist Party after a civil war (1918–22). The Empire was reconstituted within a reduced territory as the Union of Soviet Socialist Republics (USSR). The republics were created as political units to satisfy the aspirations of the minority peoples of the old Empire who had been conquered by the Russians. However, the Russian Federal Socialist Republic (RFSR) remained the largest and predominant republic. In any case all the republics and the USSR as a whole were effectively ruled by the Communist Party, the real centre of power.

The USSR was attacked by Nazi Germany in 1941 and bore the brunt of fighting over the next four years. Soviet troops gradually pushed the Germans back and occupied Eastern Germany and East-Central Europe. Communist regimes modelled on the Soviet one were forcibly installed in all these countries while the Soviet frontier was extended to take in all the territory of the old Empire.

These actions led to a break with the USA and Britain. Hostility and frontier incidents prompted the formation of a Western military alliance (NATO, the North Atlantic Treaty Organisation) covering the USA, Canada, Britain and most countries of Western Europe. NATO left troops in Europe, notably in Germany, Britain and Spain, which were confronted by the forces of the Warsaw Pact, dominated by the USSR.

The confrontation between those opposing sides was known as the Cold War and lasted from 1948 to 1989. The inefficiency of the Soviet economy brought it to an end, as the USSR was unable to sustain a high technology arms race with the USA. The countries of East-Central Europe instituted democracy while the minority republics of the USSR broke away to become independent, leaving Russia itself as the successor state.

when the American-led NATO alliance (of which Britain was a leading member) confronted the Soviet Union and its allies, sometimes violently (see Briefing 23.1).

With the end of the Cold War and the growth of intergovernmental co-operation channelled through organisations like the United Nations and the European Union, another analysis of international relations has gained support (see Briefing 13.2). Termed 'idealism', this sees countries as having many common interests which they can maximise only through full co-operation. Often such co-operation involves the setting up of international regimes and organisations which may even take over sovereign power from states in certain areas. To a considerable extent these 'idealist' assumptions are the ones which led to the formation of the EU. They also have a considerable affinity to the nineteenth century idea that countries could attain peace and prosperity by opening themselves to each other through free trade, as described in Chapter 2. Indeed, an alternative label for the idealist position is (international) liberalism.

As we shall see, both 'realism' and 'idealism' have influenced British foreign and military policy. Like most general ideas, however, they do not give complete answers to the practical decisions faced by governments.

BRIEFINGS

23.2 THE UNITED NATIONS

The First World War (1914–18) killed around 20 million people through fighting, famine and disease, mostly in Europe. To help avoid conflict in the future, the victors hoped to create a world body which would bring nation-states together and help them resolve disputes peacefully. This was the League of Nations. The League held regular assemblies but became increasingly ineffective as national conflicts intensified in the 1930s. It was also weakened by the fact that the USA and USSR were never members. It did, however, do useful work through its specialised organisations, particularly for refugees, in the 1920s and was associated with bodies like the International Labour Organisation (ILO) which tried to get world agreement on working conditions.

Such bodies were inherited by the League's successor organisation, the United Nations, set up in 1946 after the Second World War (1939–45). This tried to avoid the weaknesses of the League by having, besides a General Assembly in which all states had a vote, a Security Council of major powers: USA, USSR (now Russia), China, Britain and France. Each of these can veto UN action, but if they agree they control forces which other states cannot resist. The UN has proved a useful umbrella both for intervention where order has broken down or to police disputed borders. The intervention in Bosnia (1992–95) was a mixture of both. It was relatively ineffective in stopping fighting, however, because UN member states often disagree on objectives and are reluctant to pay for costs.

Like the League, the UN does much useful work through specialised agencies for refugees, education, children and health, and also tries to get international agreements on the environment. The Secretary-General appointed by the Assembly has become a world figure but as a result is often controversial and opposed by one or other of the superpowers. The activity of the UN marks another breakdown in the traditional view of the state as a sovereign entity controlling everything that happens within its own borders.

POSTWAR DEVELOPMENTS IN BRITISH FOREIGN POLICY

A summary of major events and developments is given in the 'Milestones' charted at the end of the chapter. For convenience they are grouped under three headings: the world, general international developments involving Britain; decolonisation, the process of disengagement from the colonial empire that in 1945 covered almost a quarter of the globe; and the European Union, already discussed in Chapters 4 and 5.

The problem of decolonisation was a major preoccupation of the first half of the postwar period, as it carried potential threats to British investment and trade and might involve the Army in unwinnable colonial wars. As the colonies became independent, however, Britain's direct involvement diminished and government attention shifted to the accelerating moves towards economic and political union in Europe, culminating in the 'deepening and widening' of the European Union in the 1990s.

Some have seen in this shift of attention from overseas to Europe evidence of the decline of Britain from a world power to a regional, European, power. But this is to ignore the major preoccupation of British governments throughout the postwar period, which was neither the Empire nor the European Union but the Cold War (1948–89), the stand-off between NATO (led by the United States and backed heavily by Britain) and the USSR.

This involved a state of constant military readiness on both sides, the stockpiling of huge nuclear and other military weapons, and the maintenance of huge armies. As part of their commitment to NATO, the Americans maintained large air and army bases in Britain and Germany, to confront the Soviet forces stationed in Central and Eastern Europe.

The Cold War sometimes erupted into local conflicts, although the Americans and Russians never confronted each other directly. Thus in Korea (1950–53) American troops, supported by Britain and other NATO allies, fought North Korean and Chinese troops backed by Russia. In Vietnam (1964–75) American troops with local support fought local communist troops backed by China and the Soviet Union. In Afghanistan (1979–89) Russian troops fought local guerrillas armed and financed by the United States.

Decolonisation

Britain's colonial wars have to be seen in this context, as an attempt to contain communist or communist-supported takeovers and leave Western-oriented regimes in their place. Sometimes local nationalists were wrongly seen as communist-inspired, as in Egypt in 1956. Intervention in Suez, in collusion with the French and Israelis, was (correctly) opposed by the Americans who did not share the British view of the Egyptian nationalists as communists. Their opposition forced an ignominious British withdrawal. On its side the British Government opposed direct American intervention in South Vietnam (1964–75) on the grounds that a jungle war there was expensive and unwinnable.

On the whole, however, the British and Americans co-operated well both in Europe and overseas. British policy in the colonies was to hand over power where a strong nationalist movement emerged, particularly if it was pro-Western in orientation and prepared to allow business and investment to continue as normal. Handovers of this kind succeeded in the Indian subcontinent, Africa and the Caribbean. Where a threat of subversion existed, most notably from Chinese communist guerrillas in Malaya, British troops generally defeated them by gaining the support of sections of the local population. Failures were Palestine and South Arabia where all the warring factions opposed the British.

By conceding power relatively quickly, and fighting limited campaigns, Britain did stabilise the situation in most former colonies and limited the military and political costs of disengagement. Their successes contrasted with the dismal record of the other European colonial powers (the Netherlands, Belgium, France and Portugal) who became enmeshed in long expensive wars which ended in humiliating withdrawals. Relics of Britain's colonial past did, however, cause some complications in the 1980s and 1990s. The rich but largely autonomous colony of Hong Kong was handed back to China, by agreement, in 1997. The remote and thinly populated Falkland Islands which had been invaded by neighbouring Argentina in 1982 were regained by a costly sea-borne expedition in the same year. Residual British responsibilities towards the black population of Southern Africa were relieved by peaceful transitions to full internal democracy in 1982 and 1994 respectively, though the British were never very directly engaged there.

Europe, NATO and the British bomb

The major process of decolonisation ended around the mid-1960s and must be seen as a major British contribution to overall Western success in the Cold War, which was then in full swing. It is artificial to separate decolonisation from its world context. The same must be said of British involvement in Europe, the main vehicle for which was NATO rather than the EU. British involvement cannot simply be seen as beginning with the first application for entry to the EU in 1962, or even with actual entry in 1973. As the main area of confrontation with the Soviet Union, Europe was at the centre of British preoccupations from 1946. Participation in the EU had economic payoffs, but was also seen as consolidating Western Europe in the face of Russian threats.

As its contribution to European defence, Britain left up to half its effective Army in Germany (BAOR, British Army of the Rhine). It also invested heavily in weapons – tanks, aircraft and ships – and in developing its own nuclear bomb.

The United States had more than enough nuclear weapons, aircrafts and rockets to deter a Russian attack on its own. British possession of a nuclear weapon, especially as it became dependent on America supplying missiles to carry it, has been criticised particularly on the left, as a childish desire to assert its 'great power' status. It was said to be a purely symbolic assertion of British importance just as the country lost its economic and strategic power.

The official justification for the 'independent deterrent', however, related it firmly to the overall question of European security. It functioned as a guarantee of American commitment to European (including British) defence. NATO would never have enough troops, the argument ran, to counter the massive superiority of the Soviet armies. It must be made very clear to the USSR, therefore, that any invasion would be met by immediate Western use of strategic nuclear weapons. America, however, might be tempted at such a point to write Europe off, hesitating to commence a nuclear war which would devastate its own territory. British nuclear weapons could then be brought in, however, to deter Soviet attack, and thus tie America irrevocably to acting in support of Britain and other NATO allies. (This view is clearly influenced by 'realist' thinking which sees even friendly states as essentially untrustworthy.)

Put in this way, the deterrent can be seen as embodying British strategic concerns with Europe since the Second World War. The fact that Britain made itself the pivot of this arrangement neatly reflects the way in which all its policies tend to be influenced by its halfway position between Europe and America. Chapter 2 has already commented on this as reflecting not just its geographical position but also cultural factors and economic interests.

The Postwar Boom 1950–73

The first half of the postwar era, up to 1973, was also a period in which a new liberal economic order consolidated itself in the West. Massive American aid to Western Europe, including Britain, succeeded in stabilising their war-shattered economies by 1950. Britain benefited both directly and indirectly from American financial reconstruction. Not only did the direct injection of capital help restore its older and damaged land, buildings and equipment, but with its infrastructure largely intact after the war it was able to meet the enhanced demand for goods from the Continent, which launched a sustained world boom till the early 1970s. During most of these years the British economy grew at a steady 2 per cent a year. This was less than other industrialised countries rebuilding from a totally shattered industrial base (Chapter 1), but it provided a surplus for increasing wages and expanding the welfare state at home, while simultaneously exporting capital abroad. British investments abroad had been liquidated to pay for the Second World War, but by the 1970s Britain had again become one of the three leading countries (with the USA and Japan) in terms of overseas capital investments. This reflected the activities of the City financial institutions described in Chapter 1.

Their activities were facilitated by the stable trading situation created in the West by the Bretton Woods Agreements (1944) which ensured that the major world currencies would have fixed exchange rates geared to the dollar. These gave world banks and financial institutions the confidence that investments would not be eroded by unexpected devaluations (sudden depreciation of one currency compared with another). The orderly process of decolonisation carried through by Britain ensured that new countries on the whole honoured these rules and also proved profitable fields for investment.

The balance of payments crises of the 1960s and 1970s

British military expenditure and capital exports increasingly tended to produce a negative balance of payments, that is, the value of British manufacturers and services exported abroad was less than the value of imports plus payments overseas (see Briefing 23.3). Increasingly during the 1960s governments raised interest rates (the price of borrowing money) so as to restrict internal demand and so reduce imports to balance the financial books. The combination of high internal interest rates and a high valued currency suited financial institutions, which saw their profits soar. But it hit manufacturing industry, forced closures of factories and firms, and increased general unemployment. This caused the direct conflict between the financial and manufacturing sectors of the British economy (Chapters 1 and 2) in which finance won out.

The obvious difficulties of British manufacturing, and frequent bouts of inflation followed by recession as a result of internal election considerations ('stop–go'), caused international money markets persistently to mark down the

BRIEFINGS

23.3 THE BALANCE OF PAYMENTS

Trade and other statistics collected on the transactions between Britain and other countries give the relative magnitude of the money earned by exports of goods and services and the money paid for imports of goods and services. For most of the postwar period Britain has imported more than it has exported. It has thus had a balance of payments deficit rather than a surplus.

The deficit is particularly evident when the British economy expands rapidly and thus imports more. In the 1960s this reduced confidence in the pound sterling, which therefore lost its value, which in turn hit the activities of the City of London. The City then pressured governments into raising interest rates to slow down expansion and restore confidence in the pound (the 'stop–go' cycle, Chapter 3).

The British balance of payments has currently been in deficit for 10 years but this has not affected financial confidence because:

- it is partly balanced by the oil surpluses in the balance of payments during the mid-1980s,
- it is also compensated by the growth in capital value of the (large) British assets abroad which are not entered into the balance of payments figures themselves,
- Britain is expected to move into surplus by the end of the 1990s.

Note that if Britain joins European Monetary Union its balance of payments will be merged with the general EU one.

value of sterling to a point when its fixed value could no longer be maintained simply by raising internal interest rates. The system of fixed rates prevented the Labour Government of the time from simply letting the value drift down, as it would do today. In 1967 the Wilson Government was forced to say that they would henceforth buy pounds for 2.40 dollars rather than the previous price of 2.80 dollars.

This devaluation was a severe shock for British financial institutions, even as it eased the situation for manufacturing industry. A major result was that the pound ceased to function as an international reserve currency in which other countries priced transactions between themselves. Buying sterling to finance such trades became too risky as the value might suddenly go down again if Britain found itself in similar financial difficulties. This deprived British banks of the profits they had made from supplying sterling to other countries. The situation was eased for them, however, by the general abandonment of fixed interest rates a few years later, when the United States found itself in the same position as Britain had been earlier and effectively devalued the dollar. Thereafter international deals were based on baskets of currencies, which London-based institutions showed themselves adept at handling, reaping large profits from doing so.

Joining 'Europe'

The financial crises of the 1960s did, however, convince British politicians of the need to strengthen manufacturing industry. Grandiose internal plans for industrial reorganisation were to be supplemented by membership of the successful and expanding European Economic Community, as the EU was then known. After two applications were vetoed by the French in the 1960s, on the grounds that Britain was too close to America, an application was finally accepted in 1972.

As opposed to most of the original six member countries, British interest in the EU was almost exclusively economic. It saw opportunities to create an expanded free trade area which would open up other markets more quickly than GATT at a world level, but which would essentially complement world free trade. From the point of view of the original members, however, the EEC was an economic means to political union. By integrating economically, the Member States would create a need for international political bodies to regulate markets and labour. Eventually this would lock European states into a political union which would prevent their ever going to war with each other again.

For the British, less directly affected by the old Franco-German rivalry, this was not immediately relevant. Moreover, increased economic co-operation was, to their minds, a way of creating a free trade zone relatively open to the rest of the world, which reflected the traditional patterns of British trade and especially finance. The French and Germans, in line with their own traditions (Chapter 2), favoured a protectionist policy in which trade would be free between members but relatively closed to the rest of the world. The model for this was the highly protectionist Common Agricultural Policy which largely closed European food markets to outsiders at the cost of high prices to consumers.

This was thus a great potential for conflict between Britain and its new-found partners within the EU, but in the 1970s this was largely masked by the crisis which hit all industrialised countries through the massive increases in the price of oil imposed by the producer countries.

The oil shock of 1973 and the world recession of the 1970s

The world economic boom from 1950 to 1970 had been largely built on cheap unlimited oil which Western dominance of the Third World had produced (see Briefing 23.4). In 1973–74 the producers created a monopoly pricing body (OPEC, the Organisation of Petroleum Exporting Countries) which massively increased oil prices and kept on increasing them through the 1970s and early 1980s. Production processes based on cheap oil suddenly became more expensive, stimulating sharp price increases. In turn this provoked factory closures, lay-offs, recession and unemployment. The quarter-century since 1975 has been marked by alternating recessions and booms, which have had major political and strategic consequences. These were mitigated for Britain by the discovery of extensive oil reserves around its own coasts, which freed governments from balance of payments difficulties until the 1990s.

BRIEFINGS

23.4 THE THIRD WORLD: UNDERDEVELOPED AND DEVELOPING COUNTRIES

The Third World essentially consists of Africa, Asia (apart from Japan) and Central and South America, in other words the areas taken over by Europeans from 1500 to 1945. Although the countries there became politically independent from the nineteenth century onwards, particularly during the 1950s, they are still financially and economically dependent on the USA, Europe and Japan. Their economies rest mainly on agriculture and mining, subject to great fluctuations in the world market, and much of their population is dependent on subsistence farming, producing their own food.

Most former British colonies are in the Third World, particularly Africa and Asia, and share these problems of 'underdeveloped' or 'developing' countries. However, things are changing fast and some countries like Brazil, Malaysia and India are developing large industrial sectors and competing with the 'First World' or 'developed' economies.

The end of the Cold War and trade liberalisation from 1979

Key term

Trade liberalisation – the process whereby international trade is increasingly opened up to market forces (free trade) by reducing trading tariffs, import and export controls, and other forms of protection.

The association of left-wing governments with recession in both Britain and the United States brought unusually rightist governments to power in both countries during the 1980s, under Margaret Thatcher and President Reagan respectively. They concurred on a massive revival of the old free-trade programme both at home and abroad. Tariffs and protection of all kinds were to be swept away and enemies of freedom (essentially the Soviet Union) were to be rigorously confronted. However, the Soviet Union was suffering from economic stagnation, which its planning programme and political controls were unable to overcome, and so was not willing to direct resources into the renewed arms race threatened by the Reagan administration. First it agreed to arms limitations in direct negotiations with the USA. Having neutralised its nuclear forces it then saw little point in continuing to prop up the authoritarian communist regimes of Central and Eastern Europe. With no internal support, these were replaced by democratic governments committed to trade liberalisation and integration with the West. Following their example, various minority nationalities incorporated inside the old USSR split away, leaving Russia proper as the successor state, still immense but within much shrunken boundaries.

These developments obviously removed much of the justification for NATO and lent a new importance to the European Union. An attempt by the Arab country of Iraq to dominate Middle Eastern oil supplies was thwarted by an American-led intervention in the Persian Gulf (1990–91). The inability of European countries to resolve fighting in Bosnia (1992–95) much closer to home – indicated that NATO might have a use in world policing even after the Cold War. This diagnosis was heavily backed by Britain, which was profoundly sceptical about Europeans being able to agree about defence on their own, and hence saw a continuing American involvement as the best guarantee for European security.

The Single European Act and Monetary Union

This attitude runs across French and German aspirations for a joint military and foreign policy as an indispensable requirement for close European Union (even if they have not been too good at agreeing what to do in Eastern Europe or the Middle East). In the 1980s Britain found a new basis of unity with its EU partners in promoting a genuine unified free market in the EU (the Single European Act 1986), which aimed at removing all barriers to internal free trade without increasing tariffs against external trade. This gave the Thatcher Government all it wanted so it agreed to the measures needed to enforce it, including greater powers for the central European institutions.

The Single Act carried through into wider agreements under GATT to liberalise world trade, in which the EU took a generally positive stand, again enthusiastically supported by Britain. One of the biggest barriers to inter-European trade was fluctuating currency rates. Britain accordingly joined the European Monetary

Reserve System in 1990, and agreed to keep the pound stable at a fixed exchange rate with the German mark, the strongest EU currency. Unfortunately it fixed the rate too high, at a level of 2.80 marks, unjustified by the relative strengths of the two currencies.

As a result, world currency speculators started using their pounds to buy marks, hoping that the British Government would eventually run out of reserves to exchange 2.80 marks for each pound. Speculators with large supplies of marks would then be able to buy much larger numbers of pounds after the exchange rate was forced down, and would make enormous profits.

This is exactly what happened on 'Black Wednesday' in September 1992. Paradoxically the cheaper pound started off a long, slow and uncertain economic recovery, with low inflation, which has lasted to the present time. But it destroyed the Conservative Government's reputation for economic competence and gave them a deficit in the opinion polls from which they did not recover up to the general election of 1997 (Chapter 15).

As a result, hostility between pro- and anti-Europeans in the Conservative Party became intense, heightened by pressures on the Government to agree to other measures for closer union (Chapters 4 and 5). To add insult to injury, the major vehicle for these was to be the adoption of a currency union of the whole European Union with a common unit, the Euro, closely related to the German mark.

As a purely economic measure, a European currency union probably makes sense for Britain just as much as for the other EU members. Financial interests would benefit from a strong currency with low inflation, as savings and investments would have a guaranteed value. Speculative profits could be retained by dealing in other currencies. Sixty to seventy per cent of British manufacturing exports go to countries of the EU and a stable currency would guarantee stable markets. For the multinationals, which now control most of British industry and have factories across the whole of Europe, accounting would be simpler and investments could be transferred more directly. Indeed their preference would probably be for locating disproportionately in Britain for cultural and linguistic reasons (English is the international language) if no barriers intervened to trading on the Continent.

As always in economic decisions, some interests would gain and others lose. European monetary policy would be dominated by intensely conservative German bankers, setting their policy by conditions in the Rhineland and concerned above all to combat inflation there. From their point of view, recession in Ireland or Scotland, or even the South-East of England, would be irrelevant. All might benefit from low inflation but the people who would pay for it in terms of higher unemployment and lower pay would be those employed in manufacturing in the peripheries. What might be new about the Euro currency is that South-East England might also become an economic periphery in this sense.

What is more likely, however, is that the European core would run from London through the Rhineland to Milan and thus the predominant British interests would actually benefit from the common currency. This makes it likely that the New Labour Government will agree in the end to currency union, in spite of its current strategic hesitations.

The difficulties of monetary union – for France particularly as well as for Britain – are also likely to produce compromises in other areas. The goal of a common European defence policy is likely to be postponed indefinitely, producing tacit acquiescence to the American involvement in Europe, which is strongly supported in Britain. Coupled with slower progress towards political integration this is likely to make it easier for British governments to get on with their partners. External pressures are also likely to make 'widening' of the EU (incorporation of the Central European countries) more prominent than ever over the next decade. This may have the effect of creating a common interest between Britain, France and Germany in retaining effective control for the larger and more powerful countries within the EU over future developments, at the expense of greater internal democratisation.

THE CHANGING WORLD CONTEXT

Clearly the developments we have traced have not taken place in a vacuum. British politics and interests have changed in response to other developments taking place around them. For example, the British would hardly have abandoned their Empire of their own volition. They got out because they sensed their presence would no longer be tolerated by the colonised populations, nor even perhaps by the two superpowers the USA and USSR. In this section we outline the major changes in the world context which influenced British responses in the postwar period.

The changing climate of ideas

Ideas are often discounted as a source of influence in politics, in part as a consequence of the realist view that what matters are resources and power. No matter what governments say, they will always try to do each other down because all they 'really' care about is maximising their own state interests.

Such a 'hard-boiled' view of international relations often attracts people because it cuts through the pretence and hypocrisy with which governments often mask their own self-interest. It is true up to a point and in many situations, but on the other hand ideas and ideals often exert an independent influence on events. For example, in order to understand how subsistence farmers were mobilised throughout the Third World against well-armed colonial armies, one needs to appreciate the force of nationalism and calls for social justice.

Not surprisingly, therefore, material changes in global economics and politics have been accompanied in the postwar period by changes in the overall climate of ideas. Three of these are worth highlighting. One was that the 'White Man's burden' view of empire – in which the colonising powers claimed to be on a civilising mission that would grant independence to colonial peoples 'when they were ready for it' – became increasingly unacceptable. It was replaced by embarrassment about the domination and exploitation of the Third World that colonialism implied. Unfortunately for the newly liberated colonial populations, however, this change in attitude was not accompanied by much of a willingness to make up for earlier exploitation.

A second change in the climate of opinion after 1945 was the apparently increasing appeal of communism as a mobilising ideology of the dispossessed. Anti-imperialists throughout the Third World frequently saw the economic and political difficulties that their countries faced, even after decolonisation, as deriving from the global capitalist system of production, distribution and exchange. Between 1945 and 1975, over 30 countries 'succumbed' to the attractions of Marxist–Leninist ideology (and, as we saw, the British were often combatting it in the colonies). After 1980, however, this seemingly inexorable tide of socialism went into rapid reverse. With the success of the Islamic revolution in Iran after 1978, with Moscow's conflict with Islamic forces in Afghanistan after 1979, and with the collapse of socialism in eastern Europe and in the Soviet Union (1989–90), communism's appeal as a vehicle for mobilising deeply felt grievances declined significantly. It was replaced by Islam in large parts of the Third World, and particularly in the Middle East and the Far East, though whether Islam will prove any more adept at removing grievances once power has been secured remains to be seen.

A third major change in the postwar climate of international opinion was an increased interest in, and commitment to, the promotion of individual human rights (see Briefing 23.5). In part this emphasis reflected a conscious rejection of the 'collective rights' stressed by communism. But it also reflected a genuine humanitarian effort on the part of Western governments and nongovernmental organisations (such as Charter 88 and Amnesty International) which sought to extend internationally the protective cover of human rights legislation.

> **Key term**
>
> **Human rights** – the fundamental and universal rights of all people, irrespective of the laws of their country, which derive from being a human being.

BRIEFINGS

23.5 THE INTERNATIONAL HUMAN RIGHTS MOVEMENT

The United Nations launched a Universal Declaration of the Rights of Man when it was founded. Although another of its principles was mutual non-interference in the internal affairs of states, in practice gross breaches of rights have led to UN or NATO intervention (for example in Bosnia from 1992 onwards).

Mutual policing of rights was in fact institutionalised by the Helsinki Accords of 1975, signed between the NATO and Warsaw Pact countries. Britain and the USA have also made protests about violation of human rights in China. Under the auspices of the Council of Europe, Britain and other members have submitted themselves to the jurisdiction of the European Court of Human Rights to which individuals and groups in Britain can appeal against the British Government. The European Court of Justice in practice applies the European Convention of Human Rights in its own jurisdiction, and Britain has agreed to incorporate it into its domestic legislation.

Supplementing these governmental initiatives, voluntary organisations like Amnesty International, with headquarters in London, have policed each country's own observance of basic rights and procedures, publicised abuses and sent observers to trials to monitor what is going on. Britain has been reasonably supportive of their efforts.

Globalisation

Key term

Globalisation – the
process whereby all parts
of the globe, no matter
how remote and isolated,
become increasingly linked
into a world system of
politics, economics, and
cultural patterns.

Key term

Imperialism – the
practice of one nation
controlling or dominating
another state or territory,
usually by military and
economic means, and to
the advantage of the
imperial power.

Nationalist movements in the old empires were not, of course, fuelled wholly by ideas. European rule produced economic development, which in turn brought social and political tensions. The process of urbanisation, together with the expansion of education and mass communications, fragmented old social networks, rendering the indigenous populations of the colonies much more susceptible to the new, radical ideas. By developing the colonies, the imperial powers created the very conditions in which anticolonial oppositions could thrive.

The British were astute enough to realise this early on, concentrating on putting the more congenial members of the opposition in power and integrating them and their newly independent countries into the Western political and trading system. In doing so they contributed to the process of 'globalisation' which has transformed the world over the last 50 years. Globalisation relates primarily to the process whereby all parts of the world, even the most remote and isolated, have been linked up by Western trade and communications. As a result, the way people live and work, the way they dress, the food they consume, the things they do – even the way they think – has become more similar. There are very few subsistence economies left which produce only for themselves. Even the largest Western economies are not self-sufficient any more but dependent on networks of traders and producers in other parts of the world.

Before 1945, countries with relatively powerful economies tended to use their economic and military muscle to extend their direct political influence beyond their current national boundaries. European imperialism in the nineteenth century, and German and Japanese expansionism in the 1930s involved precisely this sort of extension. Since 1945, however, nation-states have increasingly recognised that economic security and global influence can be achieved without direct or indirect political control, as the cases of postwar Germany and Japan have demonstrated.

A related change in the international system has been the massive increase in world trade and financial exchanges. These increases have both reflected and reinforced the revolutions in transport technology and global communications that have occurred since 1945. Although direct comparison is difficult, the available figures suggest that the volume of world trade in goods and services in 1993 was more than 20 times greater than it had been in 1950. The volume of currency exchanges and capital transfers, spurred on by trade liberalisation and deregulation, was so great by the mid-1990s that it was beyond the capability of national governments even to monitor them effectively. This expansion of the financial sector, in particular, has served to increase the significance of international markets and market forces. Economists sometimes speak about the *permeability* of national economies, meaning the extent to which capital, labour, goods and services can be either introduced into or extracted from a given country. There can be little doubt that, over the last 50 years, the average level of permeability has increased considerably. The consequence of this has been a corresponding decrease in the decision-making autonomy of national governments, which have found their economic policy strategies increasingly vulnerable to international market pressures.

An internal consequence of globalisation which is often overlooked is that the very concept of a national economy, with most exchanges going on between its component parts – all affected uniformly by national economic developments – has lost any reality it ever had. The rhetoric of British politicians about 'Great Britain plc' acting like a cohesive firm in international markets, and showing a single profit-and-loss account, is largely irrelevant. Britain, in fact, because of its pivotal position in the global economic system from the mid-nineteenth century (Chapter 2), has lacked a cohesive national economy in this sense for a very long time. What benefits London finance does not necessarily benefit manufacturing, and there are strong conflicts of economic interest between regions which are exacerbated by the different relationships each part has to the world economy.

Reflecting economic globalisation and integration one can observe a parallel growth of 'international regimes'. Regimes are sets of international 'rules of the game' accepted by states because of the importance of joint rather than independent decision making in many areas. States are prepared to accept regime-imposed restrictions on their decision-making autonomy on two conditions: first, that the benefits of any co-operation sponsored by the regime more than outweigh the costs entailed by any loss of autonomy; second, that the regime is able to ensure that states which fail to co-operate (or which 'free-ride' on the concessions made by others) are suitably penalised.

In the postwar period, international regimes have proliferated to such an extent that we cannot even attempt to describe them all here. Three examples, however, indicate the wide range of contexts in which international regimes have developed. In the economic sphere, the General Agreement on Tariffs and Trade (now the World Trade Organisation) has been remarkably successful, through a series of negotiating rounds which culminated in the Uruguay Round in the early 1990s, in bringing down trade barriers and in expanding world trade. In the security sphere, the Conference on (now the Organisation for) Security and Co-operation in Europe made an important contribution to the softening of East–West relations in the years immediately before the end of the Cold War. Finally, in the ecological sphere, the Vienna Convention (1985) and the Montreal Protocol (1987) established and extended guidelines for reducing CFC production in order to protect the earth's ozone layer.

Ensuring compliance with a regime's rules is always a difficult matter in practice. Nonetheless, the enormous growth of regime-like organisations and practices since 1945 represents an important change in the international environment in which Britain now operates. To a lesser extent, this also reflects the commitment of successive UK governments to the construction of regimes which would themselves facilitate further international co-operation (a practical application of 'idealist' principles).

The end of the Cold War

The break-up of the old Communist bloc of countries and their increasing assimilation into the Western capitalist system in the 1990s have been partly a consequence, but also a powerful facilitator, of globalisation. It is difficult to overestimate the extent to which the Soviet/Communist threat dominated British and Western strategic calculations during the Cold War. Decolonisation was pursued so as to ward off Communist takeovers. The protection of Western Europe was always a first priority and all major foreign policy decisions were undertaken with a view to the Soviets' likely reaction. In these circumstances, the abrupt termination of the external threat that, since 1949, had provided the NATO alliance with its principal *raison d'être* was bound to create difficulties for Western policy makers. In early 1996, with NATO embarking on its first (Bosnian) 'out-of-area' operation, the alliance's unity and resolve seemed undiminished. This could not hide the fact that NATO's long-term survival would always be in doubt unless a new threat, equivalent to that represented by the USSR, were to emerge.

The end of the Cold War has increased the international community's ability, acting through the UN, to intervene in local conflicts in order to protect the innocent and defend the interests of victims of aggression. Prior to 1989, the ideological divide almost invariably meant that one of the permanent Security Council members would employ its veto power in order to ensure that the Council was deadlocked. The sort of concerted action that the UN-sponsored multilateral force took in defence of Kuwait against Iraq in 1990, for example, would have been almost unthinkable. Sadly, the Kuwait crisis excepted, greater agreement within the Security Council since 1990 has not been accompanied by conspicuous success on the ground. As events in Bosnia between 1992 and 1995 demonstrated, UN-sponsored forces have found it very difficult to take the sort of decisive action that is typically required for effective and durable conflict resolution. This points to the need to develop new types of military operation geared to fighting long-drawn-out, low tech, low intensity wars. This is an area in which the British military have, of course, extensive experience and a practical training-ground in Northern Ireland.

MOTIVATIONS AND ASSUMPTIONS OF BRITISH FOREIGN POLICY

Foreign policy is largely constrained by developments in the surrounding world. No country can simply devise a policy and carry it through, unaffected by external events. Any attempt to ignore these would be self-defeating.

British foreign policy is no exception and has clearly had to respond to the developments traced above. The real question is whether it has been a good or bad response. Has it succeeded in advancing British interests as well as could be expected within the inevitable constraints or has it squandered resources while not achieving its objectives? We will be able to judge this better after analysing policy in this section and considering British capabilities, both general and military, in the following one.

The million dollar question with regard to foreign policy, as with any other policy, is whose interests are being served. It is a mistake to assume that there is any readily identifiable general British 'national interest' to be served by its foreign policy. Usually there are competing interests, one of which successfully asserts a claim to be the 'national interest' while the others lose out.

In other areas of policy the financial interests of the City of London have exerted a disproportionate influence, at the expense of other interests such as those of manufacturing industry and of the peripheral regions. So it would not be surprising to find the same influence being exerted in foreign policy, particularly as British trade and investment are so closely attuned to foreign developments.

It is only fair to say, however, that the major motivation behind postwar policy, to defend liberal democracy and the capitalist system against communist attempts to subvert it, enjoyed widespread support among all sections of the population. Thus on the major lines of British policy – managed decolonisation, staunch membership of NATO, support for international organisations and regimes operating on broadly democratic liberal lines (UN, GATT) – there was broad agreement.

On some of the more detailed implementation of policy there might naturally be dissent. Three major areas are European Union, nuclear deterrence and the relationship with the USA.

European Union

The decision to join the European Union, taken by a Conservative Government in 1972, was attacked by the trade unions and Labour Party as a sellout to European capitalist interests which would thwart left-wing plans for a radical overhaul of British society. Paradoxically, by the 1990s the EU was seen in exactly parallel terms by the Conservative right, as a leftist constraint on radical free market reform in Britain! Both reactions demonstrated the structural and cultural difficulties the British had in coping with the capitalist-protectionist traditions of France and Germany, so alien to support for a totally free market in Britain.

Nuclear Deterrence and Unilateral Disarmament

Few groups in Britain advocated a pull-out from NATO. There was considerably more support for giving up the independent British nuclear bomb, which was seen as expensive and unreliable in light of American capabilities. Protests against British nuclear, and to a lesser extent chemical, weapons reached a head in the 1960s, when the Campaign for Nuclear Disarmament could muster up to half a million people in its protest marches. In the 1980s there were other protests against the stationing of American nuclear missiles on British soil.

The 'Special Relationship' with America

A major argument of nuclear protesters was that Britain should scrap its own deterrent and rely on the American one. Paradoxically, however, there was an anti-American tinge to their arguments too. The United States was seen as too eager to risk war with Russia and as inclined to oppose radical but perfectly democratic reform as communist-inspired, particularly if it threatened business profits. This critique saw Britain as too subservient to American interests, even to the extent of sacrificing its own resources to forwarding them.

Certainly Conservative prime ministers like Churchill (1951–55), Macmillan (1957–62) and Thatcher (1979–90) were fond of referring to the 'special relationship' between Britain and the United States. With the major exception of Vietnam (1964–72), Britain generally supported US policies, while with the exception of Suez (1956) the USA generally supported British ones.

The relationship took its most concrete form inside NATO, where Britain actively backed up the US leadership. Most other NATO members were content to let the USA carry a disproportionate share of common defence costs. Britain, in contrast, allocated a significantly higher proportion of its GDP to defence. In 1979, for example, the UK spent 4.7 per cent of GDP on defence compared with Germany's 3.9 per cent. In the 1990s the purchase from the USA of Trident submarines to carry nuclear missiles still went on, even under Labour, while the new Government reaffirmed its commitment to development of a 'Eurofighter' estimated to cost 15 billion pounds.

Nuclear and other defence costs have been criticised for overstraining and distorting the economy for the sake of an overextended military role. It is claimed that Britain's reduced status as a European rather than a world power does not require this. Maintaining an expensive military capability does not advance British interests and is harmful economically and financially.

To evaluate this criticism properly we need now to look at the other basis of foreign policy, resources and capability. Even if British interests are broadly to support America and uphold a liberal-democratic world order, does it really have the economic base to push them in the way it has done? In any case, what should be the British military posture after the end of the Cold War? These are the questions we consider in the next section.

BRITISH CAPABILITIES IN THE POSTWAR ERA

Critics of British 'overextension' abroad generally emphasise the way in which 'relative decline' of the economy has diminished the resources available for a large foreign and military role. They also regard the economic demands and distortions produced by this role as an important factor producing 'decline' in the first place.

As pointed out in Chapter 1, we put 'decline' in inverted commas because in fact the British economy has actually *expanded* fivefold in the postwar period! 'Relative' decline refers to the slower growth, on average, of the British economy compared with Germany, France and Japan. It also refers to factors like the reduction of the British share of world trade from over 20 per cent in the late 1940s to under 5 per cent today. (Paradoxically this figure too actually represents an absolute *increase* in British trading activity, owing to the vast expansion in the volume of total world trade.)

If Britain overall has had ever more resources to dispose of, however, it is not obvious that it has been overstraining them by keeping up its military role. To say so is covertly to expand the meaning of 'relative' decline to absolute decline. In that case Britain would indeed have had diminishing resources each year and would be necessarily sacrificing other priorities to military ones. This was not the case, however, as it actually had *increasing* economic resources at its disposal.

Of course, had its foreign expenses been less, Britain might have chosen to put even more money into welfare or industrial reconstruction, but there is no guarantee that freed resources would have been spent there, nor that they would have been wisely spent. So it is not obvious that high levels of foreign and military expenditure have necessarily damaged Britain economically.

The one crisis that originated in part from such expenditure concerned the balance of payments in 1966–67, but this was not an inevitable consequence of foreign overextension. What brought it on was Conservative engineering of a pre-election boom in 1963–64, and Labour mishandling of devaluation from 1965–67. Again military expenditure does not seem to be the direct cause of internal difficulties.

The financial crisis of the 1960s in any case stimulated a rationalisation of military spending. This involved a withdrawal of forces from east of Suez, reasonably soon after decolonisation rendered them unnecessary, to concentrate on defending Britain's growing interests in Europe. Again, reactions to the changed situation seem to have been relatively quick and relatively effective.

A further criticism of the effects of Britain's military role has been of the distortions produced by the supporting arms industry and of the concentration of Government investment in research and development (R & D) on military equipment. This has meant, according to this argument, that investment and research in civil industry has been downgraded. It would have been better to invest money in developing the car industry or civil electronics which would have produced payoffs for a whole range of other manufacturers, rather than in the highly specialised area of military hardware, with limited civil applications.

The trouble with this argument is, of course, that it assumes that money saved from military research *would* have gone into manufacturing R & D. All the evidence we have, however, is that stock market pressures on British firms to get quick results would have precluded any more long-range investment than they actually make. 'Short-termism' and lack of basic investment is a structural feature deriving from the relations of industry with the Stock Exchange and British banks, so money not spent on military research would not have been spent constructively elsewhere. One reason why more money was spent on R & D by armaments firms was that they had stable long-term projects and assured markets which other British firms did not have, guaranteed by governments in the name of national security.

A result of this is that arms manufacture has developed as one of the more successful and largest areas of the British economy. Britain is one of the four leading arms exporters in the world. The success of this sector again illustrates the extent to which the 'British economy' is partly an empty term, the separate enterprises in Britain having little more to do with each other than the fact that they all pay tax (some more than others) to the British Government. The arms industry

Plate 23.1 Michael Cummings cartoon in *The Times*, 26 July 1997: The Government grants exports licences for more Hawk jets to Indonesia and sponsors an international arms fair – after Labour pledges that it 'would not permit the sale of arms to regimes that might use them for internal repression or internal aggression'. More than 200,000 innocent people have died in East Timor and internal dissent has been ruthlessly suppressed in parts of Indonesia

operates in a specialised international sector where its relationships with Aerospatiale of France or Krupp–Thyssen of Germany are more important than its links with British Petroleum (BP) or Courtaulds, the textile firm.

Nonetheless British armaments firms such as General Electric Company (GEC) and British Aerospace do depend heavily on British taxes to provide a protected market where they can recoup costs on weapon development and subsidise overseas sales. Their close relationships with the civil servants of the Ministry of Defence have meant that massive cost overruns and delays on weapons development have not only been tolerated, but paid for, by British taxpayers. Often these have escalated to five or six times the original cost of a project. The Ministry of Defence has been astonishingly tolerant of this and has never been held closely to account for its expenditures, even in the most cost-conscious and cost-cutting days of Conservative Government. The argument that national security is involved seems to silence critics, who may also be under pressure from the security services mentioned in the last chapter.

The case of nuclear development gives an additional twist to the argument for the distorting effects of military expenditures. For here military research costs were passed off as civil ones, necessary to develop peaceful use of nuclear power through the government-backed Atomic Energy Authority (AEA). As a result nuclear power was overdeveloped, regardless of its (well-concealed) high costs, during the 1970s and 1980s.

The argument that military investments have distorted economic ones does seem to have some validity but these effects are not unique to Britain. Exactly similar subsidies to arms firms and the blurring of civil and military expenditures have occurred in France and the United States. It seems that any country with a sizeable military force is liable to run into these problems. They have certainly produced perverse effects, but these do not constitute a unique British problem.

British military capabilities: dilemmas for the year 2000

The armaments industry is powerful partly because it has protectors and supporters right up to the highest levels of government. High-ranking ministers may have had past links with arms firms or taken up positions with them after leaving office (see Briefing 23.6). So also may retired civil servants, particularly from the Ministry of Defence. Their technical expertise may have some market value but they are more likely valued for their political and administrative contacts.

BRIEFINGS

23.6 THE CAREER OF JONATHAN AITKEN, JOURNALIST, ARMS DEALER, POLITICIAN

Jonathan Aitken is a nephew of one of the prewar media moguls, Lord Beaverbrook (Max Aitken). He was prosecuted under the Official Secrets Act in 1971, when he reported in the *Sunday Telegraph* that arms sales to Nigeria were much larger than the Government claimed. After he was acquitted he went on to engage in the arms trade himself, becoming particularly involved in the huge arms deals of the 1980s with Saudi Arabia.

At the same time he became a Conservative MP and rose rapidly, becoming Chief Secretary to the Treasury – second in command of finances – in the 1990s. He continued to accept hospitality from Saudi Arabians engaged in the arms trade. Mohammed Al Fayed, who was pursuing a personal vendetta against the British establishment, leaked receipts to the *Guardian* from a stay of Aitken's at the Ritz Hotel in Paris that had been paid for in this way. Government ministers are not supposed to accept such hospitality in case they are influenced improperly.

The case contributed to the accusations of sleaze facing the Major Government and Aitken resigned from his post in a reshuffle in order to pursue a libel charge against the *Guardian*. This had to be abandoned in 1997, amid accusations of perjury against him.

Aitken's career illustrates the close connection between the arms trade, politics and journalism in Britain, and the role of the Official Secrets Act and severe libel laws in suppressing relevant political information. It is still unclear what the influence of arms dealers over government policy really is, but their ability to gain high-level political representation and to influence aid-for-trade deals such as the Pergau Dam, indicates that it is great. What facts we have come mostly from investigative journalism to which, paradoxically, Aitken contributed at the beginning of his career.

There is also an institutionalised pressure group right at the heart of government which will always speak up for defence contracts. This is the Joint Chiefs of Staff Committee, representing the high commands of the Army, Navy and Air Force. Naturally the generals, marshals and admirals are anxious to see their forces well equipped. They have two reasons for this: first, a genuine concern that the military should have the capability for what is demanded of them, and second, the more that is spent on the armed forces the more important they and their commanders become in the governmental structure. Influence correlates with budgets, so budget cutting constitutes a major threat.

By the same token, decisions about what weapons to buy generally set off a struggle between the forces themselves. Is money to be invested on ships for the Navy, new fighters for the Air Force or tanks for the Army? Each service desperately tries to ensure that it is not downgraded relative to the others. Withdrawal 'east of Suez' in the late 1960s meant that the Navy was no longer so important for guarding extended communication routes to India and South East Asia. It was compensated to some extent, however, by the shift in delivery systems for the nuclear bomb from aircraft to submarines. The expeditions to the Falklands and the Gulf again demonstrated the importance of the Navy in carrying troops to where they were needed. However, airlifts were also very important, and air offensives were a crucial element in both these cases as also in Bosnia (1992–95). That is one reason why the Royal Air Force (RAF) has managed to retain political support for the hugely expensive Eurofighter project, despite doubts about the real need for an enhanced front-line fighter after the end of the Cold War.

The need for an effective army is unchallenged, whether to fight off a large-scale invasion of Europe or to undertake limited war or peace-keeping operations (which often in fact develop into low intensity conflicts). The question, as always, is what kind of army with what kind of equipment? Should it be equipped to fight at all levels, even if some possibilities are less likely than others? The concern of 1990s governments, Labour and Conservatives, to cut costs and reduce taxes renders this unlikely. So a choice probably has to be made between equipping the Army for limited low intensity war and for all-out, high level conflict.

One problem is that expensive equipment – like larger and more sophisticated main battle tanks – lends more prestige, swells the budget, and can most easily be justified. The kind of all-out war for which it is really required seems much less likely however than low intensity conflicts. Hence it is likely that the issue will be fudged by the generals, who will argue that large tanks overawe local populations and hence are indispensable for all types of military operation.

In fact the major resource for limited, low intensity interventions is soldiers. A major peculiarity of the British Army compared with continental ones is the fact that, having no land borders to defend, it is primarily a small professional force of highly trained soldiers. Universal conscription of young men was only practised between 1939 and 1960, and was abolished at the first reduction of tension in the Cold War. Whatever other distortions military needs may have produced in Britain, they have not taken years out of the lives of generations of young males. (The United States abolished conscription in the 1970s, after Vietnam, and France is only now considering doing so.)

The small size of the British Army is all the more surprising since it has been engaged in limited, and sometimes not so limited, warfare in some part of the world, for the whole of the postwar period (colonial wars being succeeded by a similar low intensity conflict in Northern Ireland).

The end of the Cold War stimulated reductions in Army size from 150,000 to 110,000. The moot point now is whether to supply these reduced numbers with ever more sophisticated hardware so that they will be completely equipped for every conceivable emergency or to accept that existing equipment is adequate for low intensity operations (and can be supplemented by the Americans if necessary) and to recruit more soldiers to supply the major need for bodies on the ground.

The temptation for defence planners is to argue for hardware, on the grounds that the Army must be maintained as an all-round independent force. If NATO is to be the major vehicle for military interventions designed to bolster security and prevent antihumanitarian acts, Britain could most usefully supplement American efforts by supplying more soldiers. For political reasons the USA wants to limit its own involvement of troops, but is happy to supply technology and transport for allied operations. If Britain wants to keep the United States involved as the main guarantor of European and world security, it could probably do so best by supplying experienced troops with long traditions of low intensity warfare.

The main question now is whether 'realist' aspirations for a more independent role, and the pressure of EU partners for independent European defence projects, would actually allow this. In military as in other fields, Britain is structurally and geographically torn between its European and its overseas affiliations.

BRITISH FOREIGN POLICY: SUCCESS OR FAILURE?

Two dramatic and sharply contrasting pictures can be drawn of Britain's progress in the world since 1945. The first, linked with the general 'decline' idea, contrasts the standing of Britain after the Second World War with its position today. The UK was one of the three 'great powers' which, at Yalta in 1944 and Potsdam in 1945, played a decisive role in shaping the postwar settlement. As one of only five permanent members of the UN Security Council, Britain enjoyed the privilege of vetoing any of the Council's resolutions. Under the terms of the 1944 Bretton Woods Agreement, London also found itself acting as Washington's partner in a new international economic regime (based on the IMF, the World Bank and GATT) aimed at promoting economic stability and growth in the Western capitalist world.

Governments had a clear vision of the sort of foreign policy strategy that postwar Britain would follow. In line with the analysis advanced by Churchill in 1945, the UK government would seek to preserve British interests in three 'interlocking circles': in Europe, in the Empire and in the special relationship with the USA. The received view of Britain's postwar foreign policy makers was that Britain remained a 'great power' with far-flung global interests that required protection. By the early 1950s, Britain had acquired its own independent nuclear capability. It was one of the two leading members of NATO, the military alliance which was set to guarantee the security of Western Europe and North America for the next four decades. In spite of the loss of India in 1947, it retained control of a still-extensive empire. And its share of world trade was well over 20 per cent, not much lower than the share it had enjoyed at the peak of the country's industrial and military pre-eminence in the mid-nineteenth century.

What a difference half a century can make! By the mid-1990s, although Britain retained both its membership of the 'Group of Seven' leading industrial economies and its permanent Security Council seat, its circumstances were considerably reduced. The UK's international ranking in terms of GDP per capita had declined, between 1950 and 1990, from seventh position to twenty-second. Its share of world trade had fallen to less than 5 per cent. It was experiencing stubbornly low long-term growth rates of around 2 per cent per year. And, despite having decolonised comprehensively in favour of a foreign policy strategy focused primarily on Europe, its government remained profoundly uncertain about the extent to which the UK should commit itself to the further development of the European Union.

A contrasting view stresses the positive side of British achievements in the post-war period. The colonial empire was untenable given the world developments we have outlined, in particular the growth of Third World nationalism. The UK got out cleverly and relatively easily from its colonial entanglements. The example of France in Vietnam and Algeria, and Portugal in Africa, shows how draining and politically destabilising mistakes here could have been. Britain also kept out of the major American blunder of the Cold War era, its involvement in Vietnam. In terms of its major preoccupation, the Cold War, Britain emerged on the winning side. It astutely aligned itself with the dominant Western power, the United States, and through this alliance secured the kind of liberal, democratic, capitalist world system which the interests dominating its governments wanted.

While securing its overseas interests, Britain also managed to advance its European ones by joining the EU and pushing its policies towards more liberal and less protectionist ones. It has an option to join in further developments (notably currency union) while at the same time avoiding the political and economic difficulties which France and Germany have created for themselves by their dash headlong into it. All these goals have been achieved while maintaining steady economic growth and general political stability.

Which of these two contrasting assessments is true? In part, as pointed out at the beginning of the chapter, the answer depends on the assumptions one starts off from. From a 'realist' position the important thing is how far a state can impose its policy on others or at least go ahead without having to take their reactions into account. From this perspective Britain is indeed more affected by other states' decisions, and less able simply to impose its views on others, than it was in 1945.

It is worth noting, however, that this is true of all the great powers of that period, not just Britain. The Soviet Union has collapsed. The United States has seen its unquestioned hegemony of the 1950s and 1960s increasingly challenged by China, Japan, Germany and France. We live in a more polycentric world than we used to, in which other states have to be taken into account and international decision making is more collaborative, as attested by the growing numbers of international organisations and regimes.

Such regimes, according to the 'idealist' view, help states achieve most of what they want – above all security – without going to war with each other. On these assumptions it may be better to share objectives with other states than to threaten them. This is the position Britain seems to have evolved towards over the postwar period. The aspirations of its governments for worldwide liberalism, democracy and security have attracted widespread support and so have largely been attained.

However, the extent to which they have been attained by Britain's own efforts remains problematic. Perhaps the UK has been lucky rather than powerful. Given that most of its objectives were shared by the United States, perhaps it should simply have let the Americans go ahead to win the Cold War while strictly limiting its own involvement.

That indeed is the tenor of another criticism of Britain's postwar policies. That is, that governments are too subservient to the Americans and spend much more than the country can afford on military support. Britain has sacrificed the gains it could have made from putting Europe first, to the maintenance of the largely fictitious special relationship.

Like many retrospective historical judgements, this depends on whether one thinks that the world situation would have developed in much the way with or without British participation. Like the other arguments reviewed in this chapter it thus derives very much from one's starting assumptions. Thus, no-one can firmly prove that Stalin and his successors in the USSR really had aggressive intentions towards Western Europe. It is just that where they felt they could act with impunity (as in Afghanistan in the 1970s and 1980s) they *did* try to take over. Extrapolating from this we can imagine that, if NATO had not existed, the Soviet Union would have tried to throw its weight around at the very least, in a way which in the end might well have provoked nuclear war.

Equally, Britain might have reduced its contribution to NATO and got rid of its nuclear deterrent without diminishing its external security. But equally, by maintaining its nuclear forces, Britain may have demonstrated a degree of commitment to the defence of Western democracy that was essential if the United States itself was to remain committed. There was always a strand of American strategic opinion that advocated a primarily European defence for Europe. There was thus always the concomitant danger that if the Europeans – and especially the British, given their historical role within NATO – seemed unprepared to shoulder their share of the defence burden, the Americans would effectively withdraw and leave the Europeans to face the Soviet threat alone. America remains the major guarantor of European security against more diffuse threats today, so the main argument probably still holds. In defence matters it is better to overinvest than underinvest, as the costs of a mistake are so high.

If we accept this, it is difficult to criticise the main lines of British foreign and defence policy in the postwar period. Certainly many of the details can be criticised. In particular much money has been wasted on failed weapons systems, while many of those actually developed would not have been undertaken if the true cost had been established at the start. This has resulted in a swollen arms and nuclear industry, in a symbiotic relationship with government and heavily dependent on covert subsidies. However, on the major point of whether Britain should broadly have done what it did do in the postwar period, the answer is probably yes.

1. Does the 'special relationship' really exist?

2. What consequences does the change from Conservative to Labour Government in 1997 have for British foreign policy?

3. What military role should Britain adopt in the future?

4. 'Just another aspect of British decline'. Discuss this assessment of postwar foreign policy in Britain.

SUMMARY

This chapter has reviewed British foreign and military policy over the postwar period. This has been dominated by three developments:

- decolonisation (1945–1964);

- increasing involvement with the European Union, culminating in the possibility of economic and monetary union by the turn of the millennium;

- European and world security, seen by British governments as best secured by a close alliance with the United States inside NATO.

In the light of these:

- British governments have been criticised for trying to do too much abroad in support of the United States (the 'special relationship').

- Although money could have been saved on costly defence projects, it is difficult to see what else, broadly, Britain could have done. Major mistakes have been avoided and the NATO alliance won the Cold War.

- The major problem for Britain at the beginning of the next millennium will be how to keep the Americans involved in NATO and Europe as major guarantors of peace and security, while consolidating its own membership of the European Union.

MILESTONES

MILESTONES IN POSTWAR FOREIGN POLICY

	World		Decolonisation		European Union
1945	Defeat of Nazi Germany and Japan				
1946	Foundation of UN (United Nations)				
1946–48	Growing tensions between USA and USSR initiate 'Cold War'. US Marshall aid stabilises economic situation in UK and Western Europe	**1948**	Independence of India, Pakistan, Burma, Ceylon and Palestine		
1949	Communist takeover of China	**1950–54**	Mau-Mau war in Kenya		
1949	Foundation of NATO, the US-dominated military alliance against USSR. UK leading initiator and member	**1951–60**	Guerrilla war in Malaya	**1951**	Treaty of Paris: the six – Belgium, Netherlands, Luxembourg, France, Italy and West Germany – form European Iron and Steel Community (ECSC)

MILESTONES IN POSTWAR FOREIGN POLICY (continued)

	World		*Decolonisation*		*European Union*
1950–53	Korean War: NATO confronts China				
1948–55	Britain develops nuclear bomb	**1956**	Abortive invasion of Suez by UK with France and Israel	**1957**	Treaty of Rome: European Economic Community aims at free market of six
1950–73	World economic growth and liberalisation of trade under GATT (General Agreement on Tariffs and Trade)	**1956–62**	Guerrilla war in Cyprus		
		1960	Ghana becomes first African colony to gain independence		
1962	Attempt by USSR to place missiles in Cuba brings USA and USSR to brink of nuclear war	**1960–62**	Peaceful independence of most African, Caribbean and Pacific Colonies	**1962–63**	British application to join EEC rejected
1964–75	US defeat in Vietnam War, tensions within NATO	**1960–63**	Breakdown of British rule in South Arabia	**1966**	De Gaulle establishes right of national veto within the EC (Luxembourg compromise)
1962–79	US–USSR relaxation of Cold War, mutual arms limitation	**1962–64**	Successful confrontation with Indonesia in Borneo		
1967	Devaluation of sterling	**1964–94**	White regimes in Rhodesia and South Africa first consolidate power, then negotiate handover to African majority	**1968**	British application rejected
1972	Discovery of oil in British North Sea	**1968–72**	British military withdrawal from east of Suez		
1973–77	Steep rise in world oil prices initiates inflation and periodic economic recessions	**1970–96**	Northern Irish terrorism	**1973**	UK, Ireland and Denmark join EEC
1979–88	Renewed arms race provokes economic crisis in USSR and ends Cold War on American terms	**1982**	Falklands War: seaborne British expedition reconquers islands from Argentine	**1979**	Direct elections to European Parliament
1989	Central and Eastern European regimes democratise and create free markets			**1985–86**	The Single European Act undermines national veto by introducing qualified majority voting on measures to achieve a single market
1989–93	World economic recession				

MILESTONES IN POSTWAR FOREIGN POLICY (continued)

	World	Decolonisation		European Union
1991	USSR splits between Russian, Ukraine and other successor states		**1986**	Spain and Portugal join EC
1991	Gulf War: NATO against Iraq		**1992**	Treaty of Maastricht plans for economic and political union. UK 'opts out' of social chapter
			1992	Black Wednesday: UK forced out of European Monetary System
1992–95	Bosnia crisis ended by NATO intervention		**1993**	EMS reorganised with broader exchange rate bands
1993	Further liberalisations of world trade under GATT		**1994–97**	Plans for single currency and closer union increasingly attacked by UK Conservative Government
1993–98	Gradual world recovery from recession		**1995**	Finland, Sweden and Austria join EU
		1997 UK returns Hong Kong to China	**1997**	Amsterdam Summit fails to move far to closer union. New Labour Government accepts social chapter and welcomes European Monetary Union
	Turmoil in Asian currency markets threatens economic recovery		**1999**	Monetary Union (EMU) scheduled. UK retains option to join

1. How can Britain's European interests be reconciled with its overseas ones in the next two decades? Answer in the form of a briefing which Foreign Office advisers are writing for a new government in 2001.

2. Analyse newspaper and journal critiques of the 1997 defence review to say how military spending should be directed in the next decade.

3. How far do the interests of British industry point in a different direction from those of finance in the field of British foreign policy? Base your answer on an analysis of trade flows and investment patterns from 1976 onwards.

FURTHER READING

For a critical overview of British foreign policy see David Sanders, *Losing an Empire, Finding a Role: British Foreign Policy since 1945* (London: Macmillan, 1990). Bernard Porter, *The Lion's Share: A Short History of British Imperialism* (Harlow: Longman, 1988) gives the background to decolonisation. On the broader European context, see Ian Budge, Kenneth Newton *et al.*, *The Politics of the New Europe* (Harlow: Addison-Wesley, Longman, 1997). David A. Baldwin (ed.), *Neorealism and Neoliberalism: The Contemporary Debate* (New York: Columbia University Press, 1993) gives an overview of these contrasting views of international relations, on which so many evaluations of British foreign policy depend.

http://www.awl-he.com/politics/newbritpol

Internet resources – visit *The New British Politics* Webpage for links to a specially-chosen selection of Internet resources relevant to this Chapter.

http://www.awl-he.com/politics/newbritpol

Environmental policy

Environmental problems raise important questions about the capacity of modern governments to solve difficult dilemmas. This chapter begins with an example of how environmental policies can lead to major domestic and international disputes. It then goes on to look at:

- Changes in the character of environmental problems

- The leading policy actors and networks in the UK

- The long-standing British philosophy of pollution control

- New pressures, especially from developments within the EU

- The difficulties which confront the new Labour Government in any attempt to implement its ambitious environmental goals

THE BRENT SPAR EPISODE

On 30 April 1995 a group of Greenpeace activists occupied the Brent Spar, a shell oil storage buoy due for disposal 150 miles west of Scotland in the Atlantic. Claiming that the buoy contained a 'toxic sludge' and a 'lethal chemical cocktail', Greenpeace launched a vigorous public relations campaign against Shell's plans to dispose of the buoy in the sea. For its part, Shell claimed that it had spent since September 1992 consulting with the relevant authorities about the correct method of disposal, and that all the alternative methods, including dismantling on land, carried greater environmental or health and safety risks than the sea disposal that had been planned.

The UK Government, led by John Major, supported the Shell decision. By early May, however, strong opposition to Shell policy had grown up in northern

Europe. The German Government formally protested on 9 May and John Major and Helmut Kohl, the German Chancellor, agreed to differ when they met at the G7 summit in Halifax, Nova Scotia, on 15–17 June. At the same time, Shell itself came under increasing pressure to abandon its plans, pressure which included the fire-bombing of its fuel stations in Germany. On 20 June the company announced that it was reversing its decision to go ahead with deep sea disposal, and that the buoy would be towed to a fjord in Norway, where it would stay until a satisfactory alternative disposal plan had been decided. Shell launched an international competition inviting people to come forward with suggestions, but over two years later, at the time of writing, no alternative plan has been agreed.

Every controversial policy decision is unique, but in many ways the Brent Spar episode symbolises the complex, volatile and precarious nature of modern environmental politics in the UK. In major matters of environmental policy no country is an island, particularly when decisions involve use of an internationally agreed resource like the open seas, and the widespread international interest in the decision is typical of many matters of environmental policy. The lead that the German Government took in opposing deep sea disposal, responding to strong currents of public opinion, was the latest scene in a long drama of conflict between Britain and Germany over environmental policy in Europe that had first emerged in the early 1980s. For a transnational corporation like Shell, the international dimension was the most important. No matter how much it might insist that more damage was done to European seas by the pollution coming into the North Sea from the Rhine than could ever have arisen from the Atlantic disposal of the Brent Spar, Shell simply could not withstand the damage to its sales and reputation in Europe that the incident was causing, despite the support it received from the British Government.

The events were also an object lesson in the strains and stresses that environmental issues placed upon the British political system in general and its system of environmental administration in particular. The UK has a long history of environmental policy and management, and many of those involved in policies for environmental protection point to the 'proud record' of the UK in reducing pollution and managing land use. In the case of the Brent Spar there had been extensive scientific investigations of alternative disposal options, and the regulatory authorities were convinced that in purely technical terms deep sea disposal was the best practicable environmental option. Yet, in coming to this conclusion, those responsible for environmental regulation failed to reckon with a public opinion that attached great symbolic importance to the idea of protecting nature from contamination and responded to the idea that the seas should not be used simply as a sink for human waste.

Brent Spar thus raised controversial issues and difficult choices. How should the UK deal with the pollution legacy of past industrial activity? How best can the complex and difficult choices be made between policy options, all of which, in the light of that legacy, involve environmental damage? How far can these policy choices be made in ways that pay attention to the technical scientific aspects of the issues without also engaging with broader issues of public opinion and sentiment? What role is there for European institutions in providing a forum within

---

Key term

Environmentalism – a concern with the natural environment (including many things from the physical environment affecting 'the quality of life') and the belief that its protection should be given more importance, and economic growth less.

which international differences can be discussed and resolved? How well adapted, in short, are British political institutions in dealing with the new politics of pollution?

ENVIRONMENTAL PROBLEMS

Environmental problems arise in many different ways and from many different sources (see Table 24.1). Sometimes the problem is local, as when a person's bonfire pollutes the neighbouring environment. Sometimes it occurs on a regional scale, as when a river basin is polluted. And sometimes it is worldwide, as is the case with global climate change. Human activity has had effects on the environment for centuries. At one time northern Europe was covered in forests before they were cut down for agriculture, a process of deforestation that is mirrored in developing countries today. Moreover, environmental issues inevitably arise from a large number of social activities and government policies. Industrial development causes problems of land use and pollution. Boosting agricultural crop production through incentive payments leads farmers to an increased use of pesticides and fertilisers that in turn cause the pollution of rivers and chemical residues in the food chain. Transport provision takes land for road building, and causes air pollution through the burning of fossil fuels. The specification of building regulations has implications for energy consumption, and tax law can affect how people consume resources. Environmental policy is both a separate sphere of government activity and a dimension of many government activities.

Table 24.1 Environmental problems, characteristics and causes

Pollution Problem	Main Pollutants	Human Activities	Expected Effects
Global climate change	Carbon dioxide, methane, CFCs	Power generation, transport	Temperature rise, unpredictable weather
Ozone depletion	CFCs	Aerosol use, refrigerators	Loss of protection against sun's radiation
Acidification	Sulphur dioxide, nitrogen oxides, ammonia	Fossil fuels	Crop and building damage, ill heath
Eutrophication	Phosphates, nitrates	Fertiliser, sewage	River pollution
Urban pollution	Smoke, noise	Traffic	Stress, dirt, ill health

Regulation

The term 'environmental policy' in the UK covers a wide field of government activity, including pollution control for discharges to air, water or land; the control of nuclear power; the release of genetically modified organisms into the environment; land use planning; building conservation; the protection of the countryside, including plants and wildlife; and urban regeneration. Within the UK there is a long history of public policy measures directed at some of the most serious environmental problems. Industrial air pollution in the nineteenth century led to pressure from land owners for controls, and in 1865 the Alkali Inspectorate was formed to regulate major industrial sources of pollution. In the late nineteenth and early twentieth centuries, legislation led to slum clearance and the rebuilding of housing to higher environmental standards. In 1947 the postwar Labour Government passed the Town and Country Planning legislation, which imposed restrictions on developments and created green belts around British towns. In 1956 clean air zones were established to prevent the recurrence of the urban smog that had caused 4,000 deaths in London in 1952. In 1969, in the wake of a worldwide upsurge of public concern and interest in environmental matters, a standing Royal Commission on Environmental Pollution was established to help formulate policy. And in 1974 the Control of Pollution Act was passed, which brought together previous pieces of legislation. In the 1980s the UK began to move towards the establishment of a separate Environment Agency, a move that was completed in 1995, and in the 1990s major policy initiatives began to develop in a context in which European and global concerns were becoming prominent.

In terms of the control of pollution, modern environmental policies typically take the form of *regulation*, that is to say the specification by government or a government agency of the standards of pollution control that a product or a process has to meet. For example, there are regulations governing car exhaust fumes which manufacturers have to meet, and on the volume of gases that can be emitted from a major electricity generating plant. Bathing and drinking waters are subject to quality standards, and factories are not allowed to discharge unauthorised pollution into rivers. There are controls on where waste can be dumped, as well as bans on the use of certain chemicals. Building and other forms of development are subject to planning controls, and certain areas may be designated as national parks or sites of special scientific interest because of the plants or animals they contain. The regulations may not always be enforced stringently, and there are many disputes about the standards. But the point remains that the most important policy instrument of environmental policy is regulation, and much of the substance of environmental policy concerns the content and strength of those regulations.

POLICY ACTORS AND NETWORKS

Around the politics of environmental regulation, there has grown up a varied policy community of those who take an interest in the way that standards are set and enforced (see Briefing 24.1). Until recently the Department of the Environment

BRIEFINGS

24.1 MAIN ACTORS IN THE BRITISH ENVIRONMENTAL POLICY NETWORK

Ministry of Environment, Transport and the Regions, incorporating the former Department of the Environment. The ministry is the main policy-making department, although the Ministry of Agriculture, Fisheries and Food has some environment responsibilities, as do the territorial ministries. The Secretary of State is assisted by ministers responsible for specific aspects of environmental policy.

Environment Agency, created in 1995 by a merger of the National Rivers Authority and Her Majesty's Inspectorate of Pollution. Responsible for detailed standard setting and implementation of pollution control measures and river basin management.

Parliamentary committees: Environment committee of the House of Commons and Committees on Science and Technology, Sustainable Development and European Communities in House of Lords. All have produced important reports on issues of environmental policy.

Royal Commission on Environmental Pollution: The major advisory body on matters of pollution control

policy. Responsible for introduction of major concepts of environmental policy, most notably integrated pollution control, and for some influential reports on lead in petrol and transport policy.

Other advisory bodies: Round Table on Sustainable Development; Advisory Council on Business and Environment; Genetic Manipulation Advisory Committee.

Local authorities: Important responsibilities for solid waste regulation (county and unitary authorities) and for local environmental controls (district authorities).

European Union: Important source of pressure to raise standards (Briefing 24.4).

Environmental groups, including Friends of the Earth, Greenpeace, Council for the Protection of Rural England, the Royal Society for the Protection of Birds, World Wide Fund for Nature, Surfers against Sewage, National Society for Clean Air, Transport 2000.

Affected interests: Electricity supply industry, water industry, road hauliers, farmers.

was the principal ministry in England and Wales, with its counterparts located in the Scottish and Northern Ireland Offices. The new Labour Government of 1997 merged the environment department with transport and regional planning, to create a new superministry, although environmental regulation will remain a separate function within this.

Environmental policy in the UK is embedded in a network of specialist advisory groups and committees, of which the most important is the Royal Commission on Environmental Pollution. Within Parliament there is a great deal of environmental interest and expertise in the House of Lords, arising from its unique mixture of landowners from the hereditary peerage and scientists from the life peers. Two committees in particular, that on science and technology and an environment subcommittee of the European Communities Committee, have been especially active. The Environment Committee of the House of Commons has also played an important role on various issues.

Environmental policy is an area in which there are well-established pressure groups, many with a high degree of skill and extensive resources, making them well able to take political action. Some have a long history, with well-established and influential memberships. For example, the Royal Society for the Protection of Birds is the largest wildlife protection group in Europe with an active, vocal and influential membership. As well as managing its own reserves, it also has a campaigning arm. It became increasingly active from the late 1970s on issues to do with pesticide use, farming practices like the rooting out of hedgerows encouraged by the Common Agricultural Policy, and the need to provide international protection for migrating species. Other organisations, like Friends of the Earth and Greenpeace, campaign on issues of air pollution, water pollution and waste disposal. Friends of the Earth, who started as a radical outsider group in the 1970s, have since been incorporated into the world of routinised government consultation and discussion. In addition to these formal organisations there are now many local and informal groups, many of whom are mobilised by what they see as threats to the environment. Protesters building tree houses and tunnels to stop the Newbury bypass or the new runway for Manchester airport fall into this category.

Other actors who should also be included as members of the environmental policy network include think-tanks, journalists and other opinion formers, including various scientific researchers whose work bears on policy questions. Some of the general think-tanks, like the Centre for Policy Research on the right or the Institute for Public Policy Research on the left, have published work on environmental policy from their own perspectives. In addition, there are specialist think-tanks and research organisations (for example, the Institute for European Environmental Policy or the International Institute for Environment and Development) which have played an important role in diffusing knowledge and understanding of policy problems. During the 1980s there also grew up a significant body of specialist journalists in the media, many of whom were extremely knowledgeable about environmental issues, and who kept in touch with both the developing scientific research and the work of the pressure groups.

Environmental policy is something no-one likes to be seen to be against, thus opposition to measures to protect the environment usually takes the form, not of questioning the goal of environmental protection but of questioning the costs, and in particular questioning whether the improvement in the environment justifies the costs that are incurred. During the 1980s the Central Electricity Generating Board, the nationalised industry responsible for electricity production, led the resistance to tighter international controls on air pollution (see next section). And in the 1990s doubts about the costs of water pollution regulation have been raised by OFWAT, the body for regulating water industry prices. In addition, at various times the CBI has expressed doubts about the imposition of environmental costs. Perhaps more important, however, has been the structural power of those groups, like farmers or the road construction industry, whose political clout makes it difficult to devise suitable policies to control pollution.

THE BRITISH APPROACH TO POLLUTION CONTROL

Scientific uncertainty

Policies to control pollution go back many centuries. The main lines of the British approach were laid down in the late nineteenth century with a series of measures to control air and water pollution (see the Milestones at the end of the chapter).

BRIEFINGS

24.2 PHASES OF UK ENVIRONMENTAL POLICY

Nineteenth century to mid-1970s, the 'traditional philosophy' phase: environmental control standards were entrusted to specialist inspectors, negotiating on a co-operative basis with industry.

Mid-1970s to 1988: Attempt by policy makers to hold on to the traditional philosophy in the face of domestic and international criticism. Domestically, groups like Friends of the Earth questioned the closed nature of the traditional regulatory system. Internationally, there was criticism of the slow and hesitant response of the UK government to problems of pollution, and the UK was dubbed 'the dirty man of Europe'.

1988–97, the period of transition: In September 1988 Mrs Thatcher made a speech to the Royal Society emphasising the seriousness of the problem of global warming. In 1989 the European elections showed strong support for the Green Party. UK policy began to shift, accepting the need for a precautionary approach and stressing the importance of integrating environmental concerns with all aspects of public policy.

1997 onwards The implementation of sustainable development? The new Labour Government has commited itself to action on global climate change and to action to control the harmful environmental effects of car use. There is talk of serious moves on environmental taxation.

During the last 20 years the modern politics of environmental policy has revolved around the question of how far the UK Government can accept the new philosophy of environmental protection known as 'sustainable development'.

The traditional British way of thinking about pollution and environmental policy became firmly established among key policy makers from 1900 until the mid-1970s (see Briefing 24.2). Briefly put, this tradition placed a great deal of emphasis upon the scientific understanding of environmental problems and upon the need to ensure flexibility and informality in the imposition of environmental regulation. The key idea was that pollution and environmental risk were insepa-rable from human activity, so the task of the environmental regulator was to understand the risks and to control those that were most damaging to the envi-ronment. As Lord Ashby, the distinguished biologist who first chaired the Standing Commission on Environmental Pollution, argued in the 1970s, the task of environmental policy is not to eliminate pollution, but to optimise it. In other words, the traditional approach was to regulate effectively, but in such a way as to recognise the capacity of the environment itself to assimilate a certain amount of pollution. The traditional British philosophy of pollution control was therefore built upon the principle of 'dilute and disperse'.

The record of pollution control that was built upon this philosophy was impressive for its time. However, by the late 1970s it was increasingly recognised that there were new problems that were not easy to deal with using the principle. The problem that came to symbolise these new challenges was that of 'acid rain'. When coal and other fossil fuels are burnt they give out a series of gases, most notably sulphur dioxide, which reacts in the atmosphere to form sulphuric acid. This sulphuric acid is then deposited in the form of rain, snow or mist, causing damage to crops, buildings, soils and fresh waters. As part of its policy to disperse pollutants from urban centres, the UK Government had favoured a policy of building tall chimney stacks. These stacks dispersed their plumes over long distances, crossing national boundaries and contributing to a generally worsening problem in Europe.

The difficulty with acid rain as an issue was that, unlike many of the traditional problems of pollution, the scientific understanding of the effects of acidifying pollution was uncertain and contested. For example, although sulphur dioxide is given off in the burning of fossil fuels, it is also given off naturally by volcanoes and some sea species. Determining how much was due to human sources and how much to these naturally occurring ones is a complex problem. It is equally complex to trace the effects of emissions. It was often thought, for example, that given its prevailing south-westerly winds, the UK exported most of its acid pollution to northern Europe. But research in the late 1980s showed that, with complex air currents, some acid rain was carried from northern England to the highlands of Scotland.

This story was repeated in a large number of cases throughout the 1980s and the 1990s. It was clear that rivers were suffering damage from excessive nitrates, but was this due to fertilisers, plough patterns or sewage sludge? How far was it possible to say that sewage pollution caused health problems for bathers, when those who did not go into the water when they went to the beach reported as many symptoms of gastric illness as those who did? Were very small quantities of pesticide residues in drinking water really a health hazard? How far was it correct to say that a significant rise in global temperatures could be predicted from observed trends?

These scientific uncertainties and the contestable hypotheses to which they gave rise began to undermine the traditional UK philosophy of pollution control. Where cause and effect relationships are contested or uncertain, it is difficult to base environmental regulation purely on scientific evidence. In the face of this difficulty a number of other countries, including Germany, the Netherlands, Denmark, Sweden and Norway, began to push for precautionary action to control pollutants even when the evidence of their damage was difficult to establish. The UK came under considerable pressure in the EU (see below) and also in other contexts, for example from states bordering on the North Sea concerned about sewage sludge dumping.

The cross-cutting nature of environmental issues

Issues of scientific uncertainty began to undermine the traditional British philosophy of pollution control, but another important feature of the changing politics of the environment has been the recognition that environmental considerations

Plate 24.1 Sizewell B
nuclear power reactor on the
Suffolk coast north of
Aldeburgh

Plate 24.1 Sizewell B nuclear power reactor on the Suffolk coast north of Aldeburgh

are a cross-cutting issue that have implications for all aspects of public policy. One area this affected was the privatisation policies of the Thatcher Governments. Both the water industry and the electricity industry were major sources of pollution. When they were nationalised, they had the protection of their 'sponsoring ministries' which spoke up for them in government during the making of policy. They were also prevented from making investments in pollution control by Treasury spending limits which restricted capital spending by the nationalised industries. With privatisation, however, this constraint has been lifted. In the case of water in particular, large investments have been necessary to meet various international obligations. This has led OFWAT, the government office responsible for regulating water prices, to question how far these pollution control measures are necessary. In other words, a new institutional tension has been built into the British policy system between those who favour environmental protection and those who stress the cost of stringent measures.

Another feature of this cross-cutting character of environmental issues has been the need to deal as much with problems of consumption as with problems of production. Since environmental damage arises often as the by-product of everyday activities, environmental policy also needs to deal with issues of lifestyle and the control of consumption. This is most obvious in the case of transport and the significantly increased use of cars in recent years. Mrs Thatcher favoured what she called 'the great car economy' and in the late 1980s significant increases in road building took place or were planned. Moreover, the deregulation of bus services and the withdrawal of subsidies to the railways made the car an economically more attractive option for many households. Public expenditure cuts, and a new thinking about the extent to which roads generate increased traffic, led to a serious reduction in the road building programme under the Major Government. A legacy has been laid down, however, which will make it difficult to develop alternative forms of transport to the car.

There have been important measures to control emissions from car exhausts and to limit the noise of vehicles, but the benefits of these measures are often offset by the increase in cars being driven on the road. The Royal Commission on Environmental Pollution, in an authoritative report, summarised the situation as follows:

> At present pollutants from vehicles are the prime cause of poor air quality that damages human health, plants, and the fabric of buildings. Noise from vehicles and aircraft is a major source of stress and dissatisfaction, notably in towns but now intruding into many formerly tranquil areas. Construction of new roads and airports to accommodate traffic is destroying irreplaceable landscapes and features of our cultural heritage. The present generation's cavalier and constantly increasing use of non-renewable resources like oil may well foreclose the options for future generations. This is doubly irresponsible in view of the risks from global warming.[1]

The merger of the departments of the environment and of transport by the new Labour Government is an indication of how far this perception of the problem of transport pollution has reached.

Sustainable development

Key term

Sustainable development – development which meets the needs of the present without compromising the ability of future generations to meet their needs.

The third source of pressure on the traditional style of British environmental policy is the rise of the principle of 'sustainable development'. This is an idea that originated with a UN Commission on Environment and Development in 1987 chaired by Mrs Gro Harlem Brundtland, the Norwegian Prime Minister. The Brundtland Report defined sustainable development as development that meets the needs of the present without compromising the ability of future generations to meet their needs (see Briefing 24.3). The importance of this concept is that it challenged an assumption that was strongly built into much conventional environmental policy, namely that environmental improvements had to be bought at the expense of economic growth. The Brundtland Report pointed out that economic growth not only did environmental damage but also prevented economic development in the future, for example through overfishing or the depletion of natural resources.

---

[1] Royal Commission on Environmental Pollution, *Eighteenth Report Transport and the Environment*, CM 2674 (London: HMSO, 1994), p. 233

BRIEFINGS

24.3 THE IDEA OF SUSTAINABLE DEVELOPMENT

Humanity has the ability to make development sustainable – to ensure that it meets the needs of the present without compromising the ability of future generations to meet their own needs ...

Sustainable global development requires that those who are more affluent adopt lifestyles within the planet's ecological means – in their use of energy, for example ...

The objective of sustainable development and the integrated nature of the global environment/development challenges pose problems for institutions, national and international, that were established on the basis of narrow preoccupations and compartmentalised concerns. Governments' general response to the speed and scale of global challenges has been a reluctance to recognise sufficiently the need to change themselves. The challenges are both interdependent and integrated, requiring comprehensive approaches and popular participation.

World Commission on Environment and Development, *Our Common Future* (the Brundtland Report) (Oxford: Oxford University Press, 1987), pp. 8–9

Within the UK the impact of the idea of sustainable development was first seen clearly in the Conservative Government's White Paper *This Common Inheritance*, which sought to examine how far the principle of sustainable development could form the basis for public policy measures. The problem of how to achieve sustainability in fields as diverse as agriculture, transport and energy consumption as well as the search for cleaner technologies that are compatible with the requirements for sustainability dominate much thinking and policy argument within environmental policy networks.

One important consequence of this development is that there is now no simple conflict between proponents of environmental protection and the business community. Business and industry are still responsible for a great deal of pollution. But there are segments of business, for example within the pollution control industries or in the field of mass transport, that have an interest in pushing the case for more stringent environmental protection. There is a lot of questioning as to whether proponents of more sustainable alternatives, for example the organic farming industry, are competing on equal terms, in respect of the public subsidies available, with their more established counterparts.

These three issues – the need for precaution as well as scientific certainty, the integration of environmental policy with general public policies and the implications of sustainable development – have transformed the politics of the environment in the last 15 years. The traditional assumption that environmental regulation was largely a specialist affair, limited to engineers and civil servants negotiating about technical standards of control, has given way to the idea that environmental standards are part of social and economic life. The policy networks around environmental policy are therefore more crowded, with new actors emerging on the scene, and with issues in sharper dispute. The way in which the disposal of the Brent Spar hit the international headlines is just one small illustration of the new politics of the environment. Moreover, these politics are being increasingly carried out within the framework of the European Union, as the next section shows.

THE ROLE OF THE EUROPEAN UNION

From the beginning of the 1980s the EU has been one of the principal forces operating on the British system of environmental protection, reshaping many of its main characteristics. Indeed, there is no other area apart from agriculture where the EU has been so influential in changing the assumptions and standard operating procedures of UK policy.

Environmental policy was not originally part of the Treaty of Rome and so was not one of the original functions of the European Economic Community (as it then was). There are two reasons why environmental policy came to occupy a central place in EU policies. First, there is often a connection between the creation of a single market and environmental regulation. For example, if one country imposes high standards on vehicle exhaust emissions, requiring that cars sold within its borders meet those high standards, this policy in effect erects barriers to trade in vehicles manufactured in other countries where standards are not so high. Indeed, some of the earliest EU legislation on the environment was concerned with harmonising standards on the permissible level of noise from vehicles.

The second reason for the EU's interest in environmental policy was that it could be seen as a way of securing greater legitimacy for the processes of European integration. EU leaders responded to the upsurge of public interest in the environment in the late 1960s and early 1970s, adopting a declaration on the importance of environmental protection in 1972. The declaration led to some policy developments during the 1970s and early 1980s, although environmental regulation was not formally included in the competences of the EU until the Single European Act of 1987.

There are a number of different actors within the EU (see Briefing 24.4). However, decisions on environmental policy are crucially shaped by the policy stances of the Member States, and in particular, given its size and centrality, by the position of Germany. Until the early 1980s Germany occupied a similar environmental policy to the UK, for example being sceptical of the international action to control acid rain that the Scandinavian countries had been proposing. For domestic political reasons this position began to change in 1982 and was consolidated by the conversion of the Christian/Liberal coalition Government in

1983 on the acid rain issue. From then on, Germany began to use the EU as a major forum within which to press for the imposition of higher environmental standards on products and manufacturing processes. First it pushed for measures to reduce acid rain by more stringent controls on sulphur dioxide emissions from electricity power stations and other large furnaces. This initial pressure was followed by support for a wide-ranging series of measures including higher standards on vehicle emissions, tighter control of water pollution and reductions in the volume of packaging waste and measures to control the disposal of wastes in landfill sites. On these points, Germany was often supported in the Council of Ministers by the other 'green' member states, Denmark and the Netherlands.

So by the middle of the 1980s the UK found itself in the position of opposing higher environmental standards in the EU, thus earning for itself the unenviable title of 'the dirty man of Europe'. From one point of view this was justified. The UK was always going to find it difficult to meet the high environmental standards demanded by countries which had a high per capita income (and who therefore

BRIEFINGS

24.4 MAIN ACTORS IN EU ENVIRONMENTAL POLICY

The Commission

The main part of the Commission with responsibility for environmental policy is Directorate-General XI. Its principal concern is to draft directives that govern the use of resources and control permissible levels of polluting discharges into the environment. There are now some 300 pieces of environmental legislation.

The Council of Ministers

All environmental measures have to be agreed by the Council of Ministers, representing the Member States. Since 1992 most measures can be agreed by qualified majority voting.

Among present Member States, those with the most positive environmental reputation are Austria, Denmark, Finland, Germany, the Netherlands and Sweden. Those with concerns for economic growth and development include Greece, Ireland, Portugal and (especially) Spain. In between are France and Italy. The UK has often found itself in opposition to measures proposed by the environmental 'leader' states.

European Parliament

The main actor here is the Environment Committee, which is chaired by a UK MEP, Ken Collins. It has the reputation of taking a strong 'pro-environment' line, for example on the control of car exhaust emissions or controls on landfill sites.

European Court of Justice

The Court plays a role in enforcing compliance with environmental measures, and a number of its judgements, for example, on the legality of measures taken by Member States to impose environmental regulations on products, have had a significant effect on policy.

European Environment Agency

This was established in 1995 in Copenhagen. Its brief is to collect data and information, rather than implement environmental measures. However, some see it as the forerunner of a European environment inspectorate.

could afford to spend more) and that had, especially in the case of Germany, world-class engineering and pollution control industries. Moreover, the UK government did not enhance its reputation by its poor implementation of measures to which it had agreed. For example, when it came to implementing the bathing waters directive, the UK designated only 27 beaches in the whole of the UK as places of traditional bathing. Not only did the list exclude Blackpool and Brighton, it also meant that officially the UK claimed to have fewer bathing beaches than land-locked Luxembourg!

By the beginning of the 1990s one issue had come to dominate discussions of European environmental policy. This was the question of global climate change and in particular the prediction that over the next 50 years or so the earth's atmosphere would warm up with unpredictable effects. Ironically, the issue had been thrust into prominence by Mrs Thatcher's speech to the Royal Society in September 1988, when she appeared to accept the seriousness of the problem. The difficulty as far as the UK was concerned was that the solution seemed to involve a tax on carbon fuels or on energy more generally, in order to cut consumption. The UK was not prepared to cede more tax-raising powers to the EU, thus undermining the possibility of joint action by Member States.

Yet in some ways, the reputation of the UK as an environmental laggard is one-sided. On some issues of EU environmental policy, the UK has been a pioneer. For example, it was the UK that pressed for important legislation on wildlife protection, most notably the protection of migrating birds. The UK also pioneered the policy of agricultural set-aside, by which farmers are paid to protect their land rather than farming it intensively. Similarly, the UK introduced the principle of integrated pollution control into EU environmental policy, by which emissions to air, water and soil are controlled as a whole.

On some questions, of course, the UK was not alone in opposing the measure. Spain was hostile to the control of sulphur dioxide from power stations, neither France or Italy wanted catalytic converters on small cars and France was also opposed to the proposal for a carbon/energy tax.

Despite the conflicts over environmental policy in which Britain has been engaged, there is no doubt that the effects of EU policy on UK law and practice have been considerable. For example, some of the main measures of the 1990 Environmental Protection Act conformed to the requirements of the 1984 EU directive on air pollution control. Much of the capital cost of water pollution control measures of the 1990s have been incurred through accepting EU standards on bathing and drinking waters. Over the next few years significant sums of money will be spent on replacing lead water piping in order to meet tighter standards on lead in drinking water.

Just as important as these legal and policy changes, however, have been the changes in the balance of power and influence within domestic policy networks. A clear example is provided by the opposition to the road-building scheme at Twyford Down near Winchester. Opponents of the scheme were able to claim that the scheme had not undergone the proper environmental appraisal that was required under the EU's 1988 environmental impact assessment directive, a position in which they were supported by the environmental commissioner at the time, Carlo Ripa de Meana. Although they lost the battle, the controversy with the

Key term

Environmental impact assessment – a requirement of the European Union, which came into effect in 1988, requiring all public and private projects above a given cost to be subject to environmental appraisal in which the advantages and disadvantages from the environmental point of view are laid out.

Commission not only slowed the road building itself, but also caused some political embarrassment for the Government.

Britain's future position in the environmental politics of the EU is more difficult to identify. The sharp antagonisms of the 1980s softened in the 1990s, not least because the EU itself lost momentum in the field of environmental policy after the difficulties of ratifying the Maastricht Treaty. With its own economic problems after reunification, German environmental initiatives became less pressing, particularly after the replacement of its committed environment minister Klaus Töpfer.

On the other hand, the UK failed to regain environmental powers in a number of fields under the doctrine of 'subsidiarity' which it tried for in the wake of the 1992 Edinburgh summit. Moreover, the accession of Sweden, Finland and Austria has augmented the pro-environment group of countries in the Council of Ministers, and led to changes in the proposed Treaty of Amsterdam (1998) which strengthen environmental provisions. In large part, the position the UK takes in the EU and other international forums will depend on how it is able to deal with precautionary measures, integration of environmental with social and economic policy, and sustainable development. With a new party in government, the question naturally occurs as to how far a new environmental approach will be followed.

NEW LABOUR, NEW ENVIRONMENT POLICY?

On coming into office, one of the first acts of the new Labour Government was the creation of a 'superministry' responsible for environment, transport and the regions, headed by John Prescott, the Deputy Prime Minister. The move was clearly intended to symbolise the importance of the field as well as providing the administrative capacity to deal with the problems involved in rethinking transport policy and its relationship to the environment. A few weeks later Tony Blair as Prime Minister made a speech to the United Nations special summit on sustainable development in New York, in which he asserted that governments needed to persuade their citizens to change their lifestyles if damage to the global environment was to be avoided. And in the first Labour budget the Chancellor of the Exchequer, Gordon Brown, built on the Conservative policy of increasing taxation on motor fuel in order to make driving more expensive. Taken together, these measures and policies suggest that the new Labour Government was shifting towards a pro-environment position. How well founded is this suggestion, and what are the political and institutional obstacles that are likely to be encountered in making the shift?

One obvious problem is that any government has to deal with the legacy of past generations. Expensive investment in water pollution control technology in the 1990s is simply catching up on the investment that ought to have been undertaken by the publicly owned water authorities in the 1980s. There is an equally large problem in dealing with the contaminated soil left from Britain's industrialised past. Yet another is the out-of-town development of supermarkets in the 1980s, which, lacking adequate public transport provision, lock many consumers into dependence upon the private car. No government can deal with such legacies overnight.

On the industrial front, the problems of pollution are made worse by the long tail of underperforming companies, particularly among small and medium-sized enterprises, for whom environmental improvement is difficult or costly. Moreover, in the commercial sector there is a constant temptation to use environmental measures as a form of window dressing. For example, a study of the eco-audits by which companies assess their environmental performance found that the quality of reporting is often variable. Firms often make reports in general terms, without reference to specific quantitative targets for reductions in polluting emissions or without providing monetary targets. Only 6 per cent of firms reporting provided evidence on eco-audits, and only 1 per cent published the results of such audits. Where special reports were published separately from the main accounts, only 26 per cent of those reporting provided information on external audit or verification of the environmental figures produced. In other words, it looks as though reports are more for show than for environmental protection.

Another major obstacle for the new Labour Government is the issue of taxation. Many experts believe that the only way to deal with environmental problems is to broaden the base of taxation, and in particular to place deterrent taxes on pollutants like pesticides or on energy use. The trouble for Labour is that these taxes raise prices for consumers in general, and for poor consumers in particular, thus hitting their own supporters. In the same budget that raised fuel duty, Gordon Brown also cut VAT on domestic fuel to 5 per cent, a move which encouraged greater use. In other words, even the modest concern about the distribution of income shown by New Labour threatens to pull its policies in the opposite direction to what would be indicated by a concern for the environment. If competition in the electricity sector leads to falling prices for the consumer, this will make the policy dilemma even more difficult.

Moreover, the issue of environmental taxation is closely related in some fields to the question of the UK's relationship with the rest of Europe and the EU. The previous Conservative Government opposed the imposition of a carbon/energy tax in large part because it did not want the EU to have more tax-raising powers. However, it is clear that there is a loss of competitiveness for any country that might want to go it alone on energy taxation, a problem for which the only solution is joint international agreement inside a body like the EU. So at some point, it will be difficult to solve the problem of greenhouse gas emissions without deepening the UK's participation in the EU. At present there is no indication that the new Labour Government has thought its way through to the necessary deeper commitment.

Yet, on the other side of the balance sheet, it is possible to point to features that strengthen the environmental hand of the new government. The pressure for savings on the public purse will provide an incentive for policy makers to phase out environmentally damaging tax subsidies. Thus, at present aviation fuel is untaxed and this could be a likely source of revenue. Similarly, the Institute for Public Policy Research, a think-tank close to the present government, has argued for changes to company car taxation to discourage drivers from driving more miles in order to increase tax benefits, a change that it estimated could yield some £400m a year. Most importantly, perhaps, the pressure to reform the Common Agricultural Policy as a prelude to EU enlargement could also bring considerable environmental benefits.

Much also depends upon the future performance of the privatised utilities and public services. Railtrack is seeking to upgrade both its track and a selected number of stations, and the rail operating companies are beginning to invest in new rolling stock. A successful investment strategy along these lines might help entice more people out of their cars and into the train.

Some proponents of a radical environmental strategy argue that there is a 'double dividend' to be had from a vigorous pursuit of environmental goals. By increasing taxation on the 'bads' of resource use and pollution, they argue that it should be possible to lower taxation on the use of labour, thereby encouraging higher levels of employment. There is no evidence that the new government is convinced of this line of argument, probably for the very good reason that it is only partially valid. Finding ways of reconciling human beings to their environment is not easy. How the Government copes with the task will be a significant measure of its performance.

SUMMARY

- Environmental policy raises important questions about the international dimension of public policy and the ability of the British political system to cope with the challenges of environmental management.

- Environmental policy covers a wide range of issues, but the usual way in which governments deal with environmental problems is by regulation. The politics of the environment is thus primarily concerned with the stringency of this regulation.

- The UK's system of environmental regulation has a long history. But in some ways the perception of Britain's 'proud record' of environmental policy has inhibited adaptation to new issues and approaches, especially problems of scientific uncertainty, overall policy integration and sustainable development.

- The EU has been a major force in reshaping Britain's environmental policy. At one stage the UK stood out against EU policy making, but the picture is more subtle than a simple tale of British intransigence would suggest.

- The new Labour Government is likely to find difficulties in its attempt to make environmental issues more central to the political agenda, although there are developments that it will find helpful.

ESSAYS

1. Explain the difficulties that a UK government would face in seeking to impose taxes on polluting activities. How best could these difficulties be overcome?

2. Has privatisation made it easier or more difficult for UK governments to pursue stringent environmental policy measures?

3. How important has the European Union been in the development of UK environmental policy?

PROJECTS

1. Analyse the positions of the major party manifestos on the subject of environmental policy in the 1997 election.

2. Identify all the major interests affected by a policy of stressing public transport rather than the car, and say whether each interest would be for or against the policy.

3. Assess the impact of one major EU directive on environmental policy on the UK.

FURTHER READING

The most recent general books on environmental politics in Britain are P. Lowe and S. Ward (eds), *British Environmental Politics* (London: Routledge, 1997), T. Gray (ed.), *UK Environmental Policy in the 1990s* (London: Macmillan, 1995), **and** J. McCormick, *British Politics and the Environment* (London: Earthscan, 1991). **On green political thought see the**

MILESTONES

MILESTONES IN THE DEVELOPMENT OF UK ENVIRONMENTAL POLICY

1865 Alkali Inspectorate created. The world's first national pollution inspectorate, it was responsible until the 1980s for regulating air pollution from industry

1947 Town and Country Planning Act creates the framework within which local authorities can control building and other development with the aim of protecting the countryside and enhancing town life

1952 London smog, caused by the burning of domestic coal fires, responsible for 4,000 deaths, the event which triggered the move for the 1956 Clean Air Act, by which local authorities could create smokeless zones

1969 Harold Wilson as Prime Minister establishes the Royal Commission on Environmental Pollution, a standing royal commission to report on matters of environmental policy

1974 Control of Pollution Act, the first attempt to begin to codify national pollution control standards

1983 German Government 'conversion' on the issue of acid rain. Germany begins to push for tougher pollution control standards in the EU, and the UK often seeks to resist the pressure

1986 The Alkali Inspectorate is merged with other pollution inspectorates to create Her Majesty's Inspectorate of Pollution, the beginnings of a separate environment agency

1987 Single European Act makes environmental policy a normal EU responsibility for the first time. Except when related to the single market, voting in the Council of Ministers is by the principle of unanimity

1988 Mrs Thatcher makes speech to the Royal Society in September referring to the problems of global warming

1990 Environmental Protection Act, the first major piece of legislation since 1974. Aimed to introduce a modern regime of pollution control, particularly in respect of air pollution and waste management. Conservative Government publishes *This Common Inheritance* in September, a statement of its policies towards sustainable development. Stronger on machinery of government issues than on substantive policy

1992 Government pursues the policy of regaining some EU environmental powers to the Member States under the principle of subsidiarity

1995 Environment Act establishes the Environment Agency, bringing together the National Rivers Authority and Her Majesty's Inspectorate of Pollution

book by A. Dobson, *Green Political Thought* (London: Unwin Hyman, 1990) and the short article by B. Jones 'Green Thinking', *Talking Politics*, 2 (2) (1989/90), 50–54. W. P. Grant, 'Are Environmental Pressure Groups Effective', *Politics Review*, September (1995) and M. Robinson, *The Greening of British Party Politics* (Manchester: Manchester University Press, 1992) discuss the issue from the point of view of pressure groups and parties. A useful book on environmental issues and Europe, though now rather old, is N. Haigh, *EEC Environmental Policy and Britain* (London: Longman, 1987) while A. Weale, *The New Politics of Pollution* (Manchester: Manchester University Press, 1992) provides a comparative account of environmental politics in Europe and elsewhere. T. O'Riordan and J. Jager (eds), *Politics of Climate Change* (London: Routledge, 1996) is a recent collection of essays on climate change, including a chapter on the UK. The official view of environmental issues of the previous government is laid out in *This Common Inheritance* (HMSO: London, 1990).

CHAPTER 25

Economic policy

Previous chapters showed how many aspects of security and foreign policy are insulated from democratic scrutiny and debate. This and the two following chapters will examine contrasting styles of decision making on the economy, social affairs and equal opportunities. Of all these, management of the economy is the 'master' policy area. Put simply, the level and quality of almost all government-provided services depends on public spending, and spending in turn is a product of the ways in which governments manage the economy. The chapter will first attempt to place spending in Britain in a comparative and historical context. It will then distinguish between macro and micro economic policy, and move on to discuss the institutional context and the style and substance of decision making in this area. The chapter will conclude by pointing up the extent to which international events are now a major influence and how this will affect the likely direction which policy making will take over the next few years. It therefore covers:

- The historical and comparative context of economic policy

- The basics of economic policy

- The institutional context, characterised above all by centralisation

- The style and substance of policy making: a new orthodoxy?

- The internationalisation of economic policy making

ECONOMIC POLICY IN HISTORICAL AND COMPARATIVE CONTEXT

As was shown in Chapters 2 and 3, Britain has had an unusual and fascinating economic history. It was the first country to move from a feudal agricultural economy to one based on cash crops and modern farming methods. It was also, in turn, the first economy to industrialise. By the first third of the nineteenth century Britain had established itself as the leading industrial nation and by the second

third of the century the British economy was easily the largest in the world. It is important to know how Britain came to assume this position. Even today, the making of economic policy is influenced by this distinctive past.

Three key facts relating to Britain's economic history have affected the nature of policy making in this area:

1. Britain was – and many would argue, remains – a world leader in the extension of free-market principles. In marked contrast to such countries as France, Germany, Japan and Russia, Britain's industrialisation occurred with little direct intervention from the central Government. Private capital was the driving force behind both the construction of infrastructure (canals, railways, roads, utilities) and the development of manufacturing and extractive (mining) industries. As a result, governments proved reluctant to intervene directly in economic affairs until the traumatic events of the Great Depression and the Second World War forced their hand (see Chapter 3). At the same time Britain was a champion of free international trade, so has long pursued policies that opened up export and import markets among all trading nations.

2. Britain's political system is highly centralised. From the very beginning, therefore, economic policy making has been directed from the centre. It has also been executive-led. Unlike political systems with federal arrangements or the separation of powers, in Britain lower level governments, the courts and even Parliament have played a minimal role in economic policy. Until very recently the central bank (the Bank of England), which in comparable systems plays a major role in economic management, has also been subservient to the executive.

3. Since the First World War, economic policy in Britain has been in almost continuous crisis. This has resulted in the elevation of economic policy to the top of the political agenda. Only very rarely have other policy issues overtaken economic affairs in importance. Hence it has been economic questions rather than foreign policy or social issues which have tended to make or break governments for most of the twentieth century.

When discussing public policy it is usual to distinguish between the *institutional context* and the *style and substance* of how policy is made. Before we examine these points, however, we need to provide some basic information on the nature of economic policy itself.

> **Key term**
>
> **Macro-economic policy** – the branch of economic policy which deals with total or aggregate performance of the national economy, including monetary policy (money in circulation and interest rates), inflation, exchange rates, capital, employment, and labour.

> **Key term**
>
> **Micro-economic policy** – the branch of economic policy which deals not with the total performance of the economy but with the performance and behaviour of individual economic actors, including firms, trade unions, consumers, and regional and local governments.

ECONOMIC POLICY: THE BASICS

The most fundamental distinction in economic policy is between *macro* and *micro* economic policy. Macro economics is concerned with the total or *aggregate* performance of the economy, including monetary policy (how much money is circulating in the economy, interest rate levels or the cost of borrowing) and the exchange rate of the pound in relation to other currencies. Monetary policy is in turn one of the determinants of the general level of activity in the economy and in particular the level of inflation. Micro economics is concerned not with aggregates, but with the behaviour of *individual* economic actors such as firms, trade unions, consumers, regional and local governments. Clearly the two are related. How firms and consumers behave greatly influences the amount of money circulating in the economy (the money supply) as well as the overall level of demand for goods and services and the savings rate. These in turn will inform macro-economic management.

As far as policy is concerned, many free market economists believe that most of economic policy should be confined to macro-economic management, and that governments should do as little as possible to interfere with individual firms and consumers. Such an approach implies minimal levels of taxation and of government spending and therefore a minimal level of government debt. Put another way, it implies that governments should be concerned with macro-economic policy but not with the micro economics of the economy. As we all know, however, governments in Britain have legislated to affect the behaviour of all economic actors and they are intimately involved in micro economics. Manufacturing firms,

Key term

Fiscal policy – a type of macro-economic policy which uses taxation and public expenditure to manage the economy.

for example, are taxed in several ways, their labour markets are regulated (employee safety, job security, equal opportunity), the safety and quality of their products are regulated by law, and government plays a major role in providing for or regulating their production environment (environmental controls, the provision of roads and utilities, planning law and so on). The EU and local Governments as well as central Government play some part in this process.

The policy universe covering this micro-economic environment is highly complex and the product of numerous pieces of legislation enacted at a number of levels over a period of time (see Briefing 25.1). Often these laws are contradictory or incompatible. High 'on-costs' (employer social security contributions and the like) may conflict with job security. Competition or anti-monopoly policy and planning policy may result in reduced profits and therefore reduced government revenues. Much of the time, governments are concerned to find a balance between these conflicting objectives, or they seek to find the optimal trade-offs between them. Because micro-economic policies affect the behaviour of individuals they

BRIEFINGS

25.1 CHARACTERISING ECONOMIC POLICY: INSTITUTIONS AND ACTORS IN APPROXIMATE ORDER OF IMPORTANCE

Monetary Policy (interest rates, money supply, exchange rates)

Institutions
The Bank of England
(The European Union, if Britain joins EMU)
The Treasury
International financial markets

Actors
Governor of the Bank of England
(European Central Bank, if Britain joins EMU)
Economic advisers to the Bank of England
Chancellor of the Exchequer
The Prime Minister
The Treasury
Market investors and speculators
Organised interests

Fiscal and Spending Policy (taxation, government spending)

Institutions
The Treasury
The Cabinet and Cabinet departments
The Public Accounts Committee and Parliament
The European Union
International financial markets

Actors
The Prime Minister
The Chancellor and First Secretary to the Treasury
Treasury officials
Cabinet ministers
Spending department officials
Members of Parliament
Organised interests
Local governments
EU officials
Market investors and speculators

Other Micro-economic Policies (labour market, industrial, regional, environmental, health and safety, and competition policy)

Institutions
The Cabinet
Cabinet departments
The European Union
Organised interests
Parliament
Local government

Actors
Prime Minister and Cabinet ministers
Departmental officials
EU officials
Interest group spokespersons and officials
Members of Parliament
Local government councillors and officials

tend to be highly politicised. Consumers, firms, taxpayers and workers are acutely aware of changes in taxation, competition policy or trade union law and are therefore likely to mobilise to protect their interests.

Macro-economic policy is, by definition, an easier area both to characterise and to manage. Only central authorities can direct broad changes in the economy and in practice this means the executive branch of the central Government. In addition, central banks are always closely involved in monetary policy and the more independent they are of central control, the less political monetary policy becomes. This is a point we will return to later. This said, all aspects of macro-economic management ultimately affect individuals, so they can be highly controversial. If, for example, the Government decides that the economy is overheating then it is likely to raise taxes and/or reduce government spending. Both decisions are likely to be resisted by a range of political and economic actors.

THE INSTITUTIONAL CONTEXT

As with so many other aspects of British politics, the most notable institutional characteristic of economic policy making is its highly centralised character. Part of this derives from the British parliamentary system, with its dominant executive, and part from the inherent weakness of regional and local government in Britain. In many other countries lower level governments – for example, the Länder (federal states) in Germany – play an important role in micro-economic policy. In others, for example the United States, national legislatures are intimately involved in the budgetary process.

Plate 25.2 Prime Minister Tony Blair with the Chancellor of the Exchequer, Gordon Brown

Centralisation *within* the executive is also high in the UK, so the lead actors are the Prime Minister, the Chancellor and the Treasury. It is significant that the Prime Minister is also the First Lord of the Treasury, so emphasising the important historical role of the Treasury in British politics.

The pre-eminence of the Treasury stems from the fact that it is the institution responsible not only for providing the Government with advice on general questions of economic policy, but also for enforcing government spending priorities and rules on all other departments. Hence it is the Treasury with whom the so-called 'spending departments' negotiate over the detail of their budgets. Its civil servants have the highest status in Whitehall, and the Chancellor of the Exchequer is widely regarded as the most senior minister in the Cabinet, bar the Prime Minister.

Of course 'The Treasury' is a building staffed with civil servants. Formally, it is not a decision-making body at all. Its job is to implement the policies of the government of the day. In this sense, the key institutional actors are the Prime Minister, the Chancellor, the First Secretary to the Treasury and the Cabinet. In reality, the Cabinet as a collective entity plays a relatively minor role in economic management. Even the key Cabinet committee in the area during John Major's prime ministership, the Economic and Domestic Policy Committee (EDP), was not a central player. Of course individual Cabinet ministers will lobby hard for their departments in the appropriate Cabinet forum, and of course general questions of economic management are discussed in Cabinet. But the core decision making is done by the PM, Chancellor and First Secretary. They may work in ad hoc groups, or they may be influenced by outside advisers – much as Margaret Thatcher was by Sir Alan Walters – but they are unlikely to depend on the collective will of the Cabinet.

The Treasury will have a 'view' on economic management, whose influence is very hard to measure. Treasury officials have almost always been fiscal conservatives or averse to increasing government debt. Since the Thatcher era, they have also become significantly more hostile to government intervention in industry and in the economy generally. What role Margaret Thatcher and her ministers played in this, compared with a changing intellectual mood on the role of government, is very difficult to say. But we do know that the Prime Minister made a number of key appointments to the Treasury which greatly helped her cause. She appointed an outsider, Terry Burns, as chief economic adviser (he was a professor at the London School of Economics rather than a career civil servant), and worked hard to get Peter Middleton appointed as Permanent Secretary. Burns and Middleton were both committed to fiscal orthodoxy and a reduction in the role of government and they dominated the Treasury for most of the 1980s.

Controversy on the policy role of the Treasury has waned significantly since the Thatcher era. The reasons for this relate to the rise of a new orthodoxy in economic policy which pervades not only much of British government, but also governments elsewhere.

Central banks are key players in economic policy in almost all political systems including the British. As the institutions responsible for setting interest rates, controlling the money supply and defending the national currency on the foreign exchanges, they are of obvious importance. Unusually among democracies, the

Bank of England has traditionally shared with the Government the responsibility for setting interest rates. Until the 1990s this was primarily the Government's prerogative, although the bank always gave advice. Under John Major the balance shifted towards the Bank. The Chancellor and the Governor of the Bank would meet monthly, the Chancellor would take the decision, but the minutes of the meeting were published later, so revealing any rifts between the Bank and the Government. Many previous governments used interest rate policy to manipulate the economy for political advantage (Chapter 3) and this innovation was designed to depoliticise the whole process.

On coming to power in 1997 the new Chancellor, Gordon Brown, announced that in future the Bank would be given the freedom to set interest rates, subject only to the advice of a group of experts appointed by the Government (a group of seven economists and bankers known as the Monetary Policy Committee). This unexpected change – there was no reference to it in the Labour manifesto – effectively gave to the Bank the same freedom enjoyed by almost all the other EU central banks.

While the Treasury and the Bank of England are undoubtedly the *core* economic policy-making institutions, there are numerous other institutional actors with some influence. All the major spending departments, and in particular those directly concerned with economic matters such as The Department of Trade and Industry, play some role. Trade and Industry is concerned with micro- rather than macro-economic policy, though in its liaison with numerous private sector firms over such matters as competition policy and aid for small business it is, by

Plate 25.3 The Bank of England. Gordon Brown, Chancellor of the Exchequer, gave the Bank freedom to set interest rates on coming to power in 1997 and set up a separate regulatory body for financial institutions

definition, immersed in the concerns of individual economic actors. The same is true of the role played by local authorities. Although their spending powers have been greatly reduced over recent years (Chapter 19), they continue to plan land use, which can greatly affect the investment decisions of companies.

Until the privatisations of the 1980s and 1990s, the nationalised corporations were important economic actors. Often their pricing and investment decisions were used by central governments as instruments of government policy. For example, if government wanted to rein in spending it would cut new investment in British Rail or British Steel. Similarly, the corporations were used as examples in incomes policy: pay rises for rail workers or miners might be held down to encourage restraint in the private sector. A relic of this is found in government regulation of prices charged by the privatised utilities for water, electricity, gas and so on.

The role that Parliament plays in economic policy is, in effect, a very small one. The Public Accounts Committee (PAC), which is the most important of Parliament's select committees, meets twice a week and is charged with scrutinising the Government's accounts and ensuring that government spending provides value for money. Although important, this function does not relate directly to the *formulation* of economic policy. Generally there are clear limits to the ability of Parliament to keep the Government accountable in any detailed way (Chapter 18).

Apart from the PAC, Parliament's role is limited – as it is with most aspects of public policy – to the collective power of backbench MPs. When they can muster a majority against the Government then they can be very effective, but this rarely happens. Indeed the only example in the last 20 years of a government's being defeated on a major economic question was when an alliance of Opposition and dissenting Conservative MPs rejected the rise in VAT on fuel from 8 to 17.5 per cent in the November 1994 budget.

Finally, what role do organised interests play in economic policy? It is clear from earlier discussions (Chapter 12) that interests are very rarely *directly* involved (see Briefing 25.2). Firms and unions may make comments on (say) a rise in taxation or interest rates, and they may lobby hard in favour of or against one policy or another. Sometimes their demands are heeded, as with the transitional relief from the Uniform Business Rates granted to business during the early and mid-1990s.

Business, in particular, is privileged in relation to other organised interests as it has an indirect veto on a range of economic polices. Governments are very aware that policies which challenge the free market environment can lead to recession and unemployment. It is rarely necessary for business leaders to threaten such consequences should particular policies be adopted. All of the actors in the policy process are aware of it and this in turn helps mould a pro-business policy agenda. Because of Britain's history as a trading nation, governments have been particularly deferential to the financial markets of the City of London. As will be discussed below, maintaining the value of the pound on the foreign exchanges was for long a major priority of successive governments.

BRIEFINGS

25.2 ORGANISED INTERESTS AND GOVERNMENT IN ECONOMIC POLICY MAKING

In some countries, peak associations (the equivalent of the British Trades Union Congress or Confederation of British Industry) are directly incorporated into the economic decision-making process. Such systems are usually labelled *corporatist*. Austria is usually identified as a corporatist system, and there are elements of corporatism in other countries such as Germany and Japan. Scholars agree that Britain has never had corporatist political arrangements. Major corporations or unions are rarely consulted before important decisions are taken. More often they will lobby to protect their interests, but there is no guarantee that their wishes will be heeded. For example, during the 1980s, Conservative governments systematically reduced the powers of trade unions. More revealing was the Government's rejection of pleas by manufacturing industry during the early 1980s that its policies were leading to rapid de-industrialisation. The determination to continue with monetarist policies showed just how far removed industry was from central decision making.

The American political scientist, Charles Lindblom, has pointed out, however, that businesses – but not trade unions – are uniquely privileged in economic policy because they can always threaten that anti-business policies will lead to recession and unemployment. In other words, they do not *need* to be directly involved in decision making; instead they have a hidden veto on the policy agenda. Today this seems almost like a truism, and it is certainly the case that all governments now talk in terms of maintaining a good environment for business investment and profits. Given Britain's status as a major trading nation over many generations, UK governments have been particularly keen to serve the interests of the City of London (Chapter 2 and 3).

Source: C. Lindblom, *Politics and Markets* (New Haven, Connecticut: Yale University Press, 1977)

THE STYLE AND SUBSTANCE OF POLICY MAKING

Economic policy making in Britain in the twentieth century has taken the form of almost continuous crisis management (Chapter 3). British efforts to sustain the free convertibility of sterling into gold, followed by the Great Depression, the Second World War and the near bankruptcy of the postwar years, were quickly followed by decades of 'stop–go' policies. Successive governments, intent on maintaining the value of the pound on the foreign exchanges, were forced into periodic bouts of deflation only to be followed by electorally inspired reflation.

Key term

Monetarism – a revised version of neo-classical economics which, contrary to Keynesianism, argues that government should minimise its involvement in economic matters, except for controlling the money supply as a way of holding down inflation.

By the late 1970s, controlling inflation became the top priority and, with the election of Margaret Thatcher in 1979, the fight against inflation was seen as inexorably linked to the supply of money circulating in the economy. Monetarism, as it came to be known, dominated British politics during the early and mid 1980s (see Briefing 25.3). It was highly controversial, not only because of its uncertain intellectual pedigree but also because, if implemented fully, it could be highly deflationary. At a time when unemployment was in any case rising, monetarism was viewed by many as involving increased unemployment as a deliberate tool of economic policy.

The monetarist experiment was abandoned once it became clear that the relationship between the money supply (which in any case was notoriously difficult to measure) and inflation was tenuous at best. What the episode demonstrates, however, is the extraordinarily centralised and closed nature of economic policy making in Britain. The Prime Minister, Chancellor (Sir Geoffrey Howe) and personal Downing Street and Treasury advisers (Alan Walters and Terry Burns) decided on the policy and it was implemented. Many in Margaret Thatcher's Cabinet objected, as did many Conservative backbenchers. Many Treasury officials were sceptical, as were most economists.

Since the mid-1980s there have been two more major crises. One of them is a typically insulated instance of economic policy making and the other – British membership of the ERM and of the European currency – is highly atypical. The

BRIEFINGS

25.3 MONETARISM AND BRITISH POLITICS

On coming to power in 1979, the Conservatives were converted to the belief that the control of the money supply (the amount of cash and credit circulating in the economy) was the key to controlling inflation. Margaret Thatcher and her intellectual guru, Sir Keith Joseph, accepted the analysis of the Nobel Laureate economist Milton Friedman who had long argued that rising inflation was linked to governments' neglect of monetary targets. Accordingly, the Government adopted a medium-term financial strategy which set specific targets for one of the Treasury's broader money supply indicators (M3, which denoted cash and accounts at UK banks). In order to curb the money supply, interest rates were raised and public expenditure cut. In addition the standard rate of value added tax (VAT) was almost doubled. The immediate effects of these changes was to fuel inflation and to depress the economy. Economists assured the Government that this was a short-term phenomenon, or a necessary

dose of medicine to guarantee long-term economic health. In the event, the recession bottomed out in 1982 and a slow but steady recovery set in thereafter. By 1983 it was becoming obvious that the objective performance of the economy, including the inflation rate, was only loosely linked to the money supply. The Treasury set ever higher monetary targets but these were almost always overshot. Meanwhile, inflation was falling steadily. By 1985 monetary targets, although set, were no longer the main guiding principle of government policy.

Monetarism was important because it demonstrated how a determined prime minister could almost unilaterally change the direction of economic policy. Monetarism also became a catch-all phrase to describe 'Thatcherite' policies. In fact, by the end of the 1980s Thatcherite policies bore very little relationship to the strictly economic definition of monetarism.

first crisis occurred after the Stock Market 'crash' in October 1987. The Chancellor of the Exchequer, Nigel Lawson, feared that the consequences would be deflationary and therefore stimulated the economy with interest rate cuts. The crash did not have the expected effect, however, and the fall in the cost of money further stimulated an already overheated economy. Credit became extremely easy to obtain and consumer debt soared. By mid-1988 the boom was widely recognised as inflationary; property prices were soaring and the Government was obliged to take Draconian corrective measures in 1989 and 1990. These events contributed to the deepest recession of the postwar era.

The second crisis grew in part out of a major rift between the lead policy makers in the economic policy arena: the Prime Minister Margaret Thatcher and her Chancellors, first Nigel Lawson and subsequently Norman Lamont. The issue was British membership of the Exchange Rate Mechanism (ERM) and of the European Monetary System (EMS). First Lawson and then Lamont supported membership, while the Prime Minister was vehemently opposed. Lawson's resignation in 1989 was partly inspired by this disagreement. The ERM supporters finally won the day and Britain joined in October 1990. Only the threat of a Cabinet revolt caused Thatcher to change her mind. This was, therefore, one of the rare instances when economic policy making moved beyond a small coterie of Downing Street and Treasury officials.

British membership of the ERM was, of course, a failure. In September 1992 the UK was forced out of the currency agreement. The issue continued to dominate economic debate in the 1990s, but now in the form of Britain's position in relation to the single European currency. The unusual nature of this policy issue is well demonstrated by the fact that the Conservative Governments of John Major could not make a clear commitment one way or another on the question. So deep were the divisions in the Conservative Party that the Government's hands

Plate 25.4 Nicholas Garland cartoon in the *Sunday Telegraph*, 1992: Kick-starting the Economy. British membership of ERM was a failure, splitting the Conservative Party and causing the electorate to lose confidence in Conservative management of the economy

KICK-STARTING THE ECONOMY

were effectively tied. No other economic issue in recent British political history has been diffused into the rank and file of a party in this way. The typical mode, as with monetarism and the Lawson boom, is for decisions to be taken by a few lead actors and then implemented irrespective of the political costs.

While Britain's membership of European monetary union remains a vitally important issue, it is unlikely to divide the Blair Government as it did Major's. In addition, Blair is Prime Minister at a time when an unusual degree of consensus applies to the fundamentals of economic policy (see Briefing 25.4). There are a number of reasons for this, including the almost universal perception that the primary aim of economic policy should be the control of inflation. As a result, the

BRIEFINGS

25.4 THE NEW ORTHODOXY IN ECONOMIC POLICY

When, in October 1997, the Deputy Prime Minister John Prescott announced to the Labour Party Conference that he would not re-nationalise the railways, he was conforming to what is an almost universally supported orthodoxy in economic policy. This consists of the following assumptions:

- The primacy of keeping rates of inflation low over all other objectives. It used to be the case that low rates of unemployment and high rates of growth were governments' top priority, with low inflation a poor third. Now, with the internationalisation of capital, governments almost everywhere see low inflation as the prerequisite for economic wellbeing.

- Fiscal responsibility. During the 1960s and 1970s some British governments believed that it was possible to 'spend their way out of trouble' or stimulate the economy through borrowing and spending to speed recovery. Today, governments are convinced that the only way to spend responsibly is to finance expenditure with taxation. Government borrowing is permissible but should not rise to more than 3 per cent of GDP. During periods of sustained growth, as in the late 1990s, it should be reduced well below this figure.

- Low, preferably indirect, taxation is a good thing; high direct taxation is a bad thing. At one time Labour Governments supported the idea of high

progressive personal income taxes and low indirect taxes (taxes on expenditure such as VAT). Today, economists argue that high income taxes distort consumer preferences and undermine efficiency. Indirect taxes leave the consumer the choice to save rather than spend, or to spend on low tax rather than high tax items. The Blair Government has broadly accepted this view, as did the Major Government. The main difference between them is Labour's preference for a much lower starting rate of income taxes for the low paid.

- If possible, the market rather than the state should provide goods and services. Until recently Labour Governments believed in nationalisation and the Conservatives in privatisation. Today all parties accept the advantages of privatisation. Labour accepts the need for more *regulation* of companies previously in public ownership, but does not propose any major re-nationalisation.

- A major debate in the Labour Party used to be between supporters of an economy protected from outside competition and those who believed in free trade. Today this debate is all but over. All leading Labour politicians support open international markets, with only a very minimal state role in protecting British industry. Put another way, Labour Governments are enthusiastic supporters of free and open competition at home and abroad.

controversial issues which dominated most of the postwar period – the proper economic role of the state, the extent of public ownership, the timing of stop–go policies, monetarism and the relationship between the trade unions and the Government – have all but passed from the political agenda.

This will almost certainly make Tony Blair's job easier. He is, of course, still obliged to operate in the same institutional environment as his predecessors. Let us look at the nuts and bolts of the most important part of this environment – the budgetary process – in more detail.

The budgetary process

Until the late 1960s the budgetary process was conducted in much the same way as it was 100 years earlier. It consisted of an annual round of expenditure approved by the Government on an ad hoc basis. No systematic survey of spending, or planning of future spending, was involved. On the recommendation of the Plowden Report in 1961, the Government accepted the need for annual expenditure surveys which were finally adopted in 1969. The system is known as the *Public Expenditure Survey Committee* (PESC). Over the years, and especially since the economic traumas of the 1970s, this process has become more thorough and more systematic.

Today the system works like this:

1. The process starts with the *estimates procedure* whereby officials from the spending departments report to the Treasury on their spending needs over the next three years.

2. These estimates are then summarised in the PESC which reports to the Chief Secretary to the Treasury. The Chief Secretary in turn reports to the Cabinet which makes an estimate on spending needs over a five-year period.

3. This is followed by a series of *bilaterals* or face-to-face negotiations between spending department ministers and Treasury ministers. This is the first phase of the *spending round*. It is characterised by horse trading, confrontation and intense negotiation. A great premium is placed on the quality of argument. Intellectually gifted and aggressive ministers are more likely to squeeze something out of the Treasury than their less gifted colleagues.

4. The results of these negotiations are passed on to Cabinet committees and thence to the full Cabinet for approval. If a minister fails to agree with the Treasury the request is sent to the *'Star Chamber'*. This is a Cabinet committee made up of senior Cabinet members who hear the arguments and adjudicate disputes between the disagreeing parties. The Star Chamber's decisions are usually final. Ministers may try to appeal against their decision to the full Cabinet, but they are unlikely to win much satisfaction.

5. Predictably, most disputes involve the large spending departments –
    Health and Social Security, Defence and Education – which serve large
    and politically powerful constituencies. As can be seen from Figure 25.1,
    spending has remained at a high level since 1971, accounting (today) for
    about 42 per cent of GDP. Table 25.1 puts this figure in comparative
    perspective over the period since 1870. Note the tendency for
    government spending to increase almost everywhere, although there has
    been some levelling off since the early 1980s. All governments are now
    committed to holding spending and government debt down. Given that
    the public continue to assign a high priority to health, education, housing
    and social security (Table 26.1, p. 610), the pressures for increases can
    be appreciated. Indeed, spending on social security, health and education
    increasingly dominate the national budget (Figure 25.2). Note also the
    relative decline in defence expenditure since 1981.

6. The budget is then consolidated in a *Finance Bill* which is presented to
    the House of Commons in November. Since 1993 both the expenditure
    side and the income (taxation) side have been combined in the November
    budget (previously, the taxation measures were announced in the Spring).
    The Finance Bill is then referred to House committees, and individual
    measures are debated upon before votes are taken. While this process
    takes some time, major amendments are very rare. Indeed, we earlier
    noted that the Government's defeat on the increase in VAT on fuel in
    1994 was a very unusual event and one which can partly be attributed to
    the Government's very small Commons majority at that time.

Figure 25.1 General
government expenditure as a
percentage of GDP,
1971–95

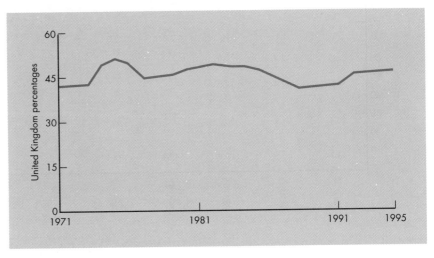

Source: *Social Trends 27* (London: The Stationery Office, 1997), Figure 6.20

Table 25.1 Government spending as a percentage of GDP, selected countries 1870–1996

	1870	**1913**	**1920**	**1937**	**1960**	**1980**	**1990**	**1996**
Austria	–	–	14.7	15.2	34.7	48.1	48.6	51.7
Belgium	–	–	–	21.8	30.3	58.6	54.8	54.3
Canada	–	–	13.3	18.6	28.6	38.8	46.0	44.7
France	12.6	17.0	27.6	29.0	34.6	46.1	49.8	54.5
Germany	10.0	14.8	25.0	42.4	32.4	47.9	45.1	49.0
Italy	11.9	11.1	22.5	24.5	30.1	41.9	53.2	52.9
Japan	8.8	8.3	14.8	25.4	17.5	32.0	31.7	36.2
Netherlands	9.1	9.0	13.5	19.0	33.7	55.2	54.0	49.9
Norway	3.7	8.3	13.7	–	29.9	37.5	53.8	45.5
Spain	–	8.3	9.3	18.4	18.8	32.2	42.0	43.3
Sweden	5.7	6.3	8.1	10.4	31.0	60.1	59.1	64.7
Switzerland	–	2.7	4.6	6.1	17.2	32.8	33.5	37.6
Britain	9.4	12.7	26.2	30.0	32.2	43.0	39.0	41.9
United States	3.9	1.8	7.0	8.6	27.0	31.8	33.3	33.3
Average	8.3	9.1	15.4	18.3*	28.5	43.3	46.1	47.1
Australia	–	–	–	–	21.2	31.6	34.7	36.6
Ireland	–	–	–	–	28.0	48.9	41.2	37.6
New Zealand	–	–	–	–	26.9	38.1	41.3	47.1
Average	–	–	–	–	25.4	39.5	39.1	40.4
Total Average	8.3	9.1	15.4	20.7	27.9	42.6	44.8	45.9

* Average without Germany, Japan and Spain undergoing war or war preparation at this time
Source: *Economist*, 20 September 1997, p. 8.

Figure 25.2 Government expenditure by function and percentage distribution, 1980/81–1995/96

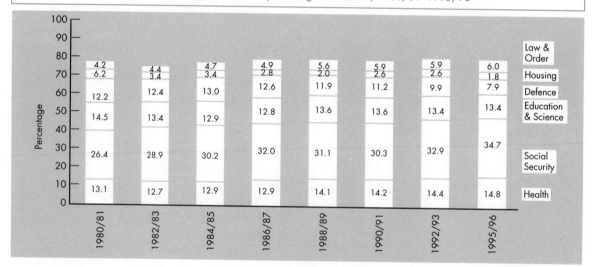

Source: Financial Statement and Budget Report 1996/97 as reproduced in P. Curwen (ed.), *Understanding the UK Economy* (London: Macmillan, 1997) Figure 8.2
Note: 1995/6 figures are estimated

Within the machinery of Whitehall, negotiations over spending are intensely political. But the same is rarely true of decisions affecting revenue. In the November budget the Chancellor announces, in a highly ritualised manner, forthcoming changes in taxation. These are deemed to be strictly confidential, with only the Prime Minister and the Treasury team privy to their contents. Indeed it is rare for even senior Cabinet ministers to be parties to these decisions. Of course much speculation surrounds the process and leaks are not uncommon. Once announced, the decisions may prove highly controversial (as with the VAT on fuel case) but they are very rarely successfully challenged. Almost all the major changes in UK taxation, including the shift from direct to indirect taxation over the last 20 years, have been the result of a relatively closed decision-making process involving very few political actors. Figure 25.3 shows the percentage distribution of tax revenues in 1996–97.

Figure 25.3 Sources of revenue by function, 1996–97

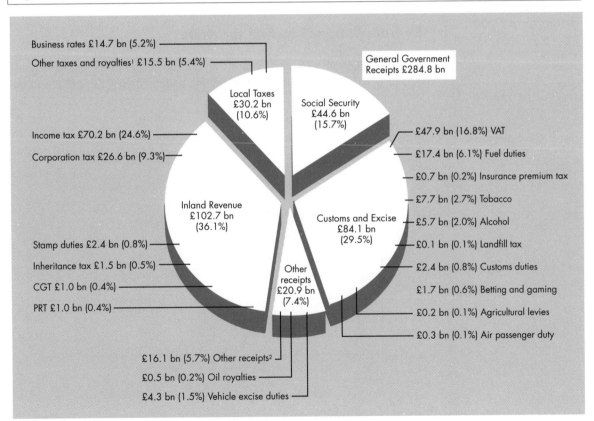

Source: Financial Statement and Budget Report, 1996–1997, as reproduced in P. Curwen (ed.), *Understanding the British Economy* (London: Macmillan, 1997), Figure 8.3

THE INTERNATIONALISATION OF ECONOMIC POLICY

Economic policy in Britain has been affected by external events for many decades. Recently, however, the constraints imposed by the international environment have grown in importance. Let us summarise these briefly.

The European Union

The EU impinges on British economic policy in a number of ways. Most of these affect micro- rather than macro-economic policy. EU regulatory, environmental and competition policy have precedence over British law. In addition, should Britain join the single currency (or European Monetary Union, EMU) then all the crucial aspects of macro-economic policy – interest rates, the money supply and exchange rate policy – would be set by the European Central Bank rather than by the Government or the Bank of England. Only fiscal (taxation and expenditure) policy would be left in the central Government's hands.

The international capital markets

Since exchange rate and other controls on the movement of capital were abolished in Britain and the other leading trading nations during the 1970s and the

Key term

Public sector borrowing requirement (PSBR) – the total amount borrowed by government to finance its annual expenditure.

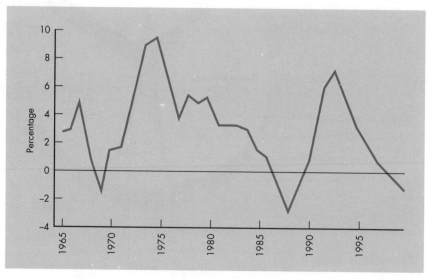

Figure 25.4 Public sector borrowing as a percentage of GDP, 1965–2000 (projected)

Source: Government data as reproduced in P. Curwen (ed.), *Understanding the British Economy* (London: Macmillan, 1997), Figure 8.4

1980s, the pressure on all economic authorities to follow certain policies has been intense. These policies include low levels of inflation and public (government) debt. If the markets sense that inflation or debt are out of control then investors will move out of what is considered a vulnerable currency. In order to maintain the value of currencies, governments will be forced into taking drastic corrective measures including cuts in spending, and raising interest rates and taxation. The alternative would be to let the currency fall which, in an import-dependent economy, would result in more inflation. As can be seen from Figure 3.1 (p. 66) the inflation picture is complex. Figure 25.4 shows the size of the Public Sector Borrowing Requirement over the period 1965–2000. Generally the PSBR rises during periods of recession and falls during booms. As of the late 1990s, the PSBR was falling quite quickly. Most commentators agree that public debt is being held at a reasonable level in Britain. Generally, the centralised and unitary nature of economic policy making in Britain gives to incumbent governments all the tools necessary to control the level of government expenditure and income, and therefore of the level of public debt.

ESSAYS

1. Distinguish between macro- and micro-economic policy. Why is micro-economic policy more 'politicised' than macro policy?

2. Identify the main actors in the British budgetary process. Which are the most important and why?

3. Why are governments under constant pressure to increase public spending? What arguments do governments use to make a case for reduced public spending?

4. What are the differences between the spending priorities of the Major Governments and the Blair Government? How do these differences compare with those prevalent in the 1960s or 1970s?

SUMMARY

This chapter has shown how highly centralised economic policy making in Britain is:

- Even within the executive, very few political actors are involved in the key decisions. This applies to both monetary and fiscal policy.

- Until recently, monetary policy was the shared prerogative of the Chancellor of the Exchequer and the Bank of England. Since 1997, however, the Bank has been the dominant influence in setting interest rates. The Prime Minister, Chancellor and the Treasury remain the key players in setting levels of government spending and taxation.

- Other Cabinet ministers play a reactive rather than proactive part in this process. Parliament's role is usually confined to approving decisions and to a limited form of supervision. Other interests such as business and the unions play an indirect role, although they may be closely involved in the detailed implementation of aspects of micro-economic policy.

- Government options in this area are, however, greatly circumscribed by the need to maintain the confidence of business. This applies both domestically and, as far as the money markets are concerned, internationally.

- In addition the European Union plays an increasingly important role in micro-economic policy. Should Britain join the single currency then the EU's role in macro-economic policy will become dominant.

MILESTONES

MILESTONES IN RECENT ECONOMIC POLICY MAKING

1961 Publication of the Plowden Report on the need for more systematic control of public spending

1969 PESC (Public Expenditure Survey Committee) system introduced to plan expenditure in advance

1976 Introduction of the 'Star Chamber' to arbitrate disputes over departmental spending

1979–80 Margaret Thatcher's monetarist experiment begins

1983–85 Monetarism quietly dropped as a guiding principle in economic policy

1987 Stock market crash followed by over-stimulation of the economy

1989–93 Deepest recession of the post-1945 period

1990 Britain joins the Exchange Rate Mechanism (ERM) of the European Monetary System (EMS)

1992 Britain is forced out of the ERM ('Black Wednesday')

1993 Spending and taxing side of the budget consolidated into one November budget

1994 Government defeated over further increases in VAT on domestic fuel

1997 New Labour Chancellor, Gordon Brown, announces that the Bank of England is immediately to be given the freedom to set interest rates

PROJECTS

1. Outline the main changes in the level of public debt in the twentieth century. Distinguish between annual and accumulated debt and provide explanations for the major fluctuations in debt levels.

2. Write a departmental brief from one of the major spending departments justifying expenditure to the Cabinet Star Chamber. Write a Treasury reply arguing for reduced expenditure.

3. Write a short history of the steps taken towards European Monetary Union since the signing of the Maastricht Treaty with a particular emphasis on the position taken by British governments in this process.

FURTHER READING

For a comprehensive statistical background and accounts of the policy-making process, see Peter Curwen (ed.), *Understanding the UK Economy* (London: Macmillan, 1997). On the Treasury and public spending, see Maurice Wright and Colin Thain, *Treasury and Whitehall: Planning and Control of Public Spending* (Oxford: Clarendon Press, 1995). Wyn Grant's *The Politics of Economic Policy* (Hemel Hempstead: Harvester Wheatsheaf, 1993) provides a good introduction to economic policy making. On the Thatcher years, see Andrew Gamble, *The Free Economy and the Strong State* (London: Macmillan, 2nd edn 1994). For a comparative account of the politics of economic policy through to the mid-1980s, see Peter Hall, *Governing the Economy: The Politics of State Intervention in Britain and France* (Oxford: Oxford University Press, 1986).

http://www.awl-he.com/politics/newbritpol

Internet resources – visit *The New British Politics* Webpage for links to a specially-chosen selection of Internet resources relevant to this Chapter.

http://www.awl-he.com/politics/newbritpol

CHAPTER 26

Social policy

Few issues in Britain arouse as much controversy as social policy. The vast majority of the population support free health care provided by the National Health Service (NHS), free high quality primary and secondary education, adequate old age pensions and unemployment benefits. Yet to a greater or lesser extent all of these benefits are perceived to have been reduced in value or quality by successive governments. Many of the problems associated with state social provision in Britain are related to the sometimes painful transition from the universal benefits promised at the inception of the welfare state in the 1940s to the much more selective system which economic and political realities have imposed since the 1970s. Much of this chapter will be devoted to explaining why this transition has occurred and why the pressures for more selectivity continue to increase. The chapter will cover:

- Problems in defining 'social policy'

- The welfare state in Britain: its foundations and principles

- The four main areas of social provision – income maintenance, housing, health and education – over the last 20 years. Each of these policy areas is examined in its institutional context and the likely direction of policy under New Labour is discussed.

DEFINING SOCIAL POLICY

What constitutes social policy depends on both historical and geographic circumstances. Within countries the definition changes over time as it does between countries. In Britain, for example, state support for housing has moved from a limited form of municipal provision before the Second World War, to near universal provision for 'general needs' housing after the war, to a much more limited level of support today. In many poorer countries state-provided benefits are limited to education. Even in rich industrialised nations such as the United States and Japan, social policy means something very different from what it means in

Key term

Universal and selective benefits – universal benefits are welfare benefits distributed to all groups and individuals who are eligible, irrespective of their particular circumstances, compared with selective benefits for which eligibility is determined according to individual circumstances such as income, age, or disability.

the UK. In the USA, for example, housing is rarely considered a part of social policy and there is no system of universal health care. Instead the market is the major provider in these areas. In Britain today the definition is changing as the political and public support for state provision of housing has fallen (see Briefing 26.1).

Very generally, social policy covers those areas where the Government (or the state), rather than the market, plays a major role in providing for the physical well-being of families and individuals. Governments came to play this role because of the failure of markets to provide acceptable standards of provision. Usually, although not always, it was electorally powerful socialist or labour parties who legislated for social provision. Often they came to power following periods of serious economic dislocation.

In Britain, for example, the Labour Government elected in 1945 legislated to create what became known as the *welfare state*, or a system of social support designed to protect every citizen from the physical insecurities of life.

BRIEFINGS

26.1 UNIVERSALISM, SELECTIVISM AND THE WELFARE STATE

In many developed modern economies, for example the United States, most state welfare benefits are provided on a selective basis, that is, eligibility is determined by individual circumstances. Income, disability and age are the usual criteria employed when potential recipients' eligibility is tested. Benefits may be selective both in terms of the *social group* legibility and in terms of the *level* of support. State pensions, for example, are obviously only available to the old and survivors (those widowed) and the amount of the pension may vary according to circumstance and past employment record.

In other systems, benefits are provided on a universal basis. *All* social groups may be eligible and the benefits may be distributed on a flat-rate basis, which means that the same benefit is given to everybody irrespective of circumstances. Elements of both systems prevail in most countries. Even in the self-reliant United States, elementary and secondary education is organised on a universal basis.

The British welfare state as implemented by the Labour Government after 1945 was based more on universal than selectivist principles. Everybody was entitled to health care, including dental care. Public housing was

for 'general need' and rents were unrelated to income. Family allowances were flat rate as was the old age pension.

The founders of the system were not so naive as to believe that it could be introduced without considerable cost. How then would it be funded? Three devices would be employed to ensure the system was viable. First, Keynesian demand management would be the dominant tool of macro-economic policy. As a result the country would enjoy full employment; the poverty, illness and dislocation associated with mass unemployment would be avoided. Second, much of the system would be self-financing through contributory national insurance stamps. Eligibility for unemployment benefit, for example, would be directly linked to this system. Third, although never explicitly stated, a system of rationing would reconcile the demand for, and the supply of, certain services. Waiting lists would prevail for some hospital treatments and for public housing.

In spite of numerous problems, the welfare state worked well for most of the postwar period. Even in the late 1990s elements of universalism – for example in the NHS and the old age pension – persist.

THE BRITISH WELFARE STATE

The British welfare system was largely a product of the Great Depression of the 1930s and of the Second World War (see Briefing 26.2). Although the rudiments of a pension and unemployment insurance system were introduced by the Liberals soon after the turn of the century, it was not until the election of a Labour Government in 1945 that the construction of the welfare state began. The mass unemployment of the 1930s had demonstrated how inadequate social protection was in the absence of comprehensive state aid. Low levels of unemployment assistance (known as the dole) were means tested or available only to families close to destitution. Families whose means were above these low levels of income had to make do as best they could. Other services, including health, housing and secondary education, had to be paid for or were freely available only on a very limited basis.

By the end of the 1940s an intellectual and political consensus was emerging in favour of a greatly enhanced role for government in economy and society. The Second World War had demonstrated how massive government spending could

BRIEFINGS

26.2 THE FOUNDATIONS OF THE BRITISH WELFARE STATE

Income Maintenance
Beveridge Report on social security, 1942
Family Allowance Act, 1945: family allowances
National Insurance Act, 1946: unemployment benefit, disability, old age and survivors' pensions
National Assistance Act, 1948: income support for those not covered by national insurance

Housing
Housing Act, 1946: central Government subsidies for local authority housing
Housing Act, 1949: council housing designated as 'general needs' and not just for the working class

Health
National Health Service Act, 1948: creation of the National Health Service

Education
Education Act, 1944: secondary education available to all, free of charge. 11-plus exam would select academically gifted for grammar schools

Employment
Employment Policy White Paper 1944: official recognition of Keynesian full employment policy. Also recognised the need for regional policy to reduce economic disparities between the regions.

quickly remove the blight of mass unemployment, and politicians became convinced that Keynesian economics, or demand management, could be used to keep unemployment at acceptably low levels for the foreseeable future. During the late 1930s and early 1940s the Government commissioned a number of reports into almost all aspects of social and economic life from land use planning to education to employment. The most famous of these, the Beveridge Report, concerned social welfare.

Beveridge argued that, with the new tools of economic management which would ensure that mass unemployment would never occur again, the Government could afford to provide a complete system of social protection for those who, through misfortune, inadequacy or dependency, could not provide for themselves. The new system would be built on the principles of universal care: the state would provide flat-rate benefits irrespective of the ability to pay. Hence public (or council) housing would be provided on a 'general needs' basis. Rents would be the same for all tenants irrespective of income. Health services and a flat-rate family allowance would be provided on the same basis. This comprehensive system of welfare would ensure that everybody was secure 'from the cradle to the grave' (see Briefing 26.3). The Labour Government legislated to produce just such a system which was fully in place by 1950.

BRIEFINGS

26.3 ANEURIN BEVAN ON HOUSING AND HEALTH

The following extracts reflect the views of the Labour politician Aneurin Bevan who was Health Minister 1945–51 and introduced the National Health Service in 1948.

I said that in my view it was entirely undesirable that on modern housing estates only one type of citizen should live. I referred to them then as 'twilight towns', and said it was a reproach to our modern social planning that from one sort of township should come one income group. I said that, if we are to enable citizens to lead a full life, if they are each to be aware of the problems of their neighbours, then they should be all drawn from the very different sections of the community and we should try to introduce in our modern villages what has always been the lovely feature of English and Welsh villages, where the doctor, the grocer, the butcher and farm labourer all lived in the same street ... I believe it is a necessary biological background for modern life, and I believe it leads to the enrichment of every member of the community to live in communities of that sort. We believe that it is essential that local authorities should also provide accommodation for single persons, for persons who are following a professional life, and that they should provide for old people.

Bevan in 1949, recalling his intentions in 1945, quoted in A. Cox and D. McKay and A. Cox, *The Politics of Urban Change* (London: Croam Helm, 1979), p. 118

BRIEFINGS

26.3 ANEURIN BEVAN ON HOUSING AND HEALTH (continued)

Allowing for all sensible administrative measures to prevent waste, the plain fact is that the cost of the health service not only will, but ought to, increase. Most of the hospitals fall far short of any proper standard; accommodation needs to be increased, particularly for tuberculosis and mental health – indeed some of the mental hospitals are very near to a public scandal and we are lucky they have not so far attracted more limelight and publicity. Throughout the service there are piling up arrears of essential capital work. Also it is in this field, particularly, that constant new development will always be needed to keep pace with research progress (as, recently, in penicillin, streptomycin, cortisone, etc.) and to expand essential specialist services, such as hearing aids or ophthalmic services. The position cannot be evaded that a nationally owned and administered hospital service will always involve a very considerable and expanding Exchequer outlay. If that position cannot, for financial reasons, be faced, then the only alternatives (to my mind thoroughly undesirable), are either to give up – in whole or in part – the idea of national responsibility for the hospitals or else to import into the scheme some regular source of revenue such as the recovery of charges from those who use it. I am afraid that it is clear that we cannot have it both ways.

Bevan in 1950, quoted in R. Klein, *The New Politics of the NHS*
(Harlow: Addison Wesley Longman, 3rd edn 1995), p. 32

Key term

Utopianism – a form of ideology which claims that it is possible to create a perfect or near perfect society. Some utopias are constructed by their creators not as feasible societies, but as models against which to compare the real world.

Given its scope – some would say its utopianism – the welfare state worked remarkably well and was soon widely admired and copied in other countries. There are a number of reasons for its initial success. First, full employment was indeed established quickly after the war, so Keynesian demand management appeared to work. Not until the 1970s did mass unemployment re-emerge. Full employment kept the cost of the welfare state down and government revenues up.

Second, benefits were established at modest levels. Unemployment benefits and old age, survivors and disability pensions were to be self-financing. Employees would pay national insurance stamps out of their wages; these stamps were to be stuck on to a national insurance card which would act as proof of eligibility for benefits. And initially, at least, benefits were low. The school leaving age was 15 and only a minority of pupils stayed on after 16, with a tiny minority going on to higher education. Health care standards were, by today's norms, low and inexpensive. Limited supplies of housing and health facilities ensured that the system worked. In effect a system of rationing prevailed which involved long waiting lists.

Third, a remarkable degree of consensus on the status of the welfare state emerged. People from all regions, ages and social classes were agreed that it was

Table 26.1 Peoples' top
priorities for extra
government spending,
1983–95

	1983	**1986**	**1990**	**1995**
Health	74	81	70	77
Education	49	57	60	66
Housing	20	21	20	14
Social security benefits	12	12	13	11
Help for industry	29	16	6	9
Police and prisons	8	8	4	9

Source: *Social Trends 27* (London: The Stationery Office, 1997) Table 6.22
Note: The table shows the percentage who gave the spending area first or second priority, when
asked: 'Here are some items of government spending. Which of them, if any, would be your highest
priority for extra spending? And which next?'

a good thing. Almost everybody used the health service, the vast majority of children
went to state schools, private pensions were available only to a minority of the
middle classes. Even council housing attracted a wide social mix, at least during
the serious housing shortages prevalent during the 1940s and 1950s.

The system worked adequately until well into the 1960s, and indeed Labour
governments legislated to extend and improve benefits during this decade. By the
1970s welfare spending had become easily the largest item on the national budget.
Politicians on the right were arguing that unless spending was curbed the system
would become untenable. During the 1980s, Conservative governments began to
roll back the welfare state, a process which continues to this day. At the same time
public support in the UK for welfare spending remained high, with health and
education the top priorities for extra spending (Table 26.1). A good way to understand how and why this transition has occurred is to examine each of the main
components of social policy in turn. In addition, we will examine the main actors
and institutions involved in these policy areas.

INCOME MAINTENANCE

Almost certainly the greatest actuarial problems in the income maintenance area
apply to old age pensions. The flat system created by Beveridge was expected to
become more expensive over time, but by the 1960s it was, in real terms, twice as
expensive as envisaged. More people were living longer and the political pressures for maintaining or increasing the level of benefit proved considerable. By
the 1970s governments were convinced that the system was in need of long-term
reform. Poverty among the old remained a serious problem, which the flat-rate
system could not solve except at huge expense. In 1975 the Government
compromised by introducing a State Earnings Related Pensions Scheme (SERPS)
which added an earnings-related element to the system. However, this too was

projected to become very expensive and in 1986 the Conservatives legislated to restrict the scope of the SERPS system.

By the 1990s, governments were under even more pressure to reduce the real value of the old age pension. In 1980 the Conservatives linked pension increases to prices rather than to earnings, so the relative value of the pension had declined over time, but even so the cost of state pensions could become prohibitive in the longer term. As can be seen from Table 26.2 the number of people in the UK likely to be dependent on the working population will increase substantially in the decades after 2020, and it is the old whose dependency will increase the most. As a result, politicians from all political parties are now committed to making the provision of state pensions *selective* by replacing them for most of the working population with private pension schemes. Given the special status that the flat-rate state pension has assumed in the minds of most voters, this proposal is bound to be politically controversial.

Family poverty was originally tackled through the provision of National Assistance or welfare payments available to all those past school leaving age not in receipt of unemployment benefit and who were in need. In addition a flat-rate family allowance was payable to second and subsequent children (it was assumed that the first child could be cared for if one parent was working). While National Assistance was selective (i.e. it was means tested), everybody from the Queen down was eligible for family allowances. Over the years this system has been modified, although, remarkably, the flat-rate element in Family Allowance (now called Child Benefit) remains. The main changes have been:

- In 1968 family allowances became taxable, but the 1975 Child Benefit Act actually strengthened the flat-rate principle by making the allowance payable to all children. One-parent families received a higher level of benefit.

Table 26.2 Projected dependency ratios, 1994–2061

	Child dependency	**Elderly dependency**	**Overall dependency**
1994	34	30	64
2001	33	29	62
2011	30	31	60
2021	28	30	58
2031	29	39	68
2041	28	43	72
2051	28	43	71
2061	29	44	73

Source: *Social Trends 27* (London: The Stationery Office, 1997) Table A.2
Note: Table 26.2 shows 1994-based projections, for number of children and people over retirement age to every 100 people of working age. The ratios take account of the change in state pension age for women from 60 years to 65 years between 2010 and 2020.

- In 1966 National Assistance was replaced with Supplementary Benefits. These means-tested payments were available to all in need, including pensioners and the unemployed who could not manage on the flat-rate pension or unemployment benefit.

- By the early 1970s it was clear that many families were in a 'poverty or income support trap'. If an adult took a job the family income could fall, given that the earned income (net of tax) could be less than the state benefits forfeited once employment began. Legislation to reduce this disincentive to work was passed in 1971 (Family Income Supplement) and 1988 (Family Credit). These laws allow benefit recipients to work without losing all their benefits. While helpful for some families, a general consensus had emerged by the late 1990s that the disincentive effect of the benefit system remained considerable for many families. Given the array of benefits (including housing benefit) individuals and families have to make complex calculations when taking employment. The system also provides an incentive for benefit recipients to work while receiving benefits without declaring their income.

- In 1982 the Government removed earning-related supplements to unemployment benefit and made such benefits taxable. Gradually during the remainder of the Conservative period in office, the relative value of benefits was reduced and eligibility criteria were tightened.

> **Key term**
>
> **Poverty trap** – the idea that the welfare state creates a vicious cycle of poverty for some social groups by imposing welfare systems that discourage people from taking responsibility for their own life or finding work. The cycle tends to continue, some claim, into the next generation of children who grow up in such a system.

Institutions and actors

Unlike economic policy, where key decisions can often be made by a few senior politicians and officials, income support policy tends to change incrementally and is often infused with interest group activity. This is particularly true of pensions policy. Given that almost all the population will eventually become pensioners, the issue is politically highly salient. In the past, politicians from all parties have expressed sympathy for poverty among the old. Groups such as Age Concern are active in keeping the issue in the public eye, and the vulnerability of the old ensures that any policy changes which occur have to be implemented over the longer term. Family support policy has a slightly different status. Public support for poor families is lower, and the Conservative legislation of the 1980s shows that relatively major changes can be wrought without serious political repercussions. This said, pressure groups (such as the Child Poverty Action Group) and individual Members of Parliament are likely to be active in support of or against particular proposals.

Given the premium on expertise in this policy area, individual Cabinet ministers and their officials are usually closely involved in income support policy making. Indeed, by the late 1990s the more than 20 different benefits available to the needy, administered by several departments, require a high level of expert input to inform any future reforms.

New Labour Policy

New Labour's stance on incomes maintenance is quite similar to that of the previous Conservative Government. As noted, they accept the need to supplement (or eventually replace) the flat-rate pension with a system of private pensions. More surprising is the Labour Party's conversion to 'workfare' or a system of family support designed to oblige parents, and particularly single parents, to work rather than depend on state help. Coupled to this objective is a commitment to expand both nursery education (which will enable single parents to take employment), and training for the unemployed. It remains to be seen how these proposals will work out in practice, but they do represent a sea change from the welfare policies Labour supported in the 1970s, which essentially were the maintenance of universal eligibility and increased spending.

HOUSING

In 1946 the Labour Government legislated to provide a new system of housing subsidies channelled through local authorities. This and later legislation identified council (public) housing as 'general needs' accommodation. In other words, the private sector was to be relegated to secondary status and most housing would be provided by local councils. Although the Conservatives later assigned a much more prominent role to the private sector, both parties accepted that council housing would be the source of new housing for the working-class population. Serious housing shortages meant that during the 1950s and early 1960s Conservative and Labour politicians vied with each other over who could build the most houses.

Unlike income support, the housing policy system closely involved local authorities. They were the recipients of Government housing grants but were left much on their own when making decisions about the location and management of housing estates. As housing was in short supply, a 'waiting list' system was created whereby local government housing departments decided on eligibility for housing. Family size and income and job status were the main criteria employed. Only in 1972 did (a Conservative) Government apply a systematic means test, whereby rent rebates were given to needy tenants both in the public and private sectors. Until that time everybody in council housing paid the same rent irrespective of income.

As can be seen from Figure 26.1, public sector housing construction remained at a high level through to the mid-1970s. Generally, Conservative governments and local authorities favoured the private sector while Labour favoured the public sector. At the same time public housing was increasingly viewed as housing for the disadvantaged, a perception that was strengthened by the construction of large, anonymous housing estates during the 1950s and 1960s which were increasingly occupied by disadvantaged families. Figure 26.1 shows how council housing construction fell from the mid-1970s on. This was initially a result of fiscal emergency, but after 1979 it was the direct result of Conservative Government policy.

Figure 26.1 Housebuilding completions by sector, 1945–95

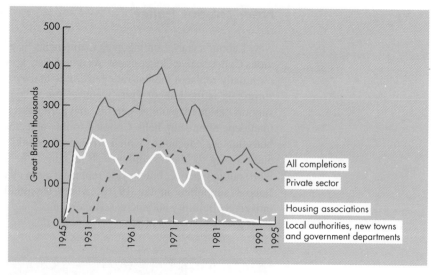

Source: *Social Trends 27* (London: The Stationery Office, 1997), Chart 10.11

Margaret Thatcher's administrations (1979–90) disliked publicly provided housing. They believed that it undermined self-reliance, encouraged local authority overspending and aggravated class divisions. As a result they progressively cut government housing grants and launched the largest single change in housing policy since the Second World War: the sale of council houses to tenants. The major changes in this and other areas were:

- In 1980 tenants were given the right to buy their houses. A system of discounts on the price was available depending on length of tenure.

- In 1982 Housing Benefits were introduced. Council rents had increased steadily although individual authorities retained some freedom to subsidise them. For those who could not pay these rents because of poverty or disability a system of rebates was available.

- In 1986 and 1988 the Government provided further incentives for council house sales. Councils could sell to housing associations and private landlords. The discounts available to sitting tenants and council flat tenants, where the property was particularly hard to sell, were increased.

- In 1989 the Government effectively ended local authority rent subsidies. In future they would have to charge an 'economic rent' with rebates available to the disadvantaged in the form of Housing Benefits.

- Throughout their tenure in office the Conservatives attempted to increase the role of private landlords. This was the smallest and least efficient part of the housing market and they believed that labour mobility would improve with a larger and more flexible private rental sector. A new form of 'regulated tenancies' was created with reduced security of tenure for tenants. Conservative efforts here were less than successful, however. Ultimately, the failure to stimulate this part of the market relates to underlying factors, including restrictive planning laws on land use and public disquiet with private landlords, which even radical Conservative governments were not prepared to challenge.

In the late 1990s social housing (as it is now called) is provided mainly by housing associations and through Housing Benefits. Local authority housing remains important (Figure 26.2) but it consists mainly of large estates occupied by disadvantaged families. Meanwhile, owner occupation has soared and now accounts for some 67 per cent of the total housing stock.

Actors and institutions

Unlike the case of income maintenance, the key actors in social housing in Britain have been local governments. They remain important as administrators of the remaining council housing stock and of Housing Benefits, although their discretion over these policy areas is now quite limited. Central Government decisions during the 1980s and the 1990s were taken with little reference to local government preferences. Organised interests in this area, including pressure groups representing the poor and homeless, have usually played a reactive rather than proactive part. In some ways it is easier to cut capital spending on social housing rather than current expenditure on such things as pensions or Housing Benefits.

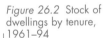

Figure 26.2 Stock of dwellings by tenure, 1961–94

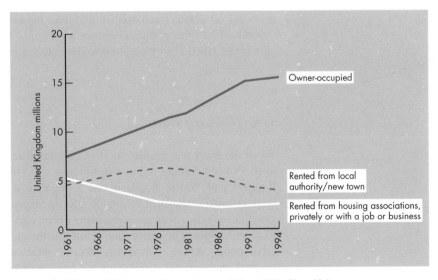

Source: *Social Trends 27* (London: The Stationery Office, 1997), Chart 10.1

The latter have numerous recipients who are highly sensitive to marginal changes in their incomes. Capital spending cuts are felt in the longer term, involve few immediate victims, and are therefore politically easier to impose.

New Labour Policy

Although housing shortages remain and many people live in poor housing conditions, the issue has slipped in political importance compared with health, education and pensions. Politicians from all parties believe the private sector should play the dominant role in housing provision. Housing Benefits are now the main means by which the state helps house the disadvantaged, and in this sense housing policy has become inseparable from income support policy. New Labour recognises this fact and does not propose a reversal of council housing sales and a return to traditional public housing. Instead it supports an extension of owner occupation to the less advantaged through tax and interest-deferred mortagages.

HEALTH

State-provided health care has assumed a very special status in British society. As noted earlier, the utopian vision of the founders of the National Health Service (NHS) was that healthcare would be provided on a universal basis. Unlike housing and many aspects of income maintenance, much of the health care system in the late 1990s, and in particular primary doctor and hospital care, remains free and universally available. However, the increasing cost has brought constant pressure for reform, and some aspects of provision, including dental care, are now provided on a selective basis. In addition, market-like mechanisms have been introduced into the system, changing what might be called the culture of health care in the UK. Let us look at the major changes in more detail.

The 1948 system

When the NHS was created in 1948 its administrative structure was a compromise between existing and new institutions. (The following description applies to England and Wales; Scotland had a separate system.) General practitioners worked much as they had before the reforms, except that their revenue came from government rather than patients; many health services remained in the hands of local authorities. The major innovation was the creation of 14 new regional hospital boards. Within each region most hospitals were run by locally appointed hospital management committees but an elite of teaching hospitals were run by boards of governors with direct links to the Ministry of Health.

The 1974 reforms

During the 1950s and 1960s a number of serious problems emerged with this structure. Regions varied enormously in size, resources tended to move towards an elite of teaching hospitals, little in the way of planning for the whole system was possible. When, during the 1960s, a major hospital building programme was launched, every regional board required major new capital expenditure but there was no means whereby priorities could be set. As a result both Labour and Conservative governments agreed that reform was needed. What transpired was a new structure which was eventually implemented in 1974. The regional boards (now regional authorities) were given the job of overall strategic planning, and a new tier of 90 area health authorities was created to manage direct care. The rationale was to facilitate better management and control of the service from the centre. At the same time democratic accountability was enhanced through the creation of a system of advisory committees and community health councils. These were made up of lay people and interest group spokespersons nominated by local governments, voluntary organisations and regional authorities.

The 1982 reforms

Among the problems with the 1974 structure was a perception that the system was run in the interests of the *producers* (the health care professionals) rather than the *consumers* (patients). At the same time, local government involvement seemed unnecessary. In 1979 the Conservative Government published a consultative document, *Patients First*, which recommended a number of changes. These culminated in the 1982 reforms which abolished area authorities and created 192 district health authorities (DHAs). Local government participation in DHAs was reduced and that of local experts and notables increased. In addition, the Government devolved greater management responsibility to the DHA level. In the ensuing decade government spending on health was reduced, at least in relation to the rest of the post-1955 period (Figure 26.3), and much of the pressure on spending was felt by the DHAs.

The 1991 and 1993 reforms

Organisational change during the 1970s and the 1980s was informed by what might be called 'managerialism', or the belief that improved managerial structures and lines of accountability would improve efficiency and therefore the quality of service provided to the public. However, during the 1980s a new administrative philosophy assumed that bringing in *market forces* rather than improving management structure would enhance efficiency. A White Paper, *Working for Patients*, argued that NHS institutions acted as both *providers* and *purchasers* of health care. In other words they might provide hospital care but

Figure 26.3 Total NHS
spending, percentage
increase per annum,
1951–89

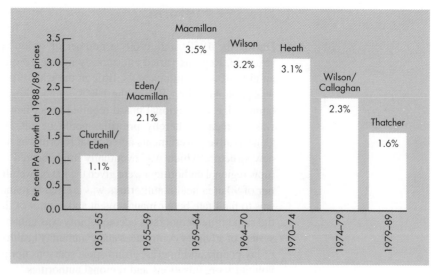

Source: J. Appleby, *Financing the NHS* (Milton Keynes: Open University Press, 1992), as
reproduced in J. Allsop, *Health Policy and the NHS* (London: Longman, 1995), Figure 4.2

they would also have to purchase hospital supplies and services. Moreover a conflict had arisen between these two functions because the health service was more
producer than it was *consumer*-oriented. Much as with the Civil Service before
the Next Steps reforms, the White Paper argued that the institutional structure of
the service gave health care professionals (doctors, nurses and so on) an incentive
to improve their status and conditions of service rather than to make patient care
the top priority.

Again as with the Civil Service (Chapter 10) the answer was to change the
incentive structure of the service by introducing market principles into the system. Accordingly, the Government designated a system of providers (NHS trusts
and general practitioners) who would bid for business (or draw up a contract)
with a purchaser (district and family health authorities, GP fundholders). These
new arrangements are shown in Figure 26.4. Note the key role played by the NHS
Management Executive which now has more control over day-to-day management than the old regional health authorities which were abolished in 1993. In
effect, these reforms increase market-like transactions between the providers and the
purchasers, but at the same time they also increase central Government control
over the resource base of the service.

The NHS reforms in perspective

Most commentators agree that the reforms of the 1990s had both desirable and
unwanted consequences. By some measures (waiting lists, outpatient services)
improvement has occurred, although *measuring* performance is notoriously difficult. The district health authorities, which are the key purchasers on behalf of

Figure 26.4 The new
structure of the NHS, post-
1993

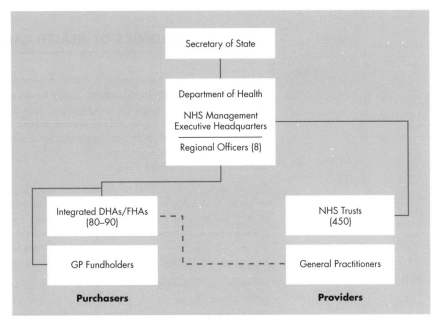

Source: Wendy Ranade, *A Future for the NHS? Health care in the 1990s* (Harlow: Longman, 1994),
Figure 5.2

consumers in the system, seem to be more attuned to GPs than to patients. Critics
also point to the rapid increase in the number of managers in the system. Perhaps
the most important change has been a shift in influence from hospital doctors to
GPs. As primary care providers, GPs are now at the centre of the system, rather
than, as before, subordinate to the priorities of hospital consultants.

As Briefing 26.4 shows, the economics of health care are such that some degree
of rationing by price or availability is necessary in any system. The reforms of the
1990s recognise this. In effect, the rationing element which has always been
present in the NHS is now more explicit. As a result health care professionals can
now order patient care priorities more rationally.

BRIEFINGS

26.4 THE ECONOMICS OF HEALTH CARE

The search for increased efficiency in some social policy areas, and especially in
health care, is beset by a structural economic problem which, unless checked,
means that the cost of health care will spiral ever upwards. With most items which
we buy as consumers, the more that is invested in the productive process the lower
the unit costs of production become. Investment in a car factory, for example,
reduces the labour input, increases productivity and ultimately reduces the real cost

26.4 THE ECONOMICS OF HEALTH CARE (continued)

of the product. Capital investment in health, however, can have perverse results. New equipment bought by a hospital usually results in an *increased* demand for labour to operate it. Worse, the complexity of such things as dialysis machines and CAT scanners requires highly trained operative staff. (In the car factory, required skill levels typically fall as capital investment increases.) Given that labour is the most expensive item in most organisations, this means that increased investment in health results in increased costs.

This problem is compounded by the fact that, in the economists' parlance, the demand for health care is highly inelastic, that is, it responds only imprecisely to variations in price. If you have the money to pay for a life-saving operation you are likely to pay for it irrespective of the cost. In addition the health professionals (doctors, nurses and so on) are in a good position to organise and negotiate higher wages. This is what has happened in the United States where health care accounts for 16 per cent of GDP.

In Britain, the Government is, in effect, a monopoly supplier and employer of health services and labour, so it has been able to hold costs down through rationing and central financial controls. An ageing and more demanding public has, however, greatly increased the pressure for more spending on health, which will almost certainly rise steadily in the future. Given the constraints on the NHS, increasing numbers of the more affluent have turned to private health care.

These problems have shifted the emphasis in health care from *curing* illness to *preventing* illness.

Institutions and actors

As can be inferred from the above, health care professionals have always been intimately involved in the politics of health care. Expertise is so crucial in this policy area that their involvement – and co-operation – is crucial. The Department of Health and its predecessors have also been a key actor, because of its intimate links with the institutional structure of the NHS. Until the 1990s, change came only slowly to the system, in part because of the entrenched power of professionals and in particular hospital doctors.

The public's role has also been crucial, not in terms of the day-to-day management of the system, but in terms of what has always been a strong public commitment to free universal health care. Conservative reforms were condemned by the Opposition as 'back door privatisation'. This was the worst possible criticism in the British context. In fact only dental care has effectively been privatised. Moves towards market-like transactions have changed the culture of the NHS but not who pays for NHS services (the taxpayer). The Labour critique was enough to disturb the electorate, however, and almost certainly contributed to the Conservative Government's defeat in 1997.

As in so many other areas, the role of local governments in health care has all but vanished, while central financial controls have strengthened.

New Labour Policy

Although, in opposition, Labour promised to abolish the NHS internal market, on coming to power they proved reluctant to implement a wholesale abolition. They are likely to make an attempt to cut bureaucracy and encourage centres of excellence. The stronger links between GPs and hospital consultants which the Conservative reforms encouraged are likely to be consolidated. In other words, Labour endorses the changed management and operating culture of the service and, like the Conservatives, is committed to maintaining free state-provided health care for the vast majority of the population.

EDUCATION

While, historically, Britain has long been regarded as a world leader in the public provision of health care, it has never been regarded as a great innovator in the provision of state education. Unlike in many countries, including France and the United States, elite secondary education has traditionally been provided by the private rather than public sector (through the perversely named public school system). Not until the passage of the 1944 Education Act did the central Government assume full responsibility for universal free primary and secondary education up to the age of 15 (16 from 1971). Since 1944 education policy has revolved around two related themes: comprehensive versus selective education, and the relationship between educational standards and the management and funding of schools. We will add a note on higher education following a discussion of these two points.

To select or not to select?

The 1944 Act formally recognised three different sorts of secondary schools: grammar for the academically gifted, modern for the mass of the population and, in some areas, technical for those with vocational skills. Very soon secondary modern schools assumed a low status and grammar schools high status. Critics pointed to the fact that entry to grammar schools, decided on by an examination at the age of 11, was closely correlated with social class. Liberal-minded Conservative ministers and local politicians were among such critics. When elected in 1964, the Labour Government pledged to reform the system by introducing one sort of school, the neighbourhood or community comprehensive, which would cater for all abilities. In October 1965 local authorities were instructed to draw up plans for the reorganisation of education by introducing comprehensive schools and, once re-elected in 1974, Labour made the change mandatory. The resulting change in school type is shown in Table 26.3.

While comprehensive schools made sense in rural areas where the provision of two sorts of schools was not viable, the reforms proved highly controversial in many urban and suburban communities. Many Conservative-controlled

Table 26.3 School pupils by type of school, 1970/71–95/96

United Kingdom					Thousands
	1970/1971	**1980/1981**	**1990/1991**	**1994/1995**	**1995/1996**
Public sector schools					
Nursery	50	89	105	85	84
Primary	5,902	5,171	4,955	5,255	5,335
Secondary modern	1,164	233	94	90	79
Grammar	673	149	156	184	182
Comprehensive	1,313	3,730	2,844	3,093	3,130
Other secondary	403	434	300	289	280
All public sector schools	9,507	9,806	8,433	8,996	9,096
Non-maintained schools					
Pupils aged 10 and under	238	n.a.	266	262	268
Pupils aged 11 and over	383	n.a.	347	338	335
All non-maintained schools	621	619	613	600	603
Special schools	103	148	114	116	114
All schools	10,230	10,572	9,180	8,714	9,813

Source: *Social Trends 27* (London: The Stationery Office, 1997), Table 3.4

authorities refused to comply, although the vast majority adopted the new system. In 1979 the new Conservative Government removed the directive and later actively encouraged authorities to maintain grammar schools.

The crucial issues in this debate were parent choice and educational standards. On the right, commentators argued that comprehensive schools drawing on poorer communities tended to develop a culture of underachievement. Gifted children from such areas were not given the chance to develop their potential as they had no choice but to attend 'dump' schools. Worse, according to the right, a new cohort of teachers infused with egalitarian educational notions were aggravating this culture of underachievement by emphasising children's development as personalities rather than as individuals trained in essential skills. Right-wing think-tanks such as the Institute for Economic Affairs and the Adam Smith Institute became increasingly vocal during the 1970s and were beginning to influence expert and political (Conservative) opinion.

The Conservatives were also keen to encourage private education and in 1980 introduced an Assisted Places Scheme which gave a small number of lower income parents a subsidised place for their child at an elite private school. Although highly controversial at the time, the scheme has remained small in cost and scope.

Standards and management

As with health care, debate moved forward rapidly during the 1980s to revolve around the question of the individual incentives of teachers and managers in the educational system. Local authorities were the traditional managers of education but the Conservatives became increasingly critical of their management standards. In two Education Acts, one passed in 1986 and the other in 1988, the Government devolved the day-to-day management of schools to school governing bodies. It also allowed schools to opt out of local authority control altogether and be maintained directly by central Government.

In combination these laws increased the power of 'managers' over educational 'professionals'. Boards of governors, which include elected parent governors, hire and fire, and manage school finances. Increasingly they have to conform to central financial directives and to central performance indicators. A national curriculum is now in place requiring pupils to study English, maths and science and seven foundation subjects. League tables on examination performance are widely published and classroom teachers are formally assessed and graded. Parents can now make comparisons between schools and, in theory at least, can choose which is best for their child. As with health care, these reforms have had good and bad consequences. By most criteria, educational attainment is improving. However, the pressures on teachers have been considerable – many have taken early retirement – and serious doubts exist as to the competence and motives of some school governors.

Higher education

Higher education escaped major reform until the 1990s. Since the Second World War, free higher education has been available to all those able to get a place at university, with maintenance grants available on a means-tested basis. Until the 1960s, when higher education was greatly expanded, this meant that a tiny minority (under 3 per cent) of 18-year-olds enjoyed university education. Expansion in the 1960s was not accompanied by any reform, so the system became increasingly expensive. Cuts in the real value of the maintenance grant helped, but were insufficient to prevent the system from experiencing a serious fiscal crisis when further expansion occurred from the late 1980s onwards. The Government instituted much tighter central controls through a newly created quango, the University Funding Council. By the mid-1990s it was clear that, for the system to survive in the absence of greatly increased funding, students would have to make some contribution towards the cost of their education. The Conservatives were already drawing up plans to this effect before their defeat in 1997. Once elected Labour promptly announced the introduction of a limited fee for all students with rebates for those on a low income.

Institutions and actors

Education is not unlike health in that it is an area where expertise is at a premium. As a result educational professionals have always been important actors in the system. Local governments, too, were important players until the Conservative reforms of the 1980s. Today, school boards of governors have assumed a new importance but they are subject to increasingly close central control. Teachers too are now more circumscribed both in the ways in which they teach, and in their role in day-to-day management. Parents, in spite of the rhetoric of 'empowerment' contained in various educational reforms, remain more passive than active actors in the system. Unlike parents in the American system, for example, they have no direct say in the financing of schools.

Again as with health, the most important decision-making institutions operate in central Government. For it is the Department for Education that sets the financial priorities and monitors school and teacher performance.

New Labour Policy

It would be misleading to talk of a consensus on education policy between the major parties on educational matters, but much more agreement exists than might be expected. Labour is committed to abolishing the Assisted Places Scheme, but the scheme is a minor part of the system. Selective schools will remain, as will the freedom to opt out. Indeed, Labour wants to persuade many middle-class parents to shift from private to state education, which can only be done by improving some state schools. In effect it means raising the standards of the better schools which implies more, rather than less, differentiation in the system.

Local governments will not be given back their management role and performance indicators will remain, so what does distinguish Labour from Conservative? It seems likely that Labour will invest more in training and vocational education and will place even more emphasis than did the Conservatives on management and leadership in individual schools. Finally, while opposed to an extension of formal selection via the 11 plus, Labour favours subject specialisation by school. Excellence in, say, music or sport will be encouraged and may become a major factor in parental choice.

In sum, however, these party differences are small. Labour's thinking on education at the century's end owes a great deal to the Conservative reforms of the 1980s and 1990s.

ESSAYS

1. Why did Britain create a welfare state during the 1940s? What remains of the original welfare state design?

2. In what ways has income maintenance become more selective over the last 25 years? What role do you think the state should play in income maintenance?

3. What role, if any, should the private sector play in *either* health *or* education? What are the major differences between the Blair Government and its Conservative predecessors in this area?

4. Outline the changes in housing policy since 1946. Why has there been such a dramatic shift from public to private provision in this period?

SUMMARY

This chapter has summarised the major changes in social policy which have occurred since the inception of the welfare state.

- In all the areas under discussion a move from universalism to selectivism has occurred. More recently, the main values underpinning reform attempts have shifted from those associated with managerial efficiency to those associated with the discipline of the market.

- More and more, policy takes heed of the personal incentives of individual actors and how reforms can harness individual incentives to particular ends such as reduced costs and improved quality in health care or education. Even in income maintenance, this transformation is under way with the prospect that private pensions and workfare will replace universal flat-rate benefits in the longer term.

- While differences between Labour and the Conservatives remain, there are few fundamental differences between the parties in most social policy areas. New Labour is committed to the state employing market-like solutions to a range of problems. In housing, the private sector is now accepted as the main provider. Income maintenance benefits are likely to become increasingly selective. Education and health will remain predominantly state-provided services for the foreseeable future, but in both areas market-like transactions will progressively replace hierarchical bureaucratic relationships.

- In terms of the institutions and actors involved in policy, central Government ministers and bureaucracies will continue to dominate, while the independent influence of professionals (doctors, teachers and the like) will likely decline.

- The unanswered question, however, relates to the power of the consumer, that is, the patient, client or parent. Reforms have promised consumer 'empowerment'. It remains to be seen whether reforms will empower the public or merely result in increased central control over the quality and price of services.

MILESTONES

MILESTONES IN POSTWAR SOCIAL POLICY

1944–49 Foundation of the welfare state

1952 Conservatives introduce charges for prescriptions and optical and dental treatment

1965 Directive calls for local authorities to draw up plans for comprehensive education

1966 Supplementary Benefits replace National Assistance

1971 School leaving age increased to 16

1972 Means-tested rent rebate scheme provides assistance to tenants in public and private sectors

1974 National insurance contributions are earnings-related. Pension increases are linked to prices or earnings, whichever is the greater

1974 Health Service reorganised. Regional and area health authorities created to co-ordinate family, hospital and community care

1975 Local education authorities directed to implement comprehensive school plans

1977 Child Allowances replaced with Child Benefit. Benefit is available to all children, with increased rate for single parents

1978 State Earnings Related Pensions Scheme (SERPS) links pensions to earnings

1980 Pensions linked to prices only, thus reducing their relative value

1980 Assisted places scheme introduced. Local authorities given right to keep selective schools

1981 Local authority tenants given the right to buy their homes. Incentive to buy is further strengthened in 1986 and 1988

1981 Housing Benefit available to provide subsidies for rent and rates

1982 Earnings-related supplements to unemployment benefit abolished. Unemployment benefits taxable

1983 NHS reforms creates district health authorities as main management units in the system

1986 and 1988 Education Acts. Day-to-day management of schools devolved to school governors. Schools given the choice to opt out of local authority control. National curriculum introduced

1988 Family Credit introduced to encourage families on income support to work

1989 Government ends subsidies for council housing. Local authorities required to set economic rents, with Housing Assistance for the needy

1991 and 1993 Major NHS reforms. Service divided into providers and purchasers. Regional authorities abolished. Central financial controls strengthened

1997 Labour Government announces introduction of tuition fees in higher education

PROJECTS

1. Evaluate the moves towards market-like transactions *either* in health care *or* education over the last 15 years. Illustrate your answer with reference to a school or hospital trust with which you are familiar.

2. What are the main economic problems associated with the future of *either* pensions *or* health care? Illustrate your answer with international comparisons.

3. Imagine that you have been given the brief of providing a plan for low income housing in your city or community. How would you use existing housing programmes to help the needy? Which *new* programmes, if any, do you think are necessary to solve housing problems?

FURTHER READING

A good analysis of the relationship between social class and benefits in the welfare state is provided by Robert Goodin and Julian Le Grand, *Not Only the Poor: The Middle Classes and the Welfare State* (London: Allen and Unwin, 1987). On the redistributive effects of the welfare state, see A. B. Atkinson, *Incomes and the Welfare State* (Cambridge: Cambridge University Press, 1996). On the politics of welfare, see Nicholas Deakin, *The Politics of Welfare* (Hemel Hempstead: Harvester Wheatsheaf, 1994). On health, see Rudolph Klein, *The New Politics of the NHS* (Harlow: Longman, 3rd edn 1995) and Judith Allsop, *Health Policy and the NHS: Towards 2000* (Harlow: Longman, 2nd edn 1995). On housing see P. Malpass (ed.), *Reshaping Housing Policy* (London: Routledge, 1990). A historical account of housing policy is provided by Brian Lund, *Housing Problems and Housing Policy* (Harlow: Longman, 1996). On recent changes in education, see Education Group II, *Education Limited: Schooling, Training and the New Right in England Since 1979* (London: Unwin Hyman, 1991).

http://www.awl-he.com/politics/newbritpol

Internet resources – visit *The New British Politics* Webpage for links to a specially-chosen selection of Internet resources relevant to this Chapter.

http://www.awl-he.com/politics/newbritpol

Equal opportunities

In contrast to the original objectives of the welfare state, which emphasised equality of condition in the provision of a wide range of benefits, policies designed to provide equal opportunity for women, ethnic minorities and other disadvantaged groups, must by definition be selective in scope. When legislation was first enacted in this area during the 1940s it was concerned with discrimination against disabled people. Since then it has been widened to embrace discrimination based on race and gender. The political salience of the issue has varied over time, and since the first legislation was passed the values underpinning public policy have changed very substantially. The chapter will outline the main legislative changes and will evaluate the effectiveness of the law in this important area. The actors and institutions involved will also be discussed and some basic data on inequality in Britain today are presented. The chapter examines:

- Some problems of definition associated with equal opportunity

- Inequality and discrimination in Britain

- Legislation to help the disabled

- Race relations

- Equal rights for women

- The future of equal opportunity legislation

Key term

Discrimination – the practice of distinguishing (usually in order to disadvantage) between individuals or social groups on grounds or criteria (such as race, religion, gender, or colour) which are not relevant to circumstances.

EQUAL OPPORTUNITY: A POLITICAL AND SEMANTIC MINEFIELD?

Equal opportunity laws are designed to reduce entrenched inequalities in society. They have come about because the income, employment, housing and educational conditions pertaining to certain social groups are persistently inferior to those of the general population. Such inequalities may result directly from *discrimination* which in turn may be *overt, covert* or *structural*. Typically, overt discrimination is easy to identify and to eradicate. Advertisements for rental housing stating 'no coloureds' – not unusual in the UK during the 1950s and early 1960s – can be identified quickly and proscribed by law. Covert discrimination is more difficult to deal with. Estate agents may have a stated policy of non-discrimination, but a tacit understanding between renter and agent might exclude minority applicants. Structural discrimination is the most problematical of all. To continue with the housing analogy, during the 1960s and 1970s many local authorities used ' housekeeping standards' as one of the criteria for eligibility for council housing. Some ethnic minorities failed to meet the prescribed standard, which was culturally biased in favour of white families.

Some feminists argue that a typical example of structural discrimination today applies in science education. Very few women enrol on engineering and science undergraduate courses and even fewer on postgraduate courses. As a result, there are very few female engineers and scientists in the job market. But the problem stems not from discrimination at entry, but from the fact that few women choose school or university courses in these areas. This may be the exercise of free choice or it may be that biases in the system discourage women from pursuing 'male' subjects and instead direct them into the more 'female' arts and humanities.

Problems with gender discrimination are sometimes rooted in biological differences. Until quite recently (and very recently indeed as far as the armed forces are concerned), pregnancy was an adequate basis for dismissal from a job. As a result, few women were able to build continuous and successful careers unless they remained childless. In order to deal with such problems, governments have legislated to ban discrimination and provide for equal opportunity.

Few subjects arouse so much passion. There are a number of reasons for this. First, policies designed to redress discrimination against the disadvantaged must focus on the circumstances of social *groups* as well as *individuals*. Because a group (e.g. women) as a whole is disadvantaged does not of course mean that all members of that group are disadvantaged. As a result, group-based antidiscrimination policies are often criticised for 'favouring' women or minorities over males or whites. This problem is particularly acute in a society where liberal, rather than collectivist, values are well established. Many of the values which make up our society are based on the worth of the individual. Individual merit or worth, not membership of a particular group, should, we believe, determine rewards. Equal opportunity policies, however well intentioned, are often difficult to reconcile with such beliefs (see Briefing 27.1).

A second and related problem concerns the nature and level of the Government's response to inequality and discrimination. Laws may be designed to combat overt discrimination or they may also tackle structural discrimination. They may go even further and attempt to reverse the effects of a long-established pattern of discrimination. In the United States such laws are called *affirmative action* measures. Their objective is to allow women and minorities to 'catch up' with whites and males. Typically they apply in employment and education and involve the use of quotas and 'balancing' to ensure that workplaces, schools and universities hire or enrol women and minorities in proportion to their numbers in the local or national population. British governments have eschewed affirmative action measures as unfair to equally qualified individuals who are not members of disadvantaged groups.

Key term

Affirmative action (positive discrimination) – policies designed to provide groups with redress for a past pattern of discrimination. Such policies often take the form of legal requirements that organisations should take positive steps to increase their numbers of minority groups.

BRIEFINGS

27.1 LIBERALISM AND EQUAL OPPORTUNITY

One of the most difficult problems associated with equal opportunity policy is reconciling rules and regulations designed to assist social *groups* with the fact that in liberal societies each citizen's worth is measured in terms of *individual* merit. When we apply for a job or a place in university we assume that what determines success is our qualifications or A level scores, not membership of a particular social group. Liberal values are offended by those collective notions of worth which prevail (or have prevailed) in some Muslim states where gender or religion determines access to employment and education, or in South Africa under apartheid where race determined access.

When there has been a long-established pattern of discrimination, however, some argue that society has a duty to seek redress for past transgressions through the use of *affirmative action*. Affirmative action can, however, mean a number of things. It can mean the use of race or gender quotas where a minimum number of places is reserved for, say, entry to a university. In such a situation it is possible that the best qualified of the minority group will have qualifications inferior to those of the majority group. In the USA the courts have effectively banned quotas of this sort, arguing that they constitute a violation of the equal protection of the law guaranteed by the Constitution. As problematical are affirmative action measures which adopt a general policy of favouring particular social groups without specifying numbers. These too have been under attack from the Courts, although their exact legal status remains unclear.

Affirmative action is often used interchangeably with the term *positive discrimination*, or the application of policies which discriminate in favour of some social groups. Generally, positive discrimination is used to create a 'level playing field' for the disadvantaged. It could apply, for example, to the provision of special English language classes for non-native speakers, or special educational help for children from poor areas. In other words it involves policies which allow certain groups to 'catch up' with the general population through special training and education.

In Britain, the use of affirmative action is rare. British anti-discrimination laws take the individual, not the group, as the basic unit, and the law's objective is to provide redress for demonstrable grievances against individuals, rather than reverse a pattern of discrimination against groups. However, there is a limited form of affirmative action for the employment of the disabled, and in one form or another positive discrimination has been a part of British social policy for many years.

The Labour Party has, however, employed affirmative action through its use of 'Emily's List' or the idea that women-only short lists for the selection of candidates should be adopted in some constituencies. By late 1997 the reforms instigated by William Hague in the Conservative Party involved similar measures for the selection of Conservative candidates.

Plate 27.1 Steve Fricker cartoon in the *Daily Telegraph*, 5 June 1997: Harriet Harman's appointment as Minister for Women signifies either girl power or tokenism

These intra-party reforms apart, British equal opportunities policy has developed incrementally. Even today it is incomplete, as the evidence on income and jobs shows. Let us examine this before we proceed to a discussion of the politics of equal opportunity legislation.

INEQUALITY AND DISCRIMINATION IN BRITAIN

All societies display a degree of wealth and income inequality. *Equality of condition*, or the same income and wealth for all, is clearly an impossibility. Most societies attempt to achieve *equality of treatment*, meaning that the same rules and standards apply to all social groups. Equality of treatment is similar to *equality of opportunity*, the main difference being the emphasis on rules guaranteeing equality of treatment rather than emphasising individuals' circumstances, which is implicit in equality of opportunity.

In fact there can never be complete equality of opportunity given individuals' widely varying inherited, home and educational backgrounds. Equality of opportunity should, therefore, be seen as an ideal goal rather than an absolute. Equality of treatment is more achievable. Rules and regulations can be standardised so that, in theory at least, all citizens are treated equally.

This distinction helps us separate out all those economic differences and inequalities which derive from employment, educational and geographic factors, from those that derive from overt, covert or structural discrimination.

Of course, in reality, discrimination may be practised against almost anyone including poor whites and the old. But our natural sense of justice is most offended by systematic and institutionalised discrimination against ethnic minorities, women and the disabled. Hence the liberal conscience was outraged at

Key term

Equality of condition – the ideal objective of providing all citizens with equal access to income, wealth, education, employment, and other aspects of social life.

Key term

Equality of treatment – the application of the same rules and standards to all individuals and social groups.

Key term

Equality of opportunity – the practice of ensuring that individuals compete on equal terms for goods, benefits and life chances, such as education, employment, or housing, even though the outcome may be unequal.

apartheid in South Africa or segregation in the American South. Similar feelings are aroused by the treatment of women in some fundamentalist Muslim states.

Measuring discrimination is difficult, to say the least. By definition, covert discrimination is not measurable and, while we may be able to identify the rules and procedures which make up structural discrimination, we can rarely measure the effects of such rules accurately.

What we can do is identify income inequalities by social group. Britain has a sizeable ethnic minority community. As can be seen from Table 27.1 almost 6 per cent of the population consists of ethnic minorities. While the definition of 'ethnic minority' is highly contentious, the categories itemised in Table 27.1 are those recognised by the Government as constituting minority groups. Note that, the Chinese population apart, ethnic minorities in Britain are much younger than the general population. As a result their numbers are likely to increase proportionately over time irrespective of future immigration patterns.

Table 27.2 shows the extent of income inequality among ethnic minorities in Great Britain. Note the very dramatic concentration of low incomes among the Pakistani/Bangladeshi population and the generally lower incomes of other ethnic groups. In fact these figures are worse than they appear when geographic location is taken into account. Most of the British minority population is concentrated in London and the Midlands where incomes are relatively high. Very few live in some of the lowest income areas: Northern Ireland, the North East, Merseyside

Table 27.1 Population by ethnic group and age, spring 1996

Great Britain	Under 16	16–34	35–54	55 and over	Total of all ages (thousands)	Ethnic groups as a percentage of total populatltion
White	20	27	27	26	52,942	94.1
Black Caribbean	23	36	24	17	477	.08
Black African	28	43	23	6	281	.05
Other Black	49	38	12	?	117	.02
Indian	27	32	29	12	877	1.6
Pakistani	40	33	19	8	579	1.0
Bangladeshi	40	35	17	8	183	.03
Chinese	16	40	30	15	126	.02
Other Asian	27	31	36	6	161	.03
Other ethnic minorities[1]	51	30	15	5	506	.09
All ethnic minorities	–	–	–	–	3,307	5.9
All ethnic groups[2]	21	27	27	25	56,267	100%

Source: *Social Trends 27* (London: HMSO, 1997), Table 1.8
Note: [1] Includes those of mixed origin
    [2] Includes ethnic group not stated

BRIEFINGS

27.2 DEFINING ETHNIC MINORITIES IN BRITAIN

Over the years, both the official and unofficial labels attached to Britain's ethnic minority population have changed considerably. During the 1950s and 1960s 'immigrant' and 'coloured' were used almost interchangeably. Both are condescending. 'Coloured' has passed from the official vocabulary and 'immigrant' is obviously inappropriate for the majority of the ethnic population born in Britain. Later, the Census used the coded term BPBNC or Both Parents Born New Commonwealth to distinguish 'black' from 'white' immigrants and their descendants. The official labels in use today are reproduced in Table 27.1. While these are more accurate and sensitive, they remain very broad categories. The use of the term 'black' is gradually being replaced by the hyphenated 'Afro-'. Using 'black' as a shorthand for *all* ethnic minorities is also passing from the political vocabulary. Of course, no-one is literally black, any more than anyone is literally white. In reality, the minority population is extraordinarily heterogeneous in its origins. West Indian or Afro-Caribbean includes people from very different island cultures. Indian applies to all those from a vast and complex medley of cultures, religions and languages. Only the Chinese population is relatively homogeneous, the vast majority having originally come from Hong Kong.

Even these distinctions can be offensive, for most of Britain's ethnic minorities have been born in Britain and are as British as the Royal Family or anyone else. By many measures the Welsh, Irish and Scots are also 'minorities', but Catholics in Northern Ireland apart, their treatment is not a political issue because they suffer from little discernible discrimination.

Labels are, however, a necessary evil. If discrimination and inequality are to be identified and dealt with it is necessary to collect the relevant statistics.

Key term
New Commonwealth – a coded term used to refer to non-white Commonwealth countries.

and the Glasgow area. Only in what used to be the textile towns of Lancashire and Yorkshire is there a congruence of high minority population and generally low local incomes.

Table 27.2 Distribution of disposable income by ethnic groups, 1994–95

	Quintile group of individuals Percentages	
	Bottom fifth	**Top four-fifths**
White	19	81
Black	27	73
Indian	27	73
Pakistani/Bangladeshi	64	36
Other ethnic minorities	36	64
All ethnic groups	20	80

Source: *Social Trends 27* (London: Stationery Office, 1997), Figure 5.20

Figure 27.1 Unemployment
rate annual averages by
gender, 1970–97

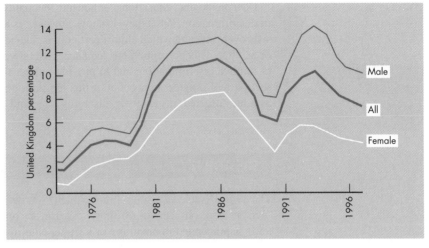

Figure 27.1 Unemployment
rate annual averages by
gender, 1970–97

Source: *Labour Market Trends*, November 1996, Table 2.1

Key term

Disposable income –
more often known as 'take-
home pay', disposable
income refers to income
after taxes have been
paid.

Income inequality by gender is less pronounced. Generally, unemployment
among women is lower than among men, although woman make up a smaller percentage of the labour force (44 per cent in 1996, up from 38 per cent in 1971). In fact,
as unemployment rose during the 1980s and 1990s so the proportion of male unemployed increased markedly (Figure 27.1). These figures disguise what has been a
large increase in lower paid, often part-time employment among women in recent
years. In the decade 1986 to 1996 part-time female workers increased by 18 per
cent to 5.3 million. Only 1.2 million men are in part-time jobs. As far as full-time
employment is concerned, women are concentrated at the lower end of the earnings scale (Figure 27.2) with more than half earning less than £250 a week in 1996.

Figure 27.2 Average gross
earnings per week by
gender, April 1996

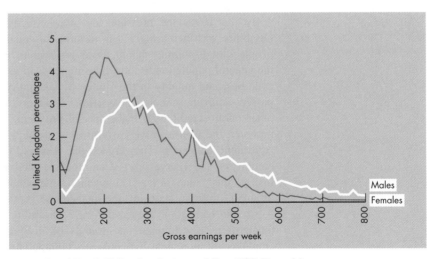

Source: *Social Trends 27* (London: Stationery Office, 1997) Figure 5.9

Data on income, educational or housing inequality in no way prove the existence of discrimination. What they do show, however, is a pattern of inequality that persists over time and which almost certainly is related to discrimination in one form or another. This perception has led successive governments to legislate to reduce or remove discrimination, and to provide redress for aggrieved parties. The next section will provide an account of this legislation and the politics surrounding it as it has affected, respectively, disability, race and gender.

DISABILITY

The 1944 Disabled Persons (Employment) Act defined a disabled individual as a 'person who, on account of injury, disease or congenital deformity, is substantially handicapped in obtaining or keeping employment'. Disabled people could, voluntarily, register under the act and, as amended in 1958, the act required employers of more than 20 people to employ a 3 per cent quota of registered disabled people. This law was widely flouted: employers could apply for exemption, and it was poorly enforced. Worse, the legislation did nothing to change the environment in which disabled people worked. Instead it assumed that disability was a permanent handicap and employers should patronise disabled people's condition by giving them 'suitable' work. Car park and passenger lift attendants were officially identified as the most appropriate work for the disabled!

By 1970 attitudes towards disability were changing and the Chronically Sick and Disabled Persons Act of that year placed on local authorities a duty to see to the general needs of the disabled. Under the act authorities are obliged to identify the local disabled population and to provide them with help. The act was well intentioned. But the actual provision of such things as suitable housing, home helps and the adaptation of facilities to the needs of the disabled was to be financed by limited local authority budgets. Local authority finances were increasingly hard pressed from the mid-1970s onwards and, as a result, provision was patchy and incomplete.

By the 1990s the pressure for more effective legislation was mounting. Disability was increasingly seen in terms of equal opportunity. In other words, people with disabilities should, as far as possible, be given access equal to that of the general population to jobs, housing, education and public facilities. In other countries, and notably in the United States and Australia, legislation had been passed *requiring* schools, universities, employers, and providers of transport and other public facilities to make special provisions for the disabled. In Britain, however, the Conservative Governments of the 1990s proved reluctant to pass equivalent legislation. They argued that it would prove an expensive burden on employers and (perversely) would be resented by the disabled themselves. Instead, they opted for legislation which, although it strengthened the rights of the disabled, fell far short of the mandatory provisions of the American and Australian legislation. Hence the 1995 Disability Discrimination Act makes it unlawful to discriminate on grounds of disability in employment; requires employers of more than 20 people to accommodate the needs of the disabled; and establishes a right of access for the disabled in transport, higher education and some other areas.

Table 27.3 Recipients of benefits for sick and disabled people

Great Britain	1981–82	1986–87	1991–92	Thousands 1994–95
Long-term sick and people with disabilities				
Invalidity benefit/severe disablement allowance	826	1,228	1,741	2,115
One of the above benefits plus income support	103	146	240	335
Income support only	n.a.	n.a.	229	425
Short-term sick				
Sickness benefit only	393	110	138	127
Sickness benefit and income support	24	16	28	40
Income support only			79	87
Disability living allowance or attendance allowance[1]	582	1,113	1,758	2,562

Note: [1] Attendance allowance and mobility allowance before April 1992
Source: *Social Trends 27* (London: HMSO, 1997), Table 8.19

The law also created a National Disability Council to provide advice on freeing the disabled from discrimination. Crucially, however, a number of loopholes in the law made most of its provisions advisory rather than compulsory. For example there is no requirement that newly built restaurants, pubs or cinemas provide access and toilet facilities for the disabled. Many do, but equally many do not.

This issue is likely to increase in importance during the next few years, partly because the number of disabled is increasing (Table 27.3) and partly because advocates on behalf of the disabled have become more effective and vocal. In the parliamentary debates on legislation for the disabled, the Labour Opposition was always more supportive of compulsion in the law than were the Conservatives. It remains to be seen how far the Blair Government will go in extending existing legislation in this direction. Interestingly, the European Union has been much less active in issuing directives in this area than it has over discrimination based on gender. This is one area, therefore, where the potential exists for the British to take a lead in providing for the disabled throughout the EU.

RACE

Race has been an important issue in British politics at least since the 1950s. For much of the nineteenth and early twentieth centuries Britain had the reputation as a haven for those subject to religious and political persecution in other European countries. Until the First World War, immigration controls were minimal and successive waves of Jews, socialists and Marxists settled in Britain during these years. Their numbers were, however, relatively small. Overt discrimination against Jews, which had become commonplace in many Continental countries during the 1930s, was relatively rare in Britain. After the Second World War a further wave of refugees arrived in Britain from the Continent. Again, numbers were limited (by official policy) and again these groups of Jews, Poles and other Eastern Europeans were assimilated with relative ease.

In 1948 the Labour Government passed the British Nationality Act which allowed Commonwealth citizens to settle in the UK. The assumption was that, with decolonisation, a new Commonwealth of Nations sharing the language and common traditions could move freely from one state to the other. At the time, it was not expected to result in mass immigration. The citizens of the 'White Commonwealth' – Australia, New Zealand, Canada – enjoyed high living standards and had little incentive to migrate to Britain. Citizens of the 'Black Commonwealth', including newly independent India, rarely had the economic resources to migrate to what was a very distant land. During the 1950s, however, the British economy suffered from shortages of unskilled labour and some employers such as London Transport actively recruited cheap unskilled labour from the West Indies and elsewhere. By the late 1950s the numbers of immigrants from the West Indies and the Indian subcontinent had increased substantially. Racist attitudes were widespread, as was discrimination. In 1958 a race riot in the Notting Hill area of London raised the political salience of the issue.

Unrestricted entry of Commonwealth citizens ceased in 1962 with the passage of the Commonwealth Immigrant's Act. Thereafter, all Commonwealth citizens were subject to immigration control except those holding British passports issued in Britain. A system of work vouchers was created which had to be issued by employers before entry was permitted.

Overt discrimination against immigrants (at the time generally called 'coloureds') was commonplace and was not proscribed until the passage of the 1965 Race Relations Act. As amended in 1968, this law banned 'whites only' advertising, prohibited discrimination in housing and employment and set up a Race Relations Board to mediate disputes concerning discrimination. Most commentators agree that the 1960s legislation was minimalist in scope. Conciliation rarely worked and large areas such as education were excluded from the law.

A much more effective law was passed in 1976 (the Race Relations Act) which banned direct and indirect discrimination in employment, education, public facilities and housing. The definition of discrimination was expanded to include nationality, citizenship and ethnic origin, and a Commission for Racial Equality (the CRE) was established to receive and process complaints. The CRE was instructed to tackle both direct and indirect discrimination and to refer unresolved complaints to an industrial tribunal for settlement.

Although the 1976 law was a great improvement on earlier legislation, the CRE's powers are quite limited. It cannot take on 'class' actions or complaints about discrimination against whole groups of complainants as opposed to individuals, its sanctions under law are limited and difficult to enforce, and its operations have been consistently underfunded. Part of its brief was to advise governments on how best the law might be improved. This it has done, but none of the Conservative Governments in the 1979 to 1997 period acted on its advice.

Against this background of antidiscrimination law, the politics of race changed dramatically from 1968 to 1997. During the 1960s, race became an important electoral issue, especially following the Conservative frontbench spokesman, Enoch Powell's 1968 'rivers of blood' speech. Powell likened the effects of immigration in Britain to the excesses of ancient Rome: 'As I look ahead I am filled with foreboding. Like the Roman, I seem to see the River Tiber foaming with much blood'. Although he was immediately sacked from the Shadow Cabinet, Powell's views were not unpopular in many parts of the country. He persisted with his scaremongering tactics and later called for a stop to all immigration, accompanied by compulsory repatriation.

> **Key term**
>
> **Racism** – the practice of discriminating between individuals or groups on racial grounds.

During the 1970s and the 1980s a racial element emerged in electoral politics. In a number of West Midlands seats race was a factor in determining electoral outcomes. As Leader of the Opposition, Margaret Thatcher said in 1978 that she understood that the 'British character' might be 'swamped' by immigrants from different cultures. And although overt cultural nationalism – some might say racism – of this kind was rare, it was apparent to most in the minority communities that the Conservative governments were at best lukewarm supporters of an enhanced state role in fighting discrimination.

A further incident in 1992 confirmed in the minds of many minority voters that some local Conservative parties held unacceptable racial views. In Cheltenham a highly qualified black candidate, John Taylor, was nominated to fight the parliamentary seat. However, he was confirmed only after an unseemly row in the local party where overt racist views were expressed. Only national publicity and pressure from Central Office facilitated Taylor's nomination. He was subsequently defeated in the general election.

Although the Conservative Party has always been identified as anti-immigrant, it has never come remotely close to endorsing discrimination and has usually been quick to condemn overtly racist attitudes and actions. Far-right parties, such as the National Front, which have racist platforms, have had very limited success in British politics. In the postwar period they have never won a parliamentary seat and have only won a few local elections. Indeed, in comparison with the major Continental states including France, Germany, Spain and Italy, Britain has no tradition of far-right political parties or far-right racist politics.

As was pointed out in Chapter 15, most ethnic minorities in Britain vote Labour. There is a class and a race element to this pattern in that minorities tend to have lower incomes. But more vote Labour than would be expected from this fact alone. In many inner city constituencies the ethnic vote has been crucial in swinging the result to Labour, so it is not surprising that as a party it has been more supportive of minority interests than have the Conservatives.

One major problem for the minority communities has been racially inspired violence by whites and a widespread perception that the police have been less than vigilant in stamping out racial attacks. Such attacks are common and should be considered a serious public order problem (see Briefing 27.3).

Antipathy towards police forces which have taken a less than firm hand in this area may help explain periodic outbreaks of rioting in British cities. These assumed serious proportions in the early 1980s and again in the early 1990s. In almost all cases, the rioting has centred around conflict between the police and ethnic minorities. As a result some police forces have instituted racial awareness programmes and have made special efforts to recruit minorities. Most commentators agree, however, that much remains to be done here.

BRIEFINGS

27.3 RACIAL HARASSMENT IN BRITAIN

Racial harassment is a serious and continuing phenomenon. The CRE defines racial harassment as verbal or physical violence towards individuals or groups on grounds of their colour, race, nationality, or ethnic or national origin, where the victims believe the aggression was racially motivated and/or there is evidence of racial motivation. Racial harassment includes attacks on property as well as people.

Levels of Harassment

- The British Crime Survey (BCS) estimated that in 1991 there were 130,000 racially motivated crimes, with nearly 89,000 against Asians and 41,000 against black groups. However, as the figure of 130,000 was based on a relatively small sample, the number of incidents could be as high as 170,000.

- Racial incidents are underreported to, and underrecorded by, the police. Pakistanis are least likely to report even serious threats to the police; only 15 per cent did so compared with 34 per cent of white and 50 per cent of Indian victims. In 1995–96, the police recorded 12,222 racial incidents in England and Wales, an increase of 3 per cent over the previous year. Four per cent of these involved serious physical violence.

- The great majority of victims are members of ethnic minority groups, with Asians the most vulnerable. Analysis of the combined 1988 and 1992 BCS data suggests that Pakistanis are the most vulnerable; nearly one-third (31 per cent) of all the crimes they had experienced had been racially motivated (compared with 18 per cent for Indians and 14 per cent for Afro-Caribbeans). For threats this rose to 72 per cent.

The Offenders

Racially motivated crimes against ethnic minorities were committed overwhelmingly by white offenders (98 per cent of those against Pakistanis, 93 per cent against Indians, and 87 per cent against Afro-Caribbeans). Men were responsible for the majority (about 80 per cent). Offenders aged 16–25 were responsible for over half the racially motivated incidents against Asians, and just over one-third of those against black people.

Assaults of any kind are covered by the existing criminal law, and most acts of racial harassment will constitute criminal offences under existing legislation. However, there is no specific offence of racial harassment in either criminal or civil law. Existing laws which can and should be used against perpetrators of these incidents include:

- Criminal Justice Act 1991
- Offences against the Person Act 1861
- Criminal Damage Act 1971
- Public Order Act 1986
- Criminal Justice and Public Order Act 1994
- Malicious Communications Act 1988
- Local Government Act 1972
- Race Relations Act 1976.

There has been a strong campaign to persuade the Government to give specific recognition to racial motivation in incidents of harassment and violence. Some, including the CRE, say that racial harassment should be a specific offence. Others say that existing laws are adequate. Racial motivation may be taken into account as an aggravating factor by courts when considering sentences. It is a matter of debate, however, whether judges should have a statutory duty to do so.

Source: Commission for Racial Equality as reproduced in Barbara Bagilhole, *Equal Opportunities and Social Policy* (Harlow: Longman, 1997), pp. 190–91

The condition of minorities in Britain is certainly not one of unrelieved gloom. Educational standards among Asian and Afro-Caribbean British are generally high. Intermarriage and cohabiting – often an indicator of good race relations – is also high as regards the Afro-Caribbean and the white population. Indeed, close to half of all Afro-Caribbean males have white partners. The 1997 intake of MPs included one per cent from ethnic minorities among their number, significantly up on the previous Parliament. Perhaps most importantly, throughout the long history of immigration into Britain, governments have never created a separate category of immigrant labour with a status inferior to that of the 'native' population. Once admitted, immigrants and their children have similar rights and privileges to other citizens. This is in contrast to countries such as Germany and Switzerland which have made extensive use of temporary migrant labour, many of whom enjoy very limited civil rights.

This is not to deny the existence of serious flaws in British immigration laws (see Briefing 27.4). All sorts of anomalies and restrictions exist and over the years governments of all political complexions have made migration to Britain more difficult. It is merely to state that the citizenship status of legal immigrants is better than in many European countries.

BRIEFINGS

27.4 IMMIGRATION LAW IN BRITAIN

Since the passage of the 1962 Commonwealth Immigrant's Act, British immigration law has gradually been tightened. In 1968 the law was changed specifically to withdraw the rights of African Asians to migrate to Britain following the granting of independence to the black majorities in East Africa. However, British citizens not born in the UK but with a parent or grandparent born in Britain (i.e. whites) could migrate to Britain. The 1971 Immigration Act abolished the work voucher system, so restricting future immigration to spouses and dependents. The law also strengthened the Government's powers of deportation.

The 1988 Immigration Act removed the right of men to be joined by dependents if they had entered the UK before the 1971 Act became effective in January 1973.

The British Nationality Act of 1981 effectively restricted immigration to those of British parents or parents settled in Britain. 'British' citizens not born in the UK and with no familial links to Britain were not permitted to settle in the UK. The vast majority of the population of Hong Kong were categorised thus.

The Refugee and Asylum Seekers Act 1996 made a distinction between 'economic' refugees, who were seeking a higher standard of living in Britain, and 'political' refugees fleeing political persecution. The Home Office draws up a list of countries eligible for political refugee status, which happens to exclude India and Pakistan. The act also denies social security and other benefits to those seeking asylum in Britain. Immigrant welfare groups condemned the law as discriminatory and leading to the break-up of families, especially those from the Indian subcontinent.

Finally it should be pointed out that, for all its flaws, Britain has a more extensive framework of antidiscrimination law than exists in most European countries. In marked contrast to its stand on gender discrimination, the EU has taken few initiatives in this area.

GENDER

Unlike race, gender has been on the political agenda for many generations. Equal pay for men and women working in the same job has been a trade union demand since the end of the nineteenth century, but it was not until 1970 that legislation was enacted to achieve this end. The Equal Pay Act of 1970 allowed women to claim equal pay if their work was of 'equal value' to that of men. This law was amended in 1983 to comply with an EC directive on equal pay which required equality of remuneration without a formal job evaluation of the work concerned and without regard to physical differences between the sexes.

In 1975 the Government acted to outlaw discrimination based on sex or marital status in employment, education, housing and public facilities. The law set up an Equal Opportunities Commission (EOC) to process complaints and refer them to industrial tribunals. As with the CRE, the EOC has limited enforcement powers, although its provisions have gradually been strengthened by European Community directives, particularly in the areas of social security and welfare.

Two major omissions in the law have been addressed in recent years. The first concerns maternity and pregnancy. European directives on maternity leave and pay were issued during the 1970s and 1980s but it was not until 1996 that these were formalised in law. Under the 1996 Employment Rights Act women have the right to paid time off both for antenatal care and after the birth of their child, with the right to return to work. The second omission concerns pension rights, which relate to the date of compulsory retirement, which typically is lower for women than for men. The Government has agreed to standardise these over time at 65. In addition, the law is being changed to allow divorced spouses a share of their former partners' pensions.

As with race, the political salience of equal rights for women has gradually increased over the years, although the women's movement in Britain has often been less vocal than in the USA and some Continental European countries. While overt discrimination in employment has been dramatically reduced, women continue to be at a disadvantage in relation to men in many workplace situations. Most senior administrative and managerial posts are held by men and women are greatly over-represented in lower paid part-time work. Sexual stereotyping in employment remains. How many students reading this text would assume they had got 'the secretary' if they phoned a college department and a man answered the phone?

With the election of a Labour administration with the largest Government and parliamentary representation of women ever, it is likely that women's issues will be given greater prominence over the next few years. Certainly, both in its response to EU directives and its stance on relevant British legislation, Labour has been more supportive of sex equality than were the Conservatives. Of all

> **Key term**
>
> **Stereotyping** – the practice of treating members of social groups as if they were all the same, often in a way which involves discrimination.

Figure 27.2 Matt cartoon in the *Daily Telegraph*, 3 June 1997: In the 'welfare-to-work' scheme Blair outlined plans to help jobless single parents by inviting them to attend job centres where they would receive advice on childcare, training and skills development.
Hector Breeze cartoon in the *Guardian*, 3 June 1997: encouraging single mothers back into the work place

'*I'm knitting a job application*'

women's issues, child care and the position of working mothers are likely to head the political agenda. Labour is committed to reforming the welfare system so as to encourage single mothers to work. Such initiatives will be difficult to achieve in the absence of state provision for child care. It remains to be seen how much money Labour is willing to devote to this important area.

THE POLITICS OF EQUAL OPPORTUNITY: WHAT DOES THE FUTURE HOLD?

> **Key term**
>
> **Political correctness** – a controversial term to describe the use of language about socially sensitive matters, such as race or gender, in a way which is designed not to give offence. Often the implication is that politically correct language is silly or absurd.

The above discussion demonstrates how attitudes have changed over time. Political discourse as it affects disability, race and gender is very different today from that prevailing in the 1970s, let alone the 1940s or 1950s. This is reflected in semantics in that we use a different language to describe the issues, and in behaviour in that discrimination is now relatively rare. Some argue that there has been a 'backlash' against tougher antidiscrimination laws. Certainly, disquiet has been expressed at what are often viewed as the strident demands of the 'politically correct'. And, as we saw in Chapter 19, a number of leftist local authorities were much derided during the 1970s and 1980s for what were considered their extreme policies in support of the disabled and sexual and other minorities.

The reality of inequality and discrimination in Britain is, however, that a framework of law was laid down in the 1970s which, although updated and amended since, in no way compares with the reach of the law in a number of other countries including the United States, the Netherlands and Australia. Many loopholes in our laws exist and discrimination on grounds of age and sexual orientation remains lawful. Given the changes that have occurred in the disability, gender and

ESSAYS

1. Why did Labour governments lay down a framework of equal opportunities law in the 1960s and 1970s? What accounts for the failure of the Conservatives subsequently to extend this framework?

2. Is there a case for affirmative action laws in Britain? Argue your case with respect to *either* race *or* gender *or* sexual orientation.

3. Write an account of the politics of immigration in Britain since 1948. How, if at all, should the existing immigration laws be amended?

4. Why is the provision of child care such an important issue in Britain today? What should be the proper role for government in this area?

race areas, it seems probable that these issues will be added to the agenda in due course. Meanwhile, the election of a Labour Government is likely to herald a generally more active official stance and stricter enforcement of existing anti-discrimination laws.

SUMMARY

- The provision of equal opportunity for women and disadvantaged minorities has become an important issue in British politics over the last 30 years. All the political parties support equal opportunity, but the Conservatives have trodden more cautiously in this area than have Labour. Indeed the framework of law that was laid down by Labour governments in the 1970s has remained largely unchanged since.

- Generally the British have eschewed affirmative action as a form of redress for past discrimination and have instead opted for redress based on proven individual grievances. Both the Commission for Racial Equality and the Equal Opportunities Commission operate on this basis.

- The framework of protective laws provided for ethnic minorities and the disabled in Britain, although flawed in many respects, compares favourably with that applicable in many European countries. Britain has tended to lag behind other EU states in the provision of equal opportunity for women, however.

- The political salience of the issue is likely to increase in the years ahead, in part because the Labour Government is likely to play a more proactive role, and in part because inequality and discrimination remain a serious disadvantage for many social groups.

MILESTONES

MILESTONES IN EQUAL OPPORTUNITIES POLICY

1944 and 1958 Disabled Persons Acts establish quotas for the employment of the disabled

1948 British Nationality Act allows access to the UK for Commonwealth citizens

1958 Notting Hill riots in London

1962 and 1968 Commonwealth Immigrants Acts restrict immigration, introduce work vouchers and deny access for African Asians

1968 Enoch Powell's 'rivers of blood' speech

1965 and 1968 Race Relations Acts provide limited redress for discrimination

1970 and 1983 Equal Pay Acts

1970 and 1976 Chronically Sick and Disabled Acts charge local authorities to see to the needs of the disabled

1975 Sex Discrimination Act outlaws sex discrimination and sets up Equal Opportunities Commission

1976 Race Relations Act outlaws race discrimination in employment, education and other areas and sets up Commission for Racial Equality

1981, 1985, 1991 Widespread race riots in British cities. British Nationality Act confines entry to UK to those with British ancestry

1986 Disabled Persons Act requires educational and other facilities to provide for the disabled

1996 Refugee and Asylum Seekers Act restricts asylum and denies social benefits to asylum seekers

1996 Employment Rights Act gives women the right to maternity pay and leave

1997 Record intake of women into the new Parliament

PROJECTS

1. Write a brief for the Blair Cabinet outlining how equal opportunity laws should be reformed. Argue your case with respect to *either* disability or race or gender.

2. Write an account of the official treatment of ethnic minorities in a local community with which you are familiar. Stress all aspects of that community including housing, policing, social services, employment and education.

3. Taking your own school or college as an example, outline how government policy affects the access to, and use of, facilities for disabled persons. Write a report on how policy might be changed to provide the disabled with a more equal opportunity to use these facilities.

FURTHER READING

A good account of the politics of race and immigration is provided by Zig Layton-Henry, *Immigration and 'Race' Politics in Post War Britain* (Oxford: Blackwell, 1992). On women and politics see Vicky Randall, *Women and Politics* (London: Macmillan, 2nd edn 1987). On equal opportunity policies, see K. Blakemore and R. Drake, *Understanding Equal Opportunity Policies* (Hemel Hempstead: Prentice Hall/Harvester Wheatsheaf, 1996). On citizenship in the European context, see Elizabeth Meehan, *Citizenship and the European Community* (London: Sage, 1993). An excellent account of equal opportunity and social policy is provided by Barbara Bagilhole, *Equal Opportunities and Social Policy* (London: Longman, 1997). Both the Commission for Racial Equality and the Equal Opportunities Commission provide good up to date reports on inequality and discrimination.

http://www.awl-he.com/politics/newbritpol

Internet resources – visit *The New British Politics* Webpage for links to a specially-chosen selection of Internet resources relevant to this Chapter.

http://www.awl-he.com/politics/newbritpol

PART VII

The New British Politics

C H A P T E R   2 8

A new politics?

This chapter cuts across the detail of previous discussions to ask if the changes of the last two decades add up to a total transformation of the British political scene? Certainly from 1979 on, Margaret Thatcher committed herself to taking the country in a new direction, with results which were not always what she expected but which certainly made an enormous difference to the way people live and how they think.

The question is: how far-reaching and permanent are these political effects? New Labour has responded to the Conservative challenge partly by developing a constitutional package of its own which could transform political relationships and the balance of power between the parties.

Most contemporary politicians like to present themselves as bold, innovative and radical. But we do not need to take them at face value. By evaluating the extent and nature of change in the various areas we have discussed we can see if they really do add up to a qualitative transformation of the whole political scene. If this has occurred, where is it taking the country? What are its implications for the quality of British democracy? This is a question posed at the beginning of the book, which we shall consider in Chapter 29.

This chapter therefore:

*   Contrasts the earlier postwar period with the later one to see if there has indeed been fundamental political change in the areas of social and economic policy, government and Europe

*   Asks whether the individual changes add up to a fundamental transformation of British politics

*   Considers whether the changes that have occurred are irreversible and, if so, where they are heading

Key term

Social democratic consensus – agreement among different political groups and parties about the general principles of social democracy, that is a generally moderate left or centre-left political programme.

BACK TO THE FUTURE?

Society and economy

In terms of ideology, Margaret Thatcher (foreshadowed by Edward Heath) broke with the 'social democratic consensus' of the earlier postwar years and substituted a 'neoliberal consensus' of her own which put promotion and expansion of the free market at the centre of everything. The Controversy contrasts the two ideologies in terms of their salient assumptions and beliefs.

If this summary of the neoliberal position is compared with the free-trade ideas which dominated British thinking in the nineteenth century, we can see that they have a lot in common. The free market is at the centre of both the old and new ideas. Government intervention is distrusted, as are interest groups and international regimes (like the EU). It is thought that both nationally and internationally free trade will guarantee the best results, and that bureaucracies and governments are best when they organise themselves like the markets and limit their own role

CONTROVERSY

VIEWS OF THE 'SOCIAL DEMOCRATIC CONSENSUS' (1948–79) AND THE 'NEOLIBERAL CONSENSUS' (1990s)

Social democratic consensus	*Neo-liberal consensus*
1. The Government knows best so will frequently intervene in the market to secure optimal economic conditions and social justice	1. The free market does best in distributing resources. The Government's role should be limited to guaranteeing and regulating markets so that they function efficiently
2. This is also true internationally (the EU and UN etc.)	2. This is also true internationally (GATT etc.)
3. The economy must be 'fine-tuned' by government, above all to avoid unemployment and to secure growth in manufacturing to support social expenditures	3. The Government should get out of the economy as far as possible. Its main role is to provide stability and control inflation. Financial considerations should thus be central
4. For planning and control purposes governments need to work through large, hierarchically organised bureaucracies	4. Excessive bureaucracy should be replaced by markets and market-like arrangements
5. Unions and other pressure groups should be consulted about policy and involved in its implementation	5. Groups outside government always want to distort policy into their own interest and should not be consulted too much

Neo-liberal consensus
– agreement among
different political groups
and parties about neo-
liberal politics, that is the
political belief that
individual rights should be
protected by maximising
freedom of choice, limiting
the powers of government,
and promoting market
economics.

Key term

Egalitarian – political
views or policies based
upon a wish to achieve
equality, or less inequality.

to upholding markets. The most characteristic policy of the Thatcherite period (1979–90) was the privatisation of government-owned industry, which fits beautifully into this set of ideas.

Of course, the Thatcher Governments, like other governments, were limited by political realities and could not do everything they wanted. The vast social schemes which they inherited – social services, social benefits, the National Health Service – could not be abolished without provoking revolution. Their existence represents a clear break with nineteenth-century thinking and provides a basic continuity with the first half of the postwar period.

The real innovation of Thatcher and her supporters was, however, to reorganise these great bureaucracies on market lines. In addition they responded to the fiscal crisis created by open-ended social demands by limiting expenditure and encouraging a shift to private provision. The idea of changing to private pension provision for old age, with state payments only for those who are unable to contribute, which was floated in the last days of the Major Government in early 1997, was a good example of neoliberal thinking on the subject.

Limiting government spending and activity of course carries social costs. The reason social democratic ideas evolved in the first place was as a solution to the poverty, disease, crime and unemployment of the nineteenth century. Cutting down government intervention even partially in the 1980s and 1990s resulted in a sharp increase in those living below the poverty line to about 20 per cent of the British population, mostly in the peripheries. These could manage more easily when the provision of health and social services was informally rationed through waiting lists and queues. When welfare depended on money – particularly when income support was being cut – they lost out. Thatcherite Britain may have been a more efficient society but it was also much less egalitarian and fair than it had been.

All the main defenders of working-class welfare, higher spending and greater government intervention were defeated or sidelined in the 1980s. The Conservatives won a famous victory over the miners' union, the NUM, in 1984–85 which prepared the way for the state coal industry to be dismantled. This allowed the Government to weaken or restrict the trade union movement as a whole. (New Labour has followed suit by keeping the unions at a distance.) Local governments were disciplined or sidelined and the Labour Party was electorally defeated until it took over many Thatcherite ideas and renounced the possibility of taking privatised industry back into state ownership.

One consequence of putting financial considerations above other economic and social ones was to consolidate the powerful position of the City of London in relation to government. If the main concern was to control inflation and strengthen the pound, retaining the confidence of the City was essential to both. Given the traditional dominance of finance over manufacturing in Britain, this was hardly a break with the past, but merely overt recognition of a long-standing power relationship.

The freeing of the Bank of England to set interest rates was perhaps the most dramatic recognition of the City's importance. This action was taken, however, by the New Labour Government in May 1997, not by its Conservative predecessors. It fits nicely with Labour's general move to the right (Figure 17.2 in Chapter 17) and shows the extent to which neoliberalism has become the dominant ideology, supported even by Labour, just as the social democratic consensus was shared by the Conservative Party of the 1950s.

However, just as the Conservatives in that period gradually whittled away at government control and extended the market (for example, to commercial television), so New Labour are less wholehearted in support of neoliberalism than the Conservatives are. Witness their windfall tax on the privatised utilities (water, gas, electricity, telephones) to pay for their youth employment programme (1997). The Liberal Democrats are far from being neoliberals themselves: their progressive political stances include widespread government intervention to protect the environment and to maintain welfare. It is quite likely that Labour will drift leftwards in their direction if Liberal support seems important at or after the next election.

However, these qualifications cannot blur the fact that Thatcher's campaign to 'roll back the state' largely succeeded. In this respect, at any rate, the British politics of the 1980s and 1990s differ substantially from what went before. She converted the previously unthinkable into the commonplace of today's politics. No government now is going to intervene in the economy to the extent that Macmillan and Heath – let alone Wilson – did. Both New Labour and the Liberal Democrats accept the new model of relations between government and society, a much less interventionist and more aloof stance than what went before.

Government

Margaret Thatcher's bold initiatives in social and economic policy were carried over to local government and bureaucracy, but not to the core executive itself, nor to Parliament. There she was content to use the existing machinery, which gave herself and her Cabinet an almost dictatorial power so long as they retained control of the majority party.

This power was used to substitute quangos for local government in many areas, to force the latter to sell off housing stock and contract out local services. Inside the central administration many services were either sold off or hived off to semi-autonomous agencies (Chapter 10). The changes are so great that some commentators have claimed that the traditional 'Whitehall model' is now defunct.[1] This has created serious problems of accountability and control of the autonomous agencies, which by definition are distanced from political intervention and scrutiny.

This compounds the general problem of the scrutiny of administration, which forms a central part of our discussion of democracy in the next chapter. One has to say, however, that the old undivided ministries were hardly models of accountability and transparency either. Matters may not have been improved by 'Next Steps' but in this respect they have not been made much worse.

---

[1] C. Campbell and G.K. Wilson, *The End of Whitehall: Death of a Paradigm* (Oxford: Blackwell, 1995), p. 314

It is also true that political organisations, particularly bureaucracies, are very resilient. The fact that prisons or payment of benefits are handled by separate agencies may not make much difference to the sponsoring ministry so long as it sets the terms of the contracts and makes overall policy. So far, at any rate, ministers and their civil servants seem to have maintained overall control of their old policy-making functions, helped by the change of government in 1997 which reduced pressure for further market-oriented reforms of administration.

The same may be said of local councils and their officials. Pushed out of many areas of local administration, obliged to follow national procedures in giving out contracts, marginalised elsewhere, they yet emerged as vibrant centres of local opposition to Conservative policies. We may expect to see the same process taking place in reverse under New Labour. With wider control over development and planning, councils may well prove to have exchanged static and declining functions for ones growing in importance. After the turbulent era of the 1980s and 1990s they are probably also in closer touch with their electorate, helped by the development of 'community politics', and with a new role as articulators of local grievances as well as providers of services.

These, of course, were consequences not intended by Thatcher. But they were provoked by her policies, even if they emerged in opposition to them. The same might be said of the growth of support for the Scottish and Welsh Assemblies. Without the insensitive imposition of full-blooded Thatcherite policies on these basically social democratic societies, Labour's devolution plans might not have had enough support to carry them through.

These plans themselves are, of course, also a backlash against Thatcherism. Not only are Welsh, Scottish and probably Northern Irish Assemblies to be put in place but London is to be given an elected executive mayor in place of the Council (GLC) abolished by Thatcher in the mid-1980s. All these constitutional developments are radical within the British context. They also include changes – in a much more proportional direction – to the way in which votes are translated into seats and, in the case of the London Mayor, a powerful directly elected executive who resembles an American state governor, rather than the traditional collective executive of local government.

Such innovations were fiercely opposed by Thatcher herself and her Conservative successors. Nevertheless, they are consequences of a style of government in which local and regional interests felt bulldozed. In reaction such interests are being entrenched politically in a way which would make them centres of opposition in the event of the Conservatives being returned nationally again.

The territorial decentralisation of power initiated by New Labour has spilled over to a limited extent into central Government. The main manifestation of this is the incorporation of the European Convention on Human Rights into British law. This extends the scope for judicial scrutiny of political and administrative decisions, thus strengthening a growing tendency which developed remarkably in the late 1980s and the 1990s, again in reaction to the 'elective dictatorship' (see Briefing 28.1).

Other constitutional innovations under New Labour are likely to be limited, however. Moves towards full freedom of information have already been inhibited

Key term

Elective dictatorship – the term used to describe the British political system, as one in which, once elected, the leadership of the majority party in the House of Commons can do more or less what it wants without constitutional checks and balances, until it faces the electorate at the next general election.

BRIEFINGS

28.1 THE 'ELECTIVE DICTATORSHIP' IN BRITISH GOVERNMENT

The 'elective dictatorship' is the shorthand term used to describe the situation whereby the leadership of the majority party in the House of Commons forms a government which can do more or less what it wants without constitutional or legislative checks. This is possible because of:

- tight internal discipline which ensures that the MPs of the majority parliamentary party will always vote to uphold the Government (Chapter 18),

- the unwritten constitution, whose conventions are more or less what the Government says they are (Chapter 7).

Although some limitations have been placed on governments through EU legislation, judicial review and investigative journalism, these are relatively weak and ineffective at the present time.

and an enhanced role has been promised for the Security Services. Tight party discipline has been enforced within the Government and the House of Commons. The 'elective dictatorship' of the majority party will be maintained as long as possible. The unwritten constitution which puts such power in the hands of a determined prime minister will remain in all its essential aspects, the only limitation on personal rule being the balance of personalities in the Cabinet.

Electoral reform could change this state of affairs almost overnight by ensuring that no majority party emerges to dominate Parliament and that governments must be coalitions. For that very reason no government with a parliamentary majority is likely to change the present system of election very radically. Only if Labour and Liberal supporters continue to vote tactically can the Liberal Democrats hope to build up their parliamentary strength under the present system. Only to the extent that they held a balance between the parties could they bargain for some change. As they would more or less be tied to Labour, however, change is likely to be limited and would retain the main features of the single-constituency simple plurality system. Even limited electoral reform will not materialise, therefore, until well into the next millennium.

The constitutional essentials have thus changed less than other aspects of politics over the postwar period. They still put massive power into the hands of the central Government. Two minor but potentially important developments have emerged which may be portents of greater flexibility in the future:

1. Greater use of referendums, whereby all or part of the British population votes on constitutional change (e.g. the European referendum of 1975, now also promised for the decision to adopt the single currency in 2002). Such exercises in direct democracy (i.e. voting directly on policy

questions rather than electing representatives to decide them) are, however, largely limited to questions that politicians want to avoid deciding for themselves and which the Government thinks it can win. Thus they are as yet largely cosmetic and do not constitute a political watershed of any kind.

2. The same may be said of the select committee structure of the House of Commons, interestingly strengthened as one of the first acts of the new Conservative Government of 1979. These do provide a potential channel for a parliamentary voice to be asserted against a dominating government. Investigative committees in combination with investigative journalism have uncovered many abuses. They have rarely affected actual government policy, however, and are unlikely to do so while the 'elective dictatorship' remains.

More administrative, constitutional and political changes thus took place after 1979 than before. They create a base for greater transformations to come. But it cannot be said that they have fulfilled that potential yet. The New Labour Government of Tony Blair functions administratively in ways that would be quite familiar to Clement Attlee and Aneurin Bevan in 1948, even if the substance of policy is very different.

Europe

The major move towards constitutional change in Britain comes, significantly, from outside the country, from Europe. In the face of the vast transformations this will entail, commenting on the small political reforms that have been made domestically may seem like describing the new decorations on the Titanic as it headed for the iceberg!

European Monetary Union (EMU) is not really about economics, though it is predominantly discussed in these terms in Britain, but is primarily about political union. Once economic and monetary policy are managed at a European level, fiscal policy (taxation) will follow. Their addition to the existing powers concentrated at Brussels will finally tip the balance away from the Member States like Britain and towards the European institutions. Pressure will grow to make these democratically responsible and accountable, by redesigning the European Commission and European Parliament along the lines of a real federal government and assembly.

As Britain becomes increasingly committed to EMU, it will have to go along this path with its partners (see Briefing 28.2 and Figure 28.1). Faced with the alternatives of withdrawing totally from the EU (on which it would still be economically dependent, however) or going along with the others, it is highly likely to go along, however virulent Eurosceptic opposition to the loss of sovereignty becomes.

Simply having political federation as a real choice to be confronted in the near future clearly distinguishes the present state of politics in Britain from what has gone before. Actual developments to date also mark out the later postwar period as different. Joining the then European Community in 1972 meant accepting all

BRIEFINGS

28.2 BRITAIN'S PLACE IN A FEDERAL EUROPEAN UNION

At present there has not been a great deal of discussion about the final institutional shape of the European Union, as the prospect of going on to a fully fledged federal structure is so recent. Very likely, however, the relationships between institutions would resemble those of the Federal Republic of Germany. The European Commission would become the Union government. Unlike now, however, it would emerge from the elected House of the Parliament – the present European Parliament – and would have to have the confidence of a majority composed of one or more European-wide political parties.

One can anticipate that, with control of a strengthened EU at stake, the European parties would become much more effective and not simply federations of national parties as they are now. Socialists, Christians and others would have their own branches in Britain as in the other Member States and would compete for votes directly through their own organisation.

The other House of Parliament would be the old Council of Ministers, composed of delegations from national governments, one being the British. The British delegation would vote as instructed by the national Government. However, decisions of the House as a whole would be made on a majority or supermajority (60–70%) basis, so the British government would have to form coalitions with other national delegations to win. If it could muster the necessary majority, the Upper House could abort legislation or veto policy, but not directly dismiss the European government. This would depend exclusively on the directly elected Lower House.

The workings of such a system are summarised in Figure 28.1. This illustrates the extent to which a European government and parliament would become 'our' government and parliament for British electors, as they would have a part in electing them.

of its established powers, an act which already subverted British parliamentary sovereignty. The European Court of Justice had established the superiority of European law, and its own interpretations of it, wherever it decided they applied. British courts accepted this principle from the outset. Their role in judging parliamentary acts and administrative decisions against a higher (European) law also encouraged them to extend the scope of judicial review even where European law was not involved. Growing judicial activism is a concurrent feature which distinguishes the last quarter of a century from the one that went before.

In foreign policy too, the EU is a factor which dominates and thus cannot simply be ignored. No longer can Britain choose between the 'three circles' of the United States, Empire and Europe. It has no choice but to concentrate on the European aspect. Left to her own devices, Thatcher would have affirmed the traditional themes of British foreign policy: support for the USA, free trade and a strong affirmation of British interests wherever they were threatened (as in the Falklands). She would have largely ignored developments on the Continent, except to expostulate about France and Germany's protectionist tendencies and lack of support for NATO.

British membership of the Union forced her, however, into an activist policy in Europe whatever her own inclinations. Certainly she devoted much energy (like her successor John Major) to trying to stem or even to roll back the transfer of powers to Brussels.

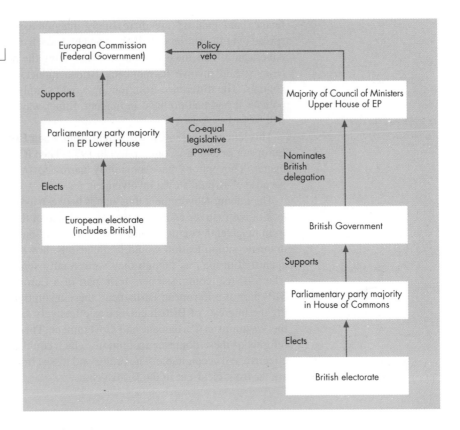

Figure 28.1 Britain's likely place in a future European Federal Union

However, the impetus towards federation forced even Thatcher into actions which strengthened that transfer. No matter that she viewed the Single European Act as essentially designed to set up a free market. It actually involved extending the autonomous powers of action of the Commission and the Court and introducing qualified majority voting into the Council of Ministers on some matters, eroding the British veto. Membership of the European Monetary System, and management of the pound to conform to the German mark, turned out to be an abortive development, though it will return with a vengeance under EMU. John Major's acceptance of the Treaty of Maastricht, even with a British opt-out in some areas, materially extended the powers of EU institutions to overrule the British Government. One of the first acts of New Labour in 1997 was to accept the Social Chapter of Maastricht, subordinating British labour regulations to European directives. Their acceptance of EMU in principle in late 1997 simply followed through the logic of closer and closer association with the EU. The drive towards a European federal state renders that the only sustainable option short of withdrawal. In a European federation, the UK would be simply one member out of 17 or 20, with all the consequences outlined above for the loss of practical sovereignty (Chapter 5).

Indeed, even if the British Government chose not to join EMU in the end, it would still be tied to it in practice. Much of British trade is now with the EU, and finance and industry are increasingly integrated with multinational enterprises spread over the Union (whether owned by French, German and Dutch firms or by Americans). This means that even maintaining the pound as an independent currency would involve harmonising British monetary and fiscal policy with the Union's. The difference from joining would simply be that Britain had to follow policies it had had no hand in making. Either way, effective British sovereignty will be lost.

This situation is radically different from when Britain joined the EU (then the European Economic Community) in 1972. Then it clearly had a choice about the matter. The options have obviously narrowed over the last 25 years, in part because of Britain's own involvement.

The Labour Government thus stands between a rock and a hard place. Britain's lack of alternatives could be taken as evidence of the country's long-term decline from nineteenth century world power to subordinate state in a larger union. This dramatic simplification would be fallacious, however, as it juxtaposes 'Britain' against 'Europe', as though they were totally separate entities. In a federation where British commissioners form part of a European government, and British MPs part of a European Parliament, these institutions may be seen as representing the interests of British citizens as effectively as, if not more effectively than, the Westminster Parliament and Government. Their influence might even speed reforms of these domestic institutions which could make them more democratic, effective and accountable. The profits and losses from finally embracing 'Europe' are far from clear-cut in the British case.

HAVE BRITISH POLITICS FUNDAMENTALLY CHANGED?

Whichever way the contemporary situation is evaluated, it is clear that the intrusion of the European dimension into the domestic one sharply distinguishes this period in British politics from anything that has gone before. The sense of difference is enhanced by the coincidental domestic shift from one ruling ideological paradigm to another: social democratic consensus to neoliberal consensus. This shift carried with it a policy revolution, as market relationships were substituted for politically planned ones. The force of this shift is shown by its ability to carry New Labour as well as the Conservatives with it, notably in increasing the independence of the Bank of England.

In terms of policy, therefore, the period from 1979 differs radically from what went before. Labour will probably prove more supportive of the welfare state than the Conservative Governments of 1979–97, more dedicated to fostering 'community' and providing for the poor. But in terms of its flagship policies for the economy it has abandoned nationalisation for private ownership, and courts business rather than trade union approval.

Only in regard to government is there some doubt whether changes have gone far enough to mark out the last two decades as fundamentally different (see Table 28.1). The reason is that no government has been willing to give up the almost dictatorial power provided by majority party discipline and government ability to

Table 28.1 Governmental and administrative continuity and change 1945–98

Institution	Reformed after 1979	By whom	Type of change
Cabinet and premiership	No	–	Continues to be 'elective dictatorship'
Parliament	Slightly	Cons.	Investigative select committees
Political parties	Slightly	Blair/Hague	More disciplined and centralised
General elections	No	–	Continue to give parliamentary majority to plurality party
Central administration	Yes	Cons.	'Hiving off' and privatisation of subsidiary and administrative functions
Local government	Yes	Cons.	More central control over administrative functions, hiving off of some, territorial reorganisation, 'community politics'
Regional assemblies	Yes	Lab/Lib. Dem	Self-government for Scotland, Wales, Northern Ireland, London Mayor; potential for conflict with centre
Quangos	Extended	Cons.	Continue to be nominated by central Government and to administer large areas of national life
Pressure groups (including unions and nonfinancial business)	Yes	Cons.	Legal curbs, marginalised in policy making, change more to market relationships
City of London, finance, banks	Slightly	Cons./Lab	New self-regulatory measures: Bank of England freed to set interest rates
Police	Slightly	Cons.	More centralised under government control
Security services	No	–	Slight moves to transparency; powers extended
Judges	No	–	Assert more autonomous powers of review
Mass media (press and TV)	No	–	Shift to market model, investigative journalism

'bend' the unwritten constitution. Thus the reforms which have been carried out are of a kind which do not affect the central power relationships: select investigative committees, more allowance for judicial review, incorporation of the Convention on Human Rights. Devolution in Scotland and Wales (and possibly Northern Ireland) removes these areas from direct control by Westminster but does not affect what goes on at the centre.

Even local government reorganisation does not alter the former situation radically. Tighter controls on local government do not remove the centre's administrative dependence on the localities, though it must be said that the councils themselves have found a new, more activist role in local representation.

Neither 'Next Steps' nor tight budgetary control have undermined the top civil servants' primary role as advisers to politicians. British ministers remain extraordinarily dependent, even under New Labour, on civil servants in the ministries.

Changes at the level of government and administration thus have a potential to destabilise and alter the British political situation. But they have not fulfilled that potential yet, even if the administrative and local reorganisations of the Thatcher era, and the decentralisation carried through by Blair, are more far-reaching than anything that happened in the sleepy decades of the 1950s and 1960s.

Together with the radical policy reversal of the 1980s and the impact of Europe, these changes certainly entitle us to regard contemporary British politics as fundamentally different from the earlier postwar period. The stakes, the goals, the strategies have now radically altered. One significant indicator of shift in thinking is the 'decline of decline'. In the 1980s political commentators were obsessed by the question of Britain's overall decline, especially what was termed 'relative economic decline', that is, the lower level of British economic growth when compared with other countries. 'Reversing decline' functioned in political debate to justify radical programmes of reform, both of the left and right, and the sacrifices they entailed. In the late 1990s, even with the same long-term growth rate, the question of decline hardly enters into political debate. Britain has made the adjustment and debate is dominated by national sovereignty versus Europe.

We can thank Margaret Thatcher for that. Her radical right policies changed the premises on which British politics were based and her energy and resolution ensured that they passed into action. Their general popularity guaranteed that Labour could not turn the clock back. The price of Labour's electoral success was acceptance of most elements of the new situation.

At the same time New Labour found its own characteristic policies in actions which reversed Thatcherite centralisation (devolution), free market individualism (a new stress on community) and Conservative Euroscepticism (acceptance of the European project and in particular EMU). By innovating in these areas it has further distanced present-day politics from the past.

The near-total transformations that have occurred are the reason why this book concentrates its descriptions and analyses of contemporary politics on the 1980s and 1990s. What happened previously has a historical interest but is not particularly illuminating about what is going on now, since things have changed so much.

NEW POLITICS, NEW DIRECTIONS?

Mrs Thatcher's revolution of the 1980s was a very Conservative one. Much of it consisted in restoring things to what they had been before the Second World War, and in some cases even to what they were like in the late nineteenth century. Thus the industries which Labour had nationalised between 1945 and 1950 – steel, coal, gas, water, electricity, rail – were all returned to private ownership. The trade unions were pushed away from government to the marginalised and somewhat suspect position they had occupied at the beginning of the century. The general predominance of financial interests in the City of London was reaffirmed.

In general a free market philosophy very much akin to that of the late nineteenth century (Chapter 2) was adopted and applied ruthlessly, not only to policies but to government structures including those of the welfare state and National Health Service. Spending on these remained at high levels owing to demographic pressures (Chapter 25), but provision was cut.

The free market revolution has now largely run its course, if only because there is little left to privatise or marketise. This is in a way a testimony to the thoroughness and extent of the changes made under that philosophy. However, as also happened a hundred years ago, the full triumph of the markets prompts a reaction against them. Reform may have produced real gains in efficiency. But these have now reached their limits. The free market also has inefficiencies, particularly where regulation is not strong and monopolies and cartels appear, or external costs like pollution and environmental degradation are passed on to others.

We can anticipate that the direction which will be taken by New Labour will increasingly involve the direction and regulation of markets. Under Thatcher and Major, regulatory agencies like Ofgas, Oftel, Ofwat and their like were set up as quangos with nominated regulators who were left largely to do as they thought right. Some regulators, like the office overseeing the privatised railways, have been notoriously lax. Over time, however, there has been a tendency to check the more outrageous price rises of the new monopolies and to enforce reasonable levels of service.

Labour has already set up a new combined administrative structure for gas and electricity. Whether it will exert more direct control is unclear. But regulators have now got the message that they should be tougher. Whether reporting directly to the Government or simply pressured by it, the new pattern of supervision will be more rigorous.

Environmental problems will push Labour into tighter regulation anyway. This cannot be said to be uncongenial to them, as intervention is the traditional ideological stance of the party. However, it is now going to be exercised through the extensive regulatory powers taken (but never fully used) by the Conservative Governments when they privatised public utilities and transport.

In one sense, therefore, the political changes made after 1979 are irreversible. Labour is not going back to nationalisation or lavish spending on social services or excessive deference to unions. Politics, however, does move on. New mechanisms of intervention will be invented and indicative planning (this time for environmental purposes rather than growth) will very likely be revived. So 2008 will differ from 1998, but probably not as sharply as 1988 did from 1968.

The European partners are in general much more interventionist than Britain, since they come from a protectionist state-directed tradition even in economics (Chapter 2). Thus the move to regulation will be strengthened by European influences, and even initiated by Brussels in many cases. Even if they wanted, New Labour could not stand out against this pressure, but they are unlikely to want to. More emphasis on fairness to workers and consumers is also likely to follow and will be strengthened by the greater ability of these groups to voice their demands through the new constitutional structures being set up.

The expectation is that New Labour – possibly in coalition with the Liberals – will be in power for a long time to oversee increasingly interventionist policies.

The continuing salience of Europe will drive the Conservative factions further and further apart, with a consequent weakening of the party electorally. Only by coming to terms with European developments and the problems of weakly regulated markets, will they become credible competitors for governmental power in Britain, let alone in Brussels. With Labour dominance and Conservative weakness, we may be seeing a new era of politics – the post-market era – emerging before our eyes.

ESSAYS

1. How will increasing integration into the EU affect the substance of British domestic policy?

2. Who is more radical and reforming, Margaret Thatcher or Tony Blair?

3. Discuss the evidence for and against the idea that we are now in a 'post-market era' of British politics.

4. How far will New Labour's 'constitutional project' change power relationships at the centre of British government?

PROJECTS

1. Write a brief for the New Labour Government on what they should do about transport and pollution up to 2005.

2. Write sections for the New Labour manifesto for the next election on welfare and pensions.

SUMMARY

This chapter has reviewed evidence that:

- Contemporary politics in Britain have been fundamentally transformed since 1979.

- Contemporary politics *are* very different, partly owing to the Thatcherite policy revolution but mainly owing to the strengthening of European Union.

- New Labour's victory in 1997 may lead to in a third era of postwar politics, when indirect regulation and control of markets will be emphasised.

- This will be congenial to Labour's general interventionist tradition but there will be no going back to state socialism.

- The EU institutions will become even more important in Britain than they are now and strengthen the tendency to government intervention and control of markets.

FURTHER READING

For an assessment of the Thatcher and Major governments and their effects see Dennis Kavanagh and Anthony Seldon (eds), *The Thatcher Effect: A Decade of Change* (Oxford: Clarendon Press, 1989) and *The Major Effect* (London: Macmillan, 1994); Dennis Kavanagh, *Thatcherism and British Politics: A Decade of Change?* (Oxford: Oxford University Press, 1987) and Stephen P. Savage and Lynton Robins (eds), *Public Policy under Thatcher* (London: Macmillan, 1990). For a broad sweep across selected topics in British politics since 1945 see Lynton Robins and Bill Jones (eds), *Half a Century of British Politics* (Manchester: Manchester University Press, 1997). An assessment of the early months of Blair's Government is to be found in Derek Draper, *Blair's 100 Days* (London: Faber and Faber, 1997), and different views of Blair and New Labour are presented by M. Perryman (ed.) *The Blair Agenda* (London: Lawrence and Wishart, 1996) and G. Kelly *et al.* (eds), *Stakeholder Capitalism* (London: Macmillan, 1997).

Two excellent books written by journalists about British politics in the 1990s are Will Hutton, *The State We're In* (London: Vintage, rev. edn 1996) and Simon Jenkins, *Accountable to None* (Harmondsworth: Penguin, 1997).

British democracy?

The 'democratic deficit' of the European Union, that is the lack of accountability of its executive bodies to the European Parliament (or to national parliaments), is often criticised. Our discussion has shown that the same criticism can be made of the United Kingdom executive in relation to the House of Commons. The executive dominates Parliament, rather than the other way round. When select committees try to hold the government accountable for its actions, as often as not they are fobbed off and their reports ignored. Whole areas of the executive, notably the security apparatus which most threatens civil liberties, are effectively screened from any scrutiny at all.

None of this implies that Britain is not a democracy, even a liberal democracy. It does show, however, that even under an old-established, democratically advanced constitution there is room for improvement.

The last chapter focused on the transformation of British political life over the last two decades. Here we examine the quality of democracy in Britain and ask whether the changes now working their way through politics will enhance or degrade this.

Liberal democracy has two aspects: popular control, and respect for individual and group rights. This chapter discusses how these stand now and how they might change. Accordingly it considers:

- Democratic control: what it is and where it operates

- The electorate's choice between left and right

- Electoral control and reform

- Pressure groups and policy

- Individual protection against administrative injustice

- Scrutiny of government and administration as a safeguard of individual rights

- A written constitution

LIBERAL DEMOCRACY: ELECTORAL CONTROL AND EFFECTIVE SCRUTINY

We are concerned with both control and scrutiny of the executive because of the dual nature of democracy as it now operates in most of the world, including Britain. Democracies tend not just to be democratic but also liberal. Their democratic character shows itself in rule by the majority, exercised by choosing between political parties on the basis of their record, candidates and programmes. The party or parties with the majority of votes should then form a government with a 'mandate' (authority) from the electorate to govern on the basis of their programme (see Briefing 29.1). In this way a rough correspondence between majority preferences and government policy is secured.

An obvious problem of British democracy is that no winning party since the Second World War has actually obtained a popular majority. Owing to the workings of the electoral system (Chapter 15), parties have obtained parliamentary majorities with only a plurality (42–48 per cent) of the votes. One could say that the majority have in fact voted against the governing party, at least in a certain sense. This might be less true where the victor has occupied a centre position, thus making itself reasonably congenial to the majority if not actually representing them directly. But where the winning party has been at one of the ideological

BRIEFINGS

29.1 THE ELECTORAL MANDATE

This is the idea that the party (or parties) getting the most votes in an election will form a government which will carry through its electoral programme, as this has been supported by electors. The details of the argument are given below:

- Electors choose between parties at least in part on the basis of their programme;

- Such programmes are distinguishable from each other so they offer electors a basis for choice;

- The party or parties which form the next government have a responsibility to carry out their programme in government, because this is a major basis on which they have been elected;

- They also have the authority to carry out their programme in government, as it has been selected by at least a sizeable number of electors as the best short-term programme for the country;

- Parties do carry through their programmatic priorities in government.

Key term

Mandate – an instruction or command which carries legal or moral force. An electoral mandate is said to give the party winning an election the right to carry out its programme.

extremes, as in general elections from 1974–92, it has seemed like a minority government masquerading as a majority one. This is a real problem for democracy in Britain which we examine below.

The liberal element in liberal democracy has some potential points of conflict with the democratic ideal that the majority should rule. Liberalism emphasises respect for individual and group rights, even when a majority might want to do away with them. Thus it sets bounds on what the majority can do.

Property rights are often involved in such a clash of principles, particularly in regard to progressive taxation where the propertyless majority may wish to redistribute wealth through special taxes on the rich. Environmental concerns might also involve restrictions on the use of property, thus limiting the owners' use of it.

Such questions often arise in day-to-day politics. In many other areas, however, liberalism and democracy are entirely compatible and even mutually reinforcing. This is because democratic principles themselves impose limits on what a current majority can do in the interests of future and possibly opposing majorities. Democratic procedures cannot, therefore, allow a current majority to punish or silence an opposing minority. Over time that minority may convince enough people of the rightness and justice of its claims to become a majority itself. In the interests of future majorities, democratic procedures have to guarantee personal immunity to minority individuals and groups, and rights of debate, assembly, discussion and voting to all, even persons holding unpopular or despised points of view.

This position brings democratic principles very close to liberal ones. Both are concerned with upholding rights even against a hostile (current) majority. Democratic procedures would, however, try to keep guaranteed rights to a minimum in order to leave a majority the maximum freedom of action. Liberalism would be more concerned with extending rights even at the cost of restricting majority rule.

In practice, civil rights tend to be under so many threats that there is little real conflict between democratic and liberal principles. This is the case in Britain with regard to official secrecy, which drastically limits not only individuals' right to know enough to claim their rights but (by the same token) also restricts full democratic debate and discussion.

In order to check on the extent to which popular majorities actually decide things in Britain we need to look at the way elections are conducted and how voting outcomes are reflected in the choice of governments and in the policies they pursue. We should also look to the future: will the conduct of elections change so as to reflect majority preferences better?

On the side of rights – both liberal and democratic – we need to see how well these are protected and how efficiently infringements are investigated and corrected. Procedurally this involves appeals against injustice and powers of scrutiny whether by courts, Parliament or media.

Electoral control and administrative scrutiny are thus the two major concerns of this chapter. At the end of the discussion we shall try to put together our conclusions about both of them, so as to form a rounded picture of the workings of liberal democracy in Britain and of its likely future development.

ELECTORAL CHOICE BETWEEN LEFT AND RIGHT

In one sense elections are a defective democratic mechanism in Britain because a majority never elects a government. Instead, the single member simple plurality constituency (or 'first past the post') system ensures that the party with the largest (but not a majority) vote gets a parliamentary majority (Chapter 15). Such a government has very wide powers even though it represents an electoral minority. There are very few restrictions within the unwritten constitution on what any government, even minority ones, can do (Chapter 7). Parliamentary sovereignty is all-important, not the popular mandate, and in practice sovereignty is appropriated by the party with the majority of seats.

This situation may not be quite as undemocratic as it seems if the party that has that majority represents the 'centre' or the 'middle ground' of politics and thus comes close to doing what most electors want anyway. To see what is involved here we need to examine the actual process of electoral campaigning and voting more closely, looking particularly at the way issues get narrowed down so as to simplify voting choices.

There are, of course, thousands of issues that could potentially enter into elections and provide a basis for choice between the political parties. It seems, however, from the evidence of the 'Essex Model' of voting (Chapter 15) that very few actually do. Basically elections focus on the economy – particularly whether there should be more or less government intervention – welfare, taxes, and peaceful international co-operation versus aggressive assertion of national interests. These are the classic issues separating left and right in Britain, as in other countries (Chapter 17).

Why should all the complex debates and issues of British politics get crushed down to a simple one-dimensional choice between left and right? The reason is simple – this is the way both parties and media present party policy positions in election campaigns. There is an inevitable element of simplification in public presentation of the political choices involved which pushes political discussion and voting decisions into this one dimension.

Of course, there is no logical reason why Labour, or the left in general, should combine internationalism with support for welfare and greater economic intervention. But it does. The Conservatives on their side combine support for (economic) freedom with hostility to a 'big' state and a nationalistic attitude abroad. Liberal Democrats support both freedom and welfare and thus tend to end up in the middle of the left–right spectrum, although in 1997 their environmentalism pushed them to the left of Labour.

We have already mapped out party positions along such a spectrum in Figure 17.2 in Chapter 17 which shows the movement of the parties to left and right over the postwar period. Representing the important election issues in this direct way helps us see more clearly which party holds the 'centre' or 'middle ground' on the most important issues and whether this is the party which gets into government as a result of the election. This is summarised in Table 29.1, in which judgements as to which party was in the middle on the most important issues of the elections are made on the basis of Figure 17.2.

Over the range of 15 postwar elections from 1945 to 1997 inclusive, the middle party got into government seven times, or at roughly half the elections. (This

Table 29.1 The middle party in government, 1945–97

Election year	45	50	51	55	59	64	66
Government party after election	LAB	LAB	CON	CON	CON	LAB	LAB
Middle party on left–right issues	LIB	CON	CON (almost)	CON	CON	LAB	LAB (almost)
Did middle party win?	NO	NO	YES	YES	YES	YES	YES

Election year	70	74(i)	74(ii)	79	83	87	92	97
Government party after election	CON	LAB	LAB	CON	CON	CON	CON	LAB
Middle party on left–right issues	CON (almost)	LIB or CON	LIB	LIB	LIB–SD ALLIA-NCE	LIB–SD ALLIA-NCE	LD	LAB
Did middle party win?	YES	NO	NO	NO	NO	NO	NO	YES

is on the generous view that the Conservative positions in 1951 and 1970 almost coincided with those of the Liberals, and so can be counted as 'middle' even though very slightly to the right of them, and that Labour in 1966 also practically coincided with the Liberals.)

What is more significant, however, is that six out of the seven occasions when the middle party, broadly defined, got into office occurred between 1951 and 1970! In 1974 a relatively extreme left-wing Labour party won both elections, then an increasingly right-wing Conservative party got into government from 1979–92. In other words, there has been a tendency for parties taking an extreme ideological position rather than one based on the 'middle ground' to win office from 1971 onwards. In that sense British governments have moved further away from reflecting majority opinion in recent years. Only New Labour, by shifting substantially rightwards, managed to reoccupy the centre in 1997 and make itself a more consensual government.

FUTURE TRENDS IN ELECTORAL CONTROL AND ELECTORAL REFORM

If Labour continues both to win elections and hold the middle ground, we should see politics becoming less adversarial than they have been recently and more reflective of majority opinion, at least on the central issues where electoral choices are made. Close relationships with the Liberal Democrats should also

BRIEFINGS

29.2 THE MIDDLE GROUND AND THE MEDIAN VOTER

The view that the popular majority is better represented by a minority government if that is formed by the party holding the 'middle ground', that is, a centrist policy position, can be expressed more generally in terms of the median voter's choice and its relationship to other voters' choices. If electoral preferences can be arranged along a left–right policy spectrum corresponding to the party positions in Figure 17.2, then the median voter is the one who pushes the count over 50 per cent, going from either left or right. A simplified illustration of this is given below, for an electorate of five voters:

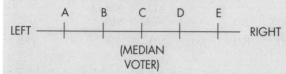

On this left–right dimension, voters are placed in terms of their policy preferences from left to right. C is the middle (or 'median') voter. For a party to have a majority, it must get C to vote for it. In order to attract C the party has to come very near to C's position, otherwise the other party will come closer, get C's vote, obtain a majority and form the government. In this situation, whatever party forms the government will always adopt a policy position closer to C's preferences in order to win a majority. Even where there is a large electorate like the British one, parties seeking extra votes will always have to move policy towards the median position (assuming they know where it is) as can be seen from the diagram below.

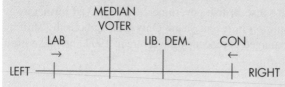

On this argument, policy will always move towards C's (the median) position. This is very nice for C of course, who will always get his or her way under ideal democratic conditions. But it is also a reasonable outcome for the other electors, indeed the best they can hope for. A and B would much prefer to have C's policies adopted than those of D and E. Similarly D and E prefer C to A and B. Thus the power of the median voter, and the adoption of that voter's preference by government, is the best way of meeting everybody's preferences under the existing distribution of opinion. The other voters do not get all they want but they get more than if the opposing wing could simply impose their preferences.

In practice, of course, Britain has three large parties, so none can hope to get a majority on its own. However, if the party which the median voter supports gets into government, the policies pursued should approximate those which a majority vote would have got anyway, given the need to attract the median voter.

Instead, from 1974 to 1992, a party not responsive to the median voter got into government. This may account for the relatively extreme policies pursued by Conservative governments during this period. It may also explain why the politics of the period from 1950 to 1970 seem more consensual than those of later. New Labour seem to have designed their policies to appeal to the median voter, perhaps ushering in a new era of (relatively) consensual politics.

strengthen these tendencies, as that party is quite likely to return to the centre position occupied during 1964–92. A coalition government of Labour and Liberal Democrats would even rest on a popular majority, producing a genuinely majoritarian government for the first time in the postwar period.

Key term

Middle ground – a political position roughly mid-way between the extremes of the political spectrum. The crucial point about the middle ground is not that it is in the middle but that it is assumed to be a position occupied by the majority of voters.

Such outcomes are very contingent ones, however, heavily dependent on the ebb and flow of electoral politics. The emergence of further nonmajority-based governments from one or other ideological extreme remains a strong possibility. Indeed they are quite likely under the workings of the present electoral system.

The rules of plurality voting, whereby the party with the single largest vote wins the seat, themselves encourage the emergence of governments with an electoral minority and parliamentary majority. This is compounded by the fact that voting takes place within small, arbitrarily drawn constituencies which, in the current state of affairs, give Labour a large, inbuilt advantage over the Conservatives in the translation of votes into seats, making it again more likely that a parliamentary majority will emerge from a voting plurality.

Minor modifications to the current first-past-the-post rules would give no guarantee that a majority-based government could be elected, particularly if they retained small constituencies. For example, the 'alternative vote' would ask voters to indicate multiple preferences (numbering candidates on their ballot papers 1, 2, 3, etc.). If no candidate had a majority of first preferences, the second preferences of the lowest-ranked candidates would be redistributed, until one of the top ones gets majority support in the constituency. (The constituencies would be the same as they are now.) Unfortunately this system of distributing seats would give virtually the same overall results as now.

Only a change to some kind of PR (proportional representation) system which deliberately tried to match vote percentages to party seat percentages in reasonably large constituencies could guarantee that all electors received fair party representation in Parliament.

Unfortunately, PR would not guarantee any one party receiving an electoral majority; only that if it did not, it could not form a government on its own. With three major parties in Britain and a number of minor ones, the probability indeed is that none could gain either a majority of votes or a majority of parliamentary seats (unless two parties formed an electoral alliance with a common programme, pledged to form a government if it got a majority).

Otherwise, parties would have to negotiate coalition governments after the election. These would certainly be based on a popular majority of votes. The problem is that electors would have voted for the different parties making up the government on the basis of their diverse policies and programmes. Even if the partners could compromise on these, it would still not be quite what the electors had voted for. British commentators have traditionally been dismissive of coalition governments, seeing them as weak and unstable and not offering electors a clear-cut choice between alternative government programmes as the British system does. However, there is much to be said for coalition governments too. The arguments are shown in the Controversy.

The saving feature about coalition governments, which predominate on the Continent, is that about 80 per cent of them over the postwar period have included the 'centre' party representing the median elector. To the extent that the middle position is the one which most fairly represents the overall preferences of the electorate, coalition governments are responsive to the democratic majority even if the actual majority on which they rest is manufactured after the election.

CONTROVERSY

COALITION GOVERNMENT VERSUS SINGLE PARTY GOVERNMENT

Arguments for single party government based on first past the post

1. The two major parties offer electors a clear-cut choice between alternative government programmes.

2. A cohesive parliamentary majority ensures that the Government programme gets through and the electoral mandate is fulfilled.

3. The largest single number of electors is represented by the party that gets into power (though this may not include the median voter).

4. The disadvantages of basing government on a popular minority are outweighed by the advantages of strong effective government.

5. Single party government encourages adversarial politics particularly between the two largest parties, as they are very much in a win or lose situation, and thus clarifies the debate on the key political issues.

Arguments for coalition government based on PR

1. Some coalition governments are formed by parties that have fought the election with a common programme of government, as an electoral alliance (Germany, Scandinavia). If they get a majority they have a mandate just as much as a single-party government.

2. Many coalitions are strong and cohesive and have a clear programme of government (Germany, Netherlands, France).

3. Coalitions are usually based on a popular majority which includes the median voter. Even though the supporting majority has not all voted for the same party, policy has a greater chance of representing majority rather than minority wishes.

4. Coalitions can be strong and effective too, as Germany and the Netherlands demonstrate.

5. Coalitions generally encourage compromise and negotiation between the partner parties, and sometimes with the opposition too. No party and its supporters will lose out entirely under coalition government because all parties have to bear in mind that they might be partners with the others in a future coalition.

If Britain is to become more democratic, in the sense of majority control being strengthened to the extent it can be under representative democracy, then the way ahead must be through a reform of the electoral system in the direction of PR. This cannot be through proportionally chosen representatives simply being added to constituency-based ones, as in Scotland. Such a system gives no guarantee of a final proportionate result. The solution lies, rather, in a system where the national vote obtained by parties determines the overall distribution of parliamentary seats between them. So far, however, there is little sign of PR in this sense being used for British parliamentary elections although it has recently been introduced for European elections in Britain.

Key term

Referendum – a vote in which only one, or a small number of issues are put to the electorate, as against a general election in which the electorate chooses between parties on a broad range of political issues.

Policy voting in referendums

Discussion so far has focused on the 'big issues' at the centre of political debate in Britain: the general left–right direction of the economy, welfare priorities and foreign policy. Voting choices between the parties focus on these, since elections are at best a blunt instrument for exerting popular control. Popular decisions cannot be fine-tuned in general elections, which take place only at four or five year intervals. They can only determine the overall direction of policy – the general priorities for governments to pursue – rather than how exactly they will be pursued. They also leave out all the other issues which do not fit on the left–right continuum – administrative reform, official secrecy, sleaze and corruption, environmental priorities, territorial management – many of which are important in their own right and have been the focus of preceding chapters.

In principle, such issues could be decided separately by popular voting in popular 'initiatives' or referendums. Many European countries do have referendums on constitutional matters and the practice is spreading in Britain (for example, the Welsh and Scottish referendums on devolution in 1997, the one on London government in 1998, and the promised all-British referendum on European Monetary Union in 2002 or 2003).

Referendums, however, are called by governments at a time of their own choosing. Either the government senses it has an advantage and the vote will go the way it wants, or the parties are themselves internally divided and pass the hot potato on to the electorate so that they can avoid the decision themselves (like the European Community referendum of 1975). Neither circumstance provides ideal conditions for unfettered popular choice.

In practice very few countries permit electors to have a vote on policy whenever a sizeable group of them wants one (a procedure known technically as a popular initiative, as opposed to a referendum, which is called by a government when it wants a popular vote). This procedure is followed in about half the states of the United States, but not at federal level. In Europe it occurs in Italy and at a variety of levels – locals, regional and federal – in Switzerland. The fact that Britain does not have popular initiatives does not make it notably less democratic than most other European countries.

Increased use of referendums from 1975 onwards does enhance the scope of popular control, but not very much, given the vast range of issues decided without reference to any kind of electoral process or popular vote. For evidence of popular influence over these we must look to other mechanisms, notably pressure group activity.

PRESSURE GROUP REPRESENTATION

As pointed out in Chapter 12, there are tens of thousands of groups in Britain representing practically every activity and interest imaginable. On issues which affect these, the relevant groups will become active, trying to influence the Government through a variety of strategies. The theory of 'pluralist democracy' emphasises the extent to which every political decision will find an advocate or defender among groups and organisations, often not primarily political ones but with interests and members affected in this particular case.

Any particular issue decision will thus tend to be a compromise or equilibrium position, attempting to reconcile the positions of the opposition groups. For example, on the right to open access to the countryside, the Ramblers' Association, who support access, will be opposed by the Country Landowners' Association and the National Farmers' Union, who oppose it. The final decision would perhaps be to allow restricted access with safeguards for crops, animals and game, giving all sides something of what they want but less than they would have preferred.

Pressure groups may thus focus popular preferences on detailed issues more precisely than political parties can. On many issues the majority of people may not be particularly involved and it is a question of two minorities confronting each other. Of course, one minority may be very much bigger than another: the Ramblers' Association, for example, has over a million members and can claim to speak for perhaps twice that number of walkers. Country landowners and farmers combined number substantially less than half a million.

If the final decision favours the larger groups somewhat more, this would be in accordance with the democratic principle that the larger number should have more weight. In such cases, pressure group activity could supplement and complement the central democratic device of elections in a way which is perfectly compatible with their pre-eminence on the issues that do fall within their purview.

There are problems, however, with the idea that group representation can supplement party representation. These have already been spelled out in Chapter 12. Basically they relate to the fact that smaller groups often have more resources and influence than larger ones. Not only can they block proposals (even ones supported by a full popular majority) but they can also work to get their own privileges and monopolies covertly extended without the majority knowing. For example the tobacco industry has been able to undermine administrative action to restrict smoking, and prevent legislation being proposed, by making large secret donations to Conservatives and Labour.

This may now be coming to light through the efforts of the Committee on Standards in Public Life. New legislation may now force the parties to disclose the amount of donations and the identity of donors. However, this will not abolish the disparity of resources between the tobacco companies and their opponents. The former will still be able to influence decisions disproportionately by advertising, wining and dining supporters, employing consultants or threatening job losses.

Disparities are even more pronounced where some pressure groups have privileged access to bureaucrats and politicians. It is an old tradition of British government to give some groups 'insider' status so that they are consulted before any action in their sphere is even formulated and are then allowed to intervene at every stage in the subsequent process. Examples of insider groups are the farmers' unions, hospital consultants, financiers, barristers. Outsiders have been trade unions (except for brief periods), manufacturers, walkers, environmentalists, consumers, the larger and more popular groups.

Insider groups have been even more fortunate where they have had an institutional sponsor within the structure of government, as farmers have had with the

Ministry of Agriculture, Fisheries and Food (MAFF) or the City of London with the Treasury and Bank of England. In the latter case, the City only needs to signal its preferences to have decision makers jumping over themselves to respond. Such is its influence over policy that the City may be said to have an inbuilt structural influence over decisions denied to mass organisations like trade unions or even to small manufacturers.

Margaret Thatcher's distancing of herself and her governments from any form of group consultation did not include the City, whose influence was rather enhanced by her reforms. Her stance has been continued by succeeding governments, including New Labour. Most pressure groups, however, are discouraged from forming a cosy relationship with a sponsoring ministry or agency.

Experience has shown, however, that this does not eliminate all group influence. Rather the practice of aloofness favours those groups, predominantly business and finance, which dispose of large resources and can threaten job losses and disruption if their interests are affected. Tobacco and arms manufacturers spring to mind here, as well as the pervasive City of London or the media proprietors.

Group representation thus seems more likely to magnify the imbalances of the electoral process in Britain rather than to compensate for them. Popular interests are able to make their voice heard and agitate on behalf of consumers, workers and environmentalists. Too often, however, they are ignored in favour of wealthy entrenched interests which can operate both covertly and overtly through threats of economic disruption to get their own way. Can scrutiny help? At least if it does not cancel out imbalances it can reveal what the richer pressure groups are up to under the cloak of official secrecy.

SCRUTINY AND RIGHTS

We associate scrutiny with defence of individual and group rights, because until decisions and their consequences are known, rights can hardly be asserted against them. The defence of rights often involves publicity to get general support, law suits to have injustices overturned, media campaigns to alert Parliament and other bodies to a wrong. All these involve some scrutiny of public decisions by organisations or individuals, which is what we concentrate on here (see Briefing 29.3).

We need to make two preliminary points. As pointed out above, the defence of rights is a defining characteristic of the liberal side of liberal democracy. But it is also closely related to the democratic element as well, since one cannot have full debate or make informed popular decisions without maintaining procedural rights. The two sides of liberal democracy are thus mutually supportive, particularly on the matter of penetrating the cloak of official secrecy under which unjust and arbitrary decisions are often made.

It might well be asked, however, why the normal practices of parliamentary democracy do not suffice for adequate scrutiny of decisions? This is the position taken by traditionalist MPs on both the Labour and Conservative side, who claim that the winning party is elected to govern and should be allowed to get on with its mandate. The Opposition should be left free to expose weaknesses in the

Government position or shortfalls in administration. If it does the job well, and the Government makes too many mistakes, it will get public opinion on its side and will win the next election, taking corrective action as the new Government.

According to this view, the adversarial relationship of Government and Opposition guarantees effective scrutiny. To work, it demands that everyone be lined up in support of their own side. Any attempt to upstage this central confrontation by select committees or judicial review or media campaigns is at best irrelevant and at worst blunts the crucial central confrontation.

We have already exposed the shallowness of this point of view (Chapter 18). It is shown up even more by what has been said about the narrow, if highly important, range of issues on which party competition focuses. We can rely on party

BRIEFINGS

29.3 SCRUTINY AND THE DEFENCE OF RIGHTS: A CASE STUDY

A recent case reveals just how much protection and scrutiny is needed against unjust administrative decisions. In 1985 most of the state-owned National Bus Company was sold off to private interests. It had run a pension scheme for its employees to which, as usual in an occupational scheme, both the employer and employees contributed. In 1985 this scheme had a surplus, over and above current obligations to members, of £114 million. Such a surplus seemed on the face of it to belong to the fund to distribute among members, particularly as they would be hit economically by the privatisation. Instead it was appropriated by the company and ultimately went to the Government's Department of Transport (DOT) as part of the profits of privatisation.

Attempts by a retired busman to query this decision were brushed off with threats of financial penalties by the DOT, by the Public Accounts Committee of the Commons, and by the first Pensions Ombudsman. It was only the support of two investigative journalists that kept the matter going, until the second Pensions Ombudsman did take it on in 1994. In late 1997 the DOT were still resisting restitution of the money, and even investigation of the case. To keep the original complainants from suing the Department directly they had got the Government Official Solicitor to instigate a lawsuit against the Department, using the Department's own lawyers! By this tactic they could keep the case going at least until the civil servants involved in the original appropriation of the surplus retired and most pensioners were dead or incapacitated.

Significantly, the change of government in May 1997 made no difference to the DOT position. Labour MPs who had criticised the Conservative Government over the case, and who had in some cases become ministers – in one case at the DOT – did not change its policy after they got to office.

Unfortunately what happened to the National Bus Company pension fund has been standard practice in the privatised utilities, where management has appropriated pension scheme surpluses wherever they could.

Source: Guardian Magazine, 15 November 1997, pp. 22–29

confrontations in the House of Commons to throw up differences on economic management, on the internal market in health, on welfare and work, and on Europe. When it comes to official secrecy, civil service incompetence or mis-management, illicit payments to parties, siphoning money from privatised pension funds, and a range of other matters affecting individual and group rights, neither of the main parties is likely to take a stand because they are both involved in the same abuses. Even if they are not, they are almost totally dependent on advice from civil servants, who are so involved. Leaving matters to ritual partisan debates in the Commons is a recipe for ignoring them altogether, which of course is just what many civil servants and Party hacks want.

THE SCOPE OF SCRUTINY

We have looked at various forms of scrutiny in the preceding chapters, notably by the courts (including the European Court, Chapter 11), parliamentary select committees (Chapter 18), and investigative journalism (Chapter 14). Encouragingly for the defence of rights, all these are on the increase.

Judicial review

The incorporation into British law of the European Convention on Human Rights in 1997 has extended the courts' powers of scrutiny and ability to reverse administrative decisions. Even before this important step was taken, the courts were extending their own jurisdiction, taking their cue from the European Court of Justice and its very wide interpretation of its own powers.

Besides their explicit scrutiny of appeals against the administration, courts are often called upon to make political decisions under the guise of legal judgements (Chapter 20). The problem here is that such decisions, based in the absence of other guidance upon their own experience and prejudices, are very much affected by the closed and privileged background of the judiciary. Though the courts are necessary and powerful defenders of rights, they often interpret them in a restrictive and eccentric way.

There are two obvious remedies for this. One is to make the ruling norms, including constitutional ones, more explicit by writing them down, so judges are not forced to make decisions beyond their own competence. The other is to reform both the legal profession and the selection of judges so as to make them more open, accessible and representative of the general population.

Unfortunately, attempts to do both of these things have been defeated. Lord McKay, the Conservative Lord Chancellor at the end of the 1980s, tried to break down barriers between barristers and solicitors, and to get the latter appointed as judges. He was defeated by the barristers. Lord Irvine, the current Labour Lord Chancellor, backed off from making the appointment of judges less arbitrary and personal by putting it through a nomination committee.

Both chancellors have responded to calls for government economy by cutting legal aid, which enabled the poor and less well off to initiate and fight cases against employers and Government. As a result both the law and legal profession are much more accessible to the rich and powerful than the poor and downtrodden, though one might feel the latter needed their help more. Overall, therefore, trends in judicial scrutiny have been mixed, giving it more scope in which to operate but restricting it to safe hands (elderly, conservative, judges) and again to insiders rather than outsiders.

Parliamentary select committees

It was one of the big surprises of the Thatcher period that a thoroughgoing reform and extension of the system of scrutiny was carried out in 1979, perhaps without proper appreciation of what the consequences might be. The predominant Conservative philosophy of the period 1979–97 was certainly that 'Government knows best' and that any scrutiny is best carried out through ritual confrontations in Parliament.

Despite this, the select committees have functioned reasonably well and extended their scope. The corresponding committees of the House of Lords have also been very active, less prone to party interference than those of the Commons, and staffed by authoritative and able figures in the shape of the life peers who carry on most of the work.

Some reports of select committees have been watered down by the majority party for fear of embarrassing their leadership. Such compromises are probably inevitable in politics, since one must always reckon with the pervasive presence of parties. The Whips have also manipulated membership and the appointment of chairs. Enough genuinely investigative work has been done, however, even when embarrassing to the parties and government, to validate the work of select committees and to identify them as one of the most genuine and worthwhile constitutional innovations of the postwar period.

The trouble with select committees, Commons as well as Lords, is not basically with what they have been able to do but with what is not within their powers to do, that is, to have their criticisms and reports attended to. In the absence of any clearly defined constitutional role being given to them, there is no obligation on the Government as a whole, or on any individual minister, department or agency, to carry through their recommendations or even to respond to them. Indeed, as we have noted, the usual reaction of ministries to a critical report is to delay replying for two or three years in the justified hope that an election will intervene or the committee will be reformed, and the matter will be lost sight of.

Only by raising a political scandal through leakages to the press can a committee hope to get some response. Even then, reactions are as likely to take the form of brazening the matter out as of redressing it. Again it appears that a remedy is to be sought in constitutional clarification. Until they are given coercive powers over civil servants, the committees are likely to remain mere talking shops, unable to effect their recommendations no matter how many abuses they uncover.

Investigative journalism

We noted that, in spite of the growing concentration of ownership of the media, market forces have encouraged a tendency to muck-raking and scandalmongering, which at the upper end has shaded over into investigative journalism. This mode of reporting has expanded steadily over the last three decades. Much of this book, in fact, could not have been written without it, as it would either have had to rely on what governments were willing to disclose (very little, possibly untrue), or have been quite unable to sort out reality from legal fiction.

Investigative journalism has made British political life much more transparent, and politicians much more accountable, in the later postwar period than before. It is, however, a fragile plant. Severe libel laws, which put the onus of proof on the reporter and paper rather than the defendant, mean that the rich and powerful can always use legal threats to manipulate what is said about them. Official secrecy can be used to censor what is said and to smother investigations, even to justify the confiscation of embarrassing material just before transmission. Media proprietors can be induced to call the hounds off in return for favours or honours.

Again what seems to be needed is the consolidation of rights to investigation, optimally as a constitutional right. Reforming the law of libel so as to allow a public interest defence for journalists – or even reversing the onus of proof in political cases, so that it is for the defendants to show that they are not doing what is alleged – would also free investigative journalism to be much more far-reaching than it is at the moment. Doing the same with the Official Secrets Act (in its latest incarnation jokingly termed the Freedom of Information Act) would be the greatest liberation of all. Forcing government, which is supposed to act on our behalf, to reveal whether it is actually doing so and how, would seem an obvious step along the road to the full informed debate and discussion to which it must surely be subject in a democracy. Secrecy should be the exception, and should need to be justified, rather than being the rule without need for justification, as it is now in British government.

The major obstacle to scrutiny: official secrecy

The blanket secrecy and obsessive defensiveness of administration and government in Britain are clearly the main obstacles to any kind of informed scrutiny. They are tempting for governments to maintain, as they act as defences against any kind of searching critique of what they are doing. New Labour, as well as the Conservatives, seems to have modified its projected reforms on finding how useful secrecy can be in this regard.

Yet to a considerable extent this judgement may be mistaken. All sorts of conflicting political and social tendencies have combined to make secrecy into a weakness of governments rather than a defence. Leaks combined with investigative journalism tend in the absence of balancing information to turn small infractions of rules into major and destabilising scandals. Not knowing what their ramifications may be, owing to secrecy and attempted news management, much more may be suspected than what is actually there.

Secrecy centres on the security services and the ramifying arms industry, even though it spreads out to encompass vast administrative areas which have very little to do with either. The Security Services indeed often seem to form a state within a state, directed by a small Cabinet clique (if indeed they are under control at all). The idea that two Directors of MI6 might have been Soviet agents, that miners in 1984–85 were secretly harassed and spied upon, that a campaign was carried out in the 1970s against the Prime Minister and the Labour Government, that left-wing student leaders are routinely put under surveillance: all these surmises are surely more destabilising to British democracy than if they were openly discussed and checked. If found to be true, precautions could be taken against their recurrence. While official secrecy hides the truth, no effective action can be taken to prevent a recurrence. In this, as in most other aspects, official secrecy is self-defeating. It is certainly inimical to British democracy.

WRITING DOWN THE CONSTITUTION

Secrecy is a relic of the time when foreign policy was the major concern of British government and Britain was the major player abroad. It was also a time when government was the King's Government, and not responsible or accountable to Parliament except for taxation. Security is still part of the Royal Prerogative (exercised now by the Cabinet) and not accountable to anyone.

To many this is illogical and absurd in a modern democracy. It might be argued that, as millions died in the World Wars, electors have as much right to know what is being done in their name in foreign policy as on welfare, the economy and other domestic matters.

There are those who laud the ambiguity and imprecision of the British constitution as a unique advantage, giving it a flexibility and adaptability which written constitutions do not have. As we have shown, however, its flexibility and adaptability are used mainly to get governments off the hook and to evade full scrutiny and democratic control.

Clearly, to extend democracy in Britain and to improve its functioning, the constitution needs to be codified and written down, so that everyone knows where they stand. Then and only then will it be possible to confront the other issues raised in this chapter: lack of clear guidelines for judicial action, absence of teeth for select committees, legal barriers to investigative journalism, reversal of official secrecy. A written constitution would also be able to tackle the issues of electoral representation and popular control, as well as relationships with European, regional, and local governments.

Writing down the British constitution would not be an enormous task, since it has already been done 40 or 50 times! Every time a British colony has gained independence a constitution heavily modelled on (sometimes an exact copy of) the British was written for it. To find the main elements of the 'Westminster model', with all its conventions and understandings, all one need do is read the Barbadian or Indian constitutions (or the Canadian or New Zealand ones) and there it is.

Of course, such documents can be modified to serve the contemporary needs of Britain. Apart from anything else, excolonial constitutions contain many of the undesirable practices taken over from Britain, which we have listed above.

> **Key term**
>
> **Codification of the constitution** – producing a written constitution which makes it clearer, and more precise, explicit, and systematic.

However, these other documents give clear testimony of the practicability of writing down the British constitution. The only thing that prevents it in the British case is not practicability and workability but political will. It is easy and tempting for governments and bureaucracy to manipulate the unwritten constitution so as to make life easier for themselves. But making life easy for governments and civil servants should not be a prime concern for a self-respecting liberal democracy.

EVALUATING CURRENT DEVELOPMENTS

To some extent New Labour have developed a 'constitutional project'. They have written the European Convention on Human Rights into British law. They have carried through their promise to give devolution to Scotland and Wales and a new local government to London. New electoral systems have been developed for each of these areas, while genuine proportional representation is to be used for European elections in Britain. All these developments, together with the rapprochement with Liberal Democrats, may indicate a more open mind towards the central question (from a democratic point of view) of electoral reform.

However, it is difficult to see Labour agreeing, certainly in the near future, to a fully proportional electoral system. The most one would expect would be an additional members' system as for the Scottish Parliament, where a certain number of MPs are elected by PR additional to a majority who sit for constituencies. The final result is not proportional but it would give Liberal Democrats more seats, while retaining the Labour lead over Conservatives in the constituencies.

If the Liberal Democrats did as well as previously in the constituencies, while getting more additional members, they would be attractive coalition partners for Labour. Government would finally be based on a popular majority to which it would be responsive on the central issues. This would enhance democratic control over the central policy process. Having two coalition partners privy to the secrets of government would also enhance scrutiny, as one party would keep an eye on the other and make sure that any administrative excesses were leaked.

Scrutiny should be helped in general by having more parliaments and assemblies. The Scottish and Welsh Offices are notoriously arbitrary and unresponsive in their attitudes and actions, part of their role in enforcing central diktats on reluctant local populations. The Westminster Parliament has had little time to supervise them. Intensified scrutiny from their local assembly will be a real gain. It might also bring the proliferating nominated quangos under control.

However, New Labour proposes to leave the central processes of government, official secrecy and all, unreformed and unchecked. Parliament is still to be dominated on all matters by the leadership of the majority party. The security services are to be retained and even enhanced in the 'War against Drugs'. Unelected quangos continue and are also given new responsibilities. The elective dictatorship is to continue. In short, very little difference is to be made to the core executive's place in the British constitution. Nor is the constitution to be written down and codified.

New Labour's reforms, therefore, advance the country a little in democratic and liberal terms, but do not take us very far. When all governments profit so much in the short term from existing arrangements it is perhaps unrealistic to think they will ever reform them radically of their own free will.

ESSAYS

1. Liberal democracy conceals a contradiction at its heart, between liberalism and democracy. Discuss.

2. Modern British democracy is party democracy. Is this true?

3. Pluralist democracy is a recipe for stalemate rather than popular 'representation'. Assess.

4. 'The power of the security services has grown, is growing, and ought to be diminished'. Can it be diminished in the modern world?

SUMMARY

This chapter has taken up the question raised at the beginning of this book: how healthy and extensive is British democracy? It has concluded that:

- Britain is a liberal democracy.

- The democratic element involves popular control.

- The liberal element involves safeguards which are secured through scrutiny of the administration and other powerful bodies in Britain.

- No postwar government has been voted in by a popular majority.

- Only seven out of fifteen have held the 'middle ground' in left–right terms and thus been broadly representative, but since 1974 only one (New Labour in 1997) has held the 'middle ground'. This means that governments from 1974 to 1992 have been less truly representative than their predecessors.

- Pressure groups cannot compensate for the defects of party representation because of the many structural advantages enjoyed by rich financial groups.

- Scrutiny by courts, select committees and investigative journalism is hampered by the lack of an adequate written constitution.

- The Constitution has been codified and spelled out many times in the form of ex-colonial constitutions. It would help British democracy if this could also be done in Britain.

- New Labour's constitutional projects usefully fill in gaps in the protection of rights and arrangements for scrutiny. It is unlikely to raise the quality of British democracy substantially if it leaves the arbitrary powers of the Government and central executive untouched.

MILESTONES

MILESTONES IN BRITISH DEMOCRACY, 1979–98

	Scrutiny	*Popular control*
1979–97	– Stretching' of constitutional conventions to increase Government power and ability to act, often secretly, without consultation	
1979	+ Parliamentary select committees reformed	
1979 onwards	+ Investigative journalism extends in depth and range, helped by increasing leaks from within the Civil Service and Cabinet	
	1979	+ Directly elected European Parliament
	1979–97	– Nominated quangos extend powers across a range of policy areas, often at expense of elected local government

MILESTONES IN BRITISH DEMOCRACY, 1979–98 (continued)

	Scrutiny		*Popular control*
1984–85	– Ad hoc national police force created to break miners' strike. Illicit surveillance and harassment by security services	**1980s**	+ Local councils become increasingly politicised and discuss and criticise government policy
1989	– Freedom of Information Act actually consolidates and strengthens official secrecy, with some minor liberalisation in unimportant areas.		
1991 onwards	+ Consumers' and Citizens' Charters force publication of performance criteria by government departments and monopolies, thus giving a limited basis for redress of consumer rights		
1990s	+ Courts extend their powers of judicial review of administrative decisions		
1990s	– Security services' role expanded domestically by both Conservative and Labour governments		
1995–98	+ Committees of investigation of corrupt links between political parties and business (Scott, Nolan, etc.)		
		1997	+ General election victory of Labour in part a reaction against arrogance and corruption of Conservative Governments
		1997	– Retention of existing quangos by Labour
1997	+ Incorporation of European Convention on Human Rights safeguards rights more and extends power of judicial scrutiny	**1997**	+ Reintroduction of referendums on important constitutional issues
1997	– Postponement of legislation to reform official secrecy		
		1998	+ Establishment of Welsh and Scottish Assemblies and all-London elected executive

Note: Positive developments for democracy are marked with +, negative ones with –. It can be see from the chart that developments are mixed and degrade as well as enhance the quality of democracy

PROJECTS

1. Do we need a written constitution (see also Chapter 7)?

2. Justify the pivotal position of the median voter and 'middle party' in a democracy.

FURTHER READING

R. Brazier, *Constitutional Reform* (Oxford: Clarendon Press, 1991) presents an account of the British constitution as it is and as it might be, while Dennis Kavanagh, *The Reordering of British Politics: Politics After Thatcher* (Oxford: Oxford University Press, 1997) assesses the current state of British government. On the new European order and the strategic choices it faces see I. Budge and K. Newton *et al.*, *The Politics of the New Europe* (Harlow: Addison Wesley Longman, 1997), Part I and Part V. H. MacRae, *The World in 2020* (London: HarperCollins, 1995) presents an optimistic account of the future but P. Kennedy, *Preparing for the Twenty First Century* (London: Fontana, 1994) is more gloomy.

http://www.awl-he.com/politics/newbritpol

Internet resources – visit *The New British Politics* Webpage for links to a specially-chosen selection of Internet resources relevant to this Chapter.

http://www.awl-he.com/politics/newbritpol

G L O S S A R Y

Accountability To have to answer for one's conduct, or to be subject to review or evaluation by a higher body. The doctrine of ministerial accountability, for example, holds that government ministers are answerable to Parliament for their actions.

Administration Either (1) the process of co-ordinating and implementing public policy through the machinery of public administration or (2) another word for government – as in 'the Blair administration'.

Affirmative action Policies designed to provide groups with redress for a past pattern of discrimination. Such policies often take the form of legal requirements that organisations, such as universities, businesses, or state bureaucracies, should take positive steps to increase their numbers of minority groups which have suffered discrimination in the past. Known as affirmative action, or reverse discrimination in the USA; the term 'positive discrimination' is often used in the UK.

Agenda-setting theory Argues that the media cannot determine what people think, but can have a strong influence over what people think about. By focusing on some issues but not others, the media can highlight the importance of some issues in the public mind.

Balance of payments A method of analysing the record of economic relations between a given country **(balance of trade)** and the rest of the world, the balance of payments measures the surplus or deficit of exports over imports over a period of time. In practice, measuring the balance of payments is a complicated matter, but it is useful as a short-hand indicator of whether a country is 'paying its way' or spending more than it earns abroad.

Bill of Rights In modern language a bill of rights is a formal statement of the rights and privileges that may be actually or theoretically claimed by citizens. The Bill of Rights passed by Parliament in 1689, however, placed restrictions on the royal prerogative, asserted some rights of parliament, and made provision for the protection of some individual rights such as the right to petition the monarch, to carry arms, and freedom from excessive fines.

Broadsheets Serious national daily and Sunday papers, so called because of their size. Daily broadsheets are *The Times*, the *Daily Telegraph*, the *Guardian*, the *Independent*, and the *Financial Times*.

Cabinet	The committee of the leading members of the government who are empowered to make decisions on behalf of the government. The Cabinet is mainly, but not entirely, formed by heads of important departments of state and others who perform important functions of state.
Cabinet collegiality	The feeling among cabinet members that they must act closely and co-operatively together, even when they conflict over policy issues and departmental interests.
Cabinet government	The theory that the cabinet, not the Prime Minister, forms a collective political executive which, therefore, constrains the power of the Prime Minister. In Cabinet government the principle of collective responsibility ensures that the Cabinet either makes or is consulted about all important political decisions.
Cadre parties	Parties of like-minded and wealthy 'notables' who used their own money to fight political campaigns and relied upon their own personal supporters. Good examples are the Conservative and Liberal Parties in Britain between about 1830 and the Reform Act of 1867.
Cause groups (promotional groups)	Promote a general cause or idea. Unlike interest groups their members are not drawn from particular occupations but may come from a wide variety of social backgrounds.
Civil liberties	The freedoms which should not normally be constrained by others, whether private individuals or the state. Civil liberties are often used as an argument against the extension of state power into areas of life regarded as private – for example, the enforced use of seat belts in cars or crash helmets for motorbike riders. Civil libertarians are those who use these arguments, or who are particularly conscious of the importance of civil liberties.
Civil servant	A servant of the Crown (i.e. the government) who is employed in a civilian capacity (not a member of the armed forces) and who is paid wholly and directly from central government funds (not local government, nationalised industries, or quangos).
Civil service anonymity	Civil servants are the confidential advisers of ministers and must not be asked questions about politically controversial matters or the policy advice they give.
Civil service impartiality	The principle that civil servants should be politically neutral and serve their Cabinet ministers regardless of which party is in power and of what they may personally feel about their minister's policies.
Civil society	The aspects of social and economic life (primarily voluntary associations and private organisations) which are outside the immediate control of the state. A strong civil society based upon a large number and wide variety of private associations and organisations is thought to be the basis for democracy.
Class	Among the many and varied definitions of class, the most useful ranks the social and economic status of people according to their occupation, most notably into manual (working class) and non-manual (middle and upper class) groups, and then into sub-groups or strata of these categories.
Coalition government	Where two or more parties combine to form the government, in contrast to single party government where all the offices of government are held by members of the

same party. Britain has had single party government for most (but not all) of the twentieth century.

Codification of the constitution
Producing a written constitution which makes it clearer, and more precise, explicit and systematic.

Cold War
The state of international relations between the West and the Communist bloc which stopped short of outright war, but involved intense hostility and the stock-piling of arms and maintenance of large armies in case war should break out. The Cold War started in a serious manner in 1947, at the time of the Berlin blockade and air-lift, but gradually died away in the 1970s as a result of international agreements and arms limitations.

Collective responsibility
The principle that decisions and policies of the Cabinet are binding on all members of the government who must support them in public, to maintain a united front, or resign their government post.

Committee of Inquiry
A committee appointed by the government, but composed of members outside Parliament, and charged with the job of inquiring into and reporting on a particular matter. Recent examples are the Nolan Committee on Standards of Public Life, the Scott Committee into 'Arms to Iraq', and the (Lord Roy) Jenkins Committee on electoral systems.

Common law
Law which is overtly made by judges and which has become part of custom and precedent.

Community Charge or Poll Tax
The local tax which replaced the rates (or property tax) in which every adult resident of a local authority paid the same amount. It came into operation in 1990 and was replaced by the Council Tax in 1993.

Community law
The treaties, legislation, and case-law of the European Court of Justice, which are the legal basis of the European Union.

Constitution
The fundamental rules (or laws) governing the relationship between the public institutions of a state. Most constitutions are written and codified in a single document, but in Britain it is partly written but uncodified. Constitutional documents set the limits and powers of government and often state the rights and freedoms of citizens.

Constitutional review
The process by which laws and other acts of the legislature can be overruled by a court if the court holds them to conflict with constitutional rules, human rights, or other laws treated as superior to legislation. Prior to joining the European Economic Community no British court had this power.

Constructionism
The practice by which the courts define and interpret the meaning of Acts of Parliament, especially where they are vague or general.

Content regulation
Regulation of the content of the media by public bodies. Regulation of political content applies mainly to the electronic media (because of spectrum scarcity), and requires that news and current affairs programmes are accurate, balanced, and impartial, but it also applies to the print media so far as pornography, violence, and public decency are concerned.

Core executive   The network of institutions, people and practices which collect at the apex of power around the Prime Minister and the Cabinet, including the most powerful civil servants of Whitehall, the Cabinet Office, and the Prime Minister's Office. The core executive integrates policy in an otherwise rather fragmented decision-making structure.

Core party support   The minimum voting support it is estimated a party can gain in a given election. The idea behind the concept is that core supporters are the die-hard voters for a party in a given election.

Corporatism   A system of policy making in which major economic interests work closely together within formal structures of government to formulate and implement public policies. Corporatism requires a formal government apparatus capable of concerting the main economic groups so that they can jointly formulate and implement binding policies. In this sense, Britain has never been a corporatist state, but had in the 1960s and 1970s a looser form of tripartite system.

Council Tax   The local tax, which replaced the Community Charge in 1993, in which, like the rates, payment is related to property values and levied on all occupants of property. Business rates are set by central government and levied on non-domestic property.

Cross-bench (non-aligned) groups   Groups which are not aligned with a party and try to maintain party political neutrality (like cross-bench groups in Parliament).

Cross-media ownership   When the same person or company has financial interests in different forms of mass media – radio, TV, and newspapers.

De-colonisation   Colonies are foreign territories dominated by stronger states by means of military and economic power. De-colonisation, therefore, is the process of withdrawing from colonial relations with foreign countries so that they gain the autonomy of a sovereign state. In the case of the British Empire, colonial countries often became members of the Commonwealth.

Deregulation   The opposite of regulation, it involves the weakening or removal of state regulations in the interests of market competition. Deregulation was accompanied by privatisation in Britain in the 1980s and early 1990s.

Democratic deficit   A phrase usually applied to the EU to describe a lack of democratic accountability in its decision-making. It is usually argued that the European Parliament is too weak in relation to the Commission, and especially the Council of Ministers.

Devolution   The delegation of specific powers by a higher level of government to a lower one. Unlike a federal system where the powers of the lower level are constitutionally guaranteed, devolved powers can always be taken back by the higher authority.

Discrimination   The practice of distinguishing (usually in order to disadvantage) between individuals or social groups on grounds or criteria (such as race, religion, gender, or colour) which are not relevant to the circumstances under consideration.

Disposable income   More often known as 'take-home pay', disposable income refers to income after taxes have been paid.

Economic management	The process by which governments assume, to varying degrees, the task of managing the national economy by means of macro- and/or micro-economic policies. Government economic intervention may become so broad and pervasive that management turns into planning. Monetarism is associated with the idea that the government's role should be limited largely to management of the money supply, but Keynesian theory advocates more interventionist economic planning.
Effective dictatorship	The term used to describe the British political system as one in which, once elected, the leadership of the majority party in the House of Commons can do more or less what it wants without constitutional checks and balances, until it faces the electorate at the next general election.
Egalitarian	Political views of policies based upon a wish to achieve equality, or less inequality.
Electoral volatility	Large and rapid changes in voting behaviour from one election to another.
Environmental impact assessment	A requirement of the European Union, which came into force in 1988, requiring all public and private projects above a given cost to be subject to environmental appraisal in which the advantages and disadvantages from the environmental point of view are laid out.
Environmentalism	A concern with the natural environment (including many things from the physical environment affecting 'the quality of life') and the belief that its protection should be given more importance, and economic growth less. Environmentalists are sometimes referred to as 'ecologists' or 'conservationists'. In the 1970s and 1980s environmentalists began to form themselves into social movements and Green Parties.
Episodic groups	Groups which are not normally political, but become so when circumstances require. For example, football clubs are politically involved only when issues such as football ground safety or hooliganism become a political issue.
Equality of condition	The ideal objective of providing all citizens with equal access to income, wealth, education, employment, and other aspects of social life.
Equality of opportunity	The practice of ensuring that individuals compete on equal terms for goods, benefits and life chances, such as education, employment, or housing, even though the outcome may be unequal. Equality of treatment does not involve treating all individuals as equals. For example, the mentally or physically handicapped should not be treated in the same way as those who are not so handicapped.
Equality of treatment	The application of the same rules and standards to all individuals and social groups.
Essex model	A method of explaining past election results and predicting future ones based on a statistical analysis of the changing economic basis of previous election results.
Establishment	A vague term referring to the elite of public and private life which, some claim, run Britain irrespective of which party is in government. The establishment consists of the small number of 'the great and the good' in the Civil Service, military, church, universities, political parties, and business. Usually with public school and Oxford and Cambridge backgrounds, they are said to follow a consensus, middle-of-the-road, and conservative approach to government and politics.

Ethnicity A mixture or combination of different social characteristics (which may include race, culture, religion, or some other basis of common origin and social identity) which give different social groups a common consciousness, and which are thought to divide or separate them in some way from other social groups.

European Monetary Union (EMU) The third and final stage of European financial integration, EMU provides for a single European currency (the Euro), to replace existing national currencies, and a European central bank. In 1997 the Blair Government announced that Britain would not join EMU, at least in 1999, when it is planned to start.

Europhiles Those who are generally well disposed to the further integration of Europe within the framework of the European Union.

Europhobes Those who are not generally well disposed to the further integration of Europe, at least within the framework of the European Union.

Exchange rate mechanism (ERM) The ERM is the first stage of a European Union plan for financial integration. As part of the European Monetary System (EMS) introduced in 1979, the ERM was designed to minimise currency exchange fluctuation among members of the EU who belonged to the system. Each currency had an exchange rate against the European Currency Unit (ECU), and was supposed to fluctuate within a band either side of this exchange rate. Britain joined the ERM in October 1990, but international currency speculation against the pound sterling drove it out again in September 1992 (Black Wednesday).

Executive One of the three branches of government (with the legislative and judiciary). The executive is concerned with making government decisions and policies rather than with passing laws. In Britain the political executive is the Prime Minister and the Cabinet; in the EU the main executive is the Council of Ministers.

Executive agencies Also known as 'Next Step agencies', these are the semi-autonomous agencies set up to carry out some of the administrative functions of government which were previously the responsibility of civil service departments.

False consciousness The state of mind induced in the working class by the ruling class in order to conceal the real nature of capitalism.

Federal A political structure which combines a central authority with a degree of constitutionally defined autonomy for sub-central units of government – usually territorial units of government such as states, regions, or provinces. In discussions about the European Union in Britain, however, the term 'federal' is sometimes used as a code-word by those critical of the idea of a 'European super-state', and sometimes as a word to describe a political structure, national or supra-national, which is decentralised.

Fire brigade groups Formed to fight a specific issue and dissolved when it is over (e.g. the Anti-Poll Tax Federation).

Fiscal policy A type of macro-economic policy which uses taxation and public expenditure to manage the economy. Fiscal theories are particularly associated with the work of J. M. Keynes (*General Theory of Employment, Interest, and Money,* 1936) who argued that fiscal tools should be used to promote economic development while avoiding the economic cycles of 'boom and bust'.

Framing effects (of the media)	The argument that the media can exercise a subtle but strong effect on how public opinion thinks about politics in a general way, and how it reacts to particular events. For example, by focusing on bad news, the media can produce 'videomalaise'.
Franchise	In its political sense, the right to vote. In Britain the male franchise was extended in 1832, 1867, 1884 and 1918. The female franchise was partly introduced in 1918 and completed in 1928, by which time Britain had a universal franchise.
Free trade	The idea that international trade should not be restricted by protection in the form of tariffs, custom duties, or import quotas which are designed to protect the domestic economy from foreign competition. Free-trade policies are sometimes called *'laissez-faire'* (allow to do) policies.
Freedom of information	Free public access to government information and records. Freedom of information is a necessary condition of open government. Under the public record acts of Britain some government records are open after 30 years.
Functional integration	A form of international integration based upon pragmatic co-operation between states in specific areas of (usually) economic activity. The European Coal and Steel Community is an example. Functional integration is often contrasted with political integration which involves more ambitious blueprints for supra-national government.
Glorious Revolution of 1688	Established the King's dependence upon the support of Parliament and is thus a first step towards parliamentary and constitutional government.
Government	A general term which refers either to the body which forms the political executive (as in 'the Labour Government'), or the institutions which form the constitutional system (as in 'the British system of government). In the second sense, the government consists of those institutions which make the binding rules and decisions in a given territory.
Harmonisation	The attempt of the EU to create common product standards and specifications among its Member States in the interests of a free and genuinely common market.
Hegemonic	In popular language the term refers to an idea or practice which is widely accepted as correct, but the term originally meant a social class (the capitalists) or nation state which is so powerful that its view of the world is accepted even by those whose interests are not served by such a world view.
Human rights	The fundamental and universal rights of all people, irrespective of the laws of their country, which derive from being a human being. Lists of such rights are a matter of controversy but the two main ones are the United Nations Charter of Human Rights and the European Declaration of Human Rights.
Idealism	The view of politics, especially international relations, which emphasises the role of ideals and morality as a determinant of state policies, and hence the possibility of peaceful co-operation.
Ideology	A system of ideas, assumptions, values, and beliefs which help us to explain the political world – what it is and why, and what it should be. Conservatism, liberalism, socialism, fascism, anarchism are main examples. Sometimes the word is used to describe a set of political ideas which are false or misleading. Marxists

use the word in this way to describe the political ideas used by the ruling class to conceal the real nature of capitalism from the workers.

Impact-based approach   The approach to judicial review which assumes that the principal task of the courts is to protect the rights and interests of citizens, rather than to ensure that public bodies act in accordance with the powers granted to them by Parliament.

Imperialism   The practice of one nation controlling or dominating another state or territory, usually by military and economic means, and usually to the advantage of the imperial power. Imperialism (as in the British Empire) is often distinguished from colonialism in that it implies a greater degree of political integration of territories and their citizens, and insofar as imperialism is sometimes claimed to be a feature of advanced capitalism. The term 'imperialism' is now sometimes loosely applied to a strong international financial or cultural influence, as in 'American imperialism' which involves American films, clothes, and speech.

Incomes policy   Government policy designed to secure economic growth and stability by regulating incomes and wages on the grounds that excess demand may be inflationary. Incomes policy was sometimes accompanied by a matching prices policy – hence prices and incomes policy.

Indicative planning   The practice of the state indicating targets or goals for such things as employment, inflation, output, without necessarily taking action of its own to achieve them.

Insider groups (established groups)   Pressure groups which are able to work closely with elected and appointed officials in central or local government.

Interest groups (sectional groups)   Pressure groups which represent the interests of particular economic or occupational groups, especially business organisations, professional associations, and trade unions.

Intergovernmental organisations   Allow national states to co-operate on specific matters while maintaining their national sovereignty. They contrast with supra-national, or federal organisations which wield some power over nation states.

International regimes   Are sets of international institutions and 'rules of the game' which are created and accepted by states in order to promote international co-operation and integration, as opposed to independent decision-making and national competition. Major examples include the General Agreement on Tariffs and Trade (GATT), the Organisation for Security and Co-operation in Europe, and the Organisation for Economic Co-operation and Development (OECD).

Investigative journalism   In-depth and often critical journalism involving research which is usually time-consuming and expensive. Examples include the *Washington Post*'s digging into the Watergate Affair in the United States, and the *Guardian*'s persistent inquiry into the cash-for-questions affair in Britain, 1995–97.

Iron law of oligarchy   The 'law' propounded by Robert Michels in 1911 whereby mass organisations cannot, by their very nature, be democratic and will always and of necessity be controlled by a small elite – the oligarchy.

Judicial review   The process whereby the courts supervise the way in which public officials and bodies carry out their duties. It includes the power to nullify actions which the courts believe to be illegal or unconstitutional.

Junior Ministers	Ministers of state and parliamentary under-secretaries.
Keynesianism	Economic theory or policy derived from the writings of J. M. Keynes (1833-1946) which advocates some government economic intervention to achieve economic stability, growth, and full employment. Keynesian policies were used widely in the Western world, including Britain, in the 1945–80 period.
Kitchen cabinet	The loose and informal policy-advice group which prime ministers may collect around them, and which may include politicians, public officials, and private citizens.
Knowledge gap	The result of the process whereby those with a good education and high status acquire knowledge faster than those with a poorer education and lower status.
Law	A body of rules enforced by the power of the state.
Left-right continuum	The continuum on which it is often convenient to locate parties, which stretches from the left-wing parties which believe in radical or revolutionary change, through the socialists and centre parties, to parties of the moderate right which oppose change, and to extremist parties of a Fascist or Nazi ideology. Although a simplification, the left-right continuum is often a convenient and accurate way of grouping and comparing parties.
Legislature	The law-making branch of government. In Britain it is the Queen in Parliament – the Queen, the House of Lords, and the House of Commons.
Legitimation	The process of making something morally acceptable in the views of the population. A government, for example, is regarded as legitimate if it has gained power by winning a free and fair election.
Liberal democracy	The form of government practised in the West which tries to combine institutions of democratic government with liberal values about individual rights and responsibilities. Britain is democratic in the sense that it has the formal institutions of representative government such as free and regular elections, government under the law, and formal political equality. It is a liberal democracy in the sense that it gives a certain independence and autonomy of government while trying to preserve the rights and freedoms of citizens.
Liberalism	Liberalism (with a capital 'L') refers to the beliefs and policies of the Liberal Party. In the nineteenth century Liberals were also liberals.
Liberalism	Liberalism (with a small 'l') is the political belief that individual rights should be protected by maximising freedom of choice by limiting the powers of government. It is therefore contrasted with socialism which believes that state intervention can increase individual freedom. To confuse matters, the term 'liberal' is sometimes applied in the USA to opponents of the neo-liberal policies of the New Right.
Lobby system	The name given to specially selected correspondents of the main newspapers, TV, and radio stations who are given confidential information by the government on a non-attributable basis. Not to be confused with 'the lobby', or pressure group system in Parliament. The lobby system for briefing journalists was widely criticised for giving the government too much influence over the news.

Macro-economic policy	The branch of economic policy which deals with total or aggregate performance of the national economy, including monetary policy (money in circulation and interest rates), inflation, exchange rates, capital, employment, and labour.
Magistrates courts	Local courts, staffed by part-time and unpaid people (Justices of the Peace or JPs), which deal with minor crimes and decide which are more serious cases to be dealt with by Crown Courts.
Mandarin power/the dictatorship of the official	The theory that, no matter which party forms the government, civil servants will exert a powerful influence over government, or even control the government, because of their ability, experience, expertise, training, and special knowledge.
Mandarins	The comparatively small number (about a thousand) of very senior civil servants who have close and regular contact with ministers in their capacity as policy advisers.
Mandate	An instruction or command which carries legal or moral force. An electoral mandate is said to give the party winning an election the right to carry out its programme. In practice, party programmes are often so broad and vague, and people vote for them for so many different reasons, that it is difficult to claim that the winning party has a mandate for any given policy.
Market regulation	Regulation of the media market by public bodies.
Market testing	The process of deciding whether a public service should be produced at all, and if so whether it should be produced by the public sector, contracted out, or privatised.
Mass parties	Are financed and organised with the help of a mass membership which both pays membership subscriptions and provides the manpower to conduct political campaigns.
Mass society	A society composed of isolated individuals who, because they have no deep roots in community and social life (civil society is weak), are liable to manipulation by political elites.
Micro-economic policy	The branch of economic policy which deals not with the total performance of the economy but with the performance and behaviour of individual economic actors, including firms, trade unions, consumers, regional and local governments, and consumers.
Middle ground	A political position roughly mid-way between the extremes of the political spectrum. The crucial point about the middle ground is not that it is in the middle but that it is assumed to be a position occupied by the majority of voters.
Ministerial responsibility	The principle that ministers are responsible to Parliament for their own and all their department's actions. In theory, ministers are responsible for administrative failure in their department, and for any injustice it may cause, whether personally responsible or not.
Ministers	The eighty or ninety most senior government members consisting of the Prime Minister, Cabinet Ministers (22-26 people), ministers of state (about 28), and parliamentary under-secretaries (about 33).

Monetarism A revised version of neo-classical economics which, contrary to Keynesianism, argues that government should minimise its involvement in economic matters, except for controlling the money supply as a way of holding down inflation. In turn, the money supply consists mainly of the amount of cash and credit circulating in the economy. Monetarism is particularly associated with the work of Milton Friedman and the Chicago school and with the economic policies of the Thatcher Government in the early 1980s.

Multi-media conglomeration When the same company has financial interests in different media and (usually) in a range of other economic activities as well.

Nationalisation The policy of taking firms, services, or industries into public ownership, either because they are key parts of the economy, or because they form natural monopolies, or because they have failed in the open market.

Nationalism Is more than patriotism in that nationalists believe in sovereign state autonomy for the people they identify as belonging to a national community.

Natural law The universal moral rules to which, it is claimed, human laws should conform.

Neo-liberal consensus Agreement among different political groups and parties about neo-liberal politics, that is the political belief that individual rights should be protected by maximising freedom of choice, limiting the powers of government, and promoting market economics. The consensus was at its strongest in Britain and the USA in the 1980s.

Neo-liberalism The ideas associated with the New Right of the 1980s that market competition is the best means of guaranteeing political freedom and economic growth. In politics, neo-liberalism is particularly associated with the policies of Thatcher in Britain and President Reagan in the USA. However, to confuse matters, the term 'liberal' is often used in the United States to describe the moderate critics of neo-liberalism.

New Commonwealth A coded term used to refer to non-white Commonwealth countries.

New Right The politicians and theorists of the 1980s who believed in the efficacy of market competition as the best means of guaranteeing political freedom and economic growth. The movement was 'new' in Britain in that it was opposed to the traditional 'one-nation' Tories (the 'wets'). It was particularly associated with the neo-liberal ideas and policies of Thatcher in Britain and Reagan in the USA.

New social movements Are organisations which emerged in the 1970s in order to influence public policy about such issues as the environment, nuclear energy and weapons, peace, women, and minorities. They have wider policy interests than most pressure groups, but are more loosely knit than political parties.

Next Steps The short title of the Ibbs report (1988) which identified serious management failure in the Civil Service and recommended far-reaching reforms in the shape of executive agencies.

Nuclear deterrent The threatened use of nuclear weapons to prevent aggression on the part of foreign states, on the grounds that the aggressor nation will suffer too much damage to make the venture worthwhile. Nuclear deterrence, counter-strike, and retaliation (all known sometimes as 'the balance of power' or 'the balance of terror') became a central feature of the Cold War.

Ombudsman	A popular word of Swedish origin (meaning grievance officer) referring to the Parliamentary Commissioner for Administration who investigates complaints of maladministration in public services.
Open government	The relatively unconstrained flow of information about government to the general public, the media, and representative bodies. Open government is relative, not absolute; all governments must keep some secrets, but critics of official secrecy in Britain claim that government is too secretive.
Orthodox economics	The dominant economic theory of the first half of the twentieth century which argued for minimal state intervention in the economy. Orthodox economics were widely practised in the Western world until the advent of Keynesian economics.
Osmotherly rules	A set of rules, named after their author, Edward Osmotherly of the Civil Service Department, for the guidance of civil servants appearing before Commons Select Committees and designed to protect civil service impartiality, anonymity, and secrecy.
Outsider groups	Do not have easy or official access to politicians and civil servants in Westminster and Whitehall, but are kept at arms length because of who they are and what they represent.
Party	An organisation of ideologically like-minded people who come together to seek power – often to fight elections with a view to gaining representation in decision making bodies.
Party democracy	Either (1) the widespread distribution of power within a political party and/or (2) a system of national democracy resting upon competitive parties.
Party factions	The sections or tendencies within parties which emphasise different features of party policy while subscribing to the overall aims of the party and its organisation. All parties contain such factions, but to varying degrees and strengths. Sometimes factions leave the main party to form their own (The Gang of Four and the SDP), and sometimes they are driven from it (Militant Tendency in the Labour Party).
Party families	Parties in different countries which share similar beliefs, principles, policies and, often, support groups. In Europe the three main party families are the Socialists (Labour and Social Democratic Parties), Conservative (Conservative and Christian Democratic Parties), and the Centre or Liberal Parties.
Party manifesto	The document which parties publish at the start of election campaigns outlining the programme of policies they intend to implement if elected to government.
Patronage	The giving of favours – office, contracts, or honours – to supporters of the government.
Peak (umbrella) associations	Co-ordinate the activities of different organisations with the same general interests (e.g. The Trades Union Congress or the Council of Churches).
Pluralism	According to pluralist theory political decisions are the outcome of competition between many different groups representing many different interests. Power is fragmented and winners and losers in the pluralist battle change and vary accord-

ing to the issue and its circumstances. Elites compete for the support of the non-elites and groups, which ensures democratic accountability.

Police
The civilian organisation established to enforce criminal law. The creation of the Metropolitan Police in London in 1829 marks the beginning of the British police force.

Policing
The processes and arrangements, usually but not always involving the police, established to maintain social order. All societies have to maintain order and so all engage in policing, although not all do so through a civilian police force.

Policy communities
Are small, stable, integrated and consensual groupings of government officials and pressure group leaders which form around particular issue areas.

Policy networks
Compared with policy communities, policy (or issue) networks are larger, looser, less integrated and more conflictual networks of political actors in a given policy area.

Political correctness
A controversial term to describe the use of language about socially sensitive matters, such as race or gender, in a way which is designed not to give offence. Often the implication is that politically correct language is silly or absurd.

Positive planning
Where the state takes direct action to achieve planning goals, as opposed to indicative planning where it sets out the goals but does not do anything itself to achieve them.

Poverty trap
The idea that the welfare state creates a vicious cycle of poverty for some social groups by imposing welfare systems that discourage people from taking responsibility for their own life or finding work. The cycle tends to continue, some claim, into the next generation of children who grow up in such a system.

Powers-based approach
The approach to judicial review which assumes that the principal task of the courts is to ensure that public bodies act in accordance with the powers granted to them by Parliament.

Precedent
A decision or practice of the past which is accepted as a guide for the present. In the law, precedents are past decisions of the courts which are thought to apply to similar legal problems or situations of the present.

Pressure groups
Private, voluntary organisations which wish to influence or control particular public policies without actually becoming the government or controlling all public policy.

Prime Minister
The head of the executive branch of government and chair of the Cabinet.

Prime ministerial government
The theory that the office of the prime minister has become so powerful that he or she now forms a political executive similar to a President. In prime ministerial government the Prime Minister is 'the efficient secret of government', the Cabinet only a 'dignified part'.

Private members' bills
Are introduced in Parliament by MPs or peers without government backing. Most (not all) fail, but in doing so they can influence future government legislation. Private members' bills may deal with any matter other than public expenditure.

Privatisation	The opposite of nationalisation, privatisation is the returning of nationalised industries wholly or partly to the private sector. Privatisation was accompanied by deregulation in Britain in the 1980s and early 1990s.
Process-based approach	The approach to judicial review which assumes that the principal task of the courts is to ensure that citizens can participate as fully and effectively as possible in the decision-making procedures of public bodies.
Progressive taxation	Where higher income groups pay proportionately more in taxation than lower income groups.
Proportional representation (PR)	A voting system which uses an allocation formula (there are many of them) which distributes seats among parties in proportion to their vote. PR tries to ensure that majorities and minorities are represented in proportion to their voting strength.
Public sector borrowing requirement (PSBR)	The amount borrowed by government to finance its annual expenditure. Keynesian theory argues that the PSBR should rise in times of economic depression in order to stimulate demand, and fall in times of rapid economic growth in order to prevent the economy from over-heating. Monetarism argues that a large PSBR fuels inflation and crowds out capital for private investment.
Public service model	The idea that radio and TV should not be commercial but used in the public interest to educate, inform, and entertain. The BBC under Lord Reith (its Director General, 1927–38) is said by some to be the epitome of public service broadcasting.
Quangos	Quasi-autonomous non-governmental organisations financed by the government to perform public service functions but not under direct government control. Examples include the BBC, and the Commission for Racial Equality (CRE). The advantage of quangos is that they can take sensitive political matters out of direct government control; the disadvantage is that they place public functions in the hands of unelected officials who are usually nominated by the government.
Racism	The practice of discriminating between individuals or groups on racial grounds.
Rate capping	The practice introduced in the 1980s whereby central government set a maximum rate level for local government in an attempt to control their control their expenditure.
Rational choice	An approach to political science which treats politics as the outcome of the interaction between rational individuals pursuing their own interests.
Realism	The view of politics, especially international relations, which emphasises the role of self-interest as a determinant of state policies, and hence the importance of power in these relations.
Referendum	A vote in which only one, or a small number of issues are put to the electorate, as against a general election in which the electorate chooses between parties on a broad range of political issues.
Regionalism	Regions are geographical areas within a state, and regionalism involves granting special forms of representation within national government to regions, or granting special powers and duties to regional forms of government. In Britain, the regions of Wales, Scotland, and Northern Ireland are examples.

Regressive taxation	Where lower income groups pay proportionately more in taxation than higher income groups.
Reinforcement theory (media effects)	Argues that the media do not create or mould public opinion so much as reinforce pre-existing opinion. This is because (1) the media adapt themselves to their consumers in their search for markets, and (2) consumers select the media and their messages to fit their own opinions, the result being that the media reflect consumer demand rather than creating it.
Representation	The process whereby one person acts on behalf, or in the interests, of another. Representative government entails the selection of representatives (usually by election) to make decisions, rather than direct participation of those represented.
Royal prerogative	Functions performed by ministers on behalf of the monarch. Before a constitutional monarchy was established, the Crown had powers which were subject to no check or veto by Parliament, but now the royal prerogative is generally exercised by ministers.
Select Committees	Committees of the House of Commons and the House of Lords which consider general political issues which are wider than a particular piece of legislation. The Public Accounts Committee of the House of Commons, which considers all accounts of money appropriated by Parliament, is a major example. Although membership is in proportion to party strength in the House, Committees try to work in a non-party political manner, and chairs of committees are often members of opposition parties.
Selective benefits	Are state welfare benefits distributed according to individual circumstances such as income, age, or disability.
Single member, simple plurality (SMSP)	The electoral system used in British general elections by which the country is divided into constituencies, each returning one Member of Parliament who need only obtain more votes than any other candidate in that constituency to be elected.
Sleaze	A popular term, much used in the mid-1990s, referring to the corrupt or improper behaviour of public officials, initially mainly members of the Conservative Government.
Social democratic	The ideology of that part of the political left which holds that political and social change can – and should – be achieved by means of peaceful reform rather than revolutionary violence. The British Labour Party is a social democratic party, as are the mainstream labour movements in Scandinavia and Germany.
Social democratic consensus	Agreement among different political groups and parties about the general principles of social democracy, that is a generally moderate left or centre-left political programme. The consensus was strong in the 1950–79 period when all major parties accepted the broad principles of the welfare state, the mixed economy, Keynesian economic policies and a NATO-based alliance against the USSR. The consensus was also known as 'Butskellism' after the left-wing Conservative leader R.A.B. Butler, and the right-wing Labour leader Hugh Gaitskell, who agreed on the broad issues of political policy, though not necessarily the details.
Sovereignty	The exclusive right to wield legitimate power within a territory. A sovereign state controls its own affairs, so far as any state can do so. Thus Parliamentary sovereignty means the power to make or repeal any law.

Spectrum scarcity   The shortage of broadcasting frequencies for radio and TV caused by the fact that the wavelengths available for public broadcasting on the spectrum are limited.

Standing committees   Committees of the House of Commons which examine bills after their second reading in order to make them more acceptable for their third reading. Committees are composed of party members in proportion to their numbers in the Commons.

State   The set of public bodies and institutions which exercise sovereign power within a territory. The state makes binding laws and policies, and claims compliance with them by virtue of its monopoly of the legitimate use of physical force. In Britain it consists primarily of Parliament, army, police, Civil Service, and local government.

State law   The sum total of laws passed by Parliament.

Statute law   Law passed by Parliament (in contrast to European law or common law).

Stereotyping   The practice of treating members of social groups as if they were all the same, often in a way which involves discrimination.

Stop-go cycle   A pattern in which the economy swings between rapid growth which becomes inflationary, out of control, and 'over-heated', followed by deflationary policies designed to slow growth and stabilise the economy.

Subsidiarity   The principle whereby decisions should be taken at the lowest possible level of the political system – that is, at the level closest to the people affected by the decisions.

Sustainable development   Development which meets the needs of the present without compromising the ability of future generations to meet their needs. The term was developed by the United Nations Commission on the Environment and Development, chaired by the Norwegian Prime Minister, Mrs Bruntland, and spelled out in its report *Our Common Future* (1987).

Tabloids   Less serious national and Sunday papers, so called because of their smaller format than broadsheets. Daily tabloids are the *Sun*, *Daily Mirror*, *Daily Express*, *Daily Star*, and *Daily Record*.

Tactical voting   The practice of voting for a candidate who is not the first preference in order to keep out a less preferred candidate.

Targeted electioneering   The practice whereby parties concentrate resources on those marginal seats which they think they have the best chance of gaining from another party, or the highest chance of losing to another party.

Think-tank   An organisation set up to develop public policy proposals and to press for their adoption by government. Since think-tanks are concerned with applied policy research and its implementation, they are often connected with governments, parties, or social movements. Major British examples include the government's own Central Policy Review Staff (1971-83), the Centre for Policy Studies (Conservative), and The Institute for Policy Research (Labour).

Trade liberalisation The process whereby international trade is increasingly opened up to market forces (free trade) by reducing trading tariffs, import and export controls, and other forms of protection.

Tripartism Compared with corporatism, tripartism is a looser, less centralised and co-ordinated system which brings together three main interests (government, business, unions) in economic policy-making. It is a consultative rather than a corporatist method of reaching and implementing decisions.

Tribunals In Britain tribunals are quasi-judicial institutions set up to resolve conflicts between public or private individuals or bodies. They are a way of avoiding the expensive and time-consuming needs of the courts, and of settling a large number of fairly small and simple cases.

Two-tier local government Where the functions of local government are divided between an upper level (counties, for example) and a lower level (boroughs or districts, for example).

Ultra Vires The doctrine whereby public bodies have only those powers granted explicitly or implicitly by Parliament, and no others.

Unilateralism The belief that a country should voluntarily and independently renounce its (nuclear) weapons, either as a moral gesture which might be followed by others, and/or because unilateralists held that nuclear weapons did not deter aggression and might even provoke it. The main unilateralist organisation in Britain is the Campaign for Nuclear Disarmament (CND).

Unitary state A state in which there is a single sovereign body, the central government. Unlike a federal state, the central government of a unitary state does not share power with smaller territorial areas within the state (states, regions, or provinces) although it may devolve some powers to them. Britain, France, Sweden, Italy, and Japan are unitary states; the USA, Germany, Austria and Switzerland are federal states.

Unitary system Where local functions are controlled by only one layer of local government.

Universal benefits Are state welfare benefits distributed to all groups and individuals who are eligible, irrespective of their particular circumstances.

Utopianism A form of ideology which claims that it is possible to create a perfect or near perfect society. However, some utopias are constructed by their creators not as feasible societies, but as models against which to compare the real world. Plato's *Republic* presents a utopia, as does Sir Thomas More's book *Utopia* (1516) from which the modern word derives.

Videomalaise The attitudes of political cynicism, despair, apathy, and disillusionment (among others) which some social scientists claim are caused by the modern mass media, especially television.

Welfare state A state in which the government ensures the basic social and economic necessities of its citizens by providing, through the revenues it raises from taxes and other sources, goods and services such as education, health, housing, and social security. In Britain the welfare state derives from the Beveridge report of 1942.

Westminster model The form of liberal democracy which is modelled on the British system of government. It is best described and analysed by Walter Bagehot in *The English Constitution* (1867), and now involves: parliamentary sovereignty and an unwritten constitution; representative democracy (rather than participatory or delegated democracy); an attempt to balance the need for strong government with the rights of citizens; an overlap between executive, legislative and judiciary; single ('winner takes all') party government; and the single member, simple plurality electoral system.

Whips Officials appointed by parliamentary parties in the Lords and the Commons to promote party discipline. A three-line whip is one requiring the voting support of all members of the party in parliamentary divisions. The whips are also said to be the 'eyes and ears' of party leaders who are too busy to maintain close and regular contact with backbench opinion.

AUTHOR INDEX

SUBJECT INDEX

Major discussions of important topics are in **bold**